The Complete Guide to

HUMAN RESOURCES

and the LAW

Dana Shilling

PRENTICE HALL

Library of Congress Cataloging-in-Publication Data

Shilling, Dana.
    Complete guide to human resources and the law / Dana Shilling.
       p. cm.
    Includes index.
    ISBN 0-13-759580-8
    1. Labor laws and legislation—United States.   2. Personnel management—
United States.   I. Title.
KF3455.S55   1998   98-5107
344.7301—dc21   CIP

Acquisitions Editor: *Susan McDermott*
Production Editor: *Jacqueline Roulette*
Formatting/Interior Design: *Robyn Beckerman*

© *1998 by Prentice Hall*

Printed in the United States of America

10 9 8 7 6

ISBN 0-13-759580-8

9 780137 595808

ATTENTION: CORPORATIONS AND SCHOOLS

Prentice Hall books are available at quantity discounts with bulk purchase for educational, business, or sales promotional use. For information, please write to:
Prentice Hall Special Sales, 240 Frisch Court, Paramus, New Jersey 07652. Please
supply: title of book, ISBN, quantity, how the book will be used, date needed.

PRENTICE HALL
Paramus, NJ 07652

On the World Wide Web at http://www.phdirect.com

Introduction

The working life of the HR professional combines elements of running the gauntlet, walking a tightrope, and walking the plank. Sometimes it seems that whatever decision the beleaguered HR department makes, it will at least be controversial and cost a lot of money. Every day there are new rules to be mastered, nervous people to reassure, policies to set, and, of course, a ream of paperwork to be processed.

The aim of this book is to explain some of the many legal issues the HR department faces, and to put those issues in context. The best case is for all HR policies to be developed and carried out in close consultation with an attorney who is experienced in and thoroughly knowledgeable about pension/employee benefit law, discrimination law, corporate law, and tax. However, this is not always possible.

The worst scenario is when the HR department, whether or not operating in good faith, promulgates an unlawful policy, violates the rights of employees, fails to make required disclosures, sends out a document in incorrect form, or makes one out of a menu of perfectly lawful choices that has the least favorable tax consequences. The upshot? A lawsuit; fines and penalties; a huge tax bill—and perhaps a mess that the company's lawyer will find it difficult or even impossible to sort out.

My hope is that this book will give the HR professional some basic tools and concepts for understanding the legal issues that arise in five areas:

- HR management (including hiring; drafting the employee handbook; creating and retaining employee records; work-family issues; workplace diversity; computer applications)

- Current compensation (including pay planning; wage and hour issues; health plans; and fringe benefits)

- Deferred compensation (including qualified and non-qualified pension plans; plan administration; disclosure to participants; distributing benefits from the plan; terminating a plan; ERISA compliance and enforcement)

- Protection of employees (including labor law; unemployment insurance; worker's compensation; occupational safety and health; privacy issues)

- Handling charges of job discrimination (based on race, sex, nationality, disability, age, etc.) and wrongful termination

The focus of this book is on private companies (not government employers or not-for-profit organizations) with 100 or more employees. The discussion of pension benefits concentrates on single employer plans rather than multi-employer plans. Because the majority of U.S. companies are not unionized, the labor law section deals in large part with preventive labor relations and the election process for certifying a union, although there is some discussion of issues within the company that is already unionized.

There are few clear answers or simple solutions in the law, and understanding the law requires constant attention to new developments. The U.S. legal system is unique in that the law develops and evolves based on input from (and tensions among) all three branches of government: executive, legislative, and judicial. Congress and the states pass laws; the Internal Revenue Service (IRS) and other administrative agencies draft regulations to carry out those laws; and the courts are often called upon to interpret those laws and regulations.

Reported court decisions are found in many places. For federal court decisions, the *Federal Reporter* (which is now in its Third Series) is the basic research tool, although decisions that are too recent or too obscure to turn up there can be found in *United States Law Week* (abbreviated LW), in "looseleaf services" such as the *Employment Coordinator and Unemployment Insurance Reporter* (published to explain and contain recent decisions about a particular specialty area), and on line on computer services such as LEXIS and Westlaw (abbreviated WL).

The federal laws passed by Congress are published in the United States Code (U.S.Code or U.S.C.). When each bill is passed, it is assigned a Public Law number such as P.L. 105-32, identifying the Congress that passed it (the 105th) and the order in which it was passed (in this case the 32nd bill of that Congress).

Federal agencies publish their new regulations in a daily magazine, the *Federal Register*. Once a year, the Code of Federal Regulations, or CFR, is updated to reflect the new regulations.

Another Code is very important to understanding HR legal issues: the Internal Revenue Code. In fact, when this book makes a reference such as "Code §411," it is that Code that's involved. The IRS publishes many kinds of documents for the guidance of people who encounter tax problems: Revenue Rulings, Announcements, Notices, etc. There are enough of these documents for the IRS to publish a weekly Internal Revenue Bulletin (abbreviated IRB). Each year, all the IRBs are collected and republished in two or three volumes as the Cumulative Bulletin (C.B.) for that year.

See the *Notes* section at the back of the book for references to important cases, laws, and regulations. You can use this information to do further research about topics that come up in your own professional life, or use it in discussions with the legal advisors for your company and its plans.

HR law offers seemingly endless opportunities to get into trouble, but the conscientious HR professional can learn to anticipate problems, operate in a lawful manner, complete all tax forms and other required documents correctly and on time, and give employees all required notices in proper form. If these proactive measures don't work, the HR professional will be able to respond to allegations of wrongdoing, by demonstrating that the company had appropriate policies and carried them out uniformly and in a timely manner. It can also show that the person making the charge does not have the appropriate evidence or has not made a timely charge in the correct form.

Thanks to the conscientious HR professional, every company can commit to equal opportunity, hire the best candidates, offer them appropriate compensation as incentives, and have a workplace that is safe, efficient, and family-friendly. Being that conscientious HR professional is an ongoing process, not a single, simple task, but I hope that this book offers some useful tools for that process.

Contents

PART II
COMPENSATION ISSUES
(Current Compensation)

Chapter 7   Compensation Planning—67

Chapter 8   Wage and Hour Issues—77

Part III
PENSIONS AND RETIREMENT
(Deferred Compensation)

Chapter 13   Plan Administration—247

Chapter 14   Plan Disclosure—273

Chapter 15 Distributions from the Plan—289

Chapter 16 Termination of a Plan—303

Chapter 17 ERISA Enforcement—317

Part IV

EMPLOYEE RELATIONS; PROTECTING EMPLOYEES

Chapter 18   Labor Law—343

Chapter 22   Privacy Issues—445

Part V

COPING WITH CHARGES OF DISCRIMINATION AND WRONGFUL TERMINATION

Chapter 23   Title VII—455

Chapter 24   The Americans with Disabilities Act (ADA)—475

Chapter 25   The Family and Medical Leave Act (FMLA)—491

Chapter 26   The Age Discrimination in Employment Act—501

Chapter 27 Procedure for Discrimination Suits—515

Chapter 28 Wrongful Termination and At-Will Employment—547

Chapter 29 Corporate Communications—569

Part I

HR Management

Chapter 1

THE HIRING PROCESS

1.1 INTRODUCTION

Efficient hiring practices benefit the company at all levels; a prompt, economical selection of the best person for the job (whether from inside the company or brought in from outside) will keep operations running smoothly, and encourage innovation that will keep the company competitive. Bad hiring practices create risks of many kinds.

The more obvious risks are charges brought by job applicants or one-time employees who claim that the company practiced some form of unlawful discrimination against them. In a worst case scenario, an employee might commit a violent crime or otherwise harm others—and the employer might be held liable for negligence in hiring or retention of such a person. Subtler risks are poorly-chosen employees who absorb too much training time, drag down the efficiency of an entire department, make costly mistakes—or who must be discharged and replaced, setting the whole cycle into motion once again. The complementary risk is that an especially productive employee will quit, to get a job somewhere else or start a business (perhaps even a business that becomes a rival of the original employer).

1.2 PRODUCTIVE HIRING

Unless the corporate objective is specifically to hire someone for a short-term or temporary assignment, an important objective is to find someone who will develop loyalty and who will want to stay with the company for a long time. Training is both a major expense and a major inconvenience, and it takes time for a new hire to get acclimated to the job, so turnover has a very negative effect on productivity.

The perfect candidate is not necessarily the one with the most impressive résumé. Indeed someone with superlative credentials might be the constant target of recruiters, and someone who will jump ship quickly—or who will have to be wooed with a constant stream of new incentives. More desirable is the one who is best suited to the job as it exists now and the way it will develop in the near future.

In order to tap the broadest possible candidate pools, it may be necessary to recruit creatively. Although current employees can provide excellent referrals, they are not a complete source—especially if you want a diverse workforce.

If you recruit at colleges and graduate schools, don't restrict yourself only to those close by (excellent candidates can be found at schools nationwide), and don't limit your search to a small class of "Ivy League" schools. True, it's expensive to send a recruiter to many campuses, or to fly strong candidates to your headquarters for interviews. Luckily, using the Internet allows you to recruit nationwide at very low cost.

⇒ TIP

Résumés posted on the Internet are no more or less truthful than those delivered by traditional means; don't forget to check credentials for online job applicants.

1.3 ANALYZING THE REQUIREMENTS

A frequent source of frustration in hiring is poor analysis of the actual requirements of the job. A candidate is chosen who matches the formal, written description of the job, and perhaps he or she would work out well if the job matched the description. However, it's common to hire people on the basis of technical skills when those skills are seldom used on a day-to-day basis, and most of the real work (and real problems) stems from close contact with other people. If the most important criterion is a sunny personality and high tolerance for frustration, a brilliant but short-tempered techno-genius will be a poor choice.

The job should be analyzed to see how much time is actually spent on tasks such as:

- Meeting and conferring with others
- Using computers (and specific programs and applications on the computer)
- Selling company products to potential customers
- Working with machinery
- Supervising the work of others

- Writing and analyzing reports
- Creating policy for the organization
- Carrying out policy set by others
- Lifting heavy objects
- Driving
- Traveling on business.

It's important to understand the physical demands of the job, in order to determine which disabled applicants are able to meet those demands without accommodation, and those who are able to meet the demands if reasonable accommodation is offered. (See page 480 for a discussion of what constitutes reasonable accommodation.)

The job's place within the organization should also be analyzed. Perhaps the entire operation would be more productive if the responsibilities assigned to the job were changed, or if the job were given a higher (or lower) level within the grading system or organization chart. Perhaps there has been conflict because the job reports to one person, when in fact it would make more sense to report to someone else.

It should be determined whether the job is exempt or non-exempt for wage and hour purposes. Sometimes it makes economic sense to restructure a job so that it becomes exempt; that way, overtime compensation is no longer required. (Of course, the restructuring must be legitimate, not merely cosmetic.)

Reasons for job turnover should also be analyzed. Factors conducive to high turnover should be studied; wherever possible, steps to promote retention should be taken.

Your company's attractiveness vis-à-vis competitors must be considered. If you're operating in an area of high unemployment, and the job opportunities you offer are above par for the area, then you can relax and expect the best candidates to come to you. However, if you are a medium-sized company in a crowded market sector, in a geographic area with a tight labor market, you may find it difficult to attract good candidates unless you can offer tangible (above-average compensation) or intangible (pleasant working environment; scope for creativity) advantages. Sometimes the way to compete is to budget extra funds for cash compensation. In a strong stock market, stock options can be a low-cost way of providing financial incentives (see page 158).

The job interview, and especially repeat interviews with various people in the hierarchy, should be used to give the potential employee strong insight into resources available and what will be expected.

Each job should have a written job description indicating what educational qualifications, skills, and experience are really required to perform effectively, and stating standards (numerical, if possible) for defining inadequate, satisfactory, good, and excellent job performance. Having strong evidence of discrepancies between explicit job requirements and actual performance goes a long way toward rebutting charges of employment discrimination.

The job description should indicate to whom the holder of the job reports, and who reports to him or her. It should explain the promotion potential for the job, including any conditions (e.g., employee has to complete a Masters' degree within two years of hiring). If your company has a grading system, the job grade should be indicated. So should its salary range.

1.4 RECRUITING FROM WITHIN

Many companies create incentives for employees to do well by stressing internal transfers and promotions. These workers don't have to leave (or threaten to leave) to advance or earn more money if they are given access to job postings and given a real chance to compete for jobs. Of course, internal recruitment also saves money that would otherwise go for advertisements and the fees of search firms, and the company can get a detailed view of the employee's past performance by consulting its own records. (However, supervisors may thwart transfer or promotion efforts by their best employees, because they don't want to lose them and have to replace them with someone who may be much less effective.)

Most companies physically post the listing on a bulletin board, leaving the notice up for five to ten days, although more and more companies are using their corporate intranet (see page 61) for this purpose. The posting should explain the nature of the job, the qualifications required, and whether there are any limitations (e.g., union seniority lists; corporate policy that does not allow employees to apply for internal vacancies unless they have held their current job for at least six months and have satisfactory performance appraisals). The usual policy is to keep applications confidential from the applicant's immediate supervisor, until there is the possibility of a job offer.

1.5 RECRUITING IN A COMPETITIVE ENVIRONMENT

Employers who face a great deal of competition have to find a way to "position" their "product": i.e., much as they would market their goods and services by identifying those who need them and discussing the value proposition of those goods and services, they must appeal to potential new hires. Attractive features may include:

- High cash compensation
- High overall compensation package, when health and other benefits are taken into account
- High job security

- Prestige within the industry
- Ability to work on cutting-edge projects
- Availability of stock options (especially in a company that might go public fairly soon)
- Pleasant working environment
- Easy commute
- Family-friendly policies (but, as page 44 shows, pro-family policies can actually create hostility among single employees).

Companies that send letters to rejected candidates often include the polite phrase, "We will keep your résumé on file." Yet few of them actually review the filed résumés when they have another position to fill; this can be a simple and inexpensive source of candidates for jobs similar to those already announced.

For lower-level jobs, and for some higher-level technical jobs, the state employment service can be a good resource. Although at first glance it seems that only people receiving unemployment benefits would be registered there, and you might be unwilling to take on workers who have lost a job somewhere else, this is not always true. First of all, unemployment benefits are not available to workers who have voluntarily quit, or who were fired for wrongdoing, so workers receiving benefits are probably not unstable or a bad risk. Second, people who are not unemployed, but who want a new job, sometimes register with the state employment office because it has contacts with a wide range of employers and because it doesn't charge jobseekers a fee.

For higher-level positions, if one of the companies in your area has had a major downsizing, it can be very worthwhile to contact the company handling executive outplacement, because a number of senior staff will be available for hiring through no fault of their own.

1.5.1 Avoiding Improprieties

Beware of hiring former employees of competitors, especially former key employees, which can have pitfalls of its own. Such individuals may be bound by a covenant not to compete that prevents them from taking a job with a company like yours. Even if there is no contractual bar, your competitor may assert (in good or bad faith) that your new hire has misappropriated the ex-employer's trade secrets or customer lists, or that he or she is inappropriately soliciting past customers or clients. Your company may be charged with interfering with the ex-employer's business prospects or contractual relationship with its former employee (if you are charged with enticement). "Stealing" a key employee could subject your company to liability, perhaps measured by the other company's lost profits; by the amount of damages specified in the employment contract; or for losses sustained because of the loss of the employee.

To avoid liability of this type, be sure to inquire if applicants are subject to any contract that prevents them from coming to work for you. If this is the case, get it on the record that the applicant approached your company for a job, and was not "enticed" or lured away.

1.6 SEARCH FIRMS

For a rank-and-file job, just putting out the word to employees, or within the neighborhood, could be sufficient to fill the vacancy. (However, you should be aware that this practice could have the effect of maintaining the current ethnic census, because peoples' neighbors and relatives tend to be a fairly homogeneous group, and this hiring pattern might be challenged by members of other groups who feel excluded.) For an entry-level job, recruiting from high schools, colleges, and vocational training programs often works well. Newspaper classified ads, ads in specialty journals, and, to an increasing extent, Internet job search sites, can result in a good match between needs and job candidates.

However, the stakes are higher when a top executive or leading professional has to be replaced. Such a person will be setting the company's policy and/or creative agenda. The right choice could strengthen the company's long-range competitive position; the wrong choice could harm the company's agenda seriously. Furthermore, a candidate could be hired who has excellent credentials and is conscientious and hard-working, but whose vision for the company is incompatible with that of the rest of management.

For all those reasons, businesses often turn to search firms when a major job needs to be filled. This is not an inexpensive proposition. Search firms may charge more than one year's salary of a well-paid executive, but it can pay off in productivity if the right candidate is selected and brought on line quickly. The problem is that, in today's low unemployment, highly competitive environment, search firms may feel that it's a seller's market, and they don't have to go the extra mile for clients. Also, many of their clients have never used a search firm before, so they don't know what to expect or how to assess quality performance. John Marra, president of Marra Peters & Partners, a recruitment firm in New Jersey, has some suggestions:

- Be clear on what your criteria will be for judging the firm's performance
- Reputable firms will usually be glad to provide references from satisfied customers—potential clients should not just collect these references but contact them to see what they have to say about the search firm
- Let the search firm know what you expect the successful candidate to accomplish in the first six months and the first year post-hiring; what benchmarks you will use to test the new hire's performance
- Ask the search firm to send only candidates who are a close fit with your specifications.

Ask the search firm to promise to keep working with you until you are satisfied with the candidate (if necessary, after the discharge of a probationary candidate and search for a replacement).

The search profession includes two main types of firms: the executive search firm (which usually gets involved only with jobs paying $75,000 a year or more) and the contingency firm (usually used to find candidates for jobs paying $40,000-$80,000 a year). A search firm works directly for the company looking for an executive, and its contracts will probably be drafted to obligate the company to pay for its services whether or not they result in hiring a candidate. In contrast, a contingency firm has both companies looking for executives and search candidates as its clients, and it charges a fee to the company only if an executive gets hired.

The search firm fee can be anywhere from 25% to 100% of the first year salary; contingency firms usually charge less, perhaps 20-33% of the first year salary. (Only cash compensation, not bonuses or stock options, is included in the calculation.) Contracts with either firm often include a provision that the company can get a refund if the new hire leaves or has to be discharged within a probationary period such as 90 days.

Other important provisions to look for in a recruitment contract:

- Clarification that the firm does not have the authority to hire someone on behalf of your company, or to promise terms and conditions of employment; only an authorized agent of your company can do that

- Statement that your company is committed to the principles of equal employment opportunity

- The firm's agreement that it will be responsible if it commits discrimination in referring candidates to you—and that it will indemnify your company if your company suffers liability because of discriminatory referrals

- A clear statement of the recruiting firm's responsibilities (including checking the references of screened candidates it sends to you)

- Recruiting expenses that your company agrees to pay

- Whether you have to pay the fee if you hire a candidate obtained through another channel, or only if the recruiter sends the successful candidate to you

- The recruiting firm's promise not to contact or solicit your new hire for a period of at least two years.

1.7 NON-DISCRIMINATORY HIRING

Of course, your company will not engage in any practices that treat people differently because of their race, sex, national origin, disability, etc. However, it can be far more difficult to avoid "disparate impact," apparently neutral practices that actually disadvantage members of one group more than members of other groups. For instance, a height requirement has disparate impact on Asians, Hispanics, and women. That doesn't mean that employers can't impose height requirements—as long as it is really necessary to be taller than 5'9" or 6' to do the job properly.

Other potential sources of disparate impact:

- Educational standards
- Preemployment testing
- Requirement of military experience
- Getting referrals from your existing workforce (who tend to know people of their own ethnicity)
- Rules about facial hair (this could disadvantage religious applicants; it also could have a disparate impact on black men, some of whom find it painful to shave because of ingrown hairs)
- Refusal to hire anyone who has ever been arrested, filed for bankruptcy, or had a child out of wedlock.

Make sure that your attorney reviews hiring practices to see if they avoid discrimination and if all requirements can be justified in terms of the practical needs of the business and skills that will actually be used on the job. For each job, you should also determine the physical capacities that are central to the job, those that are sometimes used but are peripheral, and those that are never invoked by the job.

If employees request flextime (for parenting needs, as an accommodation to disability, as an accommodation to religious observance, or simply for convenience), you should either be able to grant the request or explain why there is a legitimate business reason why conventional business hours or standard shifts must be observed.

There are two important criteria for assessing the questions asked during an interview:

- Do the questions relate to legitimate workplace issues, rather than merely satisfying idle curiosity?
- Are they asked uniformly, not only to a group of people selected based on preconceived notions? For instance, it is discriminatory to ask a woman if her husband "lets" her travel on business, but it is not discriminatory to advise all job applicants that the job includes X number of days of travel a year, including Y number of overnight or prolonged stays, and to ask the candidate if he or she is able to travel that much.

Anti-discrimination law assumes that many individuals will be interviewed for each opening, and there are many reasons why the successful candidate will be preferred. There is no reason to collect a great deal of information about candidates who have no real chance of selection. Therefore, certain inquiries are acceptable in connection with a conditional job offer that would not be acceptable as a general part of first-level interviewing.

For instance, whether a person is married or has children is quite relevant to that person's participation in an employee group health plan, but is irrelevant if the person is not going to get a job offer. Thus, this information should either be requested only after the person is hired, or collected on a separate sheet of paper and not consulted until hiring occurs.

See page 478 for a discussion of acceptable and unacceptable pre-employment inquiries and tests in the disability context. It is not acceptable to ask an interviewee about his or her history of receiving Worker's Compensation benefits, but a person who has gotten a conditional job offer can be asked about past injuries that may require accommodation.

There are also circumstances under which the company's commitment to equal employment opportunity must be put into writing. If the company is a federal contractor, EEOC rules published in 41 Code of Federal Regulations Part 60, job applications used by federal contractors must include an invitation for Vietnam veterans, disabled veterans, and other people with disabilities to identify themselves.

The application must stipulate that the information will remain confidential, and that there is no penalty for not providing the information. The application file for someone who does identify him- or herself as belonging to one of those categories should indicate the vacancy for which he or she was considered, and the reason why a job offer was not extended (including a comparison of that person's qualifications with those of the person who was offered the job).

1.8 PRE-EMPLOYMENT TESTING

It's legitimate for an employer to test job applicants to see if they have relevant skills. Title VII permits the use of professionally developed ability tests that are not designed or administered with a discriminatory motive. A valid test is one that is neither explicitly nor implicitly discriminatory against protected groups; one that tests skills that are actually used in the job (an administrative assistant has to know how to use computers for word processing, but doesn't need to know how to create original programs); and one that has been validated by psychologists or other experts so that it really offers insight into the issues needed to hire appropriate candidates.

A 1975 Supreme Court case, *Albemarle Paper Co.* v. *Moody,* holds that if a test has a disproportionate negative effect on a minority group, the test is permissible only if professionally accepted methods verify the test's ability to predict important elements of work behavior. As the Supreme Court case of *Griggs* v. *Duke Power Co.,* 401 U.S. 424 (1971) says, the point of pre-employment testing is to measure the applicant's performance vis-à-vis a specific job, not in the abstract.

⇒ TIP

Even if a company's pre-employment tests are valid, it is discriminatory to give the tests only to minorities.

The EEOC's Uniform Guidelines on Employee Selection Procedures say that an employment practice is discriminatory if the selection rate (usually, passing a test, job offers or hiring) for members of a race, sex, or ethnic group is less than 80% of the selection rate for the group that has the highest selection rate. Although these Guidelines were never promulgated as an official agency regulation, courts award them a great deal of deference.

The "bottom-line rule" is that the EEOC and other anti-discrimination agencies will not challenge ONE part of an employment screening system, even if it might have a disparate impact on a protected group, as long as the WHOLE selection process does not have a disproportionately negative impact. But this rule applies only to agency actions; a member of the group can still sue, alleging discrimination against him- or herself, even if the bottom-line result is more minority than non-minority hires or promotions. Individuals who believe that they have been discrimination victims can still sue, even if the employer can argue that the organization as a whole is not discriminatory.

1.8.1 Validating a Test

Let's say that your company adopts a pre-employment test, monitors the results, and discovers that the test does have an adverse impact on women and/or minority group members. In that case, the Guidelines give the company three options:

- Get rid of the test
- Change the test until the adverse impact is removed

⇒ TIP

The Civil Rights Act of 1991 says it is *not* acceptable to grade on a "curve" for minorities, or to have a lower passing grade for minorities.

- Do a validity study that confirms both the business necessity for using the test and the usefulness of the test because it accurately predicts good job performance.

The published psychological literature is a good place to find out which tests have already been validated. There are three methods for checking validity:

- Criterion-related (i.e., the test is an accurate predictor of work behavior or other criteria of "employee adequacy")

- Content-related (the test accurately duplicates actual duties—e.g., asking someone to use Pagemaker to lay out an advertisement, or to use a drill press or lathe under conditions similar to those of the workplace)

- Construct-related (it identifies general mental and psychological traits needed to do the job, such as ability to remain cool under pressure and respond courteously to hostile customers).

1.9 IMMIGRATION AND HIRING PRACTICES

Traditionally, the United States has been a land of opportunity for people throughout the world, and many people want to settle and work in the United States. Employers also benefit by immigration, especially of scientists, health care workers, and others who have skills for which the demand outstrips the easily available supply of U.S. workers.

According to the Immigration and Naturalization Service (INS), in 1996 employment-based immigration to the United States increased by close to 40%. In 1995, about 85,000 job-seekers immigrated to the U.S.; almost 117,500 did so in 1996. In fiscal 1996, 23% of job-related visas were issued to "priority workers": professionals with extraordinary skills in fields such as computer science.

1.9.1 Immigration Categories

Today, employment-based immigration is regulated under the Immigration Act of 1990, Public Law 101-649. Out of the 675,000 visas granted each year to all types of immigrants, 140,000 are employment-related. There are seven categories of employable immigrants:

- Priority workers: individuals of extraordinary ability and/or vocational responsibility

- Professionals with advanced degrees and/or exceptional ability

- Other workers (skilled workers, professionals without advanced degrees; unskilled workers who have DOL certification that there is a shortage of U.S. citizens with similar skills)

- Special immigrants (e.g., religious workers sent to the U.S. by a religious hierarchy)

- Immigrants who have the financial capacity to invest at least $1 million within the U.S., employing at least 10 U.S. workers

- H-1B "specialty occupation" workers who reside temporarily within the United States, and work here, but do not become U.S. citizens
- H-2B temporary non-agricultural workers.

1.9.2 Employer Responsibilities

Although it would seem that it is the responsibility of an individual who applies for a job to determine whether he or she has legal status that would justify employment within the United States, U.S. labor and immigration law places at least an equal burden on the employer. At the time of hiring, the employer must ascertain if the new hire is a U.S. citizen or a legal immigrant who is not only permitted to reside in this country but to work here.

The employer responsibilities stem from the Immigration Reform and Control Act of 1986 (IRCA), 8 U.S.C. §1324a. For all employee hiring after November 6, 1986, the employer has become responsible for checking documents presented by potential new employees to demonstrate their identity and authorization to work within the United States. (A person can be lawfully admitted into the United States, but not permitted to work in this country, so it's not a simple question of distinguishing illegal aliens from lawful immigrants.)

This information must also be ascertained in a way that is not discriminatory against, for example, dark-skinned individuals or persons whose first language is not English. Once individuals are eligible to work in the U.S., IRCA makes it an unfair employment practice to discriminate in hiring, recruitment, or retention on the basis of national origin (but this provision is applicable only to companies that employ four or more, but fewer than 15, employees). It is unlawful for any employer of four or more to discriminate on the basis of citizenship against a noncitizen who is a lawful resident, but it is permissible for an employer to hire a citizen instead of an equally qualified noncitizen.

- Documents must be checked within three days of hiring someone; and records of the document checks must be kept for three years, or one year after employment terminates. The new hire submits an I-9 form to provide the proof.

➠ **TIP**

Blank I-9 forms are available from the U.S. Government Printing Office in Washington, D.C. (202-783-3238) or the Employer Relations Officer at your local INS office; once you have some blank forms, you can copy or otherwise reproduce them.

The employer can't avoid this responsibility by having workers supplied under a contract with others (such as an employment agency or leasing company). It also won't get the employer off the hook to require new hires to indemnify the employer if they are not actually permitted to work in the U.S. However, if the employer gets referrals from a state employment service, and if the service furnishes certification that it has verified employee eligibility, that's enough to insulate the employer from liability.

Both the INS and the DOL are entitled to inspect an employer's collection of I-9 forms, but to enter a workplace they must either have a warrant or give 72 hours' notice.

Civil and criminal penalties of anywhere from $250 to $2,000 (depending on circumstances) can be imposed for a first offense of hiring persons who are not permitted to work in the United States. Repeat offenses can be penalized by $3,000 to $10,000. Even failure to maintain the appropriate paperwork and records can be penalized by up to $1,000. Anyone (including an employer) who is guilty of outright document fraud is subject to a fine of $250 to $2,000 per document per instance in which it was used, and up to $5,000 per document for repeat violations.

In addition to the penalties imposed on employers, a 1996 Ninth Circuit decision points out that aliens can be fined for using false documentation to certify their employment eligibility. The 1990 amendments to the Immigration and Nationality Act penalize "any person," not just an employer, who neglects his or her verification responsibilities.

It's illegal to knowingly hire an ineligible person, a category that includes constructive knowledge—information that can reasonably be inferred from the facts and circumstances, to the degree that a person acting with reasonable care would have to be aware of the facts. According to Immigration and Naturalization Service regulations found in 8 CFR §274a, these are circumstances creating an inference of constructive knowledge:

- The employer actually has some information that the person is not eligible for U.S employment
- The applicant refuses to complete the I-9 form, or does it improperly
- The employer acts with "reckless and wanton disregard" of the consequences of hiring ineligible persons.

However, accent and appearance are not acceptable sources of constructive knowledge.

A Presidential Executive Order, 12989 (February 13, 1996), published at 61 Federal Register 6091, debars federal contractors from getting further federal contracts after they have been caught knowingly hiring illegal aliens.

> ⇒ **TIP**
>
> Originally, the Supreme Court agreed to decide a case about whether it is legitimate for an employer to maintain "English-only" rules in the workplace, but the case was dismissed as moot (of purely academic interest) after the plaintiff employee quit the job that imposed the rule. This seems like a way of weaseling out of a controversial issue. The Supreme Court wouldn't have agreed to hear the case in the first place if it had only affected one person; and employers throughout the U.S. would benefit from a clarification of what they can and can't require within the workplace.

1.9.3 Employment Verification Documents

Hired individuals prove their eligibility to work within the United States either by showing that they are U.S. citizens (e.g., showing a U.S. passport or a birth certificate evidencing birth within the U.S.) or by showing that they have a so-called "green card." (It's so-called because the document is no longer green; it has a white background and carries a photograph of the worker, his or her fingerprint, bar codes, holograms, and other anti-counterfeiting features.) Starting on January 27, 1997, the Immigration and Naturalization Service began to issue Form I-766, a tamper-resistant card issued to aliens whose immigration status permits them to work in the U.S. It replaces the more familiar I-688B form. The INS has a fact sheet on the I-766; call (800) 870-3676. The I-766 is a Class A Employment Authorization Document (EAD): that is, it establishes both the job applicant's identity and his or her entitlement to work within the United States.

There are three categories of documents. List A documents can be used to prove both identity and employability:

- U.S. passport (even if expired; all other documents must be unexpired to be usable for this purpose)
- A current non-U.S. passport, stamped to show permission to work in the U.S.
- INS Forms N-560 or –561 (certificate of U.S. citizenship)
- INS Forms N-550 or –570 (certificate of naturalization)
- INS Form I-151 (alien registration receipt card) or I-551 (resident alien card), but only if they have photographs of the individual
- INS Form I-688 (temporary resident card), 688-A (employment authorization card)
- INS Form I-327 (permit for reentry into the United States after leaving—e.g., returning to the former country of residence to visit family members)
- INS Form I-571 (refugee travel document).

The employer is not required to engage in Sherlock-Holmes-like deductions, but must at least examine the documents to see if they appear to relate to the person offering them as proof.

List B consists of documents that prove identity only:

- A U.S. or Canadian driver's license, especially if it has a photograph
- A voter registration card
- A university photo I.D.
- A U.S. military card or draft record
- I.D. issued by a state or local government.

    List C documents prove employability only:

- A Social Security card (unless it is stamped to indicate that the person is not permitted to work in this country)
- An original birth certificate, or a certified copy of a birth certificate that bears an official seal
- A current INS employment authorization document
- INS Form I-197 (U.S. citizen I.D. card)
- INS Form I-179 (I.D. card for the use of residents).

The employee, not the employer, decides which of these documents will be presented; the employer must accept any combination of original documents that establishes both.

1.10 ADA COMPLIANCE IN HIRING

The ADA protects qualified disabled individuals. The employer must determine whether to extend a job offer to a disabled candidate, a question that includes consideration of accommodations that may be needed in the course of employment. However, there are some narrow shoals to navigate through: some pre-employment inquiries are simply unacceptable; others are permissible only after a conditional job offer is made. The EEOC's Technical Assistance Manual for implementation of the ADA defines these pre-hire questions as improper:

- Have you ever been treated for any of these diseases? (specify)
- Have you ever been hospitalized? Why?
- Are there any health factors that prevent you from doing the job you applied for? (However, if the inquiry is restricted to specific job functions, it's permissible to ask about ability to perform those specific functions, and about potential accommodations.)

- How much sick leave did you take last year?
- Are you taking any prescribed medications?
- Have you ever been treated for substance abuse?

When it comes to pre-employment testing, it is discriminatory to give a test in a form or manner that requires the use of an impaired sensory, speaking, or manual skill, unless the point of the test is the degree to which that skill is present. Thus, an assembly-line job may legitimately require manual dexterity; but if the point is to test typing speed, a hearing-impaired person may have to be given a test that includes non-verbal commands as to when to start or stop. It may be necessary to have a test read aloud to a blind or dyslexic person, or to have a sign language interpreter. Of course, every effort should be made to administer the test in a room that is wheelchair-accessible.

➡ **TIP**

Applicants should be informed if there will be a test as part of the interview procedure; then it's up to them to explain the nature of any accommodation they require to take the test.

Pre-employment medical examinations are not allowed unless the candidate has already met the other criteria and a conditional job offer has been extended. Such examinations must be required of everyone in that job category who gets a conditional offer of employment. Once the offer has been made, it's acceptable to ask about past injuries and Worker's Compensation claims.

Post-offer medical examinations are considered non-discriminatory, and therefore it is not necessary to provide proof of business necessity. But if the disabled applicant is in fact qualified for the job, and the offer is withdrawn subsequent to the examination, the employer must show job-related business necessity for canceling the offer (e.g., the would-be employee poses a safety risk), and must also prove that reasonable accommodation to the disability could not be made without undue hardship.

For active employees, medical examinations and inquiries about the nature and severity of disability can be required only if they are job-related and consistent with business necessity (e.g., if someone has been ill or been injured, and the question is fitness to return to work).

The ADA also requires disability-related information to be kept confidential; in fact, it should be collected and maintained on separate forms, and even stored in files separate from general personnel information. However, there are three exceptions to the general rule of confidentiality:

- Supervisors and managers can be informed about work restrictions or accommodations that are needed

- If emergency treatment might be required for a disabled employee (e.g., an epileptic might have a seizure; a diabetic might go into insulin shock or coma), first aid and safety personnel can be informed so they'll be prepared

- Government officials investigating ADA compliance are entitled to information about the number of employees with disabilities, and the nature of those disabilities.

1.11 CREDIT REPORTING IN THE HIRING PROCESS

The federal statute, the Fair Credit Reporting Act (FCRA), 15 U.S.C. §1681a et.seq., and the amendments made by the Consumer Credit Reporting Reform Act of 1996, P.L. 104-208 (CCRRA), govern the use of credit reports and investigative credit reports not only for making loans and approving applications for credit cards, but in the employment context as well. (The amendments became effective September 30, 1997.)

A consumer report is a written or oral communication from a consumer reporting agency, dealing with a consumer's entitlement to credit, "character, general reputation, personal characteristics, or mode of living."

An investigative credit report is different in that it involves personal interviews with people who know something about the consumer (or think they do, anyway). The CCRRA requires employers to give job applicants a written disclosure statement, and to get their consent in writing before requesting either a consumer report or an investigative consumer report. Furthermore, if the employer wants an investigative report, it must explain to the applicant (via a written disclosure mailed no later than three days after the report is requested) that this type of report delves into matters such as character and conduct.

Under the FCRA, "employment purposes" (one of the legitimate reasons for requesting a credit report or investigative credit report [see 15 U.S.C. §1681b(3)(B)]) are defined to mean "evaluating a consumer for employment, promotion, reassignment or retention as an employee." Because the FCRA specifically authorizes the use of credit reporting information in the hiring process, doing so does not constitute employment discrimination.

An "adverse action" includes "denial of employment or any other decision for employment purposes that adversely affects any current or prospective employee." When the credit report is negative, leading to adverse action, the employer must give the consumer oral, written, or electronic (e.g. , fax or e-mail) notice of the adverse action. It must also explain how to review the credit report file, correct errors (for instance, "Betty W. Barnes" may be a deadbeat, but "Elizabeth M. Barnes" is someone else entirely, with a clean credit history) and contest items that the consumer believes to be untrue. Notice must be given after the employer makes the decision, but before the adverse action is implemented.

The CCRRA also imposes an obligation on the employer: before it gets any reports from a reporting agency, it must furnish the agency with a statement that the employer complies with the various consumer protection requirements of credit reporting law.

The FCRA includes an exception for a "report containing information solely as to transactions between the consumer and the person making the report," so the FCRA does not apply to the case of an employee fired when his drug urinalysis was positive for marijuana. The employee could not sue the employer under the FCRA, because there was no third party involved.

1.12 JOB APPLICATIONS

Frequently, the first real contact between the corporation and the potential employee occurs when the employee submits a formal job application. The application is, in fact, a legal document that can be quite significant to both employer and employee, both as a source of promises that the employer will be held to, and as a source of information for whose correctness the employee can be held responsible. For example, false statements on the application can constitute after-acquired evidence of wrongdoing that can reduce the damages available to a successful employee plaintiff (see page 538).

It often makes sense to have a candidate fill out a job application even if he or she has submitted a résumé. The résumé, after all, includes only the information the candidate wants to disclose. (Also, the application form is standard, and résumés are very variable; it's easier to compare applicants for the same job if you have the same data about each.) The application might, for instance, ask for:

- Positions held with the last three or four employers
- Dates of employment
- Job title
- Salary
- Name of immediate supervisor
- Why the candidate left that job (or if he or she is still employed)
- Permission to contact the supervisor for a reference.

One focus of anti-discrimination laws is to rule out certain lines of inquiry on job applications and during job interviews. Some questions may be permissible, but only if they are asked of all applicants (e.g., questions relating to physical capacity, travel, child care arrangements). Check state law about what inquiries you can make about applicants' arrest records; some states allow inquiries about *convictions*, but not about mere arrests.

> ➡ **TIP**
>
> In many states, if you require applicants to sign their applications, state privacy laws require that you must also give them a copy of the completed application.

The application should make it clear that the form is a legal document that can have serious ramifications. In particular, it should require the applicant to state that all information given on the application is complete and accurate—and that if the applicant is eventually hired, the employer will have grounds for discipline or dismissal if it discovers that false information was given on the application.

If the employer wants to get a credit report on the applicant, the application should have a signature line for the applicants to authorize release of this information. They should also be informed when reference checks will be performed. The form should clarify that application is being made for at-will employment; where accurate, it should also state that if a job offer is made, it is conditional on the applicant's passing a physical examination, including drug and alcohol testing.

1.13 SETTING TERMS AND CONDITIONS

If your company wants to employ at will (i.e., be able to terminate employees without extensive procedures), it's important to use the interview to stress the at-will nature of employment. Make sure that the people who do the interviewing understand this point, and that they do not make statements like "If you do a good job, you'll be set for life here" or "We never lay anybody off, no matter how tough the economy gets." Interviewers should also avoid statements about corporate procedures ("We go through all the channels before we fire anybody") unless those statements are accurate and reflect company policy.

Interviewers are agents of the company, and even if the employee handbook contains statements about written contracts being required to obligate the company, in fact it is likely to be held accountable for promises made by the interviewer (e.g., vacation terms, leave availability, education benefits).

Many companies set a salary range rather than an explicit pay rate for a particular job. Interviewers should understand whether or not they can negotiate a salary with a promising candidate, or if that matter will have to be referred to a higher-up. Interviewees should always be clear on who else is involved in the interview process, and what the powers are of each.

1.14 REFERENCE CHECKS

Employers who hire without checking references may be persuaded by an effective job interview, and may hire someone who has exaggerated or even invented credentials. The candidate may even be a convicted felon, whose interest in the company and its clients is not quite what the company had in mind! There are third-party companies that will perform simple records checks for $25-$35 per inquiry, and it's worth investing at least this much before extending a job offer. (In the case of a particularly important or particularly sensitive job, a more protracted investigation, or even retaining a private investigator, may be worthwhile.)

It's tempting, but imprudent, to take applicants' statements at face value. For reasons discussed in the materials on defamation (page 569), past employers may not be very forthcoming about an applicant's past performance or reasons for leaving. Nevertheless, employers will probably be willing to confirm the fact that someone was an employee, the dates of that employment, and the position(s) held. Even if they won't be willing to discuss why Jenny Whittaker left the company, they may be willing to say that Ms. Whittaker worked as a budget analyst, a position that reports to the head of the analysis department, and that Ms. Whittaker had three subordinates who reported to her. That information can be plenty to spot someone who exaggerated the importance of his or her job and the seniority of the position.

⇛ TIP

The way you ask the question can influence the answer. If you ask about the employee's strengths and talents, past employers may be more forthcoming than if you act like you're trying to find out what was wrong with the employee and how much dirt you can dig.

Academic references are also worth checking. In addition to outright fabrications, people may claim to have completed a degree program that they attended but did not finish; or they may claim a full-fledged degree when in fact they attended a less rigorous certificate program.

Although the best-case scenario is to do reference checks before making a job offer, it can be worth doing at a later stage. Finding out that an employee was not truthful can be a good reason to deny a raise or promotion. "After-acquired evidence" discovered as late as the time for preparation of a discrimination suit can be used to reduce the recovery the employee can obtain after proving his or her case.

Employers are not allowed to ask if a job applicant has ever been arrested: first, because such inquiries have disparate impact on minority-group males, and second, because far more people are arrested than are ever convicted or even charged with a crime. It is permissible to ask about criminal convictions, however. In some contexts, employers are *required* to ask about certain convictions: potential day care center or adult facility workers must be questioned about past histories of child or elder abuse. Furthermore, there are central registries of people convicted or investigated and found to have committed abuse. Certain health care and related employers have an obligation to consult the central registry within a few days after employing a person; the offer of employment should be withdrawn if any new hire appears in the registry.

1.15 REHIRING FORMER EMPLOYEES

Sometimes the hiring process seems like "déjà vu all over again." A company realizes that it cut too deep while downsizing. Employees leave because of differences of opinion, personality conflicts, or because they have been offered another job or start their own businesses. For these and other reasons an ex-employee returns to the fold. There are some obvious advantages to rehiring a one-time employee, because he or she is already familiar with the corporate culture and won't need a lengthy transition period to learn the way your company does things.

Rehiring can create morale problems at all levels. The rehired workers may still feel resentful about their initial termination; workers who were there all along may resent the bonuses, raises, and other incentives provided to rehirees. They may feel that if they went through the revolving door, they'd earn more and get more respect and be in line for better jobs. We all remember—and sometimes identify with—the non-prodigal son, who stayed put and probably felt entitled to the occasional fatted calf himself.

Chapter 2

EMPLOYEE HANDBOOKS

2.1 INTRODUCTION

Employee handbooks are traditional in large corporations, as a means of creating a uniform culture and distributing information about what can be a very diverse and far-flung business enterprise. A handbook can be a few photocopied sheets; an attractively printed book—or even part of a Website or intranet.

At first glance, the employee handbook seems like a non-controversial, non-problematic good thing. However, it must be drafted carefully and kept up to date to avoid legal problems. Many employers have discovered that they were held to provisions against their will, because of a statement in the handbook or the way it was interpreted.

2.2 LEGAL IMPLICATIONS OF THE HANDBOOK

Handbooks can play a useful role in training employees about the employer's expectations, and furnishing a ready source of reference about work rules. An employee facing discipline or discharge can reasonably argue that it's unfair to penalize someone for rulebreaking or for substandard performance, if that person has never been informed of what was expected or what would constitute adequate performance.

However, the handbooks can definitely be more trouble than they're worth if they are carelessly drafted so that they create implied contracts that are unwanted by the employer. All too often, employers have written something that's just supposed to sound impressive but have no real binding effect, only to find that it has become obligated to do something it would rather avoid. If something is described as a "corporate credo" or a "goal," it will probably not be treated as a contract, but you never can tell. Don't express goals unless you're prepared to follow through.

Once the employer is deemed to have created a contract, some courts will rule that the employer will not be able to amend that contract freely, without providing the employees with additional consideration for the change. Although some courts will agree that continued employment is adequate consideration (i.e., value in exchange for the employee's changed position), others say that employees must be given some additional benefit if the employer wants to alter the contract.

Make sure that you understand the applicable state and federal statutes, and that you are in conformity. For instance, a policy against leaves of less than one day might violate the Family and Medical Leave Act (see page 497) or might be tantamount to refusal to make reasonable accommodation to the disabilities of qualified employees, thus violating the Americans with Disabilities Act (ADA; see page 480).

2.2.1 At-Will Employment

A first line of defense for the employer is to include a disclaimer in the handbook, stating that employees are hired at will, can be discharged as the employer sees fit, and that the handbook information is for guidance only and does not bind the employer to a contract. Such disclaimers must be clear and conspicuous. They can't be buried in small print somewhere in the back of the book; in fact, the first page is an excellent location. When a disclaimer is issued, it doesn't apply to people who were already employees and working under the old policy.

The mere fact that the employer has a system of progressive discipline, spelled out in the handbook, does not stop the employees from working at will. Nevertheless, it makes sense to include a disclaimer explaining the function of the disciplinary system.

The more specific a provision is, the more likely that courts are to construe it as creating a formal contract. However, in order to win when they charge breach of this implied contract, employees may have to show detrimental reliance (i.e., that they changed their position because of the "contract," and were harmed by the change). At the very least, they will probably have to prove that they read the handbook. It's hard to claim that provisions in an unread handbook affected employment choices!

2.3 ORIENTATION CHECKLISTS

It's a good idea to provide orientation for new employees so they understand the way you do things. It's an even better idea to standardize the orientation process, with standard documents for welcoming and instructing new employees. Both the employee and the supervisor who handle the orientation should sign the document so that later on the employee can't claim that he or she was promised lifetime employment if the document clearly states that employment is at will. The checklist should cover subjects such as:

- The company's equal employment opportunity policies
- The unions that are already recognized as bargaining units (if any); the company's position on unionization and union activity. (Make sure that the union policies are lawful.)
- The formal probation process, if there is one; if so, what the employee has to do to become permanent. (Make sure that no promises of permanent or lifetime employment are made.)
- The new employee's job title, duties, and promotion path
- Compensation and benefits for the job (including vacation days, vacation banking, disability benefits, sick leave, options under the group health plan, and severance pay).
- Work rules
- Circumstances under which the employee can be terminated.

⟹ TIP

It isn't enough to indicate that employees will be on "probation" for a certain amount of time before hiring. They are still entitled to good faith and fair dealing from the employer. In fact, some courts will permit probationary employees to sue for wrongful termination, if the employer did not offer them long-term employment after the expiration of the probation period.

2.4 WORK RULES

Some organizations are small enough, informal enough, or simple enough in operation so that it is unnecessary to express the work rules in writing. In the larger organization, however, or even in a small operation that has multiple and potentially contentious work rules, a written list of rules, set out in the employee handbook or in a separate document, can be very useful. The text of the work rules should make it clear that the rules are established unilaterally by the employer, and can be modified by the employer at any time; the rules themselves are not a contract with the employees that must be negotiated with them or preserved intact.

Work rules deal with issues such as:

- Safety and security in the workplace (not letting in unauthorized persons; wearing protective equipment in a construction area or where hazardous chemicals are present)
- Emergency procedures (what to do if there is a fire, chemical spill, etc.)

- Where, if anywhere, in the workplace smoking is allowed; limitations on smoking breaks outside the workplace if smoking is banned within the workplace
- Dress and grooming—are uniforms required for any job titles? Which days, if any, are "casual days," and what is acceptable business casual attire? Are there any bans or limitations on facial hair, hairstyles, makeup, or jewelry?

⇒ **TIP**

Make sure that rules in this area do not infringe on employees' right to reasonable accommodation of their religious practices.

- Availability of paid and unpaid leave: how to request leave. Some companies maintain a no-fault absence policy, under which employees are permitted a certain amount of time off irrespective of why it is taken, but discipline can be imposed for excessive absence. A paid leave bank is similar, but allows unused days to be carried over or cashed out. See page 183 for more discussion of leave and time off.

⇒ **TIP**

Make sure that legal requirements for accommodation of disability and unpaid family leave are satisfied.

- Ban on horseplay, substance abuse, and taking products or materials (including waste and spoiled items) without permission
- Ban on solicitations within the workplace. A "no-solicitation" rule can be very helpful, not only in restricting union activity (see page 353 for a discussion of this issue) but in improving efficiency and avoiding conflict among employees. (It can get pretty expensive to come to work if every day you're asked to contribute to someone's favorite charity, or buy a present for someone who's leaving the company, getting married, having a baby, in the hospital . . .) To be effective, a no-solicitation rule must be appropriately communicated to employees, must be non-discriminatory, and must be applied uniformly. It would look like excellent evidence of discrimination if one employee is granted permission to sell raffle tickets for a Catholic church, while another one is denied permission to raise money for the NAACP, for instance.
- The extent to which employees are permitted to inspect their own personnel records, or show them to an attorney, union representative, etc. Check your state law; most states require employees to have access to their records, and also impose limitations on the extent to which personal information can be disclosed to anyone other than the employee.

- Ethical standards: for example, when it is permissible to accept gifts from a potential supplier; use of inside information; lobbying, political activities and donations
- Where to find further work-related information: for instance, through the company's Employee Assistance Program or on its intranet. (See Chapter 6 for more information about HR computing.)

Even though the work rules are not contractual in nature, it's a good idea for the employer to have employees sign a notice stating that they have received a copy of the work rules and had the opportunity to read and understand them. This notice serves as a rebuttal if, at a later date, the employee claims that he or she never saw the work rules and therefore should not be held subject to them.

➠ TIP

If you have an employee handbook at all, you must include in it the rights of the Family and Medical Leave Act (FMLA). If you don't want to write your own explanation of this somewhat confusing statute, you can reprint information from the Department of Labor's Wage and Hour Division; there is an FMLA Fact Sheet designed for this purpose.

2.5 SYSTEMS OF PROGRESSIVE DISCIPLINE

One approach to at-will employment is for the employer to take and maintain a consistent position that the employer is the sole arbiter of the quality of work performance, and that employees can be disciplined or fired based on the employer's unilateral determination that their work is unsatisfactory. However, in a unionized workplace, the collective bargaining agreement is almost certain to require a system of progressive discipline, under which employees will be warned about work deficiencies, admonished, and disciplined, but all the steps must be completed before discharge can occur.

Even non-union workplaces may adopt a system of progressive discipline for various reasons. They may find that it improves efficiency; workers may be genuinely unaware that their work is sub-par, and it's better all around if they can be admonished and then improve performance so there is no need to discharge them. Furthermore, if the employer offers a fair compensation package and a system of progressive discipline, employees may have little incentive to unionize.

The downside of this system is that it limits the employer's flexibility. Even in a non-union setting, the system may be interpreted by the courts as a contract. Once the system is implemented, it may have to be followed in the future.

Usually, a system of progressive discipline begins with an oral warning, explaining why the supervisor is dissatisfied with the employee's performance. The next step is a written warning. If performance is still unsatisfactory, discipline proceeds to a probationary period or suspension (unpaid suspensions usually last 3-5 days), then demotion or termination.

All the steps, including oral warnings, should be documented in the employee's personnel record. The written warning should include a place for the employee to sign (indicating that the document has been read), and the employee should be given a copy for reference. It is often worthwhile to give the employee a chance to include a brief written statement giving his or her side of the story. In a unionized workplace, the employee will probably be entitled to have a union representative present during investigatory interviews that could lead to disciplinary actions. In such cases, the collective bargaining agreement also sets many of the parameters of the investigation.

Also, it's important to monitor the cause of an employee's lateness or absences. If the employee has been injured (and qualifies for worker's compensation), is disabled as defined by the ADA, or is taking care of a sick family member (and therefore entitled to FMLA leave), then discipline or a discharge could constitute a violation of a relevant statute.

⇒ TIP

It's a good idea for the employer to reserve the right to cumulate several different disciplinary matters involving the same employee; even if individual problems are trivial, the employee who accumulates several of them could deserve harsher treatment.

Before discipline becomes serious, it will be necessary to investigate the facts of the case. Of course, the investigation should be documented, because there's a chance that state or federal discrimination or wrongful termination charges will be made.

Any termination decision should be reviewed by an objective second party, preferably after tempers have had time to cool, yet promptly enough to demonstrate the employer's efficiency and involvement. Before the actual termination occurs, the threatened termination should be reviewed for adequacy of process. (Were the appropriate warnings given? Did the investigation give enough weight to the employee's explanation? Was the employee treated in the same way as other similarly-situated employees, or did preconceptions influence the supervisor's judgment?)

⇒ **TIP**

If severance policies are reduced to writing and communicated to workers, they may take on the status of a welfare benefit plan for ERISA purposes, whereas a less formal policy would not constitute a plan. If there is no plan, and the employer has not entered into an express or implied contract governing the provision of severance benefits, then it is entirely at the employer's discretion to grant or withhold such benefits. In general, employees who are discharged for cause are not entitled to severance benefits—although, for instance the employee handbook may have been written in such general terms that it constitutes a contract to pay the benefits even for discharges for cause.

Chapter 3

EMPLOYEE RECORDS

3.1 INTRODUCTION

In their most benign aspects, employee records are "fuel" for efficient operation of the enterprise. They make it possible to set compensation, make sure it is paid appropriately, and administer benefit plans. The employer uses proper records to handle insurance matters, comply with court orders, assess employee performance, and determine who gets promoted or receives a bonus. Records demonstrate the company's EEO compliance, maintain data on employee performance and how it changes over time, prove that all employees had a legal right to work within the United States, and make it possible to issue accurate paychecks, comply with tax requirements, withhold and submit taxes on the proper schedule.

All companies must confer with their attorneys and set a regular policy of document *destruction*. Of course, documents must not be destroyed if their retention is legally required, if they are still useful, or if they are the subject of ongoing litigation. (Destroying documents that are subject to discovery is at least a civil offense subject to sanctions, and may constitute contempt of court or even a criminal offense, depending on circumstances.)

However, there is nothing suspicious about a company destroying all documents of a particular class as part of a standard program. The objective of the program is to have a regular schedule for reviewing each employee's file, then removing anything that is incorrect or obsolete from that file, and relocating documents that have been misfiled. Some companies schedule a regular "Trash Bash" for record maintenance.

⇒ **TIP**

All documents in personnel files should be date-stamped when they are received; it may be necessary to be able to state what was in the file at a particular time. For instance, if the company is accused of retaliating based on something the employee did, the employer could not have taken an action in November based on facts it did not learn until December!

The risk is that an unavailable document will give rise to sinister inferences that could have been dispelled by viewing the real document. For instance, if a personnel memo is destroyed as part of a clean-out, and the memo contained an ethnic joke, the jury might have chuckled, shrugged, or winced at this evidence of the supervisor's racial attitudes, depending on their own attitudes. But if the document is unavailable, the jurors may envision it as a full-scale expression of racial hatred.

⇒ **TIP**

If it is legal and practical to destroy a document, make sure that *all* paper copies have been destroyed, as well as all computer files (including back-ups and floppy disk copies). Just because a document has been deleted from a computer system, and no longer appears on the file listing, doesn't mean that a copy is not stored somewhere in the system (where it might be retrieved by a discrimination plaintiff). Get technical advice from a computer expert about how to make sure that deletion is complete.

⇒ **TIP**

Even if the company's policy about clearing out dead files is well-known, employees may resist, figuring that sooner or later they'll get in trouble if they DON'T have a copy of those documents. So make sure that employees are not penalized for carrying out the document-destruction policy.

3.2 RECORD RETENTION REQUIREMENTS

Various state and federal laws require retention of records (both records relating to individual employees and summaries reflecting the entire corporate experience) for periods of time that may be much longer than they would otherwise be kept. Record retention policy should be drafted bearing these requirements in mind.

1. **Title VII:** Personnel and employment records must be kept for six months; EEO-1 reports (see page 36) must also be kept for six months; records relating to a discrimination charge must be retained until the charge is disposed of.

2. **Equal Pay Act:** If a pay differential based on sex is imposed, records must be kept for two years.

3. **FMLA Records:** Records must be retained for three years.

4. **FICA/FUTA:** Both FICA and FUTA records (of withholding and employer payments) must be kept for four years.

5 **ERISA:** Records must be kept for six years.

6. **Federal Contractors:** Information about the employer's contractor status must be retained for three years. Records of the employment of Vietnam veterans must be retained for a year.

7. **OSHA:** Records relating to employee exposure to toxic substances must be kept for 30 years (not 3).

8. **Tax Records:** The minimum retention period is four years.

9. **ADEA:** Under 29 CFR §1627.3(b)(2), a benefit plan that is subject to the ADEA must be kept on file while the plan is in operation, and for at least one year after its termination.

3.2.1 Employee Access to Records

More than one-third of the states have laws that provide employees with access to their own employment records.

➠ TIP

Some of the laws limit access to current employees; ex-employees (including angry and potentially litigious ex-employees) do not have access under laws of this type.

At times, one employee will want to see other employees' records—for instance, to see if the same degree of discipline was imposed on employees who were late, spoiled work, were inefficient, or were otherwise subject to discipline. Usually the employee will only be able to gain access to other records with a court order. Whether a court will grant the order depends on a balancing test: whether the seeking employee's need for the records outweighs the privacy rights of the employees whose records are sought.

3.3 EEO RECORDS

The Equal Employment Opportunity Commission (EEOC) requires companies with 100 or more employees to file an annual report, the Employer Information Report, also known as the EEO-1. The EEO-1 is a simple two-page form that tracks the composition of the workforce. The due date is September 30 of each year. A copy of the most recent report must be kept on file at every company required to file (at the "reporting unit," or at the company's or division's headquarters). Although filing the EEO-1 is mandatory, it is not necessarily the end of the story: the EEOC has the right to require other reports about employment practices if it thinks additional reports are necessary to carry out Title VII or the Americans with Disabilities Act.

Records of application forms, requests for accommodation, and other employment-related data, must be preserved for one year. The one-year period starts either with collecting the data or taking personnel action, whichever is later. The personnel records of fired employees must also be retained for one year after the termination of employment.

If the employer becomes the subject of a discrimination charge, all records relating to the personnel action that the employee complains about must be retained until there has been a final disposition of the charge: either the case is over, or it is too late for employees to sue. See 29 CFR § 1602.14.

Users of pre-employment tests must maintain records specifically relating to test validation, including statistical studies to determine if the test has adverse impact on women, blacks, Native Americans, Asians, Hispanics, or non-Hispanic whites.

3.4 FMLA RECORDS

There is no particular form for keeping FMLA records, so any paper or electronic method can be used. The information that must be recorded is:

- Basic payroll data for each employee, such as hours worked; pay rate; supplemental wages or wage deductions; total compensation paid

- Dates on which FMLA leave was taken
- Hours of leave (if less than a day was taken)
- Copies of the employee's notice to the employer of impending leave
- Copies of the employer's disclosure materials about FMLA rights
- Documentation of the employer's leave policy
- Records of payment of premiums for employee benefits
- Records of any dispute about employee entitlement to leave, or to post-leave reinstatement.

⇒ TIP

Employee medical records, including certification of serious medical condition and fitness to return to work, are considered confidential, and should be kept physically separate from the employee's other records (so that unauthorized people will not gain access to the confidential medical data).

3.5 IMMIGRATION RECORDS

See page 16 for the information an employer must collect to verify identity and eligibility to work in the U.S. The required retention period is three years after the date of hiring (or the date of recruiting or referral for applicants who were not hired or did not accept a job offer). Certifications of employment eligibility furnished by state employment services must also be retained for three years. For former employees, the record retention period is three years after hiring, or one year after termination, whichever is later.

3.6 EMPLOYMENT TAX RECORDS

A newly hired employee should always be asked to provide a W-4 (withholding exemptions) form, so the appropriate number of exemptions can be used to calculate the withholding amount. An employee about to retire should be asked for Form W-4P to determine susceptibility to pension withholding, and the amount to be withheld. (See page 104).

According to IRS Publication 15, the Employer's Tax Guide, at least the following information must be collected about employment tax, and made available for IRS review on request:

- Dates and amounts of all payments of wages and pensions

- Fair market value of any wages paid other than in cash (e.g., in merchandise or services)

- For each employee: name, address, Social Security number, and job title

- Dates each employee started and terminated employment

- Dates and amounts of any payments you made, or an insurer or other third party paid, to employees who were out sick or after an injury

- Copies of W-4 and W-4P forms (withholding exemptions)

- Whatever W-2 forms you sent to employees, but that were returned as undeliverable

- Copies of all your tax returns

- Records of when tax deposits were made, and how much was deposited.

3.7 UNEMPLOYMENT INSURANCE RECORDS

FUTA records, as noted above, should be retained for four years from the date the tax becomes due or when it is paid, whichever is later. The records must be open to inspection by the IRS. FUTA records must show the total amount of remuneration to employees in the calendar year, the amount of wages subject to tax, and the contributions made to the state unemployment insurance funds of each state in which the company does business.

Furthermore, records must be maintained and kept available for inspection by state unemployment tax officials. For each pay period, records must be compiled showing the dates the period starts and ends, and the total remuneration (including commissions) paid in the period.

Records to be kept for each worker include:

- Name
- Social Security Number
- Date hired, rehired, terminated
- Place of work
- Wages for each payroll period
- Wage rate
- Date wages paid
- Amount of expense reimbursement granted
- Time lost each week when worker is unavailable for work.

Although unemployment insurance information can be released to government agencies other than the unemployment security agency (for instance, agencies that collect child support obligations), in general the information is confidential and should not be disclosed to unauthorized parties.

3.8 EMPLOYEE EVALUATIONS

Quality expert W. Edward Deming called performance appraisals "a deadly disease"—and this sometimes literally becomes true, when performance appraisals are treated as evidence of employment discrimination. Theoretically, a performance appraisal should make it possible to pinpoint problems within an organization. The goal is to find out which employees are not performing up to par, why they're not doing well, and give them the training, encouragement, or even the equivalent of a kick in the pants to make them improve. When it's time to award merit raises and bonuses, the performance appraisal should indicate who the stars are.

However, they usually don't work this way. There are many reasons for this:

- Managers don't have time to do a thoughtful job of appraising performance, so they err on the side of generosity

- It may not seem as if the appraisals are ever used for anything, so managers put down whatever seems least controversial (or just do a little cosmetic updating on last year's forms).

- In a large work group, they may not know very much about what individual employees are doing

- Managers want the employees who report to them to like them, and are afraid that a tough-minded appraisal could create hostility and reduce motivation

- Ambitious managers may want to give themselves an indirect pat on the back: if all their subordinates are real stars, they themselves must be exceptional leaders.

- A bad appraisal could be attacked as the product of racism, sexism, sexual harassment, etc. (On the other hand, a series of unjustified good appraisals frequently dooms the employer who attempts to claim that a discrimination plaintiff was fired for good cause.)

The best performance reviews not only protect the company in case of litigation—they identify real problems in employee performance and give insights into solutions. Some of the basic issues for performance reviews include:

- Whether the quantity of work performed by the employee has been satisfactory

- Quality of work

- The extent to which the employee has demonstrated knowledge of the job
- Dependability, initiative, and adaptability
- The extent to which the employee has mastered new skills needed in the job and new skills that will be required in the foreseeable future
- Cooperation, attendance, punctuality
- Areas in which the employee needs to improve.

At a minimum, the employee should see a written performance appraisal, should have an opportunity to discuss it, and should be asked to sign indicating that he or she has read the document. (If the employee refuses to sign, there should be a way for the supervisor to indicate this.) It's preferable to allow the employee to add written comments to the record. (Some states make this a legal requirement.)

The modern form of appraisal is the "360-degree review," where workers are rated by more than one person, including co-workers and customers. However, it can be quite cumbersome to get the additional input, and favorable comments can reflect an employee's popularity rather than skills (or "you-scratch-my-back-I'll-scratch- yours" reciprocity). An alternative might be to substitute more frequent but less formal reviews: e.g., after the end of every project, or after every quarter or twice a year.

3.9 GRIEVANCE RECORDS

If your company is unionized, or if it has adopted a grievance procedure of a type similar to that found in collective bargaining agreements, then over the years various employees will assert grievances over disciplinary actions or the way they have been treated within the workplace. See page 525 for a discussion of grievance and arbitration issues when employment discrimination is alleged. Remember, though, that many grievances involve workplace disputes in which there is no allegation of discrimination.

It makes sense to buy or design standard forms for keeping track of employee grievances, although there is no specific federal requirement for making those records or retaining them for any particular length of time. The grievance form should contain:

- Identification of the CBA that creates the grievance procedure, and the specific clause of that contract that has to be interpreted
- Date the grievance was submitted
- Grievance case number
- Name, department, shift, and job title of the employee who submits the grievance

- What the employee says is wrong
- Records of statements by witnesses; documentary evidence bearing on the employee's grievances
- Whether the employee was represented (e.g., by the shop steward)
- Written decisions by the first-level supervisor and everyone else involved in higher levels of grievance processing
- A signed statement by the union representative as to whether the union considers the grievance to be adequately resolved
- Signatures of the employee and all decision-makers.

It can be very helpful to analyze grievances and see how patterns change over time—especially to see if past problems have been resolved, and to identify possible problem areas. If employees allege sexual harassment or other forms of hostile work environment, the employer has a burden of investigating the claim thoroughly, or it will become liable.

Chapter 4

WORK–FAMILY ISSUES

4.1 INTRODUCTION

Work-family issues didn't arise when most people were farmers and the whole family labored together to raise food and cash crops. The problems were muted when most family units consisted of a male breadwinner and a stay-at-home wife. But this configuration didn't work during World War II, when most of the men were needed in military service and millions of women had to be employed in paid jobs to keep defense plants and civilian industry operating. During that crisis, employers responded by offering improved transportation and child care, so working mothers could reconcile family and home responsibilities.

For a couple of decades after World War II, most (although not all) families followed the breadwinner/homemaker pattern. Since the 1970s, however, paid employment by married women, including married women with children, has increased to the point that now most married couples are two-earner couples. If, as a result of personal preference, further education, or job loss there is only one breadwinner, it might be the wife rather than the husband.

There are also new kinds of families developing, and their needs will also influence the workplace: single parents (by birth or adoption), blended families after divorce and remarriage, older parents, and grandparents raising grandchildren. More and more fathers are discovering the rewards of greater involvement in child rearing and child development, so the parent seeking leave, flexible work hours, or resigning to care for children full-time might be a married or single father. To an increasing extent, employees in the "sandwich" generation face elder care responsibilities for their aging parents as well as, or long after, their child care responsibilities.

Becoming family-friendly can enhance a company's profitability, especially by reducing turnover. A survey done by chemical company Hoechst Celanese finds that employees place great value on flexible work hours—a policy that has NO direct cost to the employer, but that promotes loyalty and longer tenure with the company.

However, work-family policies can have a downside, if single employees or married employees who do not have children feel that they are expected to do extra work to cover for employees taking family-related leave. A more constructive approach might be to find cost-effective adjustments to the benefit package so that the needs of employees with and without family responsibilities can be met. A "work-life" package could provide flexibility for a single person's hobbies, as well as a parent's involvement in youth sports or an employee's elder care responsibilities.

4.2 CHILD CARE OPTIONS AT WORK (HARRIED, WITH CHILDREN)

One option, perhaps the most appreciated by employees, is for the employer to maintain an on-site day care center. Employees would especially value a center that is open longer than conventional 9-to-5 office hours, or one that makes provision for children with minor illnesses.

It can be difficult for the employer to calculate the costs and benefits of running a day care center. Initial expenses can be high, but so can the benefits, such as greatly increased retention of experienced and valued employees who return to work after maternity leave instead of quitting.

An on-site day care center is only feasible for a large company, and probably only feasible outside big cities (because big-city rents and real estate costs are often prohibitively high). An employer-sponsored day care center must go through a licensing process, will be subject to ongoing inspections, and could create liability if, for instance, a child is injured on premises, or if a number of children develop a contagious illness.

➠ TIP

Employer-operated day care centers are also excluded under the standard Worker's Compensation insurance policy, so the none-too-exotic injuries to workers that might ensue could become the subject of expensive litigation.

Much of the inconvenience can be avoided by contracting out the daily operations to an experienced provider of high-quality child care, but this will add a further set of expenses. Or the employer can co-sponsor a nearby child care center that also cares for children of parents who work for other companies.

A much more usual option is for the employer to provide reimbursement of a portion of employees' child care expenses. (See page 179 for a discussion of dependent care fringe benefits and their tax implications.) A smaller-scale program offers information and referral to child care resources, but does not actually provide services or funds.

Creative companies don't always need elaborate, formal programs. One option that can work for very young infants (i.e., those that don't run around and get into things!) is for a parent to bring the child to work and take responsibility for feeding, diapering, and other care tasks—as long as other employees in the department choose not to exercise their veto power.

> **⇒ TIP**
> Rotating shifts are not only hard for workers to adapt to, but greatly increase their child care problems. Unless there's some reason why workers must rotate rather than have a stable first, second, or third shift assignment, merely guaranteeing a stable shift improves productivity and job satisfaction for workers with young children.

4.3 ADOPTION ASSISTANCE

Employers are taking an increasing role in assisting employees who wish to become parents through adoption. (See page 180 for the tax consequences of offering adoption assistance.)

> **⇒ TIP**
> All companies must offer unpaid leave under the FMLA for adoptions.

According to the National Adoption Center (located in Philadelphia) the average cost of an adoption is $12,000, and in some instances (if the legal situation is complex, or a child is being adopted from outside the United States), the costs could exceed $30,000—obviously sums that many employees would find difficult to pay without assistance.

> **⇒ TIP**
> A free publication, *The Employer's Guide to Adoption*, can be obtained (with additional information about creating an adoption assistance program) from the Adoption Benefits Coordinator, National Adoption Center, 1500 Walnut Street, Suite 701, Philadelphia, PA, 19102, (215) 735-9988.

Although adoption assistance might seem like a very costly benefit, in fact only a few employees become adoptive parents each year. (Adoption assistance programs usually are limited to adoption of an unrelated child, not a step-parent adoption of a new spouse's children by a former marriage.)

⇒ **TIP**

IRS Announcement 97-6, 1997-26 IRB 9, clarifies the rules for reporting employer-provided adoption benefits on the recipient's W-2 form.

4.4 CORPORATE ELDER CARE ACTIVITIES

It's well-understood that, difficult as it often is, raising children is an exciting business that involves a great deal of pride and happiness. But, even though many employees spend more years taking care of aging parents and in-laws than they do raising children, we don't even have a term for "lowering" parents.

The process of elder care is often difficult, expensive, and emotionally stressful. Instead of seeing a child gain new skills and get ready to face the world independently, the "sandwich generation" employee (caught between parental and child needs and demands) has to face the parent's physical and perhaps mental decline. A parent who once was strong, active, and proud may be unable to perform the simplest physical task, may even have forgotten who spouse and children are.

4.4.1 Productivity Impact

Caring for the disabled elderly has an immense impact on the family life of the caregivers—and on their productivity as employees. A 1995 study by AARP and the National Alliance for Caregiving estimates that U.S. industry loses at least $11.4 billion a year in productivity when employee caregivers have to take emergency time off, leave early, or are interrupted at work. The same organizations' 1996 survey estimates that there are about 14.4 million employee caregivers in the U.S.

Caregivers spend an estimated average of 15 hours a week taking care of their aging relatives, and sometimes these tasks have to be performed during working hours. In some instances, caregivers have to switch from full-time to part-time work, or quit their paying jobs entirely; and stress can make caregiver employees much less productive when they are at the office.

In 1996, Hewitt Associates found that 30% of major corporations now offer elder care benefits: 79% information and referral services (I&R), 25% had a long-term care insurance plan, and 17% provided counseling to help caregivers cope with stress and make practical plans. Under an I&R plan, the Employee Assistance Program, HR department, or other relevant department maintains listings of nursing homes, home health agencies, government agencies for the aging, and other resources.

A fairly low-cost option is for the corporation to offer employees and their parents access to long-term care insurance (LTCI). Group LTCI premiums are much lower than individual premiums. Most employment-related LTCI plans are "employee-pay-all" so the employer's only cost is a small amount for administration and employee communications.

However, the Health Insurance Portability and Accountability Act of 1996 (HIPAA) clarifies some previously murky tax questions. In effect, it places "qualified" LTCI plans that satisfy Internal Revenue Code standards on the same footing as Accident and Health (A&H) plans. So, should the employer choose to provide such coverage, the employer will be entitled to deduct the premiums, and employees will not have taxable income if they receive up to $175 a day in LTCI benefits (or a greater amount reimbursed under a plan that pays on the basis of actual costs rather than a set amount per day). Employees who pay for qualified policies themselves will be entitled to a tax deduction for the premium; the maximum deduction depends on the age of the purchaser.

> ⮕ **TIP**
>
> However, HIPAA also makes it clear that LTCI cannot be provided through either a cafeteria plan or a flexible spending account.

Chapter 5

DIVERSITY IN THE WORKPLACE

5.1 INTRODUCTION

At one time, most workplaces were quite homogeneous, with a workforce drawn from the surrounding area. Sons would follow their fathers into "the mill" or the office, joined by their brothers and cousins, then retiring at 65 with a gold watch from the appreciative employer. Handicapped people were kept out of sight. There might be a few workers who were suspected of being insufficiently masculine, or even downright homosexual—but they were at pains to deny it. They certainly didn't turn up at the company picnic with a male life partner in tow. Although the workers might be immigrants or the children of immigrants, it was a pretty sure bet that the managers would be college-educated, Anglo-Saxon white males. Whatever the problems and tensions within the operation, comparatively few of them would be caused by racial, religious, nationalistic, or cultural friction.

Today, of course, the picture has changed. Although the majority of the U.S. workforce is male, there is a high proportion of female workers, most, but not all of whom hold traditionally "feminine" jobs such as clerical work and nursing. There are many immigrants and children of immigrants in the workforce, but now they are more likely to come from Asia and the Pacific, or from Latin America, than from the European countries that dominated earlier waves of immigration. Some of them are fluent in English; some know only a few words. Black and Hispanic workers are no longer limited to segregated workspaces or menial jobs.

It would be delightful, but unrealistic, to pretend that greater workplace diversity has been achieved without a struggle, and that managing a diverse workforce is easy. Nor do all the problems come from the proverbial "angry white males." Anybody can be prejudiced, hostile, intolerant, blinded by stereotypes, ignorant of other peoples' traditions, or just plain hard to work with. Furthermore, a company can be doing its level best to offer equal opportunity—while women and minorities believe that they have little access to good assignments or promotions, and white males simultaneously feel that any advantage available will go to a woman or minority-group member.

The HR manager's mission is not to turn the workplace into a multicultural Eden where Swedish-Americans season their Russian pelmeni with Vietnamese fish sauce and there's a piñata at every Christmas party. Once they leave the workplace, employees can say vicious things about each other, laugh at deeply bigoted ethnic jokes, and associate only with people who are just like themselves. A company's workforce doesn't have to worship together, enjoy the same sporting events, celebrate the same holidays, or even like each other. What it does have to do is understand the factors shaping other peoples' behavior, strive to avoid offending others, be tolerant of unintended offensive remarks and actions, and work together harmoniously and productively.

⇒ **TIP**

For some tested techniques of diversity management, see *Career* magazine's Diversity Initiative Program website, http://www.careermag.com/diversity, or call(303) 440-3386 for more information.

5.2 THE GLASS CEILING

Unfortunately, some people are actively and consciously hostile to those different from themselves, and engage in whatever discriminatory actions they think they can get away with. However, overt hatred and resentment are not the only factors that block full advancement of qualified women and members of minority groups. There are other, subtler forces at work, and sometimes they involve people who on a conscious level are tolerant and objective.

For one thing, the prejudices of the past cast a long shadow. If law and business schools used to discriminate against women and minorities, then the supply of women and minorities with professional degrees will be reduced. Corporate hiring that makes a (reasonable) demand for a professional degree will continue to concentrate on white males.

Similarly, if a company hardly ever recruits women or minority members for its training program, and if its policy is to promote from within, then it will look to its (overwhelmingly white male) middle managers when it's time to select senior executives. Qualified people may not even bother to apply to professional schools or internships if they don't think they have a chance. Of course, people who never bother to apply never get hired.

These subtler barriers are sometimes called the "glass ceiling": women and minorities can advance to a certain degree, but come up against invisible barriers when it comes to getting the really top jobs. Is this a real phenomenon, or just a perception (or just an excuse used by people who have not achieved as much as they would like)?

The Civil Rights Act of 1991, Public Law 102-166, contains a provision called the Glass Ceiling Act. The Glass Ceiling Act established a federal commission to study the status of corporate opportunities for women and minority group members. The commission drafted several reports, which are available at Cornell University's labor law website, **http://www.ilr.cornell.edu/lib/bookshelf/e-archive/GlassCeiling**.

According to the Executive Summary of the main report, "A Solid Investment: Making Full Use of the Nation's Human Capital": "Many judgments on hiring and promotion are made on the basis of a look, the shape of a body, or the color of skin." The report agrees with Ann Morrison's conclusion in her 1992 report, "The New Leaders: Guidelines on Leadership Diversity in America," that prejudice is the single most important barrier to female and minority advancement into, and within, executive ranks.

In 1990, according to Census figures, the makeup of the overall workforce was 43.2% white males, 35.6% white females, 4.7% black males, 5.3% black females, 4.6% Hispanic males, and 3.2% Hispanic females (with smaller groups of Asian and Native American workers).

The study finds that close to 97% of male managers in leading corporations are white; less than 1% each are black, Asian, or Hispanic. Black males and females hold only 2.5% of senior positions in the private sector, and they earn much less than their white male counterparts: black women earn 60% of what white men earn, and black men earn 79% of white male compensation. Opportunities for female and minority managers and professionals are much greater in the public than in the private sector; yet such positions are typically less prestigious and far less well-paid than major corporate office.

As for glass ceiling barriers to female advancement, it should be noted that 998 of the Fortune 1000 companies have male CEOs. About 95% of executives at the Vice President level and above are male. Corporate Boards of Directors usually include only white males.

Although the Glass Ceiling report acknowledges that some factors (such as educational systems and social attitudes) are outside corporate control, the report identifies some factors that corporations CAN control:

- Whether recruitment is narrow or broad-based; whether outreach efforts are made

- Assigning female and minority new hires to marginal areas or staff jobs that have less promotion potential than more central, line jobs

- Presence or absence of mentors

- Whether access to training and prime assignments reflects individual abilities and performance, or whether prejudice is at work

- Access to social events and informal networks (e.g., social and sporting events)
- Whether colleagues are helpful and supportive, or hostile and demeaning
- Whether evaluations are objective or reflect prejudices.

The report noted that successful programs to promote corporate diversity tend to share certain characteristics:

- The CEO actively supports the program
- The program is comprehensive and inclusive; it genuinely seeks to advance the most talented people of whatever background
- Results are reviewed, and managers are accountable for results.

There are also factors that help determine whether an executive will be successful and promotable. Giving women and minorities access to broad experience in the business, in "line" (marketing, finance, production) as well as in staff jobs, giving them good initial job assignments, and giving them access to information (including information provided by mentors) will help break through the glass ceiling.

5.3 DIVERSITY TRAINING

Corporations frequently attempt to defuse hostilities within the workplace by offering, or requiring, diversity training, usually provided by outside contractors. The training might be a voluntary initiative by management, a part of a negotiated settlement with the EEOC or with a state anti-discrimination agency, or part of the settlement of a case in litigation. The mission of the training is to make employees examine their assumptions and to relate to other employees in a more professional manner.

The goals of corporate diversity training include:

- Finding areas in which the organization is defective
- Setting goals for improvement
- Creating specific steps for reaching the goals
- Training employees to carry out those steps.

5.3.1 Risks and Disadvantages

- Ironically, diversity training programs sometimes wind up as evidence in employees' Title VII suits. A well-intentioned program that was supposed to promote understanding and harmony can worsen anger and resentment that were already present, but simmered below the surface. Poorly-chosen exercises can encourage employees to vent their frustration, use the vilest racial epithets, and otherwise create breaches that are hard to heal.

- Minority employees may feel that the programs are just window-dressing, something the company does instead of hiring and promoting qualified applicants. They may also resent having to "represent" their ethnic groups in ways that are not expected of white males. There is an ongoing debate in our society over whether homogenization is possible or desirable, or whether individuals should retain distinct cultural identity and identification with a group even after many generations in the United States.

- The materials generated by the company to examine its diversity record might be ruled non-privileged, and therefore discoverable in a discrimination suit. (See page 573 for a discussion of the self-critical analysis privilege, which might protect the materials from discovery.) The attempt to reach out to traditionally disfavored groups might also be treated as reverse discrimination, or as prolongation of an affirmative action program after correction of the initial discrimination. (Affirmative action programs are discussed at page 472.)

- The advice of some management experts and of some minority-group members is different: it may be impossible to eradicate prejudices, but perhaps corporations can recognize talent and performance even in people against whom they harbor prejudices. In this analysis, what counts is hiring and promotion, not formal diversity training programs.

5.4 ENGLISH-ONLY RULES

It's easy to imagine a situation in which the ability to speak and understand English fluently is a legitimate job qualification. However, a person can be fluent in English even though it is not his or her first language, and he or she may be more comfortable speaking other languages. If the employer puts a ban on speaking languages other than English within the workplace, it's easy for national-origin minority groups to show disparate impact.

The employer who imposes such a rule must be able to demonstrate job-relatedness and business necessity: for instance, a showing that there is no other way to communicate in an emergency or to serve the needs of customers or patients. However, it would be hard to justify the business necessity of forbidding employees to converse in a non-English language during meals or breaks, or while they are in the restroom or locker room.

The EEOC's National Origins Guidelines say that merely implementing an English-only rule has disparate impact. However, the Ninth Circuit rejected these guidelines, requiring proof that the rule creates a hostile work environment for employees whose first language is not English, or proof that the rule is imposed on employees who experience difficulty in speaking English. At press time, several suits were pending.

⇒ **TIP**

Although an English-only rule is problematic, it's important for employees to be able to communicate, especially to avoid danger or cope with workplace emergencies. Therefore, a workplace English class, centering around work-related vocabulary and concepts, can be an excellent idea. This is especially true if the workplace includes employees with several or even many native languages: English becomes a means by which they can all communicate, with each other and with native English-speakers. By the same token, it makes sense for co-employees and supervisors to learn at least a few critical terms in the other employees' language(s).

Because paperwork, computer use, and documentation are so important, classes to enhance English literacy skills (of native-born as well as immigrant employees) can be productive.

5.4.1 *Bilingual Employees*

Where a large proportion of employees or customers speak languages other than English, bilingual employees (whether native speakers or those who have learned in other contexts) can be invaluable. For example, they can handle telephone inquiries by customers with limited English, or can communicate between a shop-floor worker who speaks Polish and Russian but only a few words of English, and a supervisor who is fluent in Spanish and English.

Should the bilingual employees get a higher pay rate because of this additional skill? Some say yes, others say that the pay rate should be uniform for the job, not adjusted for personal characteristics of the worker. Further, language skills may have been acquired at home or in the neighborhood, without specific training or effort on the bi- or multilingual employee's part. An employer that doesn't provide a premium for additional languages might find its employees vulnerable to recruitment incentives from companies that do.

⇒ **TIP**

If you do decide to offer a premium for language skills, make sure you budget enough—you might discover that, say, 55% of your workforce qualifies, rather than the 25% you anticipated.

5.5 PROMOTING DIVERSITY

Whether you have a genuine commitment to equality of opportunity, or simply don't want to get sued, here are some steps you can take:

- Broaden your recruitment efforts—don't just recruit at the nearest colleges, or only accept Ivy League resumes. Low-cost public colleges attract some excellent students who couldn't afford a private institution, so don't rule them out as recruitment arenas.

- Reward (with raises, bonuses, and promotions) managers who increase the diversity of their workforces; employee surveys can be an interesting (or humbling) way of testing the success of diversity programs

- Check your diversity efforts against those of competitors

- Make sure that newly hired female and minority candidates get the training, access to information, and networking that they need to succeed

- Remind everyone that, even though it might further their prejudices to sabotage someone else's career, it will probably hurt the corporation's efficiency and bottom line (even if it doesn't lead to an expensive lawsuit!)

- Remind everyone that written documents, recorded phone messages, and e-mail can be found at a later date (or discovered as part of a suit), so discretion is especially important in these media.

Chapter 6

THE ROLE OF THE
COMPUTER IN HR

6.1 INTRODUCTION

Corporate human resources functions have always been number-intensive, from calculating a payroll to preparing reports on the nature of the workforce. Hence, the HR department was an "early adopter" of all kinds of technology, from tabulating machines to mainframe computers using punched cards, to the desktop PC, to today's networked systems (that, ironically, have something in common with the old-style mainframe and "dumb terminals").

In addition to computer usage within the operation (or outsourcing of functions such as payroll preparation and compliance with tax reporting), computer communications are gaining importance. As discussed in this chapter, the Internet offers vast information and calculation resources for the HR department.

Furthermore, a corporate intranet can be developed to communicate effectively with employees. Instead of having to print a lengthy manual, then reprint new pages as laws and corporate policies change, the material can be input into computer-usable form (whether by keying it in, transferring it from disk or tape, or scanning it) then displayed on the intranet, which is a private network available only to authorized persons. (There can be various levels of security within the intranet, perhaps safeguarded by passwords, so all employees have access to basic information like the corporate policy manual, but only those who need to know have access to salary information and employee performance ratings.) Corporate intranets can also be used for training, for job postings within the organization, and for advice about how to deal with the health plan and save for retirement.

Congress has recognized the important part that computers play in pension administration. The 1997 tax law contains a provision giving the Department of the Treasury and the Department of Labor from August 5, 1997 to December 31, 1998 to issue guidance on the way to use "new technologies" (e-mail, voice response, computers) to keep records, make disclosures, and give notices under the Internal Revenue Code and ERISA. The guidance will also explain the extent to which required "writings" can be done electronically.

6.2 DOING RESEARCH ON THE NET

In addition to the immense online bookstores (such as Amazon, **http://www. amazon.com**) that have books about everything, and therefore have books about HR topics, there are specialized sites that concentrate on the HR function. The Society for Human Resources Management (SHRM) has a secure commerce server for online book orders (in other words, it's safe to give your credit card number) at **http://shrmstore.shrm.org**. HRMagazine's site, **http://www.hrhq.com**, has a "conference room" for on-line chat with other HR professionals.

Many law firms maintain websites and, as a means of showing off their expertise, they offer important information about legal developments and how to apply them in practice. Publishers are also a good source of online information. Fidelity Publishing has a subscription newsletter, the Independent Contractor Report; but to publicize the newsletter, it has a site at **http://www.webcom.com/ic_rep** with lots of free, useful information.

Organizations frequently use the Web to post information and increase their visibility. If you need information about outplacement, or need to find an experienced, professional outplacement firm in your area, check the Association of Outplacement Consulting Firms' site, at **http://www.aocfi.org**. The International Foundation of Benefit Plans hangs its hat in cyberspace at **http://www. ifepb.org**. ADIA, a consulting firm that concentrates on temporary services, has a site with much information about temporary work, and links to many other sites, at **http://www.adia.com**.

The Department of Labor has an immense bank of information on the web, but the site doesn't always run quickly, and finding the specific information you need can be difficult.

> ➠ **TIP**
>
> HRMagazine's home page has a site map that helps users be more productive in accessing government information: **http://www.shrm.org/cyberspace/**).

The main site is **http://www.dol.gov**. The Bureau of Labor Statistics reports the relative strengths of various employment sectors and employment cost trends: **http://stats.bls.gov/blshome.html**. It also disseminates statistics on occupational safety and health: **http://stats.bls.gov/oshhome/htm**; OSHA's home page is

http://www.osha.gov. Federal contracting compliance information is available from the Employment Standards Administration, **http://www.dol.gov./dol/esa/public/ofcp_org.htm**).

The Pension and Welfare Benefits Administration's online site is **http://www.dol.gov/pwba/**. For Workers' Compensation information, see **http://www.dol.gov/dol/esa/public/owcp org.htm**. The Wage and Hour Division's subsection in the DOL page is **http://www.dol.gov/dol/esa/public/whd org.htm**. See **http://www.ttrc.doleta.gov/citizen/** for the DOL's Corporate Citizenship Resource Center that profiles companies which have implemented exemplary work-family programs.

Private sites that may be of interest to HR professionals include:

- Work/Family Forum, **http://www.workfamily.com/forum/default.htm**
- Labor Base (records of petitions filed for union representation), **http://www.cin.ix.net/anh/nlrb-db.html**
- AboutWork (career development advice and strategies), **http://www.aboutwork.com**
- Work & Family Connection (including descriptions of programs at model companies), **http://www.workfamily.com**
- Wageweb (survey data on typical compensation level for various jobs, designed for use in setting salary levels), **http://www.wageweb.com**

There are so many HR resources available on-line that it would be too time-consuming to use an ordinary search engine to find and work through them all. Therefore, "meta-indexes" have been developed: World Wide Web home pages that offer links to information-rich sites that are free of ads, or at least offer objective content in addition to advertising. Sites that may repay your interest include:

- HR Links (Society of Human Resources Management), **http://www.shrm.org/hrlinks/**
- Cornell University's School of Industrial Labor Relations, **http://workindex.com**
- HR Professional's Gateway to the Internet (compiled by Eric Wilson), **http://www.teleport.com/~erwilson/**
- Human Resources Management Resources on the Internet (Nottingham Trent University) **http://www.nbs.ntu.ac.uk/staff/1yerj/hrm link.htm**

The Internet works very well for delivering content prepared by someone else, but its real strength is interactivity. Sometimes you can get involved in real-time "chat" (so far, this usually involves typing in your queries and responses, although speech and videoconferencing are becoming more popular, less expensive, and easier to use). In other instances, you use e-mail to pose a question to a group of HR professionals; their answers may come directly to you, be shared with all other participants, or both. HR-oriented chat and messaging can be found, for example, at:

- HR Talk (limited to SHRM members), **http://www.shrm.org/hrtalk**
- Sobeco Ernst & Young (emphasis on Canadian topics, but significant US content), **http://htnews.idirect.comhrnews.html**

6.3 THE INTERNET AS A RECRUITING TOOL

According to consulting firm The Internet Business Network, more than 1.2 million job postings are already available online, and there are more than a million resumes available for search. Many of the postings and resumes involve computer and other technical jobs, but more and more people (especially recent graduates) are computer and Internet-savvy even if they were liberal arts majors!

There have been comparatively few instances of actual hiring based on these ads and resume postings, but the potential of the Internet for recruiting is becoming better recognized. In 1996, for instance, Coopers & Lybrand estimates that it saved about $200,000 in executive search fees by adding an electronic component to its recruitment process.

➟ TIP
___

If your corporation has a Website, you can easily and inexpensively add an area for posting job opportunities, and you can include an electronic "form" to fill out so even candidates who don't have a resume in electronic form can submit their qualifications. (Those who do have an electronic resume should be asked to submit it in ASCII form to avoid format incompatibilities.) The form can be used to screen out hopeful would-be applicants whose qualifications are not appropriate for the job at issue.

➟ TIP
___

For a copy of SHRM's "Net Working '97: A Research Study on Employment and the Internet," contact Tena Olson, Marketing Director, JWT Specialized Communications, at 6500 Wilshire Boulevard, Los Angeles, CA, 90048, (213) 655-4262.

6.4 CREATING AND MANAGING AN INTRANET

There's nothing mysterious about the Internet: it's just a "backbone" that links millions of computers worldwide that use a common method of dividing information into "packets," then send the packets to other computers and reassemble them at the destination computer. The method of sending the information packets is a program called TCP/IP. Originally, documents sent on the Internet tended to be written in a computer language called the Hypertext Markup Language (HTML). The World Wide Web is a subsection of the Internet, the part that uses Graphical User Interfaces (GUI) to display rich pictorial content. To an increasing extent, sounds and video are being added to the pictorial resources of the Web.

Internet/Web technology has many advantages: it's mature enough so that many tools are available for every price range, skill level, and design objective. Many people have the computer equipment and skills to access this content and even to contribute their own interactive content.

However, there are many reasons why corporate content should not be placed on the public Internet. Some of the information is confidential, and could lead to the loss of privacy, premature revelation of corporate plans, exposure of corporate trade secrets, securities law violations, etc., if it were to be generally revealed. Corporations also generate an immense amount of information that is not security-sensitive, but that is simply not interesting to anyone outside the organization.

For a growing number of corporations, the answer is a corporate intranet: a small computer network that uses TCP/IP, HTML, and Web technology, but where access is limited (for instance, with passwords) to authorized users. There could be several levels of password protection so that, for instance, everybody in the corporation would have access to the employee handbook and information about the health plans, but only top HR executives would have access to the full set of salary data.

> ⇒ **TIP**
>
> The more decentralized a company's operations, the more likely it is to be interested in, and benefit from, intranet utilization.

Companies usually begin intranet deployment by posting their employee handbooks and internal job openings. An intranet of this type can pay for itself in as little as two years, by reducing printing and distribution costs. A common next step is to add benefit enrollment and reporting changes in marital and family status to corporate intranet functions.

How much does it cost to implement an intranet? It depends how modest or how sophisticated your needs are. Can you use off-the-shelf software "as is," or with minor modifications? Or do you need intensive tune-ups or even custom-built software? It also matters whether your Information Technology (IT) staff or other technically-minded employees can handle the job in-house, or whether a consultant must be retained. About half of the companies in the Watson Wyatt survey spent under $50,000 for their intranets.

⟹ TIP

Make sure that all materials on the intranet carry a date that will appear on pages that are downloaded and printed out; otherwise, employees might continue to rely on outdated materials that have been replaced by other materials on the company site.

6.5 LEGAL IMPLICATIONS OF E-MAIL

Companies that provide employees with e-mail access through modems or the network have facilitated communication because employees can zip off a message instantly, without the bother of typing a letter or getting caught up in "voice-mail hell" or endless rounds of telephone tag.

However, e-mail is not secure; it is much more like a postcard that can be read by anybody than like a sealed letter (much less a coded message). Also, the mere fact that a reader clicks a "delete" icon doesn't mean that the message is completely and permanently deleted from the entire computer system, network, or service provider that offers the e-mail service. So a message that is embarrassing (or worse such as sexually harassing or racist material) can easily be found by hostile parties—including plaintiffs' lawyers.

A reasonable strategy is for companies that install e-mail capacity to also inform employees of the company e-mail policy:

- Restriction of e-mail to business use (special software can be used to un-install or disable games on workplace networks or office computers)
- No forwarding of copyrighted materials (e.g., newspaper cartoons)
- No use of suggestive, obscene, or racist language
- No discussion of matters that might have adverse legal consequences (e.g., price fixing; industrial espionage)
- Require employees to ask themselves before they communicate if there is anything in the message that the employee would not want publicly revealed, or that would put the employer in a bad light if it were revealed.

- Inform employees that the employer retains the right to monitor employees' e-mail messages on the company network.

As the discussion of privacy on page 445 shows, it's hard to define the extent of employees' privacy rights in the workplace. Probably the best summary is that employees do not have a right to consider their e-mail correspondence personal, confidential, or protected against viewing and supervision by the employer.

However, there may be labor law implications. In the view of the NLRB, employee e-mail communications about work-related topics (such as complaining about employer policies) can be a concerted activity among employees that constitutes "mutual aid or protection." (See page 344; a workplace doesn't have to be unionized for its employees to be allowed to engage in protected activity without retaliation.) So it would be illegal for an employer to fire, or otherwise act against, an employee who has engaged in such activity. Threatening or inflammatory messages are not protected by labor law, but a direct protest to management certainly would be, and employee-to-employee communication probably would be unless there was an outright threat to harmonious operation of the workplace.

It's not a serious technological challenge to add monitoring devices to the network, so it's possible to detect when employees are playing computer or on-line games or doing recreational Net surfing. It would probably not be a First Amendment issue to ban these computer uses (because employees are not engaged in politically-tinged communications). However, leisure activities can be harmless or even enhance productivity by acting as a safety valve for fatigue and frustration. Furthermore, employees may resent what they see as infantilization or a "1984" atmosphere, and the resentment itself can depress productivity.

Part II

COMPENSATION ISSUES

(Current Compensation)

Chapter 7

COMPENSATION PLANNING

7.1 INTRODUCTION

In many businesses, and especially in service businesses, payroll is the largest, or at least one of the largest, corporate expenses. Increases in payroll will therefore have immense bottom-line impact. In order to succeed, the corporation must attract and retain skilled, hard-working employees, and must motivate them to do their best. Yet at the same time the company must run economically. There are also "ripple effects" to worry about: the raise of one employee, or group of employees, is likely to enhance the expectations of other employees. They are usually skeptical if they are told that they must sacrifice raises and enhanced benefits for the overall good of the company—and will be particularly skeptical if they find out that the CEO has been paid several million dollars, with millions more in stock options!

If a company has many unions, negotiations with each union become nerve-racking, because the contract with the first union will trigger a demand for parity (or higher compensation) by the other unions whose contracts must be negotiated later. The temptation is to draw a very hard line with the first union, but that creates a serious strike risk.

Salary is an important element in compensation, of course, but it must be considered in the context of an entire compensation package. Taxes must be paid by the employer, and withheld by the employer from the employee's salary, based on all or a percentage of compensation. Benefits such as group health insurance will be offered. The employee may be entitled to participate in a qualified pension plan, a nonqualified executives-only plan, or both. Perhaps the employee will be required to, or allowed to, place some of his or her compensation into a pension plan instead of receiving it immediately in cash. Top managers may receive a minor or even a major portion of their overall compensation in the form of shares of company stock or stock options rather than in cash.

In a very small corporation (especially a family-owned business), the ownership group will represent a noticeable percentage of all the employees, and the ownership group's compensation will be a significant part of the overall payroll. In the larger corporation, such as the one that is the target audience for this book, there will be many more rank-and-file employees than top executives, although the compensation package for a top executive may be many times that of the average employee.

7.2 DECISIONS IN SETTING COMPENSATION

A business' policies in setting compensation depend on many things:

- How much the business can afford to pay!
- Competitive factors—in a high-cost area, where unemployment is low, employers will have to pay top dollar to attract workers. If unemployment is high and living costs are low, workers will be able to accept a lower-paying job, especially if the alternative is no job at all.
- Impact on cash flow. If a corporation has little current cash but a bright future (e.g., a technology start-up), it may be possible to pay less in cash by offering a generous stock option package.
- Effect on future financing: venture capitalists who want to receive one-third of a new business' stock won't be too happy to hear that employees already own most of the stock and have been promised options that limit the venture capitalists' potential profits in an Initial Public Offering.
- What employees want. Young, single people may prefer a raise to enhanced benefits; married people with families may derive more benefit from child care or improved health insurance than from a cash raise.
- Tax factors—for both employer and employee. The employer will probably want to be able to deduct the full amount spent on compensation in the year it was spent, and will probably resist any compensation form that is not eligible for a full current deduction. Before 1986, highly-paid employees were especially interested in deferred compensation, because they had to pay income taxes at rates much higher than their expected post-retirement rate. Since 1986, tax rates have been fairly "flat" (not much difference between the highest and the middle bracket), so employees may push for more current cash and less deferral.

7.3 MERIT INCREASES

During the 1950s and 1960s, employees grew to expect an annual raise (and annual increases in benefit packages as well). However, there were some recessionary years in the 1970s, and in the 1980s and 1990s a new pay paradigm emerged.

Instead of routine increases, performance-based pay became more common, with raises keyed to the workers', work team's, or division's attainment of pre-set goals. Some companies are eliminating merit raises altogether; instead, employees get a bonus each year. The size of the bonus reflects performance; but a bonus, unlike a raise, does not affect future years' compensation. Rather it is computed independently each year.

In 1990, 47% of medium-sized and larger companies had a variable pay program (including profit-sharing and bonuses); by 1997, close to two-thirds of such companies had a variable pay program in place. Variable pay is seen as a better motivator than routinized merit increases. (After all, not all employees achieve at the same level of merit.)

7.4 INNOVATIVE PAY SYSTEMS

Written contracts, such as collective bargaining agreements and contracts negotiated by executives, do obligate the company to pay particular wage rates or to calculate compensation in particular ways. But for companies that do not have such written contracts, pay planning is usually a tradition-oriented, seat-of-the-pants process. There is no requirement that the old practices be continued; and today, some companies are innovative in ways to calculate compensation.

7.4.1 Value-Based Systems

Economic Value Added, or EVA, is a pay planning measure that reflects a public company's enhanced stock value by calculating the net operating profit (after taxes), adjusting the figure to take the cost of capital into account, and then raising or lowering employee compensation accordingly (at the top executive level only, or throughout the company). The company sets a target; if the target is met, EVA participants get a two-part bonus. One part is paid out immediately. The other part goes into a "bonus bank," and each year the part of the bonus bank that can be paid out depends on satisfying further targets.

One thing that makes a company's stock attractive to stockholders is that the company is above average in the productive use of capital. In 1993, a *Wall Street Journal* survey performed by William M. Mercer Inc. showed that 2.3% of survey respondents used value-based incentives to pay their CEOs; by 1994, 8.6% of companies had a value component in CEO pay. (Of course, these were also years of an active bull market, so CEOs were far more likely to be pleased than threatened by this development.)

There is a downside to EVA. Companies that implement it need a lot of expensive consulting time to set the system up and calibrate it. The system is also hard for employees to understand. Furthermore, it may accentuate the trend, already viewed as negative by some observers, for executives to focus on quarterly results and short-term changes in stock prices rather than on developments that will keep the company evolving and competitive in the long run. Some commentators feel that the company's EPS (Earnings per Share) is a more meaningful measure than after-tax operating profits.

7.4.2 Broadbanding

Traditionally, companies set up a grade system, under which each job is assigned to a pay grade; companies can have two dozen or more grades to assign workers to. Everyone holding the same job will earn approximately the same amount, with variations based on the length of their tenure with the organization, how well they have performed, and special factors such as additional relevant education and in-service training. A more recent development reflecting "flatter" organization charts (with fewer levels of hierarchy, greater use of teams, and more lateral equality of people with different tasks and skillsets) is salary "broadbanding." In other words, the organization might go from having 25 categories, each with a pay scale ranging from $5,000-$10,000, to four or five categories, within which pay could vary as much as $30,000.

Buck Consultants has been monitoring broadbanding for several years. In 1994, about one-sixth of companies they reviewed used this compensation model. By 1996, 29% compensated in broad bands, and another 27% were considering switching to this method. In a traditional organization, promotions from one grade to another would be frequent, and each promotion would almost certainly require a pay increase.

A broadbanded organization can be more egalitarian, because the employees fall within a small number of bands instead of a lot of hierarchical grades. However, they do not necessarily like this—the distinctions may have been a source of pride to those who achieved promotions. Managers have to spend extra time letting employees know what their goals are within the bands, and what they have to do to achieve a higher pay level within the band.

7.5 BENEFITS AS AN ELEMENT OF COMPENSATION

The Society of Human Relations Management's 1997 study (available at **http://www.shrm.org**) shows that benefits now represent about 40% of the compensation package. Nearly all employers responding to the survey provided health insurance. More than half (55%) offered medical flexible spending accounts and 44% offered FSAs that pay health care premiums. Paid vacations were also more or less universal (offered by 94% of respondents); 86% provided sick leave, 60% maternity leave, 60% dependent care FSAs, and 46% flextime.

Hewitt Associates' survey of 1996 benefits offered by 1,050 major U.S. employers indicates that 86% offered some form of child care, usually in the form of Information and Referral (I&R) services (40%), versus only 6% that offered discounts to employees who took their children to local child-care providers, and 13% that provided emergency care or care for sick children. In this survey, flextime was much more common (available in 72% of the workplaces); part-time work was available in 64% of respondents, 22% offered compressed schedules (a full-time schedule of four ten-hour days a week), and 36% offered job sharing.

The size of the benefit package is often directly related to the size of the company, with large companies in a position to offer better benefits. According to Bureau of Labor Statistics (BLS), in 1994 97% of employers with 500 or more employees offered paid vacations, versus only 86% for smaller companies. Health insurance was provided by 82% of large, 62% of small companies; short-term disability plans were found at 87% of large, but only 56% of small companies, long-term disability programs at 41% and 14% respectively. About half of the larger companies had 401(k) plans, versus only 29% of smaller companies. Even if smaller companies did provide benefits, they typically offered a more stripped-down form of the benefit and/or required higher employee copayments. Health care coverage for dependents was far more common in large-company plans than in their small-company counterparts.

7.6 SEVERANCE PAY

Although there is no federal mandate to do so, employers frequently provide severance pay when a job ends, of one or more weeks additional compensation (often defined as a certain number of days or weeks pay for every year of service with the employer). However, this usually does not occur if the termination is the result of employee wrongdoing.

The key to characterizing a payment as severance is that it is over and above the normal salary or wages earned for past services. Employers must pay the compensation that terminated employees have already earned; severance payments are by and large discretionary. However, if the employer enters into an explicit or implied contract to provide severance benefits, that contract must be obeyed.

7.6.1 *Severance Trends*

1996 was the third straight year in which average severance pay for mid-level executives increased. In 1994, the average was 8.5 months' compensation, versus 9.9 months in 1995 and a much higher 14.6 months in 1996. Furthermore, the generosity of the average severance package increased, not just its basis of length. In 1994, the average award was 2/3 of a month's pay per year of service; in 1995, it was 4/5; and in 1996, it was 1.1 months per service year. Because of downsizing, it was more likely that experienced, highly-paid employees would lose their jobs (or would become redundant in the course of a merger or acquisition); many companies felt it was more economical to offer generous severance packages than to get sued.

7.6.2 Severance Arrangements as a "Plan"

ERISA will not be involved in a one-time decision by the employer to grant or enhance severance benefits, or in an employer's payroll practices or payment to active employees of extra money for overtime or holiday work. However, ERISA must be obeyed if severance payments are made in connection with a "plan"; and even an unwritten or informal arrangement might be interpreted by the DOL or the court system as a plan.

Once the severance payment comes under the ambit of ERISA, the degree and nature of regulation depends on whether it is characterized as a pension plan or a welfare benefit plan. The arrangement will not be a pension plan if:

- Payments are not contingent on the recipient's retirement (i.e., if the recipient is free to seek another job and still retain the payments)

- The total payments do not exceed twice the recipient's compensation for the year immediately preceding the termination

- The payments are completed within 24 months of the termination (or 24 months of the time the employee reaches normal retirement age, if that is later, and if the termination is part of a "limited program of terminations" rather than an individual response by the employer to the employee).

See DOL Reg. §2510.3-2(b) and 29 CFR §2510.3-1(a).

Sometimes an employee accepts a severance offer, only to discover that a better offer was made later on. In this situation, as page 325 explains, the employee is not entitled to disclosure of possible plans that might be offered in the future, until and unless the proposal is under "serious consideration" by the employer company.

See page 509 for a discussion of the interaction of severance pay with retirement (especially early retirement) and how the Age Discrimination in Employment Act handles severance issues.

7.6.3 Parachute Payments

A specialized form of severance, the "parachute" payment, comes into play in the course of a hostile takeover or takeover attempt. The best-known form is the "golden parachute" for executives (the counterpart of "golden handcuffs" that are supposed to discourage top executives from leaving companies that prize their services highly). However, a few states mandate the payment of "tin parachutes" to rank-and-file workers to compensate them for job loss that arises out of a corporate transition.

A "single-trigger" agreement gives the executive the right to additional compensation whenever there is a merger or acquisition of the employer company. A "double-trigger" agreement doesn't come into play unless there has not only been a corporate transition, but the executive has been terminated or demoted and therefore has a real economic injury.

A golden parachute arrangement compensates top employees very generously if the takeover costs them their jobs—so generously, in fact, that the acquirer must cope with a depleted corporate treasury once the acquisition has been consummated. In addition to cash severance, golden parachute agreements could include stock, enhanced pension benefits, and insurance.

7.6.4 Taxing "Excess" Payments

There are two dimensions to the question of whether a parachute payment is excessive. If it is so large that it drains the corporate treasury, stockholders might sue, claiming "corporate waste." However, the corporation (and the directors who voted in the parachute arrangement) will probably win in court, because the "business judgment" rule protects compensation-related decisions that do not involve fraud, bad faith, abuse of discretion, or gross overreaching.

In this analysis, the parachute arrangement is a legitimate business decision because it both deters unwanted acquisitions and allows executives to be more productive because they are less fearful of a sudden takeover attempt.

The other implication is the excise tax that the Internal Revenue Code imposes on excess parachute payments (Code §§280G(b) and 4999). Those in response to a change in corporate ownership or control cannot be deducted by the corporation if they are excessive (because the compensation deduction is limited to that which is "reasonable compensation" and an "ordinary and necessary business expense"). Payments from qualified pension plans are not considered parachute payments. There is also an excise tax equal to 20% of the excess parachute payment.

⥤ TIP

S Corporations are not subject to the excise tax. Nor does the tax apply to those corporations whose stock is not publicly traded on an exchange, if the owners of 75% of the company's voting stock approved the parachute agreement.

An excess parachute payment is any amount that: (1) is not reasonable compensation for work done either before the change in ownership/control, or (2) for work that is scheduled to be done after the change, and (3) that exceeds three times the "base amount" (see top of the next page).

A parachute payment is one that is contingent on change in corporate ownership or control, or the ownership or control of a significant portion of the corporation's assets. If the executive and corporation entered into a compensation agreement within the year before an ownership or control change, the payments are presumed to be parachute payments unless there is clear and convincing evidence of another motivation for the payments.

The base amount is the average annual compensation of the executive for the five years just before the corporation's ownership or control changed. Cash salary is not the only factor here; bonuses, fringe and pension benefits, and severance pay are included.

When the change-of-control transaction is structured as an asset sale, the buyer might not assume the seller's responsibilities for its unfunded deferred compensation plans. Non-qualified plans often have change of control provisions that make the benefits immediately payable when the company changes hands—but these funds might be characterized as excess parachute payments when they are made.

> ⇒ **TIP**
>
> One way to cope with both problems is to draft the parachute agreement to provide that payments will be reduced if they are ever large enough to trigger the excise tax. It also helps to include or attach documentation of severance arrangements reached by other companies comparable to yours, to show that you acted reasonably in furtherance of corporate needs.

> ⇒ **TIP**
>
> If a company makes severance payments in connection with downsizing, those payments will probably be currently deductible. However, if the *buyer* is obligated to make severance payments in the course of an acquisition transaction, those payments will probably have to be capitalized and not deducted currently.

7.7 COMPENSATION DEDUCTION

The Internal Revenue Code, in §162, allows a corporation to deduct its ordinary and necessary business expenses, including "reasonable" salaries for personal services. A salary may be challenged if, in fact, the recipient really hasn't rendered substantial services, or if payment is being made for something he or she is not qualified to do (naming a teenage offspring as Vice President, Marketing, or placing a former homemaker with no special training in charge of sophisticated management financial functions).

For tax years beginning after 1993, §162(m) provides that public corporations (those whose stock is traded on public markets, as distinct from closely-held private companies) are not allowed to deduct any portion of an employee's compensation exceeding $1 million. In this context, compensation means salary plus benefits, but does not include qualified retirement plans. Even a public company can deduct compensation in excess of $1 million if:

- It constitutes commissions paid on sales.

- It is paid pursuant to a contract that was already in effect on February 17, 1993 and that was not materially modified after that date and before the compensation was paid.

- The compensation is based on performance, and performance is measured by objective goals set by a Board of Directors compensation committee consisting of at least two outside directors (and no interested directors). Furthermore, the performance-based arrangement must be disclosed to the stockholders, and approved by a majority vote of the stockholders. The money can't be paid until the compensation committee certifies that the goals (e.g., an increase in the price of the company's stock; solving a difficult production problem; increasing revenues by a certain percentage) have been met.

- If vacation pay is treated as deferred compensation, it is not deductible until the year it is actually paid: Code §404(a)(5).

7.8 DIRECT DEPOSIT

Many companies enter into arrangements with banks under which employees' earnings are deposited directly into designated bank accounts. The employee benefits by getting immediate electronic availability of the funds, and by saving a trip to a crowded bank branch(which would usually occur at lunchtime on payday—of course, just when everybody else goes to the bank). Paper checks are much more vulnerable to theft, loss, and forgery than direct deposits.

⇒ **TIP**

If there is a problem, employees can use a federal banking rule called Regulation E to protest, but must be careful to follow all of the Reg. E procedures, including giving timely notice.

The employer, of course, benefits by *not* having to issue, print, and distribute dozens, hundreds, or thousands of paper checks. This is so significant a benefit that the National Automated Clearinghouse estimates that close to half of all U.S. employees get paid via direct deposit.

Direct deposit authorizations often contain a clause allowing automatic deductions of amounts mistakenly placed into an employee's account. This authorization is sometimes used by employers to withdraw disputed amounts (e.g., excess vacation time taken by a departing employee). To employers, this is an additional benefit of direct deposit (disputed amounts can be collected, putting the ball in the employee's court to protest).

Understandably, employees are less enthusiastic about this aspect, and state laws may be enacted requiring employers to give notice before taking an automatic payment. Check with your attorney to make sure your system continues to conform to state law requirements.

Chapter 8

WAGE AND HOUR ISSUES

8.1 INTRODUCTION

The responsibilities of the HR department are many and varied. They usually include pay planning and compliance, setting work schedules for employees, keeping track of hours worked, and handling payroll matters. This latter responsibility comprises preparing paychecks that reflect both work (at the appropriate salary or hourly rate) and deductions (tax withholding and both employer and employee share of FICA and FUTA).

The Fair Labor Standards Act (FLSA), 29 United States Code §201-219 and 251-262, regulates wages and hours in both the private and public sectors. It forbids sex discrimination in compensation, sets a minimum wage, requires extra pay to be given if hourly workers put in overtime, and mandates recordkeeping and record retention. The FLSA does not preempt state laws that do not conflict with it, which also provide additional protection for employees, so you should check your state law to see if it imposes additional compliance burdens or covers employees who are excluded from the scope of the FLSA. The Department of Labor's Wage and Hour Division is responsible for administering the FLSA.

Employees have a private right of action (i.e., they can sue the employer) for unpaid minimum wages and/or overtime, plus liquidated damages, attorneys' fees, and court costs. Courts have the power under 29 U.S.C. §216 to order legal and equitable relief against employers who discharge their employees, or who otherwise discriminate or retaliate against them for making an FLSA complaint or participating in a Wage and Hour Division proceeding.

In addition to employees' private right of action, the Secretary of Labor has the power to sue for unpaid minimum wages and overtime. The funds in question are paid directly to the employees who should have received them. The court can enjoin the employer against committing further violations. Willful violations of the FLSA are criminal rather than civil in nature, so prosecution by the federal Attorney General's office is possible, in addition to DOL actions or civil suits by employees.

8.2 MINIMUM WAGE

On Labor Day, 1997, the minimum wage was increased for the 25th time, from $4.75 an hour to $5.15. It was estimated that there were 6.4 million minimum wage workers who would have an immediate pay increase because of the change. Ripple effects were also expected, because if a company's lowest-paid workers get a raise, other workers who are slightly higher paid expect the same to maintain the salary differential.

8.2.1 Internships

Under some circumstances, a company can have work done by people who do not get paid at all, much less get paid at the minimum wage rate. The Department of Labor permits unpaid internships for trainees, on the assumption that it could make sense for a person to work without pay if he or she acquires usable job skills.

Criteria for an acceptable internship program include:

- Even though the employer's facilities are used, the training is similar to the curriculum of a vocational school
- The trainee, not the employer, derives the real benefit from the training (in fact, the employer's operations may even be slowed down by the efforts of the novices)
- Trainees get close supervision, but do not replace regular employees
- The trainee explicitly agrees to work without pay
- There is no guarantee that the trainee will be hired for a paid job.

From the DOL perspective, the most valid training program is one where the trainee is prepared for a new career, but doesn't embark on it until a paid job is secured. A structured curriculum will be viewed more favorably than an unstructured one, classroom training more favorably than work in the plant, and the less skillful the trainee's work, the more likely he or she is to be considered an intern rather than a new employee "learning the ropes"—at regular salary.

8.3 FREELANCERS AND INDEPENDENT CONTRACTORS

Given the extremely high cost of employee benefits, and the risk that even a person hired as an at-will employee may have a degree of protection against termination, the appeal of part-time, contingent, contract, temporary, and other non-full-time workers is evident. In fact, a number of employers follow a downsizing process under which full-time jobs are eliminated, but the former holders of those jobs are re-hired, this time at a lower pay rate and with fewer or no benefits; almost 12% of workers provided by contract firms, and 22.3% of independent contractors who earn a salary were re-hired by companies that employed them in the past.

Yet employers must step cautiously: if they are not careful, they may achieve a short-term saving that is very costly in the long run. They may be forced to "make up" for wages, benefits, taxes, and penalties that should have been paid in the past but were not because of an incorrect characterization of the status of particular workers. Such mischaracterization can render the company liable to the worker, to tax and regulatory authorities, or both.

There is no simple alignment of interests; sometimes the individual seeks to be treated as an employee in order to qualify for benefits (and in order to avoid the heavy burden of paying both the employer and employee shares of the FICA tax). At other times, the worker prefers independent contractor characterization in order to receive a check that is not diminished by deductions. (This is particularly true if the individual does not intend to make the tax payments on a current basis, or at all.)

An individual who performs services but is not a conventional employee of the company might actually be a common-law employee, albeit of some other company (such as a temporary personnel service or leasing company). In other situations, the worker is not an employee at all, but an independent contractor, and thus personally responsible for making tax payments and for securing insurance and other benefits.

The real test of employee or independent contractor status is control; the more discretion the individual has in deciding how and when to perform services to reach an agreed-upon result, the more likely it is that he or she will be an independent contractor.

In 1996, the IRS provided some help in IR-96-44, "Independent Contractor or Employee?" It permits relief from federal employment taxes if a business consistently treats a group of similarly-situated workers as independent contractors, has a reasonable basis (and not just wishful thinking) to support this characterization, and files information returns (Form 1099) with the IRS on a consistent basis.

Characterizing sales staff can be difficult. A person who sells big-ticket equipment can have a high degree of independence and earn over $1 million a year; a store clerk can earn a low wage for highly-supervised tasks like re-stocking store shelves.

The clerk is clearly an employee; the elite salesperson is probably an independent contractor. There are special rules in various areas of law (such as tax compliance and unemployment insurance) for sales staff. It is quite relevant whether the individual works at the business location of the employer, whether he or she receives a salary irrespective of the amount sold, or whether commissions are a significant factor in compensation.

8.3.1 Leased Employees

It should also be noted that, under Code §414(n), long-term employee leases (where a person who is formally employed by a leasing company nevertheless spends a year or more working full-time for your company) may not be effective to save pension costs for your company. As page 239 explains, your company may be required to take the long-term leased employees into account when testing your company's pension and fringe benefit plans for discrimination.

There is a safe harbor if you get less than 20% of your non-highly-compensated employees through leasing services, and if those services provide excellent pension coverage for their employees. Needless to say, the second part of the test occurs less often than the first part!

8.4 THE CONTINGENT WORKFORCE

Figures from the Bureau of Labor Statistics show that in 1982 there were about half a million temporary workers in the U.S. This number has risen steadily from 1982, when there were only about 417,000 "temps," until 1990 (when there were close to 1.5 million such workers). It stayed stable until 1992, then picked up growth at a faster pace, until there were about 2.25 million temporary workers in 1995 and 2.3 million in 1996.

In 1996, employers paid $93 million to staffing companies, about two-thirds of that for temporary help, 24% for staff leasing, 12% for permanent placement, and 1% for outplacement of employees who had been discharged.

According to Staffing Industry Analysis Inc., the fastest-growing areas within the staffing business were "temp-to-permanent conversions" (i.e., hiring employees short-term, then offering them permanent employment if and when their performance was particularly satisfactory). Other areas involved staff leasing, technical temporary workers (especially in computer fields) and professional and specialty temps, reflecting the generally more upscale image of temporary workers, who now include corporate executives and professionals as well as clerical and factory workers.

See page 158 for a discussion of the eligibility of workers other than full-time, permanent employees, for benefits that are deemed "welfare benefits" for ERISA purposes.

8.4.1 Alternative Staffing

The BLS says that about one-tenth of the U.S. workforce is employed in some arrangement other than traditional, permanent, full-time employment for a single employer. The typical pattern is for the core corporate group, about 60% of the workers, to hold traditional jobs; the rest work under a variety of other arrangements, e.g.,:

- Temporary employment, where the worker is actually employed by a "temp agency" that recruits, trains, and sends workers to companies that are clients of the agency.

- Long-term temporary assignments: the arrangement is that a temporary worker will stay at one location for weeks or months, instead of being hired on a daily basis and often moving from company to company

- Master vendor, on-site programs, or vendor-on-premises: a single staffing firm handles many temporary placements for an employer, and places one of its own employees at the business location to coordinate all work by the "temps."

- Floaters: people who are actually employees of the company, not of a temporary agency, but who have no fixed job assignment within the company. Instead, they are assigned to various tasks and departments, depending on what the company needs at a given time (e.g., someone to process documents to get ready for an audit; someone to fill in for vacationing permanent employees).

- Payrolling: the company wants to hire a specific person (not just whomever the temp agency refers), and gets that person hired by the temporary agency, which then becomes that person's formal employer and takes responsibility for payment, taxes, and other employment-related matters.

- Part-time work.

- Independent contractors—individuals who are genuinely self-directed and have clients, rather than employers who control their work.

- Contract workers—an arrangement usually made for technical workers, such as engineers who install machinery at a new plant and make sure it works, and systems analysts who craft a new computer system. The contract workers are formally employed by a technical services firm (in effect, a high-powered temp agency), not by the company where they work. This arrangement is often used for long-range projects, including those that require the contract worker to relocate to the employer's site.

- Leased employees—including one-time common-law employees who are discharged by their one-time employer, rehired by a leasing company, and then leased back to the original employer. They may be back in the same worksite, doing the same job, but they are now paid by the leasing company, which also handles administrative tasks like tax and Worker's Compensation compliance.

- Outsourcing—a company that specializes in a particular function performs that function (perhaps processing payrolls, operating an employee cafeteria, or guarding a store or worksite) and is paid by the company that requires the services.

- Temp-to-lease programs—the company makes a deal with both a temporary agency and a leasing company. (Often, the two companies will be affiliated.) The temporary agency provides a kind of "audition" for workers. They start out as temporary workers at the jobsite; if they do their jobs well, they are transferred to the leasing company, which bills the worksite company for their long-term or permanent services.

- Temp-to-permanent programs—a similar arrangement, although this time if the temporary workers perform well, they will become permanent employees of the underlying worksite company.

There are subtle questions to be explored in each of these alternatives; for instance, which of these workers are entitled to pension and welfare benefits? For which workers must FICA and FUTA taxes be paid, and who is responsible for making these payments and withholding the employees' share? If the individual harms someone else, who is liable for his or her conduct? Who owns intellectual property created by these individuals? Who decides if the individual's job performance is satisfactory, and who is authorized to grant a pay increase or a bonus—or, on the other side of the scale, who is authorized to discipline or fire the individual?

The relationship between the worksite company and the individual worker is not always the only relationship that requires thought (or that must be coordinated by the worksite company's HR department). For instance, will temporary or leased employees be considered for permanent employment with the worksite company? If they are, can the initiative come from either side, or can only the worker apply for the job or only the worksite company offer it? Does the temporary agency or leasing company have to be notified? Is it entitled to any kind of commission on the placement, or to any compensation if it loses the services of a much-in-demand worker?

Typically, recruiting a temporary, part-time, or leased worker as a full-time permanent employee will reduce his or her raw hourly rate, because the past rate had to compensate the agency and cover various risks. On the other hand, the worksite company will have to take on responsibilities delegated to the supplier. These questions should be addressed in the contract between the worksite company and the supplier of its less-than-permanent staff.

8.4.2 Co-Employers

Sometimes, whether or not it is the intention of either the worksite company or the company that furnishes staff, both of them will be treated as "co-employers" for legal purposes; the responsibility for payments as well as liability when something goes wrong may be allocated between the two. If they are jointly and severally liable, either can be required to assume full responsibility for all adverse consequences, although it can then turn to the other for reimbursement.

To avoid co-employment, review the contract with your supplier, and demand to see the contracts the supplier has with the people who work for it. Make sure that responsibility is allocated to your liking. (Remember, however, that the more responsibility your supplier takes on, the more you will have to pay for its services!) Make sure that the supplier, and not your company, has long-range responsibility for the worker's training, promotion, benefits, and work-life problems. If the worker wants a permanent job at your company, feels entitled to a promotion, or wants to change working arrangements, those matters should be referred to the supplier rather than handled in-house by your department.

8.4.3 Part-Time Work

Although traditionally part-time hours have been correlated with low-skilled jobs, today 4.5 million of the 23 million part-time workers in the U.S. hold executive and professional jobs. In the late 1980s and the 1990s, the percentage of part-time workers has remained fairly steady, at or near 18%, but the skill level of part-timers has grown. Furthermore, most of the growth in part-time work came between 1968 and 1975; the percentage of part-timers in the workforce has been fairly steady since then.

The Conference Board's 1996 Work/Family Research and Advisory Panel found that 73% of the 102 companies surveyed have part-time workers who used to be employed full-time. In most instances, they are mothers who would have quit their jobs if they couldn't get part-time hours, but they could also be older workers making a gradual transition to retirement, or individuals with a personal project (such as training for the Olympics or writing a novel). Employers liked having part-timers in their workforce because it improved flexibility of staffing (cited by 86% of respondents), improved morale (73% said this was true), cut turnover (71%) and costs (52%); half the respondents associated part-time workers with higher productivity. (The Conference Board in 1995 cited other rationales for part-time hiring, including acquiring specific expertise, filling in for workers who were on leave or otherwise absent, "auditioning" workers who might later get a full-time job offer, and buffering the company's best workers against job loss in a downturn.)

The Conference Board found that 97% of the survey respondents offer benefits to part-time workers, as long as they work at least a minimum number of hours and had a certain number of years of full-time tenure before adopting the shortened schedule. A common tactic was to have part-timers pay a higher proportion of health costs than full-time workers do.

According to the same Conference Board study, 84% of respondents provided health benefits to their part-timers. EAPs, paid time off, and retirement benefits were all made available to part-time workers in 80% of the companies. About three-quarters of the companies offered life insurance and paid sick leave to part-time workers. About two-thirds of the employers provided dental, disability, and savings plans, and flexible spending accounts. However, only 40% gave part-timers access to the company's stock purchase plan.

Only about one-third of the respondents reported that their census included involuntary part-timers (those who would prefer to work full-time but did not have that option). Eighty-five percent of respondents said their part-timer workers were permanent employees, and that the employee census included voluntary part-timers. Seventy percent had part-time workers who were job-sharers (i.e., two employees divide a conventional full-time schedule); 49% had part-time employees who telecommuted (worked part-time at home, relying on telephones and modems for communications with the office).

In a company that uses part-timers extensively, it makes more sense to set staffing requirements in terms of FTEs (Full Time Equivalents) rather than a certain number of workers. If staff has to be reduced, the reductions should not automatically begin with the part-timers. (In fact, it might make more sense to keep them on and lay off the full-time workers!) Employees who ask for a shortened schedule as a transition to retirement should be counseled about the impact of a cut in hours (and therefore a cut in salary), and on their retirement benefits, because many plans base post-retirement compensation on that earned in the last few pre-retirement years.

One way to increase the number of part-time workers is to adopt a one-year pilot project. Assess the reaction of full-time workers: do they feel that their own jobs are threatened? Or do they think that they'll have to work harder to make up for the others' shorter schedules? Determine the busiest times, when staffing needs are greatest, and have as many part-timers available then as possible. Continue to assess the success of the program; don't renew it unless it is cost-effective and keeps productivity at acceptable levels.

8.5 WORK SCHEDULING

Although the conventional working hours are nine to five (or perhaps eight to four), there are many reasons why work hours may have to be extended, either for particular workers or for the enterprise as a whole. Sometimes the company's product or service involves emergencies and public safety, so staffers must be present around-the-clock: nobody would want to report a fire and be told to call back the next morning. Hospitals must stay open day and night. Planes fly and buses roll in darkness as well as during daylight hours. Sometimes equipment is so delicate that it must be operated constantly, or at least must have constant attendance in case a problem develops. Demand for a factory's products might be so high that the only way to cope is to work two or three eight-hour shifts a day. Demand might be high but unpredictable, or predictably seasonal, so that the plant runs at full steam for several months, then phases down, resulting in layoffs and terminations.

For all these reasons, some employees will have to work overtime and weekend hours occasionally; some will have to work unconventional hours as a long-range or permanent condition of employment.

8.5.1 *Shift Work*

Shift work is usually defined as a system under which the workplace operates two or three eight-hour shifts a day, or where coverage must be obtained for weekends. It is a complex subject, with complex effects on the human body. Rotating or split shifts are especially hard on employees, because they can't find a new pattern of sleep and waking and adjust to it. Shift workers are at higher risk than others for on-the-job fatigue, sleep disorders, health complaints, and depression. When workers are less alert than normal, they are more likely than normal to get injured, cause injuries to others, damage products and machinery, and make bad decisions. Therefore, the adjustment problems of shift work are not just personal to the employees; they are major productivity problems for employers as well.

Workers who don't feel well and don't enjoy their jobs (in part because they don't feel supported by management) are likely to have higher rates of absenteeism and turnover. The Conference Board recommends the adoption of measures such as making information and referral and Employee Assistance Program services available around the clock, and training not just shift workers but managers to understand and cope with the stresses of shift work.

Some employees prefer the second or third shift to conventional working hours, because they are "night owls"; because they can get free or low-cost child care if they work at unconventional hours; because of the higher pay in overtime or shift differentials; or because they are combining shift work with going to school, auditioning for acting roles, or for other reasons why conventional hours don't work. On the other hand, employees may feel pressured into shift work if those with more seniority get to bid on the more popular shifts, or if the choice is between an undesirable shift and no job at all. Furthermore, it can put stress on a marriage if the spouses only see each other for a short time, so that marriage seems more like a relay race than a partnership.

8.5.2 *Same Hours, Fewer Days*

There's nothing sacred about a 40-hour week. When factories first became prevalent, much longer workweeks were common (even for child laborers). The 40-hour week was a union demand that eventually gained acceptance, even for non-union workers. The five-day week is also a fairly recent innovation: a six-day schedule prevailed for part of the twentieth century.

A schedule that works very well in some environments: a 40-hour workweek, but one in which employees come to the office only four days a week (although these four days might include one or two weekend days). It's easier for employees who need child care to arrange it four days a week rather than five; the "extra" day gives them more time to spend with the children; and employees are often more productive because it takes them time to get focused on work each morning.

Conventional working hours often end when employees feel they're "in the swing of things." Then they leave for the day, and come back and have to get focused all over again. Fewer, longer workdays allow them to take advantage of this feeling of being in control.

8.5.3 *Fewer Hours, Same Pay*

Employers in a tight labor market, or those with especially heavy turnover, sometimes offer a "30-40" schedule as a hiring incentive: that is, the employee receives the normal salary for a 40-hour week, but is expected to work only 30 hours (perhaps at an unpopular shift, such as midnight to 6 A.M.). An executive whose company uses this schedule was quoted as saying that running four six-hour shifts a day increases the employee census and payroll, but cuts turnover by 50% and improves productivity by 25% while greatly reducing the cost of returns (because more-satisfied employees do better-quality work).

The 9/80 workweek is another compressed schedule: this time, the employees put in 80 hours in a nine-day period, with a three-day break between weeks, but no consistent "weekend."

8.5.4 *Flextime*

Another possibility is flextime, a flexible work schedule under which employees commit to working at least a certain number of hours per day, week, or month, and commit to be present at certain agreed-on times (e.g., a monthly staff meeting; times when customer demand is highest). Otherwise they can work at any schedule that suits their needs and permits them to meet their work goals. In 1992, about half of the companies surveyed by Hewitt Associates allowed employees to adopt a flexible schedule; this was increased to 68% by 1996. (Flextime is distinct from a company that is so understaffed or so pressured that employees can "work any 80 hours a week they feel like," as the Microsoft joke goes.)

Flextime can work well for employees who have caregiving responsibilities (for children, or for disabled or elderly family members). In these situations, flextime can allow the employee to retain his or her job (and gives the employer the continued benefit of his or her skills and experience), at little or no additional cost, as long as the flexible schedule is consistent with performing the necessary job tasks on time.

8.6 TELECOMMUTING

To do many modern jobs, it's not necessary to have a lot of face-to-face contact with co-workers or customers. The employee often works alone completing various tasks, or communicates with others by telephone or e-mail. For many jobs, the "tools" are not sewing machines or lathes, but computers. Under those circumstances, it might seem ideal to shift the main location of the job from an office to the telecommuter's home computer. He or she can work at home, confer by telephone, e-mail, or video-conferencing, send in work by modem, and appear at the office only when necessary for essential meetings.

Telecommuting sounds perfect for many reasons. Employees can work on their own schedule (taking the time they need to care for children, or for elderly or sick relatives). They don't have to spend hours a day on a crowded highway or packed commuter train. (In fact, the state of Arizona implemented a major civil service telecommuting program, to cut down on air pollution caused by the twice-a-day drive between home and office.) Workers can be more relaxed, creative, and productive. The employer, in turn, doesn't have to pay for immense amounts of expensive office space, because the employees furnish their own workspaces.

➠ **TIP**

Management guru Tom Peters says that all CEOs should ask themselves why they *don't* telecommute at least one day a week, so they can tackle projects or make phone calls with fewer distractions.

Employees who are recovering from a serious accident or illness may be able to work at home (with or without adaptive devices provided by the employer) before they are able to return to the regular workplace, or even if they are never able to return to the regular workplace.

An employee might work at the office on specified days, and telecommute the rest of the time; or the employee might normally work at home, coming in to the office (or visiting clients) only on an as-needed basis, scheduled in advance. Another possibility (currently more common in Europe than in the United States) is for employers to maintain "satellite offices" that contain sophisticated equipment, such as videoconferencing, located away from the main office (and probably carrying a much lower per-square-foot rent). After all, if a company has customers and clients worldwide, an employee in the office is no closer to a Singapore customer than one who works at home.

In 1995, Olsten Corporation found that 33% of survey respondents permitted telecommuting; this figure went up to 42% in the 1996 survey. However, for the past four years, only 7% of employees in these companies have actually been involved in telecommuting. Estimates of the number of U.S. telecommuters vary widely, from 5 to 42 million; one commonly-reported figure is that 11 million American workers telecommute at least one day a week on a regular basis.

> ▥➡ **TIP**
> ___
>
> Minimize problems by setting up formal agreements with telecommuters that will specify:
>
> - how often they will be expected to appear at the office;
> - how much notice they need to be called to the office at other times;
> - how many hours they will work;
> - what their schedules will be;
> - whether telecommuting is expected to be temporary or permanent;
> - who the worker reports to;
> - who reports to him or her;
> - what the promotion possibilities are.

The agreement should clarify whether the telecommuter is an independent contractor or a common-law employee. This is an unsettled area legally. Certainly, providing a place to work and tools to do work are important "control" factors in deciding employee status. However, it is certainly possible for a telecommuter to be under the employer's control (both as to what should be done and how to do it) sufficiently to be a common-law employee. Get legal advice on this point; you can be sure the IRS will not supinely accept an agreement between telecommuter and employer company that characterizes the telecommuter as an independent contractor if the control tests are satisfied.

The company should also train both employees and managers in telecommuting basics, including how to maintain lines of communication. Initial experiences with telecommuting should be treated as experiments, with both parties showing willingness to adapt and patience to work out the problems.

Despite the potential of telecommuting, an estimated 20% of telecommuting arrangements fail, for various reasons. Not everyone enjoys working at home; some find the home environment too distracting, or miss the interaction with co-workers. Employees in the office may resent telecommuters who they think "have it too easy." Computer glitches can lead to lost or corrupted data. The Worker's Compensation status of injuries that occur at home, but while doing tasks for the employer's benefit, is unclear.

8.6.1 Planning for Successful Telecommuting

A telecommuting arrangement that satisfies both employer and employee depends on good planning, but also on the characteristics of the job and the worker.

A project that is suitable for telecommuting is one that can be handled by one person, with limited input from others (and with that input working efficiently by telephone or electronically; for example, a computer professional could conduct a telephone help line for beleaguered computer users from his or her home). It should be clearly defined and easily measured, so the supervisor will be able to assess if performance is adequate.

Personality characteristics of successful telecommuters include being comfortable working essentially alone, without office social contacts; being able to schedule tasks and hold to a schedule; being able to get the job done whatever the demands of family; and having the discipline to perform without a supervisor literally looking over his or her shoulder.

Because telecommuting relies so heavily on electronics, care must be taken to safeguard devices and information. If possible, the telecommuter should have extra equipment (perhaps a desktop computer and a laptop computer that can be used while traveling and in emergencies). Telecommuters should be required to back up their data frequently, to have a high-quality Uninterruptible Power Source to give them time to save work before the computer goes down, and should be required to keep back-up disks and other media in a safe location (such as a fireproof safe or a safe deposit box)—preferably somewhere other than the home.

Make sure the telecommuter has homeowner's insurance (by rider or separate policy, if necessary) that covers the computer equipment against theft and damage—especially if it is supplied by the employer, not the employee. A "consequential damages" provision that covers lost data and business opportunities is especially valuable, although it can be costly and hard to get.

Because telecommuting is so heavily dependent on computers, it's only natural that there are several sites giving advice about creating an effective telecommuting program. Check these out:

- Pacific Bell's guide to "moving the work instead of the worker": **http://www.pacbell.com/products/business/general/telecommuting/ tcguide/index.html**
- Consultant Gil Gordon's guide to effective work-from-home programs: **http://www.gilgordon.com**
- Job ads for telecommuting positions: **http://www.tjobs.com/**

8.7 LEGAL ISSUES OF WORK SCHEDULING

As discussed in the context of overtime (page 90), there is a basic division between salaried employees whose compensation does not vary if they work more or fewer hours, and hourly employees who do get a larger paycheck if they put in more hours. Therefore, a time clock or other system must be used to record the hours worked by hourly employees. It is less usual for salaried workers to keep time records, although they may be asked to do so if the management wants to analyze task and time performance. Another possibility is that, even though the employees earn a salary, the company or firm bills their time out to clients, and therefore paper time sheets or their computerized equivalent will be needed for accurate billing.

It is customary (although not legally required) for hourly employees to clock out when they leave the workplace (e.g., for lunch breaks or to do personal errands), and for them not to be paid for this non-work time. Salaried employees are usually not charged for this non-work time, although personal time is sometimes charged against their entitlement to sick leave. In unionized workplaces the Collective Bargaining Agreement will determine matters such as scheduling of meal breaks and when employees have to punch in and punch out.

⇒ **TIP**

There may also be state laws requiring at least minimal meal breaks during a work shift.

In July, 1997, the Second Circuit ruled that, if the employer requires employees to stay at the outdoor workplace during their lunch breaks (to protect the safety and security of the jobsite), then the employees are working and must be compensated for the time. Although the work was not arduous, it still benefited the employer and had to be paid for. The upshot was that 1,500 employees were awarded close to $5 million in overtime and nearly $10 million in damages; the misinterpretation of the work rules was a costly one!

⇒ **TIP**

Under Private Letter Ruling 9635002, the employer can add the value of any unused vacation days to an employee's 401(k) plan account; payroll taxes need not be paid or withheld, income tax on the value of the vacation days is deferred until the 401(k) account is accessed, and the full amount of current compensation can still be deferred and placed into the account. (For 1998, the 401(k) limit is $10,000.)

8.8 OVERTIME AND OVERTIME PLANNING

One of the centerpieces of the FLSA is its guarantee of "time and a half for overtime." That is, non-exempt hourly employees who put in more than 40 hours during a "workweek" are entitled to receive 150% of their normal rate for the additional hours. (Although the FLSA does not require it, many companies offer "comp time"—additional time off—if an hourly employee works more than his or her normal schedule, but less than 40 hours during a workweek.)

Certain categories of employees are exempt from the FLSA's minimum wage and overtime provisions under 29 USC §213(a)(1).(However, since qualifying for the exemptions depends on earning more than a certain amount, the exemption from the minimum wage doesn't have much practical effect.) Although payment of overtime to exempt employees cannot be mandated, some courts allow voluntary overtime payments to them, on the theory that the payments are the equivalent of bonuses.

The major exempt categories that readers of this book will encounter are executives, administrators, professionals, and outside salespersons. The availability of the exemption depends on the actual work activities performed, not the job title or even the nature of the employer's business. Exemption is based on "primary duties"—i.e., what work the employee does during 50% or more of the work time. The percentage calculation is based on the standard workweek for the employer's *non-exempt* employees.

The exemption can be lost if the employee devotes too much time to non-exempt, rank-and-file duties (although it's permissible for a white-collar worker to pitch in when there's an emergency). Exempt employees must also satisfy the minimum compensation standards of 29 CFR Part 541, but the dollar amounts are laughably low: $155 a week, or $250 a week if the employee's exemption is calculated based on the less-complex "short test."

It's not necessary to pay exempt workers for weeks in which they do not work at all, but otherwise their salary can't be reduced based on the number of hours worked or the number of hours of absences. (See 29 CFR §541.118(a).) The employer is not allowed to deduct from the wages of exempt employees for absences that were caused by the employer or the operating requirements of its business. Nor can the employer take deductions to penalize an exempt worker for workplace infractions, other than violations of major safety rules.

Specifically, docking a worker for "variations in quantity or quality of work" is appropriate for hourly workers entitled to overtime, but not for exempt workers. But the real test is whether reductions are ever made in practice. In 1997, the U.S. Supreme Court ruled that police officers were salaried and exempt, even though the employee manual said that pay could be docked for various disciplinary infractions; the mere possibility of salary reductions did not convert them to non-exempt workers.

⇒ TIP

If an exempt employee is absent for less than one day for sickness, disability, or personal reasons, the employer is not permitted to reduce the employee's paycheck, although some courts will allow the employer to reduce the amount of leave available to the employee.

The FLSA includes elaborate provisions for defining executives, professionals, etc., based on what their main job is (for instance, an executive manages a whole enterprise, or a recognized department or subdivision of an enterprise, and regularly directs the work of the equivalent of two or more full-time employees). The definition also limits the amount of time that can be spent on tasks outside the definition, such as the amount of time an executive can spend on non-managerial tasks. An administrator uses discretion and independent judgment to perform office or non-manual work.

A professional is an exempt employee whose primary duties are the practice of a learned, artistic, or educational profession. The work is primarily intellectual and varied in character, calling for constant exercise of judgment and discretion, and output cannot be standardized according to time. Not more than 20% of the workweek can be devoted to non-professional activities.

An outside salesperson is one who operates outside the employer's place of business, securing sales or orders for sales. The individual has received special sales training, spends less than 20% of the workweek on non-sales tasks, and commissions are a significant part of his or her compensation. The salesperson works with little direct supervision, and has a written contract designating him or her as an exempt employee. See 29 CFR §779.415(b) if you need detailed information about treatment of various sales commission arrangements for FLSA purposes.

Furthermore, overtime pay is not required for employees of retail or service establishments who are paid partly or entirely on a commission basis (i.e., commissions represent 50% or more of compensation for a representative period of at least one month). To qualify for this exemption, the employer must pay a regular rate of at least 150% of the minimum wage.

8.8.1 Payment of Overtime

Non-exempt hourly employees must be paid time-and-a-half (i.e., 150% of their normal pay rate, including commissions) when they work more than 40 hours in any workweek. Work time is all the time when the employer controls the employee's actions, including times that the employee is required to be on duty or at a prescribed place; but bona fide meal periods are not considered work time. Ordinary commuting to work is not work time, but work-related travel, such as an assignment to deliver something or go to a meeting at a client's office, is.

The rules given in 29 CFR §778.602(a) say that as long as the whole workweek is less than 40 hours, it is not necessary to pay overtime if a particular workday was more than eight hours, or if weekend work was required. (However, the union contract may require such payments in a unionized workplace.)

Generally speaking, overtime must be paid in cash, on the regular payday for the pay period in which the overtime was worked, although allowing $1^1/_2$ hours off for every overtime hour worked is permissible, as long as the comp time is given in the same period and is not carried over.

The workweek is not necessarily Monday–Friday, 9–5; it can be defined as any consecutive 168 hours, beginning at any time. It doesn't have to be the same as the payroll period. The workweek can be the same for all employees in the plant, or it can be different for different work groups or individuals. Usually, once an employer sets a workweek, it must abide by it, but a permanent change that is not a subterfuge to elude the FLSA's overtime requirements is lawful. Employers are not allowed to average two weeks' hours to see if overtime is payable (see 29 CFR §778.104).

A premium rate, such as differentials for Sunday or holiday work, is not included in the calculation of the regular rate, as long as the premium rate itself is at least 150% of the non-premium rate. Similarly, a "clock pattern" premium (pre-scribed by many collective bargaining agreements) for working past basic hours is not included in the basic rate if it satisfies the 150% test. However, a shift differential, such as additional payment for working the night shift, IS included.

8.8.2 Scheduling Workers for Overtime

Depending on the circumstances, it may be necessary to go to extremes to get workers to put in overtime hours. For instance, employees may have to be given incentives in the form of meal vouchers or free meals in the employee cafeteria if they work overtime (and it may be necessary to add late-night cafeteria hours for this purpose). Or employees who work past a certain time, or more than a certain number of hours may be reimbursed for cab rides or given a car-service ride home at company expense.

More likely, however, employees will be competing to be able to put in the highly paid extra hours. It is quite lawful to assign overtime to employees in order of seniority: i.e., to let employees bid for the right to work overtime, with priority to the most senior. Employers are permitted to maintain a policy under which employees are not allowed to work overtime hours unless the extra time is specifically authorized. (Otherwise, employees would have an incentive to goof off during the regular working day, then cite their own low productivity as a reason to put in more hours at time-and-a-half.) But if the employer permits or even is aware that the employee is working, overtime payment will be required.

⟱➡ TIP

The amount of overtime can be reduced by:

- planning further in advance;
- being more realistic about schedules;
- coordinating tasks better (so that raw materials and intermediate products are available throughout the production cycle, rather than alternating between slack times and times of heavy overtime);
- coordinating vacation and leave schedules so that there will never be a time when a few hard-pressed employees have to work overtime to make up for the absences of others.

In unionized workplaces, the CBA determines issues such as the amount of notice the company must give when overtime will be required, the extent to which overtime is voluntary (and, if so, who gets to bid on it) or compulsory, meal and rest breaks during overtime, and maximum overtime hours. The general rule is that employees get to bid for overtime in seniority order. If the employer imposes an obligation to work overtime, the disciplinary procedure should be drafted to make it clear that refusal to work mandatory overtime is a legitimate subject for discipline.

8.9 GARNISHMENTS AND DEDUCTIONS FOR SUPPORT ORDERS

An "assignment" is an action undertaken by an individual to direct some of his or her future compensation to creditors. A "garnishment" is a deduction from wages made pursuant to a court order. Various kinds of debts can give rise to assignments and garnishments: consumer debts; student loan debt; and, perhaps most important, obligations to support children and/or an ex-spouse.

Federal law doesn't say anything about wage assignments, although many states do. Several states limit the amount or percentage of each paycheck that can be assigned, permit assignments only for certain classes of debts (such as debts incurred to pay for necessities), or require spousal consent to the assignment.

It should be noted that strict limits are placed on "alienation" (i.e., transfer of future payments) of pensions, except in the context of a divorce-related court order. (See page 296 for a discussion of these "qualified domestic relations orders.") Once a pension payment is made, the recipient can do whatever he or she wants with it, but creditors cannot divert future payments before they are made.

The federal Consumer Credit Protection Act (CCPA), 15 U.S. Code §1671 et.seq., puts limits on garnishment. Generally, the maximum permitted garnishment will be 25% of the employee's "disposable" earnings. (Stricter limitations are imposed for very low-income workers.) Broadly speaking, "disposable earnings" means gross income minus Social Security taxes and withheld income taxes, but health insurance premiums and spousal and child support are *not* deducted, even if the support is ordered by a court. Thus, serious problems can occur if the same individual is subject to garnishment for consumer debt and also for support payments.

If the garnishment is for support rather than consumer debt, 15 U.S. Code §1673 allows a higher level of disposable earnings to be garnished:

- 50%, if the employee is supporting a spouse or child other than the subject of the order, and the garnishment order covers less than 12 weeks' worth of arrears
- 55%, if conditions are the same but more than 12 weeks of arrears are involved

- 60%, if the employee does *not* have a new family to support, and arrears are 12 weeks or less

- 65%, if there is no second family and arrears are over 12 weeks.

There is no limit whatsoever on garnishments in response to an order issued by a bankruptcy court in Chapter 11 or Chapter 13, or on a debt due for any state or federal tax. The general rule against alienation of plan benefits doesn't prevent the IRS from garnishing a taxpayer's (or, rather, non-taxpayer's) vested interest in qualified plan benefits when the agency has a judgment for unpaid taxes.

The federal Fair Debt Collection Procedures Act, 28 U.S.Code §3001 et.seq. (FDCPA), lets the federal government collect its judgments by garnishing property held by a third party when the debtor has a "substantial non-exempt interest" in the property. According to the Sixth Circuit, the IRS Regulations for qualified plans do not consider tax levies to violate ERISA's anti-alienation provision.

The CCPA says that, if state law limits garnishment more than the federal law does, employees are entitled to the protection of the stricter state-law limits. In other words, the company must reduce the amount garnished if state law requires this.

Under the CCPA, it's illegal to discharge an employee because he or she has *one* garnishment but it's lawful to fire if additional garnishments are imposed. (See 15 United States Code § 1674.) A willful violation of this provision can be punished by a $1,000 fine and/or one year's imprisonment.

8.9.1 Student Loan Garnishments

Separate federal rules appear at 20 United States Code §1095a dealing with garnishment to repay student loans. Up to 10% of disposable earnings can be garnished to repay those loans. The employee can sign a written document agreeing to a higher garnishment level. Before the garnishment order is submitted to the employer, the employee has the right to contest the garnishment and suggest a voluntary payment schedule. There is an unusual provision in this situation: if a person is fired or laid off from a job, and is re-hired by that employer or by another company less than 12 months after termination, student loan garnishment is deferred until the person has been back in the workforce for 12 months.

The federal provisions do not require employers to change or depart from their normal payment mechanisms to comply with student loan garnishment orders, but if they fail to comply with the order entirely, they can be penalized by the amount that should have been withheld to satisfy the garnishment, plus costs, fees, and punitive damages.

It is also contrary to federal law to discharge, refuse to hire, or discipline a person because he or she is subject to a student loan garnishment. Violative employers can be ordered to reinstate the affected employee with back pay, and can also be ordered to pay punitive damages and attorneys' fees.

8.9.2 *Child Support Collection*

If parents don't support their children, then it's much more likely that the children will become welfare recipients—an outcome that welfare programs are eager to avoid! A federal statute, the Child Support Enforcement Amendments of 1984, obligates states to enact laws requiring wage withholding for support arrears. If states fail to do this, their federal funding will be cut. In order to get federal Medicaid funding, states are obligated to have a procedure for Qualified Medical Child Support Orders (QMCSOs; see page 153), under which parents who are covered by an EGHP are required to take whatever steps are necessary to get the child covered under the health plan (and thus not enrolled in Medicaid).

Another aspect of the federal law is that all state-court child support orders are supposed to contain a withholding provision. That way, as soon as the parent who is supposed to pay support falls behind, the withholding order can be issued without separate court proceedings. The state child support enforcement agency mails the employer a notice that a particular employee is in arrears of child support; the employer's duty is to impose withholding as of the first pay period after 14 days from the date the agency mailed its notice.

➧ TIP

Once the employer begins withholding in accordance with the order, and the employee quits or gets fired, the employer has an obligation to notify the child support agency promptly, giving the termination date, the employee's last known address, and the address of the new employer (if known).

The CCPA percentage limits discussed above apply to child support orders, i.e., depending on circumstances, up to 65% of disposable earnings may be subject to support withholding. The Child Support Enforcement Amendments allow states to impose a late payment fee of 3-6% of the overdue support. Support withholding takes priority over other legal process (e.g., for consumer debts or student loans) applying to the same income.

As of October 1, 1997, employers will have a further reporting responsibility: within 20 days of hiring a new employee, the employer will have to submit data about that employee to the state unemployment insurance agency, so that the information can be aggregated into a National Directory of New Hires and used to find "deadbeat dads" (and any moms who are ordered to pay child support but fail to do so).

The basic federal report (which can be made by mail or magnetic tape; state support enforcement agencies can accept telephoned, faxed, and e-mailed reports) consists of the employer's name, address, and Taxpayer Identification Number, plus the employee's name, address, and Social Security Number. States may impose additional disclosure requirements, such as telephone numbers, driver's license numbers, and information about the group health plan (to be used in connection with medical child support orders).

Once hiring is reported, the employer will be further obligated to make a quarterly report of wages paid to its staff, for use in instituting withholding orders before major arrears accumulate. The Department of Health and Human Services will maintain a register of child support obligors, and will correlate the new-hire information with the obligor database. Employers can be fined $25 per employee for failure to make a required report, or $500 if they conspire with an employee to avoid the requirement.

8.10 TAX ISSUES IN EMPLOYEE COMPENSATION

Employees are subject to income taxation on their "wages," and the employer is required to withhold income taxes and submit them both to the IRS and to state and local taxing authorities. All remuneration (whether in cash or in kind) is considered to be "wages" unless it is specifically excluded. Therefore, not only salary but also vacation pay, commissions, bonuses, and certain fringe benefits are wages. Severance pay is considered wages and thus taxable, but payments for cancellation of an employment contract are not wages. The tax status of employment-related judgments and settlements is complex (see page 544), but the general rule is that personal injury damages are not taxed as wages, but back pay and other amounts that replace wages that should have been earned are taxed as wages and are subject to FICA and FUTA and withholding in the same way as normal wage payments.

Certain amounts operate as exclusions from taxable income:

- Worker's Compensation benefits
- Contributions that the employer makes to qualified pension plans. However, pretax deferrals placed into 401(k) plans are considered wages for FICA and FUTA purposes (see below). Also, a distribution from a qualified plan that is eligible to be a rollover (see page 294), but that is not rolled over to an IRA or another qualified plan is subject to withholding at a 20% rate.
- §79 group-term life insurance coverage up to $50,000. If the employer provides a higher level of coverage, the cost of the additional coverage is taxable income that must be reported on the W-2 form, but withholding is not required. Both the employer and employee share of FICA is required on the excess coverage, but it is not subject to FUTA tax.
- Certain fringe benefits are excluded—e.g., employee discounts; working condition and de minimis fringes (see page 182), qualified transportation fringes; employer-provided parking; qualified moving expenses; qualified dependent care assistance that does not exceed $5,000 a year ($2,500 a year for a married employee who does not file a joint return).

- Cash tips are not subject to FICA or FUTA if they are under $20 a month; tips over $20 are subject to FUTA to the extent reported by the employee. Amounts designated as tips on credit card vouchers are considered cash tips.

8.10.1 Tax Issues of Employment and Self-Employment

There are many contexts in which it is necessary to decide if someone is an employee or an independent contractor (e.g., whether that person is entitled to health insurance and qualified plan participation; if he or she is entitled to unemployment benefits upon termination of work; coverage of anti-discrimination laws), but perhaps the most salient is the tax context. If the individual is an employee, the employer will be responsible for paying its own share of FICA and FUTA tax, and must withhold income taxes.

However, the individual who is an independent contractor is responsible for his or her own tax compliance, and the employer does not have to pay employment taxes. Although the analysis of employee versus contractor status is similar, no matter what the context, the tests used for various purposes are not identical, and it is conceivable that a person will be an employee for some purposes but not for others.

The Internal Revenue Code specifically identifies some groups as statutory employees, and others as statutory non-employees. A licensed real estate agent who is compensated on the basis of output, not hours worked, and who has a written contract identifying him or her as an independent contractor is a statutory non-employee. So is a "direct seller" who sells consumer products outside of a permanent resale establishment, who is paid on the basis of output, and who has a written contract stipulating non-employee status.

In contrast, the following groups of workers are statutory employees:

- Agents or commission drivers who deliver food products, laundry, or dry cleaning
- A full-time traveling salesperson who solicits orders for merchandise to be delivered later (unlike the direct seller who delivers the merchandise at the time of sale)
- Full-time life insurance salespersons
- Corporate officers
- Persons who work in their own homes, but under the supervision of someone who supplies the materials to be used in work (e.g., assembling clothing components).

8.10.2 The 20-Factor Test

Internal IRS documents used to train tax auditors to identify 20 factors in deciding whether a person is an employee who is subject to income tax withholding. The factors are:

- If the potential "employer" gives instructions that the "employee" has to follow
- If the employer trains the employee. Independent contractors should not be asked to attend training sessions with regular employees.
- If the person renders services that are specific to him or her and can't be delegated to someone else
- If any assistants in the task are provided by the employer, not by an individual who is therefore more likely to be an independent contractor
- If the services are integrated into the employer's ordinary work, not separate
- If the work relationship continues over time. Independent contractors should not be asked to be "on call"
- If there are established, structured work hours or a work schedule (such as a shift system)
- If the employer requires full-time commitment from the worker
- If the worker works for other companies at the same time; if the answer is yes, it tends to imply independent contractor status (although someone could be a part-time employee and could have more than one part-time job)
- If work is done on the employer's premises
- If the employer determines the order or sequence of tasks to be done to accomplish the overall task
- If the worker has to submit regular reports (even regularly scheduled oral reports)
- If payment is by time (hour, week, or month) rather than by the project
- If the tools and materials come from the employer
- If the worker doesn't have to make a significant investment to accomplish the tasks
- If business and travel expenses are paid by the employer
- If the worker doesn't have a profit-and-loss interest in the employer's underlying business, and doesn't get paid by the employer's customers
- If the worker regularly offers services to the public; this suggests that the worker is an independent contractor
- If the employer has the right to fire the worker, it suggests an employment relationship; getting rid of an independent contractor usually involves exercising termination provisions of a contract (or refusing to renew the contract), not firing
- If the worker might have liability to the employer if he or she quits; if so, this suggests independent contractor status (because it is consistent with remedies for breach of contract).

If the IRS examines employment records and decides that one or more persons who were treated as independent contractors were actually employees, the employer will certainly have to make up the taxes that should have been paid but were not. The question is whether additional penalties will be imposed. If the employer filed all required information returns (W-2s and 1099s), and did not "intentionally misclassify" (i.e., lie about) worker status, then the penalty will be limited to 1.5% of the employee's wages, plus 20% of the FICA taxes that were not paid because the person was not treated as an employee.

However, those penalties are doubled if the information returns were *not* filed (unless there was reasonable cause for non-filing, and there was no willful neglect). Even heavier penalties are assessed if the employer made a deliberate attempt to avoid taxation, rather than merely making a mistake about who was supposed to get what information return on what schedule. (See page 105 for a discussion of the heavy penalties for failure to remit "trust fund" taxes.)

⇒ **TIP**

The employer is not allowed to go to the reclassified employee and demand reimbursement of the unpaid taxes or penalties, and these amounts cannot be deducted from the worker's future salary.

8.10.3 Safe Harbor Treatment

Of course, applying the long list of factors is complex, and reasonable people might differ (especially if one of them is an IRS agent in quest of back taxes!). Congress passed a safe harbor in 1978, in the form of §530 of the Revenue Act of 1978. Under §530, if an employer treats a person as an independent contractor, the IRS will not be able to re-classify that individual as an employee (or, more to the point, will not be able to assess back taxes and penalties or require payment of back FICA and Medicare taxes) as long as the employer acted reasonably and in good faith in treating that person as a non-employee. Employers can seek a refund of penalties already paid that they believe were improperly assessed.

There are three safe-harbor tests of reasonableness:

- There is published authority from the court system or the IRS (such as decisions, IRS rulings, or IRS Technical Advice Memorandums or even Private Letter Rulings) justifying independent contractor treatment in a situation like the employer's

- The IRS has already audited the employer, and didn't find any problems about employee characterization during the audit

- A significant segment of the employer's industry has an established practice of treating individuals who do similar work as independent contractors. For example, a 1996 Tax Court case finds that a used car dealer was entitled to use the safe harbor because a significant percentage of all used car dealers treated their sales staff as independent contractors.

However, to use the safe harbor, the employer must have been consistent about treating the person as an independent contractor, including filing the required 1099 forms. If, however, the person was treated as an employee at anytime after December 31, 1977, the safe harbor will not be available.

Some technical workers (for example, computer network administrators) are in a peculiar situation: although they work for one company, they spend a lot of work time doing assignments for client companies. Does that make them independent contractors, because they travel from site to site doing skilled work with little supervision? The IRS position is that the regular 20-factor test determines if the technical worker is an employee of the technical services firm that is hired by outside clients. If that firm has a direct contract with the worker and there are no clients involved, then the safe harbor might be available.

8.10.4 Other Tests of Employee Status

The common-law test of employee status is ability to control work behavior (both as to methods and as to results). This is the test applied in determining employee status for ERISA purposes, for instance.

State unemployment insurance coverage typically depends either on the common-law right of control, or supplying a worker with a workplace, tools, and materials in addition to control. Most states use an "ABC test": in other words, a person who performs services is an employee, and the employer must pay unemployment insurance premiums on behalf of that person, unless:

- The person is customarily engaged in an independent trade, business, profession, or occupation
- No direction or control is given in performing the services
- The services are not performed in the usual course of the employer's business, or are not performed within any regular business location of the employer.

If the employer fails to treat an employee as such, it has to pay unemployment insurance plus penalties and interest for the misclassified workers.

The Fair Labor Standards Act test is one of economic reality. In other words, a person who is not economically dependent on a company, and who is not an integral part of its operations, would not be an employee. The decision factors include:

- If the worker has made an investment in facilities or equipment

- Presence or absence of opportunity to earn profit or loss from managerial or special skills
- Control others have over his or her work
- Permanence of the work relationship
- Skill required to perform the services.

In this case, misclassification requires payment of any unpaid minimum wages and overtime that should have been paid if employee status had been acknowledged, plus liquidated damages, attorneys' fees, and court costs.

If it is questionable whether a person who charges violation of Title VII, the ADEA, or the ADA is actually an employee, three tests might be applied: common-law right to control; economic realities and dependence; or a hybrid of the two.

8.11 INCOME TAX WITHHOLDING COMPLIANCE

Once it is determined that someone is indeed an employee, the amount of income tax to be withheld is usually determined under either the percentage method or the wage bracket method. (If payroll tasks are outsourced, the payroll preparation contractor will do the calculations.)

The main factors in tax withholding are the amount of wages paid, the person's marital status (which determines his or her tax rate), and the number of exemptions claimed on the W-4 (the form the employee uses to claim withholding exemptions).

> ⇒ **TIP**
>
> If it has no W-4 on file for a particular employee, the employer can calculate deductions as if the employee were single with zero withholding exemptions.

The percentage method involves tables of withholding allowances and wage rates.

> ⇒ **TIP**
>
> Official tables are published in Circular E, the IRS publication dealing with the employer's tax compliance duties. (It's IRS Publication 15, supplemented by 15-A.) If you need more detailed information about scheduling tax payments, see Publication 509, updated each year to explain the tax calendar for that year.

The number of allowances claimed is multiplied by the amount from the allowance table. The product is subtracted from the employee's wages; then the wage rate table gives the actual amount to be withheld.

Under the wage bracket method, tables are used to compute withholding per pay period (weekly, semiweekly, monthly, etc.) based on wage level, marital status, and number of claimed exemptions.

8.11.1 Withholding in Special Circumstances

In addition to the fairly straightforward techniques to be used for ordinary wages and salaries, the HR department may encounter some more complex withholding challenges. For income tax purposes, "supplemental wages" means compensation other than or in addition to ordinary cash compensation: bonuses, commissions, overtime pay, severance pay, back pay, taxable fringe benefits, and payments for accumulated sick leave.

If supplemental wages are simply combined with ordinary compensation in a paycheck, with no allocation between the two, withholding should be done as if the supplemental wages were actually ordinary compensation. However, if the supplemental amount is paid in a separate check, or as part of the regular paycheck but with an explicit allocation, then either the supplemental and regular wages can be treated and withheld as a single payment (with a credit for amounts already withheld), or you can apply a 28% flat rate to the supplemental wages.

8.11.2 Expense Accounts

It is quite common for employees to incur expenses on behalf of the employer (e.g., buying tickets for business travel, using a personal automobile for business travel, charging a hotel bill to a personal credit card, or buying meals during a business trip or when entertaining a customer or potential customer). If legitimate, these are all expenses that the employer could have paid at the outset. But it is usually more convenient for the employer to require the employee to forward the money and submit a claim proving the nature and amount of expenses to be reimbursed.

Legitimate reimbursement of business expenses is not income for the employee, and therefore the withholding system must differentiate between compensation paid to the employee and expense reimbursements. For tax purposes, expense accounts are characterized as either accountable or non-accountable plans. Amounts paid under an accountable plan are not wages for the employee, so they are not subject to FICA or FUTA taxes and withholding is not required.

Employees must meet three tests under an accountable plan:

- They paid or incurred deductible expenses in the course of their employment
- They have to provide adequate accounts of the expenses within a reasonable time of incurring them

- They have to give back within a reasonable time any amount they receive over and above their expenses.

If these tests are not met, the money is treated as if it were paid under a nonaccountable plan (one which does not require documentation of expenses). Such a consideration makes the money wages for the employee, to be included in income and subject to withholding in the first payroll period after the expiration of a reasonable time to return the excess funds.

The general rule is that it is reasonable for employees to get their reimbursement within 30 days of spending the money; to provide an expense account within 60 days after spending the money; and for them to return excess amounts within 120 days of advancing the money initially.

⇒ TIP

Accounting for a per diem or fixed allowances (e.g., X cents per mile) is considered adequate as long as the payments are within the government per diem rates for meals and lodging (see IRS Publication 1542) and the standard mileage rate for travel (see Publication 553).

8.11.3 Pension Withholding

Pension plans that make payments to retired employees are required to withhold income tax from the taxable portion of each payment. Retirees can elect NOT to have withholding performed, but withholding is mandatory in some circumstances. For ordinary payments in annuity form, the plan can use ordinary withholding procedures, based on the number of withholding exemptions on the Form W-4P filed by the retiree. If no W-4P is submitted, the plan should withhold as if the retiree is married with three withholding allowances.

If, on the other hand, the distribution is not an annuity but a lump sum or other non-periodic payment, the question is whether or not it is an "eligible rollover distribution." If it is not, the basic rule is 10% withholding, although the person receiving the lump sum can use the W-4P to claim exemption from withholding; or, if he or she expects to be in a high tax bracket, the person can ask for withholding at a rate higher than 10%.

However, certain amounts are eligible for placement in the retiree's IRA or for transfer to another qualified plan. If these amounts are not rolled over, then withholding must be made at a rate of at least 20%. The recipient of the distribution can increase the withholding rate, but cannot lower it below 20% or claim a withholding exemption. See the instructions for the IRS Form 1099-R. Within a reasonable time before making the distribution, the plan is obligated to notify the recipient of the option to roll over the funds, and the withholding consequences if he or she prefers not to roll over.

> ⇒ **TIP**
>
> IRS Notice 92-48, 1992-2 C.B. 377, provides the text of a sample notice you can use to explain withholding on lump sums.

Withholding from lump-sum pension distributions is *not* reported on Form 941; instead, it belongs on Form 945, the Annual Return of Withheld Federal Income Tax. The pension withholding amounts should be combined with the other Form 945 amounts, but for non-payroll withholding only, not payroll taxes. See the Form 945 instructions for further information. The recipient of the distribution receives a Form 1099-R, Distributions from Pensions, Annuities, Retirement or Profit-Sharing Plans.

> ⇒ **TIP**
>
> Because of a 1996 Treasury Decision (T.D. 8672), it is not necessary to file Form 945 in every calendar year, only in years in which federal income tax is withheld from non-payroll payments.

8.12 TRUST FUND TAX COMPLIANCE AND THE 100% PENALTY

Employers are required to make payments of FICA (Social Security/Medicare taxes), which can be substantial. Employers must also withhold the employee share of FICA tax and withhold income tax on employee earnings. (Also see pages 104 and 295 for discussions of withholding in the pension context.)

FICA tax consists of two parts. One of them funds old age and disability benefits (OASDI component); the other one funds Medicare Part A (HI component). The OASDI component is charged on only part of the employee's wages; it is not collected after the employee's compensation reaches the "wage base." (The 1997 wage base is $65,400, and 1998's is $68,400.)

> ⇒ **TIP**
>
> The new wage base for each year is published in the Federal Register by November 1 of the preceding year. (Publication usually occurs in late October.)

Employer and employee are each responsible for payment of OASDI tax at a rate of 6.2%. The HI component, at 1.45% each for employer and employee, is charged on the employee's full salary; it does not stop when the employee's compensation reaches the wage base. If an employee has more than one employer during a calendar year, the wage base applies to compensation from each employer. If this results in over-withholding, it's up to the employee to claim a credit for the excess payments.

The amounts withheld from employees are referred to as "trust fund taxes"; although the employer's FICA share, and Federal Unemployment Tax Act (FUTA) taxes must also be paid, they are not trust-fund taxes. Frequently employers will collect such amounts at every payroll, yet will not have to make deposits until the end of the quarter. The temptation for a cash-strapped company to "borrow" that money for its own immediate needs is immense.

To stem temptation, Code §6672 subjects "responsible persons" to a 100% penalty (not dischargeable in bankruptcy) for willful failure to submit withheld trust fund taxes to the government. That is, in addition to having to pay over the money owed to the government, the responsible person must pay a penalty of the same size, and all of his or her personal assets can be attached to satisfy the debt.

The definition of "responsible persons" is quite broadly drawn. It includes the corporation's officers, shareholders, and directors, based on their level of responsibility within the corporation. For example, factors include authority to hire and fire, to choose which creditors will be paid in what order, control over payroll, and power to deposit federal tax amounts. Top management will probably be liable because of the degree of control it exercises over corporate financial matters. Lower-level managers will probably not be liable unless their duties include actually writing checks (and thus actual knowledge of amounts disbursed or not disbursed). Even parties outside the corporation, such as its bankers and accountants, can be liable if they have the real control over corporate funds.

If a penalty is due, the government has the option of collecting it all from one responsible person, or dividing it among several responsible persons. To escape liability, it is necessary to prove that the individual was wrongly characterized as a responsible person, or that the failure to pay over the funds was not willful. The provision can operate quite onerously: for instance, if a corporation's treasurer or other officer wants to submit the taxes as required, but gets orders "from above" to use the money to pay creditors instead, the courts have a history of penalizing the corporate officer in addition to, or even instead of, the higher-up who gave the order.

In the legal system's view, the corporate officer in effect chose between keeping his job and fulfilling his tax obligations; if the job meant that much, he should be prepared to pay the penalty. Even if he quits his job in protest, he is still liable for payments that should have been made prior to resigning.

But the IRS, upheld by the court system, doesn't just penalize corporate officers; lower-level managers with day-to-day financial powers and check-writing authority can be subject to the 100% penalty as well.

Only "willful" failures to pay over the taxes are subject to the 100% penalty, but in this context willfulness merely means knowledge that the taxes were not submitted, added to a failure to correct the situation. And if a responsible person finds out that payments were omitted for one quarter, that creates a duty to investigate and find out if other payments were missed as well.

When a business is in trouble, the trust fund taxes aren't the only financial problem. Sometimes the company has already defaulted on a loan, which then gives the lender the right to take over the company's finances. If the lender neglects or refuses to submit the trust fund taxes . . . you guessed it, the borrower corporation's staff can still be treated as responsible parties who "willfully" allowed the payments to be omitted (even if they ordered, urged, or pleaded with the lender to pay the trust fund taxes).

Some courts are tough, saying that the borrower corporation should have filed for bankruptcy protection to keep the lender from applying the trust fund tax money to other debts, although others will accept the argument that failure to pay is not willful if someone else prevented the payment from being made.

The responsible person's duty is to use all of the corporation's "unencumbered funds" to take care of the trust fund taxes. Unencumbered funds are those that have not already been assigned to a debt that existed before the tax liability arose. The courts ask a lot before they consider amounts "encumbered"—a perfected security interest doesn't always count, although the creditor's seizing funds and putting them in its own lockbox would probably be considered an encumbrance.

How can you protect yourself in this situation? Press strongly for a corporate policy that allocates funds to the trust taxes first. In fact, if the company owes money to the IRS under various tax provisions, it's essential to make sure that tax payments are allocated first to the trust fund taxes, then to other amounts owed, because the other penalties are lower than 100%.

When a company makes voluntary payments of withholding taxes (i.e., payments made routinely, not in response to a suit by the IRS or IRS collection proceedings), it can give the IRS specific instructions that the funds are applied first to the trust fund taxes. But without clear instructions, the IRS is likely to apply the taxes in the way that yields the highest, not the lowest, penalties. Furthermore, once the IRS undertakes collection, it will not take instructions from the debtor about how to allocate the funds.

If somebody else is supposed to forward the money to the IRS, don't just assume that it was done; check to see that trust fund taxes are submitted on time. Make sure your loan agreements stipulate that the lender will forward trust fund taxes before making payments to itself or other creditors.

Thanks to the Taxpayer Bill of Rights 2, the IRS must give the responsible person advance written notice before imposing the penalty; the notice must also disclose who else is supposed to be a responsible person, what collection efforts the IRS has made against that party, and the success of those efforts. The responsible person can pay the penalty and sue for a refund, or contest the penalty in federal court (collection efforts will be suspended until the case is resolved). For penalties assessed after July 30, 1996, if there is more than one responsible party but the IRS pursues only some of them, the responsible parties who actually pay the penalty can sue the other responsible parties to make them pay their fair share.

8.12.1 Other Tax Penalties

Even for companies and responsible parties who steer past the shoals of the trust fund taxes, the Internal Revenue Code offers plentiful opportunities for getting into trouble. Criminal penalties are imposed for willful acts of fraud and evasion.

There are five potential sources of criminal liability:

- Willful failure to collect or pay over federal tax; the penalty is up to $10,000 and/or up to five years in prison, and the defendant also has to pay the costs of prosecution.

- Willful failure to pay tax, make a return, keep records, or provide mandated information to the IRS *is* only a misdemeanor (not a felony), but can still be penalized by up to a year in jail and/or a $25,000 fine (individual) or $100,000 fine (corporate). Here, too, the defendant has to pay prosecution costs.

- Willful furnishing of a false or fraudulent tax statement, or willful refusal to furnish a required statement, carries a penalty of up to $1,000 and/or one year per violation.

- Willful tax evasion can be punished by up to five years in prison and/or $100,000 (for an individual) or $500,000 (for a corporation).

- It's perjury to willfully sign a return or other tax document that you know is false or inaccurate, and the penalty can be up to three years' imprisonment and/or $100,000 (individual) or $500,000 (corporate).

In practice, the IRS often goes for civil penalties instead, because it's easy to prove that taxes weren't paid, but hard to prove the mindset of the person or organization that was supposed to do the paying.

8.13 TAX DEPOSITS: PAPER FORMS

The standard method of paying FICA and Medicare taxes, and of forwarding income taxes withheld from employees' pay, is to send cash, checks, or money orders to a Federal Reserve Bank or other financial institution that is authorized as a tax depository. As the next section shows, the IRS plans to phase out this paper-based method in favor of mandatory electronic payments. However, for smaller companies, or for larger companies that have some trouble implementing the electronic system, paper forms will continue to be used for at least a few more years.

The very smallest firms do not have to make tax deposits; they can pay their entire deposit liability, of $500 or less, once a year when filing Form 941. However, it is very unlikely that a company with 100 or more employees, the target audience of this book, would fit into that category.

The basic paper form for deposits is Form 8109, the Federal Tax Deposit (FTD) Coupon. (It cannot be used to pay delinquent taxes assessed by the IRS; those have to be sent directly to the IRS, with copies of the IRS notice assessing the delinquency.) Employers get their first supply of FTD coupons when they first apply for an Employer Identification Number; after that, the IRS sends a continuing supply of coupons to replace the ones used to deposit taxes.

It's important to make a clear allocation of amounts deposited with the FTD coupon, so your account can be credited correctly. The FTD coupon and the money to pay the taxes must be mailed or delivered to a Federal Reserve Bank or other financial institution authorized to receive tax deposits. In other words, the coupon and money do NOT go to the IRS, and the check should be made payable to the bank, not the IRS. Make sure your check includes the company's Employer Identification Number, the type of tax, and the time period for which the payment is being made.

Unless you can show that you were not willfully neglectful, and there was good cause for the delay, you may be subject to late-deposit penalties, ranging from 2% if the deposit is one to five days late, to 10% if your deposit is over 16 days late, or if 10 days elapse after the IRS notifies you that tax is due and it still remains unpaid.

Income tax withheld on non-payroll amounts is not reported on Form 941; it is reported on Form 945, and 941 and 945 amounts should not be combined in a single deposit.

8.13.1 The Deposit Schedule

Depending on the amount at stake, tax deposits are required either monthly or semi-weekly (i.e., once every other week), keyed to the company's payroll period (which is the time at which the liability to pay taxes arises). However, it is perfectly possible for a company that pays its personnel twice a month to be a monthly depositor, or for a company that pays weekly to deposit on either the monthly or the semi-weekly schedule.

Companies that reported $50,000 or less on Line 11 of Form 941 during the look-back period deposit once a month (no later than the 15th of the following month), using Form 941. Those who reported more must deposit semi-weekly. Deposits relating to payments made on a Wednesday, Thursday, or Friday are due on the following Wednesday; those for Saturday through Tuesday are due on the following Friday. The look-back period is a 12-month period running from July 1-June 30 a year and a half earlier: i.e., for 1997, the look-back period is July 1995-June 1996.

Theoretically, employers are supposed to deposit 100% of their tax liability. An underpayment penalty of 5% of the unpaid tax per month of non-payment is required, subject to a maximum of 25% of the unpaid tax. There is also a penalty on late payments: 0.5% per month, up to a cap of 25%. However, the penalty will be waived if there was good cause for the failure, or if the shortfall is less than 2% of the taxes due (or is less than $100, whichever is greater), and the employer catches up by the special catch-up date (the due date of the Form 941 for the quarter, for monthly depositors; by the Form 941 due date, or close to the 15th of the month after the month of the shortfall).

8.13.2 Nonpayroll Withholding

It is common for employers to have to perform withholding on nonpayroll amounts in two situations: pension payments in annuity form, and backup withholding. The rules for pension withholding are discussed at page 104; the appropriate tax return is Form 945 Annual Return of Withheld Federal Income Tax, which is due on January 31 of the year following the year for which taxes are being reported. All tax withholding that was reported on Form 1099s must be summarized on Form 945.

⇒ TIP

If an individual receives distributions from a non-qualified pension plan, that money is considered to be wages and should be disclosed to the individual on Form W-2 and summed up on Form 941. However, if the payments are not made directly to the employee or ex-employee, but to a beneficiary or to the ex-employee's estate, disclosure should be made on Form 1099-R and Form 945.

Backup withholding is required if a payor does not have a valid taxpayer identification number on record for a payee; this sometimes happens if independent contractors or individuals entitled to royalty payments or commissions forget or refuse to submit TINs. (The payor can use Form W-9 to request the payee to provide a TIN; see IRS Publication 1679, *A Guide to Backup Withholding*, for more information.) Because the payor lacks adequate information, it cannot make an accurate determination of withholding, and consequently must withhold at a default rate of 31%. Because this is higher than most people end up paying, it serves to encourage payees to provide the data!

8.13.3 W-2 Forms

The W-2 form, in its conventional paper form, reports employee compensation for the year and is in six parts. Copy A is submitted to the Social Security

Administration. Copy 1 goes to the state, city, or local tax department; Copies 2, B and C go to the employee, who files one with the federal tax return, one with the state tax return, and keeps the other. Copy D is retained by the employer for its own records.

➠ TIP

Companies with 250 or more employees are supposed to file their W-2 forms on magnetic media, but if it is more convenient to file on paper, you can file Form 8508 before the due date for the W-2s and the W-3 transmittal form. See the W-2 Instructions for more information on how to get an exemption.

8.14 PAYING TAXES ELECTRONICALLY

Employers whose deposits of FICA, Medicare, and withheld income taxes for calendar 1995 were greater than $50,000 are supposed to use the EFTPS system. This provides for electronic deposit of taxes due on Form 720 (quarterly federal excise tax), 940 and 940-EZ (Federal Unemployment Tax Act form), and 941 (employer's quarterly federal tax return). Those whose deposits were over $50,000 in 1996 but not in 1995 are supposed to start using EFTPS by 1/1/98, and even those with deposit liability of $20,000 for 1997 are supposed to switch to the electronic system no later than 1/1/99. The switch to EFTPS is permanent—no matter how low a company's responsibilities fall, they cannot go back to using paper tax deposit forms.

EFTPS is also supposed to be used by employers with depository tax liability other than employment taxes (e.g., corporate income tax), if they had to deposit over $50,000 in calendar 1995 or 1996 (EFTPS required by 1/1/98), or over $20,000 in 1997 (EFTPS required by 1/1/99). However, because the IRS has had a lot of trouble getting its own electronic filing systems to work, penalties will not be imposed in 1997 on employers who make appropriate and timely deposits but continue to use paper forms.

The IRS doesn't charge a fee for using the system, but bank fees are a distinct possibility for on-line debit and credit or FEDWIRE transactions. Employers have to take affirmative steps to enroll in the EFTPS system. Forms are available from the two EFTPS Customer Service Centers, First Chicago/Mercantile Services for the Northern U.S. (1-800-945-8400) and NationsBank for the South (1-800-555-4477). The IRS set up the system based on voluntary enrollment rather than automatically transferring everyone with large enough tax deposits into the system, because the payments are based on bank account information, business structures, and the business' preferred method of payment. Companies already using TAXLINK are required to convert to EFTPS.

⇒ **TIP**

Internal Revenue Bulletin 1997-30 contains several IRS pronounce-ments explaining various aspects of electronic filing.

8.15 TAX COMPLIANCE CALENDAR

Tax compliance is a blend of one-time or uncommon events and recurring ones. For instance, when a new employee is hired, he or she should submit a W-4 form so you will be able to determine his or her withholding allowances and thus the amount to be withheld from each paycheck.

As explained above, most employers will have to make tax deposits of trust fund taxes and withheld income tax either monthly or 26 times a year. Employers whose payroll is too small to require regular tax deposits can make quarterly pay-ments in conjunction with the Form 941 filing. Quarterly filing and deposits are also required for FUTA tax.

Employees are entitled to receive a W-2 (Wage and Tax Statement) form by January 31 of the year after the year being reported. If it is inconvenient to distrib-ute the forms in the workplace, they can be sent by first class mail. Individuals (e.g., independent contractors) who received miscellaneous compensation must get a Form 1099-MISC; retirees get a Form 1099-R.

January 31 is also the due date for Form 945 (Annual Return of Withheld Federal Income Tax) and the FUTA tax form, which could be either Form 940 or Form 940-EZ, depending on circumstances.

⇒ **TIP**

Filing this form can be delayed until February 10 if all FUTA tax was deposited when due. (The dates for quarterly FUTA deposits are April 30, July 31, October 31, and January 31; quarterly filing is required if the tax is over $100, a small enough amount to make quarterly filings virtu-ally universal.) The FUTA deposit goes to the local Federal Reserve Bank or other authorized financial institution, using IRS Form 8109.

No later than February 15, all employees (other than those who did not claim any withholding exemptions) should be asked for a new W-4 to update the number of their withholding allowances. (It's proper to ask for the new form in January, or even in December of the preceding year.) Withhold on the basis of a single taxpay-er with no allowances for all employees who do not submit the form by February 16.

February 28 is the due date for filing the employer's copy of all 1099 forms, accompanied by Form 1096, Annual Summary and Transmittal of U.S. Information Returns. The appropriate place for filing is your local IRS center. The employer's copy of all W-2 forms is due on the same date. The summary transmittal form is the W-3, Transmittal of Wage and Tax Statements, but in this case the destination is the Social Security Administration.

The quarterly filing dates for Form 941 are April 30, July 31, October 31, and January 31, with a 10-day extension permitted if all taxes have already been deposited under the monthly or semi-weekly plan.

➠ **TIP**
_____

IRS Publication 509, revised annually, gives the latest tax calendar.

EMPLOYEE GROUP HEALTH PLANS (EGHPs)

9.1 INTRODUCTION

Given the high cost of medical care, very few people would be willing to pay out of pocket for all the care they and their families require. And, given the high cost of health insurance, employees consider health insurance furnished under an employee group health plan (EGHP) one of the fundamental and most valued components of the compensation package. Although many small companies refrain from providing such coverage for their employees, health insurance of some sort is virtually universal for employees of larger companies (including those with 100 or more employees).

Of course, employers are not unaffected by the high cost of health insurance, and there has been an increasing trend to limit the scope of coverage, limit coverage of dependents, require employees to pay (or pay more) for insurance, and increase deductible and coinsurance amounts so that employees undertake a higher proportion of the costs themselves. There has also been a shift from indemnity insurance to managed care, so that virtually all employees who are covered by EGHPs either have managed care as an option or as the sole health care coverage mechanism in the plan.

The central feature of EGHPs is provision for employees' hospital bills, doctor bills, and perhaps recuperative home care, physical therapy, and related treatments. Generally, prescription drugs, dental care and vision care will either not be covered by an employer plan, or will be covered by a fringe benefit plan separate from the EGHP. See p. 119.

There is no legal requirement that employers offer health benefits at all, although once offered, there may be limitations on alteration or termination of the benefits. For ERISA purposes, EGHPs are welfare benefit plans, and therefore employees do not become vested. However, in many (if not most) circumstances, the employer will have some degree of contractual obligation to maintain the plan. In a unionized company, the CBA will impose further limitations on the employer's ability to terminate or alter its health plans.

9.2 CONTENT OF THE PLAN

Federal regulation of pension benefits via ERISA is extremely thorough and detailed; ERISA regulation of welfare benefit plans is far less extensive. The employer has immense leeway in designing a health plan (or, indeed, in deciding not to offer health benefits, or to limit them to non-qualified plans for key employees). However, certain federal laws outside ERISA, state laws, and court cases do impose some constraints on complete freedom of health plan design.

9.2.1 Mental Health Parity

A 1996 statute, the Veterans' Affairs, Housing and Urban Development and Independent Agencies Appropriations Act (P.L. 104-204) imposes a requirement of parity between benefits for mental ailments and benefits for physical ailments provided under an EGHP. The parity requirement applies to employers of 50 or more employees. If a plan does not impose lifetime or annual limits on medical and surgical benefits, it cannot do so for mental health benefits.

If, like most plans, the plan does impose a limit, the limits must be the same for mental and physical ailments. In 1996, Congress put this requirement into ERISA; in 1997, as part of the 1997 tax and budget bill, the mental health parity requirement was made part of the Internal Revenue Code, for services furnished between January 1, 1998, and before September 30, 2001, when the mental health parity provision phases out.

At first glance, this is a crippling burden for employers. However, the statute contains a number of relief provisions. First of all, it does not require plans to *add* mental health coverage if such is not already part of the plan. Second, it excludes substance abuse treatment from the definition of health coverage. Third, it permits employers to have different deductibles, coinsurance amounts, numbers of visits, or days of coverage for mental and physical ailments, as long as the limits are the same. Finally, perhaps most important, a plan is exempt from the statute if parity would raise the costs of the health plan by 1% or more. Thus the financial impact of the statute is limited, not infinite. The statute is also time-limited: as noted above, it phases out in September, 2001 (unless Congress renews it).

In December, 1997, the Clinton Administration announced a new policy: companies would have to comply with the mental health parity requirement for at least a year before seeking an exemption.

9.2.2 Maternity Stays

The Newborns' and Mothers' Health Protection Act of 1996, P.L. 104-204, and the Taxpayer Relief Act of 1997, P.L. 105-35, combine ERISA and tax code provisions in the same way as the mental health parity provision described on the previous page. Group health plans must provide at least a minimum hospital stay for childbirth: 48 hours after a normal delivery, 96 hours after a C-section.

The mother and child can be discharged from the hospital earlier than this if the patient's attending physician allows it (after consulting the mother), but the plan is not allowed to offer financial incentives (to mother or, especially, to health care provider) to shorten the stay. Both insured and self-insured EGHPs are subject to this requirement, no matter how few or how many employees are covered. But if the plan does not provide hospitalization benefits for childbirth, it is not required to add those benefits because of this legislation. If the plan operates in a state that requires coverage of an even longer maternity stay, this legislation does not preempt the more protective state law.

Failure to abide by this requirement is subject to the Code §4980D penalty of $100 per participant per day from the occurrence of the failure to the time of its correction. If the failure to provide an adequate postpartum stay is unintentional, and is corrected within 30 days, no penalty will be imposed. If the failure is unintentional and not corrected, the maximum penalty is $500,000 a year, or 10% of the EGHP's expenses for the year before the failure—whichever is less.

9.2.3 Other Inclusion Issues

The Eighth Circuit view is that it is lawful to exclude infertility treatments (both male and female) from plan coverage without violating Title VII, the PDA, or the ADA, on the theory that nobody (fertile or infertile) could receive fertility treatments under the plan, so there was no discrimination.

EGHPs are forbidden to discriminate against employees and their dependents who suffer from end-stage renal disease (ESRD). Code §5000 imposes a heavy penalty for violating this requirement: 25% of the employer's expenses (not just the amount they should have paid for ESRD benefits). Also note that ERISA §609(d) requires plans to maintain their coverage for pediatric vaccines at least at the May 1, 1993 level.

9.2.4 Domestic Partner Benefits

Although the usual categories are "married" and "single," a number of employees have non-marital domestic partners, whether same-sex or of the opposite sex but involved in a cohabitation rather than a marital relationship. Initially, dependent care benefits were restricted to legal spouses. Today, an increasing number of companies are offering health benefits to the domestic partners of their employees.

> ⇒ **TIP**
>
> For same-sex couples, some states and cities have a provision for "registered domestic partnerships." Although they are not the civil equivalent of marriages, they do make it easier to distinguish between long-term relationships that are marriage-equivalents and other relationships. Registration of the partnership, or the fact that the domestic partners have gone through a commitment ceremony, could be evidence of the quasi-marital nature of the relationship.

The general rule is that it's up to the employer whether to offer or refuse to offer domestic partner benefits. The advantages: management may feel that it's only fair to recognize more than one type of relationship; it may be worthwhile as a way of attracting and retaining top-flight employees who are involved in nonmarital relationships. The disadvantages: all health benefits are expensive; some managers, fellow employees, customers, or suppliers may feel that recognition of non-marital relationships is contrary to their moral and ethical values. As of mid-1997, about 500 companies and non-profit employers (e.g., universities) offered domestic partner benefits.

The Society for Human Resources Management did a mini-survey on domestic partner benefits and found that about one company out of every ten either had or was considering adding benefits for domestic partners. Of the companies that do provide partner benefits, 85% provide medical benefits, 74% dental benefits, and 55% offer vision care. About one-third of the companies offer benefits for non-marital partners in heterosexual couples; 21% offer the benefits for same-sex couples only (after all, heterosexual couples have but presumably rejected the option of marriage); and 43% cover all domestic partnerships.

However, that doesn't mean that these companies are patsies: as a condition of granting benefits, 42% require proof that the alleged partners share a home, and 38% ask for a notarized affidavit of partnership status. The organizations that do not offer domestic partner benefits tend to reject this option because of lack of interest on the part of employees (56%), moral objections (21%), and fear of cost increases (30%). Eighty-five percent of the companies with partner benefits report, however, that the cost impact of adding these benefits was small.

Employers that actually implement domestic partner benefits are often surprised at how *unpopular* these benefits are. Although the expectation has been that 3-4% of a company's workforce would sign up, in practice only about 1/2 of 1% have done so. Perhaps their partners already have adequate health insurance; perhaps the premium and copayments required for domestic partner coverage are not affordable, or are not competitive with other insurance alternatives; or perhaps the individuals involved prefer not to disclose the fact that they are living with a non-marital partner (especially a same-sex partner).

In a 1997 Private Letter Ruling, the IRS said that the fair market value of group-term life insurance provided to employees' domestic partners, and the children of the domestic partners, constitutes taxable income to the employee. This is also the case for medical, hospitalization, dental, and prescription drug benefits for domestic partners and their dependents. On the other hand, once benefits are paid under the insurance policies, the insurance benefits do not constitute taxable income at all (if they are made because of the death of the domestic partner). For medical and allied insurance, the benefits are not taxable income for the employee to the extent that the employee paid for the coverage, or the fair market value of the coverage was included in his or her taxable income.

9.2.5 Dental Plans

The traditional definition of health insurance does not include the care provided by dentists, although it is obvious that the implications of tooth and gum problems go far beyond the cosmetic. It is quite common for medium-sized and large employers to offer some form of dental coverage: in 1993, about two-thirds of such companies did so. As with most health-related benefits, the prevalence of the benefit increases directly with the size of the company actually or potentially offering it.

> ⇒ **TIP**
>
> Companies that decide to implement a dental plan often find that claims in the first few years are very heavy, as employees and their families satisfy a previously unmet need for dental procedures that they couldn't afford on an out-of-pocket basis.

Dental plans usually follow patterns currently or formerly found in EGHPs. For instance, about six out of every seven dental plans are fee-for-service plans; only about one-seventh of the plans use HMOs or PPOs (in about equal proportions). Dental plans are subject to COBRA's continuation coverage requirement (see page 142).

The basic structure of a dental plan is a schedule of covered procedures and payments for each (which might be defined as dollar amounts or percentages). The general rule is that the percentage of coverage is inversely related to the expected cost of the service, so low-cost procedures like X-rays and examinations get a higher percentage of coverage (often, 100%, but it's also typical for only two exams and cleanings to be covered per year) than fillings, root canals, and dental surgery (typically covered at 80%), and only 50% coverage for prosthetics and orthodontia. Typical dental-plan exclusions: cosmetic dentistry; hospitalization for in-patient dental procedures; and amounts that would be covered by other insurance (including Worker's Compensation).

It is usual for dental plans to provide care subject to an annual maximum amount (in 1993, the most common was $1,000 a year, the second most common $1,500 a year), with employee copayment responsibilities. It is typical for the copayment to be low for preventive procedures such as examinations and cleaning, but higher for expensive treatments. In addition, many plans are controlling their costs by increasing the copayment expected of employees. The dentist who renders the care is paid for each service to covered employees (in a fee for service plan) or receives capitated or other pre-arranged compensation under an HMO or PPO plan.

Dental plan claims administration is usually similar to EGHP claims administration. That is, both the covered employee and the dentist rendering the service complete claim forms. Depending on the way the plan is drafted, the dentist might be paid directly, or the employee might pay and be reimbursed for the covered portion of the amount spent on treatment. A common provision is to limit reimbursement to a percentage of the least expensive commonly accepted treatment method, even if this does not have the best cosmetic result. (Employees who choose alternate procedures that are more cosmetic-oriented will thus have to pay a large percentage of the cost of the actual treatment.) There is an increasing trend to require advance approval of large non-emergency claims (e.g., treatments costing $200 or more).

9.2.6 Prescription Drug Coverage

It is very common for a company's ordinary EGHP to provide at least some coverage of prescription drugs; after all, medical treatment would be incomplete if patients could not afford to take the drugs prescribed by the physicians whose services are covered by the plan. However, some employers offer separate prescription drug plans to achieve cost savings (by ordering in bulk), to save employees the burden of saving receipts and filing multiple small claims, or to cover prescriptions that would otherwise be excluded before the employee met the plan deductible or a separate deductible for each spell of illness.

Depending on the employer's preferences, the prescription plan may also cover dependents. Employees might have to pay part of the cost of dependent coverage, or it could be an optional, employee-pay-all extra.

The typical prescription drug plan covers only outpatient drugs—i.e., drugs prescribed and taken while the employee is a hospital patient are covered under the benefits for hospital care. The plans are usually limited to drugs; medical equipment such as wheelchairs and oxygen tanks are typically excluded, and generally speaking, non-prescription drugs are not covered (although insulin generally is covered and some plans exclude contraceptives). The usual plan requires a copayment for each prescription, but this is generally less than $10.

Even if an employee is chronically ill and has a predictable continuing need for prescription medications, most plans limit the amount of the drug that can be dispensed at any one time under the plan: usually 100 doses or about one month's supply, whichever is greater. However, the prescription can be repeated as needed. Overall dollar limitations on reimbursement per plan year are fairly common, but far from universal.

Mail order plans, another cost control device, allow negotiations for major bulk cost savings on prescriptions that can be dispensed by mail—e.g., a heart patient's always-renewed prescription for cardiac drugs. This arrangement allows for centralized claims processing, thus cutting that cost, but the mail order plan is not well-suited to acute-care drugs that are required immediately, and for only a short time (e.g., antibiotics to treat an infection that clears up quickly).

Mail order plans can be combined with nationwide panel plans which can also operate independently. The nationwide panel plan creates a network of pharmacies who agree to sell prescription drugs at the panel's schedule prices. A prepaid drug plan administrator (similar to a TPA firm; see page 138) coordinates the plan. All participating pharmacies accept membership cards from employees who are enrolled in the nationwide panel plan; they submit their claims for payment directly to the plan.

9.3 ERISA PREEMPTION

Employees who charge the employer with some form of impropriety often prefer to sue in state rather than federal court, because cases often get to court faster in the state system, and for various technical legal reasons, the employees are likely to be entitled to a broader range of remedies in state than in federal court.

However, cases involving EGHPs often have to be tried in federal court, because of a legal doctrine called "ERISA preemption." That is, the federal law replaces state regulation of many benefit-related issues. However, it can be quite difficult to decide whether or not ERISA preempts state law. Sophisticated legal concepts are involved, and the complex rules carry a host of exceptions.

ERISA always preempts state laws that "relate to" employee benefit plans that are covered by ERISA Title I. Health insurance is usually part of a welfare benefit plan covered by Title I, so ERISA preemption is common in this context.

There's an important exception: states, not the federal government, are assigned the major role in regulating insurance, so state laws might not be preempted if the legal system interprets the case as involving insurance rather than plan benefits.

It makes a big difference whether the employee charges medical malpractice or questions the quality of care provided under the plan (which will probably not be preempted) or whether he or she seeks benefits under the plan (when preemption will probably occur). In the latter case, it is necessary for courts to interpret the language of the welfare benefit plan, so ERISA preemption is triggered. In the former case, the conduct of the health care provider, not the content of the plan, is at stake.

9.3.1 ERISA Preemption of HMO Claims

If a person chooses a doctor and goes to the doctor's office for treatment, and if the doctor's carelessness injures the patient, the malpractice case is fairly straightforward. The patient sues the doctor, and wins if adequate evidence of negligence is presented. The situation becomes more complex if the treatment occurs in a hospital. In that situation, both doctor and hospital might be liable; the hospital's liability might come from hiring an unskillful physician, retaining one whose carelessness was on the record, or failing to supervise the staff.

If the employer simply pays the doctor or hospital bill, then it's unlikely that the employer will be implicated in any way in the malpractice case. But if the employer has a role in selecting the physician or restricting the care, then the employer might become a potential defendant. An insurer or managed care entity that sets rules for treatment (such as the need to see a gatekeeper before a specialist referral; imposing a limited formulary of drugs that can be prescribed; limiting the number of visits or hospital days that can be covered) might also be a defendant. Thus, the question of ERISA preemption of malpractice claims asserted by employees becomes important.

In the most dramatic cases, the survivors of an insured employee file a wrongful death suit, claiming that the death was a direct result of limitation of care by the HMO, or of poor care received by an HMO-connected doctor or medical facility. Courts have reached varying decisions about ERISA preemption of these claims.

The Eighth and Ninth Circuits have ruled that ERISA preempts wrongful death malpractice claims against an HMO. A District Court found that ERISA preempts a suit attempting to establish the HMO's vicarious liability for medical malpractice.

Of even greater relevance to the plan administrator: several cases find that ERISA preempts a suit against a plan administrator or administrative entity because of medical malpractice by a health care provider rendering services under an EGHP.

But see *Shea* v. *Esenstein*, 65 LW 2593 (8th Cir. 1997), holding that under ERISA, a widow has standing to sue an HMO in its role as a fiduciary, for failing to disclose the financial incentives doctors were given to avoid referring patients. The state wrongful death action *was* preempted by ERISA, but the HMO was liable because, in effect, it cost the plaintiff's husband the chance to get specialty medical treatment, survive, and exercise ERISA rights on his own behalf. A fiduciary has a duty to disclose whenever silence could be harmful, so the HMO has to disclose facts that are material to participants who make health care decisions.

There is another line of cases that says, on the contrary, that ERISA does *not* preempt malpractice claims, because the connection between the plan and the claims is too tenuous to justify preemption.

Another theory is that employees can sue in state court if they charge that a plan's limitations on length of hospital stays constitute medical malpractice, and that financial incentives to providers to discharge patients more quickly undermine the quality of care. The state suit was permitted because there was no claim for plan benefits, only a challenge to the way the plan was designed and run.

Some courts take the position that Congress never intended ERISA enforcement to deal with HMO malpractice cases, so preemption is not proper.

The "any willing provider" law is another controversial area of state lawmaking. As the power of managed care networks grows, health care providers often fear that they will be excluded from these networks (perhaps for discriminatory reasons) and thus be unable to sustain their practices or business operations. The purpose of "any willing provider" laws is to require the network to accept all qualified providers who are willing to abide by the network's rules. Several cases find that these state laws are preempted by ERISA.

The Fifth Circuit says that these laws "relate to" plans, and do not constitute insurance regulation (an area where the states are permitted to operate) because they govern health care organizations rather than insurance companies. The Eastern District of Arkansas' rationale for preemption is a little different: it says that ERISA preempts the Arkansas "any willing provider" law because the state law changes the terms of ERISA plans by limiting their gatekeeper function and preventing them from setting up limited panel networks.

The Washington State statute that added a twist to the "any willing provider" law (by requiring HMOs and other health carriers to offer coverage for non-traditional health care providers' services, including chiropractors and acupuncturists) was also found to be ERISA-preempted.

In the summer of 1997, Texas became the first state to pass a state law explicitly subjecting HMOs to malpractice liability; at that time, similar legislation had been introduced in several other states. A similar bill passed in Florida in 1996, but was vetoed by the governor, who was concerned about the effect such a law would have on HMO premiums. Governor Bush of Texas did not veto the bill, but permitted it to be enacted without his signature, thus withholding his approval for similar reasons. However, it is uncertain whether such state legislation will survive a challenge based on ERISA preemption arguments. See page 136 for a further discussion of state laws regulating (or attempting to regulate) managed care organizations.

In addition to questions of whether federal or state courts should handle a particular health-insurance-related case, there may be questions about whether the case should be in court at all, rather than arbitrated. The extent to which HMO agreements with subscribers can mandate arbitration is an unsettled legal issue. On the one hand, our legal system favors arbitration as being comparatively speedy and inexpensive. On the other hand, employees have little choice about the text of their HMO agreements, and don't have much negotiating power, so there's an argument that it's unfair to prevent them from suing (and perhaps getting a large jury verdict or settlement) if they have a grievance.

9.4 LABOR LAW ISSUES IN THE EGHP

A 1996 NLRB Ruling holds that an employer's reservation of the right to "amend or modify" the health plan did not give the employer the power to replace the existing fee-for-service plan with a managed care plan. The change was so sweeping that the employer could not institute it unilaterally without bargaining.

When negotiations reach an impasse, the employer cannot replace the union-sponsored health (and retirement) plans with employer-proposed plans that were not discussed during the pre-impasse negotiations. (In this case, the negotiations involved only the size of the contributions the employer would make to the union health plan, not the substitution of a completely different plan, one more favorable to the employer's interests.)

9.5 CLAIMS PROBLEMS

Claims administration is a fiduciary duty, and it is an abuse of discretion merely to reject a claim without explanation or without getting the necessary information to determine if a desired procedure is covered. If a participant doesn't provide enough information for the plan to make a sound decision, more must be asked for.

Even if a particular service is not covered by a plan, the employer may be estopped from denying coverage if the employee asks about coverage and is informed that the service is covered. Furthermore, once treatment begins, benefits vest, so continuing coverage has to be provided for the rest of the course of treatment.

The plan will have no obligation to pay at all in situations where a physician waives the copayment. Although the doctor's motivation is usually to help out the employee, courts have found that copayment obligations serve a valuable function (controlling overutilization and inappropriate utilization of health services). To discourage the waiver, courts have ruled that the patient has to pay 20% of the bill. If the waiver reduces the employee's share to $0 (20% of $0), the plan's obligation is also defined as 80% of $0—i.e., the plan has no liability.

9.6 COORDINATION OF COVERAGE

There are various reasons why a person might have actual or potential coverage under several plans. A very young employee might still be covered by a parent's policy. Both spouses in a married couple might each have employment-related coverage that covers dependents. A newly-hired employee might have purchased individual health insurance which he or she has not discontinued. (For instance, the employee might be afraid that there would be a period when certain conditions would be excluded as pre-existing by the new EGHP; or the employee might be uncertain whether the job would last long enough to qualify for coverage.)

Some employees will be entitled to Medicare or Medicaid coverage for certain amounts and under certain circumstances (although generally speaking, the EGHP will be primary and the public benefits only secondary). Last but certainly not least, the need for medical treatment might stem from an automobile accident or other situation in which liability or no-fault insurance is involved.

Coordination of coverage provisions exist to make sure that the employee receives less than 100% of the cost of treatment, from all sources. These provisions also exist so that each EGHP will pay only its proportionate share of the cost when several plans are involved. Plans have many options in drafting their coordination clauses; there are state laws on the subject; and there is a potential for ERISA preemption—with the overall result that what seems on the surface to be a simple coordination problem may be very difficult indeed to resolve.

There are two main structures for coordination provisions. An "escape clause" says that there is no coverage under the plan if the participant is covered by another plan or insurance policy. (Imagine the problems if BOTH policies have escape clauses!) At least for a single-employer plan, it is permissible under ERISA to amend an existing plan to add an escape clause. An "excess clause" says that this policy is only secondary if other coverage is available. A coordination of benefits (COB) provision is a kind of excess clause that defines when the plan will be primary coverage and when it will be merely secondary.

State COB rules might even be applied when two self-insured plans have potential responsibility for coverage. Such rules might provide, for instance, that primary coverage for a child comes from whichever parent is older; if both parents are the same age, the primary coverage might be from the one whose birthday is earlier in the year. The Sixth Circuit says that if both plans have COB clauses but one is an ERISA plan and the other is no-fault auto insurance, the ERISA plan will be the secondary coverage and the auto insurance will be primary.

9.7 THE EMPLOYER'S RIGHT OF SUBROGATION

Subrogation is a legal concept under which a party that advances expenses can later recover them once the person who received the advance is eventually reimbursed for those expenses. More specifically, if an EGHP covers the medical treatment of an injured employee (or family member of an employee), the EGHP will have a legal right to part of the verdict or settlement that the employee receives by suing the party who caused the accident or manufactured the dangerous product (or by going through the relevant no-fault procedure for an auto accident).

It is typical (and, when you think of it, only sensible) for plans to be drafted to give the plan the right of subrogation. The plan or insurance policy must make explicit reference to subrogation for this right to be available, and state law must be consulted to see if limits are set on the subrogation right, or if the state law actually promotes the employer's position. For instance, state law may require the participant to consent to subrogation as a condition of receiving plan benefits.

9.8 HEALTH CARE COST TRENDS

In the late 1980s, health care cost increases were greater than the price changes in almost any other sector. In the years 1988–1990, for instance, the annual cost increase hovered close to 20%. In 1990, there was a dramatic change: the rate of health care cost increases trended strongly downward each year, especially between 1993 and 1994, when there was essentially no cost increase. Costs increased very modestly between 1994 and 1995 and stayed approximately level from 1995 to 1996. In 1996, however, the upward trend began again. With health care costs in check, overall inflation rates were also brought into line.

This is not to say that health care costs were *modest* in 1996. (According to the Foster Higgins annual survey, providing health coverage for an employee cost an average of $3,915.) But cost increases were minimal or small. In 1988, the average small-firm (under 200 people) employee paid about one-third the cost of family health coverage, and only one-eighth of the cost of individual coverage. In 1996, not only the absolute amount but the allocation of costs had changed dramatically. Employees in small firms paid one-third of the individual premium, 44% of the family premium. (Their counterparts in companies with more than 200 employees paid an average of 22% of the premium for individual coverage and 30% of the cost of family coverage.)

As discussed below, one of the most important reasons for the change from exploding health costs to fairly level costs was an ever-increasing adoption of managed care plans. These plans can control expenditures for very costly medical equipment, a control which is beneficial if institutions are buying equipment they don't really need merely for reasons of prestige, but very harmful if patients lose access to worthwhile diagnostic and treatment technologies.

Ironically, in 1997, fears began to be expressed about the rising cost of HMO premiums. A quote from a spokesperson for the New York State HMO Council was that most plans would increase their rates by 5–8%, although some small firms were faced with 15–20% projected increases.

9.9 INDEMNITY INSURANCE

Before the Great Depression, health insurance was almost unheard of. Whatever comparatively modest services doctors could provide were in exchange for small sums of cash (and, sometimes, literally in exchange for chickens or fresh-baked pies). During the Depression, health insurance gained some currency as a means of coping with two problems: doctors' and hospitals' well-grounded fear of not getting paid at all, and patients' well-grounded fear of being unable to pay their medical bills.

Health insurance became a common and popular fringe benefit during World War II, when the federal government imposed stringent controls on wage increases (to "freeze" civilian workers in place, and to avoid excessive competition among private employers seeking to recruit the scanty supply of potential employees) but did not impose the same degree of control on fringe benefits. In prosperous post-war America, it seemed to make sense to maintain, and indeed continually to upgrade, health plans . . . until cost increases got out of hand in the 1980s.

Originally, there were significant differences between not-for-profit Blue Cross/Blue Shield plans and commercial insurers, but the differences (in terms of costs, services offered, and methods of operation) are diminishing. Usually, indemnity plans are divided into "basic" and "major medical" models. Basic coverage encompasses surgery, hospitalization, and care by physicians during hospitalization. A major medical plan pays when other coverage is exhausted. A comprehensive major medical plan has both basic and major medical features; a supplemental plan is pure excess insurance.

> ⇒ **TIP**
>
> See the discussion of fringe benefits on page 119 re allied health plans such as dental and vision care. Also see page 142 for the extent to which former employees and their families must be given access to "continuation coverage" once they are no longer entitled to coverage under the EGHP.

The standard model for indemnity insurance calls for the patient to be responsible for paying a deductible each year (e.g., $100; $500; $100 per family member) before the plan is required to make any payments. Patients usually also have a coinsurance responsibility, e.g., a duty to pay 20% of the bill (or 20% of the plan's "schedule amount" for the service or procedure, plus the full difference between the actual charge and the schedule amount). Although some plans pay all, or a percentage, of the provider's actual charge, reimbursement to health care providers under traditional, indemnity plans is typically based on "usual, customary and reasonable" charges, i.e., historical figures, or on a schedule of per-item charges. A typical provision of an indemnity plan is a limitation on employee copayment responsibilities, e.g., an out-of-pocket maximum that stops the employee's loss once it reaches a certain amount. After that point, the plan will pay covered charges in full. According to figures compiled by the Employee Benefit Research Institute (EBRI) in 1995, the average employee who had family coverage under an indemnity plan would not have to pay more than $2,642 no matter how large the expenses grew. For individual coverage, the average stop-loss was $1,319.

On the other hand, plans usually limit their exposure by setting overall limits on each employee's coverage, whether by the year or over a lifetime. (See page 116 for the requirement of parity between maximums for mental health care and physical ailments.) Refusal to pay for treatment of preexisting conditions is another traditional means of controlling the cost of an indemnity plan; but see page 148 for the treatment of preexisting conditions for which earlier coverage is "creditable" and therefore cannot be used to deny treatment under the current plan.

Employers have also tended to increase employee copayment responsibility, i.e., to make the employee pay a greater share of the recurring premium, and to impose higher deductibles and coinsurance. In 1995, for example, the average employee paid $61 a month for indemnity plan participation, a figure that increased to $71 a month in 1996. The theory is that employees will become more informed health-care consumers, and less wasteful, if they are responsible for a significant part of the cost of care.

9.10 MANAGED CARE

In the 1970s and 1980s, employers found themselves faced with explosive increases in the cost of providing medical care. Some employers coped by terminating their health care plans (or by deciding not to implement a plan that was under consideration). For instance, in 1993, 82% of the full-time workers employed in medium or large-sized companies were EGHP participants; 40% of these plans provided coverage at no charge to the employee, and 20% provided dependent coverage at no charge. In 1994, only 62% of full-time employees in small companies had health coverage. By 1997, there were over 40 million Americans who did not have health insurance; many of them were employees of companies that never, or that no longer, maintained EGHPs.

However, the most common response to health care cost increases was a shift from indemnity-based plans (where employees select their own health care and file claims for reimbursement after they encounter health costs) to managed care plans. However, there was a backlash, and the late 1990s showed increasing popularity of Preferred Provider Organizations and Point-of-Service plans, which require employees to pay more but give them a greater choice of providers than strict Health Maintenance Organizations (HMOs).

The general concept of managed care includes various kinds of entities and relationships with patients, employers, and health care providers. The theory is that adding management skills to the health care equation will cut costs by removing patients' incentives to consume excessive quantities of medical care, and providers' incentives to overtreat.

A common feature of managed care plans is utilization review. Patients may have to consult a primary care physician who acts as gatekeeper before they can be referred to an expensive specialist (that is, if they want their care to be covered by the plan wholly or in part). Non-emergency procedures may have to be approved in advance by a claims reviewer. Patients' surgeries and hospital stays will be assessed for medical necessity in another part of the review process.

In one managed care model, the trade-off for the employee is that he or she must get all care within the network; there is no reimbursement available for non-network care (except for emergencies and situations in which services are required that are not included within the network). However, the employee either pays nothing for health care within the network, or pays a small amount per visit, per prescription, or per service.

Managed care plans typically have their own payment schedules, which may be significantly lower than actual health care costs encountered in the community. The managed care plan's reimbursement to the patient may be defined in terms of a percentage of its own schedule—with the result that the patient may have to make a significant copayment. For instance, consider a patient who has satisfied his or her deductible and who actually pays $1,000 for a procedure. The health plan pays 80% of the schedule amount, but this amount is $800, so it will pay only $640 (80% of $800). The patient will have to pay the other $360. If the patient had not satisfied the deductible before having the procedure, his or her responsibility would have included the deductible amount as well.

9.10.1 Health Maintenance Organizations (HMOs)

The Health Maintenance Organization, or HMO, is the most popular form of managed care organization within the U.S. employee group market, although many other structures and hybrid structures are available. EBRI reports that, as of July 1, 1995, about 593 HMOs and POS (point-of-service) plans (see page 131) covered almost 53.5 million employees and dependents. There were also several hundred Medicare HMOs providing care to senior citizens.

The HMO is both a network of providers and a mechanism for financing health care. The theory is that participating providers will be paid a capitation fee, i.e., a fee (usually annual) "per head" that covers all medical services under the plan for the individual member (e.g., employee or dependent of an employee). Because they do not earn more money if patients consume more health care, the theory is that providers will have an incentive to provide excellent care and thus keep their patients healthy and outside the medical system. (Another, more cynical, interpretation could be placed on the incentives that HMOs offer to providers.)

In a "staff-model" HMO, the doctors and other health professionals are salaried employees of the HMO. In the more prevalent Individual Practice Association (IPA) model HMO, the health professionals enter into contracts with the IPA, and the IPA negotiates with the HMO to set a reimbursement schedule with a price for each service on the schedule. Under the group model, the HMO enters into contracts with independent group practices. These practices are responsible for handling administrative tasks; they are usually paid on a capitated basis. Under the network model, doctors practice primarily in the fee-for-service mode, but also agree to provide certain services to HMO patients, once again generally in exchange for a capitation fee.

Employees who want HMO coverage can sign up with the HMO, during a stated open enrollment period each year. There are also rules for switching from one

HMO to another (if several are available in the relevant geographic area) and for disenrolling from an HMO and returning to an indemnity plan—if the employer continues to offer one, and has not adopted an HMO-only health plan.

A federal law, the Health Maintenance Organization Act of 1973, imposes some degree of uniformity and federal regulation (by the Department of Health and Human Services) on HMOs that want to describe themselves as "federally qualified." (HMOs that do not meet these qualifications can still lawfully do business, as long as they are licensed by the states in which they offer services.)

As of January 1, 1995, there were 270 federally qualified HMOs. They are all subject to minimum standards for the services they offer, their reserves and other financial measures, and the quality of their services (as determined by uniform, standardized quality assessment surveys). They also must adhere to rigid disclosure requirements; when they solicit membership directly, or run advertisements, they must provide accurate descriptions of the services they offer and the costs subscribers encounter.

The plan must include an annual open enrollment period, during which employees can elect between the various plans the employer offers. Employees who enroll during this time are not subject to waiting periods, exclusions, or preexisting condition limitations. Before 1988 changes in the federal law, employers had to pay the same amount to federally qualified HMOs as they did to their most expensive non-HMO plan. Of course, this requirement made it impossible to use HMOs to achieve cost savings. Under current law, employers are not allowed to discriminate in benefits by contracting with HMOs, but there is no discrimination as long as the contributions for each employee (fee-for-service or HMO user) are reasonable, and as long as employees have a fair choice among differing benefit plans.

Solicitation of employers by HMOs is also subject to disclosure rules. The HMO must communicate in writing, rather than orally, and must send information to a managing official of the company at least 180 days before the employer's collective bargaining agreement or existing health benefit contract expires or is subject to renewal.

➡ TIP

Until October 24, 1995, employers were subject to a "dual choice" requirement, i.e., if any federally qualified HMO wanted to be made available to employees, the employer had to offer that HMO as an option to the indemnity plan already being made available. Since that date, however, employers have been free to turn down overtures from federally qualified HMOs.

A federally qualified HMO must offer certain obligatory services:

• Physician services (both primary and specialty)

- Hospital services (inpatient and outpatient)
- Emergency medical treatment
- Outpatient mental health treatment (short-term only)
- Referrals and treatment of substance abuse
- Home health care
- Preventive health care.

Various other services are optional with the federally qualified HMO: long-term care at home or in an institution; longer-term mental hygiene services; dental and vision care; physical therapy and rehabilitation; and prescription drugs. These optional services do not have to be provided on a capitated basis; the HMO can require fees for such services.

9.10.2 Preferred Provider Organizations (PPOs)

A PPO is an administrative structure. Health care providers can become "preferred providers" by affiliating with the structure. Employers negotiate with the PPO to set a rate schedule for specified health services.

PPOs do not have set enrollment periods for employees to join. There is no single centralized entity that has complete financial responsibility for the employee's care, and therefore sponsorship of PPOs is quite diverse. It might be created by a hospital or other health care provider, a health insurer, entrepreneur, or group of doctors.

9.10.3 Point of Service Plans (POS)

A point of service plan is an indemnity/HMO hybrid. Participants are not required to select their health care providers from within the "network" of the managed care plan. However, if they get care within the network, their only copayment responsibility is a small amount per visit. For out-of-network care, indemnity concepts such as an annual deductible and a copayment percentage for each service are applicable. Patients must be advised to make sure that they follow the network's referral requirements; otherwise, the care is likely to be treated as out-of-network services for which the employee has a larger copayment responsibility. Although the typical coinsurance percentage for an indemnity plan is 20%, out-of-network care from a POS can carry a coinsurance requirement as high as 40%.

9.10.4 Carve-Outs and Global Case Rates

A carve-out is a discount mechanism under which particular forms of medical expense, or high-cost conditions, are given separate management from the rest of the health plan. For instance, pharmacy benefits, mental health/substance abuse, cancer care, and cardiac treatment are common subjects of carve-outs. In an oncology carve-out plan, for instance, an insurer and one or more health care providers could agree to a set price for the complete management of all of the insurer's cancer cases; the cancer patients are all referred to a particular network, which in turn offers a flat fee (also known as a global case rate). Various problems remain to be settled under these mechanisms: for instance, does the global case rate include the treatment of other conditions a patient happens to have (such as a cancer patient's unrelated heart problems)? Carve-out plans also add an additional layer of bureaucracy for the patients (and the employer offering the health plan) to deal with.

9.10.5 Cost Cutting Mechanisms Under Managed Care

Utilization review is a cornerstone of managed care cost-cutting. In traditional fee-for-service medicine, the health care provider determines which interventions will be used, and the payor simply reimburses for part or all of the care ordered by the provider. Managed care plans add "gatekeepers," reviewers (who may be physicians, but are usually nurses or administrative staff with no scientific background) who determine the validity of claims. In many instances, the plan will require prior approval of claims, and will reduce or deny reimbursement of non-emergency claims where such approval was not obtained. Managed care utilization review (UR) also includes concurrent review (e.g., reviewing the need for continued hospitalization while the patient is still in the hospital) and retrospective review (after completion of treatment).

Procedural controls are common. For instance, reimbursement of a hospital stay (unless admission was through the emergency room) often depends on having preauthorization. Most plans will pay for a second opinion before surgery, but will not pay for the surgery unless the recommendation for surgery is confirmed by the second opinion. (However, such a provision requires the plan to have an appeals procedure if the patient wants to accept the first doctor's recommendation for surgery.)

Cost-cutting techniques also include adopting a fixed payment schedule, usually with the intention of increasing payment for office treatment but decreasing reimbursement for surgery and high-tech diagnostic procedures. There is also a trend toward favoring outpatient and home care rather than hospitalization.

9.10.6 Choosing a Managed Care Plan

In most geographic areas, employers will not only have access to a managed care contract, but will be approached by many vendors, most of whom will have a multiplicity of options. If the employer has decided to contract with a plan rather than self-insure, it will have to decide the type(s) of plan(s) to offer, then shop for price and quality. Low price is, of course, important, but it doesn't tell the whole story.

Employees may initially be glad to sign up with an HMO that has low copayments, but they will be dissatisfied if they have to travel too far or wait too long for appointments, if they have trouble getting referrals to specialists, and if they are denied access to prescriptions, tests, and treatments that they and their doctors think are likely to be beneficial. Furthermore, they are likely to express their dissatisfaction to the employer—ranging from a thoughtful missive in the Suggestion Box to a suit in federal court!

Account representatives of HMOs that seek your company's business should have a great deal of information about the plan, its history, and its results (including other customers who will provide references). You should be able to arrange a face-to-face or telephone appointment with the plan's medical director to learn about staff quality. He or she can let you know how the HMO chooses its affiliated physicians and how much input they have on HMO policies; also find out whether the plan is good at retaining physicians or has a problem with excessive turnover. An important issue to explore as well is how network physicians resolve differences among themselves, and with the HMO, about preferred treatment methods.

The state insurance department will probably have information about the HMO's operations, loss ratios (amount of premium devoted to paying claims vs. profits and administrative expenses), and past complaints and how they were resolved.

There are various objective measures of HMO quality. The National Commission on Quality Assurance accredits HMOs, and an established HMO should certainly be accredited; a new HMO should have applied for accreditation. (It's important to follow up and see what became of its application.) The standard survey instrument for managed care plans is HEDIS (Health Plan Employer Data and Information Set) reports, and plans should provide their HEDIS results for comparison with others.

- Number of health care providers involved in the plan or its network

- Qualifications of health care providers (board certification or board eligibility; hospital affiliations; any past complaints)

- Suitability of provider ratio to employee base (e.g., whether there are not enough obstetricians but too many cardiologists, or vice versa)

- Quality of hospitals and other facilities affiliated with the plan or its network (including available equipment and extent of investment in patient service)

- Cost effectiveness (i.e., degree of utilization review)

- Availability of primary care physicians at off-hours (otherwise, patients will either have to go to an expensive emergency room or defer treatment until conventional office hours, by which time a condition may have deteriorated significantly)

- Use of claims management to coordinate treatment of a serious illness or injury as the employee recovers and is rehabilitated as much as possible

- How premiums compare to premiums of other MCOs (Managed Care Organizations)

- Consumer satisfaction measures, such as telephone help lines, clear explanations of claims procedures, swift resolution of claim disputes, periodic surveys to find out what consumers like and dislike about the plan

- Quality of care (NOTE: The employer could be liable for selecting or maintaining affiliation with a low-quality plan).

Treatment protocols (standardized information sets based on retrospective studies of the effectiveness of various treatment methods) are controversial. The more treatment is standardized, the easier it is to compile statistics on results, and the more uniform the experience of various HMO patients will be. Treatment protocols also allow some cost-cutting through "de-skilling": instead of having patients go to see a primary care physician whenever the patients think they need treatment, a nurse can use the treatment protocols to decide whether the patient can be adequately treated with home remedies or needs to see a doctor or go to the emergency room.

Doctors usually dislike treatment protocols, for both good and bad reasons: they tend to resist having their performance monitored, and they make the valid point that clinical judgment does more for patients than "cookbook medicine." However, treatment protocols are very beneficial for the patients of below-average doctors, or those who haven't kept up with medical developments, because the protocols ameliorate some of the doctors' clinical deficiencies. If an HMO uses treatment protocols, they should be developed in consultation with the plan's doctors who should be given a chance to contribute to their evolution.

A good HMO should have plenty of staff to respond to patients' questions (about whether to go to the doctor; what to do for a minor ailment or accident; and about claims and benefits).

If the employer and its HR department feel that the selection process is too complex, plenty of specialty consulting firms are available to assist. Major accounting and consulting firms maintain a huge base of current data about health care utilization and costs, allowing them to compare multiple health care providers in terms of costs, cost increases, qualifications of doctors, number of days of hospital care utilized, and similar measures. A skillful consultant understands which options are the most practical, what the bottom-line impact of each will be, and the legal and tax implications of each potential choice.

➠ **TIP**

Sometimes health plans retain consulting firms (and pay their fees) so you can get information from the consulting firm without charge. Of course, you'll only be getting one side of the story!

However, the cost of consulting itself can be significant: anything from $25,000 for a simple analysis of the change from indemnity-based to managed care, to over $1 million if the creation of a new benefit plan (including record-keeping and employee communications) is fully outsourced.

9.10.7 Administration of Managed Care Plans

Generally, the employees will be given one open enrollment period a year. During this time employees who have just become eligible will be able to select one of the options available under the plan, or employees who have already selected a plan option will be able to change their selection. Once made, a decision is usually irrevocable until the next open enrollment period, which is usually in the autumn, although there is no legal requirement mandating this.

If the employer pays the full cost of the premium, there is no need for a mechanism for collecting from the employee. However, it is increasingly prevalent that employees are expected to pay at least a portion of the premium (and perhaps a higher proportion if they elect a fee-for-service or high-option plan, or if they wish coverage of their dependents). Many plans have increased the amount of cost-sharing that employees must assume for dependent coverage, and it is not uncommon for employees to have to pay both a premium for their own coverage and 100% of the cost of coverage for their spouses and children. In these plans, arrangements must be made for payroll deduction or other collection mechanism.

In addition to full-scale health plans, there may be flexible spending accounts, Medical Savings Accounts, long-term care insurance plans, separate dental and/or vision care plans, and other quasi-medical plans requiring administration.

9.10.8 Employer Liability for HMO Actions

The managed care relationship has three parts: the HMO or other managed care organization that provides care; the employer that enters into a contract with the HMO; and the employee who receives care (or uses the HMO to get care for a family member). When there is a bad result of treatment (whether or not malpractice occurred), the employee might wish to sue the employer as well as the HMO.

To reduce its liability exposure, the employer should negotiate and draft its contracts with managed care organizations accordingly:

- An acknowledgment by doctors and other individual health care providers that they are independent contractors, not employees of the sponsor corporation, and that they are fully responsible for their own professional actions
- An alternative dispute resolution provision for patient complaints
- A feedback mechanism so providers can discuss the need for care when reimbursement is denied

- A requirement that providers maintain at least a specified minimum level of malpractice coverage (the less insurance the provider has, the more likely the patient is to feel that additional defendants must be brought into the dispute)

The administrative structure of the health care plan can be created to reduce the likelihood of employer liability:

- Specify formal criteria for denial of reimbursement
- Have medical specialists review the criteria before they are implemented
- Don't permit a claims reviewer's decision to become final until all of the relevant medical records have been reviewed AND the treating physician has been consulted
- Add an informal appeals procedure before the claim goes to arbitration
- Make sure that medical specialists are consulted about all decisions involving specialty referrals
- Maintain adequate documentation of the disposal of each claim.

9.10.9 State Regulation of Managed Care Plans

As discussed above, there are situations in which only the federal government, under ERISA, can regulate EGHPs. Nevertheless, states frequently pass laws (which may or may not survive an ERISA-preemption challenge) to regulate the relationship between managed care providers and employees who receive health services under managed care.

One stumbling block for state legislation is the legal doctrine that only individual human beings can practice medicine, not a corporation. This doctrine often preserves HMOs from liability, because they take the position that they are mere agents that administer the medical care provided (or malpracticed) by individuals, and that the individuals and not the HMO are responsible for the quality of the care. Sometimes this argument is met by suing the HMO not for malpractice, but for negligent hiring and supervision of the allegedly substandard doctors.

More than 400 bills dealing with managed care were introduced in the state legislatures in 1996, although many of them were very similar and few actually achieved passage. States with managed care laws passed in 1996 and 1997 alone include Connecticut, Colorado, Florida, Minnesota, Nevada, New Hampshire, New Jersey, Ohio, Oregon, and Texas. These laws strive to protect managed care patients against potential abuses and to give them more information (including state-created "report cards") about managed care quality so they can make an informed choice of plan.

For instance, several of the statutes forbid "gag clauses" (provisions in contracts between managed care organizations and doctors that forbid doctors to discuss treatments that are not covered by the MCOs). Limitations may be imposed on financial incentives that plans can give doctors for restricting treatment. States often require managed care plans to cover emergency treatment without pre-approval under any circumstances that would induce a reasonable layman to believe that an emergency is occurring (for instance, unexplained chest pain).

The laws may require patients to be given the option of seeking care outside the network if they assume a larger portion (but not full responsibility for) the cost of care. States often require MCOs to strengthen the grievance procedures available to patients. Regulations in some states define the maximum geographic distance between patients and care providers and/or require managed care networks to include a minimum number of specialists. The plans may also be required to submit their coverage denials to an independent review panel, in all contested cases or only in cases involving treatments that might be deemed experimental and hence not covered.

9.11 SELF-INSURED PLANS

Managed care cost savings and increased employee responsibilities notwithstanding, purchasing health insurance can be quite costly for a company. Yet health care coverage is one of the most appreciated aspects of the entire compensation package, and it can be hard to attract, motivate, and retain high-level employees (especially in a time of low unemployment) without offering such coverage. An employer might also have applied for insurance but been turned down, because in a small group, a few or even one employee with a preexisting health condition could make the entire group uninsurable.

> ⇒ **TIP**
>
> For companies with under 50 employees, the Health Insurance Portability and Accountability Act of 1996 imposes some limits on insurers' ability to deny applications or cancel policies (see page 151); but these limitations are not fully applicable to companies with 100 or more employees, the target audience for this book.

Some companies, especially large ones, adopt a policy of bypassing health insurance and offering a self-insured plan. That is, the company sets aside reserves that can be invested and used to pay reimbursement claims submitted by employees. Given enough market power and a favorable state legislative climate, large employers can even cut their own deals for "discount pricing" with hospitals and other health care providers. The likelihood of obtaining concessions depends, for example, on whether a hospital has a high or low patient census, and how many patients the self-insured plan can be expected to channel to the hospital.

Of course, that means that the employer is saddled with the burden of reimbursement paperwork normally handled by the health insurance company. As a hybrid between full self-insurance and a (perhaps unaffordable) full insurance package, insurers and employers may enter into a Third-Party Administration (TPA) arrangement. Under the TPA deal, the insurance company handles the paperwork but does not provide actual health reimbursement.

Yet another option is direct contracting. Although the predominant model is for insurance companies to create managed care networks, and to enter into contracts with both health care providers and insurers, it's possible for doctors to organize their own networks, known as Physician-Sponsored Organizations (PSOs). Employers can then sign contracts with these doctor-controlled networks and eliminate some of the middle-man costs. Employees may also feel more positive toward PSOs (run by the doctors they know and trust) than toward managed care organizations, which may be perceived as cold, insensitive, and unduly profit-motivated. However, PSOs don't always work well; doctors who offer excellent clinical care are not necessarily equally adept at management.

The American Medical Association estimates that there are 3,000 health plans controlled by providers, although the Health Insurance Association of America identifies only 500 provider-controlled plans, with applications for another 1,000 in the works. An employer considering signing on with one of these plans should consider:

- What are the management skills and backgrounds of the plan's administrators?
- Are the plan's financial reserves adequate—not just enough to satisfy statutory minimums, but large enough to meet practical demands?
- Does the plan have a sound reinsurance agreement?
- Will the plan release its balance sheets and does it pay participating physicians enough to keep them satisfied?
- What will the plan do to promote employee health?
- What are the plan's strategies for improving its results in the future?
- How many physicians are involved? The average EGHP needs to have 25 or more physicians available on a 24-hour-a-day basis.
- Does the plan have enough subscribers ("covered lives") to spread the impact of a large claim filed by a very sick employee? Estimates of the necessary number of covered lives vary wildly—experts have named any figure from 1,200 to 100,000 as the minimum for efficient PSO operations.

9.12 MEDICAL EXPENSE PLANS

Maintaining a medical expense plan is yet another option that employers have for coping with the health care needs of employees. A medical expense plan must cover employees, though not necessarily all employees. The plan can be informal; there is no requirement that the plan be in writing, unless it is also a welfare plan within the ERISA definition. Nevertheless, employees must be given reasonable notice of the plan's existence and how it operates.

Typically, the employer will reimburse employees directly for their medical expenses, and the reimbursement will come from the employer's resources, not from an insurance policy. Most medical expense plans have a plan maximum—e.g., only claims of $X per year will be covered. Some plans are coordinated with insurance, in that the employer pays up to $Y of employee claims, with insurance covering the rest. Sometimes the plan acts as an informal PPO (see page 131 for discussion of formal PPOs) by negotiating discount rates that employees can take advantage of.

For tax purposes, the most important inquiry is whether the plan shifts risk to a third party (neither employer nor employee). A plan is still self-insured if an insurance company is involved merely to provide administrative services or book-keeping, but does not take on any risk.

Code §105(h) governs self-insured medical expense reimbursement plans, those whose benefits are not payable exclusively from insurance. Plans of this type are required to satisfy coverage and nondiscrimination tests to qualify:

- The IRS issues a determination letter stating that the plan is not discriminatory
- 70% or more of *all* employees are covered under the plan
- 70% or more of all employees are eligible; 80% or more of the eligible employees are actually covered.

The plan need not count employees who are younger than 25 years old, those with less than three years' service, part-time or seasonal employees, or employees covered by a collective bargaining agreement under which accident and health benefits were the subject of good-faith bargaining.

Nondiscrimination in benefits is assured if the benefits provided for HCEs (highly compensated employees) and their dependents are also provided for other employees. This is interpreted to mean that the plan can impose a dollar maximum on benefits paid on behalf of any individual, but can't set the maximum at a percentage of compensation, because this would unfairly favor the HCEs.

If the self-insured medical expense reimbursement plan discriminates in favor of highly-compensated employees, then they (but not the rank-and-file employees) will have taxable income deriving from the employer's plan contributions on their behalf. In this context, highly compensated employees are the five highest-paid officers, 10% stockholders, and the top 25% in employee salary. HCEs do not have taxable income from plan benefits if the plan satisfies §105(b); otherwise, they will. If taxable income does result from a self-insured medical expense reimbursement plan, the income will be subject to income tax withholding, but not to FICA or FUTA: see Code §3121(a)(2)(B). The employer will probably be entitled to deduct its costs of maintaining a self-insured plan, because they will probably be ordinary and necessary business expenses.

9.13 401(h) PLANS

In addition to providing health plans for current employees, some employers offer some coverage as well for retirees. This is especially important because many individuals, by their own choice or in response to early retirement incentives offered by the employer, retire before they become eligible for Medicare coverage. (Eligibility for Medicare is not related to income or asset levels, or to employment status; it depends upon reaching age 65 or having been disabled for a two-year period.)

A 401(h) plan is a pension or annuity plan that also provides incidental health benefits for retirees: i.e., benefits for sickness, accident, hospitalization, and medical expenses. The health-type benefits must be subordinate to the plan's main business of offering retirement benefits. All incidental benefits (insurance and health) must not cost more than 25% of the employer's total contributions to a defined benefit plan.

An employer that maintains a 401(h) plan must maintain separate accounts for retiree health benefits and pension benefits. The employer must make reasonable and ascertainable contributions to fund the retiree health benefits which must be distinct from the ones made to fund pension benefits.

The distinctive feature of the 401(h) plan is that, for tax years beginning during the time period 1/1/91–12/31/2000, an employer that maintains a fully-funded pension plan can transfer money from the pension account to the retiree health benefit account once a year. (See Code §420(b)(5).) A transfer of this type is not penalized: it is neither a reversion nor a prohibited transaction.

It is a precondition of the transfer to the 401(h) account that the pension plan have excess assets. Excess assets are the extent to which the fair market value of the plan's assets exceeds the largest of these amounts:

- The plan's accrued liability, including normal cost
- 150% of the plan's current liability
- 125% of current liability (all liabilities under the plan to employees and beneficiaries)

Assets transferred to the 401(h) account must be used for only one purpose: to pay the employer's qualified current retiree health liabilities. Whatever amounts are not needed to satisfy current health benefit obligations to retirees must (not may) be returned to the underlying pension account.

➡ TIP

Returning the assets to the pension account will be treated as a reversion—so the employer should be very careful to transfer only the appropriate amount into the 401(h) account.

9.14 TAX IMPLICATIONS OF HEALTH PLANS

For both employer and employee, the major tax issues for EGHPs are covered by Code §§104-106. In many instances, both prefer that the medical benefits offered by the employer derive from a plan of accident and health insurance. This result is desirable because the employer can deduct its costs of providing such a plan, and the employee does not have taxable income either because the plan exists or because he or she receives benefits under it.

Section 104 provides that employees do not have gross income on account of amounts received from a plan of accident and health insurance (A&H) that was paid for by the *employee* or that derives from employer contributions that were already taxed to the employee.

⮕ **TIP**

For years after 1996, amounts paid under arrangements having the EFFECT of A&H plans will be taxed as if they did, in fact, come from an A&H plan.

Code §105 says that the amounts an employee receives from an A&H plan are taxable if they are paid by the employer or stem from employer contributions that have not previously been taxed to the employee. However, if the employer reimburses medical expenses incurred by the employee for him- or herself and family, if the expenses would be deductible under §213 (e.g., they cover medical diagnosis and treatment, not cosmetic or experimental procedures), and if they have not already been deducted by the employee, then the employee has no gross income as a result of the medical expense reimbursement. (See page 138, above, for more discussion of medical expense reimbursement plans.)

The employee can cite §105 to exclude amounts that were not received from an insurance policy, as long as they were received under a "plan." For this purpose, a plan is a structured arrangement, although it need not be legally enforceable or even written. The purpose of the plan must be to pay employees (common-law employees, not independent contractors or self-employed individuals) in the event of personal injury or sickness.

⮕ **TIP**

If the plan is not legally enforceable, Reg. §1.105-5 requires that it must be communicated to employees before they encounter covered health expenses.

The third section in the trilogy, §106, says that employees do not have gross income if their employers provide them with A&H insurance.

> ⇒ **TIP**
>
> If a company offers benefits to non-marital domestic partners (see page 117, above), the employee will have taxable income as a result of the coverage, unless the domestic partner is also a dependent of the employee for tax purposes (i.e., the employee provides at least half of the partner's support).

Because of 1996 statutory changes, the IRS issued new codes for Form W-2. Code R is used for employer contributions to MSAs, Code 8 for salary reduction contributions to a SIMPLE plan (see page 218), and Code T for employer payments to an adoption assistance plan.

9.15 COBRA CONTINUATION COVERAGE

As anyone knows who has ever tried to purchase health insurance (whether for his or her own family or for an entire corporation), this coverage is quite expensive. It is even more expensive for an individual than for a member of a large group. Congress' response includes the Comprehensive Omnibus Budget Reconciliation Act (COBRA), which added a new planning device: continuation coverage.

Continuation coverage is the right of a "qualified beneficiary" (i.e., a one-time employee or his or her spouse and dependents) to maintain coverage under the employer's group health plan. When the employee is fired (other than for gross misconduct), laid off, quits, or retires, the employee can take over premiums for the coverage.

> ⇒ **TIP**
>
> For retirees, the employer corporation's Chapter 11 filing is also an event that triggers the right to COBRA continuation coverage.

The employee's spouse and children may also have independent rights to maintain coverage, e.g., after a divorce, upon the ex-employee's death, or when the ex-employee becomes eligible for Medicare (although once the ex-employee becomes eligible for Medicare, he or she can no longer have personal continuation coverage).

> ⇒ **TIP**
>
> Continuation coverage is available if the ex-employee's child is no longer a dependent as defined by the terms of the plan (e.g., reaches age 19 and is no longer a full-time student). A "qualified beneficiary" is anyone who has a right to make a COBRA election (one-time employee; family member of a one-time employee).

The general rule is that the employer charges the employee the equivalent of the employee's premium for the coverage; adding an administration charge is permissible, as long as it is no more than 2% of the premium. (On the other hand, the employer can choose to pay part or all of the cost, for example as an early retirement incentive or if the employee has negotiated an exit package.) The premium level is set once a year, in advance.

Self-insured plans are subject to COBRA, too; for them, the "premium" is a reasonable estimate, using reasonable actuarial assumptions, of the cost of providing health coverage for employees similarly situated to the qualified beneficiary.

> ⇒ **TIP**
>
> Continuation coverage cannot be conditioned on producing evidence of insurability: see Code §4980B(f)(2)(D). The coverage must be the same as active employees receive, so a person electing continuation coverage begins with his or her original type and level of coverage, but that coverage can be changed as the underlying plan changes.

If an employer terminates or reduces coverage of a group health plan that is subject to COBRA, qualified beneficiaries (ex-workers and their families) must be allowed to elect coverage under any plan that the employer continues to maintain for similarly-situated active employees.

The Revenue Reconciliation Act of 1989 (P.L. 101-239) amended COBRA continuation coverage requirements in several ways. First of all, anyone who performs services for the employer and who is covered under the group plan must be given COBRA rights after a qualifying event. This includes partners, self-employed people who are nevertheless plan participants, and eligible independent contractors.

> ⇒ **TIP**
>
> Make sure you understand who is entitled to participate; the rights of non-conventional employees are being extended in this area.

The basic duration of COBRA continuation coverage for ex-employees is 18 months. The rules are more complex when there are special situations (such as the employer corporation's bankruptcy) or when the qualified beneficiary is a family member rather than the ex-employee. Sometimes if there is a second qualifying event, the employee will be entitled to 36 months of continuation coverage (i.e., two 18-month periods).

➠ **TIP**

COBRA defines obligations that the employer must meet; the employer can choose to offer longer periods of continuation coverage.

When an employee is disabled, within the Social Security Act definition (basically, when he or she is incapable of substantial gainful activity), at the time of termination, the employee is entitled to 29 months of continuation coverage, as are the employee's family members. However, for the 11 months after expiration of the normal 18 month continuation coverage term, the employer can charge the employee 150% of the premium, not just the normal 102%.

If the qualifying event is the ex-employee's eligibility for Medicare, the covered employee's qualified beneficiaries are entitled to 36 months of continuation coverage.

COBRA entitlement ends if:

- the employer terminates and does not replace the EGHP for active employees (in effect, there is no longer a plan whose coverage can be continued);

- the qualified beneficiary fails to pay the premium;

- the employee becomes Medicare-eligible (although family members are still eligible for coverage);

- the qualified beneficiary gains coverage under another EGHP and is not debarred from receiving medical benefits by a preexisting condition limitation. In 1997 and later years, "creditable coverage" under the earlier plan becomes a factor: see page 149.

Businesses are subject to COBRA if they have 20 or more employees on a typical working day, and a group health plan (whether insured or self-insured), so the readers of this book are subject to COBRA unless they have declined to maintain a health plan at all. If a cafeteria plan includes health benefits, the COBRA continuation coverage requirement applies only to benefits actually elected by a plan participant, not those that he or she declined.

> ⮕ **TIP**
>
> COBRA requirements are not imposed on plans substantially limited to qualified long-term care services. (See page 47 for more about the employer's role in LTC coverage.)

Benefits under an EGHP are divided into "core coverage" (everything except vision and dental benefits) and "non-core coverage." If the EGHP provides both types of coverage, a qualified beneficiary can elect continuation of the whole package, or of just the core coverage.

> ⮕ **TIP**
>
> Employers don't have to offer this choice if the premium cost of the core coverage is 95% or more of the cost of the whole benefit package, or if the employer has a core-coverage-only plan for employees who are similarly situated to the qualified beneficiary.

9.15.1 COBRA Administration

Running a COBRA plan combines the usual tasks of any insurance plan (selecting a carrier, selecting a plan of coverage, making sure premiums are paid on time, making sure that coverage is renewed as necessary or that substitute coverage is purchased) with specific tasks, involving disclosure to employees, and management of COBRA elections made by employees and their beneficiaries.

> ⮕ **TIP**
>
> A one-time employee can exercise the COBRA election for his or her spouse and children; a spouse can exercise it on behalf of the children.

The employer has an obligation to notify the plan administrator when employment-related qualifying events occur, e.g., when an employee is terminated or laid off, or when the company makes a Chapter 11 filing. The responsibility for reporting personal qualifying events, such as divorce or separation, rests on the qualified beneficiary. The notice is due within 60 days of the event. The plan administrator then has 14 days from receiving notice from the employer to notify the qualified beneficiary.

9.15.2 COBRA Notice

Employees must get a written notice explaining their COBRA rights as soon as they are covered by the statute. The notice requirement comes from Code §4980B(f)(6)(A) and ERISA §606. The notice should explain:

- Who fits into the class of qualified beneficiaries
- What events trigger the right to continuation coverage
- How and when to elect continuation coverage
- The right to turn down the coverage
- Rights of other qualified beneficiaries if one qualified beneficiary waives the election
- Obligation to pay the premiums on time
- How long the coverage will last
- Events that will allow the employer to terminate continuation coverage.

Qualified beneficiaries must be given a period of at least 60 days to either accept or waive continuation coverage. The election period must begin no later than the time coverage would end under the EGHP. In other words, notice must be given early enough to prevent any gap in coverage, if the qualified beneficiary takes up the option of continuing coverage, and there must be a full 60-day period for consideration.

⇒ **TIP**

According to the Eleventh Circuit, if the notice fails to specify the 60-day period, then the right to make the election extends indefinitely.

The first premium payment is not due until 45 days after the election. Qualified beneficiaries get an automatic grace period of at least 30 days, during which coverage cannot be terminated for nonpayment of premiums—even if the underlying EGHP has a shorter grace period. However, if the plan provides a longer grace period, the employee must be allowed to take advantage of it.

If the qualified beneficiary does make a COBRA election, then continuation coverage relates back to the date that coverage under the EGHP would have been lost if there were no election. However, employees get a second chance: until the election period ends, a qualified beneficiary who waives COBRA coverage can revoke the waiver and opt for continuation coverage after all. But in that case, coverage is not retroactive; it begins on the date the qualified beneficiary sent the waiver to the employer or plan administrator. (Remember, if the ex-employee waives for him- or herself, family members still have the right to elect continuation coverage for themselves.)

⟶ **TIP**

COBRA notices must be written, but a federal District Court has found an oral waiver of the election to be valid and enforceable.

The Internal Revenue Code imposes a penalty of $100 per day per beneficiary for noncompliance, subject to a maximum of $200 per family per day. (In other words, if a covered employee has a spouse and three children, the penalty cannot be $400 per day for that family, even if the family does not receive its rights under COBRA.) There is also an aggregate maximum of the smaller of $500,000 or 10% of the amount the employer paid (or incurred obligations for) for its EGHPs in the preceding year. Furthermore, a health plan that fails to conform to COBRA does not generate "ordinary and necessary" business expenses (Code §162) and therefore the costs of such a plan are not deductible to the employer.

The penalty is imposed on the employer, but also on individuals responsible for administering the plan or providing benefits under it, as long as those individuals have contractual responsibility for running the plan. For instance, a third party administrator (TPA) would fall into this category unless there were factors beyond the administrator's control that prevented the notice from being given. An administrator who fails to satisfy all the COBRA requirements, but who is not guilty of willful neglect, and who had reasonable support for his or her decisions, will not be penalized more than $2 million for all plans administered.

In appropriate cases, the penalty can be reduced or waived if no one had reason to know that the appropriate notices were not given, or if the failure to notify was corrected within 30 days after a responsible person became aware of the failure.

In addition to the official penalties imposed by statute, any person or organization whose actions result in someone's loss of COBRA coverage can be sued (under ERISA Title I) by the person who lost coverage.

9.15.3 COBRA and the FMLA

A frequent scenario: an employee applies for unpaid leave under the Family and Medical Leave Act, either because he or she is sick, because he or she must care for a sick family member, or because a new baby has been born or adopted. The employee fully intends to go back to work after the leave, but is unable to do so (because of deterioration in health or failure of child care arrangements). Once the employee becomes an ex-employee, COBRA continuation coverage becomes available. At the end of 1994, the IRS published a notice explaining the way COBRA and the FMLA work together.

Merely taking an FMLA leave is not a COBRA-qualifying event. But there is a qualifying event if the employee, the employee's spouse, or employee's dependent child was covered under the EGHP when the FMLA leave began; the employee doesn't go back to work after the leave, and the employee, spouse, or child is at risk of losing EGHP coverage if COBRA is not invoked. On the other hand, if, while the employee is on leave, the employer eliminates EGHP coverage for the whole group of workers the employee belonged to, there is no qualifying event (because the worker wouldn't have had health coverage even if he or she had not taken leave).

The qualifying event occurs on the *last* day of the FMLA leave, and the regular COBRA notice must be given. There has been a qualifying event even if the employee had an obligation to pay health insurance premiums during the leave but failed to do so. Although the employer may have a right to get the employee to pay back premiums if he or she quits instead of returning from leave, this obligation doesn't prevent a COBRA qualifying event from occurring. (In other words, the employee gets another chance to preserve health coverage for him- or herself and family.) State laws that require a longer leave than the 12-week FMLA period are also disregarded in determining the occurrence of a qualifying event.

9.16 HEALTH INSURANCE PORTABILITY

COBRA (IRC §4908B: see page 142) has done a lot to smooth the situation of the ex-employee who is at risk of losing personal and family health coverage because of a job transition. However, COBRA didn't address the problem of the employee who ceases to be employed by Corporation A, later gets a job with Company B, and experiences catastrophic health expenses during the waiting period to join the Company B group health plan, or whose health claims are rejected by the Company B health plan on the grounds that they are preexisting conditions.

It took more than a decade for COBRA to be supplemented with HIPAA, the Health Insurance Portability and Accountability Act of 1996, also known as the Kennedy-Kassebaum Act (KK). HIPAA's main focus is health insurance portability (the ability to become eligible for benefits under a new plan by transferring experience from a former plan). It adds a new Chapter 100, §§9801-9806, to the Internal Revenue Code. Although the HIPAA has a general effective date for plan years beginning after June 30, 1997, the effect of portability will not be seen for several years, because employees do not have "creditable coverage" that can be transferred from one plan to another except for services rendered in and after July 1, 1996, and employers will not be subjected to HIPAA penalties before January 1, 1998.

HIPAA does not prevent plans from controlling costs by imposing preexisting condition limitations on new plan members. However, the plan cannot define a preexisting condition more stringently than as a mental or physical condition for which medical advice, diagnosis, care, or treatment was sought during the six-month period before the enrollment date.

In other words, the plan can't say that the new employee's cancer (which was not discovered until after his or her plan participation began) must already have damaged the employee's health, unless he or she was actually seen by a doctor in the six months before the enrollment date.

Furthermore, the fact that someone underwent genetic testing is not a "pre-existing condition" (even if susceptibility to a disease or condition is revealed) as long as there is no actual diagnosis of an existing illness.

Preexisting condition limitations cannot be imposed on pregnancy, and there are very few situations in which they can be applied to employees' newly born or adopted children. Furthermore, if the plan includes dependent coverage, and a plan participant gains a new dependent because of marriage, birth or adoption, the group health plan must offer a "dependent special enrollment period" lasting at least 30 days.

The general rule is that the maximum duration for a preexisting condition limitation is 12 months from the enrollment date for the current health plan. (The enrollment date is defined as the date of actual enrollment, or the first day of the waiting period for enrollment—whichever comes earlier.) However, late enrollees (those who fail to enroll in the plan during the open enrollment period, or in the first period of eligibility) can be subject to an 18-month preexisting condition limitation.

"Creditable coverage" is defined as coverage from another EGHP, from individually-purchased health insurance, from Medicare Part A or B, or from Medicaid (except for §1928 benefits).

Fortunately for the financial soundness of EGHPs (although unfortunately for employees who suffer health problems as well as a lengthy period of unemployment), health plan participation is not considered "creditable," and therefore is not portable to a new plan, if there is a break of 63 days or more when the employee was completely without health insurance. (Of course, this is an incentive to ex-employees to maintain COBRA coverage, so they will not have an uninsured period.) The so-called affiliation period (the waiting period after a new employee enrolls in a new health plan) is not considered a period of being uninsured.

⇒ TIP

Under HIPAA, EGHPs have an obligation to provide a certification of the dates creditable coverage began and ended, whenever a one-time participant becomes entitled to, or loses entitlement to, COBRA continuation coverage. The ex-participant also has the right to request the certification at any time within 24 months of the COBRA event (so that he or she can submit it to a new plan and prove portability, of course). However, if your plan is an insured plan and not a self-insured plan, then you are exempt from the certification requirement if there is a procedure in place for the insurer to issue the certificates.

9.16.1 Nondiscrimination Requirements

In addition to the pension plan nondiscrimination requirements (see page 206), HIPAA imposes health insurance nondiscrimination requirements. It is unlawful under HIPAA for a plan to base its rules for eligibility or continued eligibility—or its definition of the waiting period—on an employee's or dependent's:

- Health status
- Physical or mental health condition
- Claims experience
- Past receipt of health care
- Medical history
- Genetic information
- Evidence of insurability
- Disability.

None of these factors can be used by a plan to obligate anyone to pay a premium or other contribution that is greater than that required from any other similarly situated individual. HIPAA just requires plans to charge the same amount to similar classes of employees. It doesn't limit the amount of contribution (whether in terms of premiums or copayments) that an employer can require of plan participants. (After all, Congress is in favor of keeping health care costs increases within bounds.) It is also legitimate to offer employees discounts, rebates, or reductions in their copayment obligations based on their participation in health promotion and disease prevention programs (weight loss and sensible exercise, or quitting smoking, for instance).

9.16.2 Exceptions to the Portability Rules

The requirements for portability, access to health benefits, and renewability do not apply to plans that cover only a single current employee.

Various other plan types are not covered, because they are not deemed to be health benefit plans:

- Plans offering accident and/or disability insurance
- Liability insurance
- Plans whose insurance policies provide medical benefits that are secondary or incidental to other benefits
- Plans covering limited-scope benefits such as dental, vision, or long-term care
- Coverage limited to a specified disease or illness
- Fixed-indemnity plans (e.g., for hospitalization)
- Medicare supplementary (Medigap) insurance.

9.16.3 Special First-Year Requirements

For the first plan year beginning after July 1, 1997 (which, in many cases, will be the year you are reading this book), HIPAA requires administrators to set up procedures for implementing HIPAA. You must include a way to issue certificates of creditable coverage, a way to tell employees how to get these certificates, a way to use certificates to reduce the impact of the plan's preexisting condition limitations, and a way to issue notices of reductions of benefits and services not more than 60 days after the reductions are implemented.

9.16.4 Penalties and Enforcement

Failure to comply with HIPAA's portability rules (IRC Chapter 100) can subject a health plan to a penalty tax. The basic penalty rate is $100 per person per day of noncompliance, so a large or even medium-sized plan can quickly rack up a lot of penalties. The maximum liability that can be incurred by a single-employer plan is $500,000 or 10% of the amount paid or incurred for the EGHP in the preceding year—whichever is less.

Plans can escape liability (or have the penalty tax reduced) if the person responsible for the error or omission didn't know—and could not have known—of the defect, if the cause of the failure was reasonable, and no willful neglect was involved, or if failure is corrected within 30 days of the first date it could have been detected.

As long as the EGHP or insurer makes a good-faith effort to comply with the statutes' objectives, no enforcement actions will be taken before January 1, 1998 (or whatever later date that interpreting Regulations are issued).

Small employers (those with 2 to 50 employees) are not subject to the penalty tax if the real cause of the problem is insurer error or misconduct.

On the other hand a minimum tax, which cannot be waived, is imposed if the failure to comply with HIPAA is found after the plan has received notice of income tax examination. In that case, the tax is $2,500 or the tax that would otherwise be imposed, whichever is less.

9.16.5 Insurer Responsibilities Under HIPAA

Employers aren't always the bad guys in the story. One of the reasons motivating Congress to pass HIPAA was the difficulty many employers (especially small companies) had in purchasing insurance—and, once purchased, maintaining coverage against the threat of cancellation or massive premium increases in later years.

HIPAA imposes obligations on insurers to group health policies, with different rules for "small employer" coverage (2 to 50 employees) and "large employer" coverage (for groups of more than 50). There are also rules about mandatory provision of individual coverage, but they are beyond the scope of this book.

HIPAA's basic rule is that an insurer who sells small employer coverage in a state has to sell to all small employers who want to purchase the coverage (with some exceptions, and with modifications for network plans). There is no corresponding obligation of large-group insurers to sell to would-be large-group buyers, so this HIPAA provision is of little practical use to most readers of this book. However, large-group insurers are required to collect information on insurance availability and submit it to Congress, presumably so that Congress can legislate further if it is discovered that large groups are deprived of access to coverage.

In either the small or the large-group market, the insurer is obligated to renew coverage or continue it in force as long as the purchaser chooses, unless, of course, the purchaser:

- stops paying the premiums;
- commits policy-related fraud;
- the insurer leaves the state market;
- plan enrollees move outside the network plan's service area;
- enrollees are no longer association members in a plan mandating association membership;
- purchaser violates the rules on participation or contribution to the plan.

There are additional requirements on small-group insurers, but they are beyond the scope of this book.

If an insurer discontinues one kind of group coverage but maintains others, all affected plan sponsors, participants, and beneficiaries must get 90 days' notice of the discontinuance. The plan sponsor must be given the option to purchase the other coverages that the insurer offers in that market.

The insurer must act uniformly, without considering the existing or potential health problems of plan participants and beneficiaries, or the claims experience of the plan sponsor. An insurer that chooses to discontinue all of its coverage in the small or large group market must give the state insurance regulators 180 days notice of intent to discontinue. The decision is a very serious one, because the insurer will be barred from re-entering the market for five years. In other words, they can't choose to "sit this one out" and return to the market as soon as conditions appear more favorable.

9.17 MEDICAL SAVINGS ACCOUNTS (MSAs)

Another HIPAA provision adds a new Internal Revenue Code §220, and amends §62, to add a new category to the health plan arsenal for taxable years that begin after 12/31/96: the "Medical Savings Account," or MSA. A small-scale pilot project is created for four years, 1997-2000, under which a limited number of individuals will be allowed to set up IRA-like MSAs and take a tax deduction for their contributions. If the experiment is successful, it may lead to an even greater shift in responsibility for health care payment from the employer to the employee (although the U.S. Treasury might potentially lose a lot of revenue if MSA tax deductions become widespread).

The discussion of MSAs in this book will be brief, because the pilot project deals with those for individuals who are self-employed or whose employer has an average of 50 or fewer employees, and the assumption behind this book is that most readers administer plans for employers of 100 or more.

MSAs can be maintained by people who are covered by a "high deductible health plan," but are not covered by other health plans. Individuals make MSA contributions in much the same way as they make IRA contributions. MSA contributions are usually tax-deductible, and the account itself remains tax-free as long as it remains an MSA. Funds can be taken from the MSA to pay for medical expenses, but they are not tax-deductible (they've already received favorable tax treatment). Funds taken from the MSA for any other purposes are taxable income, and are also subject to a 15% excise tax.

9.18 QUALIFIED MEDICAL CHILD SUPPORT ORDERS

As discussed on page 296, it is quite common for divorce courts to issue orders stipulating how an employee spouse's retirement benefits will be shared with the non-employee spouse. These orders are called Qualified Domestic Relations Orders, or QDROs. There is an EGHP counterpart: the Qualified Medical Child Support Order (QMCSO), which supplements the COBRA continuation coverage option as a supplementary means of ensuring that children do not lose health coverage as a result of their parents' divorce.

When it receives a document that is supposed to be a QMCSO, the plan has an obligation to review it to see if it is a valid order. (For instance, courts don't have the power to order benefits that are not ordinarily a part of the plan; if the plan doesn't cover dependents under any circumstances, a QMCSO can't create this coverage.)

Health coverage is an important component of child support, and a parent who is covered by an EGHP can be ordered to take steps (e.g., notifying the plan; paying premiums in a contributory plan) to make sure that the child is enrolled. In legal lingo, the child is described as an "alternate recipient."

The QMCSO has to identify:

- Every plan it applies to
- The period of time covered by the order
- The type of coverage the plan must give each alternate recipient (or a method of determining the coverage)
- The name and last known mailing address of the employee parent and of each alternate recipient.

A plan administrator who receives a QMCSO has a duty to notify the participant and the alternate recipients that the order has been received, and how the plan will analyze it to determine its validity. Usually, of course, the plan will determine that the order is valid; this decision, too, requires notice to the participant and alternate recipients. (The alternate recipients are children, of course, so the notice probably won't mean much to them; they can designate someone else, like a parent, step-parent, or attorney, to get copies of these notices.) EGHPs have a legal duty to draft a procedure for validating QMCSOs, and to express the procedure in writing.

9.19 MEDICARE AS SECONDARY PAYER (MSP)

Given the employer's wide latitude to design the health plan, it might seem obvious that employers could draft their plans to coordinate benefits, and to give Medicare primary responsibility for employees and dependents who are over 65 when they use medical services. After all, if the employer's plan didn't exist, then Medicare would have to reimburse their medical care.

However, this has not been the case for over a decade and a half. Federal legislation called the Tax Equity and Fiscal Responsibility Act of 1982 (P.L. 97-248; TEFRA) required employers who have health plans to provide coverage for active employees aged 65-69, and to their spouses, on the same terms as for employees younger than age 65. TEFRA instituted "Medicare Secondary Payer" rules (MSP) under which the employer group health plan has primary responsibility for paying for the medical care, and Medicare's role is only secondary. The Deficit Reduction Act of 1984, P.L. 98-369, known as "DEFRA," made the EGHP the primary payer for employees' spouses who are aged 65-69 (even if the employees themselves are younger).

The Comprehensive Omnibus Budget Reconciliation Act of 1985 ("COBRA"; P.L. 99-272) pushed the MSP concept even further, by requiring employers who provide health insurance to ANY employee to offer coverage to ALL employees and spouses, irrespective of age, on comparable terms. However, employees can elect to be covered by Medicare rather than the EGHP.

Medicare's secondary payment rules are found in Social Security Act §1862(b)(3); the regulations are in 42 CFR Part 411. The rules for who pays what are quite complex—and the complexities increase even further if liability, medical malpractice, or automobile no-fault insurance could be involved. Let's say that a 67-year-old employee is injured in a car crash. The potential payers are the EGHP, Medicare, the medical component of the employee's own auto insurance, and the other driver's liability or no-fault insurance. (In practice, what often happens is that health care providers get a windfall: they get at least some payment from multiple payers, adding up to more than the total they are entitled to, instead of getting a single payment that combines the amount actually required from each potential payer.)

Plan provisions that purport to limit the plan to offering "complementary coverage" (only items such as deductibles and coinsurance that are not covered by Medicare) are void. After all, employers can't draft a contract that alters federal law, and federal law makes the EGHP the primary payer. In fact, a federal District Court has found that an EGHP was the primary payer for the wife of an independent contractor sales representative who was covered by the plan: the MSP rules are not limited to common-law employees.

The employer has an economic incentive to attempt to get Medicare to pay amounts that are properly covered by the employer plan. To combat this incentive, the federal law permits the Medicare system to recover from the EGHP any amounts that Medicare paid when the EGHP should have paid. An individual who has been harmed by the employer's failure to pay has a private right of action against the employer for double damages: See 42 U.S.C. §1395y(b)(3). Furthermore, Code §5000 imposes a tax of 25% on the calendar-year expenses of a "nonconforming" group health plan, i.e., one which does not conform to the Social Security Act §1862(b)(1) provisions dealing with Medicare as secondary payer and coverage of older employees.

FRINGE BENEFITS

10.1 INTRODUCTION

The major factors in employee compensation are current compensation, pension plans and other deferred compensation, and health benefits. However, there are additional benefits provided by some or all employers. These fringe benefits raise questions of state law, taxation, and ERISA (to the extent that they are part of a "plan" and that plan provides "welfare benefits").

The relevant Code sections include §162 (which permits a deduction for all ordinary and necessary business expenses, including the employer's contributions to unfunded welfare benefit plans) and §419 and 419A, which set limits on the deduction. The general rule is that contributions will be deductible insofar as they represent direct payments of benefits or expenses. Employers can make contributions that bear a reasonable actuarial relationship to the future needs to pay benefits under the plans. In some cases, there is a statutory safe harbor allowing contributions.

The income that a funded welfare plan earns will probably constitute taxable income for the employer that maintains the plan. If the plan earns unrelated business taxable income, this almost certainly will be taxed to the employer.

10.2 ELIGIBILITY FOR BENEFITS

Within limits, the benefit plan can determine who is eligible for participation. However, the employer's characterization of workers is not necessarily the last word. Several Microsoft workers were characterized by the company as freelancers and independent contractors, in large part because they were paid through invoices submitted to the Accounts Payable department rather than through the payroll process.

After an IRS ruling that these workers were actually common-law employees, they sought participation in Microsoft's savings and Employee Stock Ownership plans. The court's judgment was that eligibility for participation depends on being a common-law employee; the form in which payment is rendered is not relevant. The court also disregarded the agreement signed by the workers indicating that they were ineligible for plan participation, on the grounds that the employees' real status as common-law employees could not be altered by the agreement.

The case created widespread apprehension among corporate planners. However, it might be a legal anomaly. In June, 1996, the Fifth Circuit ruled that Exxon's leased employees were not eligible for participation in the company's benefit plans; and in January, 1997, the Fourth Circuit found that DuPont's leased employees were not entitled to participate in the company's insurance plans. Perhaps, therefore, the main difference between these companies and Microsoft was not so much the design of their plans but the existence of an IRS ruling characterizing workers as common-law employees rather than independent contractors.

⇒ **TIP**
_____

It might be worthwhile to amend your welfare benefit plans to clarify the ineligibility of leased and part-time workers for participation.

10.3 STOCK OPTIONS

One measure of a publicly traded corporation's success (and of the performance of its managers) is the price of the company's stock. Awarding stock options can be an easy way for the corporation to reward excellent performance and motivate continued hard work and creativity. To a certain extent, stock prices rise simply because of inflation, or because a bull market increases the price levels of stock overall; but there is a potential for additional appreciation because the company's financial results are above-par for the industry.

The company may also maintain a more generalized stock option or stock purchase plan that operates as a qualified plan for tax purposes, and that is available to a broad range of employees. Furthermore, a company that issues stock options can provide additional compensation to workers (and take a deduction for providing it) without actually giving the employees cash from the corporate coffers. In 1995, 43% of all publicly traded companies had stock option plans covering at least some employees; in the late 1980s, only about one-third of public companies made use of this compensation measure.

Stock options also have a place in the privately held start-up company, where the pay scale may be far below industry standards, but employees are awarded stock options in the hope that eventually there will be an IPO, and "insiders" will be able to earn a great deal of money by exercising their options and then selling the stock. Some venerable computer industry success stories feature millionaire secretaries and warehouse workers who prospered because of their stock options.

⇒ **TIP**

On the other hand, the motivating effects of a stock option plan can be strictly temporary. As soon as employees are in a position to exercise options and then sell stock, they may quit their jobs (very possibly using the stock windfall to start up a company that competes with the original employer!). Some long-time Microsoft employees sport "FYIFV" buttons (IFV stands for "I'm fully vested"; you can guess the rest) — they won't stand for much guff, because they can live off their Microsoft stock.

Depending on the company's circumstances, and the incentives it wants to provide, stock options could be a perk available only to a few top executives (e.g., those earning $60,000 or more), or to all employees.

Generally speaking, the employer will have both practical and tax motivations for imposing some limitations on the stock options. A typical restriction is the employee's obligation to put (re-sell) the stock back to the corporation on termination of employment. Such an arrangement will provide a means of calculating the put price, such as book value or a set P/E ratio.

Under the labor and tax rules, a stock bonus plan is a form very similar to the profit sharing plan. However, the distributions are generally made in the employer's common stock, not in cash. Employees must be given put options obligating the employer to re-purchase shares of stock that is not readily tradable on an established market.

An Employee Stock Ownership Plan (ESOP) is a stock bonus plan or one combining stock bonus and money purchase features. ESOPs invest primarily in the employer's common stock. The Code contains additional rules for leveraged ESOPs that borrow the funds used to purchase the stock. ESOPs can be used as defensive tools against hostile takeovers of the issuer corporation, although this strategy is beyond the scope of this book. There are many ESOP variations, so consult your plan's financial advisor if you think an ESOP elaboration could work well for your company and its employees. The KSOP is a 401(k) plan that is a stock bonus plan investing in qualifying employer securities. An HSOP is a leveraged ESOP combined with a 401(h) retiree health plan account (see page 140); the plan borrows to buy employer securities, and as they are allocated to benefit plan accounts, they go to fund retiree health benefits for plan participants.

> ⇒ **TIP**
>
> Administering a stock purchase plan, especially a broadly-based ESOP, can be difficult if employees are allowed to select their own stockbrokers (since each brokerage firm has its own paperwork requirements). Some companies negotiate with a major securities firm to act as a "captive-broker" to process all stock option transactions. The captive firm reports to the employer when employees sell the shares they acquired through options, thus enabling the employer to claim a compensation deduction related to the employee's acquisition of taxable income.

Although a full discussion is beyond the scope of this book, it should be noted that federal securities laws and state Blue Sky laws must be consulted before offering stock options or other compensation in the form of stock. If the company is a public company, option transactions will probably have to be disclosed to the shareholders at large and reported both on the company's SEC filings (10-K, 10-Q, etc.) and on its proxy statements. "Insiders" are also forbidden by the Exchange Act to take short-swing profits.

10.3.1 Incentive Stock Options (ISOs)

For tax purposes, Code §422 creates a specially favored category, the Incentive Stock Option (ISO). An ISO plan is permitted to discriminate in favor of highly compensated employees. However, favorable tax consequences are available to the employee only if he or she retains the shares for at least one year from the exercise of the option or two years from the grant of the option.

The Tax Code (see §422(b)) requires ISOs to be granted pursuant to a plan that states the aggregate number of shares that can be issued under option, and indicates which employees qualify to receive them. The plan must be approved by the corporation's shareholders, during the time period running from 12 months before to 12 months after the adoption of the plan. Options can only be granted during the 10-year period after adoption of the plan (of course, a corporation can simply adopt further plans in later years).

The option price must be at least equal to the fair market value of the stock at the time the option is granted—in other words, ISOs can't be issued at a bargain price (although NQSOs can be); the employees have to wait for the stock's value to increase to benefit from the options. ISOs can only be exercised by employees themselves, during their lifetimes, and they are not allowed to transfer ISOs except by will or intestacy. If, at the time of the grant, the grantee owns 10% or more of the corporation's stock, the option price must be set higher, and only five years can be given to exercise the option—not ten.

Furthermore, the aggregate fair market value of each employee's stock cannot exceed $100,000 (measured as of the date of the grant of the option) in the first calendar year for which the options are exercisable.

⇒ **TIP**

It is not necessary to write this provision into the ISO plan document; it is applied automatically, and amounts over $100,000 are simply not characterized as ISOs.

10.3.2 Nonqualified Stock Options (NQSOs)

Yet another possible option mechanism: NQSOs are non-qualified stock options that fail to satisfy the §422 rules. Sometimes NQSOs are issued "in the money," that is, the price at which the option can be exercised is lower than the current value of the stock, not just the anticipated future value of the stock at the time the option can be exercised.

The tax treatment of NQSOs is somewhat different from that of ISOs. There is no tax effect at the time of the grant, provided that the option does not have a readily ascertainable market value (i.e., the options are not traded actively). When the option is exercised, the employee has taxable income, equal to the FMV of the stock minus the consideration paid for the option. However, if the stock received by exercising the option is not transferable, and is subject to a substantial risk of forfeiture, then income is not taxed until the condition lapses. At that time, the amount of gain is determined according to the then-current FMV of the stock.

⇒ **TIP**

The fair market value of the stock at the time of the exercise of the option, minus the price of the option is a "preference item" for which Alternative Minimum Tax may have to be paid.

10.3.3 Stock Appreciation Rights (SARs)

Stock Appreciation Rights (SARs) are really a form of cash compensation. The grantee of SARs gets money from the corporation, based on the price of the company stock. If, for instance, a corporate Vice President has SARs for 1000 shares, the corporation will pay him or her the difference between the FMV of those shares at the time of exercise and the FMV at the time of grant. SARs are not usually issued in isolation; generally they accompany qualified or non-qualified stock options. Often they can be exercised with the stock options, so the employee receives some of the cash needed to pay for the optioned shares.

10.3.4 Junior Stock

Another motivational device is the junior stock plan, under which the executive is given the right to purchase junior stock, which is stock in the employer corporation that has reduced dividend rights and voting powers. The employee is given the right to convert the junior stock to ordinary common stock if he or she satisfies specified performance goals.

10.3.5 Option Taxation Under §83

When stock options are discussed, it's important to look at Code §83 (which governs all transfers of property in exchange for performance of services; it's broader than just stock options). Under this section, the person who performs the services has taxable income (at ordinary income rates) at the time that the rights in the property become transferable or are no longer subject to a substantial risk of forfeiture. The amount of ordinary income to be recognized equals the fair market value (FMV) of the property minus any amount the employee paid for it.

> **➡ TIP**
>
> This means that options can be made forfeitable if the employee leaves before a certain number of years of employment, thus both motivating the employee to stay longer and improving his or her tax position, because there is no taxable income until the restriction lapses.

The point at which an option comes under §83 depends on whether it has an ascertainable fair market value (basically, whether it is actively traded on an established market, or otherwise has a determinable value). If so, and if the option is vested, it is taxed as soon as it is granted—not at the later point when it is exercised. Options that have no ascertainable FMV do not become subject to §83 until they are exercised. The legal theory behind the distinction is that an option with a fair market value can be sold as a separate asset.

Note that the employee faces taxation at two stages: once when the option can be exercised and stock purchased, and again when he or she sells the stock. (The sale of the stock gives rise to capital gains, not ordinary income.) Stock options are vested when there is no longer a substantial risk of forfeiture and the stock is transferable. (In some instances, employees will be awarded stock that is endorsed on its face to prevent transfer.)

Under §83, property is subject to a substantial risk of forfeiture if the right to the property is conditioned on future performance of substantial services. This is called an earn-out restriction. There's no hard and fast test of when services are substantial; the decision uses factors such as the regularity with which services are supposed to be performed and the amount of time needed to perform them.

A retiree's consulting agreement with his or her former employer does *not* constitute substantial services, if the retiree could fail to perform the consulting services and still keep the stock. Refraining from performing services (for instance, under a noncompete clause) can also give rise to a substantial risk of forfeiture.

If the employer company has publicly traded stock and is a "reporting" company under the Exchange Act of 1934, major executives who are corporate officers, directors, or 10% shareholders are likely to be subject to the Exchange Act's ban on "short-swing" profits earned by corporate insiders who trade in the company's stock. Code §83(c)(3) provides that rights are not vested at any time that the person receiving stock options is unable to sell the stock without violating the short-swing profit rules. That means that the insider who gets a stock option has no income either for six months or until the first day that the stock can be sold.

In the usual stock option situation, until the option vests, the corporation is still considered the owner of the stock. The dividends that the stock earns are considered additional compensation to the employee. On the other hand, the corporation can deduct these dividends (because they constitute employee compensation) where it would not be able to deduct regular dividends paid to stockholders under ordinary circumstances.

Even if tax would not be due under §83, the employee has the right to elect immediate taxation in the year of the transfer of the property. This is a reasonable choice where otherwise the appreciation on the stock would be taxed as compensation.

⇒ **TIP**

If the employee pays the tax right away and later has to forfeit the options (e.g., by leaving the company early), there is no provision for getting a refund of the tax already paid.

From the employer's viewpoint, it can deduct the amount of compensation that the employee includes in income under §83 (subject, however, to the requirement that the compensation must be reasonable). The deduction is taken in the employer's taxable year that includes the year in which the employee includes the sum in income. (It is typical for employers to have fiscal years; it is almost inevitable that employees will pay their taxes on a calendar-year basis.) The employer gets an immediate deduction if the property is vested as soon as it is transferred, or if the employee exercises the §83 election for immediate taxation.

Prior to 1995, the employer couldn't take the deduction unless it also withheld taxes based on the employee's gross income. This is no longer true, but the employer is still required to comply with W-2 and 1099 reporting requirements in connection with stock options and other property transfers.

To sum up the ISO/NQSO distinction, when an individual is granted NQSOs:

- (At time of grant) if there is no readily ascertainable FMV, there is no tax effect

- (At time of grant) If there is an ascertainable FMV, §83 determines taxation

- (At time of exercise) The employee has taxable income equal to the FMV of the stock minus consideration paid for the option; but if the stock received on exercise of the option is non-transferable and subject to a substantial risk of forfeiture, taxable income is not a factor until the condition lapses. At that point, gain is determined based on the FMV at the time of the lapse. If the employee actually sells the stock purchased under the option, then he or she will have capital gain or loss on the sale

- The employer gets a deduction equal to the individual's gain.

If the grant is of ISOs rather than NQSOs:

- (At time of grant) The employee has no taxable income

- (At time of exercise) The employee has no income

- (At time of disposition of stock) The employee has capital gain or loss, long- or short-term depending on how long the stock was held

- The employer does not get a deduction (Code §421(a)(2)).

The basic rule for ISOs is that the employee cannot dispose of the shares within two years of the grant of the option or one year of exercising the option. If he or she does so, any gain constitutes ordinary income, and the employer is entitled to a tax deduction equal to this income.

If corporate income tax rates are higher than individual tax rates, the corporation will have an incentive to prefer NQSOs to ISOs, but employees will probably prefer ISOs. If the corporation is especially interested in satisfying the employees' expectations, it can adopt an NQSO plan but provide additional incentives for the employees in the form of Stock Appreciation Rights or extra cash.

⇒ **TIP**

If ISO characterization is unwelcome, an option can simply provide that it is *not* an ISO; in that case, it will be treated as an NQSO.

10.3.6 Bad Boy Clauses

An increasing trend in the late 1990s is for stock option packages to be drafted with "golden handcuff" provisions: clauses that call for forfeiture of stock options if the executive optionee quits his or her job and subsequently engages in competitive activity, participates in a takeover bid, or carries out any other activity that is considered detrimental to the company that granted the options. An even tougher variation requires forfeiture of stock options if the executive quits before the contract expires, even if post-resignation activities don't hurt the corporation. Or, the number of years for which stock options must be surrendered could vary from one to three, depending on the nature of the conduct. Toughest of all: a contract that says that if an executive is awarded *new* stock options, he or she has to agree to these stringent terms for options that were already granted under an earlier employment contract.

10.4 LIFE INSURANCE FRINGE BENEFITS

Because of its favorable tax characteristics, life insurance is an important estate planning device. It is a valued employee benefit, whatever the employee's stage in the life cycle, or the size of his or her estate. Younger employees or those with limited savings find life insurance valuable to safeguard the financial position of their survivors. Older and/or more affluent employees value the ability to structure insurance proceeds so that they are received free of estate tax.

The Code authorizes several mechanisms under which employers can provide life insurance to employees at little or no income tax cost to the employees. The basic rule is that if the employer pays the premiums and the insurance proceeds go to the beneficiary designated by the employee (i.e., not "key-person" insurance that is payable to the corporation to compensate it for the loss of a top manager), the employee will have taxable income and the employer will be able to deduct the cost of providing the insurance (but only if, and only to the extent that, it is an ordinary and necessary business expense). Nevertheless, group-term life insurance plans and "split dollar" plans are worthwhile employee benefits and motivational devices because they permit employees to receive insurance coverage at small or no income tax cost.

10.4.1 Employer Pays; Employee Owns

It is common for employers to provide employee-owned life insurance for which the employer pays the premiums. Reg. §1.1035-1 gives the employer a deduction for the cost of such plans, provided that the employer is NOT the beneficiary of the insurance, and also provided that the cost is a §162 ordinary and necessary business expense. The premiums are taxable income for the employee, but the insurance proceeds conform to §101 and thus do not constitute income to their recipient. If the employee borrows against the policy, interest on the loan (unlike most forms of personal interest) is deductible.

➠ **TIP**

Employer-pay life insurance plans are not subject to nondiscrimination requirements, so it is perfectly legitimate for the employer to furnish insurance to certain employees whom the company wishes to motivate, without offering a plan that is open to all employees.

10.4.2 Section 79 (Group-Term Life)

Code §79 authorizes written, nondiscriminatory plans that provide term life insurance policies (pure insurance, with no cash value) to a group of employees. The employee who participates in such a plan has no taxable income when up to $50,000 worth of coverage is provided under the plan. When employer-paid coverage exceeds that amount for a particular employee, he or she does have taxable income. The calculation is made based on the Uniform Premium Table contained in the IRS Regulations; costs are set out in five-year age brackets. The excess coverage is subject to FICA (Social Security taxes), but not to FUTA or income tax withholding: Code §3121(a)(2).

The §79 plan must either be available to all employees, or to groups of employees defined in a way that does not permit selection of some individual employees and exclusion of others because of individual characteristics. In other words, the plan can condition eligibility on age or employment-related factors, but not on the amount of the corporation's stock that an individual owns. The amount of coverage provided to each employee must be based on a formula that does not permit individual selection. For instance, age and length of service are permissible factors. As a general rule, §79 plans must cover at least ten employees.

There are IRS Regulations explaining how to prevent a §79 plan from discriminating in favor of highly compensated employees. A nondiscriminatory §79 plan has three criteria: (1) it is one which benefits at least 70% of the employees; (2) no more than 15% of the participants are key employees; and (3) is a plan for which the Treasury finds the class of beneficiaries to be nondiscriminatory. If the §79 plan is part of a cafeteria plan, it is further necessary to satisfy the §125 rules.

➠ **TIP**

In assessing the plan, it is not necessary to count employees with less than three years of service, part-time or seasonal employees, or those covered by a collective bargaining agreement where the bargaining involved negotiation over benefit coverage.

The §79 plan must make whatever benefits are available to key employees available to all employees, although it is permissible to make the amount of insurance proportionate to compensation. It's also acceptable to set different benefit levels for active and former employees.

If a §79 plan is discriminatory, key employees are required to include the full cost of the coverage (even the portion up to $50,000) in gross income. In practical terms, this won't be a problem: a few hundred dollars' additional income is not a tax burden for a highly compensated person. In this context, a key employee has several definitions:

- an officer who earns more than 50% of the defined benefit plan limit;
- one of the ten employees earning more than the defined contribution plan limit and who also have the largest holdings of the employer corporation's stock;
- employees who are 5% owners of the employer corporation's stock;
- 1% owners who earn $150,000 or more a year;
- retirees who were key employees at the time they separated from service. (If the plan is discriminatory, only the key employees, not the rank-and-filers, are penalized.)

The employer must "carry" the policy, directly or indirectly. That means that the employer pays for part or all of the insurance, or that the employer arranges for the employees to pay for the insurance—and at least one employee pays more than the actual cost of coverage, while at least one employee pays less.

⇒ **TIP**

Group-term life insurance plans do not have to provide coverage for employees who continue to work after age 65. However, if the plan does cover senior citizen employees, it must either offer them the same type of coverage as younger employees get, or must satisfy alternative standards set out in Reg. §1.79-1 (c) (2) (11).

⇒ **TIP**

The cost of retirees' group-term life insurance that is subject to payroll taxes can be reported by the employer on Form W-2; the employee has the responsibility for paying the employee share of the taxes.

There is a special rule for former employees whose employment is terminated because of disability: the $50,000 limit does not apply to the cost of insurance provided by the employer after the disability termination.

Coverage of the life of the employee's dependents is not taxed under §79, but in most instances the employee will have noncash compensation that is taxed under §61. No tax is imposed on incidental coverage (i.e., a death benefit of under $2,000 per dependent) because it is considered a de minimis fringe benefit.

10.4.3 Split-Dollar and Reverse Split-Dollar

Under a split-dollar plan, the employer and employee enter into an agreement. Each year, the employer contributes an amount equal to the policy's increase in cash value for that year. (In some split-dollar plans, the employer pays the entire premium, but owns only the cash surrender value portion of the policy.)

If the "endorsement method" is used, the employer owns the policy, and an endorsement to the policy describes the employer/beneficiary allocation. Under the "collateral assignment" method, the employee or a third party owns the policy, which is then assigned to the employer via the collateral endorsement.

When the employee dies, the employer receives an amount equivalent to the premiums paid (or representing the cash value); the beneficiary designated by the employee gets the rest of the benefits. For income tax purposes, the employee has to determine the cost of pure life insurance (i.e., simple term), using either the actual premiums or the IRS tables for this purpose, and then subtract all the premiums paid by the employee. The difference constitutes taxable income for the employee. Employers are not entitled to deduct their costs of providing this type of insurance.

In a reverse split dollar plan, the employee owns the policy and its cash value; the employer receives the basic death benefit (the death benefit minus amounts attributable to any investment portion of the life insurance contract). When such arrangements are undertaken, the employer usually reimburses the employee for the annual term costs of the death benefit (roughly equal to the PS 58 cost). The employee's current compensation might also be increased so he or she has funds to pay the premium.

The additional compensation is, naturally, taxable income for the employee; so is any premium payment by the employer that is compensation-equivalent. The employer can't deduct any payment representing the annual term cost of the policy, but the rest of the cost of the plan probably would be deductible as compensation as long as they are ordinary and necessary business expenses. Once again, Code §101 is applicable, so neither the employer nor the employee's beneficiary has income when the proceeds are received.

10.4.4 Company-Owned Life Insurance (COLI)

Company-Owned Life Insurance (COLI) is yet another variation. The policies are owned by the employer company, and can be used to finance death benefits provided by the employer's plans. If the insurance has a cash build-up value, it can even be used to finance retirement benefits. In this variation, the beneficiary or estate of the deceased employee does have income under §101(a), because the death benefits are deemed to be paid directly by the employer, rather than by an insurance policy.

When the employer owns the COLI policy and uses it only to fund the death benefit, the employee does not have taxable income during his or her life from the policy's cash surrender value or the premium payments that the employer makes—as long as the employee's beneficiary is only an unsecured creditor vis-à-vis the policy proceeds.

The employer can borrow from the COLI policies to pay current benefits under a nonqualified plan, but cannot deduct the interest if more than $50,000 is borrowed from a policy covering an individual: see Code §264(a)(4).

The general rule is that premiums that the corporation pays for COLI are not deductible, because of the employer's interest as a beneficiary. However, there is an exception to this rule for premiums paid for certain annuity contracts used in connection with COLI plans. If the company borrows to purchase the COLI, the general rule is that it is not entitled to an interest deduction (again, because of its insurable interest in the life of the covered executive, and the company's eventual share of the insurance proceeds). For a corporate (or other non-human) taxpayer, no interest deduction is allowed for the part of interest that can be traced to policy cash surrender values net of amounts borrowed under the policy.

However, an interest deduction is allowable if an entity engaged in a trade or business owns a policy covering only one individual (or an individual and spouse) if that individual is either a 20% stockholder in the entity, or is an employee, officer, or director of the entity. The interest provisions derive from the Taxpayer Relief Act of 1997, §1084(a)(1), and are effective for contracts issued after June 8, 1997 and for tax years that end after June 8, 1997.

10.4.5 *Accelerated Benefits*

Although, naturally, the most important function of life insurance is to provide benefits to the insured person's survivors, there are various ways that the benefits can be accessed during lifetime. If the insurance has cash value (i.e., is whole life, universal life, or variable life, rather than term insurance), policy loans are a possibility. A terminally ill person, or a person who is seriously ill enough to require a significant amount of medical care, has other options: viatication and acceleration of the death benefit.

Viatication, also known as viatical settlement, is the practice of assigning the policy's benefits to a third-party settlement company. In effect, the policy is sold at a discount; the amount the insured person receives for the policy depends on his or her life expectancy (and thus the degree of risk the settlement company undergoes).

⇒ **TIP**

The Health Insurance Portability and Accountability Act of 1996 clarifies the tax treatment of viatication and accelerated death benefits.

In contrast, accelerated death benefits are paid directly by the insurance company that issued the policy. According to LIMRA's (the Life Insurance Marketing
Research Association) 1994 survey, about five million Americans had access to some
accelerated benefits provision in their life insurance, usually in the form of a rider
issued at no additional cost.

10.5 CAFETERIA PLANS

The benefits that the employer selects for a plan are not always the ones on which
employees place the greatest value. Furthermore, not every employee will have the
same preferences in a benefit plan. Cafeteria plans, as provided by Code §125, allow
the employer to offer a "menu" of benefits, thus attracting employee loyalty by permitting the work force to choose the benefits that each one finds most worthwhile.
The advantage of receiving cash is, of course, that it can be spent immediately or
invested by the employee. However, cash has its disadvantages as well, including
income tax liability and being subject to employment-related taxes such as FICA
and FUTA.

A cafeteria plan is a written plan that provides a choice of two or more benefits: cash and at least one taxable and one non-taxable benefit. It can include a
CODA (401(k)) component, but no other deferred compensation. The potential
benefits include:

- Accident and health plans
- Group-term life insurance (the $50,000 limit—see page 166—does not apply
  in this context)
- Disability coverage, including accidental death and dismemberment (ADD)
  plans
- Dependent care assistance
- Benefits that lose qualification because they fail non-discrimination tests
- Vacation days
- Group automobile insurance or other taxable benefit that the employee uses
  his or her own after-tax dollars to purchase.

➠ **TIP**

Provisions in the Health Insurance Portability and Accessibility Act of 1996 about long-term care insurance as an employee benefit make it clear that LTCI cannot be included in a cafeteria plan (or, for that matter, provided under a Flexible Spending Account, because FSAs are specifically precluded from paying insurance premiums). Nor can a cafeteria plan include scholarships, education assistance, or employee discounts.

The non-taxable benefits that can be included in a cafeteria plan are group-term life insurance, medical expense reimbursement, accident and disability benefits as defined by Code §106, dependent care assistance, and paid vacation days.

The Code §125 requirements for a valid cafeteria plan are:

- All plan participants are employees

➠ **TIP**

The Proposed Regulations say that it's all right to include former employees in a cafeteria plan, as long as it is not predominantly for their benefit. Employees' spouses and children can receive benefits under the plan, but can't choose the benefits or otherwise actively participate.

- The participant chooses between cash and one or more benefits.

➠ **TIP**

Prop. Reg. §1.125-1 says that the amount of cash need not necessarily equal the entire cost of the nontaxable benefit

- The plan does not discriminate in favor of highly compensated employees
- Benefits provided to highly compensated employees do not exceed 25% of the total benefits for the year
- The election to take benefits rather than cash must be made before the beginning of the plan year
- The election can only be changed on the basis of a change in family status (e.g., marriage, divorce, birth or adoption of a child), not because the employee changes his or her mind about the comparative value of benefits and cash.

In a pre-tax premium plan, a "mini cafeteria" salary reduction plan is used to provide after-tax dollars for the employee to pay insurance premiums. The most common application is health insurance coverage for dependents, in plans where the employer pays for employee coverage but dependent coverage is "employee-pay-all." The employer adopts a plan that allows the employee, before the start of the plan year, to elect to have compensation reduced enough to pay the employee's share of the premium.

> ⇒ **TIP**
>
> The employer share of FICA tax is not due on these salary reductions.

A cafeteria plan must be designed as a "use it or lose it" plan: unused benefits cannot be carried over to subsequent years. Participants can be given a chance to use their vacation days, sell them back to the employer for cash, or buy extra vacation days—as long as the plan is not used to defer the receipt of compensation into a later plan year. This is explained in IRS' Proposed Regulation §1.125-1, Q&A 7.

> ⇒ **TIP**
>
> In a 1996 Private Letter Ruling, the IRS said that employers can contribute the value of unused vacation days to an employee's 401(k) plan, and such a contribution will not reduce the amount of compensation that the employee can defer, or that the employer can match.

If the cafeteria plan is not operated in a non-discriminatory manner, the highly compensated employees will have taxable income as a result. Under the Code, the test for discrimination in benefits is whether contributions are made for each participant in a uniform relationship to compensation; if contributions for each participant are equal to the cost of coverage that the plan incurs for highly compensated employees; or if contributions for each participant are at least equal to 75% of the cost of the similarly-situated plan participant who has the highest cost of benefits.

Neither employer nor employee FICA taxes are due on non-taxable cafeteria plan benefits, although amounts placed into a 401(k) plan are subject to FICA and FUTA (both employer and employee shares).

Generally, participants will be given a 30-day period at the end of each year to make the election for the following year. It might close a few days, or even one month, before the end of the year to give the plan administrators time to process the election requests. The basic ERISA rule, found in §403 (which might be altered by the terms of the plan itself) is that cafeteria plans do not have to be managed by a trust. However, if the plan permits after-tax contributions for the purchase of benefits, those contributions must be placed into trust unless they are used to purchase insurance policies.

10.6 FLEXIBLE SPENDING ACCOUNTS (FSAs)

An FSA is an arrangement under which an employee diverts some cash compensation into a separate account which must be identified for specific use for either medical expenses that are not reimbursed by other means (e.g., insurance; an employer-paid medical expense reimbursement account) or for dependent care expenses.

The amount that can be placed into a dependent care FSA is limited by the Internal Revenue Code's limits on deductible dependent care expenses. Moneys targeted for medical care cannot be used for dependent care, and vice versa. A medical expense FSA must last at least twelve months (but a short first year, when the plan is initially adopted, is permissible). As noted above, reimbursable expenses under an FSA cannot include premiums for other health coverage.

Depending on circumstances and preferences, an FSA can be part of a cafeteria plan (see previous page) or can be a separate plan. Stand-alone FSAs are subject to the same nondiscrimination requirements as cafeteria plans.

The §125 Proposed Regulations define an FSA as a benefit program that reimburses an employee for specified, incurred expenses. The maximum amount of reimbursement that can be made "reasonably available" to a participant during a period of coverage is limited to 500% of the total premium for the coverage. FSA reimbursement must be made available at least monthly, or when the level of expenses reaches a reasonable minimum amount such as $50.

In order to receive reimbursement, the FSA participant must submit a written statement from an independent third party (i.e., the doctor or medical office administrator) to confirm that a medical expense of $X has been incurred, and that this expense was neither reimbursed nor reimbursable by any other plan.

> **⇒ TIP**
>
> This IRC requirement can lead to an "endless loop" if each spouse works for a company that has an FSA!

FSA plans, whether or not contained within cafeteria plans, operate on a "use it or lose it" basis. In other words, if an employee puts $3,000 into a medical expense FSA, but has only $1,000 in unreimbursed medical expenses, the other $2,000 is forfeited. Forfeitures can be refunded to the participants as a whole, based on a reasonable and uniform method of allocation, based on the amount of contributions to the plan, but not based on reimbursement from the plan. The IRS has made informal statements to the effect that forfeitures can be used to pay the plan's administrative expenses or can be returned to participants pro rata.

10.7 SICK LEAVE

It's a rare employee indeed who can go through an entire career without so much as a minor illness. Employee benefit plans usually recognize this fact by providing for "sick days" during which the employee will receive full pay. Usually the plan provides for X days of sick leave per year, but an alternate plan design is to allow a certain number of days per illness rather than per year.

A sickness and accident plan provides coverage (either a certain number of dollars or a certain percentage of income replacement) for employees who have used up their sick leave for the year. The level of income replacement is usually low (e.g., 33-50%) because the company does not want to create an incentive for employee absences! (In a company with no sickness and accident plan, employees can use their vacation days to take time off at full pay; they can also take unpaid FMLA leave, as described on page 491, that will nevertheless preserve their seniority and benefit eligibility.)

Some companies have a "leave sharing" plan under which employees can donate unused leave on behalf of other employees who have medical emergencies. According to the IRS' Publication 15-A, page 11, the pay that donees receive is considered wages, is included in the gross income of the leave recipients, and is subject to Social Security, Medicare, and FUTA taxes. Withholding of income tax is also required. The amounts should not, however, be included in the income of the employees who donate vacation time.

10.8 DISABILITY PLANS

As a result of acute illness, chronic illness, and injuries (work-related or otherwise), many individuals of working age will suffer brief, extended, or permanent periods during which they are unable to perform their normal job tasks. Studies published in 1993 by UNUM Corporation and the Department of Commerce show that about 30% of workers have a disability period of 90 days or more at some time between age 35 and the conventional retirement age of 65. In fact, one-seventh of individuals will have a disability of five years or more during the period of expected worklife.

Close to one-eighth of people in the age group 16-65 had a physical problem that limited their work capacity in some way (in the nation as a whole, that means close to 20 million people), and more than five percent of adults, or almost nine million people, were disabled enough to be unable to work. On the whole, between 6 and 12% of the average corporate payroll goes to disability-related costs.

➡ **TIP**

Downsizing increases workplace stress, and is associated with increased disability claims among the remaining workers (who may be taking on additional tasks subsequent to layoffs). Cigna Corp. performed a survey for the American Management Association in 1996, finding that the more drastic a company's layoffs had been, the greater the number of subsequent stress-related disability claims, including mental health disabilities, substance abuse claims, heart ailments and high blood pressure.

Furthermore, the average duration of disability claims was higher in downsized firms: 155 days versus 12 days (no doubt there was less incentive to recover quickly, because there was less chance of being rehired and a less pleasant working environment if rehiring did occur). So layoff plans should be drafted carefully, and allowances should be made for compensating increased costs of disability,

The potential for disability is addressed by both the public sector (the Social Security system includes benefits for totally disabled persons; Worker's Compensation replaces part of the income lost to work-related disability) and the private sector (by disability insurance and self-insured plans offered by employers).

Whether because state law makes it mandatory, or as an employee incentive, it is quite common for employers to maintain plans that provide coverage of employees' short- and/or long-term disability. As of 1993, the Bureau of Labor Statistics found that 87% of employees of medium-sized and larger companies had some form of short-term disability coverage. That breaks down to 25% sickness and accident insurance, 49% paid sick leave only, and 26% with both. Long-term disability coverage was less common, available to 41% of the employees of those businesses.

There is no hard-and-fast dividing line, but plans usually define a short-term disability as one that lasts less than six months or less than a year; long-term disability benefits typically end after a period of years (e.g., five years) or at age 65 (at which time it is presumed that the employee would be retiring anyway, disabled or not; and at which time he or she almost certainly qualifies for Social Security retirement benefits even if he or she was unable to satisfy the tough criteria for Social Security disability benefits).

A typical arrangement is for the employer to self-insure for short-term disability, but to purchase coverage for long-term disability (perhaps with an employee contribution component). Often, the two types of plan have different definitions of disability (more restrictive for the long-term plan because its exposure is greater). An "own occupation" definition (a person is disabled when unable to carry out the duties of the pre-disability occupation) makes it easier to qualify for benefits than an "any occupation" definition (benefits stop as soon as the employee is able to return to any work, or any work suitable to his or her education and training).

Another frequent design is for the definition of disability to begin as "own-occ" but switch after two years to inability to perform any occupation for which the individual is suited by education and training. The typical income replacement ratio under a long-term disability plan is 60-70% (60% is the most common), and the plan may also provide that income replacement from all sources, including Social Security disability benefits and Worker's Compensation does not exceed a percentage such as 75% of pre-disability income.

As an incentive to rehabilitation, the plan may continue benefits at a low level while the individual engages in a trial period of re-employment, or undertakes part-time or lower-level work in an attempt to re-enter the workforce. See page 513 for a discussion of Age Discrimination in Employment Act implications of disability plans.

In five states (California, Hawaii, New York, New Jersey, Rhode Island), employers are required to provide TDI (Temporary Disability Insurance) coverage for 26-52 weeks of non-occupational temporary disability to industrial and commercial workers. Either the state administers a fund from which employer contributions are disbursed to disabled employees, or the state maintains a fund but gives employers the option of self-insuring, purchasing insurance, or working with a union-sponsored disability plan.

TDI benefits are offset by Worker's Compensation and unemployment benefits. In the other states, TDI plans are a common employee benefit, but are optional with the employer; sometimes employee contributions are a mandatory feature of the plan. A "Taft-Hartley" plan is a temporary disability plan jointly run by employers and a union. The goal of the plan is to assist employees who are in financial need because of a disability, but to help them to return to work as soon as possible (if they can be rehabilitated adequately).

The plan should offer substantial income replacement, but not a windfall; usually the plan replaces 70% or less of pre-disability income. Many plans offset (reduce) disability benefits to account for government benefits such as those under the Social Security system and damages received from tort suits or settlements (e.g., if the employee was injured in an accident or by a defective product).

Another cost-saving measure is to have benefits start after a waiting period, so that the plan covers situations in which work ability is impaired for a long time, but not run-of-the-mill illnesses and minor injuries. (The employee will probably have paid sick leave for the initial portion of the disability anyway.)

The employer's tax deduction depends on satisfying §162 (ordinary and necessary business expenses). If the plan is tax qualified, the employer's contributions must also satisfy §404 to be deductible. Vis-à-vis ERISA, most disability benefit arrangements are welfare benefit plans, and therefore subject to disclosure, filing, and fiduciary requirements. Some, however, are top-hat plans for executives, and thus have more limited disclosure obligations.

> ⇒ **TIP**
>
> Plans that are maintained *only* to comply with Worker's Compensation or state disability laws are exempt from these ERISA rules: ERISA §4(b)(3); so are situations under which an employer makes payments out of its general assets to an employee who is out of work for medical reasons (29 CFR §2510.3-1(b)(1).)

Disability benefits are not considered "medical care," so when an employee is terminated, the right to COBRA continuation coverage (see page 142) extends to the employee group health plan but NOT to the long-term disability plan.

From the employee's viewpoint, the key tax section is §106, which excludes employer coverage under an accident and health insurance plan from the employee's gross income. This section is usually interpreted to include the premiums that the employer pays for an insured disability plan, as well as the value of coverage under a self-insured disability plan (i.e., one where the benefits are paid directly by the employer out of funds it has set aside for this purpose, or out of the employer's general assets if there are no reserves). Subsequent to a disability, the benefits received by the employee under accident and health or disability insurance must be included in income to the extent they are attributable to previously-excluded employer contributions. Amounts paid directly by the employer to the employee are also includible in gross income.

Different treatment is accorded to payments made for permanent loss or loss of use of a body part or its function, or for disfigurement; these are not included in the employee's income (as long as they are computed without regard to absence from work).

> ⇒ **TIP**
>
> There is a tax credit for elderly individuals that also applies to individuals who retired on disability at a time when they were permanently and totally disabled (Code §22).

See page 491 for a discussion of the Family and Medical Leave Act, under which the employee is entitled to claim unpaid leave for personal medical needs, or medical and care needs of family members. The FMLA is not the only statute that can interact with a disability plan.

For instance, a disability plan that imposes lower limits on mental health care than on care of physical ailments may violate the Americans with Disabilities Act. (See page 116 for a discussion of the requirement that EGHPs be amended to provide some degree of parity with physical ailments; but this provision did not take effect until 1997, and is scheduled to expire in 2001, so there will be many claims involving plan operations before the effective date and, if it is not extended, after its expiration.)

Disability insurers seldom litigate mental disability claims until the second year; they may take a more proactive stance if they face the potential of claims with the same limits as physical disability claims, or without any limits at all.

If your company is not in a position to add a new benefit to the package, but employees show high interest in disability coverage, it may be possible for the employees themselves to form a "list billed" small group disability plan, which your company can administer via payroll deductions (but not otherwise finance). In a group of four or more, rates may be as low as 50% of the rates for individual policies.

⇒ TIP

According to the Eighth Circuit, former employees must go through all the internal review procedures provided by a disability plan before bringing suit to collect disability benefits. This is true even if the plan doesn't have explicit instructions about exhausting internal remedies; the court's position is that employees can be expected to know that the plan's rules have to be followed before invoking the legal system.

10.9 EDUCATION ASSISTANCE

The progression from high school to college to the workforce is not inevitable. Some people drop out of high school and later qualify for equivalency certificates. Others start work right after high school, with the intention of combining work and college study. Many employers applaud employees' efforts to get more training (especially if the training is work-related and enhances productivity) and provide material assistance to help. As of 1993, about three-quarters of the medium-sized and larger private-sector companies offered educational assistance for courses related to the job.

The tax status of employer education assistance is tenuous. There were no Code provisions until 1978, the year in which §127 was enacted as a five-year pilot provision; under this Code section, employees would not have taxable income as a result of qualified employer educational assistance. On several occasions, §127 has expired but has then been re-enacted retroactively by Congress. The Small Business Job Protection Act of 1996 permitted employees to exclude qualified educational assistance received during the period January 1, 1995–May 31, 1997; the Taxpayer Relief Act of 1997, effective for tax years beginning after December 31, 1996 extends the exclusion from income yet again, for courses that begin before June 1, 2000.

Qualified employer education assistance consists of up to $5,250 per year for tuition, fees, and related expenses (but not dormitory room and board or education-related transportation), paid for an undergraduate-level course. Any amount paid by the employer as assistance for graduate-level courses is taxable to the employee.

For the employee to receive assistance money tax-free, the employer must establish a separate written educational assistance plan, and must communicate the existence of the plan (and how to use it) to employees. The education assistance plan can't be part of a cafeteria plan, because §127 forbids the employer to make the employee choose between education benefits and taxable benefits. Education assistance plans must not discriminate in favor of officers, shareholders, or highly compensated employees. At least 95% of the benefits under the plan must go to rank-and-file employees, and not to corporate shareholders or owners of five percent or more of the company's stock—and not to their dependents, either.

Employers maintaining educational assistance plans are required to submit an information return to the IRS each year, disclosing:

- Employer's name, address, and Employer Identification Number
- Employer's line of business
- Total number of employees
- Number of employees eligible for participation in the education assistance plan
- Number actually participating
- Total cost of the education assistance plan.

10.10 DEPENDENT CARE ASSISTANCE PLANS

Plans of this type are governed by Code §129. The employer can make direct payments to provide dependent care to employees; or the employees can pay for the care themselves, and then receive reimbursement from the employer. The employer is not obligated to pre-fund the plan; it can pay benefits as they arise out of current income, with no need to maintain a separate account. However, the employer is required to provide reasonable notice to eligible employees that the program is in existence and how it operates.

Employees who are covered by §129 plans do not have taxable income because of the plans. However, the plan cannot pay more for dependent care than the employee earns. (In other words, the plan can't be set up as a perk for employees who are, in essence, on parenthood leave and earn very little.) Furthermore, in effect the plan only assists employees who are single parents, or who are part of a two-career couple, because the employee will have taxable income if §129 benefits exceed the income of the employee's *spouse* unless that spouse is a full-time student or disabled. In addition to these limitations, the maximum employer contribution to a §129 plan that can be excluded from income is $5000 per employee (or $2500 per employee who is married but filing a separate return).

For this purpose, dependent care expenses are household services and other expenses that are incurred so that the employee will indeed be able to work. In this context, dependents are dependent children under age 15, or a spouse or other dependent (e.g., an aging parent) who is physically or mentally incapable of self care.

The Code defines a qualified dependent care assistance plan as a written plan, for the exclusive benefit of employees, subject to a classification created by the employer but approved as non-discriminatory by the IRS. To be considered non-discriminatory, not more than 25% of contributions to the plan or benefits received from the plan may relate to shareholders, 5% owners, or their families. The average benefits provided under the plan to employees who are not highly compensated must be 55% or more of those provided to highly compensated employees.

⟹ **TIP**

If the plan is not qualified, highly compensated employees (but not ordinary employees) will have taxable income on account of the plan. Each year, by January 31st, employees must be given a written report of the amounts paid or expenses incurred by the plan in order to provide dependent care to that employee in the previous year.

⟹ **TIP**

An employer-provided day care *center* is deemed to be a welfare benefit plan, but a dependent care plan that involves reimbursement of employees' dependent care expenses is not.

10.11 ADOPTION ASSISTANCE

For years after 1996, employers can establish a written adoption assistance program, providing benefits of up to $5,000 total (or $6,000 if the adoptee has special needs) to compensate employees for their "qualified adoption expenses." (Code §137) Qualified adoption expenses represent adoption agency fees, court costs, and associated attorney's fees. See page 45 for a discussion of the work-family implications of corporate adoption assistance.

⇒ **TIP**

If the adoption is occurring from outside the United States, the plan cannot pay adoption expenses until the adoption is final.

As a general rule, the employer's provision of this assistance does not generate taxable income for the employee, but the exclusion is limited if the employee's Adjusted Gross Income is over $75,000, and phases out at AGI of $115,000. See IRS Announcement 97-6, 1997-26 IRB 9, for an explanation of how to reflect adoption assistance on the W-2 form.

Adoption assistance plans must be non-discriminatory, and not more than 5% of assistance under the plan can go to 5% shareholders. The employer has an obligation to notify employees if a plan is put into place. However, the employer is not obligated to fund the plan in advance.

10.12 EMPLOYEE ASSISTANCE PROGRAMS (EAPs)

The mission of the EAP is to help employees cope with stress and other problems. The theory is that in many, or even most, cases, merely listening with a sympathetic ear, and providing information and referrals for more sophisticated services, will make employees less anxious and more productive. EAPs might offer any combination of one-to-one counseling, information and referral to appropriate community resources (e.g., an adult day care center for an employee's disabled elderly parent; an Alanon or Alateen meeting for a family member of an alcoholic), hotlines and crisis intervention, and informational seminars.

EAPs typically deal with problems such as substance abuse, dependent care, and problems with spouses and children. Many companies have found that early intervention makes it possible to shorten the damage and amount of time that would otherwise be involved, for instance, when the employee "hits bottom" with a drug or alcohol problem, or when an untreated mental illness requires inpatient hospitalization in a crisis. Each dollar invested in EAP services is estimated to return anywhere from two to eight dollars in health and productivity savings.

EAPs also take a role in coordinating an employee's return to work after recuperating from an accident or illness (which may include a shortened or flexible schedule, intermittent FMLA leave, or other accommodations).

The typical company with an EAP finds that 5-10% of the employees consult the EAP each year; a much higher or much lower pattern of utilization could indicate either that the EAP is so comprehensive that it replaces services employees would otherwise pay for, or that it is perceived as not very useful or not willing to keep employee information confidential. EAP services can be provided in-house, by the HR department, or contracted out to outside vendors. The latter course is more expensive, but may make the EAP more credible to employees, or may reassure employees that their confidentiality will be protected.

10.13 MISCELLANEOUS FRINGES

Code §132 provides that employees do not have taxable income as a result of certain minor fringe benefits provided by the employer on a non-discriminatory basis to all employees:

- No-additional-cost services of the employer company—e.g., a simple will prepared by a law firm for a clerical employee, or air travel for an airline employee. The employee must get access to the same services normally sold to customers, but the employer must not incur any substantial cost; in essence, the employees are given access to the business' excess capacity.

- Employee discounts—e.g., designer clothing sold at a discount to boutique employees; the discount must not exceed the gross profit percentage for goods, or 20% of the cost of services.

- De minimis fringe benefits—e.g., a company-sponsored coffee pot or small Christmas presents; anything too trivial to account for separately.

- An on-premises eating facility such as a low-cost cafeteria that prepares meals on premises for the convenience of the employer (because employees can take shorter meal breaks while enjoying the subsidized cuisine). However, to qualify under §132, the facility must be owned or operated by the employer, must generate revenue at least equal to its direct operating costs, and must provide meals during the workday or right before or after it. It must also be in or near the workplace, and must be operated by the employer (possibly through a contract with a third-party management company).

- Working condition fringe benefits—goods or services the employee could deduct if he or she paid for them personally. Typical examples are business travel and the use of company cars. A full discussion of the elaborate rules governing the taxation of company cars is outside the scope of this book, but check with your attorney AND accountant before creating a program of this kind.

- Qualified transportation fringes—e.g., a van pool; a transit pass; parking spaces.

- An on-premises gym for the exclusive use of employees and their families.

- Reimbursement of employment-related moving expenses that would be deductible if the employee paid them directly (but have not in fact been deducted by the employee). The move must be at least 50 miles from the employee's former personal residence, and the employee must be a full-time employee for at least 39 weeks in the 12 months after his or her arrival at the new job location.

The effect of §132 is that the benefits are not taxed to the employees, and so FICA, FUTA, and federal income tax withholding are not required, and the employer share of these taxes does not have to be paid. The employer generally gets to deduct the cost (which is supposed to be nominal) of these benefits, as long as it fits within the definition of an ordinary and necessary business expense.

Another provision, this time found in §119, governs meals and lodging furnished on premises for the convenience of the employer: e.g., a room for a hotel manager who must be around to handle problems as they arise. When these benefits are provided, they do not generate taxable income for the employee.

Employers can offer qualified parking subsidies of up to $170/month tax-free to employees. For tax years beginning after December 31, 1997, employees can be given a choice between non-taxable parking benefits and the equivalent in taxable cash. The cash option for parking plans was added by Taxpayer Reform Act of 1997 §1072. However, parking subsidies cannot be offered as part of a cafeteria plan.

10.14 VOLUNTARY EMPLOYEE BENEFIT ASSOCIATIONS (VEBAs)

The Code also defines Voluntary Employee Benefit Associations, or VEBAs, in §501(c)(9). A VEBA is a trust that is funded by employer contributions (with or without employee contributions) and is used to pay benefits to employees who voluntarily exercise the option to participate in the association.

VEBA benefits constitute taxable income to the employee unless they are specifically exempted, but the trust itself is not a taxable entity.

VEBAs provide life, sickness, accident, or similar benefits to employee members and their dependents and designated beneficiaries. The permitted benefits are those that safeguard or improve health or protect against a contingency that threatens the employee's earning power. On the other hand, VEBAs are not permitted to offer commuting expenses, profit shares, or stock bonuses.

The VEBA must be controlled by its employee membership, by a bank or other independent trustee, or by fiduciaries chosen by or on behalf of the membership. A VEBA is considered a welfare plan under ERISA, and therefore is subject to ERISA Parts 1 (notice and reporting), 4 (trust and fiduciary responsibility) and 5 (enforcement).

10.15 VACATIONS AND VACATION BANKING

Some degree of paid vacation time, including major holidays and an entitlement of about two to four weeks, is almost universal in U.S. corporations. (European entitlement to vacation time is both greater and more formal; the practice is usually a matter of labor law, not left up to employer discretion.) Certain companies shut down on summer Fridays, or close for a week or more each year; others must stay operational day-long and year-round.

Furthermore, the needs of employees have gotten more complex. An employee might prefer to take a day or two at a time to decompress or spend time with his or her family, as opposed to a multi-week chunk of vacation time. On the other hand, brief absences might be harder for the company to work around than a solid block of time when projects can be postponed or delegated to an "understudy."

According to Hewitt Associates, employees who have worked for the company for a year are usually entitled to 10–14 days of vacation: this is the policy in 83% of the firms surveyed; 13% give 15–19 days off after a year of service. Employees with five years of tenure usually get 15–19 days off (this is true in 75% of companies; 20% offer two weeks of vacation or less, though.) After ten years' tenure, 62% of companies surveyed offer 15–19 days, 37% offer 20–24 days. The 20–24 day allotment is standard for employees with 15 years service: 88% of companies provide this much.

> ⟹ **TIP**
> ___
> Audit requirements may *force* employees with access to the firm's cash and books to take vacations of at least two consecutive weeks. An employee who never uses his or her full allotment of vacation time could be a conscientious person who wants to cope with a backlog, a workaholic who really needs to "get a life" outside the office, a sub-par employee who needs a full 52 weeks a year to do 48 weeks worth of work, or an embezzler who has to hang around so his or her schemes don't come unraveled.

By far the most popular method for dealing with unused vacation time is the carry-over, permitted by 51% of employers. Only 14% allow cash-outs; only 11% have buy-sell plans, and only 8% allow employees to donate vacation time (e.g., if a sympathetic friend is willing to give vacation days so a co-worker who has used up FMLA leave can continue to care for a sick family member). These figures come from a 1994 Hewitt Associates survey of 360 companies with fewer than 1,000 employees.

The buy-sell option creates a "bank" of vacation days. Employees who want more time off can "buy" vacation days from the bank by giving up equivalent other benefits; those who are short of cash can work more or "sell" vacation days in exchange for enhanced health benefits. (Hewitt Associates' 1995 survey showed that 24% of workers who have the choice buy more vacation days, choosing greater leisure over higher compensation; 6% sell vacation days.)

> ⟹ **TIP**
> ___
> Even if you don't want employees to buy extra vacation time (when you're short-staffed), you might let employees sell vacation time in exchange for cash or health benefits.

Vacation banking is usually cost-neutral, because the number of days bought and sold is approximately equal. However, if a company's workforce disproportionately chooses extra vacation time, it may be necessary to hire some temporary workers or outsource some tasks to compensate.

> ⇒ **TIP**
>
> If the vacation plan is contained within a cafeteria plan, don't forget that Code §125 imposes a ban on carryovers, so cafeteria plan vacation time is on a "use it or lose it" basis.

10.16 FRINGE BENEFIT PLAN COMPLIANCE

The reporting requirements for fringe benefit plans are set out in Code §6039D. The plan must report:

- The number of employees the employer has
- The number of employees eligible to participate in the plan
- The number actually participating
- The number of highly compensated employees in each of the above categories
- The plan's total cost during the year
- The employer's name, address, and Employer Identification Number; the nature of its business.

If there are any taxable fringe benefits, the employer can either add them to the regular wages for a payroll period, or withhold federal income tax at the 28% flat rate used for supplemental wages.

10.17 EMPLOYER TAX DEDUCTION FOR FRINGE BENEFIT PLANS

In the pension context, the tax rules are devised to make sure that the employer contributes enough to the account. In contrast, in the welfare benefit context, the tax focus is preventing excessive prefunding of benefit plans. Therefore, the relevant Code sections (§419 and 419A) specify a maximum funding level for welfare benefit trusts; if this level is exceeded, the trust ceases to be tax-exempt.

Although the employer receives a tax deduction for maintaining a welfare benefit trust, the deduction is limited to the "qualified cost" of the benefit plans for the year—i.e., the direct cost of funding benefits, plus whatever amount §419A permits to be added to the account for the year as a safety cushion.

Reference should also be made to Code §4976, which imposes a 100% excise tax on disqualified benefit distributions made from funded welfare benefit plans. For instance, retiree health and life insurance benefits for highly compensated employees are supposed to be kept in a separate account from comparable contributions for rank-and-file employees.

Therefore, benefits paid to HCEs from the general account would be disqualified. VEBA payments to HCEs that violate nondiscrimination requirements are also disqualified, as are amounts that revert to the employer. (An erroneous contribution which is withdrawn by the employer after a determination that it is not deductible is not considered a reversion.)

10.18 ERISA REGULATION OF WELFARE BENEFIT PLANS

Although most of the attention goes to ERISA's regulation of pension plans, ERISA also covers "welfare benefit plans"—roughly equivalent to fringe benefit plans. A welfare benefit plan is one created (generally by a corporate resolution passed by the Board of Directors and administered by the relevant corporate officials) and administered to provide one or more of these benefits to plan participants and their beneficiaries:

- Medical benefits
- Health care
- Accident insurance
- Disability benefits
- Death benefits
- Supplemental unemployment benefits
- Vacation benefits
- Training (e.g., apprenticeship)
- Day care centers (but not dependent care reimbursement spending accounts)
- Scholarships
- Prepaid legal services
- Any benefit described in the Labor-Management Relations Act §302(c) other than death benefits, pensions, or insurance coverage for pensions or death benefits.

> **TIP**
>
> The participants who receive the benefits must be common-law employees, and not independent contractors; for this purpose, whether a person is an employee or independent contractor depends on agency principles such as who controls and supervises the individual, and whether the individual can recognize profit or loss from the work relationship. It does not depend on the "reasonable expectations" of the parties: *Mutual Insurance Co. v. Darden*, 503 U.S. 318 (1992).

Welfare benefit plans are subject to ERISA Title I. The Eleventh Circuit has ruled that a Title I plan exists if circumstances lead a reasonable person to ascertain the intended benefits, intended beneficiaries, financing sources, and procedure for receiving benefits under the plan. A plan can be deemed to exist even if the ERISA rules are not observed, and, indeed, even if there is no written instrument.

Depending on the circumstances, a plan that provides severance pay might be treated as a pension plan, but it is more likely to be characterized as a welfare benefit plan. DOL Advisory Opinion 84-12A says that a severance pay plan is not a pension plan if:

- Its benefits are not contingent on the employee's retirement
- Total payments do not exceed twice the employee's compensation for the year before the termination
- Payments are completed within 24 months after termination of service for the employer.

Under a similar analysis, bonus programs are not treated as pension plans for the purposes of ERISA Title I unless the payments are systematically deferred at least until termination of employment. DOL Regulation §2510.3 says that an employer plan that supplements retirement benefits (e.g., until early retirees can qualify for Social Security benefits) can be either a pension or a welfare benefit plan, depending on its terms and how it is administered.

ERISA Title I does *not* apply to certain payroll practices:

- Extra pay for non-standard working hours (overtime, shift premiums, holiday premiums)
- Compensation paid while the employee is on sick leave, taking a sick day, or otherwise medically unable to work
- Compensation paid for other absences, such as vacation days, sabbaticals, and military leave.

Part III

PENSIONS AND RETIREMENT

(Deferred Compensation)

Chapter 11

EARLY RETIREMENT AND RETIREE HEALTH BENEFITS

11.1 INTRODUCTION

Although some individuals want to continue to work well into later life (and civil rights law and the tax code take the possibility of employment past 65 into account), in fact only about one-eighth of all persons over 65 are in the labor force, and many people retire several years in advance of this conventional retirement age.

Early retirement can occur at the impetus of the employee, who wants to switch careers or simply leave the workforce, or at the impetus of an employer who wants to reduce the payroll and thinks that the least contentious way to do so is through attrition. Early retirement programs should be planned carefully, and documents signed by participants should be drafted with due attention to the Older Worker's Benefit Protection Act (OWBPA): see p. 559.

11.2 EARLY RETIREMENT INCENTIVES: ADEA ISSUES

At what point does an incentive offered to motivate early retirement turn into "constructive discharge" (the equivalent of firing the employee)? Clearly, the employee can choose to retire at any time, although the employer can try to shape this decision by improving the worker's economic position if he or she retires at the time most convenient to the employer.

The relevant statute is the Older Worker's Benefit Protection Act, which allows voluntary early retirement incentives but requires the incentive programs to conform to Congress' initial objectives in passing the ADEA: promoting employment opportunities for willing, qualified older workers. Under the OWBPA, employers are permitted to subsidize early retirement via flat dollar benefits, extra benefits, or percentage increases. Employees who retire early can be offered a more favorable formula for computing benefits (e.g., assuming that they worked three years longer than they actually did). The incentives can also be limited to a "window" period without violating the OWBPA.

A defined benefit plan can pay a "Social Security supplement" starting at the date of early retirement and ending on the first date of eligibility for reduced Social Security benefits (or, at the employer's discretion, eligibility for unreduced benefits).

➠ TIP

It's permissible for an employer to amend a pension plan to raise the normal retirement age from 65 to 67, as long as accrued early retirement benefits, including subsidies, are preserved. The Tenth Circuit ruled in 1997 that there is no requirement that "normal retirement age" be 65 or earlier, although the change cannot remove benefits employees have already become entitled to.

A 1993 Eighth Circuit case involves a plan amendment saying that work for the predecessor company, before the sale of a corporate division, counts for pension vesting but not for other purposes. The amendment was given effect by the court, so work for the former employer did not count toward satisfying the requirements for an early retirement subsidy.

Medicare eligibility depends on age (65 or over) or disability, not employment status. Furthermore, the Medicare system does not provide spousal benefits: each spouse must qualify independently. Therefore, a savvy potential early retiree who is younger than 65 will negotiate hard for additional medical coverage, especially if there is a gap between the end of COBRA coverage and Medicare eligibility.

11.2.1 Eligibility for Incentives

Employers should be aware that early retirement incentive plans can generate litigation in two ways. First, employees who are eligible may charge that the plan is a subterfuge for forcing them out of the company. This argument is unlikely to succeed: a 1992 case from the Fifth Circuit, for example, finds that an attractive early retirement offer is not tantamount to constructive discharge.

Second, employees who are *not* offered the incentives may charge that they are the victims of discrimination because they could not gain access to the incentive plan.

Furthermore, a company that alters its strategy over time can be attacked. If incentives are offered, and later a better package is offered, those who accepted the first offer may charge that the employer affirmatively misled them, or failed to meet its obligation to disclose the superior offer that would be made in the future.

11.2.2 ERISA Preemption

Although it is very likely that state court cases involving group health plans will be found to be preempted by ERISA (see page 121), preemption is less likely to be found in the early retirement context. According to the Sixth Circuit, ERISA does not preempt claims of age discrimination merely because the plaintiff retired early and was collecting a pension at the time of the suit

The Ninth Circuit said that ERISA does not preempt claims that the employer was guilty of fraud and negligent misrepresentation in the information it gave the employee about the tax consequences of electing early retirement. In contrast, the Eleventh Circuit found preemption of state law claims of fraudulent misrepresentation about the availability of an early retirement program.

Also see *Lockheed* v. *Spink*, #95-809, 116 S.Ct. 1783 (Sup.Ct. 6/10/96), finding (among other issues) that setting up an early retirement program that is conditioned on waiving enforcement of employment claims is not a prohibited transaction as defined by ERISA §406. In this analysis, paying benefits (under whatever circumstances, and for whatever reason) cannot be penalized as a prohibited transaction.

It's hard to say what ERISA fiduciaries are required to do in connection with early retirement programs. The Seventh Circuit said that it is not a violation of ERISA fiduciary duty for early retirement benefits to be available in only one of the employer's locations. This was deemed a business decision about plan design, not a decision taken in the capacity of an ERISA fiduciary. But a year later, the District Court for the Southern District of New York held that a benefit committee that delegates to the employer the power to decide which business units can have early retirement programs is guilty of a violation of fiduciary duty. (Not making the early retirement program available to all units was also deemed a violation of fiduciary duty.)

Another important question is what happens if the terms of the offer change. People who were not eligible for the improved terms, or who elected early retirement without knowing that they could have gotten a better deal by waiting longer, might charge the employer with fraud, and might charge various parties involved with the plan with violation of fiduciary duty. (See page 325 for a discussion of this issue in connection with retirement at normal retirement age, as distinct from early retirement.)

A 1991 Eleventh Circuit case says that, where early retirement incentives were presented to the workforce as a one-time offer, it does not constitute a breach of fiduciary duty to offer another incentive package several years later—provided that there was no intention to offer the second set of incentives when the first was made available.

In other words, the employer can change its mind without rendering the initial decision deceptive. It is not permitted to lie when an employee asks about the company's future plans, but there is no obligation to discuss alternatives that the company might perhaps adopt but does not have under serious consideration. It is a very bad idea to try to pressure employees to adopt a package by telling them that this is their last chance for incentives, or at least incentives of this caliber.

11.3 RETIREE HEALTH BENEFITS

Whether as a general offer to all retirees or all early retirees, or as a special negotiating "carrot" to motivate a particular retirement, it is common for employers to offer retiree health benefits (although much less common than it used to be). These benefits could be part of the regular EGHP, or a separate benefit package. The most common form that this benefit takes is "lifetime health benefits at no cost."

> **➠ TIP**
> _____
>
> A retiree health benefit program should not be undertaken lightly. Poor health is a motivating factor that could lead an employee to elect early retirement—and the more health care a person expects to require, the more attractive he or she will find a retiree health benefit package. So adopting a plan of this type may subject the employer to costs far in excess of the projected amount. In fact, the overall lifetime cost of providing retiree health benefits may actually exceed that of paying the same individual's pension.

The general rule is that, as long as the employer retains the right to amend, modify, or terminate the health benefits, it can do so unilaterally. Although ERISA is quite explicit about the circumstances under which pension benefits vest (become nonforfeitable), ERISA fails to provide for vesting of welfare benefits such as retiree health benefits. As discussed on page 329, ERISA preempts state regulation in this context, so states do not have the power to draft their own laws calling for vesting of welfare benefits.

However, there are circumstances under which a promise of retiree health coverage can be converted into an enforceable contract, e.g., if the employer makes an unambiguous promise of lifetime benefits that terminates the employer's right to change the plan. This is referred to as a "promissory estoppel" theory.

A limitation on this theory is that the plaintiff might be required to prove that he or she would have obtained comparable medical insurance at his or her own expense if the plan had not been misleading about the future availability of retiree health benefits. Employers might also be bound by a promise of lifetime no-cost retiree health benefits if employees actually gave up cash compensation or some other benefit in exchange for the employer's promise.

Another argument that employers can make to cut back or eliminate retiree health benefits is that they were provided by a particular collective bargaining agreement, and thus do not survive the expiration of that agreement—unless the agreement itself is drafted to provide for survival of benefits. Retirees are no longer employees, and therefore are not part of the union's bargaining unit

Retiree benefits are not included among the mandatory subjects of bargaining (see page 356 for a discussion of this issue). In fact, the bargaining agent does not have a duty to represent retirees; indeed, there is a real potential for conflict of interest if the employer strives to cut health costs and the union strives to maintain benefits for its members who are active employees (very possibly at the expense of the retirees).

A mere course of conduct by the employer (such as a practice of increasing health benefits for retirees in tandem with benefits for active workers) will probably not prevent the employer from changing its policy, especially if the benefit increases were gratuitous on the employer's part, and workers did not have to surrender anything to get them.

A 1988 case from the Second Circuit takes the Summary Plan Description (SPD) as the major source of information about plans. So booklets issued by the employer, promising "lifetime benefits at no cost" [to the retirees] could not serve to modify the SPD and other plan documents that reserved the employer's right to amend or terminate the plan.

Similar analyses are applied when the employer seeks to increase retirees' costs (premiums, deductibles, coinsurance) rather than eliminate the entire plan; retaining the right to terminate the plan is likely to be interpreted as a retained right to increase employees' copayment responsibilities, unless there is a contractual or promissory estoppel issue that prevents this characterization.

See page 509 for a discussion of the Older Worker's Benefit Protection Act (OWBPA) provisions about reductions in severance pay based on the availability of retiree health benefits to early retirees.

11.3.1 Implications of the Employer's Bankruptcy

The basic rule, as created by *In re White Farm Equipment Co.*, 788 F.2d 1186 (6th Cir. 1986) is that vesting of welfare benefits is not automatic. It is a subject of bargaining, to be contracted for. The company was bankrupt; the case dealt with a noncontributory, non-collectively-bargained plan that provided retiree benefits. The plaintiffs in this class action were retirees who asked the court for a declaratory judgment (an official statement) that their claims were both valid under ERISA and allowable as bankruptcy claims.

They also asked the court to order the employer to reinstate the plan retroactively, and to resume funding it. But the court found that employee benefit regulation is exclusively a federal concern; and, if the plan documents gave the employer the power to terminate the plan, the employer could do so.

Ironically, retirees of bankrupt companies may have more protection for their benefits than retirees of solvent companies (and, conversely, bankruptcy may solve some of a company's problems, but it will generate others).

A company that is in Chapter 11 bankruptcy proceedings can ask the bankruptcy court for the right to reject an existing collective bargaining agreement, including provisions covering retiree health benefits (see 11 United States Code §1113). To use this provision, the company must disclose the relevant information to the union and bargain in good faith about the termination.

If a company with a Chapter 11 reorganization plan was already paying retiree benefits, P.L. 100-334, the Retiree Benefits Bankruptcy Protection Act of 1988 (RBBPA) requires medical and disability payments to retirees to continue on their original terms either until the parties agree to modify the benefits or the bankruptcy court orders a modification.

The Act includes standards for bankruptcy courts to use in deciding whether a modification is appropriate; the modifications proposed by the bankruptcy trustee must be equitable, not just to current and former employees, but also to the company's creditors. The retirees must not have had good cause for rejecting the proposals, and the proposed modifications must be necessary to permit the employer's bankruptcy reorganization on fair terms.

The RBBPA also requires the employer to negotiate with retiree representatives, and to disclose the best available information about the employer's financial condition. Generally speaking, the union will serve as the representative of the retirees, unless it refuses to do so or unless the court finds that a different representative should be designated. Any party can petition the court for the appointment of a committee of retirees to represent benefit recipients who are not covered by a collective bargaining agreement.

When the court considers the trustee's proposal, it will not have the power to order benefits LOWER than the proposed schedule. Once the parties reach an agreement, or once the court orders changes in the benefits, the authorized representative of the retirees has status to petition the court for an increase. It will be granted if it appears clearly just to do so.

⟾ **TIP**

The RBBPA protection does not apply to retirees or their spouses or dependents if the gross income of the retiree was $250,000 or more for the year before the employer's bankruptcy petition. The only exception is if they can prove that they are unable to get comparable insurance coverage on their own. The RBBPA does not require an employer to maintain retiree health benefits that were provided by the union rather than the employer prior to the bankruptcy.

11.3.2 SFAS 106: Accounting Issues

Before January 1, 1993, Generally Accepted Accounting Principles (GAAP) did not require the cost of providing retiree health benefits to be treated as a current liability or cost of doing business. A retiree health benefit plan (although it can be quite costly—as much as 10% of corporate net income) did not have to have any impact on either balance sheet or income statement. The usual pre-1993 treatment was to consider the retiree health benefit obligation an unfunded liability.

In December 1990, the Financial Accounting Standards Board (FASB) released Statement of Financial Accounting Standards (SFAS) No. 106, entitled "Employers' Accounting for Postretirement Benefits Other Than Pensions." January 1, 1993 is its effective date.

SFAS 106 requires corporations to accrue the costs of future retiree health benefits; it is no longer sufficient to reflect the actual costs paid each year in the records and publicly disclosed financials. The result of accruing the future costs is a decline, perhaps a serious one, in reported profitability. The cost of deferred compensation in the form of postretirement benefits should be matched with the years of service over which the compensation is actually earned.

The buzzword for this purpose is the EPBO, the expected postretirement benefit obligation (i.e., an estimate of the total costs). The EPBO is the actuarial present value, as of a particular date, of the benefits that the corporation expects to pay on behalf of a particular employee. The EPBO is attributed (charged) to each year of service until the date of full eligibility for the retiree health benefit. In many instances, the employee will be eligible for benefits several years before he or she actually retires.

The ABPO, or accumulated postretirement benefit obligation, is the actuarial present value of benefits attributed to employee service rendered up to a particular date (i.e., the benefits already earned, as distinct from the benefits the employer expects to pay after further service by the employee).

The corporation's income statement should include:

- The net periodic postretirement benefit cost
- The service cost (current period's share of EPBO)
- The interest cost used in discounting the entire obligation
- The return on the plan assets funding the obligation
- Amortization of the actuarial gains and losses
- Transaction obligation (the APBO on the date FAS 106 was implemented in the plan, minus amounts already expensed to prefund the obligation). Of course, in most corporations, the pre-FAS 106 prefunding was limited or nonexistent.

The transaction obligation can either be recognized immediately or stretched out—usually over a 20-year period.

11.3.3 Retiree Health Benefit Tax Issues

In many instances, the tax treatment of an item is different from its accounting treatment. Generally speaking, for tax purposes corporations will not create actual cash reserves to pay future retiree health benefits. Instead, when benefits are actually paid to the retirees, a deduction is taken under Code §162 (ordinary and necessary business expenses). The somewhat laissez-faire attitude the Code takes to retiree health benefits is, of course, in contrast to the high degree of regulation of qualified pension plans and their financial implications.

Code §419A(c)(2) permits the employer to deduct the cost of retiree health benefits as part of a funded welfare plan which must be nondiscriminatory. Key employees' retiree health benefits must be drawn from separate accounts, not the main account. (Failure to maintain the separate accounts, or discrimination in furnishing retiree health benefits, leads to a 100% excise tax on disqualified benefits, imposed by §4976.)

A funded welfare plan can maintain a reserve for future retiree health benefits, funded over the work lives of employees, without violating the account limit. The reserve must use a level-basis actuarial determination, using reasonable assumptions and current medical costs.

Voluntary Employees' Beneficiary Association (VEBA) trusts, as defined by Code §501(c)(9), are a possible funding vehicle for retiree health benefits. Use of the VEBA requires caution, however: first, because the trust is a tax-exempt organization, and thus will be taxed on its investment income; second, because VEBAs are required to use current health costs to calculate the contributions to be made for future retirees. So if costs increase more than anticipated, or if retirees use more health care than expected, the VEBA may be exhausted.

➡ TIP

If you need more information on this subject, Michael Canan and William Mitchell's *Employee Fringe and Welfare Benefit Plans* (West 1997), Chapter 10, contains an excellent detailed exploration of the accounting issues.

11.3.4 Other Tax Issues

Under 1994 tax legislation, the General Agreement on Tariffs and Trade (P.L. 103-463), Congress imposed rules governing the interest rate assumptions to be used in the actuarial reduction of lump sum benefits paid before age 62. (Actuarial reduction is required to equalize the treatment of early, normal, and late payouts.) Under the GATT, the interest rate had to be at least equal to the rate specified in the plan. If the plan rate was below the interest rate paid on 30-year Treasuries, the Treasury interest had to be used instead.

In 1996, the Small Business Job Protection Act §1449 amended Code §415(b)(2)(E) to repeal this requirement. The SBJPA requirement is that the interest rate must be the plan rate (the same rate as for non-lump-sum benefits), but must be at least 5%. The Taxpayer Relief Act of 1997 §1604(b)(4) further amended the interest-rate rule for early retirement lump sums, in a manner too complex to spell out here; it is merely noted so you can ask your tax counsel if your plan complies with the current rules.

11.3.5 Funding Retiree Health Benefits With 401(h) Accounts

As discussed on page 202, the primary purpose of a qualified pension plan must always be the provision of retirement benefits to participants and their beneficiaries. However, a qualified plan can provide certain ancillary benefits that are clearly subordinated to the pension benefits, and retiree health benefits can be furnished as one of these. The aggregate contributions the employer makes to provide all ancillary benefits (including retiree health benefits, other health benefits, and life insurance) cannot exceed 25% of the overall contributions to the plan.

The plan must maintain a separate account for health benefits, and further separate accounts for each key employee who receives retiree health benefits from the plan. Furthermore, the employer's contributions to the separate account must be reasonable and ascertainable. The employer is entitled to reversion of the contents of the separate accounts once all liabilities for retiree health benefits have been paid. (In fact, the amounts *must* revert to the employer.)

Employers whose defined benefit plans are fully funded and indeed have excess assets can transfer the excess assets (not to exceed amounts reasonably necessary to provide retiree health benefits) to a §401(h) account: see Code §420(a). Under current law, this provision is scheduled to expire for tax years beginning after December 31, 2000. For all transfers made after December 8, 1994, the employer must maintain substantially the same level of retiree health benefits for the year of the transfer and for the four succeeding years.

11.3.6 Disqualified Benefits

Yet another excise tax is imposed, this time by §4976, equaling 100% of the "disqualified benefit." A disqualified benefit is any one of three things:

- Post-retirement medical or life insurance benefit provided for a key employee that is supposed to be provided through a separate account, but is not
- A post-retirement medical or life insurance benefit provided on a basis that discriminates in favor of highly compensated employees
- Any part of the fund that reverts to the employer.

Chapter 12

THE SUBSTANTIVE LAW OF PENSIONS

12.1 INTRODUCTION

The reasons that Congress instituted ERISA, the Employee Retirement Income and Security Act of 1974, are easy to comprehend. There was widespread corruption and mismanagement in the way company pension plans were drafted and operated. In too many cases, employees' income during worklife was reduced by contributions made to the pension plan—yet rank-and-file employees never got to collect. The rules for collection from such plans were so restrictive that only a small inside management group ever succeeded in drawing benefits.

ERISA changed the situation by establishing a detailed series of rules for "qualified" plans, i.e., plans for which employers can deduct contributions. If the employer wants a tax deduction for the significant cost of funding and managing a plan, it must abide by two related series of rules: one prescribed by the Department of Labor, the other falling under the Internal Revenue Code.

ERISA governs the way that qualified plans are set up, the form in which they are administered, which employees are entitled to participate, and how much must be contributed on behalf of each employee. Its rules also specify how contributions must be managed, invested, and distributed. Fiduciaries—individuals with responsibility for supervising beneficiaries' plan interests—have a duty to act exclusively in the interests of plan participants and their beneficiaries. Certain conduct is prohibited, and fiduciaries can be penalized (individually as well as in their corporate roles) for ERISA violations.

Qualified plans must be non-discriminatory, that is, although the plan can favor highly compensated individuals in some ways, and to a certain extent, nevertheless the bulk of the plan must benefit the rank-and-file.

ERISA, supplemented by other legislation (such as the Retirement Equity Act and Small Business Job Protection Act, and 1997's Balanced Budget Act and

Taxpayer Relief Act), determines how payments can be made to retirees and how those payments will be taxed.

> ➡ **TIP**
>
> The general rule is that a married retiree will receive the pension in joint and survivor annuity form, unless the non-employee spouse signs a valid consent form agreeing to another distribution mechanism.

ERISA also makes pension law an exclusively federal subject. It preempts state law on related subjects. That is, the states are forbidden to enact their own laws in any area covered by ERISA. This contrasts with many other federal laws, which specify that they establish a minimum standard, and that states are free to enact their own rules if they are more protective of the interest of consumers, employees, or other potentially vulnerable groups.

The bulk of ERISA deals with pension plans. However, it has less extensive provisions dealing with other types of plan, including profit-sharing plans, stock bonus plans, and welfare benefit plans (e.g., health plans, vacation plans, cafeteria plans).

ERISA requires that a qualified pension plan be more or less limited to providing pension benefits. Most non-pension benefits (e.g., layoff, accident, health) must be kept outside the pension plan and administered separately. However, a pension plan can legitimately provide retiree health benefits, incidental death benefits (but not full-scale life insurance), and pensions that are triggered by disability rather than by the recipient reaching retirement age.

> ➡ **TIP**
>
> The Small Business Job Protection Act of 1996 eliminated the favorable tax treatment formerly given to recipients of pension plan death benefits who got a death benefit of $5000 or less.

ERISA gives employers a choice. There is no requirement that an employer maintain any pension plan at all. If the employer wants to benefit its top executives, but not the average worker, the employer can take a trade-off: it can establish one or more non-qualified pension plans, limited only to executives (or even only to certain executives), but it will not get a tax deduction for the cost of funding the plan. If the employer chooses to have a qualified plan whose cost is tax-deductible, then the employer must satisfy the panoply of ERISA regulations.

As a general rule, the employer's tax deduction relating to a qualified plan is taken on a cash basis. In other words, the deduction is taken for the year in which money was placed into the plan. When the employer maintains non-qualified plans instead of or in addition to its qualified plans, the employer does not get a deduction until the employee receives benefits from the non-qualified plan and includes them in income.

12.2 THE STRUCTURE OF ERISA

ERISA is not an easy law to understand. One reason for the confusion is that the law allows a vast variety of funding and benefit structures. Another reason is that plans often involve complex mathematical formulas, and a trivial change in the formula can have immense financial implications for the sponsoring corporation and for those who expect to receive plan benefits. Another problem is the division of authority: ERISA includes a lot of complex tax law (administered by the IRS) as well as a lot of complex labor law (under the control of the Department of Labor).

Title I of ERISA, also referred to as the "labor title," deals with issues such as plan structure, fiduciary conduct, and prohibited transactions.

Title II is the tax title, covering the requirements for plan qualification and tax deductions. There is some overlap between the two; for instance, although prohibited transactions are defined by Title I, a penalty excise tax on such transactions is imposed under Title II. The provisions of Title II appear in the Internal Revenue Code as well as in ERISA.

From the plan administrator's viewpoint, perhaps the most significant provisions of ERISA are found in Title I, Subtitle B, which, in turn, is divided into six Parts:

- Part 1: Reporting and Disclosure
- Part 2: Participation and vesting standards
- Part 3: Funding standards
- Part 4: Fiduciary responsibility
- Part 5: Administration and enforcement
- Part 6: Continuation coverage (for health insurance).

Subtle distinctions arise as to which plans are subject to which provisions of ERISA. The safest way to operate is just to assume that any pension or benefit arrangement does constitute a "plan" subject to all ERISA requirements. However, exemptions are available in various contexts.

For example, a welfare plan (one which provides benefits such as health insurance or severance pay, but not pension benefits) is covered by most (but not all) of the Title I, Subtitle B, Part 1 reporting and disclosure rules, and is also subject to the Parts 4 and 5 fiduciary, administration, and enforcement rules—but is not required to satisfy the rules about participation, vesting, and funding.

12.2.1 What's a Plan?

A corporation's payroll practices (such as rules for overtime, shift premiums, holiday pay, vacation pay, and disability pay) are not considered welfare benefits as long as any payment that is required is made from the employer's general assets. Because there is no ERISA plan, these programs are not subject to any of the Title I requirements. However, if the employer sets up a funded program to pay wages when the employee is not at work, then there is a plan and Title I must be obeyed.

A plan of group insurance, or group-type insurance, is not a welfare plan for ERISA purposes as long as the employer's only involvement is in administering the plan, and all contributions are made by the employees themselves, none by the employer or a union ("employee pay all" system). To be exempt from ERISA, employee participation in the arrangement must be completely voluntary. The employer cannot endorse the program; it merely allows an insurer to publicize the program, and the employer merely collects the premiums by payroll deduction, then remits the collected premiums to the insurer.

A plan that is maintained only to comply with laws about Worker's Compensation, unemployment compensation, or disability insurance is not a plan subject to Title I; neither is an unfunded excess benefit plan. An unfunded scholarship program that pays the scholarships out of the employer's general assets is not a plan.

An arrangement for paying severance benefits is a welfare plan for ERISA purposes, but is not a pension plan, as long as the payments made to the employee are not directly or indirectly contingent on his or her retirement. The payments can't exceed twice the employee's annual compensation for the year before termination, and payments must be completed within two years after termination. (If these rules can't be met, the inference is that the plan provides retirement rather than severance benefits, and therefore must be regulated as a pension plan.)

The rules for avoiding characterization as a pension plan are slightly different when severance pay is provided under a limited program of terminations (e.g., if the company has to reduce its payroll to operate more efficiently). The payments must be made within two years after the termination, or two years after the employee reaches normal retirement age, whichever is later.

An employer's program of paying bonuses to employees is not a pension plan unless the payments are systematically deferred until or after termination of employment. If bonuses are usually or always paid to active workers, then the arrangement is not an ERISA plan.

If employees maintain their own IRAs, based on their own voluntary choice, and the employer does not contribute but merely administers payroll deductions, the IRAs are not a pension plan. (There are several ways for the employer to contribute to employees' IRAs, and thus to maintain a stripped-down pension plan, but these ways are not discussed in this book because they are primarily for small companies, and the focus of this book is on the company with 100-500 employees.)

Frequently plans provide an "early retirement window," which grants two extra years' age and service credits on behalf of employees who retire during a particular six-month period during which the employer wants to reduce its workforce. Employers might also subsidize early retirement via Social Security supplements, which provide monthly income, but only until the employee qualifies for Social Security benefits (probably at slightly over age 62 for a reduced benefit). Its purpose is to assure a steady income stream; without it, employees might turn down the early retirement incentives and stay at work, contrary to the employer's staffing requirements.

Confusingly, an employer plan that supplements retirement benefits might be treated as a welfare benefit plan, not a pension plan (and therefore would be subject to fewer ERISA requirements). To qualify as a welfare plan, the supplemental plan must make payments either from the employer's general assets or from a single-purpose separate trust. The payment must be made on or after the last day of the month for which it is calculated. It also can't exceed the "supplemental payment factor," which is computed based on the pension benefit plus a cost of living adjustment. (See DOL Reg.§2510.3-2(g)).

12.3 FACTORS IN QUALIFICATION

In order to receive the status of a qualified plan, and continue in that status, plans must satisfy a broad range of labor law, tax, and accounting rules. (Many of these rules will be explained in much greater detail in other places in this book.)

- The plan must be written and communicated to participants.
- The sponsor must intend the plan to be permanent when it is adopted (although there are rules for amending and terminating plans).
- The plan must be funded by contributions made by the employer and/or employees; in turn, the employee contributions can be either mandatory or voluntary.
- The plan must be operated for the exclusive benefit of participants and their beneficiaries.
- All employee contributions and 401(k) salary deferrals must be placed into the plan trust as soon as possible, and in no event later than 90 days after receipt (or after the salary would have been payable in cash if it had not been placed into the 401(k) plan instead). After the 90 days have expired, the money is characterized as "plan assets" subject to the rules on fiduciary responsibility. (DOL Reg. §2510.3-102)
- Plan benefits must vest according to an approved schedule, and back-loading is limited. See Code §411(b). That is, it is not necessary that benefits accrue at the same rate each year, but limitations are imposed to prevent a situation

in which there is so little accrual in the early years that employees would not be able to qualify for significant benefits unless they remain with the same employer until retirement age.

- If the plan is a defined benefit plan, it must satisfy the "minimum participation" rule: on each day of the plan year, the plan must benefit either 40% of all the company's employees, or 50 people, whichever is less. (A very small plan can satisfy the rule by covering only one or two employees, but that exception is not relevant to the concerns of this book.)

> ⇒ **TIP**
>
> Before 1997, defined contribution plans were also subject to the minimum participation rule, but this requirement was eliminated by the 1996 Small Business Job Protection Act (SBJPA).

- Both defined benefit and defined contribution plans must satisfy the §410(b) "minimum coverage" rules:

  1. the plan must either cover a percentage of the rank-and-file that is equal to or greater than 70% of the percentage of highly compensated persons covered by the plan; or

  2. it must cover a "reasonable classification" of employees that is nondiscriminatory;

  3. contributions made on behalf of, or benefits provided to, the rank-and-file must equal at least 70% of the ratio for the highly compensated.

- Qualified plans must be non-discriminatory (although non-qualified plans are permitted to discriminate in favor of the highly-compensated: see page 219). The general rule of non-discrimination is that allocation to the rank-and-file, measured as a percentage of their compensation, must be equal or greater than the allocation to the highly compensated as a percentage of *their* compensation. (See page 227 for a discussion of plan integration: the use of Social Security employer contributions and benefits to offset the amount the employee must spend on behalf of employees who earn less than the FICA maximum.)

- Under the non-discrimination rule, the employer is entitled to various safe harbors. Social Security integration, also known as "permitted disparity," is one of them. The employer can use a point allocation formula that is uniform for all participants. It can also make a uniform allocation of the same percentage of compensation, the same dollar amount, or the same dollar amount per day or week for everybody.

- Age-weighting and cross-testing are permitted. That is, a plan can still be qualified if it favors older employees (who have less time to accumulate a retirement fund). It's permissible to use an allocation factor based on the present value of a single-life annuity.
- If a plan is "top-heavy"—60% or more of its benefits going to highly compensated employees—certain especially strict rules apply.

> ➠ **TIP**
>
> Nearly all top-heavy plans have only a few employees, so in a plan covering hundreds of employees, even if the top management earns much more than the average worker, it is unlikely that the plan will be top-heavy. Consequently, these rules are not discussed in detail in this book.

- Not only must plans cover certain percentages of employees, as described above, but a qualified plan must *not* cover independent contractors. (If it does so, it violates the rule that plans must be maintained for the exclusive benefit of participants and their beneficiaries.) However, a §457 plan (a deferred compensation plan for a state or local government or for a tax-exempt organization) can legitimately cover anyone who performs services for the employer. Be aware that, if a person is treated as an independent contractor but is later identified as a common-law employee, he or she must be taken into account for coverage purposes for qualified plans, and probably will have to be covered retroactively.
- For married plan participants, the basic form of pension benefit is the Qualified Joint and Survivor Annuity, and a Qualified Pre-retirement Survivor Annuity must be made available if a married employee dies before pension payments begin.
- Before a pension payment is made, the benefits cannot be assigned to anyone else.

> ➠ **TIP**
>
> An exception is made for court orders on behalf of an ex-spouse or children of a divorced employee.

- A plan participant must be allowed to receive benefits within 60 days of the end of the plan year in which he or she reaches the plan's normal retirement age or age 65, terminates service, or has 10 years of service, whichever is latest. However, because of the Small Business Job Protection Act of 1996, employees no longer *have* to start collecting their pensions at a specific age; they can defer the first pension payment until they actually retire, at whatever age that might be.

- Social Security increases can't be used to reduce the benefits of vested participants who no longer work for the employee, or participants already receiving plan benefits. See Code §§401(a)(15) and 404(a)(2).

- If the plan is covered by ERISA §4021 (Code §401(a)(33) determines whether this is true), the plan cannot be amended to increase benefits at any time that the sponsor is a bankruptcy debtor, if the amendment increases the plan liability due to the benefit increase itself, any change in the accrual of benefits, or a change in the rate at which benefits become nonforfeitable. (§401(a)(33)).

- For years after 1987, plans must continue to accrue benefits on behalf of older participants who choose to work after normal retirement age or age 65. A defined contribution plan is not permitted to stop making contributions because of the participant's age, and cannot reduce allocations to his or her account on this basis. A defined benefit plan can't stop or reduce the rate of accrual because of age. However, it *is* permissible to stop accruals when a participant has attained the plan's maximum number of years of creditable service, e.g., 30 years. It's also permissible to increase the normal retirement age steadily, to keep pace with the Social Security normal retirement age (which is gradually being increased to 67).

- The tax code sets maximum amounts of contributions that can be made to a plan for each employee, and maximum benefits that each employee can receive. Under current law, the maximum contribution to a defined contribution plan is $30,000 a year; the maximum defined benefit is $125,000 a year for 1997 and $130,000 for 1998. For 1997 and later years, the definition of compensation for this purpose includes elective deferrals under §§401(k) and 403(b) (CODA and annuity plans), §457, and amounts placed into a §125 cafeteria plan. (Under earlier law, deferred amounts were not included in the calculation.)

- Furthermore, calculations made by the plan only use the first $150,000 (adjusted for cost of living increases) of a participant's compensation; for 1997 and 1998, the relevant figure is $160,000.

- Employees must always have the right to withdraw their own voluntary contributions to the plan at any time, without their accrued benefits attributable to employer contributions becoming forfeitable: Code §401(a)(19). But if a plan requires mandatory employee contributions, §411(a)(3)(D) allows it to provide that the employer contributions are forfeited if a participant who is less than 50% vested withdraws any of the mandatory employee contributions. The benefits must be restored, however, if the contributions are repaid on time. In this context, "on time" means within five years after the withdrawal, or two years after the employee returns to participation under the plan, whichever comes first.

- If a plan allows employee contributions or elective deferrals, a person who comes back to work after military service must be allowed to contribute to the plan, or defer receipt of cash compensation, for the period of military service.

(The theory is that service for Uncle Sam counts as service for the employer.) Make-up contributions and deferrals can be made for five years, or for three times the length of the military hitch, whichever is greater.

- The employer must not have discretion over the actuarial assumptions of a defined benefit plan.

- Defined benefit plans must maintain separate accounts for voluntary contributions, and Code §411(b)(3)(A) mandates that a separate determination be made (using the rules otherwise applicable to defined contribution plans) of the accrued benefit deriving from the voluntary-contribution account.

- A defined contribution plan (other than a profit sharing plan) that is more than 10% invested in the employer's securities that are not readily tradable on an established market must satisfy additional requirements as to voting those shares of stock. (Code 409(l))

- Participants who receive distributions that are eligible for rollovers must be given the option to transfer those distributions to an IRA or another qualified plan.

- Benefits must become nonforfeitable when the plan terminates or partially terminates. Defined contribution plans become nonforfeitable upon complete cessation of contributions to the plan. However, for this purpose, money-purchase plans are treated like defined-benefit and not defined-contribution plans.

- A defined benefit plan must have liquid assets equal to at least three times the amount paid out in the past 12 months. If the plan has less than this amount ("liquidity shortfall"), it is required to make quarterly payments to increase assets and remove the shortfall.

Theoretically, a 10% excise tax is imposed on employers who fail to make the payment, and a 100% excise tax is imposed on employers who have a shortfall as of a calendar quarter and also of the four following quarters. However, yet another SBJPA change is that, effective for years going back to 1994 (not the 1997 effective date of most SBJPA provisions), the IRS can waive part or all of the excise if the shortfall was due to a reasonable cause, there was no willful neglect involved, and the employer is taking reasonable steps to remove the shortfall. (Code §4971(f)(4))

Defined benefit plans are subject to full funding limitations (see page 255), and the Taxpayer Relief Act of 1997 increases those limitations from 150% to 155% (for plan years that begin in 1999 and 2000), 150% for 2001-2002 plan years, 165% (2003-2004 plan years), and 170% (for plan years that begin in and after 2005). Congress' rationale in amending Code §412(c)(7) was that the 150% limit was too restrictive, and prevented employers from placing enough into a plan to guarantee that benefits would be paid.

The Taxpayer Relief Act of 1997 §1502 adds a new ERISA §206(d)(4)(5) and Code §401(a)(13)(C), permitting "bad boy" clauses. In other words, an individual's pension can be reduced to reimburse the plan if the individual has breached his or her fiduciary duty to the plan, commits a crime against the plan and is convicted, loses or settles a civil case, or settles charges with the Department of Labor or PBGC.

➠ **TIP**

For the compliance schedule under which employers will be required to amend their pension plans to conform to the Tax Reform Act of 1997, see TRA '97 §1541(b)(2)(A); it's too complex to explain in detail here.

12.4 PENSION PLAN STRUCTURES

The traditional pension plan form is the defined benefit plan, under which the employer agrees to a formula for determining each employee's individual pension based on factors such as age at retirement, number of years of service, and compensation. Compensation can be defined as that of the year of retirement, or average compensation for the employee's entire career, or for a number of years in which earnings were highest.

More specifically, if the plan uses a "fixed benefit," the employee is promised $X per month as a pension. If it's a "flat benefit" plan, the pension is Y% of compensation. If it's a unit benefit plan, the benefit equals a percentage of final average compensation times years of service.

The employer's contribution for each year is the sum total of contributions for each employee in satisfaction of the formula. Naturally, the calculation is not a matter of simple arithmetic. Professional actuaries must be involved in choosing the correct formulas and making the calculation. Employer contributions for all employees are placed into a single account or trust for the entire plan. However, if voluntary employee contributions to the plan are accepted, IRC §411(b)(2)(A) mandates a separate account balance for each participant who contributes.

Forfeitures (account funds contributed on behalf of individuals who terminate employment without being vested) cannot be used to increase the benefits of other participants. (This provision was enacted because, pre-ERISA, many plans were explicitly designed to benefit top management via forfeitures of rank-and-file employees who were not permitted to vest.) However, the plan's investment earnings have the effect of reducing the amount that the employer must contribute; in a defined contribution plan, investment success increases the employees' accounts.

Under normal circumstances, distributions will not be made from a defined-benefit plan until retirement. Plan loans are a possibility, but they are circumscribed by many requirements.

The defined contribution form (which can be used for profit sharing, money purchase, 401(k) and stock bonus plans as well as conventional pension plans) is conceptually much simpler. Each participating employee has a separate account that potentially belongs only to him or her. (Ownership is just potential, because of the vesting rules: see page 236.)

The accrued benefit for each participant equals the balance in the account, which in turn consists of employer contributions plus mandatory employee contributions (if they are required) and any voluntary contributions made by the employee and accepted by the plan.

⇒ TIP

Plans usually maintain separate sub-accounts for the employer and employee contributions for each participant, but this is not a legal requirement.

The employer's annual contribution to each account is based on a formula, such as X% of the employee's compensation.

⇒ TIP

401(k) plans and money purchase plans, where the employer's contribution is fixed and determinable, not discretionary, are also defined contribution plans for tax purposes.

Under ERISA §404(c), a defined contribution plan can allow the participant to control the assets in the account. If this is done, the plan's fiduciaries will not be liable for losses that result from the control exercised by the participants. Section 404(c) requires that the plan must give participants adequate information about their investment alternatives. At least three investment types must be offered. They must be diversified, with materially different characteristics with respect to risk and return. Consult the DOL regulations for the procedures under which participants give instructions about the investment of their account balances.

A study published by pension consulting firm RogersCasey [sic] shows that 25% of amounts invested in participant-directed accounts are invested in actively managed equity funds, 21% in Guaranteed Investment Contracts and other stable-value instruments, 10% in the employer's own stock, 10% in balanced funds, 7% in money-market funds, 6% in index funds, 6% in bonds, and 5% in non-U.S. investments. Many employers were worried that their employees would not have adequate post-retirement income, either because they did not participate in voluntary plans, did not save enough, or did not allocate their funds appropriately.

Code §411(d)(6) permits the plan sponsor a great deal of freedom to amend the stated contribution rate, but no amendment can ever reduce a benefit which has already accrued. A plan can be amended to change the allocation rate until 15 days before the end of the plan year. However, the amendment must go through the corporate formalities of adoption (e.g., a resolution by the sponsor corporation's Board of Directors) before the participants are notified, and the notices to participants must be sent 15 days before the amendment takes effect, so changes can't be left until the last minute.

12.4.1 Money Purchase Pension Plans

A money purchase pension plan provides definitely determinable benefits, funded by fixed employer contributions. Such plans can also offer incidental death benefits. A money purchase plan has a single allocation formula that sets both the amount the employer must contribute and the amount allocated to a given participant's account. (In contrast, a profit-sharing plan, as discussed below, has a separate formula for each.)

A corporation can deduct its contributions to a money purchase pension plan as provided by Code §404(a)(1). There is a limitation: 25% of the compensation of the employee for whom contributions are made. This is the same limitation as that applied to defined contribution plans, but money purchase plans are not subject to the 15% of compensation limitation imposed on profit sharing plans.

Money purchase plans, but not profit sharing plans, are subject to the minimum funding standard set out in Code §412: in other words, the employer must contribute at least the amount required by the plan's funding formula. The general rule is that contributions must be made in quarterly installments; if the sponsor misses a contribution date, it must pay interest. The vesting and forfeiture rules are the same for money purchase and profit-sharing plans (see below). All defined contribution plans can use their forfeitures to increase the benefits to non-forfeited participants.

Money purchase plans and profit sharing plans can accept employee contributions, and both can make loans to plan participants on more or less the same terms: see page 214 for the factors involved. Both of them must have the QPSA and QJSA as standard payment forms for married employees who receive plan distributions.

12.4.2 Profit Sharing Plans

Under ERISA, a profit sharing plan must be drafted with a definite formula, set in advance, for allocating the employer's total contribution among the plan participants. There must also be a set formula for distributing the account money to participants. Distribution can be made after a certain number of years of accrual in the account (ERISA requires that the money spend at least two years in the account before distribution), attainment of a stated age (not necessarily retirement age), or an employment-related event such as layoff, retirement, termination, disability, or illness. Generally an employee's entitlement to profit sharing money depends on factors like length of employment and compensation.

Note that formulas are required only for allocating and distributing the employer's contributions—not for the actual level of contributions for each year. A profit sharing plan can legitimately allow the corporation's Board of Directors to pass a resolution each year, setting the level of contributions.

Calling the plan a profit-sharing plan is something of a misnomer because it is not necessary for the corporation to have profits in a particular year for which plan contributions are made. (Until 1986, contributions did have to come from profits.) Most companies structure their profit sharing plans as a trust for legal purposes. However, ERISA does permit profit sharing annuity plans, i.e., funds are used to buy retirement annuities for employees, purchased directly from an insurance company.

Profit sharing plans (except for those that are fully insured) have to provide a specified inventory date, once a year or more often, for valuing the fair market value of the investments held by the profit sharing trust. The method must be used consistently and uniformly. Once completed, the valuation must be used to adjust the value of participants' accounts at least once a year, in accordance with the increases or decreases in value.

Once made, contributions are allocated among the individual accounts of the participants. The plan must have definite predetermined formulas for distributing the funds. Generally distribution occurs after a certain number of years (the Internal Revenue Code requires that the number be at least two), once the employee attains a stated age, or once a particular event—retirement, death, illness, layoff, or termination—has occurred.

However, unlike a defined benefit plan, the profit sharing plan has no obligation to set a formula in advance for making the contribution. The amount can be completely discretionary, and it is not even mandatory to make contributions in every year. Watch out: if the plan fails to make recurring and substantial contributions, it will not retain its qualification as a plan.

The maximum amount that an employer can place into a profit sharing plan and deduct is 15% of the participant's compensation for the year. If a contribution in excess of that amount is made, it can be carried forward and deducted next year (subject to the 15% limitation for that year). However, the nondeductible portion is subject to a 10% excise tax.

Unless the profit sharing plan is fully insured, it must have a specified inventory date, scheduled at least once a year, for determining the fair market value of the trust's investments. The plan must use a method that is "consistently followed and uniformly applied." At least once a year, participants' accounts must be adjusted to reflect the valuation.

Most profit sharing plans permit employees to receive a distribution of their entire vested balance when their employment terminates. It's permissible for the plan to defer the distribution until the plan's normal retirement date. If an employee prefers an annuity payment, the plan cannot force him or her to "cash out" (accept a lump sum instead of the annuity) unless the balance is very small ($5,000 or less). No particular form of distribution is required, as long as there is no discrimination in favor of highly compensated employees.

In addition to distributing benefits to participants who have satisfied the requirements, profit sharing plans can make loans to participants. (Thus, they can have access to funds even prior to the earliest time an outright distribution would be permitted.) Beware: the Code imposes various limitations on loans from these plans:

- Loans must be made available to all participants on reasonably equivalent terms

- Loans must not be available in greater amounts to highly compensated employees

- Loans must be made pursuant to specific provisions contained in the plan document

- A reasonable rate of interest must be charged

- Loans must have reasonable security. Not more than 50% of the participant's account balance can be used as security, so the upshot is that any loan must be less than this amount.

The general rule is that plan loans are taxable to the employee-borrower, but Code §72(p) specifies the circumstances under which the loan will not be taxable:

- Level payments must be due at least quarterly to repay the loan

- Loans must be repaid within five years, unless the purpose of the loan is to buy a principal residence (not a vacation home or investment real estate) for the participant—in which case, repayment must be made within a reasonable time

- The loan must not exceed the limits specified in the Code. It cannot exceed the greater of $10,000, or 50% of the vested account balance; and it cannot exceed $50,000 minus the highest balance for the preceding year, minus the balance outstanding when the loan was taken.

The vesting and forfeiture rules are the same for money purchase and profit sharing plans. Like all defined contribution plans, they can use forfeitures to increase the benefits available to other participants. Loans are permitted on the same terms in both plan types. Both can provide incidental life insurance and health benefits, and both must provide Qualified Joint and Survivor Annuities and Qualified Preretirement Survivor Annuities as the basic payment options for married participants.

A profit sharing plan is allowed to offer incidental benefits, such as life and accident and health insurance covering participants and their families. The employer can pay the insurance premiums, but not more than 25% of the employer contribution can be used to provide incidental benefits rather than the core benefit of deferred compensation.

12.4.3 401(k) Plans

Cash or deferred arrangements (CODAs), commonly known as 401(k) plans, give employees a choice: either they can receive a certain amount of compensation immediately in cash, or they can have it placed into an account whose appreciation in value will be tax-free until funds are withdrawn from the account. Employees must be permitted to participate in the company's 401(k) plan on the first entry date after they have completed one year of service.

A 401(k) arrangement can either contain nothing but the compensation that the employee has agreed to defer, or can contain both the deferred amounts and an employer "match." The general rule is that the maximum deferral permitted in a 401(k) account is $10,000 per year. (The 401(k) plans of small companies can also contain a "SIMPLE" feature, under which the employee defers up to $6,000 in compensation, and the employer makes a 2% payment or 3% match.)

⟹ TIP

In many companies, 401(k) plan participation, especially on the part of lower-paid employees, falls below employer expectations. One alternative some companies are using is automatic enrollment: instead of requiring employees to take steps to participate, they are signed up in the plan unless they opt out. Employees have an automatic deduction of a stipulated portion of pretax salary invested in one of the plan's options, unless they make a different choice. Another alternative is to simplify the enrollment form to make it more user-friendly.

In effect, the deferrals placed into 401(k) plans are employee contributions. Therefore, they must be 100% vested at all times. If the employer chooses to match employee contributions (e.g., by contributing $1 for every $2 or $3 deferred by the employee), that match will be subject to the Code's anti-discrimination rules. A different rule is applied depending on whether the match is 100% vested as soon as it is made and whether distribution of the matching funds is subject to the same limitations as ordinary 401(k) account amounts.

In addition to deferral of compensation (i.e., contributions made from pretax income) it is theoretically possible for 401(k) plans to accept after-tax contributions. The employee does not get a tax deduction for after-tax amounts contributed to the plan, but there is no penalty on after-tax amounts withdrawn from the plan, even if the worker has not yet reached age $59\,^1/_2$. However, both income tax and the 10% premature withdrawal penalty must be paid if the worker withdraws *appreciated earnings* on after-tax contributions before age $59\,^1/_2$; after $59\,^1/_2$, income tax is due but there is no penalty.

This is not a common feature of 401(k) plans. According to the Profit Sharing/401(k) Council of America, almost three-quarters of 401(k) plans accepted only pretax contributions. Only a minuscule 4.7% accepted only after-tax contributions, and 21.7% accepted both types.

Initially, most 401(k) plans offered three or four mutual funds as investment options. In the late 1990s, in response to employee demands, companies offered a larger number of fund alternatives, or turned to a brokerage option: putting the employee in full control of the money.

For plan years beginning after December 31, 1998, employers are entitled to use a new safe harbor rule to determine whether a 401(k) plan is nondiscriminatory. The safe harbor replaces the tests that would otherwise be required, but employees must be given written notice disclosing the terms of the 401(k) plan as it applies to both rank-and-file and highly compensated employees.

⟾ **TIP**

PLR 9530038 permits a 401(k) "wraparound": before the beginning of the plan year, participants can elect to have excess 401(k) funds that would otherwise be returned to them placed into a nonqualified plan instead.

The Taxpayer Relief Act of 1997 imposes an additional diversification requirement on 401(k) plans, effective for plan years beginning after December 31, 1998. Employers are not permitted to force employees to invest more than 10% of their 401(k) accounts in the employer's own stock, although employees can purchase as much stock for their 401(k) plans as they see fit. The new law is a limitation on employer coercion, not employee investment choices.

401(k) plans can make loans to participants on the same terms as profit sharing plans: see page 214. Theoretically, the loan is not supposed to exceed 50% of the balance, but in practice a participant can take a loan, pledge 50% of the account, and take a hardship withdrawal, thus reducing the actual security for the loan below the 50% level.

A hardship distribution can be made from the deferred compensation placed into the 401(k) account, but not from the earnings on those deferrals. These distributions can be made only if the participant demonstrates an immediate and heavy need for the funds, for a serious purpose (not just taking a vacation or purchasing ordinary consumer goods, for instance). However, the need can be voluntarily incurred; it need not be an unhappy accident the participant is subject to. The need must be one that can't be met by using savings and other personal and family assets reasonably available to the plan participant.

Possible motives for a hardship distribution include:

- Medical expenses incurred by the employee or the employee's spouse or children

- The purchase of a principal residence (but not ordinary mortgage payments)

- Staving off eviction or mortgage foreclosure on the principal residence

- Tuition and room and board for the succeeding 12 months of post-secondary education for the employee, spouse, or dependents. (In other words, private primary or high school tuition doesn't count.)

➠ TIP

If the employee applies for a hardship withdrawal but is turned down, he or she is entitled to use the ERISA §503 appeal process.

The employer's deduction for its "matches" to a 401(k) plan is calculated similarly to the deduction for a profit sharing plan (see page 213). However, the employer is not entitled to a deduction for contributions attributed to service after the end of the employer's tax year.

The employer has to pay FICA and FUTA tax on the employee's pretax deferrals. After all, the employer would have had to pay these taxes if the employee had received the amount in the form of current cash compensation. The employee is also responsible for employee-share FICA tax on the deferred amounts.

Although a 10% excise tax is imposed by Code §4972(c)(6)(B) on amounts that the employer contributes to the plan but cannot deduct (i.e., "excessive" contributions), the Tax Reform Act of 1997 eliminates the excise tax in the situation in which the contributions exceed the combined plan deduction limit, but do not exceed the elective deferrals to the 401(k) plan, plus the employer's matching contribution.

12.4.4 Target Benefit Plans

A target benefit plan is something of a hybrid. It is a money purchase plan, and therefore subject to rules for defined contribution plans, but contributions are calculated so that they can fund a specific level of retirement benefit at the plan's normal retirement age. At that time, the plan participant receives the aggregate of contributions made for him or her, plus their earnings; the actual benefit may be either higher or lower than the target. In other words, like all defined contribution plans, target benefit plans shift investment risk to the participant.

12.4.5 SEP and SIMPLE Plans

The requirements of maintaining a full-scale plan are quite complex, and can be onerous for a small company. Thus, ERISA and the Internal Revenue Code do have various small-scale programs (similar to the simplified 1041A and 1120A tax forms) for companies with a limited number of employees. They are not really relevant to this book, which concentrates on the 100-500 employee plans. Nevertheless, a mention is in order, in case you have heard of these mechanisms and do not know if they can be adopted by your company.

The SEP, or Simplified Employee Pension, plan is an IRA sponsored by the employer. Contributions are made by the employer under a written plan whose contribution formula does not discriminate in favor of highly compensated employees. The employee can make the maximum IRA contribution to his or her SEP; in addition, the employer can make additional contributions, which do not disqualify the employee's contribution. SEP plans must have trustees, but the requirement of disclosing information to employees is simplified from the normal pension plan requirements.

The maximum employer contribution to a SEP is 25% of compensation or $30,000 (whichever is less). Furthermore, the employer's deduction is limited to 15% of the employee's contribution. The contribution is determined by the plan formula, which must bear a uniform relationship to the first $160,000 of compensation for all employees. Integrating a SEP plan with Social Security is permitted.

Once the contribution is made, the employee can exclude from income up to $30,000 in contributions or 15% of compensation, whichever is less. SEP participation must be provided to all employees who have reached age 21, worked for the employer in at least three of the last five years, and who have earned $400 in the current year.

The most recent small business pension plan form is the Savings Incentive Match Plan for Employees (SIMPLE), enacted in 1996 by the SBJPA. It is available only to companies with 100 or fewer employees. Instead of setting up a plan trust or purchasing insurance, the employer relies on the employees' own IRAs as a funding vehicle. Either the employer makes a contribution to the IRA of at least 2% of the employee's compensation, or matches the employee's contributions to the IRA in an amount equal to at least 3% of employee compensation. The 1997 Taxpayer Relief Act increases the maximum SIMPLE limit to $6,000 per year.

> ⇒ **TIP**
> ───
> The SIMPLE plan replaces the SARSEP, an earlier IRA-based form of simplified pension plan. SARSEPs already in existence can continue to be maintained, but no new ones were created after 12/31/96.

Check the provisions of the Taxpayer Relief Act of 1997 for further details about the most recent amendments to the SIMPLE plan rules.

12.5 NONQUALIFIED PLANS

We tend to think of pension plans as the qualified plans that cover most or all of the rank-and-file workforce. However, corporations that are willing to establish a non-deductible plan for a "select group of management or highly compensated employees" can do so. These plans do not have to have a plan trust the way qualified plans typically do.

Instead, the plan can be unfunded (the employer makes the payments as they come due, out of its general assets rather than a dedicated fund) or insured (with a financial structure based on the purchase of insurance contracts). Nonqualified plans are exempt from ERISA's funding requirements, so they can be financed with various promises and forms of securities that would not be acceptable in the context of a qualified plan.

Furthermore, nonqualified plans can have "bad boy" clauses (calling for forfeiture of plan benefits if the covered employee leaves the company's employment); such provisions are forbidden in qualified plans (other than the more drastic situation in which the "bad" behavior consists of fiduciary breach or embezzlement, not just simple change of employment).

Under a qualified plan, the employer makes contributions each year, and gets a deduction for that year. Under a nonqualified plan, the employer is not entitled to take the deduction until the favored employee receives money from the plan and includes it in income. Furthermore, if the employer reserves funds to be able to pay claims under nonqualified plans, the corporation's general creditors are allowed to make claims against those funds—but not against the funds set aside in a qualified pension plan. Thus, if the corporation runs into financial trouble, the creditors may get access to money that was supposed to be used to pay nonqualified plan benefits.

Various structures have evolved for non-qualified plans. A Supplemental Executive Retirement Plan (SERP), also known as an excess-benefit plan, can defer amounts greater than those permitted by the qualified plan limits. A rabbi trust sets aside assets to pay the nonqualified benefits, although the separate amounts are subject to the claims of the employer corporation's creditors. A secular trust offers more protection for the executive's right to receive deferred compensation, but is less convenient for the corporation.

A top hat plan is an unfunded deferred compensation plan limited to managers and/or highly compensated employees. If the top hat plan is a pension plan, a brief notice has to be filed each year with the Department of Labor, although the disclosure requirements are more modest than for qualified plans. If the top hat plan is not a pension plan, then it is probably exempt from ERISA Title I.

An unfunded top hat pension plan does not have to satisfy the ERISA rules for participation, vesting, funding, or fiduciary responsibility, but it is covered by Title I's administration and enforcement provisions. The plan must have a claims procedure. Furthermore, even this modest ERISA role is enough to preempt state law, so suits cannot be brought in state court involving claims to benefits from these plans.

An excess benefit plan exists simply to provide benefits greater than Code §415 would permit under a qualified plan. An unfunded excess benefit plan is not subject to ERISA Title I. The trade-off is that the absence of ERISA coverage permits the states to regulate plans of this type.

A "rabbi trust" is one way to provide reassurance for nonqualified plan participants. (There's nothing specifically Jewish or religious about the trust; that's just a nickname because the first one was done to provide retirement benefits for a clergyman.)

A rabbi trust is an irrevocable trust set up by an employer as an advance funding mechanism for deferred compensation. The assets in the trust can't revert to the employer until all of the obligations to pay deferred compensation are satisfied. However, the corporation's general creditors have a right to press their claims against plan assets, so the executives whose benefits are funded by the trust still have enough risk to escape current taxation; they are not taxed until they receive benefits from the plan.

➡ **TIP**

Any plan that wants an IRS ruling on the validity of its rabbi trust arrangement *must* use the model rabbi trust form published in Rev.Proc. 92-64, 1992-2 C.B. 422. Except to the extent that the standard form contains options, the model plan must be adopted verbatim. However, additional provisions can be added to the standard form as long as they are not inconsistent with what is in the standard plan.

A "springing" rabbi trust is permissible: the employer can set up the trust with only minimal funding, but if a change in control of the corporation occurs (e.g., merger or acquisition), the employer provides funding for payment of benefits under the trust. The "spring" provision does not make the trust "funded" for ERISA purposes.

Unlike a rabbi trust, a secular trust is an irrevocable trust whose assets cannot be reached by the employer's creditors (including its bankruptcy creditors). Such trusts usually provide for payment of benefits on the occurrence of events such as a certain number of years' tenure, retirement, disability, or death.

The price of increased protection for the employee is that the employee has taxable income equal to the employer contributions to the trust on his or her behalf, and perhaps on the income those contributions earn within the trust. Taxation follows the annuity rules of §72. The employer benefits by deducting contributions to the trust (to the extent that they constitute ordinary and necessary business expenses) that are allocable to the trust accounts of participants in the secular trust, in the taxable year in which the contributions are taken into the employee's taxable income.

In instances in which a trust or escrow arrangement is involved (rather than a pure unfunded arrangement where the employer makes payments out of its current funds), there are complex factors (centering around the extent of the employer's contributions and control) used to determine who "owns" the trust, and therefore who should be taxed on the trust income. The potential taxpayers are the employer, the employee, and the trust itself.

⇒ **TIP**

If the employer is concerned about having to pay income tax, funding could be done with a low- or no-income method such as zero-coupon bonds or insurance policies.

12.5.1 Taxation of Participants of Nonqualified Plans

Nonqualified plans can create some subtle tax problems for the plan participants. The mere fact that the employer promises to pay benefits in the future doesn't create income for the participant in the nonqualified plan. The employee doesn't have income until plan benefits are either actually received or "constructively" received. (Constructive receipt is a tax concept that covers the situation in which a person deliberately turns down money he or she is entitled to.)

➠ TIP

Tax planning for nonqualified plan participants requires a look at Code §83, too; sometimes employees have to include amounts that have not been distributed from the nonqualified plan in their income. Section 83 says that, whenever property is transferred to anyone except the employer for the provision of services, the employee has to include in income the fair market value of the transferred property, minus anything paid for the property. Section 83 doesn't apply to transfers to qualified plan trusts, or to many stock option transactions, or to a deferred compensation arrangement that gives the employee a mere contractual right to receive compensation in the future. However, it does apply to assets set aside in trusts, escrows, or similar arrangements and that are not subject to the claims of the corporation's general creditors.

Where §83 applies, the employee's tax before distribution is based on the value of the employee's income in the plan trust at the time of taxation, and not on the fair market value of the employer's contributions to the trust.

Employees will certainly be taxed on benefits from the nonqualified plan when they are distributed; if they had to pay tax on amounts not yet distributed, they are entitled to compute an exclusion ratio. (An exclusion ratio is a percentage of a distribution that can be disregarded for tax purposes, because it has already been taxed or because Congress has decided to award favorable tax treatment to a particular type of transaction.)

While the nonqualified plan is in operation, the income on the employer's contributions is usually taxed to the trust. (In some situations, it will be taxed to the employer corporation itself.) This is in contrast to the result for a qualified plan trust, which is a tax-exempt organization. The participants are not considered "owners" of the trust, so they are not taxed on the trust income.

The executive or other participant in the nonqualified plan recognizes taxable income in the year in which rights to the property are transferable, or the substantial risk of forfeiture ends, whichever comes first.

Sometimes property rights depend, directly or indirectly, on the plan participant continuing to perform services for the sponsoring employer. Sometimes they depend on the participant *not* performing services, (if there is a covenant not to compete). IRS Regulations say that each case must be checked for its own facts to see if there is a substantial risk of forfeiture because of a requirement of continued employment or non-competition.

A participant in a qualified plan has a good deal of assurance (though not absolute certainty) that benefits will be paid as promised, because the plan is supposed to be fully funded to pay out the promised benefits. Participants in nonqualified plans, on the other hand, are taking some risk, because there is no requirement that the employer set aside money in advance to provide the benefits. If the employer doesn't fund the plan, a time may come when benefits are supposed to be paid, but the employer is short of cash. (Indeed, the existence of this risk is one reason why executives are not taxed each year because of their participation in these plans.)

12.5.2 Tax Deduction and Compliance Issues

Although the purpose of maintaining nonqualified plans is to motivate the company's leaders, the company will generally want to receive a tax deduction for the cost of the plan. Code §404(a)(5) gives the rules for deferred compensation plans for employees; similar rules are found for the deferred compensation of independent contractors in §404(d)(2).

⇒ **TIP**
_____

Contributions that an employer makes to a plan that provides deferred compensation for *shareholders* who are not employees or independent contractors are not deductible. Reg. §1.404(a)-12(b)(1) provides that the employer deducts only the amount it actually contributes, even though the employee may have to report a larger sum in income (because of appreciation of amounts within the plan).

When deferred compensation is paid directly to the employee under an unfunded arrangement, the employer gets the deduction in the year of the payment (in contrast to the deduction in the year of contribution to a qualified plan). If the deferred compensation obligations are merely contractual, and not funded or otherwise secured, then the employer doesn't get a deduction until the compensation is actually received. If it exceeds a reasonable amount that would be an ordinary and necessary business expense, the excess is not deductible.

For funded deferred compensation arrangements that are not qualified plans, and where the employer makes contributions to a trust covering more than one employee, the employer cannot receive a deduction unless it maintains a separate account for each covered employee.

Most businesses use an accrual method of accounting, not the cash method that is used by nearly all employees. If an accrual-basis employer defers payment of compensation to a year other than the year in which it was earned, the deduction must be delayed until the year of actual payment—unless the company is financially unable to pay, or unless it is impossible to determine the correct amount to be paid until after the year ends. See Reg. §§1.404(a)-1(c), 1.404(b)-1.

As for tax compliance, distributions from nonqualified plans (other than distributions made on account of death, sickness, accident, disability, or disability retirement) are wages for FICA and FUTA purposes. Code §3121(v)(2) provides that, for the purposes of paying the employer share and withholding the employee's share of FICA and Medicare tax, amounts deferred under a nonqualified deferred compensation plan are taken into account only once, at the time the services are performed or when there is no longer a substantial risk of forfeiture, whichever occurs later. (Of course, if the plan is drafted to make forfeiture a significant risk, the risk will generally end at some time after the services are performed.)

The general rule is that income taxes must be withheld on benefits from nonqualified deferred compensation arrangements at a rate of 10% of the lump sum of benefits paid within the year, when the amounts are constructively received by the employee. However, Code §3405 gives the payee of the benefits the option of instructing the plan not to withhold on the benefits.

⇒ **TIP**

It's fairly common for nonqualified plans to contain a provision that makes benefits payable immediately if the corporation goes through a change in control (i.e., someone else merges with the corporation or purchases its stock or assets). However, it's possible that the deferred compensation that becomes due at this time will be treated as an "excess parachute payment" and subjected to a 20% excise tax (see page 73). Thus the value of this provision in reassuring (and thus motivating) senior management must be balanced against the risk of increased corporate excise tax liability.

12.6 FACTORS IN CHOOSING A PLAN FORM

Participants in a defined benefit plan know what their eventual pension will be, if they stay with the plan until normal retirement age. (If their employment terminates earlier, the vesting rules also control the size of the eventual pension—which will be paid at retirement age, not at the time of termination.) The certainty is valuable, but the participants have the problem of retiring with a fixed income, which is especially worrisome in a time of high inflation. Their pension doesn't reflect investment results, either, which is of concern when the stock market is booming.

In contrast, participants in a defined contribution plan know how large their account is at any given time (and can project the size of the account at any time in the future, based on a projection of future compensation). They do not know the size of the pension, because that is dependent on the plan's success in investing the account. Therefore, market risk is shifted from the employer (who would have to contribute more to keep the pension level in a declining market) to the employee/future retiree.

Another important distinction between defined benefit and defined contribution plans is that defined benefit plans are subject to a federal insurance program run by the Pension Benefit Guaranty Corporation (PBGC). The PBGC insures that employees will receive at least part of their pension benefits (up to a maximum of $2,761.36 per month) if the plan terminates. Employers that maintain defined benefit plans must pay PBGC premiums to fund the insurance program.

If an underfunded defined benefit plan is terminated (see page 255 for a discussion of funding requirements, and page 303 for a discussion of plan termination), the PBGC takes over part of the obligation to pay benefits. The result is that some participants will lose their pensions, and some will receive less than the amount stipulated in the plan.

Defined contribution plans offer much more portability. That is, if an employee quits, is fired, is laid off, or otherwise stops being employed by Company A, and is later hired by Company B, the employee can simply "roll over" his or her individual pension account from Company A's defined contribution plan to Company B's.

If the company has a cadre of highly valuable older employees and if it seeks to motivate them, a defined benefit plan may be preferable, because it is possible to put far more into a defined benefit plan on their behalf than into a defined contribution plan, subject to the $30,000 contribution maximum.

In contrast, a profit sharing plan offers the greatest degree of flexibility because no specific amount of contributions is mandated, and contributions can be made as late as the due date (including any extensions) for filing the business tax return. But flexibility is not indefinite: a profit sharing plan will lose its qualification if substantial contributions are not made on a recurring basis.

The preferred form for the company may not be that preferred by its employees; or employee preferences may vary widely. Typically, young participants have more positive feelings about defined contribution plans than older participants. One of the important functions of maintaining a pension plan at all is to motivate employees, so it may make sense to shift plan form based on the preferences of the age group you wish to appeal to.

12.7 BASIC REQUIREMENTS FOR AN ERISA PLAN

This section of the chapter is intended as a summary to put the basic ERISA requirements into perspective. Many of the issues briefly discussed here will be discussed in greater detail later.

The first requirement is that all ERISA plans must be in writing; they can't be informal understandings or "handshake deals." The plan must either be set up as a trust (a plan trust is a tax-exempt organization) or as an insured plan funded by insurance policies. The plan must name at least one fiduciary who is responsible for its management and must specify the mechanism for amendment—including who has the authority to amend. (This becomes very important when the employer wants to cut back on plan benefits, which can only be done with a proper amendment.)

All plans must also spell out who can participate, the schedule on which benefits become vested, the schedule when benefits accrue, how the employer will fund the plan, and when benefit payments to an individual can commence. They must have an administrative structure; it must be clear who has responsibility for operations and administration. This is an immense job, probably too big for any one person to handle, so the named fiduciaries are allowed to delegate certain plan responsibilities to others (e.g., investment managers)—but only if the plan specifically gives them this power.

If a plan is sponsored by a corporation, the corporation's Board of Directors is permitted to appoint an administrative committee. In a large plan, it's common to have a separate committee of the Board that oversees the way the plan's assets are invested. If the plan is collectively bargained (part of a union contract), then the joint board of trustees for the plan supervises both administration and investment.

All plans must spell out the procedure for making a claim, considering claims from participants, and resolving disputes when a participant does not accept the administrator's judgment in denying a claim.

> ⇒ **TIP**
>
> The claims procedure must be disclosed in the Summary Plan Description (SPD), but need not be included in the plan document itself.

Although ERISA and the tax code accept the possibility of amending a plan in response to changed conditions, plans can be amended only if the employer reserves the right to amend, and indicates (though not necessarily in detail) who has the power to make the amendments.

ERISA imposes a requirement of non-alienation. That is, nobody can tap into his or her own pension benefits before the commencement date provided by the plan (although loans may be allowed). More to the point, the employee's creditors can't put a lien on the pension account; they have to wait until each payment is made, and then try to collect from the employee at that point.

12.7.1 Employee Communications

An employer can't set up a "stealth plan" that is kept in secret: the existence of the plan, and its terms, must be communicated to employees. The plan administrator is responsible for reporting and disclosure, and can be held liable if appropriate disclosures are not made.

ERISA provides three permissible communications methods:

- Giving each employee a copy of the plan itself
- Giving each employee an SPD (Summary Plan Description) booklet that describes plan features in understandable language
- Posting a bulletin-board notice that informs employees that the company does have a plan, and where copies of the plan can be consulted.

In practical terms, nearly every company chooses the second alternative. The full-scale plan itself is a very lengthy document, chock-full of dense legal verbiage. It doesn't really communicate very much to the average rank-and-file employee. (Actually, it doesn't communicate very much to the average Senior Vice President, either.) The more practical alternative, and the way that gives employees the most real data about their retirement alternatives, is to give them an SPD, notifying them that it contains important legal information that should be kept for reference.

12.7.2 *Fiduciary Duty*

Any fiduciary—a person or business placed in charge of someone else's property or finances—has certain legal duties. The fiduciary must act in a moral manner, and must not make use of the other person's assets for the fiduciary's personal benefit. The fiduciary must act prudently: investment (in this case, the assets of the pension plan trust) must be placed into a diversified portfolio of well-chosen investments that produce a level of return appropriate for contemporary market conditions, but do not involve an excessively high level of risk.

ERISA fiduciaries have a special duty: they must administer the plan exclusively in the interests of the plan's participants and their beneficiaries. Specifically, if there is a situation in which one strategy would be most beneficial to the participants, and another strategy would be most beneficial to the corporation sponsoring the plan, the fiduciaries must take the first course of action, not the second.

There are some difficult questions of fiduciary duty that arise when many individuals (some within, others outside the corporation) are involved in making decisions for the plan. See page 327 for a discussion of the distribution of responsibility when, for instance, the plan hires professional investment advisors.

If there is more than one named fiduciary, they are jointly and severally liable. That is, someone who charges fiduciary impropriety can sue any one fiduciary, all of them, or any combination, and can collect the entire amount of liability from each or from any combination of fiduciaries—no matter whose fault the actual violation was. This is supposed to be a tough standard, and it is, but the harshness is relieved a little by the fact that fiduciaries who are sued can bring fiduciaries who aren't sued into the lawsuit, and can make them pay their fair share.

12.7.3 *Trusts and Insurance*

For legal purposes, the basic rule is that employee plans must be set up as trusts. That is, there must be a written trust document that explains how the funds will be administered, who the trustees will be, and what the rights of plan participants and their beneficiaries will be. A few special kinds of plans can be created without trusts: top hat plans for a corporation's major executives, unfunded plans that provide employee benefits rather than pensions, and some insured plans.

An insured plan is one that involves the purchase of annuities and other policies from insurance companies. The employer pays for the policies; the insurance company then takes over the routine administrative tasks.

12.7.4 *Plan Integration*

In a sense, the Social Security system is a kind of pension plan. Both employer and employee make contributions during the working lifetime, so payments will be made after retirement. (At least that's the way it's supposed to work; there is widespread skepticism that it will continue to work that way once the unusually large and prosperous Baby Boom generation reaches retirement age.)

However, contributions to FICA (Social Security taxes) phase out at a level that changes each year (for 1997, $65,400 for 1998, $68,400). Higher levels of compensation are subject to Medicare tax, but not to FICA tax. The result is that the employer makes FICA contributions on all or nearly all of rank-and-file employees' compensation, but on a smaller proportion of the compensation of top executives.

The Internal Revenue Code contains "permitted disparity" rules under which qualified plans can be "integrated" with Social Security. That is, within limits, the employer can reduce its plan contributions on behalf of rank-and-file employees to take the FICA contributions into account. As long as the permitted disparity rules are satisfied, the plan will retain its qualification, and will not be treated as discriminatory, even though the practical effect is to reduce contributions on behalf of rank-and-file workers and thus the size of their pensions from the qualified plan.

▪➡ TIP

Disparities are not permitted in ESOPs, 401(k) plans, or SARSEPs (Salary Reduction Simplified Employee Plans).

12.7.5 *Minimum Coverage*

These are general, basic rules; examining all the exceptions and details is beyond the scope of this work. The Code has two tests of minimum coverage under a qualified plan: the ratio percentage test and the average benefit percentage test. The ratio percentage test examines the plan in operation to verify coverage of 70% of rank-and-file employees, or a percentage of rank-and-file employees at least equal to that of executive or highly compensated employees who are covered by the plan.

The average benefit percentage test has two parts. The employee benefit percentage for rank-and-file employees must be at least 70% of that for non-rank-and-file employees, and the plan must benefit a classification of employees that is not discriminatory.

> ⇒ **TIP**
>
> Employers who have bona fide SLOBs (separate lines of business—it's not a value judgment) can apply the coverage tests separately to the employees in each business. Furthermore, employees who are covered by a collective bargaining agreement which made retirement benefits the subject of good faith bargaining can be omitted when making the minimum coverage calculations.

12.7.6 Minimum Participation

To be qualified, a plan must benefit at least 50 employees. (Remember, as noted above, minimum participation requirements are now imposed only on defined benefit plans.) For very small companies, an alternate test is permissible: the plan can benefit 40% of *all* employees.

> ⇒ **TIP**
>
> Leased employees are considered "employees" when calculating compliance with the minimum participation requirements.

The SLOB (separate line of business) technique can be used to calculate participation for each line of business. Certain plans—those that are not top-heavy and do not benefit any highly compensated employee or former employee who was highly compensated—are exempt from having to satisfy the minimum participation requirements.

12.7.7 Age and Service Requirements

One simple approach is just to have the plan cover all employees. However, the Code does not require qualified plans to do this; employee turnover can be accommodated by requiring employees to be at least 21 years old and to have completed one year of service before they are eligible for plan participation. Part-time employees must be covered if they can complete a year of service (defined as 1000 hours) within a 12-month period. Since this equals only 40 weeks of 25 hour-a-week employment, it is not unlikely that part-time employees will have to be covered under this requirement.

⇒ **TIP**

A plan (unless it is a 401(k) plan)) can require two years of service as a condition of plan participation, if plan benefits are 100% vested after only two years. In other words, the employer can defer employees' participation in the plan, if it speeds up their vesting.

Although plans can impose a minimum age for participation (21), they can't impose a maximum age. On the other hand, you can make employees wait until the fifth anniversary of their plan participation to be fully vested, if they were hired comparatively late in life and became plan participants within five years of normal retirement age.

For tax code and ERISA purposes, a year of service is a 12-month period including 1000 hours of service. The term "hours of service" is something of a misnomer, because it includes time that the employee is getting paid but is not working (vacations, holidays, illness, layoffs, jury duty, military duty, leave of absence, and times when the employee is receiving back pay). However, if there is a continuous period without duties, the employer doesn't have to credit more than 501 hours of non-working service. Up to that much time of maternity or paternity leave must be given service credit.

The employer is not required to give service credit when the one-time employee receives payments under unemployment compensation, Worker's Compensation, or disability laws, or when he or she is reimbursed for medical expenses.

The service credit rules are significant in many pension contexts: who is eligible for participation, who is counted in testing the plan's minimum participation and whether it is discriminatory, determining the employee's seniority, and determining who is entitled to benefits and, often, the size of the benefits.

If an employee has already met the plan's participation standards, but is separated from service on the plan entry date, he or she must be allowed to participate immediately upon a return to service after the plan entry date but before the break in service has lasted for a full year.

However, if there is a one-year break in service (defined to mean a 12-month period in which the employee has less than 501 hours of service credit), the prior service before the break does not have to be considered in determining the employee's eligibility for plan participation.

If an employee has a one-year break in service before he or she has met the plan's participation standards, service before the break does not have to be taken into account until the employee has been re-hired and completes another year of service.

12.7.8 Benefit Accrual

Plan design has many variables; one of the most significant is the way the plan allocates contributions and/or benefits to participants. ERISA and the tax code specify minimum rates at which benefits must accrue (i.e., be contributed on the individual's behalf, or be added to the pension account so that the participant's defined benefit will eventually become payable).

Vesting (see page 236) is a separate but related concept. Vesting determines the extent to which employees are entitled to *receive* their accrued benefits (or defined benefit pension payments based on their accrued benefits) when they retire or otherwise terminate employment.

The basic rule for qualified defined benefit plans is that benefit accrual must take place in accordance with one of the three permitted mechanisms:

- The 3% rule: at all times, the accrued benefit must be at least 3% of the maximum benefit calculated under the plan's formula, multiplied by the number of years of participation.

- The $133\frac{1}{3}$% test: the accrued benefit payable at Normal Retirement Age equals the normal retirement benefit, and accrual in any plan year does not exceed $133\frac{1}{3}$% of the accrual for any prior plan year. (In other words, benefits must accrue in a more or less level manner over time.)

- The fractional rule: the annual benefit an employee has accrued at the time of separation must be proportionate to what he or she would have received by remaining employed until normal retirement age.

➠ TIP

There is an exception for insured plans that satisfy §412(i) as long as the accrued benefit is always at least equal to the cash surrender value of the insurance.

12.7.9 Vesting

For a single-employer plan that is not top-heavy (and very few plans with large numbers of participants are top-heavy), for plan years beginning after 12/31/88 there are only two permissible vesting schedules.

One is five-year cliff vesting: participants are not vested at all for the first five years of service, but then they are immediately 100% vested as to employer contributions. The other is 3-to-7 graded vesting: there is no vesting for three years; participants must be fully vested by seven years; and vesting increases proportionately in years 4, 5, and 6. (Multi-employer plans are permitted to have a 10-year vesting schedule.)

The normal retirement benefit must always be nonforfeitable at the normal retirement age (see below). These vesting schedules are minimum requirements; there is nothing to stop a plan from vesting faster.

For vesting purposes, a year of service is a period of 12 consecutive months during which the employee performs at least 1000 hours of service. An employee who performs less than the 1000 hours does not have to receive any credit for the year, i.e., the plan doesn't have to award fractional years of service credit.

⇒ **TIP**

A year of service for vesting purposes, or a year of participation for accrual purposes, can be any period of 12 consecutive months that the employer designates. On the other hand, a year of service for eligibility purposes has to start on the first day of employment. A plan can have more than one year for vesting purposes, and if the plan selects a single vesting year for convenience, it doesn't have to be the same as the plan year.

12.7.10 Break in Service Rules

A one-year break in service (a concept with many implications) means a year in which 501 or fewer hours of service for the employer were rendered. If hours of service for the year fall between 501 and 1000, the employee does not have to be credited with a year of service, but cannot be penalized for a break in service.

Subsequent to a one-year break, pre-break service can be disregarded for vesting purposes until the employee has returned to work and completed a year of service. A defined contribution plan (as well as certain insured defined benefit plans) can treat vested benefits as forfeited, and allocate them to other participants, after five consecutive one-year breaks in service. If a participant was 0% vested before the break in service (e.g., someone who had worked for only two years in a plan with five-year cliff vesting), the "Rule of Parity" requires the plan to add up the number of years of service prior to the break. If the number of consecutive one-year breaks is at least five, or is greater than or equal to the aggregate number of pre-break years of service (whichever is greater), the rule permits the pre-break years to be disregarded for vesting purposes, even if the participant is later re-employed.

⇒ **TIP**

Due to the Retirement Equity Act of 1984, a break in service that is caused by parenting leave probably cannot be counted against the employee.

12.7.11 Nondiscrimination Rules

Especially in small plans, there is a constant risk that the pension plan will be drafted and operated in a way that makes it difficult or even impossible for rank-and-file workers to gain significant benefits. The Code contains elaborate provisions for determining if a pension (or welfare benefit) plan is "discriminatory," i.e., if it is unduly favorable to owners and executives and unduly punitive toward ordinary staffers.

- Plans must be operated for the exclusive benefit of participants and beneficiaries; and within that group, limitations are imposed on the extent to which highly-compensated employees (HCEs) can be favored by the plan. No matter how much the individual earned before retirement, the maximum contribution that can be made to a defined contribution plan is $30,000 per year. In appropriate circumstances, the employer can spend more than that to fund a defined-benefit plan (especially if the favored employee is middle-aged or older, and especially if there is a small number of years before retirement to complete the funding). However, the maximum defined benefit that can be paid under a qualified plan is $130,000 per year.

⇒ **TIP**

Originally, the Internal Revenue Code contained "family aggregation rules" under which the compensation of several members of the family owning a family business could be combined in testing whether the plan was qualified in terms of coverage, nondiscrimination, limitations on compensation, and deductions. However, the rules were abolished by the Small Business Job Protection Act (SBJPA) of 1996, effective for plan years beginning on and after January 1, 1997.

- The SBJPA also simplifies the Code §414(q) definition of HCEs. Someone who now owns (or owned in the past year) 5% or more of the company's stock is by definition an HCE. So is someone who earned $80,000 or more from the company in the preceding year. (The $80,000 figure will increase in response to inflation.) The employer can elect to limit the application of the $80,000 test to individuals who were in the top 20% of the company's earnings structure in the preceding year.

- Qualified plans are, however, permitted to be "integrated" with Social Security. Because FICA taxes phase out (for 1998, they are imposed only on the first $68,400 of compensation income), in effect FICA taxes are assessed on low-paid employees' entire salary, but on only a portion of highly-compensated employees' salaries. Furthermore, Social Security benefits replace a higher percentage of pre-retirement income for rank-and-file workers than for the highly compensated. This is the rationale for the permitted disparity rules of Code §401(l), which control the extent to which Social Security taxes paid by the employer, or Social Security benefits paid to the retiree, can be used to reduce the employer's contribution or the pension that will eventually be received.

- The Code's anti-discrimination rules require qualified plans to avoid discrimination in contributions OR in benefits, not necessarily both. Furthermore, it is permissible for a defined contribution plan to satisfy the tests for nondiscrimination in benefits, or vice versa.

⟫ **TIP**

The calculations are made *excluding* employees who are part of a bargaining unit with a collective bargaining agreement that was the subject of good faith bargaining about pensions and benefits.

Many highly complex formulas can be used to prove non-discrimination, as well as simplified "safe harbors" that can be found in Reg. §1.401-1-13. (These rules are effective for private sector plans for years beginning on or after January 1, 1994; government and nonprofit plans got additional years to come into compliance.)

To sum up, the safe harbor for non-discrimination in contributions means that either a uniform allocation formula is used for all employees, or a uniform formula is used for allocating points. Non-discriminatory benefits must be designed uniformly. When "general testing" of either a defined benefit or defined contribution plan is done, the employer must prove that each "rate group" satisfies Code §410(b).

The maximum defined benefit payable by a qualified plan is the equivalent of a straight life annuity, with no ancillary or incidental benefits, rollovers, or employee contributions, of $130,000—or, technically, $90,000 as adjusted for inflation. The $90,000-as-adjusted limit must be reduced for participants who had less than 10 years of service at the time of retirement. The maximum benefit is subject to an additional limitation: it cannot exceed 100% of what the employee earned in his or her three highest-paid years. For years after 1997, compensation for §415 purposes includes §125 (cafeteria plan) elections and elective deferrals made under §§401(k), 403(b), and 457.

If the plan provides ancillary benefits, the limit is reduced actuarially to account for the ancillary benefits. Certain of these can be provided without triggering an adjustment: a qualified joint and survivor annuity that provides more than a single life annuity (but lump sums cannot exceed the value of the single life annuity), benefits that are not directly related to the pension—e.g., retiree health benefits, and post-retirement cost of living increases that comply with §415(d). An upward adjustment is required if the employee made voluntary contributions to the plan or rolled over amounts from another plan into that plan. In other words, the employee can receive the full employer pension, plus rollover amounts and voluntary contributions.

For years before 1999, employers that maintain both a defined contribution and a defined benefit plan must keep the combined plan amounts within limits, but those limits are repealed for 1999 and later years.

12.7.12 Normal Retirement Age

Many of the ERISA and tax rules are based on the concept of drawing a pension at Normal Retirement Age (NRA)—or perhaps either drawing a reduced pension at earlier than the normal age, or an enhanced pension later. The typical NRA is 65, but under appropriate circumstances, a plan can define an NRA that is either earlier or later.

> ⟶ **TIP**
>
> If the plan fails to name an NRA, it is deemed to be the age at which accrued benefits no longer increase solely on account of age or service.

A plan can set the NRA lower than 65 if this is customary for the company or the industry, and if the choice is not a device to accelerate funding. However, if the NRA is set lower than 55, §415(b) requires reduction of the maximum pension that is payable under the plan.

> ⟶ **TIP**
>
> A profit sharing plan is allowed to have an NRA lower than 55 even if this is below the industry average.

If the plan sets the NRA higher than 65, or if there is no definition in the plan, then individual NRAs are computed for each participant: either the 65th birthday, or the fifth anniversary of plan participation, whichever is later. Hours that fall under the break in service rule can be disregarded in determining the occurrence of the fifth anniversary.

12.7.13 Normal Retirement Benefit

The Normal Retirement Benefit (NRB) is another key concept. It is defined as the greater of the early retirement benefit (if the plan provides for one) or the benefit commencing at the NRA.

> ⮕ **TIP**
>
> For this purpose, the early retirement benefit is NOT adjusted actuarially even though it will continue for more years than the benefit commencing at the NRA. Early retirement subsidies are not counted if they do not exceed the Social Security benefit, and if they end once the retiree becomes eligible for Social Security.

Participants retire throughout the year, of course, not necessarily on their anniversaries of plan participation. So, if the benefit depends on average compensation for a certain number of years (e.g., three years or five years) rather than on compensation for the highest-paid years, Reg. §1.411(a)-7(c)(5) requires that the last partial year of service be treated as a full year.

> ⮕ **TIP**
>
> If an employee retires and begins to collect benefits, then returns to work with the same employer, the benefit payments can be suspended until the employee retires once again.

12.8 MINIMUM VESTING RULES

One of the abuses that led to the drafting of ERISA was some employers' use of vesting to prevent the majority of workers from earning a pension. Twenty or more years' service might be required, perhaps in conjunction with other requirements that were unrealistic for rank-and-file employees to satisfy. Pre-ERISA, not only did many employees lose out on pensions—but the "forfeitures" (amounts deposited in rank-and-file employees' accounts, but not paid to them) usually went to enhance the pensions payable to the companies' top executives.

Under ERISA, defined benefit pension plans are subject to strict requirements on vesting. (Vesting is not a problem for defined contribution plans because, as long as the employer makes the necessary contributions, the worker will have an individual account available to him or her at retirement.) Vesting means that the right to a particular benefit has become irrevocable, nonforfeitable, and not conditioned on any event in the future (including continuing to work for the same employer).

The accrued benefit under a defined benefit plan is the benefit that is payable, at the normal retirement date, in the form of a single-life annuity or its actuarial equivalent. (But see page 290: the actual benefit will probably be paid in the form of a joint and survivor annuity.) Vesting is the minimum rate of accrual at which benefits become non-forfeitable.

As a general rule, the employer has to choose between two vesting schedules: five-year cliff or three-to-seven year graded. If the employer chooses the first, employees can be required to work for five years without any vesting—but as soon as they pass the five-year mark, their pensions are fully vested. If the employer chooses the second, vesting must begin after three years' service, and must be complete after seven years (20% vesting at three years, 40% at four years, and so forth).

However, the employer has another choice: deferring employee eligibility to participate in the pension for two years (instead of the regular one year), but vesting 100% after two years. This combination of deferred participation and faster vesting might be chosen in a workplace with a very high turnover.

There is another exception: if the plan is "top-heavy" (devotes a high percentage of its benefits to top-compensated employees), vesting must be faster than usual: three-year cliff vesting, or six year graded vesting.

⇒ **TIP**
_____

If an employer is allowed to, and does, change its vesting schedule, employees with three years or more of service have the right to elect to have their vesting calculations made on the basis of the old rules.

12.9 FORFEITURES

When an employee leaves, his or her non-vested benefits are forfeited. ERISA and the Internal Revenue Code also control the way plans must handle forfeitures.

If a worker leaves employment, then is later re-employed by the same company (after a layoff, or after quitting or being fired), the employee's eventual retirement benefit must be adjusted actuarially to reflect both periods of employment (except where the break in service rules make this unnecessary). Another option is for the plan to give timely notice of its provisions for suspension of benefits, so there is no forfeiture: Reg. §2530.203-3(b)(4).

When an employee dies, the plan can call for forfeiture of his or her unvested benefits, except to the extent that a Qualified Preretirement Survivor Annuity (QPSA) is required. See page 291.

12.10 EMPLOYEE CONTRIBUTIONS

Although the employer's role in the pension plan is certainly dominant, plans can be drafted to accept voluntary contributions from employees, or to require mandatory contributions from employees as a condition of participation or receiving an employer "match." (Code §411(c)(2)(C) characterizes the employee contribution as mandatory if it is a precondition of the employer match.)

The defined-contribution limit of the smaller of $30,000 a year or 25% of compensation applies to all annual additions, whether they derive from the employer or the employee.

Employee contributions are also important in determining whether or not a plan discriminates in favor of highly-compensated employees (HCEs). Employees never get a tax deduction for contributing to qualified plans (although they may for IRA contributions, depending on their income, the type of IRA they prefer, and whether they are simultaneously participating in a qualified plan).

Nevertheless, employees do have an incentive to contribute to the plan because they are not taxed on the appreciation of the value of their contributions until after retirement. Yet HCEs have more disposable income than rank-and-file employees, and thus are better able to save; and the higher an individual's tax bracket, the more appealing he or she will find tax deferral or tax savings. Thus, employee contributions must be tested for non-discrimination.

Code §414(q) contains the formulas for testing whether the employer's aggregate contributions to the plan on behalf of HCEs are too high. If the plan fails to satisfy the requirements of this section, it will be disqualified, unless the excess contributions made on behalf of the HCEs, plus the earnings on the excess contributions, are returned to the company's employees by the end of the plan year after the year of the excess contribution. A 10% excise also applies to excess *employee* contributions (e.g., made by HCEs) that are not distributed within two and a half months of the end of the plan year.

12.10.1 Withdrawal of Employee Contributions

It's permissible for plans to be drafted so that employees can withdraw some or all of their voluntary contributions, plus accumulated earnings, while they remain employed and continue to participate in the plan. (In contrast, benefits deriving from the employer's contributions cannot be anticipated or alienated, except in the form of a QDRO, although participants can take plan loans. The employer's contributions are subject to elaborate vesting rules; employees are always 100% vested as to their own contributions.)

Code §411(a)(3)(D) permits forfeiture of employer contributions if a participant who is less than 50% vested in employer contributions withdraws his or her own mandatory contributions from the plan. However, the participant must be given the right to return his or her contributions and have the forfeiture reversed.

12.11 LEASED EMPLOYEES

As Chapter 8 shows, there are many ways to get work done other than by hiring full-time permanent employees. One reason for exploring new forms of work is to reduce the proportion of the workforce that is entitled to participate in the company's benefit plans (and, of course, to reduce the amount that the company must contribute to such plans). But such arrangements must be approached with caution: it's quite possible that Code §414(n) will require that some people be treated as "employees" eligible for plan participation even though they are formally employed by a leasing company rather than by the company for whom they perform services each day.

Section 414(n) refers to "leased employees," who are nominally employed by a "leasing organization" (e.g., an organization that furnishes temporary and contingent workers) but who "perform services" for a "service recipient." Instead of paying the leased employees directly, the service recipient pays the employees' wages (and an agency commission) to the leasing organization which handles payroll functions (including tax withholding).

However, the leased employees will be considered "employees" of the service recipient when it comes to determining whether the service recipient's pension plans discriminate in favor of highly-compensated employees (HCEs). If the leasing organization maintains a pension plan for the employees it leases out, its contributions or benefits are treated as if they were made by the service recipient for the service recipient's discrimination tests. The leasing organization's plan must count all service by leased employees for the leasing organization (even when they're leased out to a service recipient) with respect to coverage, vesting, contributions, and benefits under its own plan.

Service recipients have to count leased employees when they test their plans under the minimum participation, age and service, vesting, and top-heavy rules. They must be taken into account when computing limits on compensation and benefits and whether contributions to the plan are deductible. Furthermore, the leased employee will be treated as an employee under the Code's rules for fringe benefits such as group-term life insurance, accident and health insurance, cafeteria plans, and dependent care assistance. Leased employees also have COBRA rights (continuation of health coverage after termination of employment).

Leased employees are defined, for §414(n) purposes, as those who provide services to a service recipient in conformity with the service recipient's agreement with the leasing organization, and the services last more than a year. The next test depends on when the services were performed. For services before January 1, 1997, the question is whether the recipient's industry conventionally uses employees rather than independent contractors to do the work.

Because of the Small Business Job Protection Act of 1996, the test for 1997 and later years is whether the service recipient provides the primary direction or control for the work. (Service for related companies, such as the service recipient's controlled group of corporations, is aggregated with service for the service recipient.)

These rules relate to "substantially full-time service," which is defined as 1500 hours of service in a 12-month period, or a job that is equivalent to 75% of the hours that the service recipient's actual employees put in during a 12-month period. In other words, after a year of the equivalent of full-time work, the leased employee is treated as the service recipient's employee for pension testing purposes.

It is certainly inconvenient for employers to treat their leased workforce as employees; and, in certain circumstances, it would be unfair to make them do so. Therefore, §414(n) contains a safe harbor, under which service recipients can avoid counting leased employees for pension plan testing purposes.

➠ **TIP**

But if the worker is a common-law employee for other purposes, the safe harbor cannot apply.

Even if leased employees have to be counted in determining whether the service recipient's pension plans are discriminatory, they do not have to be offered participation in the plan until they satisfy any conditions for plan participation lawfully imposed by the plan (e.g., if the employer imposes an age-21 minimum for participation, and a leased employee starts working for the employer at age 19, completing a year of service at age 20, participation can be delayed until the leased employee reaches 21).

To qualify for the safe harbor, the service recipient must get 20% or less of its rank-and-file workforce (i.e., workers who are not HCEs) through leasing—and the leasing organization must have its own qualified pension plan that fits a particularly stringent set of criteria. The leasing organization's plan must be a money purchase plan. It must not be integrated with Social Security, the leasing organization's employees must be able to participate as soon as they are hired by the organization, and they must be fully vested immediately. Furthermore, the leasing organization must contribute at least 10% of compensation for each plan participant.

> ➠ **TIP**
> _____
>
> If you're not sure whether contingent employees fit the definition of leased employees, and if so how this affects your plan's qualification, you can request an IRS determination letter on this point. A user fee will be imposed.

See page 79 for a discussion of IR-96-44, an IRS document defining independent contractors and employees, and for a discussion of the control factors used to determine employee status.

Although it is helpful to have individuals you believe to be independent contractors sign waivers agreeing that they will not participate in pension and benefit plans, these waivers will not be sufficient if, under otherwise applicable legal principles, those people really are common-law employees.

12.12 PLAN AMENDMENTS

In order to preserve flexibility, it's a good idea for the plan sponsor to draft the plan reserving the right to amend the plan in the future. For example, plan sponsors are permitted to amend plans to eliminate:

- Ancillary life insurance provided as an accessory to the plan
- Accident or health insurance (remember, this is the context of a pension plan, not a welfare benefit plan)
- Some supplements paid to Social Security
- Availability of loans
- The ability to direct investment of the plan account or balance
- The actual investment options available under the plan
- Employees' ability to make after-tax contributions to the plan, or have elective salary deferrals made
- Administrative procedures for the plan (although even after the amendment, participants must have the right to fair redress of their grievances)
- Dates used to allocate contributions, forfeitures, earnings, and account balances.

However, Internal Revenue Code §411(d)(6) forbids plan amendments that reduce accrued benefits, including early retirement benefits and retirement-related subsidies, even if the affected employees consent. Furthermore, the protected benefits generally cannot be reduced or eliminated when the plan is merged or its benefits are transferred to another plan.

There's an exception to this rule. A plan that is subject to the minimum funding standard of Code §412 can be amended retroactively to reduce accrued benefits. To qualify, the plan sponsor must be able to prove to the DOL that the sponsor is undergoing substantial business hardship that makes it necessary to cut back on benefits. Amendments of this type must be adopted within $2\,^1/_2$ months of the end of the plan year, so respond promptly to business hardships.

Also, Code §412(c)(8) and ERISA §302(c)(8) permit certain retroactive amendments that reduce accrued benefits. The amendments must be adopted within $2^1/_2$ months of the end of the plan year, and the amendment must not reduce anyone's accrued benefit for plan years before the beginning of the first plan year that the amendment applies to. IRS approval is required for such amendments, and the DOL may have to be notified.

A plan can be amended to change the vesting schedule as long as no participant loses any non-forfeitable accrued benefits. Nevertheless, even if an amendment is permissible, participants who have at least three years of service with the plan must be given the chance to choose between the new and old schedules: see Code §411(a)(10)(B). Once made, the plan can specify that the election is irrevocable. The period during which employees can make the election must start by the date the amendment is adopted, and cannot end before 60 days after the date the amendment is adopted, the date it becomes effective, or the date the participant gets written notice of the amendment—whichever comes last.

12.13 WHICH PLANS ARE MOST POPULAR?

The larger the employer, the more likely it is to offer a pension plan (as well as other benefits, such as health insurance). The defined-benefit plan is the traditional pension form, but defined contribution plans have become by far the more popular, because of their simplicity of administration, greater popularity with participants, and shift of investment risk to the participants. In 1993, there were about 565,000 businesses that had single-employer pension plans; 88% of them reported that they had only defined contribution plans; 9% of employers had only defined benefit plans, and 3% of employers had both types of plan. In the same year, there were about 19.9 million employees covered only by defined contribution plans, 5.4 million covered only by defined benefit plans, and 18.9 million covered by both types of plan. (These percentages are very different from the percentages of total plans maintained in each form because some pension plans have only a few participants, others more than 100,000.)

Just about all pension plans covering fewer than 500 employees are defined contribution plans, but most employers with 500 or more employees had at least one defined benefit plan (often offered in conjunction with one or more defined contribution plans).

Either kind of plan can accept employee contributions (and either kind can require employees to contribute in order to participate in the plan). Employee contributions are a much greater factor in defined contribution plans than in defined benefit plans. In 1993, for instance, employers contributed $1.80 for every $1.00 that employees put into defined contribution plans—but there was almost $20 in employer contributions to every $1 of employee defined-benefit plan contributions.

The GAO report discussed above finds that a defined-contribution-plan-only package was the least expensive to administer, at $103 in expenses per employee per year. The cost of a defined benefit plan only averaged $157 per participant-year. Arrangements that included both defined benefit and defined contribution plans cost an average of $71 per participant for the latter, $125 for the former, for a total of $196 per person.

Despite the increased number of defined contribution plans, at all times since 1976 there have been more total assets in defined benefit plans. The disparity was greatest in the early 1990s; by 1995, defined-contribution aggregate assets topped $1,400 *billion*, but even that immense amount was dwarfed by nearly $1,700 billion in defined benefit plans. Yet, although the amount of money invested in pension plans is colossal, employers actually spend less (in real dollars) on all retirement plans than they did in 1977. In 1977, employers put 84 cents per employee hour worked into all pension plans; by 1996, the inflation-adjusted equivalent was 53 cents per employee-hour.

When Buck Consultants, Inc. analyzed the annual reports of about half of the Fortune 1000 companies, they found that in 1995 there was a sharp decline in the percentage of major companies whose defined benefit plans were fully funded (i.e., possessed enough assets to cover the plan's accumulated benefit obligations). In 1994, 75% of the defined benefit plans were fully funded; less than half were fully funded in 1995. The funding ratio (the plan assets as a percentage of accumulated benefit obligations) declined from 121% in 1994 to 103% in 1995.

"Voluntary benefits"—employee-pay-all products sold by insurance brokers at the worksite, with the consent of the employer—are gaining in popularity. When 554 benefit specialists were surveyed in 1997, 25% said that there is little or no additional administrative work in setting up such a plan. Forty-two percent said that the employer had to devote minimal or no additional administrative time to running the plan, and 45% said that there was a moderate to heavy workload associated with maintaining the plan. Life insurance for employees' dependents was the most popular voluntary benefit (57% of the plans offered it), followed by term life insurance offered by 52%, disability insurance by 34%, dental benefits by 23%, long-term care insurance by 20%, auto insurance by 20%, and homeowner's insurance by 17%.

12.14 PBGC PREMIUMS

The PBGC maintains its precarious equilibrium by charging a premium to employers who maintain defined benefit plans. (In fact, the obligation to pay the premium is another factor in the declining popularity of defined benefit plans.) The

PBGC premium is $19 per plan participant, plus $9 for every $1000 of vested but unfunded benefit for which the plan is responsible. The premium is charged for each participant, terminated vested participant, and beneficiary already receiving benefits, but not individuals for whom an insurance company has an irrevocable commitment to pay all the benefits.

Until June 30, 1996, employers were entitled to a safe harbor: there was a ceiling on the variable portion of the premium (the part related to unfunded vested benefits). Since that date, the ceiling has been removed, and the sky's the limit. Unfunded benefits are defined as unfunded current liabilities determined by counting only vested benefits. The plan can use the information from Schedule B of Form 5500 instead of making a separate calculation.

⇒ TIP

If a plan has fewer than 500 participants, it can submit a certificate from an enrolled actuary stating that there are no unfunded vested benefits. Nor is it necessary to calculate unfunded vested benefits if the plan is fully insured, or if the plan was fully funded in the year before the year in question. When a plan terminates, the PBGC premium is payable until the plan assets have been distributed, or until a trustee is appointed (whichever comes first). This is an incentive to finish winding up the plan, so the PBGC will refund any unearned part of the premium for the year of the termination.

12.15 REVIEWING PLAN DECISIONS

It's easy to imagine situations in which a plan participant applies for benefits, but the plan administrators decide that the participant is not entitled to the desired benefits. As noted above, each plan must have a claims procedure and an appeal procedure.

Can dissatisfied participants and beneficiaries head to the courthouse and sue the plan, or the plan fiduciaries and administrators as individuals? Yes, but only under strictly controlled circumstances. The general rule is that the participants and beneficiaries can't use the state court system, because ERISA preempts (takes over) the entire field of plan administration. Therefore, if a suit is possible at all, it may have to go through the federal court system. Just getting a case into federal court involves lengthy delays, which may be enough to discourage a potential litigant.

Another general rule: before bringing a lawsuit, participants and beneficiaries must "exhaust administrative remedies." In other words, they have to use all of the plan's grievance mechanisms before starting litigation. On the other hand, if they can prove that it would be useless to go through the administrative procedures (for instance, if the plan administrators are so prejudiced that they cannot make a fair judgment) then they can go right to court and bypass the plan's own procedures. They can also sue directly if they can prove that they were denied "meaningful access" to the plan's appeal procedures.

Federal courts use one of two standards when they review a plan administrator's decision: "de novo" (new, from the beginning) and "abuse of discretion." The general rule is that the court can review de novo—that is, it can examine the plan administrator's decision to see if it is a valid decision, using all the facts of the case to make the determination.

However, if the plan instrument specifically gives the fiduciary the discretion to determine eligibility for benefits and to interpret the terms of the plan, then courts can only review for "abuse of discretion." In other words, all they can do is see if the plan administrator made improper use of discretion. The court can't consider whether the plan administrator made a good decision, or whether some other decision would have made more sense.

12.16 PENSION PLAN FORMS

The plan administrator's job involves the compilation and submission of plenty of IRS and DOL forms (as well as internal forms and records required by the sponsor corporation and its accountants and auditors).

Form 5300 is filed with the IRS in order to get a "determination letter" that proves that the plan is qualified (and tax deductions can be taken). Form 5310 is used to re-determine qualification when a plan is terminated. If a plan merges, consolidates, or transfers its assets, it must give the IRS notice on Form 5310A.

Pension plans must file an annual report with the IRS, choosing the appropriate form from the Form 5500 series. For readers of this book, it can be assumed that the appropriate form is the full-scale Form 5500, not one of the shorter ones for small plans. The multi-page 5500 form requires several attachments, depending on the company's circumstances:

- Schedule A: insurance information
- Schedule B: actuarial information
- Schedule C: information about the plan's service providers and trustees
- Schedule E: information about the annual results of the company's ESOP (there isn't any Schedule D)
- Schedule F: annual information return of the fringe benefit plan (it's an information return because fringe benefit plans are generally organized as tax-exempt entities)
- Schedule G: financial schedules (assets, loans, leases, etc.)

- Schedule P: annual return rendered by the fiduciary of the employee benefit plan trust
- Schedule SSA: identification of separated participants who are entitled to deferred vested benefits under the plan.

The information on the 5500-series form must be summarized briefly; this quick summary, officially known as the SAR (Summary Annual Report) must be distributed to the employees when the plan files its annual report. That isn't the only document that plan participants get: they get an SPD (Summary Plan Description) when they join the plan. (Beneficiaries get an SPD when they start receiving benefits.)

The SMM (Summary of Material Modifications) is both an internal document which must be given to plan participants whenever the plan is modified significantly, and an official filing which must be made with the Department of Labor, to notify the Department of the changes.

⇒ TIP

IRS Announcement 96-53 contains revised application forms for getting IRS determination letters with respect to qualified plans. New Schedule Q, documenting that the plan is not discriminatory, must be attached for Forms 5300, 5305, 5307, and 5310.

Chapter 13

P LAN ADMINISTRATION

13.1 INTRODUCTION

ERISA is a very wide-ranging statute. If a plan is subject to ERISA (and it's safe to assume that anything intended as a plan—and even some informal measures that were not so intended—will be subject to ERISA), then not only must the plan be drafted to satisfy ERISA, it must be administered by its fiduciaries in compliance with ERISA. There are additional requirements, written into the Internal Revenue Code or added by court interpretations, that will also have to be met.

This chapter deals with some of the day-to-day tasks involved in setting up and administering a plan. See Chapter 14 for the rules about required disclosures to plan participants, Chapter 15 for making routine distributions from the plan, and Chapter 16 for termination of a plan. Chapter 17 deals with enforcement of ERISA, including penalties that can be imposed on fiduciaries and plan administrators.

13.2 CREATING A PLAN

Most of the people reading this book work for a company that already has one or more plans. Nevertheless, it is worth spending a little time to discuss the process under which plans are set up, qualified with the Department of Labor and the IRS (if qualification is sought), and especially the procedures for amending an existing plan.

In all cases, employers adopting a plan have an obligation to notify the employees. The Department of Labor has to be notified of any intention to adopt a plan subject to ERISA Title I. Interestingly, even if the employer wants to establish a plan that is qualified for tax purposes, it is not strictly necessary to notify the IRS, but the agency does have to be contacted if a determination letter is sought. However, the determination letter is merely evidence of a plan's qualification (it isn't even conclusive on that point), and a plan can certainly generate legitimate tax deductions if it is operated in accordance with the Code but has never secured a determination letter.

If the plan nevertheless wants a determination letter, employees must be notified of the intention to apply for the letter. The application is made to the IRS District Director's office; if the letter is not issued based on the company's request, there are several levels of review within the IRS, followed by appeal to the Tax Court.

The Summary Plan Description (see page 273) for a newly created plan must be filed with the Department of Labor within 120 days of the plan's adoption (or 120 days of the first time it covers common-law employees and therefore becomes subject to ERISA Title I, if this is later than the date of establishment).

ERISA §104(a)(4)(A) gives the Department of Labor the power to reject an incomplete SPD filing. After such a rejection, the plan administrator has 45 days to refile in response to the DOL comments. Omitting the refiling is a very bad idea: DOL has the power to sue for legal or equitable relief or any other remedy authorized by ERISA Title I.

A similar process is required when a plan is materially modified or the information called for by ERISA §102(b) changes. The DOL must receive an updated SPD when the participants and beneficiaries do. The DOL can reject a submission on the same terms as an initial plan description. In addition, the 5500-series form filed with the IRS calls for annual reporting of plan amendments and changes in the plan description.

➡ TIP

Don't forget that many tax-law changes require conforming plan amendments, so annual or nearly-annual amendments may be necessary even if the employer doesn't initiate any changes in the plan's provisions.

13.2.1 Prototype and Master Plans

Drafting an ERISA- and tax-compliant plan is a very difficult matter. Yet, paradoxically, the problems encountered by one plan are very much like the problems of others. In response to both these factors, the IRS publishes prototype and master plans. A company can clearly meet its compliance burden by adopting, and sticking to, one of these "official" plans. There are several, to suit various employer needs. They either integrate the basic plan and the trust document into a single document, or have a trust agreement separate from the plan, with an adoption agreement that covers matters such as participation, benefit formulas, and vesting.

➠ **TIP**

In this context, the plan "sponsor" is not the employer whose employees are covered by the plan, but instead an institution such as a bank, insurance company, trade organization, or professional organization.

The difference between prototype and master plans is that a prototype plan has a separate funding mechanism for each employer. A master plan has a single trust or other funding mechanism that covers multiple employers.

13.2.2 Determination Letters in Detail

Although prototype and master plans offer convenience, it is quite permissible to draft a plan individually. Most determination letters are sought for such "custom" plans.

Determination letters are requested on official IRS forms. User fees of $50-$3600, depending on the nature of the application, are charged. (Creating a plan may require filing several applications, so it's hard to say what the overall fee structure would be.) The appropriate form numbers are:

- 4461: Application for a determination letter for a master or prototype defined contribution plan
- 4461-A: " " defined benefit plan
- 5300: Individually drafted defined benefit plan
- 5302: " " defined contribution plan
- 5309: ESOP
- 5307: Prototype or master submission.

➠ **TIP**

Rev. Proc. 96-8, 1996-1 CB 561, contains a list of user fees for the various applications and rulings. See IRS Manual Supplement 77G-14 for the guidelines the IRS imposes on staffers who review applications. You can use the guidelines to make sure that originally-drafted language in a plan satisfies IRS requirements. Also see Announcement 96-53, showing the revised application forms for seeking a determination letter for a qualified plan. This Announcement adds a new Schedule Q, demonstrating conformity with the non-discrimination requirements. Schedule Q must be attached to Forms 5300, 5303, 5307, and 5310.

Before the request for a determination letter is submitted to the IRS, all "interested parties" have to be notified, in other words, the current employees who are eligible for plan participation if the plan is implemented. If the plan is collectively bargained, all employees covered by the collective bargaining agreement are entitled to notice which can be given in person (e.g., printed and handed to all employees; slips placed in all pay envelopes), by mailing, or by posting in the usual place for posting employer and/or union notices.

The appropriate time for employee notice is 7–21 days before the IRS gets the application. If the employees are notified by mail, the notices should be mailed 10–24 days before submission of the application.

Employees must be notified because interested parties have the right to comment directly to the IRS about the application. The PBGC or a group of interested parties can also invite the Department of Labor to comment on the application; the PBGC has the right to submit its own comments directly. The comment period is either 45 or 60 days after the IRS receives the request.

After 60 days have elapsed, the IRS does its own investigation of the qualification of the proposed plan (including consideration of any comments that have been submitted). A reviewing agent in the relevant IRS Key District Office issues the determination letter (or refuses to do so); if there are questions about the application, the agent tries to work them out by telephoning or writing to the company that applied for the determination letter.

Determination letters can also be obtained for plan amendments. The "interested parties" who must be notified are the eligible current employees. If the proposed amendment changes the rules for participation, all employees with the same principal place of business as the eligible employees must be notified.

Although in most instances IRS approval will be required to change a retirement plan's plan year, approval of the request (which must be made on Form 5308) is automatic as long as:

- No plan year is longer than 12 months. In other words, a year can be broken up into two short years, but two short years can't be consolidated into a long one.

- The change doesn't have the effect of deferring the time at which the plan becomes subject to changes in the law

- The plan trust (if any) remains tax-exempt and doesn't have any Unrelated Business Taxable Income in the short year

- Legal approval for the change is granted before the end of the short year

- If the plan is a defined benefit plan, the deduction taken for the short year is the appropriate prorated share of the costs for the full year.

13.3 CLAIMS PROCEDURE

All plans (pension and welfare benefit) that are subject to ERISA Title I must maintain a reasonable claims procedure. DOL Reg. §2560.503 defines an appropriate claims procedure as one which is described in the SPD, does not place undue restrictions or inhibitions on claims processing, and complies with the relevant regulations about filing claims, reviewing submitted claims, and informing participants when claims are denied. At a minimum, the procedure must give claimants or their authorized representatives the right to apply to the plan for review, see the pertinent documents, and submit written comments and issues to be resolved.

If the claim is denied, there must be a specific reason for the denial. Claimants must be referred to the plan provision that requires denial, and must be given information about how to appeal. The administrator must make a decision about the claim within 90 days of receiving it. However, if there are special circumstances justifying an extension, up to 90 more days can be given to review the claim, but the claimant must get a written notice disclosing the extension before the original 90-day period expires. The notice to the claimant must be sent within a reasonable time of the submission of the claim. If this is not done, then the claim is deemed denied, thus giving the claimant the right to appeal.

Plan participants must be given at least 60 days to appeal the denial of a claim to the appropriate named fiduciary or to the person he or she has designated. The plan document must either name the reviewer or describe how the reviewer will be chosen. The reviewer gets 60 days from the receipt of the review request to issue a decision. In special circumstances, such as those where an in-person hearing rather than a paper review is needed, this period can be extended, but not to more than 120 days.

13.4 STANDARD OF REVIEW

If and when a case involving a plan gets to the courts, a basic question is what its role should be. Should the court look at the underlying decision and see if it is the correct one that the administrator should have made ("de novo" review—as if the matter were a new case), or only see if the administrator abused his or her discretion? Of course, many more plan decisions will be reversed (and many more employee claimants will prevail) if the court can look at the underlying decision rather than only proper or improper exercise of discretion.

In the case of *Bruch* v. *Firestone Tire & Rubber* (489 U.S. 101 (1989)), the Supreme Court set the standard: the basic rule is that decisions will be reviewed de novo. However, plan sponsors have the power to draft the plan so that it gives the fiduciaries discretion over plan operations. If this is done, the courts review only the presence or absence of an abuse of discretion.

But if the fiduciary who made the decision has a conflict of interest (e.g., his or her personal interest is contrary to that of the plan and its beneficiaries), then de novo review might be imposed; or the conflict might be used as a factor in determining if discretion was abused.

Under the de novo standard, the court treats the plan's and the claimant's interpretation of the plan language the same way; neither is entitled to special deference. In contrast, if the plan reserves Bruch-type discretion to the fiduciary, then the fiduciary's interpretation of the plan language will, in all probability, prevail with the court.

13.5 ADMINISTERING THE CLAIM

Health plan fiduciaries have a duty to consider all pertinent available information, and to make a decision based on substantial evidence. A recent District Court case found that an employer did not provide the necessary "full and fair review" when it relied on its Utilization Review firm and therefore approved payment for only 30 days of a four-month psychiatric hospitalization. The plan administrator's duty was to review the medical records and make an independent determination of the correctness of the Utilization Review firm's decision. Furthermore, the administrator's fiduciary duty called for full and fair review of the case; it wasn't enough to permit an appeal after a claim was denied.

Although a number of cases have required managed care plans to pay for high-dose chemotherapy and bone marrow transplants for cancer patients (probably because the patients would almost certainly die without the therapy and transplants, and saving money for the plan seems much less important), a mid-1997 Fourth Circuit case says that a plan did not abuse its discretion in denying reimbursement for these treatments (which it deemed experimental). The plaintiff applied for pre-authorization, was refused, and not unnaturally went ahead with the treatment anyway; she also signed a medical disclosure statement to the effect that the treatment was experimental, not conventional and accepted.

13.6 PLAN AMENDMENTS

No matter how carefully a plan was drafted, there are many reasons why amendments might be prudent—or, indeed, mandatory. As labor and tax laws change, plans are required to keep in step. A company's economic situation might make it possible to expand benefit availability—or necessary to contract it! The nature of the company's business, and therefore of its workforce, might change over time.

The general rule is that plan amendments can be adopted either prospectively or retroactively. Retroactive amendments can be made until the last day (including extensions) to file the income tax return for the year the plan was adopted.

A defined benefit plan can lose its qualified status if it adopts an amendment that increases plan liabilities, if the result is that the funded current liability falls below 60% for the plan year. The employer can preserve the plan's qualification by posting "adequate" security. Either the corporation must place cash and securities in escrow, or it must secure a bond from a corporate security company that is acceptable under ERISA §412. See Code §401(a)(20)and ERISA §307.

In most instances, employees do not have to be notified in advance that the plan will be amended. (This means that they have no right to comment on proposed amendments, either—in contrast to their right to comment on a plan's application for a determination letter; see page 250 earlier.) Advance notice is required if the amendment changes the vesting schedules of participants who have three years or more of plan participation, because they have to be given the right to choose between the new and the old schedules.

Once the amendment is made, ERISA requires the plan to give participants a Summary of Material Modifications within 210 days of the end of the plan year in which the change is adopted.

13.7 INVESTMENT-RELATED COSTS

Most plans outsource many plan administration and investment decision-making tasks. The costs of various plan management alternatives differ greatly. A more expensive management alternative is certainly worthwhile if it leverages the HR department's time, offers greater convenience, or delivers better investment performance than its competitors.

The analysis usually involves Total Plan Cost, Total Benefit Cost, or both. (Costs are much more predictable than returns.) Plan costs comprise investment management costs, trustee costs, and administrative costs.

Trustees charge general processing fees, plus custody costs for each asset. The cost of administration includes such items as recordkeeping and loan initiation fees. Investment costs can either be calculated based on an individual portfolio or for a commingled pool of investments from several pension plans. The basic fees for an individual portfolio usually decrease as the size of the portfolio increases (because of economies of scale), but the more actively the portfolio is traded, the higher the fees will be.

13.7.1 Duties When Participants Control Investment

To an ever-increasing extent, plans are shifting toward forms that transfer investment decision-making to the participant. Typically, the plan will select a palette of investment choices (e.g., four or five mutual funds with differing portfolio styles, risk profiles, and objectives) and indicate how often a participant can make or change elections (although some very large plans allow daily switches between funds); within those parameters, the participant controls the investment of his or her account balance. It is permissible for the plan to require participants to pay reasonable transaction fees.

DOL Reg. §2550.404c-1(b)(3)(i)(B) requires the plan to offer at least three diversified categories of investments, each with materially different risk and return characteristics, which in the aggregate permit the participant to choose the risk and return characteristics that are appropriate for his or her individual account.

In effect, in an individual account plan the power (and the risk) then shifts from the plan administrator and other fiduciaries to the participant. Plan fiduciaries are not liable if the participant's own investment choices result in losses (unless the fiduciary violates the terms of the plan by obeying the participant's investment instructions). Technically speaking, the participant does not become a fiduciary him- or herself because of the transfer, although participants who are disqualified persons are subject to the prohibited transaction rules.

The shift in authority takes place in "participant directed individual account plans"—i.e., profit sharing, stock bonus, and money purchase plans. Individual account plans should be drafted to forbid participants from engaging in prohibited transactions or in any that give rise to Unrelated Business Taxable Income for the plan trust.

13.7.2 Mandated Disclosures

Participants are entitled to receive a great deal of information relative to individual account plans. They don't have to make a specific request for the information because the burden is on the plan to supply it. The mandated disclosures include:

- The fact that fiduciaries are not liable if they follow participants' investment directions, even if losses result

- A description of the investment alternatives available under the plan, including the general risk and return characteristics and objectives of each (including the assets within the portfolio of each investment alternative and how these portfolios are diversified)

- The designated investment managers for the investment alternatives

- When and how participants can give investment instructions

- Any limitations (e.g., only four switches a year) that the plan imposes on the instructions

- Fees and expenses that affect the participant's account balance

- The name, address, and phone number of the fiduciary (or designee of the fiduciary) who can provide additional information on request

- (If employer securities are an available investment alternative) how information about the participant's voting, tendering of shares of the employer's stock, etc., will be kept confidential; the name, address, and telephone number of the fiduciary who monitors the confidentiality provisions.

> ⇒ **TIP**
>
> If the participant invests in assets that are subject to the Securities Act of 1933 (e.g., publicly traded securities), he or she must be given a prospectus for each such asset either before or right after making the investment. If the plan "passes through" the rights to vote and/or tender shares of the investment alternatives, the plan must submit the relevant materials to the participant and also must inform him or her how to exercise these rights.

Participants are entitled to at least this much information (given directly to them, or upon request), based on the latest information available to the plan:

- The fees and operating expenses of each of the available investment alternatives, expressed as a percentage of the average net assets of that alternative
- Any prospectuses, financial statements, or reports the plan has about the alternative
- A description of the portfolio of each alternative. If it is a fixed-rate contract issued by a financial institution, the name of the institution and the term and rate of return of the contract
- The value of shares (or units, if that's how the alternative is sold) in each alternative available to plan participants; the current and past performance of each alternative, after expenses, calculated on a "reasonable and consistent basis"
- The value of shares or units in the individual participant's account.

13.8 MINIMUM FUNDING

It's quite simple to determine how much to spend to fund a defined contribution plan: it's a certain percentage of compensation, but not more than the Internal Revenue Code ceiling (currently $30,000 per person per year). No discretion is involved. In contrast, funding a defined benefit plan is a subtle process of predicting long-range economic and employment trends in order to deposit money now into an account that will provide the correct stream of future benefits to the work force.

The plan must rely on sophisticated professional advice from actuaries, who will make calculations based on various assumptions (about when employees will retire, how much they will earn in each interim year, what prevailing interest rates will be). The temptation is obvious: either to disregard the actuaries' advice and deposit less into the account (to save money) or more into the account (to increase the tax deduction). If too many mistakes are made, or if the system is manipulated too far, then the plan will not have enough money to make benefit payments at the appropriate times, increasing the stress on the PBGC even further.

Therefore, defined benefit, money purchase, and target benefit plans are subject to Code §412's minimum funding requirements. Section 412 does not apply to a profit sharing or stock bonus plan, or to a §412(i) plan—that is, one that is exclusively funded by purchase of individual insurance or annuity contracts.

An excise tax of 10% is imposed for failure to meet the standard, increasing to 100% of the deficiency if the plan fails to correct it in a reasonable time after receiving IRS notice. A 1996 Supreme Court case says that this amount is a penalty (and therefore an ordinary unsecured claim), not an excise tax entitled to seventh priority, if the company files for bankruptcy protection.

The implications of underfunding spread more broadly: if the plan is covered by PBGC insurance, the PBGC must be notified whenever the minimum funding standard is not met. If the plan is terminated, underfunding could make it liable to the PBGC for accumulated funding deficiencies.

Avoiding a violation of the minimum funding standard doesn't solve all of the employer's problems. An excise tax penalty is also imposed by Code §4972 for *excess* contributions to a qualified plan. See page 262.

The funding standard has another function. It sets an upward limit on the amount of the employer's income tax deduction for the plan (§404). Furthermore, Code §6662 imposes a 20% accuracy-related underpayment penalty if income taxes are underpaid by 20% or more as a result of an excessive §404 deduction that stems from an overstatement of pension liabilities. The penalty will be suspended if the pension overstatement is under $1,000, or if the plan relied on substantial authority such as Revenue Rulings and IRS Notices.

A lien arises in favor of the plan, and against the employer, when the employer fails to make a required contribution on time (generally quarterly) if, at the time the contribution was due, the plan's funded current liability percentage fell below 100% and the unpaid balance plus interest exceeded $1 million. See §412(n) for the lien provision.

However, only plans that come under ERISA §4021, and thus under PBGC jurisdiction, are subject to the lien which covers all of the employer's real and personal property and starts on the date the payment should have been made, running to the end of the plan year in which the liabilities top the $1 million mark.

➠ **TIP**
_____

If a payment is missed, the person responsible for making the payment has an obligation to notify the PBGC within 10 days of the due date that the payment was omitted.

ERISA §4003(e)(1) lets the PBGC sue in federal district court to enforce those liens against the employer at any time until three years after the PBGC knew or should have known of the failure to make the necessary payment (six years after, if the employer committed fraud or concealment), or six years after the required payment was not made.

In short, the employer will want the plan contribution to fall within a narrow range. It should not be small enough to constitute underfunding, generate excise tax liability, be a reportable event that the PBGC must be told about, and especially not be inadequate enough to cause the PBGC to terminate the plan. On the other hand, the employer will not want to contribute amounts so large that they are not fully deductible, and will particularly want to avoid the excise penalties on excessive contributions.

13.8.1 Plan Valuation Issues

Plans that are subject to §412 must perform an actuarial valuation at least once a year: the assets and liabilities of the plan are determined, and the contributions level is set. This information is also used to prepare Schedule B on the Form 5500 or 5500-C. Within limits, the employer can issue instructions to the actuary about years in which it expects to have more or less cash to devote to the plan.

The basic factors in setting assumptions include:

- Employee turnover
- The rates of disability and mortality (both before and after retirement)
- Life expectancy of the employee's spouse (if the default QJSA is elected)
- Employee compensation
- Rate at which employees retire before normal retirement age
- Expected investment revenue of the plan's investments (expressed as a percentage). After a few years of plan experience, it may be necessary to adjust the interest assumptions to reflect the plan's investment history.
- Administrative expenses expressed as either a certain number of dollars per participant or a reduction in the rate of return assigned to the plan.

As long as §412 and other relevant provisions are not violated, the amount of contributions can be increased or decreased somewhat based on corporate needs; but the plan's actuarial assumptions must always be reasonable (not just the aggregate of the assumptions as they work together, but each individual assumption).

> ➠ **TIP**
>
> Although the average age at which employees enter the plan is significant, technically it is not an assumption.

Courts have the power to overturn a plan's actuarial assumptions, even if the assumptions are not unreasonable. This result is especially likely if the plan applies its own assumptions inconsistently.

Code §412(l) sets the parameters for the interest rates used to determine the employer's contributions to the plan and the plan's current liability. The "permissible range" set by the Code is within 10% of the weighted average of rates on 30-year Treasury obligations for the four years ending the day before the beginning of the plan year. (One has to wonder who dreams this stuff up.) The Department of the Treasury has the power under §412(b)(5) to issue regulations lowering the permissible range, but it is not allowed to fall below 80% of the weighted 30-year average Treasury rate.

The interest rate assumption is another multi-factorial decision involving, e.g.,

- Long-term economic trends, especially those in the money supply and interest rates
- The economic components of interest rates
- Current long-term interest rates (because the plan operates over a term of decades, not just one quarter or even one year)
- Actuarial factors, and factors specific to the plan (such as its investment history) that justify adjustments.

> ➠ **TIP**
>
> The IRS has a history of auditing small benefit plans with deductions over $100,000 a year, if the plan maintains a normal retirement age under 55 and sets its interest rate assumptions below 8%.

13.8.2 Calculating the Contribution

Calculating the contribution the employer must make is no simple matter. The plan's actuary can use either of two basic methods to compute the contribution; each one has variations.

The accrued benefit method (also called the unit credit cost method) defines the plan liabilities on the basis of benefits that accrue in that particular year. In contrast, the projected benefit cost method (and its variations defined by ERISA §3(31), such as the entry age normal method, aggregate cost method, attained age normal cost method, and frozen initial liability cost method) calculates benefits using an assumption that they accrue as long as each plan participant remains a participant.

Furthermore, the contribution must take into account both normal cost and supplemental liability. The normal cost for each participant is the actuarial value of the benefit units assigned for that year. The supplemental liability provides benefits for service before adoption of the plan, or between the time of the plan's adoption and an amendment that has the effect of increasing coverage.

Code §412(b) and ERISA §302(b) require maintenance of a "minimum funding standard account" in all plan years until the end of the one in which the plan terminates. The minimum funding standard is met if, at the end of the plan year, there is no accumulated funding deficiency. In turn, the deficiency is avoided if, for all plan years, the credits to the funding standard account are at least equal to the total charges.

The minimum funding standard account consists of charges for normal costs, past service liabilities, experience losses in investments, and funding deficiencies. (Experience losses and funding deficiencies generally have to be amortized, over a 5- to 30-year period, depending on each item's categorization, rather than being deducted currently.) The credits that offset the charges include, e.g., the employer's contributions to the plan, investment experience gains, and funding deficiencies that are waived by the IRS.

If a single-employer plan with 100 or more participants has a "funded current liability" percentage below 80% for this year (and 90% for the preceding year), §412(l) imposes even more detailed rules. Furthermore, the underfunded plans have to notify their participants and beneficiaries of the funding deficiency. The funded current liability percentage is a simple ratio: the value of the plan assets divided by current liabilities.

13.8.3 The Full Funding Limitation

The plan must always be aware of its "full funding limitation" (FFL). The employer risks excise tax liability whenever its contribution falls below the FFL. (But there will be no excise tax if the contribution exceeds the FFL, even if the funding standard account has a deficit for the year.) Another implication: the employer's income tax deduction for plan contributions cannot exceed the FFL. When contributions dip below the FFL and the plan must pay the extra PBGC premium for underfunded plans, ERISA §4011 requires notice to participants and beneficiaries about the plan's funding status and the limits of the PBGC guarantee.

A simple way to think of the FFL is as (A) – (B). In this formula, (A) is either the accrued liability or a percentage of the current liability, whichever is less. (B) is the smaller of the fair market value of plan assets or the value of the assets calculated based on the Code §412(c)(2) fixed debt obligation. At all times, the FFL must be at least equal to 90% of the plan's current liability.

The current liability, in turn, is defined as all liabilities to participants and beneficiaries, calculated without regard to "unpredictable contingent event benefits." Such benefits are contingent on an event other than age, service, compensation, death, or disability—i.e., are outliers that fall outside the normal range of plan benefits.

For plan years beginning before 1998, the percentage was a flat 150%. But for later years, Taxpayer Relief Act of 1997 §1521(a) amends Code §412(c)(7) to phase in a higher percentage limit. For plan years that begin within the calendar years 1999 or 2000, the limit is 155%; it's 150% for 2001-2002 plan years, 165% for 2003-2004 plan years, and 170% for plan years that begin in and after 2005. Congress found the prior limit too restrictive, and therefore chose to increase it.

13.8.4 Funding Procedures

To actually fund the plan, the employer can make contributions in cash, non-cash property, or its own securities. Cash raises few problems: its value is obvious, and (despite the existence of inflation) it is not deemed to appreciate or depreciate in value. For the other two funding tools, the valuation of the contributions must be established. Furthermore, non-cash transactions must be handled so that prohibited transactions (see page 329) do not occur. If possible, transactions should be structured so that the plan trust will not have Unrelated Business Taxable Income (UBTI). (Plan trusts generally are exempt from income taxation, except on UBTI.)

Non-cash transactions have other implications. If the employer uses appreciated property to fund its contributions, Code §267(b)(4) says that the employer will have taxable gain, which could be capital or ordinary, depending on circumstances. Unfortunately, losses on depreciated property are not recognized, because there is a transfer between a trust grantor and the trust's fiduciary. Therefore, wherever possible, contributions of depreciated property should be avoided.

➠ **TIP**

If for some reason a contribution of depreciated property seems desirable, the employer can sell the property to a third party, recognize the loss for tax purposes, and use the cash from the sale as a plan contribution.

Thanks to PBGC Technical Update 97–4 (May 8, 1997), certain small or fully-funded plans that fail to make required quarterly contributions to defined benefit plans are entitled to file a single notice that covers all missed payments for the 1996 or 1997 plan year, and due on or after July 1, 1997. The notice is due on the same day as the PBGC Form 1 that is used to pay the 1997 PBGC premium. The notice form is PBGC-10, "Post-Event Notice of Reportable Events." Eligible plans are those with fewer than 100 defined-benefit plan participants, or fewer than 500 participants if they do not have to file the §4011 notice (i.e., the plan is at least 90% funded).

13.8.5 The Contribution Deduction

The main reason why an employer would undertake the significant costs and inconvenience involved in having a tax-qualified plan is the chance to take a tax deduction for its cost. However, it would be simplistic to assume that all plan-related costs are automatically fully deductible in the year they are paid or incurred. The Internal Revenue Code imposes various limitations on the amount and timing of the employer's deduction. Pensions are a form of deferred compensation, and any form of compensation is deductible if, and only if, it is reasonable and if it constitutes an ordinary and necessary business expense.

If the plan includes particularly highly-paid employees, part of their compensation may have to be disregarded, because several calculations under the Code involve only the part of an employee's compensation that falls below a stated limit. Under §401(a)(17) and §404(l), for instance, only $150,000 (as adjusted for inflation) can be taken into account. The 1997–1998 figure is $160,000. (The adjustment must be made in $10,000 increments, rounding downward, so the next possible adjustment is to $170,000.)

Even legitimate compensation may have to be deducted over a span of several years, not all at once. Code §263A requires capitalization of employee compensation, including benefit and retirement plan costs, incurred in connection with either in-house production or purchase for resale of real property or tangible personal property.

The next hoop to jump through is Code §404, whose objective is to differentiate pension and annuity plans from profit sharing and stock bonus plans. Under §404(a), to deduct a contribution in the year it was made, the plan must have been in existence by the end of the employer's tax year.

If the plan exists by the end of the year, actual contributions made after the end of the tax year, but before the due date for that year's tax return (including any extensions the employer has obtained), can be deducted for the previous year. This rule may seem familiar because it is used in other contexts; for instance, a 1998 IRA contribution is deductible if it is made before the due date (sometime in 1999) of the IRA holder's 1998 tax return. However, contributions made to a defined contribution plan after the end of the employer's tax year cannot be based on compensation paid between the end of the tax year and the due date of the return. Similar considerations apply to benefits attributable to service in a defined benefit plan between the end of the tax year and the return due date.

> **⇒ TIP**
>
> Not only are excessive contributions non-deductible, but they can become the subject of excise tax penalties, under Code §4972 for excess contributions, and under §6659A for excess contributions to a defined benefit plan.

Section 404(a)(1) defines three basic methods, each of which can be used to compute the maximum deduction for the year's plan contributions. In general, the upper limit on the deduction is the full funding limitation for the year. However, a single employer plan with 100 or more participants can deduct up to the §412(l) unfunded current liability. Once the full funding limitation has been calculated, the plan selects the method that gives the largest deduction for the year:

- The minimum funding standard
- Individual level premium (the amount needed to provide either the remaining unfunded cost of past service credits and entry age normal method current service credits distributed as a level amount, or a level percentage of compensation over the remaining future service of each participant).
- Normal cost plus 10-year amortization (deduction of the normal cost of the plan, plus an annual 10% of any supplementary cost).

The limit for profit sharing and stock bonus plans is 15% of the compensation paid to, or accrued by, the plan's participants in the employer's tax year. Two things should be noted. First, if any compensation paid to participants is unreasonable, that compensation is not included in calculating the 15% limit. Second, if the employer's tax year is different from the plan year, it is the tax year rather than the plan year that is used in this calculation.

Thanks to §404(a)(1), otherwise deductible contributions that exceed the permissible limit for deductions can be carried forward indefinitely and applied to as many future years as it takes to use them up.

13.8.6 Adaptations when Minimum Funding is Impractical

It's easy to imagine a situation in which a corporation's minimum funding obligation is $X, yet the company's assets are tied up, or expenses exceed revenues, to an extent that it is difficult or impossible to find the $X to contribute to the plan without making it impossible to satisfy pressing current debts.

The Internal Revenue Code and ERISA specify various means of avoiding an accumulated funding deficiency without actually making the inconveniently large payments that would normally be required. Under appropriate circumstances, the funding method can be changed. The plan can be amended retroactively to reduce accrued benefits, or a variance from the minimum funding standards can be obtained. Another way is that the amortization periods used in the funding standard account can be extended.

The general rule is that IRS approval is required to change funding methods. But see Rev.Proc. 95-51, 1995-2 C.B. 430, which permits certain changes to be made without the approval: a change to the unit credit method; valuing assets at their FMV; or changing the valuation of ancillary benefits.

A retroactive plan amendment can be adopted within two and a half months after the close of the plan year, with the effect of reducing benefits which accrued during the plan year for which the amendment is effective: Code §412(c)(8). The IRS, and the plan's interested parties, must be informed of the amendment; a model notice for this purpose can be found in Rev.Proc. 94-42, 1994-1 C.B. 717. The IRS has a 90-day period to review the proposed plan amendment (to see if it is necessary because of substantial business hardship, at a time when a variance is unavailable or inadequate). The amendment takes effect when the 90 days expire, if the IRS has not disapproved.

Employers can apply for a waiver of the minimum funding standard in any year: see Code §412(d). Details about application procedure and a model notice to be given to interested parties appear in Rev.Proc. 94-41, 1994-1 C.B. 711. The due date for the application is the fifteenth day of the third month after the end of the plan year for which the waiver is requested. The employer's task is to prove to the IRS that satisfying the standard would give rise to "temporary substantial business hardship," so that in the long run participants will actually be helped by giving the plan some breathing space.

The IRS considers factors such as:

- If the waiver is the only way to continue the plan
- If the employer has an operating loss
- Conditions within the employer's industry.

If the IRS grants the application, part or all of the funding deficiency is waived for the year. (If the amount in question is substantial, the employer may have to provide security to the plan.) However, the IRS lacks the power to waive amortization of funding deficiencies that were waived in earlier years.

Yet another relief measure is extension of amortization. The IRS can grant up to ten additional years to amortize items such as unfunded past service liability and net experience losses. To grant this relief, the IRS must conclude that the extension carries out the purposes of ERISA, and that participants and beneficiaries receive adequate protection—in fact, they would be harmed in the long run if the extension is NOT granted, because there is a substantial risk of plan termination or substantial curtailment of pension benefit levels absent the extension.

Note that ERISA §302(c) provides that a defined benefit plan that is subject to PBGC termination insurance must get IRS approval to change its actuarial assumptions, if all of the employer's plans (and all plans of its controlled group) have an aggregate unfunded benefit in excess of $50,000,000, or the proposed change in assumptions decreases the unfunded current liability by $50 million or more for the current plan year (or more than $5 million, representing more than 5% of the current liability).

Plans can't have it both ways. If they are granted minimum funding relief (other than a change of funding methods), as long as the relief continues the plan is limited in its ability to adopt plan changes that increase benefits, change benefit accrual, or change the rate at which benefits become nonforfeitable. See Code §412(f).

Nonetheless, amendments are permitted if the IRS agrees that they are reasonable and increase plan liabilities only by a minimal amount, if they are actually required for the plan to remain qualified, or if the amendment merely repeals one that would have retroactively decreased accrued benefits under the plan.

13.8.7 Quarterly Payments

The employer has to be concerned about the schedule on which funding payments are made, not just the amount of the payments. Defined benefit plans that fall under Code §412 or ERISA §302 have a duty to make quarterly payments to fund the plan liability: §412(m)(1). For calendar-year plans, the due dates are April 15, July 15, October 15, and January 15 of the following year (i.e., not the same dates as the corporation's estimated income tax payments). Fiscal year plans modify this schedule—e.g., if the plan's fiscal year ends on March 31, the dates are advanced by three months because the fiscal year ends three months later than the calendar year.

This obligation is waived if the funded current liability percentage for the prior plan year was 100% or greater (i.e., if the plan was fully funded). If and when payments are required, they follow rules very much like the rules for estimated tax payments. The payments for the year must either add up to 90% of the §412 funding liability for the current year, or 100% of the funding liability for the previous year (whichever is smaller).

As noted on page 255, failure to make required contributions can give the plan a lien on all of the employer's assets, and the PBGC can get involved in collecting the lien.

Plans with 100 or more participants must calculate the payments to reflect any "liquidity shortfall," but it is not necessary to fund the plan beyond 100% of the funded current liability percentage, including any expected increase for benefits accruing in the current year. The liquidity shortfall is the "base amount" minus the plan's liquid assets on the last day of the quarter.

The base amount, in turn, is three times the total adjusted disbursements from the plan for the 12 months ending on the last day of the quarter. The plan's liquid assets are cash, marketing securities, and other assets specified by the IRS Regulations. Adjusted disbursements are distributions of benefits and payment of expenses, minus the total benefits distributed for the plan year multiplied by the funded current liability percentage.

13.8.8 Funding-Related Penalties

A plan whose funded current liability fell below the mandated 100% level in the preceding year, and whose employer fails to make a quarterly installment payment on time, is entitled to have the employer pay interest to the plan. The interest rate is the higher of the §412(b)(5) interest rate, or 175% of the federal mid-term rate (i.e., the rate the federal government pays on mid-term bonds and other government obligations). This interest payment is probably deductible on the employer's income tax return.

A plan with an "accumulated funding deficiency" is subject to an excise tax of 10% per year of this deficiency. The employer is responsible for paying this tax, and is not entitled to deduct it for income tax purposes. See Code §§275(a)(6) and 4971. If the deficiency is detected by the IRS, but is not corrected (by depositing enough money to eliminate the accumulated funding deficiency into the plan) pursuant to the IRS notice within 90 days, the penalty increases to a potential 100% of the deficiency. (If the employer chooses to appeal the notice of deficiency to the Tax Court, the deficiency doesn't have to be corrected until and unless the Tax Court rules against the employer and in favor of the IRS on this issue.) The IRS has the power to waive the 100% penalty.

To simplify the calculation somewhat, an accumulated funding deficiency exists if the plan's accounting "Charges to Account" exceed the "Credits to Account." If the plan is allowed to use an alternative minimum funding standard account in general, it can use it for this purpose also.

Everyone wants to get into the act: the IRS, DOL, and PBGC are all involved in assessment of the penalty. The IRS has to notify the DOL, which is allowed to "comment" on the proposed penalty. The DOL or PBGC can ask the IRS to investigate a company that might have incurred a 10% or 100% excise tax.

Code §4971 also imposes a 10% excise tax on plans that have a liquidity shortfall in any quarter. If a shortfall continues for five consecutive quarters, a 100% tax is theoretically imposed on the amount that should have been but was not paid. The 100% penalty can be reduced or waived at the discretion of the IRS, for plans that acted reasonably, absent willful neglect, and which took reasonable steps to clear the shortfall.

At the other end of the spectrum, §4972 imposes an excise tax, at the familiar 10% rate, on *excess* contributions to a qualified plan, defined as a contribution for the current year that exceeds the deductible amount, plus any excess contributions from the preceding year that remain in the plan.

> ⇒ **TIP**
>
> This penalty is not due on certain plans in their year of termination. Excise taxes on excess contributions are not charged on amounts that fall within the §4980(c)(2)(B)(ii) safe harbor—for instance, contributions that were made only because of a mistake of fact- as long as the excess amounts are removed from the plan before the last day that contributions could be deducted under §404(a)(6).

13.9 ACCOUNTING ISSUES FOR PENSION PLANS

Exploring plan accounting in full detail is beyond the scope of this book, but certain important issues should be mentioned. Above all, the plan administrator and HR department must be aware that corporate Generally Accepted Accounting Principles (GAAP) sometimes require income and costs to be reported and treated differently for accounting than for tax purposes. So it's not sufficient to collect and report information as required by the IRS and DOL; additional work may be required to properly account for plan costs on the company's income statement, balance sheets, securities law filings, and communications with stockholders.

Since 1985, the central documents in plan accounting have been the Financial Accounting Standards Board's (FASB) FAS 87 (pension accounting) and FAS 88 (accounting for termination benefits, settlements and curtailments of defined benefit plans).

FAS 87 and 88 apply to funded and unfunded executive deferred compensation plans as well as tax-qualified retirement plans. However, they do not apply to fully insured benefits (which are accounted for on a cash basis) or retiree health benefits (which are subject to FAS 106 instead; see page 197). Theoretically, FAS 87 applies to defined contribution plans, but the treatment of these plans is fairly straightforward; most of the problems relate to defined benefit plans.

ERISA gives plans six options to choose from for actuarial funding methods, but FAS 87 requires the use of a single method, the Projected Unit Credit (PUC) method. The expense of providing a pension plan is recognized over the working lifetime of each covered employee (although the benefits naturally begin after worklife ends). Benefits must be funded for each participant as they accrue. An estimate is made of the expected final pension the employee will receive; this amount is divided into one unit for each year of service. Units must be funded in the year to which they are credited.

"Service cost" is the fundamental FAS 87 concept. An employer's pension expense consists of service cost plus interest cost plus amortization, minus the return earned on the plan's assets. Service cost, in turn, is the PUC actuarial normal cost (the value of the pension benefit earned in the year under discussion). Interest cost is the plan's past service liability multiplied by the appropriate discount factor.

Amortization is the process of "stretching out" costs that cannot be deducted in one year. Under FAS 87, the basis for amortization consists of transition amounts (relating to the time the plan adopted FAS 87), prior service costs (when a plan is amended to change future benefits), and accumulated gains and losses that occur when the plan's investment returns are either higher or lower than the assumptions the plan used to project them.

FAS 87 provides "guideposts" for selecting assumptions (such as interest rates) to be used in plan accounting. FAS 87 takes the position that the plan's assumptions will change frequently to reflect changing conditions. This is the opposite tack to the one ERISA takes; for ERISA purposes, changes in funding assumptions are supposed to occur only in exceptional circumstances.

FAS 88's accounting rules center around plan terminations. In that situation, there is no future useful lifetime of the plan, so all items that are the subject of an amortization schedule must be recognized at one time. Various costs relating to the termination itself must also be recognized: for instance, irrevocable settlements of plan liabilities by paying out lump sums or buying annuities, and early retirement incentives.

13.10 ROUTINE TAX COMPLIANCE

Day-to-day administration of a plan involves creation of tax records and submission of numerous forms to the IRS and state taxing authorities. The forms include:

- W-2—for each individual employee, this lists the compensation paid. The form must be submitted to the IRS and also to the employee. The normal due date for employee W-2s is January 31 following the end of the year of employment, but employees who leave during the year have a right to demand that they receive a W-2 form within 30 days of the last paycheck (or of the request, if it is made at a later date). The employer can use Form 8809 to request additional time to file the W-2s.

- W-3—a transmittal form filed with the Social Security Administration with all of the W-2 and W-2P forms for the entire company. The regular due date for any year's W-3 is February 28 of the following year.

- W-4P is used by employees to opt out of withholding or increase withholding on their pension and annuity payments. (See page 104 for the withholding requirement.) This form is transmitted only between employer and employee; an IRS filing is not required.

- 941/941E—these are the forms for quarterly returns of federal income tax; 941 is used if there are FICA taxes withheld or paid, 941E otherwise. The due date is the end of the month after the close of the calendar quarter being reported on.

- 945—the report on withheld taxes that are not payroll taxes, such as withholding on retirement plan distributions.

- 1041—trust income tax return; required if the plan's trust becomes disqualified, or otherwise does not operate as a tax-exempt organization, and if it also has income equal to or greater than $600. The due date is the 15th day of the fourth month after the end of the trust's tax year.

- 1099-R—1099-series forms are used to report miscellaneous sums that might otherwise escape the attention of the taxing authorities. The 1099-R is used to report lump sum and periodic distributions. The entire group of a company's transmittal forms requires a transmittal form, 1096. The filing is due by February 28th each year for the preceding year.

⇒ **TIP**
_____

Within two weeks of making a distribution, the plan administrator must provide each recipient with a written explanation of the tax consequences of taking a lump sum, including how to elect lump sum tax treatment and how to roll over the sum to another qualified plan or to an IRA.

- 5308—when a qualified plan or trust changes its tax year, this form must be filed.

- 5330—the employer files this excise tax form when it fails to meet the minimum funding standard or when it receives an impermissible reversion of plan assets. Disqualified persons who engage in prohibited transactions are also required to file this form. There is no fixed due date; timing is based on the nature of the transaction subject to excise tax.

⇒ **TIP**
_____

Form 5558 is used to request additional time to file this form.

- 8109—the quarterly estimated tax return when a plan trust has unrelated business taxable income (UBTI). The form is the Federal Tax Deposit Coupon which the employer uses to identify the deposit made either to a Federal Reserve bank or to a commercial bank authorized to accept such deposits. Interest, at a rate of the short-term federal rate plus two percent, is required if quarterly installments are omitted.

Theoretically, businesses are supposed to report and pay their taxes electronically, rather than on paper, but the IRS has experienced significant difficulties in standardizing and implementing electronic filing. Under the rules, plan sponsors and plan administrators whose 1995 withholding tax liability exceeded $50,000 are supposed to have filed Form 9779, Application for the Electronic Federal Tax Payment System (EFTPS) and started electronic deposits no later than July 1, 1997.

However, on June 2, 1997, the IRS announced it would not penalize failure to file in electronic form before December 31, 1997. Two banks are responsible for coordinating the EFTPS program: the First National Bank of Chicago, (800) 945-8500, and Nationsbank, (800) 555-4477. See IRS Publication 966 for instructions for electronic filing.

13.10.1 UBTI

In most cases, the plan will be formally administered through the medium of a trust. Once again normally, the plan trust will be a tax-exempt organization. However, if the plan trust regularly carries on an unrelated trade or business, Code §512(a)(1) imposes a tax on the income from the unrelated trade or business (UBTI). The UBTI characterization is limited to net income from a business (after deducting the costs of producing the income); it does not include dividends, interest, annuities, loan fees, or royalties.

13.11 ROUTINE PBGC COMPLIANCE

The PBGC is formally organized as a corporation, but it's really a quasi-government agency that draws its powers from ERISA §4002. The PBGC's Board of Directors consists of the Secretaries of Labor, Treasury, and Commerce. The federal court system is supposed to grant the agency special deference: PBGC cases are supposed to get the earliest possible calendar dates, and part or all of the PBGC's litigation costs in plan termination cases can be assessed against the plan sponsor.

As discussed on page 304, the PBGC guarantees that participants in defined benefit plans will receive a "basic benefit" even if their plan is insufficiently funded or if it terminates. As a last resort, the PBGC can borrow from the Treasury to make good on this pledge, but the agency's general source of revenue is the premium paid by employers. The baseline premium is $19 per year per participant, with an additional premium of up to $53 per participant calculated based on the level of the plan's unfunded vested benefits.

The premium is due $8^1/_2$ months after the beginning of the plan year (note that most due dates are calculated from the end of a year), and is paid with Form 1-ES (if the plan has more than 500 participants) or with Form 10-SP (short form for smaller plans). The contributing sponsor and the plan administrator are both liable for the PBGC premium.

> ⇒ **TIP**
>
> Premiums should be mailed to the PBGC, Post Office Box 105655, Atlanta, GA, 30310, or to the NationsBank Retail Lockbox Processing Center, PBGC Lockbox 105655, 6000 Feldwood Road, 5 Southside East, College Park, GA, 30349.

If the premium is not paid on time, interest runs from the due date, plus a late charge of 5% per month (capped at 100% of the original unpaid premium). The penalty, but not the interest, can be averted by getting a waiver from the PBGC; the waiver extends the time to pay by up to 60 days: PBGC Regulations §4007.8(b). The PBGC is also empowered to collect unpaid premiums from what would otherwise be the employer's federal tax refund. If the employer is a federal contractor, the PBGC can seize federal contract payments.

> ⇒ **TIP**
>
> PBGC Proposed Regulations permit the penalty to be waived if payment is made within 30 days of the due date.

All defined benefit plans that are subject to PBGC insurance must file Form PBGC-1 each year as a combined annual report and declaration of premium payments.

When a defined benefit plan fails to satisfy the minimum funding standard (see page 255), and there has been no waiver of minimum funding granted, then participants must be notified. Form 200 must be filed with the PBGC within 10 days of the time a failure to meet the minimum funding standard involves $1 million or more.

13.12 REPORTABLE EVENTS

The PBGC doesn't want to be caught by surprise when a plan fails. To this end, plan administrators have a duty to report unusual events to the PBGC that might eventually require it to make insurance payments. Depending on the seriousness of the event, the PBGC might merely maintain a watchful attitude; or it might seek the appointment of a temporary trustee to manage the plan, or even go to the appropriate federal District Court and seek authority to terminate the plan.

The PBGC Regulations list 17 reportable events. Some of them must be reported 30 days *before* the event occurs; others may be reported retroactively:

- The plan's bankruptcy or insolvency
- The sponsoring employer's bankruptcy or insolvency

- The sponsoring employer or a member of its controlled group of corporations liquidates under the Bankruptcy Code or any similar law
- Notice from the IRS that the plan has ceased to be a qualified retirement plan
- An IRS determination that the plan has terminated or partially terminated
- Failure to meet the minimum funding standard—or even receiving a minimum funding waiver from the IRS
- The plan's inability to pay benefits as they come due
- A DOL determination that the plan fails to comply with ERISA Title I
- Adoption of a plan amendment that has the effect of decreasing any participant's retirement benefit (except for certain decreases relating to Social Security integration)
- Reducing the number of active participants in the plan, so that the number is below 80% of the census at the beginning of the year, or 75% of the number of active participants at the beginning of the preceding plan year
- Distributing $10,000 or more to a participant who is a "substantial owner" (basically, a 10% shareholder in the employer corporation) if, after the distribution, the plan has any unfunded, non-forfeitable benefits. (Distributions made on account of the death of the substantial owner don't count for this purpose.)
- The plan's merger, consolidation, or transfer of its assets
- Having the DOL prescribe an alternative method of compliance under ERISA §110
- A change of plan sponsor (or the same plan sponsor leaving a controlled group of corporations), if the plan has $1 million or more in unfunded non-forfeitable benefits
- A "person" involved with the plan leaving a controlled group of corporations
- The controlling sponsor, or a member of its controlled group, engages in a highly unusual transaction, such as declaring an extraordinary dividend or redeeming 10% or more of its stock
- Within a 12-month period, a total of 3% or more of the plan's benefit liabilities are transferred outside the sponsor's controlled group (whether or not the transferee is another plan).

Initially, the sponsoring employer had a duty to report the events to the plan administrator, but now it is only mandatory to report the events to the PBGC.

Under ERISA §4043, advance notice is required of liquidating bankruptcy, extraordinary dividends, transfer of 3% of plan liabilities, and leaving the controlled group.

Chapter 14

PLAN DISCLOSURE

14.1 INTRODUCTION

ERISA does not require corporations to maintain plans at all, but if they do, they must conform to numerous rules, including rules of procedure. Furthermore, they must communicate with plan participants so they can understand their benefits and particularly any benefits which are available in multiple forms and for which informed choices must be made (e.g., choosing between lump sum and annuity forms of pension payout).

The primary communication mechanism is the Summary Plan Description (SPD), although other documents may also be required (e.g., when the terms of the plan are altered).

If the plan is materially modified, or if there are changes in the information given in the SPD, the plan administrator has a duty to give participants and beneficiaries a Summary of Material Modifications (SMM).

In addition to documents given to them, participants and beneficiaries have a right to inspect other plan documents.

14.2 SUMMARY PLAN DESCRIPTION (SPD)

The SPD must be understandable, accurate, and comprehensive, and must disclose (not omit or play down) exceptions or limitations to the availability of plan benefits. The information in the SPD must be accurate as of 120 days before the date the SPD is released.

ERISA requires the following items to be included in the SPD:

- The formal and common names of the plan

- The name and address of the employer (or of the organization maintaining the plan, if it is a collectively bargained plan)
- The employer's EIN and the plan's number issued by the IRS
- What kind of plan it is
- How the plan is administered, e.g., by contract or by an insurer
- The name, address, and telephone number of the plan administrator
- The name and address of the agent for service of process (the person designated to receive summonses, complaints, subpoenas, and related litigation documents)
- A statement that process can be served not only on this designated agent, but also on the plan's administrator or trustee
- The name, address, and title of each trustee
- Disclosure of whether the plan is a collectively bargained plan, as well as a statement that the participant can examine the collective bargaining agreement or get a copy of the agreement from the plan administrator
- Rules of eligibility for participation
- The plan's normal retirement age
- Circumstances under which plan benefits can be altered or suspended
- How to waive the normal payment mechanism (the qualified joint and survivor annuity)
- A clear description of the circumstances under which the plan can be terminated, the rights of participants and beneficiaries after termination occurs, and the circumstances under which benefits can be denied or suspended
- If the plan benefits are insured by the PBGC; if they are not, the reason why insurance is not required; if they are, a disclosure that PBGC insurance is in place, how it works, and where to get more information (from the plan administrator or the PBGC; the PBGC's address must be given in the SPD)
- An explanation of the plan's rules for determining service to calculate vesting and breaks in service
- The procedure for amending and terminating the plan

⟶ TIP

If, as usually happens, the sponsoring corporation retains the power to amend the plan, and chooses to amend, it's vital to make sure that the necessary corporate governance steps (such as having the Board of Directors adopt a resolution) be taken.

- Where the contributions to the plan come from: exclusively from the employer, or are employee contributions accepted or mandated?
- Method of calculating the amount to be contributed; for a defined benefit plan, it's OK just to say that the amount is "actuarially determined"
- The funding medium and entity for the plan—usually a trust fund, but sometimes an insurance company
- The plan's fiscal year
- How to present a claim for plan benefits
- If the plan will use the "cutback" rule to change the vesting or accrual rules described in the SPD, participants must be informed which provisions of the plan are subject to modification; when modified, the nature of the modifications must be explained
- Remedies that are available if a claim is denied
- A statement of the rights of participants and beneficiaries, and what protections are available for those rights. You can find a model statement in 29 CFR §2520.102-3.

➡ TIP

If benefits are different for different groups of employees, it's OK to have a separate SPD for each group.

SPDs must be given to participants and beneficiaries within 90 days after they achieve that status. For a new plan, all participants get an SPD 120 days after the plan becomes subject to ERISA reporting and disclosure requirements.

How can SPDs be distributed to employees? The best methods are handing the SPDs to the employees at the workplace, or mailing them to employees' homes. It isn't enough to stack them in the workplace, because there's no guarantee that employees will take them.

The SPD can also be distributed as an insert in an employee periodical, such as one published by the company or the union. If you choose this option, be sure to put a prominent notice on the front page of the periodical stating that this issue contains an insert that has important legal consequences, and that should be retained for reference, not discarded.

➡ TIP

The statement of participant rights required by ERISA can be incorporated into the SPD.

14.2.1 Updated SPD

If the plan is amended at all (and it probably will be!), every five years (measured from the time the plan first became subject to ERISA) the plan administrator must issue an updated SPD that reflects the changes of the past five years. In fact, even if there are no changes at all, every 10 years (also measured from initial ERISA coverage) the administrator must issue an updated SPD to all participants. Probably the theory behind this requirement is that many corporations have plenty of long-stay employees, and nobody can be expected to remember where they kept the plan booklet for a decade at a time.

ERISA §104(b)(1)(B) requires that plan participants and beneficiaries be notified within 60 days of a material reduction in the services provided under an Employer Group Health Plan (EGHP). As an alternative, the plan's sponsor can simply provide notices at regular intervals, not more than 90 days apart, of changes in the interim. The SPD for an EGHP (as distinct from a pension plan SPD) must indicate if a health insurer is responsible for financing or administration (including claims payment). If an insurer is involved, the insurer's name and address must appear in the SPD.

⇒ **TIP**

If this requirement is unfamiliar to you, it could be because you've been working in this area for a while; this requirement took effect June 30, 1997.

14.2.2 False Statements

If the SPD contains any false statements, this constitutes a violation of the ERISA disclosure regulations, and the employer (or other sponsor) might get into a tangle with the Department of Labor.

⇒ **TIP**

If any employees bring a suit involving the plan provisions, another risk is that the court will declare that the SPD is confusing and therefore must be interpreted in favor of the employees, because the employer is responsible for the confusion and can't be allowed to benefit from it.

Why does it matter what the SPD says, when it comes to construing the plan? Because generally speaking, plan participants see the SPD but never see the full plan document. So, as far as the employees are concerned, the SPD is the major means for getting information about how the plan operates.

> ⇒ **TIP**
>
> According to a 1994 case, an employer that distributes plan literature is considered to have discretionary authority in plan administration. That makes the employer at least potentially liable for affirmative misrepresentations that appear in the documents.

14.2.3 1997 Disclosure Changes

The Taxpayer Relief Act of 1997, effective August 5, 1997, reduces the amount of paperwork that the plan administrator has to process. Prior to that date, plan administrators had to submit copies of SPDs and SMMs with the Secretary of Labor. The TRA eliminates routine filing of these documents (although they must still be given to plan participants). The Secretary of Labor has the right to demand copies of particular plans' SPDs and SMMs, and the administrator must submit the documents within 30 days or face a civil penalty of up to $100 per day, capped at $1,000 per request. The penalty is waived if factors beyond the plan administrator's reasonable control prevent submission of the documents.

14.3 SUMMARY ANNUAL REPORT (SAR)

One of the administrator's more onerous tasks is preparing the plan's annual report, using a form from the Form 5500 series. But doing this does not completely discharge the duty. Summary Annual Reports (SARs) must be distributed under the same rules as SPDs.

The administrator has nine months from the end of the plan year (or two years after the end of the extension, if an extension was granted for filing the underlying 5500-series form): 29 CFR §2520.104b-10. But the administrator definitely doesn't have to worry about being William Shakespeare, or even being able to write a note to the milkman: the DOL regulations (at 29 CFR §2520.104b-10(d)) contain a simple "fill-in-the-blanks" form whose use is mandatory. (It's not mandatory to fill out the entire form; inapplicable portions can simply be left blank.)

The form consists of a basic financial statement about the plan (including the plan's expenses), the net value of plan assets, and whether the plan's assets appreciated or depreciated in value during the year. If the plan is subject to minimum funding standards, the plan must disclose either that contributions were adequate to satisfy the requirement, or the amount of the deficit. Participants must also be informed of their right to receive additional information, including a copy of the full annual report, a statement of the plan's assets and liabilities, or a statement of the plan's income and expenses.

➠ **TIP**

Plans that have simplified reporting requirements can use alternative compliance methods to satisfy the SAR requirement.

Certain plans are not required to furnish SARs:

- Welfare plans that are totally unfunded
- Small welfare plans that are either unfunded or insured
- Top-hat plans
- Pension or welfare plans that are financed by employee dues and not employer contributions
- Day care centers.

These are also plans with limited reporting requirements, so it makes sense that if they are excused from the comprehensive report, they are also excused from the report summary.

14.4 OTHER NOTICES

1. Notice of Deferred Benefits   Frequently an employee will leave for one reason or another (technically, this is known as separation from service) at a time when he or she is entitled to a deferred vested benefit, but is not yet entitled to a retirement pension. Everyone in that situation is entitled to a notice containing:

- The name and address of the plan administrator
- The nature, form, and amount of the deferred benefit for which the person is eligible
- An explanation of any benefits that are forfeitable if the employee dies before a certain date.

The schedule must be delivered no later than the date Schedule SSA is to be filed with the IRS.

> ⮕ **TIP**
>
> An IRS penalty of $50 per erroneous statement or willful failure to furnish a statement can be imposed.

Thirty to ninety days before the annuity start date of a benefit that is immediately distributable before the participant reaches 62 or normal retirement age, the participant must also be given notice of any right he or she has to defer distribution. See Reg. §1.411(a)-11(c)(2).

2. Withholding Certificate   Before a plan makes a distribution that is not an eligible rollover distribution, the plan must send the participant IRS Form W-4P, Withholding Certificate for Pension or Annuity Payments. The W-4P informs the participant of the choices he or she can make about withholding:

- Elect against federal income tax withholding on the distribution
- Direct withholding based on marital status or number of allowances
- Increase withholding on periodic payments (e.g., if the participant has extensive outside income and might otherwise owe a large balance at the end of the tax year).

3. Break in Service Notice   As you can see from the discussion on page 230, ERISA's break in service rules are complex, even for a skilled administrator. The difficulties posed to participants are easy to imagine! Therefore, participants have the right to make a written request (although only one request per year) when they are separated from service, or have a one-year break in service. The notice defines their accrued benefits under the plan, and the percentage of the benefits that is nonforfeitable.

4. Notice of Claims Denial   Within 90 days after a claim is filed (or other reasonable time), the participant and beneficiary(ies) must be given a detailed written notice explaining exactly why the claims were denied.

5. Notice of Amendment   If a plan amendment has the effect of reducing future benefit accruals (amendments are not allowed to tamper with benefits already accrued), then participants and beneficiaries must be given notice at least 15 days before the amendment's effective date.

6. Rollover Notice   Not more than 90, and not less than 30, days before making a distribution, the plan administrator must notify the participant of the potential consequences of receiving a distribution that could be made the subject of a rollover. The notice should inform participants that they can have the distribution sent right to an IRA, or to another qualified plan that will accept it.

Participants must be warned about the 20% withholding that will be imposed on all taxable distributions that are neither rolled over nor transferred—and that the sums that are received are taxable in the year of receipt. They must also be told that they can roll over the distribution within 60 days of its receipt to an IRA or to another qualified plan. The notice must also provide information about capital gains treatment of lump sums, and about the limited continuing availability of five-year averaging for lump sums.

IRS Form 1099-R is used to report the taxable amount from a designated distribution (taxable benefits that are subject to withholding).

7. QJSA/QPSA Notice Not more than 90, but at least 30 days before receipt of benefits, if the plan (like most plans) permits payouts in annuity form, all participants must get a statement. The statement must be written in easily understandable terms. All participants are entitled to the statement, even if they are not vested. See Code §417(a)(3), Reg. §1.401(a)(11), and 1.417(e)-1(b)(3). The contents of the notice should be:

- The terms and conditions of the joint and survivor annuity
- The participant's right to waive the annuity, including a description of the consequences of the waiver
- Rights of the participant's spouse
- Description of the right to revoke the election, and consequences of the revocation.

A comparable explanation must be given of the Qualified Preretirement Survivor Annuity. The timing requirement is more complicated here. The notice is due by the latest of these:

- The period that begins on the first day of the plan year in which the participant reaches age 32, and ends at the end of the plan year before the participant reaches 35
- A reasonable time after a person becomes a plan participant. (A "reasonable period" is deemed to mean a year after an event occurs)
- A reasonable time after the employer stops subsidizing the survivor benefit (see below)
- A reasonable time after the Code §401(a)(11) survivor benefit provisions become applicable to the participant, which might happen, for example, if a single or divorced person gets married and therefore acquires a spouse who could get a QPSA

- A reasonable time after separation from service. If the employee leaves before he or she is 35, then the period runs from one year before to one year after the separation.

> ⮕ **TIP**
>
> Plans are permitted to accept waivers at earlier stages (as long as the spouse consents). But the plan must give the participant a written explanation of how QPSAs work. Furthermore, the waiver becomes void at the beginning of the plan year in which the participant reaches age 35. If a new waiver is not signed, and the participant dies before retirement age, then the spouse gets a QPSA despite the attempt to waive this form of benefit.

A plan can skip the notice of the right to waive the QPSA/QJSA if the benefit is fully subsidized by the plan, and the participant can neither waive the QPSA/QJSA nor name a person other than a spouse as beneficiary. The benefit is fully subsidized if *not* waiving the QPSA/QJSA neither lowers the benefit nor results in higher costs for the participant.

8. Notice of Termination   Between 60 and 180 days before the scheduled date of a standard or distress termination (see page 303 for a discussion of plan termination), the administrator must give written notice to the parties affected.

For a standard termination, the written notice must be drafted in understandable language. It must disclose the amount and form of the benefit due as of the proposed termination date, and must explain how the benefit was calculated (e.g., length of service, participant's age, interest rate and other assumptions, and any other factors that the PBGC requires to be disclosed).

9. QDRO Notices   The general rule is that no one can garnish or otherwise get hold of plan benefits before they are paid. The exception to the rule is that a plan administrator not only can but must obey court orders that direct part of the benefit to the participant's separated or divorced spouse. However, not every divorce-related order is considered a Qualified Domestic Relations Order (QDRO).

Therefore, once a court order is delivered to the plan, Code §414(p) obligates the administrator to review it to see if it is qualified. The plan participant and the alternate payee (nearly always the spouse) must be notified that the plan has received an order, and what the plan will do to assess its qualification. Then the administrator carries out that procedure, and sends another notice to the participant and alternate payee if the order has been determined to be qualified and therefore must be obeyed by the plan.

> ⇒ **TIP**
>
> These notices should be sent to the addresses given in the court order; if there is no address, they should be sent to the last known address on file for the employee and alternate payee.

10. Notices re Funding Problems   If the plan is underfunded, ERISA §4011 generally requires the administrator to notify participants and beneficiaries of the funding standards and the limitations on the PBGC's guarantee of payment of benefits. A model notice that can be used for this purpose can be found at 29 CFR §§2627.1–.9. The notice must be given within two months of the plan's deadline (the extended deadline, if an extension has been obtained) for filing its annual report for the prior plan year. Certain plans are exempt from delivering this notice, even if they are underfunded:

- A new plan, in its first year of being subject to PBGC coverage
- Plans that are not required to make ERISA §302(d)(2) deficit reduction contributions because they are relieved of this requirement by §302(d)(9).

ERISA §502(c)(3) states that failure to give this notice can be penalized up to $110 a day, or whatever relief the court hearing the case deems proper. (The amount was $100 a day, but for violations after July 29, 1997, it was increased by the Pension and Welfare Benefits Administration. See 62 *Federal Register* 40696, 7/29/97.)

14.5 DISCLOSURE ON REQUEST

In addition to disclosures that must be made to all participants and/or beneficiaries in a specific situation, ERISA and the Code call for disclosures that must be made on request by a particular participant or beneficiary.

> ⇒ **TIP**
>
> If a request is made, the information should be mailed within 30 days to the last known address for the individual making the request. Material that can be requested includes:

- A complete copy of the latest annual report (5500 series)
- The plan instrument (e.g., CBA or trust agreement)

- The latest updated SPD
- Report on termination of the plan
- Statement of accrued benefits (but the administrator has to furnish this only once in every 12-month period)
- Percentage of vesting; if the participant is not fully vested, the schedule on which full vesting will occur.

The plan is permitted to make a reasonable charge for this information, which is one based on the least expensive available means of reproducing the documents.

The plan description, latest annual report, and plan documents must also be kept on file for participants who want to inspect them. They must be made available at the plan administrator's principal office. The documents must also be made available for review at the employer's principal office and at each of the employer's locations where 50 or more employees work, if there is a request to provide them.

⇒ **TIP**

If the plan fails to make a required disclosure within 30 days of a document request, a civil fine of up to $100 per day (starting from the date of the failure or refusal to disclose) can be imposed. In fact, if the violation is willful, criminal penalties of up to $100,000 can be imposed on entities, and individuals can be fined up to $5,000 and/or imprisoned for up to a year.

14.6 ANNUAL REPORTS

Qualified plans must report each year to the IRS, DOL, and PBGC so that these agencies can monitor plan operations and determine if they remain qualified, are financially sound, and are operated in accordance with all applicable requirements.

The report is made on one of the IRS forms in the 5500 series. Most readers of this book will use the basic Form 5500, which covers plans with 100 or more participants. Smaller plans can use the less complex, easier-to-complete 5500-C/R or 5500-EZ. A plan with under 100 participants at the beginning of the plan year is required to file Form 5500-C for its first plan year, the year of its final annual report, and any year in which it does not file a Form 5500-R.

> ⇒ **TIP**
>
> Only one filing is necessary; the IRS transmits the necessary information to the DOL and PBGC.

Code §6039, which can be satisfied by the 5500 filing, requires employers to disclose: employer's name, address, Taxpayer Identification Number, and line of business; the number of its employees; the number of employees eligible for plan participation; the number of employees actually participating; and the total plan cost.

Like the familiar 1040 and 1120 forms, the 5500-series forms often require that Schedules be completed and attached to the basic form to give more details about line items. For the 5500 series, important schedules include:

- A: insurance information
- B: actuarial information
- C: disclosures about trustees and service providers
- E: ESOP data
- F: annual information return about fringe benefits
- G: financial schedules
- P: fiduciary annual return of an employee benefits trust
- SSA, annual statement identifying the separated plan participants who are entitled to deferred vested benefits.

The annual report covers four main subjects: the plan's financial statements, actuarial data, administrative data, and information about any insured benefits provided by an insurance company.

14.6.1 The Annual Report in Detail

The major line items on Form 5500 include:

- Lines 1-7: administrative information such as the name of the plan, the name and address of its administrator, the number of participants, and how many participants are nonvested, partially vested, or fully vested.
- 8–10: plan status (has a merger, consolidation, amendment, or termination occurred?)
- 11: funding type (if the plan is insured, Schedule A must be attached to disclose the premiums, benefits paid, commissions paid, and amount held to pay future benefits)

- 15: funding standards. Some plans must file Schedule B, prepared and certified by an enrolled actuary, to provide actuarial information about the plan.

- 16: whether the plan observes the requirement that only $160,000 of compensation be taken into account for any given individual

- 21: information about plan coverage and qualification

- 22: if the plan is supposed to be qualified under Code §401(a); if so, the date of the IRS determination letter

- 25a: details about all individuals receiving $5,000 or more for providing services to the plan. Plan employees who earn less than $1,000 a month don't have to be listed here

- 25c-g: changes in identity of the plan's service providers. Schedule C, part III may have to be completed to flesh out this information.

- 27: reportable items such as transactions that might be questionable.

⇒ TIP

Schedule G or other financial schedule satisfying the DOL regulations found at 29 CFR §2520.103-10 must be filed to flesh out Line 27. An opinion from an independent qualified public accountant must also be filed, unless the annual report is for an unfunded plan or some insured plans. See the AICPA's guide, "Audits of Employee Benefit Plans," for details about the auditor's-eye-view of plan operations.

⇒ TIP

Item 28 asks about changes that result from material disputes or disagreements with service providers, in case a provider resigned because of improprieties in plan administration. Also, if a plan fires an accountant or enrolled actuary, the financial expert must be notified of his or her right to contact the DOL and register an explanation of the termination on the record.

- 29: information about the plan's bonding

- 30: disclosure of whether or not the plan is covered by PBGC termination insurance

- 31-32: detailed financial information (balance sheet and income statement for both the beginning and end of the year; net assets; changes in financial position; and change in the net assets available to pay plan benefits.

14.6.2 Due Date

The annual report is due at the end of the seventh month following the end of the plan year. If it appears that the plan will not be able to complete the annual report in time, it should file IRS Form 5558, Application for Extension of Time to File Certain Employee Plan Returns, to get an extension of up to $2^1/_2$ months. It will be granted automatically, until the due date for the employer's income tax return, as long as the plan year is the same as the employer's tax year, the income tax deadline has been extended to a date after the normal due date for the Form 5500, and a copy of the income tax extension is attached to the plan's 5500-series form.

In June, 1997, the IRS and the Pension and Welfare Benefit Administration announced an initiative to redesign the 5500-series forms, removing some items that are not legally mandated and are not necessary to monitor pension and health benefits. The paper form will be reprinted so that it can be scanned electronically, and electronic filing (currently available but little-used) will be promoted. The agencies also seek funding for a "help desk" to assist filers. The new form will probably be adopted early in 1998 for use in reporting the events of the 1998 plan year.

Under current law, the IRS divides the forms among three processing centers (with a fourth for the 5500-EZ short form); the proposal calls for outsourcing the processing to a single private firm with centralized operations.

14.7 MISCELLANEOUS REPORTING REQUIREMENTS

For pension plans and other plans subject to the ERISA Title I, Part 3 vesting requirements, Code §6057 requires annual reporting on Form SSA.

As a general rule, plans that are administered in trust form are not taxable entities. However, if the plan trust has Unrelated Business Taxable Income (UBTI), IRS Form 990-T must be filed to report the UBTI.

Even though contributions cease to be made, or benefits cease to be accrued, annual reports must still be filed if the plan is not terminated. See IRS Publication 1048.

14.8 EXCEPTIONS TO THE REPORTING REQUIREMENTS

ERISA §104(a)(1) provides that certain welfare benefit plans need not file an annual report: plans that are fully insurance-funded, and those that make all their payments from the employer's general assets rather than from a specialized plan trust.

But for plan years beginning on or after January 1, 1989, Form 5500-series forms *are* required of fringe benefit plans such as group term life insurance plans, accident and health plans, and dependent care assistance plans (Code §6039D).

14.9 PENALTIES FOR NONCOMPLIANCE

A civil penalty of up to $1,100 per day can be imposed, under ERISA §502(c)(2), for failure to file the 5500-series form. First, the DOL sends written notice to the plan administrator that the agency intends to assess a penalty, why the agency believes a penalty is due, and the period of time involved. Receipt of the notice gives the administrator 30 days to submit a written response showing that there was reasonable cause not to file.

➡ TIP

If the 30 days elapse without this statement being submitted, the administrator has waived the right to appear and contest the DOL penalty. If the statement is submitted, the DOL has the right to get a hearing by an Administrative Law Judge.

ERISA §502 also imposes a penalty of $110 per day when a plan administrator refuses to comply with a participant's or beneficiary's request for information that ERISA gives them access to. When a reporting or disclosure failure occurs but does not cause harm to participants, if the case ever gets to court, the court might order equitable relief, such as an injunction against further failures, but might reject the option of monetary damages. Under certain circumstances, reporting and disclosure failures might also be treated as breaches of fiduciary duty.

Effective August 11, 1997, the ERISA §4071 penalty for failure to provide notices or material information required by law or Regulation was increased from $1,000 to $1,100. The penalty for failure to furnish information, or to keep proper records, is $11 per day per employee.

Last but certainly not least, it should be noted that under 18 United States Code §1027 (not part of ERISA), a fiduciary, employer, or even a plan participant can be subject to criminal penalties for making false statements or concealing facts in any ERISA-mandated document.

The DOL's Delinquent Filer Voluntary Compliance Program can reduce the civil penalties that would otherwise be imposed on plan administrators who filed late when the plan sponsor failed to file timely annual reports for years beginning on or after January 1, 1988. However, the administrator must approach the DFVC program before being detected by the DOL as a late filer. Furthermore, protection under this program is limited: the IRS can still impose penalties on the administrators of pension plans (but not of welfare benefit plans) if filings are omitted.

14.10 DISCLOSURE CALENDAR

For a calendar-year plan that has undergone a material modification, the SMM must be sent to participants and beneficiaries by July 27 of the following year; fiscal-year plans have until the 210th day after the end of the plan year.

The 5500-series form is due on July 31 for calendar-year plans, and on the last day of the seventh month of the plan year after the plan year being reported.

This is also the due date for individual statements of deferred vested benefits, to be sent to plan participants whose employment terminated during the plan year and who had deferred vested benefits at the time of termination.

For defined benefit plans only, the PBGC Form 1 is due on September 15 (calendar year plans) or eight-and-a-half months after the close of the plan year being reported on. For all plans, the Summary Annual Report must be given to participants and beneficiaries by September 30 (or the last day of the ninth month of the plan year after the plan year in question). That is also the date that participants and beneficiaries of defined-benefit plans that are less than 90% funded should be given notice of the plan's funding status and the limits on the PBGC guarantee.

Distributions From the Plan

15.1 INTRODUCTION

One of the major tasks of plan administration is distributing plan benefits on the correct schedule and in the correct amounts. Of course, from the participants' point of view, this is the entire rationale of the plan, and participants are often unaware of the sheer amount of hard work that goes on behind the scenes.

Most defined contribution plans, and some defined benefit plans, permit participants to receive their benefits in the form of a single lump sum (or distributions of several lump sums) which the participant can elect to receive at or after the earliest date annuity payments could begin under the terms of the plan.

Participants cannot be forced to take a lump sum unless their balance is so small ($5,000 or less; before the Taxpayer Relief Act of 1997, the amount was $3,500 or less) that it is more economical for the plan to cash them out than to make continuing structured payments. A Proposed Regulation, §1.402(e)-2(e)(3), says that an employee must put in at least five full years of plan participation before taking a lump sum pension payout.

> **➠ TIP**
>
> Plans that offer lump sums should specify whether early retirement subsidies can be built into the lump sum, or whether they have to be received in annuity form.

> **➠ TIP**
>
> The plan administrator's duties include notifying participants of the various payment options available under the plan, and how to elect a payment method other than the standard life or joint life annuity form.

Generally speaking, defined contribution plans take care of their distribution responsibilities by using the contents of the employee's account to buy a commercial annuity for the appropriate term (which is usually the employee's life or the joint lives of employee and spouse). However, the plan might undertake payments itself in the simpler case of an annuity for a term of years (e.g., 10, 20) where the plan's financial exposure is more predictable.

> **➠ TIP**
>
> DOL Interpretive Bulletin 95-1 (adopted after a number of pension plans ran into trouble with defaulting Guaranteed Insurance Contracts (GICs)) says that choosing the annuity payer is a fiduciary decision, and includes a list of criteria that plan administrators must use in making the choice.

It is also common for defined benefit plans to buy annuities, although some plans prefer to handle the distributions in-house to save some fees. In that situation, the plan is at risk if participants live longer than anticipated, because the payments will be greater than the amount the plan expected to pay.

15.2 QJSA/QPSA PAYMENTS

For a married plan participant, the normal method of paying plan benefits is as a QJSA (Qualified Joint and Survivor Annuity); for an unmarried participant, the normal method is a single-life annuity.

A QJSA is payable for the lives of both the employee and his or her spouse. Once the first spouse dies, the plan can reduce the annuity payable to the survivor, although it cannot be reduced to less than 50% of the initial payment. Employers can also choose to subsidize the survivor annuity at some level between 50% and 100% of the initial joint annuity payment.

The normal payment method for a profit sharing plan or stock bonus plan is the lump sum, not the QJSA or other periodic payment. However, when a participant in a profit sharing or stock bonus plan dies, the entire vested balance remaining in his or her account must go to the participant's designated beneficiary.

Furthermore, a married participant must designate the spouse as beneficiary unless the spouse consents in writing to a different beneficiary being named.

Single-life annuities and QJSAs are not the only periodic payment options that plans can offer. They can also offer annuities for a term of years (such as 10 or 20), and/or life annuities with or without a term certain guarantee. But plans are required to offer QJSAs and single life annuities; the other payment options are, indeed, options.

Furthermore, if a participant is married, the payment must be made in QJSA form unless the employee's spouse consents to payment in a form other than QJSA. The size of each annuity payment fluctuates depending on the amount of risk the plan is taking: the more payments the plan is required or is likely to make, the smaller each payment will be. Some married couples may want to increase the amount of the pension payment, especially if they have ample life insurance on the employee spouse's life, so the absence of a survivor annuity, or reduced payments after one spouse's death, will be less of a hardship.

Because of a 1984 law called the Retirement Equity Act, the employee spouse cannot make a choice to take a non-QJSA payment form without a spousal waiver. This must be in writing, must be made within a period beginning 90 days before, and ending 30 days before, the annuity start date (the first day of the employee spouse's first benefit period under the plan), and must either be notarized or witnessed by a representative of the pension plan.

⇒ **TIP**

IRC §417 provides that the QJSA can be waived only during that 60-day window, not, for instance, when the employee is first hired.

Technically, the QJSA need not be provided unless the participant was married for one year or more before plan payments begin (see §417(d)), with an exception to the exception if a participant gets married during the year before benefit payments begin and stays married for one year. In practice, the plan usually offers a QJSA to everyone who is married at the time of retirement, irrespective of the duration of the marriage.

A Qualified Preretirement Survivor Annuity (QPSA) must also be provided if a vested plan participant dies before benefits begin. The QPSA for a person who was eligible to retire with a defined benefit pension at the time of death must be equal to or greater than the amount the spouse would have received by retiring with the QJSA on the day before he or she actually died.

The calculation is different if the decedent was not eligible for retirement when he or she died. In that case, the plan has to calculate the survivor annuity that the surviving spouse would have been entitled to on the date of death—but based on the assumption that the employee had separated from service on that date, but did not die but instead survived to the plan's earliest retirement date. The calculation must further assume that the employee retired on that date with a QJSA, but died the following day. The QPSA must be at least equal to the survivor annuity calculated based on all those assumptions.

The QPSA for a defined contribution plan must be actuarially equivalent to at least 50% of the account balance in which the participant had nonforfeitable rights at the time of death. Although the relevant IRC section, 417(c)(2), does not make it clear, the plan participant probably has the right to designate any beneficiary he or she chooses for the other 50%, and the surviving spouse does not have to consent to the designation and cannot veto the employee spouse's choice.

Qualified plans are allowed to reduce their pension benefits to fund the QPSA. Participants (with consent of their spouses, if they are married) must be given the right to waive the QPSA in order to prevent their pensions from being reduced accordingly.

> **➠ TIP**
>
> Pension plans are subject to Code §412. Those deferred compensation plans that are not subject to §412 and do not have to provide a QPSA nevertheless must pay the balance in the account of a married participant to the participant's surviving spouse, unless the surviving spouse waives (or unless the balance was distributed before the death).

> **➠ TIP**
>
> See IRS Notice 97-10, 1997-2 IRB 40, for sample language that can be used by a spouse to consent to waiver of the QJSA or QPSA. (The waiver might be desired in order to increase the current payments, especially if it is anticipated that the non-employee spouse will have adequate funds, from insurance and other sources, after the death of the employee spouse.)

15.3 TIMING OF PAYOUT

Unless the participant elects otherwise, payments from pension, annuity, profit sharing, and stock bonus plans are required to begin within 60 days after the end of whichever of these plan years is latest:

- The participant reaches age 65 (or normal retirement age, if that is set earlier than 65)

- The tenth year the employee has been a plan participant
- Termination of the employee's service with the company.

IRS Reg. §1.401(a)-14(b) allows the participant to delay the commencement of benefits by furnishing the plan administrator with a signed statement describing the benefit and the date on which payment is requested.

15.4 EXCISE TAXES

The basic tax rule is that employees have to pay income tax for each year on whatever they receive from the plan in that year. (That's why it's important for participants to be allowed to use income averaging to lessen the impact of a big lump sum on their tax liability.) Plan participants are discouraged from some courses of action that Congress thinks are unwise by having to pay excise taxes in addition to income tax on the same amounts.

Plan participants who get "premature" distributions must pay a 10% excise tax in addition to the normal income tax on the amounts they receive from the plan. The general rule is that premature distributions are those made before age $59\frac{1}{2}$. However, a distribution is not considered premature if it is made to an employee who has reached age 55 and separated from service. Distributions made after the employee's death are not subject to the 10% penalty. Neither are those made to employees who are sufficiently disabled to be incapable of engaging in any substantial gainful activity.

The premature distribution excise tax is also excused if the distribution is not a lump sum, but is made over the life, lives, or joint life expectancies of the participant or participant and beneficiaries. (Special, particularly complex rules apply to defined benefit plans in this situation.) Distributions made under a Qualified Domestic Relations Order (QDRO) are not subject to the excise tax. Finally, if a plan participant has medical expenses large enough to be deductible (higher than 7.5% of his or her adjusted gross income), plan distributions are not considered premature—even if, in fact, the participant does not use the distributions to pay medical bills.

⇒ TIP

If the participant made after-tax contributions to the plan, those contributions were not deductible when they were made. Therefore, the participant is allowed to calculate an exclusion ratio: he or she will not be taxed again on the part of the distribution that can be traced to those after-tax contributions.

Retirement plans are supposed to be used to meet the retiree's needs after leaving the workforce. Building an estate is only a secondary reason why qualified plans exist and are given favorable tax treatment. Therefore, prior to 1996, excise taxes were imposed on both the rock and the hard place: that is, excess withdrawals from a pension plan during lifetime would generate a 15% excise, but so would excessive accumulations of pension benefits within the estate.

The Small Business Job Protection Act of 1996 (SBJPA) suspended the "excessive distributions" excise tax for three years, 1997–1999, but retained the tax on excessive accumulation within the estate (i.e., failure to withdraw enough). The Taxpayer Relief Act of 1997 permanently repealed both excise taxes, thus giving taxpayers much more flexibility to choose any withdrawal schedule that makes financial sense, without worrying about tax consequences.

The SBJPA also made another change, removing the excise tax on failure to start receiving plan distributions by April 1 of the year following that in which the participant reaches age 70 1/2. In other words, because of the SBJPA, a plan participant (unless he or she owns 5% or more of the sponsor corporation's stock) can defer plan distributions and need not start receiving them on any particular schedule. See IRS Notice 96-7, 1996-53 IRB 121, for guidance on complying with this change in the law. By the way, the employer can allow older employees who remain in the workforce to defer their initial pension payment, even before the plan has been amended to reflect the SBJPA: see IRS Announcement 97-24, 1997-1 IRB 24.

⇒ TIP

IRA participants are still required to take their first distribution no later than April 1 of the year after the year of reaching age $70\frac{1}{2}$; or else the excise tax penalty kicks in.

If deferral is elected, the plan is required to make an upward actuarial adjustment to the benefit (because the employee will be receiving benefits for fewer years).

15.5 ROLLOVERS

The plan administrator's job also includes dealing with employees who are entitled to receive a plan distribution but who, for one reason or another, don't want an immediate payout. In that situation, the employee is entitled to roll over the distribution, i.e., to place it into an eligible retirement plan. A qualified plan under §401(a) is such an eligible retirement plan; so is an IRA or a §403(a) annuity plan.

⇒ **TIP**

Oddly enough, although the employee has a right to do this, the other qualified plan that the employee wants to receive the rollover is not obligated to accept it. So it is permissible, and good policy, for the plan to require the employee to submit a statement that the potential recipient is not only qualified to receive the potential rollover, but is willing to do so. Furthermore, even if the second plan does accept the rollover, it does not thereby become obligated to offer the same payout options as the original source plan. The recipient plan can also set its own rules for the form in which it will accept rollovers (e.g., cash only, not securities) and the minimum amount it will accept as a partial rollover.

When the employee wants to make a rollover, the plan administrator can either write a check or wire payment to the trustee or custodian of the plan to which the funds will be transferred, or can give the participant a check payable to the IRA, plan trustee, or custodian. The plan administrator should inform the participant how to make the rollover, and point out that if the funds are not rolled over within 60 days, they will become taxable income in that year.

A distribution made to a spouse, or a distribution under a QDRO to an ex-spouse, can also be rolled over. But in this situation, it can only be made to an IRA, not a §401(a) or §403(a) plan. Although, in general, withdrawals from an IRA are not entitled to favorable taxation as lump sums, a balance distributed under a QDRO can be treated as a lump sum and five- or ten-year averaging elected. Code §402(D)(4)(j) allows averaging to be used in a QDRO situation. However, an alternate payee, or a beneficiary who is not a spouse, is not entitled to make a rollover at all.

Reg. §1.401(a)(31)-1 provides that a direct rollover is deemed to be a distribution rather than a transfer of assets. Therefore, it may be necessary for the participant and spouse to waive payment of the plan benefits in qualified annuity form.

15.6 WITHHOLDING

Code §§ 401(a)(31) and 3405(c) require plan administrators to withhold a mandatory 20% of any "designated distribution." (A designated distribution is an amount of $200 or more that is eligible to be rolled over, but is not in fact rolled over.) The entire balance, or part of an employee's balance in a qualified retirement plan, is eligible for rollover except:

- A series of substantially equal periodic payments, with at least one payment made each year, for the life of the employee or the joint lives of the employee and spouse or other beneficiary

- Payments made for a term of years, lasting at least ten years (e.g., a 15-year annuity qualifies, a 5-year annuity doesn't). These payouts are exempted from withholding by §402(c)(4).

- The required minimum distributions mandated by Code §401(a)(9) for officers, directors, and 5% stockholders. (Before the SBJPA, all employees had to commence distributions from the plan no later than April 1 of the year following the year in which they attained age $70^1/_2$, but the SBJPA eliminated this requirement for rank-and-file participants in qualified plans, retaining it for IRAs and for non-rank-and-file qualified plan participants.)

If the employee takes part of a distribution in cash and rolls the rest over, withholding applies only to the part that is taken, not to the rollover.

Non-mandatory withholding at a 10% rate applies to "nonperiodic distributions" (i.e., those that are neither annuities nor eligible rollover distributions). Withholding is not mandatory in that employees can direct the plan *not* to withhold, and in fact the plan has an obligation to inform employees who are close to retirement that they have the right to make, renew, or revoke a withholding election. Notice must be given during the six months immediately preceding the first payment, and notice must be repeated at least once a year after that.

The general rule is that the plan administrator is responsible for withholding (see Reg. §31.3405(c)-1), unless the administrator informs the payer of the benefits to take care of withholding chores. The employer can include the withheld amounts when it files Form 941 each quarter, or can use Form 941E to report withholding.

Making designated distributions (i.e., those eligible for withholding) obligates the employer and plan administrator to make returns and reports to the IRS, participants, and beneficiaries. There is a penalty of $25 per day, up to a $15,000 limit, under §6047(e) if the reporting requirement is not met. The penalty can be waived if, for example, the plan had good cause for failing to report. Section 6047(b) details the records that employers must keep; record-keeping violations can be penalized by $50 per failure per year, up to a maximum of $50,000 per year.

⇒ TIP

See IRS Notice 92-48, 1992-2 C.B. 377, for information about rollovers (including text that can be used to explain the rollover process to employees).

15.7 QDROs

Plan administrators are often asked to comply with court orders incident to separation or divorce. After all, for many couples, an employee's pension plan interest is one of the few truly valuable assets available for division. Difficult problems can arise for the plan administrator when an employee remarries after a divorce and attempts to name the new spouse as plan beneficiary (despite the rights of the prior spouse), or if a beneficiary dies at a time when it is unclear who is the appropriate beneficiary.

> ⇒ **TIP**
>
> The Department of Labor released a 91-page guidebook in July, 1997, "QDROs: The Division of Pensions Through Qualified Domestic Relations Orders." Free copies are available by calling the Pension and Benefit Welfare Administration's toll-free number, (800) 998-7542. The text can also be downloaded from the DOL Website, http://www.dol.gov/dol/pwba. Further current language for sample QDROs can be found in Notice 97-11, 1997-2 IRB 49.

ERISA imposes strict limitations on alienation of employee benefits. In other words, ordinary creditors can't seize plan benefits before they are paid out. However, ERISA contains a significant exception to this rule for Qualified Domestic Relations Orders (QDROs) and Qualified Medical Child Support Orders (QMCSOs).

A QDRO is a court order dealing with child support, spousal alimony, or marital property rights. These orders are promulgated based on a state domestic relations law (including community property laws). A QDRO must contain at least this much information:

- The recipient's right to plan benefits
- The names and addresses of the parties
- The amount or percentage of the plan benefit to be paid out to the alternate payee (e.g., the divorced or divorcing non-employee spouse) named in the order
- The time period or number of payments covered by the order
- The plan(s) it applies to. For instance, an employee might be covered by both a defined benefit and a defined contribution plan, or a qualified plan and a top-hat plan, or a pension plan and a welfare benefit plan.

> ⇒ **TIP**
>
> No court is allowed to use a QDRO to order a plan to make payments in any type or form not allowed by the plan. The order can't force the plan to increase the actuarial value of the benefits, or to pay benefits that have already been assigned to someone else under another QDRO.

In general, distributions will be made to the alternate payee under a QDRO on the date the employee would be entitled to them. However, sometimes the distribution will be made earlier: on the earliest date when the participant could get the distribution after separating from service, or when the participant reaches age 50 (whichever is later).

⮕ TIP

If the plan is drafted to permit it, a QDRO can order distributions immediately, or at a time that has no relation to the participant spouse's age.

If the participant is still working when the QDRO is issued, the size of the payments is based on the present value of the normal retirement benefits accrued to date. Early retirement subsidies (if the employer offers any) are not considered. If, when the participant actually retires, he or she receives a retirement subsidy, the QDRO can provide for recalculation at that time.

⮕ TIP

A 1997 Fourth Circuit case says that unless the QDRO is entered before the date of retirement, benefits vest in the current spouse, not the divorced spouse. This is because the pension will be distributed as a QJSA unless there is a QDRO or a proper waiver by the participant and spouse during the 90-day period before the "annuity starting date" for the pension. The annuity starting date is often, but not necessarily, the date of retirement.

An administrator who receives a document that purports to be a QDRO must:

- Make a prompt notification to the participant and proposed alternate payee (usually a separated or divorced spouse of the employee) that the order was received

- Explain to them how the plan will determine if the document is a valid QDRO

- Make the determination within a reasonable time, then notify the participant and potential alternate payee

- Keep the funds segregated, and account for them separately, until the determination is made.

> ⇒ **TIP**
> _____
> ERISA Opinion Letter 94-32A says that it is improper to charge either
> the participant or alternate payee a fee for processing a QDRO.

If the employee is in the process of divorce and has not designated another
beneficiary, and dies before a QDRO is issued, it is difficult to determine how to dispose of the funds; consult the plan's attorney in this situation.

15.8 POST-DEATH PAYMENTS

Under certain circumstances, the death of the retiree will terminate the plan's
obligations entirely—if the employee was unmarried, and received the pension in
life annuity form, or if the employee was married and validly opted out of the joint
and survivor annuity, for instance.

Usually, however, benefit payments will continue after the employee's or
retiree's death. In most instances, there will be an individual who, for ERISA and
tax purposes, is properly designated as the beneficiary (either by action of the
employee/retiree or automatically, pursuant to the terms of the plan).

The designated beneficiary can also be an irrevocable trust that is valid under
the law of your state and has identifiable beneficiaries; the employee must provide
the plan with a copy of the trust instrument if he or she wants to go this route. If
the employee fails to make adequate arrangements, his or her heirs under state law
or the law of intestacy are *not* considered designated beneficiaries.

According to Code §401(a)(9)(B), if an employee dies *after* payment of an
annuity or installment pension has begun, then the plan simply continues the distributions in the same manner (unless, of course, they are supposed to end at the
employee's death).

The general rule is that the plan has five years from the death of the employee to complete distribution of the decedent's entire interest. However, the plan
does not have to satisfy the five-year rule if the decedent's interest is payable to a
designated beneficiary in life annuity form, or in installments that do not extend
past the beneficiary's life expectancy. In this situation, the plan must begin the distributions no later than December 31 of the year following the date of the employee's death.

Furthermore, if the designated beneficiary is the decedent's surviving spouse,
the distribution can be delayed until the later of December 31 of the year following
the employee's death, or April 1 of the year following the year in which the employee would have attained age 70 1/2.

Should the surviving spouse die before the distributions are required to
begin, they must be completed within five years of the survivor's death. That is,

unless the surviving spouse also designated a beneficiary and the distributions are made in the form of an annuity or installment payments for a period that does not exceed the life expectancy of that designated beneficiary.

A mid-1997 Supreme Court case directly affects the nine community property states, and has implications for the other states as well. The Supreme Court ruled that ERISA preempts a state law permitting the non-employee spouse to use his or her will to transfer an interest in the employee spouse's undistributed pension benefits. The rationale is that leaving the benefits by will is an assignment or alienation, but it is not a QDRO, the only permissible assignment form.

In a pension, annuity, profit sharing, or stock bonus plan that accepts (or requires) employee contributions, the general rule is that the employee's own contributions must be 100% vested at all times. However, Code §401(a)(19) permits a plan to make the employer contributions forfeitable if the employee withdraws his or her own contributions from the plan at a time when he or she is less than 50% vested.

15.9 ANTI-ALIENATION RULES

The primary rule of plan administration is that the plan is run for the exclusive benefit of its participants and beneficiaries—and no one else. This is expressed in ERISA §206 and echoed by Code §§401(a)(13) and 404(a)(2). Therefore, in most circumstances plan benefits cannot be anticipated or alienated. That is, benefits that are not yet in pay status must remain within the plan, protected from the claims of creditors. In fact, the IRS position is that a plan can be disqualified if its trustees allow benefits to be attached, or even distributed directly to an employee's trustee in bankruptcy. Pension plans are subject to anti-alienation rules, but welfare benefit plans are not.

A 1990 Supreme Court case even prevents attachment of pension benefits of a participant who was both a fiduciary and an embezzler (although he embezzled union funds rather than pension funds). According to the Fifth Circuit, even a claim made by the pension plan itself cannot be used to offset pension benefits, although the Third Circuit does allow offsets in this specific, somewhat uncommon, circumstance.

Courts are also divided as to whether creditors can reach plan funds where benefits have been distributed, but the check itself is being held for distribution to the beneficiary. In this situation, a Maryland court has ruled that attachment is improper, but a New York court has allowed it.

Once benefits have unequivocally been distributed, state law takes over to determine whether attachment is permitted. However, a 1995 Fourth Circuit decision says that attachment of benefits distributed before retirement is permissible, but ERISA protects post-retirement benefits from attachment even after their distribution. One major exception, enforcement of court orders (QDROs, QMCSOs) is discussed above.

Once the benefits are in pay status, a participant or beneficiary can make a voluntary revocable assignment of up to 10% of any benefit payment, as long as the assignment is for a purpose other than paying the costs of plan administration.

Creditors of plan participants and beneficiaries often get tired of waiting to collect their debts, and would frequently like to approach the plan administrator to get hold of benefits that have not yet been paid. In almost all circumstances, non-QDRO creditors will be disappointed. As page 94 explains, creditors are sometimes entitled (within limits) to garnish the wages of debtors, but they cannot garnish future plan benefits.

15.9.1 Bankruptcy Questions

If the employee files for bankruptcy protection and if an ex-spouse has already been awarded an interest in the employee's retirement plan, that interest is generally treated as belonging to the non-employee ex-spouse; therefore, it does not enter the bankruptcy estate of the employee spouse.

Otherwise, all the property in which the debtor has an interest goes into the bankruptcy estate, other than an interest in a trust that is subject to transfer restrictions that are imposed by "applicable non-bankruptcy law." The Fourth Circuit reads this to mean that ERISA keeps all qualified plans out of the bankruptcy estate, but several other Circuits disagree.

Even if the pension benefits do enter the bankruptcy estate, they may be protected for the employee based on various other theories. The federal Bankruptcy Code itself (at §522(d)) has an exemption for certain payments made under qualified pension, profit sharing, stock bonus, or annuity plans.

Bankruptcy law is a tricky joint federal/state system. States have the option of drafting their laws so that, within the state borders, both federal and state bankruptcy exemptions can be claimed—or only the state exemptions. If only the state exemptions are usable, then pension funds do become part of the bankruptcy estate unless they qualify for either a state exemption or an exemption under a law that deals with a subject other than bankruptcy.

In 1992, the Supreme Court settled a much-disputed question as to whether ERISA's ban on alienation of pension benefits constitutes "applicable non-bankruptcy law." *Patterson v. Shumate*, 504 U.S. 753 (1992) says yes, at least for qualified plans that are subject to Title I. However, if the plan has not received an IRS determination letter affirming its qualified status, then creditors probably can attach employee-debtor's interest in the plan.

Many states have statutes protecting qualified plans. However, a 1988 Supreme Court case says that ERISA preempts state laws that forbid garnishment of benefits. In other words, pension plans are protected, but welfare benefit plans are not.

If the plan itself is terminating, creditors cannot garnish employees' interests in the plan, even if they will receive lump sums rather than periodic payments as a consequence of the termination.

TERMINATION OF A PLAN

16.1 INTRODUCTION

In general, pension plans are started with the intention that they will continue indefinitely. However, for various reasons (usually involving negative financial factors), a corporation may choose to terminate its pension plan. The corporation itself may be terminated, or may lose its identity in the course of a merger or acquisition. The Pension Benefit Guaranty Corporation (PBGC) may step in and ask a federal court—or demand that a federal court—close down the pension plan and supervise the orderly distribution of its assets.

Under some (albeit rare) circumstances, the employer can even benefit financially by terminating an over-funded pension plan, distributing its assets, and retaining the surplus.

The basic rule is that, as soon as a plan is terminated or partially terminated, the accrued benefits must vest fully even though, under the normal schedule, a significant portion of the accrued benefits would still be unvested. This acceleration takes away some of the financial incentive for terminating unwanted pension plans.

⟹ **TIP**

Depending on the circumstances, a Reduction in Force might be considered a partial termination that accelerates vesting—be sure to get legal advice on this point before scheduling a RIF.

16.2 THE PBGC'S ROLE

The PBGC's job is to supervise terminations and make sure that participants receive the protected portion of their benefits, if necessary, by paying out benefits itself. (That's why the PBGC charges premiums—see page 243 to fund the shortfalls.)

The general rule is that the PBGC guarantees payment of all nonforfeitable benefits under single-employer plans. The agency has the power to maintain a separate trust fund for non-basic benefits, but has chosen not to do so.

The basic benefit, for this purpose, is a monthly life annuity for the participant's life (*not* a joint and survivor annuity, although this is the default payment method for an ongoing pension plan), commencing at age 65, set at one of two levels: the lesser of $750 adjusted for changes in the FICA covered wage base since 1974, or the employee's average monthly gross income for his or her five consecutive years of highest income. ERISA §4022(a) specifies a maximum guaranteed amount (a monthly benefit of $2542.05, for 1996 and $2761.36 for 1997).

The PBGC doesn't guarantee benefits that become nonforfeitable only because a plan has terminated. There is also an exception: benefits from a plan that was in effect for under 60 months are usually not guaranteed in full. Neither are benefit increases put in place by a plan amendment that was made or took effect within the 60-month period before the plan termination, or benefits of "substantial owners" (e.g., 10% shareholders in the employer corporation).

First, the PBGC determines whether a benefit is a guaranteed basic benefit (one that is nonforfeitable and payable in periodic installments). The next query is what percentage will be guaranteed. Actuarial calculations will be performed to convert benefits that are not straight life annuities commencing at age 65 to that form.

Terminating a plan involves both the Department of Labor and the IRS, and it's necessary to consult both ERISA and the Tax Code to be aware of all of the requirements that must be satisfied. Forms must be filed; consents must be obtained; and plan participants and their beneficiaries are entitled to be kept up to date on what's happening to the plan and their benefits.

The PBGC insurance protects the plan's employees, not the company that established the plan. In fact, if a plan terminates at a time when its assets are insufficient to pay basic benefits, the PBGC will make the payments and then go after the employer for reimbursement. The employer's potential liability to the PBGC is capped at 70% of its net worth with a separate cap of 75% of the unfunded guaranteed benefits.

16.3 TERMINATION TYPES

There are two kinds of voluntary terminations: standard and distress. The basic form, the standard termination under ERISA §4041, is used by plans that have enough assets to pay the PBGC-guaranteed benefits. (Of course, the preferable state is a plan that is able to pay all of its liabilities.)

ERISA §4044 sets up six categories of accrued benefits entitled to priority in distribution of the plan's assets. First, all Category-1 claims must be paid, then all Category-2 claims, until the plan's assets are exhausted; the assets are *not* distributed proportionately among all the classes. Interestingly, the categories do not parallel the tests for PBGC-guaranteed benefits.

The categories, in descending order of priority, are:

- Voluntary employee contributions made to the plan. Although these amounts take first priority, they are not guaranteed by the PBGC because they fall outside the definition of "basic benefit."

- Mandatory employee contributions made to the plan; employees are entitled to 5% interest on these contributions.

- Annuity benefits stemming from employer contributions, if the annuity was or could have been in pay status three years or more before the termination of the plan. "Could have been" refers to situations such as employees who continued to work after eligibility for early retirement.

- All PBGC-guaranteed benefits that are not in a higher category.

- All other non-forfeitable benefits.

- All benefits that are accrued but forfeitable.

Before actually making any distributions, the plan administrator is obligated to determine that the plan can pay benefits at the level deemed appropriate by the PBGC. If the administrator determines that the plan is unable to pay the guaranteed benefits, the plan termination process comes to a halt as the administrator notifies the PBGC, which then makes its own determination and issues notices. On the other hand, if the administrator's judgment is that the plan is sufficient to pay the PBGC-guaranteed benefits, but not all guaranteed liability, the administrator must still notify the PBGC, but should continue to distribute the plan's assets.

If the PBGC agrees with the administrator's characterization of the situation, it will issue a notice of inability to determine the sufficiency of the plan. The plan administrator must provide a new valuation, certified by an enrolled actuary, of the plan's liabilities and guaranteed benefits.

16.3.1 Standard Termination

Unless the PBGC gives permission for the less-demanding "distress termination," the plan will be wound up under the standard termination rules.

At least 60 days, but not more than 90 days, before the proposed date of a voluntary termination, the plan administrator must notify participants and their beneficiaries, alternate payees under domestic relations orders, and any collective bargaining representative of the employees, that a termination is contemplated.

The notice must give the date of the termination and must explain that the PBGC's guarantee ends as soon as benefits are distributed. The notice must also give the name and address of the insurance company selected to provide annuities for participants. (If the plan hasn't made a choice yet, the participants and beneficiaries must be given the names of insurers that might be chosen as annuity providers.) There must be an identified contact person who can be approached to answer questions about the termination process.

Once the plan files Form 500 (Standard Termination Notice) with the PBGC, participants and beneficiaries must be given another notice, this time explaining their benefit entitlement and how payment will be made. The notice must explain the factors (e.g., age, length of service, wages, interest assumptions) used to determine the benefit. The notice must be expressed in a form understandable by the ordinary participant.

Within 120 days after the proposed termination date, the plan administrator must send the PBGC a certificate compiled by an actuary who is enrolled with the PBGC. The actuary's certificate is Schedule EA-5 of PBGC Form 500, the Standard Termination Notice for a Single-Employer Plan. It estimates the value of the plan assets and the present value of the plan's liabilities. The actuary certifies that the assets are large enough to satisfy the liabilities.

The plan administrator has a duty to furnish any other information called for by PBGC regulations, and also has to certify (i.e., can be held liable for perjury for lying) that the actuary's certificate is correct and the information given to the PBGC has been accurate and complete.

The PBGC has a review period of 60 days (or longer, if the plan administrator agrees to let the PBGC extend the time). The purpose of the review is for the PBGC to identify any proposed terminations that would be improper.

If the review period ends without the PBGC voicing an objection, then the plan's assets must be distributed "as soon as practicable"—which generally means within 180 days of the end of the PBGC review period.

Pension plans are supposed to be wound up in an orderly way, with assets usually going to purchase annuities that will pay participants' pensions once they reach retirement age or are otherwise entitled to payments. The assets are supposed to be distributed within an "administratively reasonable time," which generally means within one year. The plan is supposed to satisfy all its benefit liabilities this way—or all benefits to which assets are allocated, if this amount exceeds the benefit liabilities.

If the process drags on too long, the plan may be treated as if it has not terminated, and must continue to report under Code §§6057-6059. (Section 6059 applies only to defined benefit plans.)

> **⇒ TIP**
>
> The date of the final distribution can be extended by filing IRS Form 5310, Application for a Determination Letter. Don't forget to notify the PBGC of the IRS filing. See IRS Announcement 97-81, 1997-34 IRB 12 for the latest versions of the 5310 and related forms.

Once all the assets are distributed, the administrator must file PBGC Form 501 within 30 days of the final distribution, to prove that assets were distributed. The penalty for a late Form 501 can be up to $1000 per day. Furthermore, a late filing can reduce the refund of the PBGC premium that the employer would otherwise be entitled to (because the termination gives the plan a last, short year).

16.3.2 Distress Termination

What if the plan doesn't have enough assets to pay all the benefit liabilities? In that situation, the beleaguered plan can apply to the PBGC for a distress termination. It is available only if the plan's sponsors (and any corporations that are fellow-members of a controlled group of corporations) can prove financial hardship.

A sufficient degree of hardship would be a situation in which the sponsor is involved in bankruptcy or insolvency proceedings (whether voluntary or involuntary). If a voluntary petition has been filed seeking a bankruptcy or insolvency reorganization (i.e., Chapter 11 rather than a Chapter 7 liquidating bankruptcy), a distress termination is available only if the bankruptcy court decides that terminating the plan is necessary, or the company can't pay its debts as they come due and stay in business if it maintains the plan.

A distress termination might also be available if the sponsor proves to the PBGC that it must terminate the plan to pay its debts and keep operating. Finally, a distress termination might be available if pension costs have become unduly burdensome solely because of the decline in the covered workforce. (For instance, a stock market decline would not be an adequate excuse).

PBGC Form 601 must be filed, not more than 120 days after the proposed termination date, to request a distress termination. Participants and beneficiaries must be notified on more or less the same terms as for a standard termination. An actuary's certificate is also required, this time Schedule EA-D on the Form 601. Once the PBGC receives an application for a distress termination, it is supposed to determine as soon as it can whether it can be granted. If the PBGC turns down the applicant, and the plan has enough assets to satisfy its liabilities, then the plan simply carries out a standard termination. However, if the assets are insufficient, but the PBGC won't go along, then it is impossible for the plan to go through a voluntary termination at all.

If the plan's assets are sufficient to pay the guaranteed benefits, the PBGC issues a "distribution notice." Within 15 days after receiving this notice, the plan administrator has an obligation to give each participant and beneficiary a notice of impending distribution, and to begin the actual distribution within 60 days and complete it within 240 days (unless an extension has been given). After the distribution is complete, PBGC Form 602 (Post-Distribution Certification) must be filed within 30 days of the completion of the distribution.

16.3.3 Involuntary Termination

If the plan assets are lower than the total of guaranteed benefits, then ERISA §4042 governs the PBGC's involuntary termination proceedings. In this situation, the plan administrator is deprived of control over the distribution process. Instead, the PBGC can ask the District Court to appoint a trustee.

Under ERISA §4062(b)(1), the employer sponsoring a plan is liable to the PBGC for the total amount of unfunded plan liabilities (measured as of the termination date), plus interest running from the same date.

The PBGC has discretion to apply to the District Court for a decree of involuntary termination if:

• The plan has failed to meet its minimum funding standards
• The plan can't pay benefits when due
• One or more reportable distributions to "substantial owners" (basically, to 10% shareholders of the sponsoring corporation) have occurred
• Termination is necessary to prevent an unreasonable increase in the fund's liabilities.

It's up to the PBGC to decide whether or not to apply for a decree in those circumstances. The PBGC has an obligation to start the proceedings if the plan's situation is even more dire:

• The plan doesn't have sufficient assets to pay its *current* benefits (as distinguished from benefits as they fall due)
• The plan has applied for a distress termination but doesn't have enough money to fund the guaranteed benefits.

A PBGC termination begins with notice to the administrator, and a District Court petition for a decree that the plan must be terminated to protect the plan's participants, to prevent an unreasonable increase in the PBGC premium, or to prevent an unreasonable deterioration in the PBGC's financial condition. Although the bankruptcy "automatic stay" prevents virtually all forms of litigation against a company that has applied for bankruptcy protection, the PBGC is empowered to apply for termination even if a bankruptcy case is pending. In fact, the bankruptcy case might be stayed long enough to sort out the pension situation.

16.4 THE TRUSTEE'S ROLE

In situations in which the District Court appoints a trustee, the plan must be terminated. The PBGC can also force termination of a plan without such an appointment.

If a trustee is appointed, his or her duty is to furnish information about the termination to the plan administrator, each plan participant, the beneficiaries of each deceased plan participant, all unions representing those employees, and all employers potentially subject to ERISA liability. The trustee can demand that some or all of the plan's assets and/or records be transferred to him or her. The trustee has the choice of either limiting payment of benefits to the basic benefits, or continuing whatever pattern of payments was in place before his or her appointment.

ERISA §4062(d) makes the employer liable for the unpaid contributions to the trusteed plan. By the date of termination, the employer must give the trustee cash or securities acceptable to the trustee, equivalent to:

- The balance of the accumulated funding deficiencies defined by Code §412(a)
- Any funding deficiencies that were waived by the IRS, under §412(c), prior to the date of termination
- All decreases in the minimum funding standard allowed under §412(e) before the termination date, plus interest running from the termination date.

➠ TIP

ERISA §4069(b) makes the successor corporation or corporations liable for the above amounts if the contributing sponsor reorganizes (changes its identity, form, or place of organization; engages in merger, consolidation, or division; is a subsidiary that is liquidated into its parent). If the purpose of the reorganization was to evade liability, and the reorganization occurs within the five years prior to a plan termination that would have caused liability, the party intending to evade liability becomes a contributing sponsor for liability purposes.

Furthermore, under ERISA §4062(b), an employer who ceases operations at a facility with the result that 20% or more of the total number of plan participants are separated from service, the employer must either fund the guaranteed benefits immediately, or make provision for their funding.

16.5 PLAN REVERSIONS

Before ERISA, employers could simply wind up a plan and take back its assets. In the current post-ERISA climate, a plan provision that calls for reversion (or increased reversion) cannot become effective until the end of the fifth calendar year following the year of adoption. In other words, employers have to wait at least five years to take advantage of a reversion opportunity. Furthermore, if the plan called for mandatory contributions, after the benefits are paid off, assets must be allocated to mandatory employee contributions before the reversion is made.

And even after the employer is entitled to a reversion, it must pay 50% of the reversion amount as an excise tax. However, if the employer establishes a qualified replacement plan or amends the terminating plan to increase benefits, the excise tax is reduced to 20%. IRS Form 5330 is used to pay the excise tax. It's due the last day of the month after the month in which the reversion occurred.

16.6 IRS REPORTING

When a plan is terminated, IRS Form 5310 is used to request an IRS determination letter stating that the associated plan trust did not become disqualified or lose its exempt status. In conjunction with this form, Form 6088 must be filed, listing up to 25 owners or 5% shareholders of the employer corporation who received any distribution from the plan during the preceding five years.

If plan assets are transferred to another qualified retirement plan because of a merger, consolidation, or shift in ownership of assets or liabilities, Form 5310-A must usually be filed 30 days or more before the transfer. When two defined contribution plans merge or a defined contribution plan is spun off, or if a defined benefit plan engages in a merger or spinoff that has only limited (de minimis) effects, the 5310-A filing is not required.

In the somewhat unlikely case that the trust of a terminating plan has more assets than are needed to pay all the plan benefits, and thus the employer recovers these excess assets, Form 5319 must be filed by the last day of the month after the month in which the employer recouped the assets. This is also the form the employer uses to pay the excise tax on the recouped funds.

Remember that the Form-5500 series annual report must be filed for the year of the merger, consolidation, division, or termination. If a trust is frozen (the plan maintains its assets, although benefit accruals have stopped), the 5500-series filing is required in every year until all the assets have been distributed.

16.7 EFFECT ON BENEFITS

When a plan terminates or partially terminates, benefits become nonforfeitable. A defined contribution plan's benefits become nonforfeitable if and when the employer completely ceases making contributions to the plan. However, for this purpose, a money-purchase plan is deemed to be a defined benefit rather than a defined contribution plan. Termination makes it impossible to reallocate nonvested amounts. In practice, this ban usually favors the plan's highly-compensated employees (HCEs) because they typically have the longest service with the plan. In a defined benefit plan, termination means that funds that might otherwise have been forfeitures have to be allocated to the employees.

These plans are subject to Code §412, so the test is not whether there has been a complete discontinuance of contributions or accrual of benefits, but whether the plan is adequately funded.

> ⇒ **TIP**
>
> If funding is inadequate, penalties under Code §4971 are likely to be imposed. Benefits continue to accrue, and thus funding requirements and potential employer exposure to penalties continue, until the plan is formally frozen or terminated. There is also the possibility that the PBGC will force involuntary termination of the plan (see page 308).

As for a profit sharing or stock bonus plan that is not subject to Code §412, when there is complete cessation of employer contributions (not just a temporary discontinuance) affected employees immediately become 100% vested as to benefits accrued up to the date of the complete discontinuance.

Calculating that date can be difficult. It's a factual determination involving factors such as employer's intent to prevent full vesting, whether recurring, substantial contributions are made, and the probability of contributions being resumed in the future. Of course, if the plan is drafted to call for contributions to be made out of corporate profits, it is not a "discontinuance" to avoid making contributions in a year when there are no profits.

If a defined benefit plan terminates within 10 years of its creation, §411(d)(2) imposes limits on the benefits that can be paid to the 25 highest-compensated individuals covered by the plan. This rule prevails even if it results in the loss of some accrued benefits.

16.8 PLAN CUTBACKS

One situation, already discussed earlier, is the employer's determination to close down a pension plan. Another situation is an employer's cutback in a plan, or scaling it down—whether deliberately or inadvertently (lacking funds to make a required deposit into the plan; neglecting to become informed about what is required to maintain the plan).

It's important to know that the consequences of such actions or inactions are not always those intended by the employer. The worst-case scenario is that the plan is deemed to be partially terminated, and then is retroactively disqualified, forcing the employer to pay heavy back taxes for prior plan years. Retroactive disqualification is also harmful to employees: not only are they likely to owe back taxes, but distributions from a disqualified plan cannot be rolled over to a qualified plan, and the use of five- and ten-year averaging is also denied.

A plan is frozen if it is amended to keep the plan trust in existence, but ending contributions or accrual of benefits. A frozen plan is still subject to the top-heavy plan rules, including the requirement of a faster vesting schedule, and is still obligated to provide QJSAs and QPSAs on the same terms as if it had not been frozen.

For the majority of plans, those that are subject to Code §412, immediate 100% vesting is required when a plan is partially terminated as defined by §411(d)(3)(A). However, full vesting for employees makes the plan more likely to be accused of prohibited discrimination or reversion to the employers. Often, employers who freeze a plan give employees the choice of either withdrawing their accrued benefits immediately, or keeping them within the plan until the normal time for distribution. However, if too many rank-and-file employees take the withdrawal option, the unintended result could be that the plan becomes discriminatory, because an excessive proportion of HCEs keep their benefits within the plan.

Generally speaking, the plan will probably be deemed partially terminated if over 20% of the plan's participants lose their jobs. A "vertical partial termination" occurs when a group of employees lose coverage under the plan; a "horizontal partial termination" is deemed to occur when the potential for reversion of plan assets to the employer increases unduly.

⇒ **TIP**

If it's uncertain whether a partial termination has occurred, Form 5300 can be filed with the IRS to get a determination letter. If the IRS rules that a partial termination has taken place, then reporting to the PBGC is required. (See page 306). Other reportable events include a 20% cut in the workforce, and a plan amendment that reduces the accrual of benefits by 50% or more for 50% or more of the workforce.

16.9 DISCLOSURE TO PARTICIPANTS

Once the decision is made to terminate a PBGC-insured plan, this triggers an obligation to give each "affected party" between 60 and 90 days' notice of the future termination. See ERISA §4041(a)(2). In general, affected parties are participants, the beneficiaries of deceased ex-participants, ex-spouses who are alternate payees under QDROs, and unions representing employees of the company sponsoring the soon-to-be-terminated plan.

The information that must be included in the notice is:

- The name of the plan and of its sponsor
- The plan's tax number; the sponsor's Employer Identification Number
- Contact information (name, address, telephone number) for a person who can give affected parties information about the termination
- Disclosure that the plan administrator intends to put the plan through a standard termination; either the date set for the termination, or the factors that go into setting the date
- Either a statement that service credit and benefits will continue to accrue until the termination, or that benefit accruals have been frozen or will be frozen on a specified date
- A promise to provide written notification of the benefits each affected party will receive under the termination
- A promise to each retiree that their retirement benefits in annuity form will not be affected by the termination
- Reassurance that a standard termination is available if and only if the plan has enough assets to satisfy plan liabilities to all participants and all beneficiaries of deceased participants
- Disclosure that the PBGC's role in the termination ends once the assets have been distributed
- A statement that if the termination does *not* occur, further notice will be given
- If the sponsor intends to purchase annuities or other irrevocable commitments from an insurance company, the name and address of the insurer or how the insurer will be selected.

⇒ TIP

Selection of the insurer is a fiduciary decision, subject to the normal standards of fiduciary duty.

If a distress termination rather than a standard termination is intended, the disclosure requirements are basically similar, but parties are told whether or not the plan's assets are great enough to pay all benefit liabilities or, at least, all guaranteed benefits. They must also be informed of the extent to which the PBGC guarantees payment of benefits, and given an explanation of reductions in benefits that may have to be imposed because of the limitations on the PBGC's obligations. See ERISA §4041(c).

A second notice, Notice of Plan Benefits, must be given to every affected party on or before the date the standard termination notice is submitted to the PBGC. PBGC Reg. §4041.23 sets the form of the notice, which duplicates many of the items from the Notice of Intent to Terminate, but also includes disclosure of an estimate of the benefits the affected party will receive under the plan that is undergoing termination. (For estimated benefits, the affected parties must be informed that benefits might be either higher or lower than the estimate.)

For benefits already in pay status, disclosure must be made of the amount and form of benefits that will be payable. For individuals who have indicated a retirement date and elected a payout form, but whose benefits are not yet in pay status, the projected benefit start date must be announced, with disclosure of the form and amount of benefits payable as of that date, and the date for any scheduled increase or reduction in benefits. The interest rate assumptions must be disclosed for lump-sum benefits. Finally, if the benefit start date is not known for benefits not in pay status, disclosure centers around the benefits available at normal retirement age (or after the death of a participant), with special attention to any benefits payable in lump-sum form.

Yet another notice is required when underfunding is very significant: for instance, if the aggregate vested but unfunded benefits of the sponsor (and all members of its controlled group of corporations, if it is part of such a group) were $50 million or more in the plan year before the year of the notice. Notice is also required if a lien could be imposed on plan assets, or the IRS granted a minimum funding waiver covering more than $1 million.

The notice informs plan participants about the financial status of the plan, its sponsor, and the sponsor's controlled group of corporations. The information must be provided within 105 days of the end of the filing corporation's information year. See PBGC Reg. §4010.

ERISA §4011 and the related PBGC Regulations (which include a model notice) call for notification of funding status when plans fail to meet their full funding limitation and their PBGC premium is increased to compensate for the underfunding. Participants and beneficiaries must be warned of the underfunding, and on the limitation on the PBGC's obligation to insure benefits. This notice is due two months after the deadline for filing the annual report for the year in which the plan was underfunded.

16.10 QDROs IN PLANS UNDER PBGC CONTROL

Given the high prevalence of divorce in our society, and the occasional phenomenon of plans terminating with inadequate funding, it's easy to see that situations will arise in which the PBGC will supervise plans some of whose benefits must be paid out to alternate payees (separated or divorced non-employee spouses and ex-spouses).

The PBGC has created two standard Qualified Domestic Relations Order (QDRO) forms to be issued by courts to cope with this situation. (See page 281 for a general discussion of QDROs.) PBGC QDROs specify (or give the alternate payee discretion to control) the time at which benefits begin, how the benefits are paid, the percentage of the pension payment that goes to the alternate payee rather than to the employee who would otherwise receive it, and how long the alternate payments continue.

QDROs cannot be used to require the PBGC to provide any benefit type or option that would not otherwise be available, or would otherwise be provided by the PBGC. Nor can the court order increase the amount that the PBGC would have to pay relative to the employee spouse's pension account.

The two standard PBGC QDROs are the Model Separate Interest and Model Shared Payment forms. The separate interest form (which can be used only if the order is entered before the employee's pension is in pay status) is used when the alternate payee gets benefits that are fixed and do not depend on when the participant starts to get benefits or the form in which the participant receives them. In effect, the pension account under the PBGC's control is divided into two parts: one for the participant, one for the non-employee alternate beneficiary.

In contrast, the Shared Payment form operates at the level of each individual payment. It takes practical effect only after the benefits are in pay status, although it can be issued earlier. Once each payment comes due, it is divided between the employee and the alternate beneficiary. The alternate payee will not receive benefits after the employee's death unless the order specifically provides for survivor benefits.

16.11 PAYMENT OF TERMINATION EXPENSES

It is appropriate for fiduciaries to use the plan's own assets to pay expenses of an ongoing plan. However, the decision to terminate a plan is a business decision made by the plan's settlor, not a fiduciary decision, and therefore some of the expenses of termination derive from "settlor-type functions." For the plan to pay settlor expenses would violate ERISA.

Therefore, it becomes necessary to allocate expenses between legitimate plan expenses and those that belong to the settlor.

⇒ **TIP**

The Department of Labor recommends having an independent fiduciary make the allocation. See ERISA Opinion Letter No. 97-032A (February, 1997).

Termination expenses that are fiduciary expenses properly paid by the plan include:

- Getting an audit and paying its costs
- Preparing and filing the final annual report
- Amending the plan to carry out the termination
- Figuring out the benefits and preparing benefit statements
- Giving notice to participants and beneficiaries about their rights incident to termination.

On the other hand, the settlor, not the plan, is responsible for the cost of maintaining the plan's tax-qualified status (including getting any needed determination letters).

Chapter 17

ERISA ENFORCEMENT

17.1 INTRODUCTION

In many contexts, enforcement is a simple, straightforward matter. Get caught committing a burglary? You'll be arrested by the police and put on trial by the state. In a dispute with your neighbor over a spite fence? You'll sue him, he'll sue you, or one will sue and the other will file counterclaims.

ERISA enforcement is far more complex. In a limited range of instances, criminal penalties can be imposed. Usually, it is a civil matter, but one that takes place on many levels. The Department of Labor and/or the IRS might challenge the plan's qualification or the way it operates. Whether as an administrative matter within the agency or within the federal court system, the plan itself or the employer sponsoring the plan might be told to start doing something, stop doing something, reimburse someone for something, pay a fine, pay an excise tax penalty, or some combination of all of them. A plan could lose its qualification for future years, or even for past years (which will require the employer to make large tax payments to compensate for plan-related deductions that were taken improperly).

That doesn't end the enforcement story. Plan participants and their beneficiaries might sue the plan, or the employer as a corporation, or plan administrators as individuals. Claims might be brought by or against a health care provider such as a hospital or HMO. The plan, its participants and beneficiaries, and/or enforcement officials might take steps against a fiduciary who has breached trust (see pages 326–7). One fiduciary might sue another fiduciary in effect for getting the first one into trouble.

A pension plan is an entity that can sue or be sued under ERISA Title I (see §502(d). The plan is responsible for paying all money judgments—unless somebody is found liable in his or her individual capacity.

This chapter discusses many issues: who is an ERISA fiduciary; how fiduciaries are required to act; which parties are subject to prohibited transaction rules; which transactions are prohibited; and who has the right to sue whom in order to carry out ERISA's rules and prohibitions.

17.2 WHO IS A FIDUCIARY?

In general legal terms, a fiduciary is anyone with responsibility for another party's funds or property. Because fiduciaries are trusted, they are expected to behave honestly and conscientiously, and to avoid promoting their own self-interest at the expense of the owner of the funds or property.

Under ERISA, pension and benefit plans are required to be managed for the exclusive benefit of plan participants and their beneficiaries. Many types of people who deal with the plan are considered fiduciaries under ERISA—including some people who may not necessarily think of themselves in that class or understand their responsibilities and possible liabilities. There's more to fiduciary liability than punishing embezzlers: it's possible to get into trouble without having any criminal intent. It's even possible for one fiduciary's mistake or wrongdoing to get a handful (or even dozens) of other fiduciaries into trouble.

Someone who deals with a plan becomes a fiduciary whenever, and to the extent that, he or she:

- Exercises any discretionary authority (i.e., is able to make decisions) or control over the management of the plan

- Exercises *any* authority (even if it isn't discretionary) over the management and disposition of plan assets. The distinction is understandable: the greatest potential for abuse exists where money is concerned.

- Receives direct or indirect compensation for giving the plan investment advice about plan assets

- Has any discretionary authority or responsibility for day-to-day plan administration (as distinct from plan management).

In other words, if a plan hires attorneys, accountants, or actuaries to provide advice, those professionals will usually not become plan fiduciaries, because they do not control the direction that the plan takes; they merely provide technical information that the administrator and other fiduciaries use to make decisions. In the same way, a stockbroker is not a fiduciary if he or she simply executes the fiduciaries' orders to adjust the plan's investment portfolio, but an investment manager (see page 323) who has a role in setting the plan's investment policy is very definitely a fiduciary.

> ⇒ **TIP**
>
> If the professional adviser is *not* a fiduciary, then ERISA will probably not preempt state law malpractice suits brought by the plan.

Fiduciary conduct is examined on two levels. First, the fiduciaries have to satisfy their affirmative duties (choose proper investments for the plan; diversify investments unless diversification itself is imprudent; maintain proper liquidity so the plan can meet its needs for cash; secure a reasonable yield on plan investments; and make proper administrative decisions). Second, they cannot engage in prohibited transactions.

> ⇒ **TIP**
>
> Although Code §4975's excise tax penalties apply only to qualified plans and IRAs, ERISA Title I imposes a similar schedule of civil penalties even on plans that are NOT subject to §4975.

17.2.1 *Trustee Duties*

The normal form of organization for a pension or welfare benefit plan is a trust, and every trust must have at least one trustee. The trustee can be named in the instrument itself, appointed according to a procedure set out in the plan, or appointed by a named fiduciary. See ERISA §403(a).

The trustee has exclusive authority and discretion to manage and control the plan's assets. (If there are multiple trustees, they must jointly manage and control the assets, although ERISA §403(a) permits them to delegate some duties. ERISA Title I explains which fiduciary duties can be delegated; this issue is not taken up by the Internal Revenue Code. The crucial question is whether trustee responsibility or other duties are involved.

A plan can be drafted so that its trustee is subject to a non-trustee who is a named fiduciary. This is often done to make the trustee subordinate to an administrative committee. If this is done, the trustee is subject to "proper" directions given by the named fiduciary, if they are in accordance with the plan's procedures and not contrary to law.

If there has been a proper appointment of an investment manager (see page 323), the trustee doesn't have to manage or invest whatever assets are placed under the investment manager's control, and will not be liable for the acts or omissions of the investment manager. The trustee has a duty to make sure the manager's fees are reasonable. (Performance-based fees, rather than flat fees determined in advance, are permissible.)

17.2.2 *Fiduciary Eligibility*

ERISA §402(a)(1) requires all plans to have a named fiduciary or, in the alternative, to explain in the plan document how fiduciaries will be selected. Under ERISA §411, a convicted felon can't serve as a plan administrator, fiduciary, officer, trustee, custodial, counsel, agent, consultant, or employee with decision-making authority for 13 years after his or her conviction or the end of his or her prison term, whichever comes later.

17.3 FIDUCIARY DUTIES

Fiduciaries have four major duties under ERISA:

- Loyalty
- Prudence
- Acting in accordance with the plan's governing instrument and other relevant legal documents
- Monitoring the performance of other individuals to whom fiduciary responsibility is delegated.

The duty of loyalty stems from the ERISA requirement that plan assets have to be held for the exclusive purpose of providing benefits (pensions, health insurance, etc.) to participants and their beneficiaries. Once placed into the plan trust (or used to buy insurance), the assets can't be used for the benefit of the employer.

> ➡ **TIP**
>
> The duty of loyalty is breached if the plan is amended to reduce benefits—and the amendment was adopted arbitrarily, capriciously, or in bad faith.

The duty of prudence requires fiduciaries to behave with the level of care, skill, prudence, and diligence that a hypothetical prudent person would use to handle the same tasks. The hypothetical prudent person is one who is familiar with the plan and its situation, not the "man on the street" who does not have this level of specific knowledge.

The "prudent person" rule that is applied in the ERISA context is not identical to that applied in analyzing trusts. Every asset within a trust must satisfy the prudent person test. But DOL Reg. §2550.404a-1(c)(2) allows the fiduciary to choose assets by considering the relevant facts and circumstances, including the role of the individual investment within the portfolio. Relying on expert advice is considered a positive factor, but it doesn't guarantee that an investment choice will be considered prudent.

17.3.1 Diversification

Although Mark Twain said that it's fine to put all your eggs in one basket—if you watch the basket!—diversification is one of the most basic investment principles. There are fashions in investments, just as in clothes, and fiduciaries often experience pressure to invest in the fashionable stocks of the moment. Another form of pressure is the sponsoring corporation's endorsement of its own stock as a suitable plan investment.

The general rule is that ERISA imposes a duty on fiduciaries to diversify unless it's prudent *not* to do so. It's up to the fiduciary to prove that diversification was unwise under the circumstances.

The fiduciary is supposed to select a balanced portfolio that is responsive to current conditions. The fiduciary must consider the portfolio's liquidity and current return as compared with the anticipated needs for cash flow. The projected return of the portfolio must be appropriate in light of the plan's funding objectives. It's all right for a fiduciary to include investments that do not yield current income, as long as overall, the plan has adequate income from all sources. Furthermore, plan fiduciaries are no longer limited to a "legal list" of stodgily safe investments. They are allowed to take SOME risks, as long as the risks are reasonable in the context of the portfolio as a whole.

If the plan invests in the employer's own securities, they must be "qualifying employer securities" such as stock and eligible debt instruments. (Defined benefit plans are subject to even stricter limitations on which employer securities they can hold.) The base rule is that the plan must not be more than 10% invested in employer securities. In fact, to invest in these at all, the fiduciaries must make an independent judgment that owning *any* employer securities is good for the plan. However, an ESOP or an individual account plan (e.g., profit sharing, stock bonus, thrift, and savings plans) can have more than 10% in employer securities, even if the normal rule of prudence would require greater diversification, provided that the plan document explicitly allows the greater concentration.

Current ERISA rules prohibit plans to invest in no-load mutual funds affiliated with banks; but in November, 1996, the DOL proposed regulations that would allow funds to be transferred from the bank to the mutual funds, thus saving a lot of fees, and making the plan's investments more productive.

Under a mid-1997 case, a pension administrator did not breach fiduciary duty by investing 63% of the plan's assets in undeveloped land. The Fifth Circuit decided that there was no real risk of a large loss, so the investment was prudent at the time it was made. Most of the plan participants were young, so there was enough time to make up for losses if they did occur, and plenty of time for appreciation in the land's value. The fiduciary was familiar with the local real estate market, and thus able to select good investments; historically, real estate has played an important portfolio role as an inflation hedge.

17.3.2 Bonding

The basic rule of ERISA §412(a) is that all fiduciaries, and any plan officials who are not fiduciaries but who do handle plan assets, must be bonded. The exceptions are some banks and insurance companies with assets over $1 million, and administrators, officers, and employees who deal with unfunded plans (plans whose assets are paid only from the general funds of the employer or a union, even if the funds derive in part from employee contributions). Nor is a bond required for funds characterized as general assets of the employer until they are transferred to the insurance companies that pay the actual benefits.

Various forms of bond are acceptable: a blanket bond (covering all the fiduciaries and everyone who handles the plan's money); an individual bond; a name schedule bond (covering a group of named individuals); and a position schedule bond (covering whoever fills certain named jobs and relationships to the plan). The bond must be issued by a corporate surety that holds a Department of Treasury Certificate of Authority. An acceptable bond must not carry a deductible, and must cover claims that were discovered within one year or more after termination or cancellation of the bond.

The bond must be large enough to cover potential losses to the plan caused by fraud or dishonesty of plan officials. In general, the bond must be 10% of the funds handled, but not less than $1,000 or more than $500,000.

Generally speaking, the employer will maintain a single bond covering all its plans that are subject to ERISA Title I. Recovery on behalf of one plan must not be allowed to reduce the amount available to the other plans below the minimum requirement.

⇒ TIP

To save the cost of the bond, a company whose financial condition is sound can ask the DOL to issue an opinion that payments are not at risk, and therefore administrators of funded plans need not be bonded. In a way, this is ironic: after all, the more financially stable a plan is, the easier it is for it to afford the cost of the bond!

17.4 RIGHTS AND DUTIES OF PARTIES INVOLVED WITH THE PLAN

In addition to the sponsor corporation, the fiduciaries, and the employees whose full-time responsibility is to carry out tasks for the plan, many other individuals may be involved. ERISA and the body of court cases spell out their mutual responsibilities and duties to one another (which, of course, fit within their duties to the participants and beneficiaries of the plan).

17.4.1 The Employer's Role

It might seem obvious that the heaviest liability for plan misconduct would fall on the company that sponsors the plan. However, that's not always the case. The people who made the decision might be held responsible. Even if corporate decisions are challenged by plan participants and beneficiaries, the court might well determine that the corporation is not liable because it was not a fiduciary.

In cases of this type, the court first determines what role the employer was playing. If it wore its "business hat," so to speak, and made business decisions (such as amending or terminating an unduly expensive plan), it might escape ERISA liability because it was not acting in any fiduciary capacity that ERISA regulates. For instance, the decision not to provide benefits to laid-off workers under a severance plan has been found to be a non-fiduciary business decision and thus not covered by ERISA.

However, it should be noted that the Ninth Circuit found that employees have a viable claim under ERISA when they say that the employer misappropriated the surplus of the pension plan for its own benefit. In a jointly funded plan, the employer does not have sole discretion over plan assets that derive in part from employee contributions.

To prevent conflicts of interest, ERISA §§403, 4042, and 4044 allow fiduciaries to perform certain employer-oriented actions without violating the duty to operate the plan in the sole interests of participants and beneficiaries. Employer contributions can be returned if:

- The contributions were made based on a mistake of fact
- The plan is not qualified under Code §§401(a) or 403(a)
- The income tax deduction for part or all of the contribution is disallowed
- The contribution could be treated as an excess contribution under Code §4975.

The fiduciary can also follow PBGC requirements for a distribution incident to a plan termination without being guilty of conflict of interest.

17.4.2 Investment Managers

Not every plan fiduciary is also a highly skilled investment expert. If the plan permits it, the fiduciaries are allowed to delegate their investment duties to a qualified investment manager.

> ⟱➡ **TIP**
>
> ERISA requires the manager to acknowledge in writing that he, she, or it has become a fiduciary. There are four categories of qualified investment managers:
>
> - Investment advisers who are registered under the federal Investment Company Act—whether they are independent consultants or in-house employees of the plan
> - Trust companies
> - Banks
> - Qualified insurance companies.

The significance of delegating authority and responsibility to an investment manager is that, as long as the fiduciaries were prudent when they chose the manager (and in retaining the manager's services, after enough time passed to review the manager's performance), then the fiduciary will *not* be held responsible for acts and omissions committed by the manager.

DOL Reg. §2510.3-21(c) explains who will be deemed qualified to render investment advice:

- Those who give advice about the value of securities or recommend investing, buying, or selling securities (or other property, such as real estate)
- Those who are given discretion to buy or sell securities for the plan
- Those who give advice, on a regular basis, pursuant to an agreement (which can be oral as well as written), that is intended to serve as a primary basis for investing plan funds. Furthermore, the advice given must be specific and individualized, not general (e.g., "Sell 10,000 shares of Apple and re-invest the proceeds in the following five health care stocks," but not "We're cautious about the high-tech sector this quarter.")

The DOL Regulations make it clear that a broker-dealer, bank, or reporting dealer does not become a fiduciary if its only role is to take and execute buy and sell orders for the plan. See §2510.3-21(d)(1). Furthermore, the investment manager is a fiduciary only with respect to whatever percentage of the overall investment he or she can influence (except in situations where ERISA §405(a) makes the investment manager responsible for breaches by co-fiduciaries).

17.4.3 The Role of the Insurer

In 1993, the Supreme Court decided *John Hancock Mutual Life Ins.* v. *Harris Trust*, 510 U.S. 86 (1993). This case's holding is that assets held in an insurer's general account, and not guaranteed by the insurer, are plan assets subject to ERISA's fiduciary requirements.

DOL was ordered to issue conforming regulations not later than 12/31/97. The effective date of the regulations is tricky: they are retroactive to 1/1/75 (i.e., the entire period of ERISA applicability) but they do not apply to lawsuits commenced before 11/7/95, and they are not applicable to insurance contracts sold after 12/31/98. (However, new policies sold after that date will be subject to the ERISA fiduciary rules.)

DOL's responsibility was to draft rules requiring a fiduciary independent of the insurance company to authorize the purchase of any policy other than life insurance, health insurance, or annuity contracts exempt from the prohibited transaction rules. Furthermore, the insurer, and not just the plan fiduciaries, has an obligation to act prudently.

DOL's Interpretive Bulletin 95-1 says that a fiduciary who chooses annuities to distribute plan benefits has a fiduciary duty to choose the safest available contract, based on factors such as the insurer's size and reputation, the insurer's other lines of business, and the size and provisions of the proposed contracts.

17.5 DUTY TO DISCLOSE

Employees will often ask for facts or advice about their benefit options. If they choose an option that later proves imprudent, or if the plan later changes to offer more favorable alternatives, the employees may charge the employer with misrepresentation or concealment.

Clearly it is wrong for an employer or a representative of the employer to lie to an employee about plan rights or the current provisions of the plan. At some point, the employer will have to mention the pendency of new plan rules. The hard part is drawing the line between vague possibilities and proposals that have already been discarded, at one end, and proposals that are certain to take effect in the future, at the other.

In March, 1997, the Second Circuit held an employer guilty of a breach of fiduciary duty for making material misrepresentations to employees about the future of the plan—whether or not the changes (including the amendments that the employer said it wouldn't adopt) were under "serious consideration" or not. But, just a few days later, the Tenth Circuit decided that misrepresentations can't be material unless a specific proposal was being discussed for implementation by senior managers who, in fact, have that power. In this reading, it is not necessary to disclose early exploration and evaluation of potential plan amendments.

There is a clear fiduciary duty to provide employees with copies of required documents. According to the Second Circuit, although ERISA §104(b)(4) requires the plan administrator to provide copies of "plan documents" on request, actuarial evaluation reports do not fall into this category, and don't have to be disclosed because they are more like non-binding advisory opinions than plan documents; however, the Sixth Circuit disagrees.

The Third Circuit ruled in mid-1997 that an employee can sue under ERISA §502(a)(3) for breach of fiduciary duty for failure to disclose pertinent information even where the employee had not specifically asked for it. In this case, a married employee opted for a joint and survivor annuity, but was not advised that this election was irrevocable. He divorced and remarried; the pension plan agreed to remove Wife #1 as an annuitant, but refused to either substitute Wife #2 or recast the annuity as a single-life annuity for the employee's life. The Third Circuit examined trust law concepts and decided that a fiduciary has a duty to speak up where silence could be harmful to a beneficiary's interests, and decided to apply that principle to ERISA plans.

ERISA §502(c) allows the Department of Labor to impose a penalty of $110 per day (dating from the date of failure or refusal to send the documents) on a plan administrator who doesn't comply with a participants or beneficiary's request for plan documents within 30 days. Administrators can be penalized even if their failure is not deliberate, but cannot be penalized if it is due to matters beyond their reasonable control.

17.6 PENALTIES FOR FIDUCIARY BREACH

If a fiduciary breaches the required duties, he or she or it can be sued by plan participants, plan beneficiaries, and/or the Department of Labor. Penalty taxes can be imposed for improper transactions involving the plan.

A fiduciary who is guilty of a breach of duty is personally liable to the plan, and has to compensate it for any loss in value caused by the violation. If the fiduciary benefited financially from the breach, he or she must also "disgorge"—give up—the ill-gotten gains. (See ERISA §409). However, liability only occurs if there is a causal connection between a breach and loss or improper profits; fiduciaries don't have to (and couldn't anyway) guarantee that the plan will never, ever lose any money.

The plan can get a court to order that the faithless fiduciary be removed from office, and that he or she pay the plan's attorney's fees and interest on the money involved. However, even if the fiduciary behaved outrageously, the plan's participants can't get an award of punitive damages, but some courts will award punitive damages to the plan itself. In egregious cases, the fiduciary might face criminal penalties instead of, or in addition to, civil penalties. Generally speaking, §409 grants relief to the plan itself; participants and beneficiaries find their relief under §502(a)(3).

Another penalty section, §502(i), requires DOL to impose a civil penalty on fiduciaries who violate the fiduciary responsibility provisions of Title I. A non-fiduciary who knowingly participates in a fiduciary violation can also be penalized under this section. The base penalty is 20% of the court-ordered penalty under ERISA §502(a)(2) or (a)(5). In a case where the fiduciary or helper settled with the

DOL to avoid being taken to court, the base penalty is 20% of the amount of the settlement. The penalty can be reduced or even waived if the person acted reasonably and in good faith. The main objective is to safeguard the plan, so a reduction or waiver can also be obtained if the fiduciary or helper would not be able to reimburse the plan without severe financial hardship if the full penalty were assessed. (See page 334 for a discussion of the various enforcement-oriented sections of ERISA.)

The Taxpayer Relief Act of 1997 §1502 adds a new ERISA section, 206(d), and new Code language at §401(a)(13)(C) permitting "bad boy" clauses: i.e., fiduciaries who are plan participants can have their pensions reduced if they are guilty of breaches of fiduciary duty, if they commit crimes against the plan and are convicted, if they lose or settle a civil suit, or enter into a Department of Labor or PBGC settlement.

17.7 INDEMNIFICATION OF FIDUCIARIES

ERISA §410 says that language in a plan (or a side agreement with a fiduciary) is void as against public policy if it limits the fiduciary's liability for breach of fiduciary duty. However, the employer (as distinct from the plan) can permissibly indemnify the fiduciary or buy insurance covering him or her; the fiduciary can also buy insurance personally.

Where the plan itself is the insured, the insurer can sue the fiduciary to collect the amount that it had to pay out. Fiduciary liability insurance is usually available only in limited amounts, and on a claims-made basis (see pages 583–4 for a discussion of claims-made policies). Another option is for the sponsor corporation to agree to use corporate assets to indemnify the fiduciary; the Department of Labor permits this, and does not consider it a prohibited transaction.

17.8 LIABILITY OF CO-FIDUCIARIES

As you have seen above, the average plan has a great many people and individuals connected with it who (whether they know it or not) have the status of fiduciaries under the plan. In certain instances, all of them will be liable if a breach occurs; but in most instances, only certain of them will be liable.

If a plan's assets are held by more than one trustee, the general rule is that all the trustees are jointly responsible for management, unless the plan's trust instrument either makes a specific allocation of responsibility, or sets up a procedure for allocating the responsibility. Every trustee has a legal duty to use reasonable care to make sure the other fiduciaries aren't breaching *their* duties. To avoid liability, it simply isn't enough for a fiduciary to prove that he or she acted properly; any fiduciary's misconduct implicates all the others.

ERISA §405(c) (1) permits a plan to make an explicit allocation of fiduciary responsibility (other than the responsibility of trustees) among the named fiduciaries. The plan can also have procedures for fiduciaries to designate a party who or that is not a named fiduciary to carry out fiduciary responsibilities under the plan. The general rule is that the fiduciary who designates someone else will not be responsible for the acts or omissions of the designee. There are two major exceptions: first, if making or continuing the designation violates the designor fiduciary's duties under ERISA §404(a)(1); and second, if ERISA §405(a) makes the designor responsible for the co-fiduciary's breach.

Fiduciaries are liable for the acts and omissions of their fellow fiduciaries under several circumstances:

- They either knowingly participate in or knowingly conceal an act of another party that they know to be a breach

- They fail to perform their own general fiduciary duties as stated by ERISA §404(a)(2) with respect to the specific responsibilities that make them fiduciaries, if the result of poor performance is that someone else is therefore able to commit a breach

- One fiduciary knows about another fiduciary's breach, but fails to make reasonable efforts to remedy it.

⇒ **TIP**

If the first fiduciary is comparatively free from blame, it's possible that he or she will be entitled to indemnification from the fiduciary who actually committed the breach.

If a fiduciary and a non-fiduciary cooperate in committing a breach of the fiduciary's duty, the Supreme Court has decided that the plan can get equitable remedies against the non-fiduciary. For instance, he or she can be enjoined against further participation in improprieties. The non-fiduciary cannot be held jointly and severally liable with the fiduciary. (See page 318 for more discussion of joint and several liability in the context of claims made by ERISA plans.)

Some courts have applied this case to prevent any claims by plans against non-fiduciaries. This only puts more pressure on the fiduciaries, because then they are the only potential defendants if something goes wrong. On the other hand, *Brock v. Gerace*, 635 F.Supp. 563 (D.N.J. 1986) does make even a nonfiduciary liable to the ERISA plan if he or she knowingly participated in a prohibited transaction for personal profit. Fiduciaries cannot be liable for other fiduciaries' conduct occurring before they themselves become fiduciaries, nor do they have a duty to remedy breaches that occurred before their tenure or after they cease to be fiduciaries.

17.9 ERISA PREEMPTION

The question of ERISA preemption of state regulation arises frequently with respect to health plan claims, and is discussed in that context on page 121. Preemption analysis is also necessary in the context of pension and benefit cases. The Tenth Circuit says that ERISA does not preempt claims about promises of job security, but it does preempt claims relating to promises about employee benefits. The Fifth Circuit applies ERISA preemption to claims of intentional infliction of emotional distress via alleged wrongful denial of disability benefits. But the Sixth Circuit found that ERISA does not preempt a state business tax that covers all employee compensation including ERISA plans; in this view, the tax really doesn't have anything to do with the plans.

In the view of the Eleventh Circuit, the employer cannot get the case removed to federal court (even for the limited purpose of deciding the preemption issue) where the employee-plaintiff's state claims relate to benefits that are bundled into an ERISA plan but are not covered by ERISA; in a multi-benefit plan, ERISA preemption is limited to the ERISA-covered benefits.

17.10 ERISA LITIGATION

In early 1997, the District Court for the District of Colorado ruled that plan participants' ERISA claims to recover benefits under a severance pay plan are legal, not equitable, so jury trial is available, although nine Circuits previously ruled to the contrary.

For a suit under ERISA §409 (breach of fiduciary duty), the statute of limitations derives from ERISA §413. Thus, the suit must be brought within the earlier of three years of the time the plaintiff became aware of the alleged wrongdoing, or six years from the date of the last incident of breach or the last date on which the omission could have been cured.

17.11 PROHIBITED TRANSACTIONS

ERISA imposes a ban on certain types of transactions between the plan and parties who cannot be expected to be objective about these transactions. ERISA defines "parties in interest" and "disqualified persons" who are not allowed to deal with the plan in certain ways, even if the transaction itself is fair.

Title I of ERISA describes a prohibited transaction (between the plan and a party in interest; see below) as follows:

- Sale, exchange, or lease of property (including the plan's assumption of a mortgage, or a mortgage placed on the property by the party in interest during the 10 years before the transfer of the property to the plan)

- Extensions of credit
- Furnishing goods or services
- Transferring or using plan assets for the benefit of a party in interest
- Acquiring or holding employer securities that are not qualified, or in excess of the normal limit (usually 10% of the fair market value of the plan assets)

⇒ **TIP**

An "eligible account plan" (profit sharing, money purchase, or stock bonus) can be up to 100% invested in qualifying employer securities or real property, subject to the general fiduciary duties (other than the duty to diversify, which is excused in this context).

- A fiduciary dealing with the plan's income or assets in his or her personal interest or for his or her own account
- Payments to a fiduciary for his or her own account, from anyone who deals with the plan
- Fiduciary conflict of interest: the fiduciary acts (whether in individual or any other capacity) on behalf of a party, or representing a party, in any transaction involving the plan if the represented party's interests are adverse to the interests of the plan or of its participants and beneficiaries.

The IRS collects the excise taxes on prohibited transactions. In addition, if a plan that is not qualified under Title I engages in a prohibited transaction, the Department of Labor can assess a civil penalty that is more or less equivalent to the excise tax.

The definition of "party in interest" can be found in ERISA §3(14). The scope of the definition is quite broad, and everyone with a central or even a peripheral relationship to the plan (and especially to the plan assets) will be swept in. Any of these is a party in interest (PII):

- Any fiduciary or relative of a fiduciary
- Plan employees or counsels to the plan, or their relatives
- The plan's service providers and *their* relatives
- Any employer or employee organization (e.g., union) whose members are covered by the plan
- Anyone who has a direct or indirect 50% ownership interest in the employer corporation (measured based on the combined voting power of all the classes of voting stock, or the total value of the shares of all classes of stock) or relatives of the 50% owner

- A corporation, partnership, trust, or estate that is 50% or more directly or indirectly controlled by the people in the above categories (but not those who appear on the list only as relatives of people involved with the plan)

- Employees, officers, and directors (or those with similar powers and responsibilities) of organizations in the list

- Employees, officers, and directors of the plan

- Anyone who has a direct or indirect 10% share ownership in the plan or in an organization that is closely related to the plan (e.g., one that provides services to the plan; an employer whose employees are covered by the plan)

- Anyone who has a direct or indirect 10% interest in the capital or profits of a partnership or a joint venture with anyone on the list.

Of course, a PII who is also a plan participant or beneficiary is entitled to receive benefits under the plan, as long as the same rules apply to PIIs as to the other participants and beneficiaries.

A disqualified person who engages in a prohibited transaction can be required to pay an excise tax even if he or she didn't know that the transaction was prohibited. The excise tax is 15% of the amount involved per year, (increased from its prior level of 5% in 1996 to 10%, then increased to 15% by the Taxpayer Relief Act of 1997). This is in addition to 100% of the amount involved when the IRS sends a notice informing the disqualified person that the transaction is prohibited, and that person does not rescind the transaction within 90 days of receiving the notice.

The 1996 amendment also narrows the scope of transactions exempt from the excise tax. Under earlier law, any transaction exempt under ERISA §408(b) was also exempt from excise tax; but the current rule is that only transactions exempt under §408(b)(12) will escape excise taxation.

17.11.1 *Prohibited Transactions of Welfare Benefit Plans*

The rules covering fiduciaries of welfare benefit plans are slightly different from those for pension plans, but the similarities are more compelling than the differences. (ERISA §502(i); a cumulative surtax is imposed on breaching parties in interest.) The tax is 5% of the amount of the prohibited transaction. Consult Code §4975(f)(5) to measure the amount involved in a prohibited transaction. The tax is cumulative in that, if a transaction lasts for several years (e.g., an improper five-year lease between the plan and a party in interest), the tax is imposed each year: for instance, for the first year, the tax would be 5% of the annual rent times 5, for the second year, 5% of the annual rent times 4, and so on for the five years.

For welfare benefit plans, as for pension plans, there is a 100% excise tax on the failure to correct a prohibited transaction within the correction period which begins with the first day of the prohibited transaction and ends 90 days after the

DOL (or other relevant federal agency) order relating to the transaction becomes final. (If the plan enters a timely challenge to the order, the 90-day period does not begin until the order is upheld by the last court to hear the case.)

17.12 PROHIBITED TRANSACTION EXEMPTIONS

The scope of the prohibited transaction rules is extremely broad—so much so that transactions that are, in fact, advantageous to the plan and not abusive might generate liability for their participants. In recognition of this fact, ERISA allows the DOL to respond to plans' requests for "Prohibited Transaction Exemptions" that allow otherwise forbidden transactions to be carried out without penalty.

The exemptions fall into two main classes. First are the specific exemptions set out in ERISA §408. The second class is the general authority that the Departments of Labor and Treasury have to issue exemptions after the agencies have conferred.

> ➠ **TIP**
>
> Retroactive exemptions are difficult, but not impossible, to achieve; see DOL Technical Release No. 85-1 for the procedure.

There is no single form of prohibited transaction exemption. They can be conditional or unconditional, granted by either Department or by both, relating to a particular disqualified person or party in interest, and covering one transaction, a class of transactions, or a class of disqualified persons or parties in interest. The exemption could relieve the deal participants from all the consequences of entering into a prohibited transaction, or only some.

Before granting the exemption, the DOL or DOT must decide that the proposed exemption is administratively feasible, whether it serves the best interests of participants and beneficiaries, and whether it protects participant and beneficiary rights. An individual exemption requires not only an application to the agency, but also notice to affected parties and publication in the *Federal Register*.

Affected parties can place their comments (positive or negative) on the record. In certain instances, a hearing may be required—for instance, when a fiduciary seeks to deal with the plan for his own account or to represent an adverse party.

> ➠ **TIP**
>
> For application procedures, see ERISA Procedure 75-1, Revenue Procedure 75-25, and IRS Announcement 79-6.

17.12.1 Statutory Exemptions

With respect to plan loans, ERISA exempts loans to participants and beneficiaries who are also Parties in Interest if:

- The plan is drafted to grant the specific authority to make loans to participants and beneficiaries
- All participants and beneficiaries have reasonably equal access to loans
- Officers, shareholders, and highly compensated employees are not granted access to larger loans than rank-and-file participants
- The plan receives a reasonable rate of interest on the loans
- The loans are made on reasonable security, which can include up to (but not exceeding) 50% of the borrower's nonforfeitable accrued plan benefits

The statutory exemption relating to securities and property exempts:

- Professional services (e.g., legal and accounting) and office space provided by a PII—as long as the plan actually needs the services, and pays a reasonable market rate for them

⇒ **TIP**

The fees charged by the preceding service provider who was *not* a PII make a good benchmark.

- Depositing funds in a financial institution that is a fiduciary, if it pays a reasonable rate of interest on the deposits
- Buying insurance from an insurance company that is the employer sponsoring the plan, or is owned by the employer or by a PII, if the premiums are reasonable. There is a further requirement that insurance sales to the plan must not exceed 5% of total premium income.
- Paying reasonable compensation to a PII for services to the plan; reimbursing reasonable expenses the PII incurred while taking care of plan business

⇒ **TIP**

Someone who receives full-time pay from the employer or from a union is only entitled to expense reimbursement, not compensation.

- Investment in qualifying employer securities and real property in excess of 10% of plan assets—as long as the plan purchases these items with adequate consideration, at a reasonable price, and does not have to pay a commission to acquire them from the employer.

A qualifying employer security is either stock or a marketable obligation such as a bond, debenture, or note. Depending on the type of security, the plan cannot hold more than 25%–50% of the entire issue.

17.12.2 Class Exemptions

It would be unduly burdensome on the agencies to have to make an individual determination in every case of a commonplace and harmless transaction. To cut down on the caseload, the DOL and DOT have adopted class-wide exemptions. Anyone who qualifies can take advantage of the exception without making an individualized application for a prohibited transaction exemption.

Many class exemptions have been granted; some of the most commonly used include:

- PIIs who provide investment advice to the plan
- Transactions that are specifically required, or at least authorized, by a federal court
- Interest-free loans
- Paying loan fees to a fiduciary that is a lending institution
- Mortgage loans to PIIs
- Sales of insurance by companies related to the employer
- Transactions involving plan assets that are managed by a qualified professional asset manager.

17.13 PROHIBITED TRANSACTION PENALTIES

In addition to the §4975 penalties, ERISA §502(i) gives the DOL power to assess a civil penalty against a party in interest who is involved in a prohibited transaction with a plan that is not subject to §4975 (which covers qualified plans and IRAs). The §502(i) penalty, which is usually assessed in connection with top-hat plans, is 5% for every year or partial year in which the transaction occurs, with an additional 100% penalty if the DOL issues a notice of violation, but the violation is not corrected within 90 days (or any extension granted by the DOL).

17.14 ENFORCEMENT UNDER ERISA SECTION 502

One section that is central to enforcement is ERISA §502, which gives participants and beneficiaries, the Department of Labor, and fiduciaries access to many legal and equitable remedies for a variety of causes of action (to be examined in more detail below). In fact, a major task for litigators can be deciding which subsection of §502 to use to bring a claim; and defendants can get claims dismissed if an attempt is made to get remedies that are unavailable under a particular subsection, or if a party ineligible to be a plaintiff brings the claim.

Under §502, "participant" is defined to mean an employee or ex-employee who is or may become eligible to receive any benefit under the plan. "Beneficiary" means someone designated by either a participant or the plan terms as entitled or potentially entitled to benefits. A 1989 Supreme Court case limits the class of people who "may become eligible" to those who have a colorable claim to vested benefits, or a reasonable expectation of return to covered employment.

The Eighth Circuit has a somewhat more expansive interpretation: it says that people who claim they would have been participants if the employer hadn't violated ERISA and deprived them of the right to participate, can bring suit under §502.

Participants and beneficiaries (but *not* the DOL, the employer, or the plan itself) can use §502(a)(1)(B) to bring suit to recover benefits due under the terms of the plan, to enforce rights under the terms of the plan, or to clarify rights to future benefits under the terms of a plan.

⇒ **TIP**

The plan administrator is so important to a suit for disability benefits that the suit can be dismissed if the plan administrator is *not* named as a defendant. However, the plaintiff will probably be allowed to start over again, naming all the proper parties.

Civil actions under §502(a)(2) can be brought by participants, beneficiaries, or the DOL to enforce ERISA §409 (breach of fiduciary duty). If recovery is ordered on behalf of the plan rather than of one or more individuals, it can be higher than what individuals would receive.

The DOL, participants, beneficiaries, and fiduciaries can sue under §§502(a)(3) and (a)(5) to enjoin violations of ERISA Title I (i.e., to get a court order telling someone to stop doing something that violates Title I) or get equitable relief under Title I (such as an order to someone to carry out the terms of the plan). Prejudgment interest can be granted under this subsection. It can also be used to penalize parties in interest for engaging in prohibited transactions (see page 334).

The remedies under §502(a)(3) can include ordering return of misappropriated plan assets, plus the profits improperly earned on them; but this remedy is not available in situations where the defendant did not hold plan assets or profit from their use. In 1993 the Supreme Court found that this subsection cannot be used to sue a non-fiduciary for money damages based on a claim that the non-fiduciary knowingly assisted a fiduciary in a breach of fiduciary duty. The types of relief that are available include imposing a constructive trust (for instance, on insurance proceeds that were wrongly withheld) and equitable estoppel.

In 1996, the Supreme Court pointed out that fiduciary obligations cannot be satisfied while lying to participants, so it permitted a §502(a)(3) suit for individualized equitable relief against a company that told its employees that their benefits would be safe if they transferred to a new division that the company spun off. In fact, the new corporation was created to collect money-losing divisions; it was insolvent from its creation. The Supreme Court ruled that the corporation was acting as a fiduciary when it lied about benefit security; a reasonable employee would have believed that the company was speaking in its joint roles as employer and fiduciary.

If ERISA §105 (requirement of providing benefit statements) is violated, the DOL, participants, or beneficiaries can sue under §502(a)(4). Plans that fail to supply the information required by Title I can be sued, under §502(a)(1)(A), for a penalty of $110 a day; in this instance, only participants and beneficiaries are permitted plaintiffs.

Section 502(a)(6) authorizes civil actions by the Department of Labor to collect the excise tax on prohibited transactions or the penalty tax on fiduciary violations. State governments (not the federal DOL) can sue under §502(a)(7) to enforce compliance with a Qualified Medical Child Support Order (QMCSO; see page 153). The states have a role to play here because they have traditionally been empowered to deal with family law, including child support.

Funds from an insurance contract or annuity purchased in connection with termination of participant status (e.g., at retirement; when someone ceases to be an employee; when a plan is terminated) can be secured by a suit under §502(a)(9). The potential plaintiffs are the DOL, plan fiduciaries, or persons who were participants or beneficiaries at the time of the violation. However, suit can only be brought if the insurance or annuity purchase violated either the terms of the plan or ERISA's provisions on fiduciary responsibility.

Both the federal and the state courts have jurisdiction under §502(e) when participants or beneficiaries bring suit to recover benefits, clarify their rights to future benefits, or enforce rights under any plan that falls under ERISA Title I. Any other type of Title I claim can only be heard by a federal court, not a state court, if the case goes to court. (ERISA doesn't rule out binding arbitration of claims.)

As discussed on page 329, Code §4975 penalizes prohibited transactions in a qualified plan or IRA. In other types of plan (for instance, top-hat plans for executives), ERISA §502(i) gives the DOL power to assess a civil penalty against a party in interest who engages in a prohibited transaction. The base level of the penalty is 5% per year or portion of a year, but the level increases to 100% if the DOL issues a notice of violation, yet the violation remains uncorrected within 90 days (or a longer period, if the DOL grants extended time for compliance but the plan still fails to return to compliance).

Section 502(k) permits plan administrators, fiduciaries, participants, and beneficiaries to sue the Department of Labor in District Court (not the other way around) to require the agency to undertake an action required by Title I of ERISA, to prevent the Department from acting contrary to Title I, or to review a final order of the Secretary of Labor. Section 502 also allows fiduciaries to seek an injunction against anyone who has violated the plan's terms, or ERISA Title I. Under this section, fiduciaries can ask the court to remove another fiduciary from office.

The Department of Labor is not only allowed but required to impose civil penalties under §502(l) against a fiduciary who violates the Title I provisions on fiduciary responsibility, and also on anyone who knowingly participates in the violation. The basic penalty equals 20% of the amount the court orders to be paid pursuant to §§502(a)(2) or (a)(5), or of the settlement the fiduciary reaches with the DOL to avoid a trial. Any penalty imposed under §502(i), or any penalties or taxes imposed on prohibited transactions, can be used to offset this penalty. The Secretary of Labor has discretion to reduce or waive the penalty if the fiduciary acted reasonably and in good faith—or, on the other hand, if the waiver makes it possible for the fiduciary to return the losses to the plan without suffering undue financial hardship.

17.15 SECTION 510

This section of ERISA imposes civil and criminal penalties for interference with anyone's Title I rights. The typical example is firing an employee to prevent benefit accrual, or in retaliation against someone who has made a claim for plan benefits. An employee who claims he or she was fired for this reason must bring an ERISA suit, not a state-court suit for wrongful termination, because ERISA preempts wrongful termination litigation in this context.

Other forbidden acts are suspending, expelling, disciplining, or discriminating against employees with the objective of interfering with the attainment of benefits or the exercise of rights under the plan. In 1997, the Supreme Court clarified that this section covers welfare benefits as well as pension benefits—it's not necessary that the benefits be subject to vesting for this section to be triggered.

➠ TIP

The First Circuit says it's also unlawful to fire a participant because a beneficiary (e.g., the participant's spouse) makes a claim for benefits. Altering records of the date of an employee's discharge, in order to deny medical benefits, also violates §510. To win, the employee has to prove that benefit discrimination was *a* determining factor (not necessarily that it was the only motivation for the discharge).

However, the plaintiff must show that the defendant specifically intended to interfere with protected rights. For instance, if an employee was fired for good cause, one natural consequence of the discharge is loss of future employee benefits—but that doesn't mean that the employer did anything wrong.

The Title VII "burden-shifting" analysis discussed in Chapter 27 applies to ERISA cases as well. That is, first the plaintiff proves a prima facie case; if he or she can't do that, the case is dismissed at an early stage. If a prima facie case is proved, then the defendant gets a chance to give a clear, specific explanation of (a) legitimate, nondiscriminatory reason(s) for the action that the plaintiff claims was motivated by discrimination. Finally, the plaintiff gets another chance, this time to prove by a preponderance of the evidence (i.e., not beyond a reasonable doubt, but by proving his or her explanation is more likely than not) that the employer's explanation sounds good but is just a pretext for discrimination.

17.16 OTHER ENFORCEMENT ISSUES

The main ERISA criminal penalties are imposed by §511, which provides that it is a crime, punishable by up to one year's imprisonment and/or a fine of $10,000, to use or threaten force, fraud, or violence to restrain, coerce, or intimidate a participant or beneficiary, in order to interfere with or prevent exercise of any right to which that person is or may become entitled under either ERISA Title I or the terms of the ERISA plan itself. Criminal penalties can also be imposed under §501, for willful violations of the Title I reporting and disclosure regulations. An individual can be fined up to $5,000 and imprisoned for up to five years (or both); a business entity can be fined up to $100,000.

Under ERISA §409(a), a breaching fiduciary is personally liable to the plan to make up for losses caused by the breach (i.e., the amount the plan would have earned from appropriate investments, minus the amount actually earned), and also for whatever other legal and equitable remedies the court chooses to impose: for instance, removal of the fiduciary from office, and an order to disgorge the profits improperly earned at the plan's expense. Relief under this section goes to the plan itself, not to individual participants (they can use §502(a)(3) to press their claims).

But see the Supreme Court case of *Peacock* v. *Thomas*, #94-1453, 116 S.Ct. 862 (2/21/96). In this case, the plaintiff won an ERISA case against his employer, but could not collect the judgment, allegedly because a corporate officer who was not a fiduciary misappropriated the funds that could have been used to satisfy the judgment. The plaintiff could not "pierce the corporate veil" and make the corporate officer personally liable, for various technical legal reasons. For one thing, the case wasn't closely enough related to ERISA for federal courts to get involved; and a federal court can't enforce a judgment against someone who was not liable for it in the first place.

The Department of Labor has authority under §504(a)(1) to investigate whether a Title I violation has occurred, so the employer might be ordered to submit books, papers, and records for DOL examination. This can be done only once in a 12-month period unless the Department has reasonable cause to believe that Title I was violated.

Under §504(c), the DOL has subpoena power over books, records, and witnesses for its investigations. Such a subpoena can be enforced in federal court, but only if the agency shows that the investigation has a legitimate purpose, the inquiry is relevant to that purpose, and the government doesn't already have the information it is seeking.

ERISA §515 permits a civil action against an employer for delinquency in making contributions. This section does not contain an express statute of limitations; most courts that have considered the issue treat the statute of limitations as six years (typical for an action to enforce a written contract).

The statute of limitations is clear under a similar provision, ERISA §4003(e)(1) (which correlates with Code §412(n)). If the employer fails to make a required contribution to the plan, at a time when the plan's funded current liability percentage is lower than 100% and the employer owes the plan more than $1 million (including interest), then all of the employer's real and personal property becomes subject to a lien in favor of the plan.

The party that was supposed to, but didn't, make the payment has an obligation to notify the PBGC within 10 days of the payment due date. The PBGC has six years from the date of the missed payment, or three years from the time it knew or should have known about the missed payment, to go to federal District Court and sue to enforce the lien. Fraud or concealment on the part of the employer extends the statute of limitations to six years from the PBGC's discovery of the true state of events.

17.16.1 Exhaustion of Remedies

The court system is supposed to handle major conflicts, not minor, everyday disputes that could and should be addressed in less complex and socially expensive manners. Therefore, in many instances plaintiffs will be subject to a requirement of "exhaustion of remedies"—i.e., they will not be permitted to bring court cases until they have pursued administrative remedies within the system they are challenging. As noted on page 251, ERISA requires every plan to have a system for pursuing claims and appealing claim denials, and would-be plaintiffs generally must go through these steps before filing suit. ERISA itself doesn't say in so many words that exhaustion of remedies is required, but judges have looked to ERISA's legislative history and other labor laws to determine when this requirement should be implied.

Plaintiffs will be required to exhaust their remedies within the plan when their case involves benefits, but courts are split as to whether §510 plaintiffs (interference with protected rights) are required to exhaust their remedies. Exhaustion of remedies will not be required in certain special circumstances:

- Going through channels would be futile
- The defendant wrongfully denied the plaintiff access to the claims procedure under the plan, so it was impossible to pursue plan remedies

- There would be irreparable harm if exhaustion of remedies were required
- Participants and beneficiaries were deprived of information about claims procedures, so they didn't know how to enforce their rights.

17.17 PROCEDURAL ISSUES IN ERISA LITIGATION

Some of the basic litigation issues are not explicitly settled by the text of ERISA, so courts have to draw analogies with other relevant laws. Most decisions say that jury trials are unavailable in §§502(a)(1)(B) and (a)(3) cases (see page 334 for a discussion of the various subsections of §502). Another possibility is that a jury will be empanelled in those cases, but it will only determine the part of the case relating to breach of contract; claims of breach of fiduciary duty will be resolved by the decision of the judge in the case.

ERISA specifies what the statute of limitations will be for actions for breach of fiduciary duty, but not for other actions. Those for fiduciary breach must be brought either three years from the time the plaintiff finds out about the breach, or six years after the last improper action by the fiduciary—whichever comes first. If the source of the suit is an omission by a fiduciary rather than a wrongful action, the time limit is six years from the last date the fiduciary could have cured the problem. If the case was complicated by fraud or concealment, the limitations period is six years from the plaintiff's discovery of the breach, rather than the three-year period that applies when there has been no fraud or concealment.

In cases where the court must imply a statute of limitations, it will probably use one applicable in contract cases, or in other labor law cases.

By and large, ERISA cases are treated like contract cases, so the damages available to a successful plaintiff basically put the plaintiff in the same position he or she would have been in if the contract had been complied with. That means that "extra-contractual" damages (for instance, damages for negligent or intentional infliction of emotional distress) probably will not be permitted. In most ERISA cases, punitive damages are also ruled out.

In any ERISA action brought by participants, beneficiaries, or fiduciaries, the winning side (whether plaintiff or defendant) can be awarded reasonable costs and attorneys' fees if the court thinks this is appropriate. The amount of attorneys' fees awarded by the court usually starts out with the "lodestar" figure: the number of hours the winning lawyer spent on the case, multiplied by an hourly rate the court deems reasonable. In rare cases, the lodestar is reduced (if the court thinks the lawyer could have expedited matters, for instance); sometimes it is enhanced (because the case was especially difficult, the lawyer broke new ground with innovative legal theories, or because the lawyer took some risks, such as challenging the main employer in a "company town").

Part IV

EMPLOYEE RELATIONS; PROTECTING EMPLOYEES

Chapter 18

LABOR LAW

18.1 INTRODUCTION

At one time (especially during the period of prosperity shortly after the Second World War), labor unions were an immensely powerful bloc within American industry and American society. During that time, a body of federal labor law developed. (As will be discussed below, the acts of Congress have such a strong preemptive effect that states have very little power to make their own labor laws.)

Since that time, unions have become much weaker, and much less influential, for many reasons. In 1983, about one-fifth of U.S. wage and salary workers were union members. That percentage fell to 14.9% in 1996, and fell slightly more in 1997, to 14.5%—i.e., only about one worker in seven. For about two and a half decades (1972–1997, with the exception of 1980), the percentage of unions gaining election victories declined, and the number of decertification elections (to remove the union's authority to negotiate) increased.

The easiest kind of operation for a union to organize is a large factory with many well-paid blue collar workers who are eager to join together to enhance their salary and benefits and improve their working conditions. The workers must be secure enough to be able to make a credible threat of striking; they must believe that they will not descend to poverty during the strike, that they will be re-hired, and that the employer's interests will be gravely harmed by a suspension of production.

Over time, manufacturing has become less and less significant in the U.S. economy, and international operations have become more significant. In many instances, employers have found it economically worthwhile to shut down unionized operations. They either relocate in a state where unions have little power, or indeed leave the United States and operate factories in countries where labor costs are very low, and safety and environmental regulations far less onerous than in the United States.

In fact, as discussed in Chapter 8, permanent, full-time, salaried employment is becoming less significant, and part-time, contingent, per-project, and other forms of employment and utilization of independent contractors are becoming more important. However, the summer of 1997 marked something of an upswing for U.S. unions, with the Teamster victory in the UPS strike and a slight reversal in the downward trend of union membership.

Section 7 of the NLRA says that employees have the right to engage in "protected concerted activities"; in other words, they can act together to form or join a union, present grievances, bargain collectively, go on strike, and picket.

In many instances, employees either feel powerless, or feel that unions can or will do little to protect them. They may feel that unionization will obligate them to pay dues, but will provide few real benefits, or that unions often have ties to organized crime or take such hard-nosed bargaining positions that employers will close their facilities rather than submit. Unions may put short-run retention of jobs ahead of adoption of new technology that will make the enterprise competitive in the long run.

For any and all of these reasons, employees may feel that unionization will harm rather than further their best interests.

➠ TIP

Once a union is certified, the employer is justified in discarding its entire benefit package and negotiating "from scratch" with the union. The result might be a LESS generous benefit package, if the union makes concessions in this area to get a better deal in other areas. The employer is entitled to give an accurate explanation of this phenomenon while workers are considering whether or not to vote for the union.

Federal labor law determines what is legitimate and illegitimate conduct—by both management and labor—during the campaign to certify a union (unionize a workplace). In essence, the employer can use its power to present an honest statement of its arguments to the workers, but must allow would-be unions a certain amount of latitude to present their case. (As page 351 shows, employers are not obligated to give unions a full-scale soap box, to the detriment of efficient operations.)

Labor law also determines the process of bargaining for a Collective Bargaining Agreement (CBA), and the settlement of disputes through its interpretation. In situations that involve such an interpretation, only federal law applies, and the states are powerless to impose their own rules.

Once again, labor law determines when a lawful strike can be called, what tactics are lawful during the strike, the extent to which the employer can hire replacements for strikers and can or cannot refuse to reinstate strikers after a strike. Labor law also has a procedure for decertifying a union if it is not truly representative of worker interests, or if the union is guilty of misconduct.

Either an employer or a union can be guilty of an "unfair labor practice" by violating the rules of engagement. The National Labor Relations Board (NLRB) has the power under federal law to issue "cease and desist" orders if it deems that an unfair practice has occurred. The NLRB's powers also extend to issuing mandatory orders—for instance, ordering an employer to bargain with a union.

More specifically, NLRA §8 defines unfair labor practices to include:

- Refusal (by either employer or union) to engage in collective bargaining

- An employer's domination of a union

- Retaliation against employees because they file charges with the NLRB, or testify before the NLRB

- Discrimination against employees based on either their union activities or their refusal to join a union. However, if a "union security" clause is in place (see page 359), employees can be required to pay union dues or the equivalent, but not actually to join the union. In this context, discrimination includes firing, refusal to hire, refusal to reinstate, demotion, discrimination in work assignments or compensation, and the like.

- Featherbedding (deliberately inefficient work practices that require the employment of excessive numbers of workers)

- Certain practices in relation to strikes and picketing.

18.2 SOURCES OF LABOR LAW

Most labor law is federal law. During the Depression, the Wagner Act (1935), also known as the National Labor Relations Act (NLRA), established the National Labor Relations Board (NLRB) and made it clear that unions are an accepted part of the legal landscape.

The Labor-Management Relations Act (LMRA) of 1947, popularly known as the Taft-Hartley Act, extends the powers of the NLRB. It outlaws certain kinds of strikes, including strikes to enforce (rather than to protest) unfair labor practices, jurisdictional strikes, and secondary boycotts (pressure on a neutral company to keep it from dealing with a company that the union has a dispute with). The LMRA brings parity into labor law by penalizing not only unfair labor practices by employers, but those by unions, including:

- Restraining or coercing employees when they exercise their right to bargain collectively, choose a representative, or vote against unionization

- Causing an employer to discriminate against any employee

- Once the union becomes the authorized bargaining representative for the employees, refusing to participate in collective bargaining

- Strikes or concerted activity undertaken for the purpose of boycotting one employer, forcing another employer to recognize an uncertified union, forcing any employer to recognize a particular union when another union is actually the authorized bargaining representative, or in the course of a jurisdictional determination

- Requiring union members in a union shop (see page 360) to pay excessive initiation fees or excessive dues

- Featherbedding (demanding that the employer overstaff operations, merely to create or maintain jobs for union members).

The next major labor statute was the Landrum-Griffin Act, the Labor-Management Reporting and Disclosure Act (LMRDA) of 1959. It forbids hot-cargo agreements (agreements not to carry the merchandise of a company involved in a labor dispute), allows pre-hire agreements in the building and construction industries, and makes it an unfair labor practice to picket in order to force an employer to recognize or bargain with a union.

While most labor laws are federal, states do have a limited role in protecting their own legitimate interests, so they can pass certain labor laws that will not be preempted by federal law. For instance, states can regulate how and when picketing can be done, because of the legitimate state interest in preserving order and preventing violence.

States can also cope with issues that are only peripheral to the main purposes of the LMRA (for instance, defamation suits brought by employers against unions; whether companies have to continue providing welfare benefits to strikers; and internal union management). Another important state law area is union security. About a dozen states have right to work laws (see page 360) that forbid union shops and agency shops.

18.3 EMPLOYEE STATUS

The NLRA defines the rights of "employees," so it's important to determine who fits into this category. The basic rule is that someone who is a common-law employee (i.e., under the employer's control in terms of hiring, firing, work methods and results, provision of tools and materials, employee discipline) will also be an employee for this purpose. Independent contractors are not "employees."

The text of the NLRA (29 U.S.C. §152) says that "supervisors" (e.g., foremen and –women) are not "employees," for the common-sense reason that the supervisors promote management interests and therefore make an uncomfortable fit with rank-and-file workers who have different and often opposing interests.

A supervisor has a formal job title indicating supervisory status, has been held out as a supervisor by management, or is perceived as a supervisor by rank-and-file workers. A supervisor makes independent, individual judgments, can reward or discipline employees (including firing them) and has authority to adjust employee grievances. Supervisory authority must exist (whether or not it is exercised) on a consistent basis; sporadic or limited authority (e.g., in an emergency) will not make a rank-and-file worker into a supervisor. Courts have expanded this statutory requirement, so that managers are not considered employees either. Managers have similar discretion, with the additional ability to set corporate policy.

> ⟶ **TIP**
>
> In May, 1997, the First Circuit held that a TV station's technical directors were not "supervisors," and should have been included in the bargaining unit. The rationale was that they don't have to make important emergency decisions, and they're not held responsible if the production crew does sloppy work.

Part-time workers are considered employees, although sometimes it is inappropriate to place them in a bargaining unit with full-timers, if their interests are adverse. Employee status is maintained during a temporary layoff where there is a reasonable expectation of recall in the future. A sick or injured worker continues to be an employee until he or she either takes another permanent full-time job, or is permanently physically unable to return to work. Temporary or casual workers will probably not be considered employees.

Perhaps surprisingly, retirees are *not* considered employees once they are off the company's active payroll and have no right to be rehired or any reasonable expectation of rehiring. The non-employee status of retirees has implications for the treatment of retiree health benefits: see page 195.

18.3.1 Status of Professional Union Organizers

It is perfectly lawful for an employer to maintain a nondiscriminatory, uniformly applied policy against moonlighting—i.e., not employing anyone who also holds another job (or another full-time job). If there is such a policy, it does not constitute unlawful discrimination for the employer to refuse to hire someone who also works as a paid union organizer. However, the union can prevail by showing that the policy is in fact not neutral, if the employer accepts non-union forms of moonlighting while refusing to hire organizers.

Nevertheless, a paid union organizer can qualify as a protected employee who is covered by the NLRA; the fact that he or she is paid a salary by the union does not deprive him or her of the protection of federal labor law.

This concept has been extended to treat a volunteer union organizer who is not paid by the union as an employee, even one who engages in conduct that is adverse to the employer.

If the NLRB general counsel charges that employees were fired for pro-union activity (rather than, for instance, poor performance, or because the employer was short of money and had to reduce the payroll), the NLRB has the duty of proving the anti-union motivation; it's not up to the employer to prove legitimate motivation for the discharge.

18.4 ELECTIONS, CERTIFICATION, AND RECOGNITION

A union becomes the employees' bargaining agent, and the employer becomes obligated to deal with it, if the union gains "certification" by winning a union election under the supervision of the NLRB. The employer is then obligated to negotiate in good faith with the certified union. From the union's perspective, there is a one-year period during which no rival union is entitled to seek certification itself.

An organizing campaign begins with a petition for certification. Typically, the petition is filed by the union or by an individual employee who is a union supporter. If there are two or more unions seeking to organize the same workplace, the employer can verbally express a preference for one over the other.

A certification petition is valid only if at least 30% of the employees in the particular bargaining unit indicate their interest. Acceptable indications of interest are authorization cards, union membership cards or applications for membership, records of union dues, or employee signatures on certification petitions. Usually the main work of organizing is done by employees who are pro-union, because employers can and usually do bar non-employees from soliciting on business premises during working hours (but see page 354 for limitations on this right).

It is a serious unfair labor practice for employers to retaliate against workers *because* of their union activism, so it's important to document good business reason for any disciplinary action taken against less-than-optimal workers who also happen to be union activists.

> ⇒ **TIP**
> ───
> It is also an unfair labor practice for an employer to recognize a union that does *not* represent the majority of workers, so it must at least examine the authorization cards before agreeing to a consent election. However, if you anticipate an NLRB hearing, it is better *not* to examine the cards. If you don't know an employee expressed pro-union sentiments, then you can't retaliate against him or her on this basis, and disciplinary actions will be less vulnerable to challenge.

18.4.1 Consent Elections

The NLRB is responsible for determining the validity of the representation petition. If the employer does not oppose the holding of the election, the election is held on consent: the employer and union sign a contract permitting an election. The NLRB will probably have to accept the consent agreement's definition of the appropriate bargaining unit, unless it violates the law (e.g., includes guards in a mixed bargaining unit).

⇒ **TIP**

Within seven days of the time the NLRB's local Regional Director approves the consent agreement, the employer has to submit the "Excelsior List" to the Regional Director. This is a list of the names and addresses of every worker eligible to vote in the consent election; the Regional Director then distributes the list to all interested parties. (The name comes from the NLRB case of *Excelsior Underwear Inc.*, 156 NLRB 271 (1986).)

18.4.2 NLRB Hearings

Should the employer object, and if the NLRB finds that there is reasonable cause to believe that the union might be an appropriate representative for the employees, the NLRB holds a non-adversary hearing to determine if there is a question of representation.

⇒ **TIP**

This hearing cannot be used to raise claims of unfair labor practices by either side. In most instances, the hearing will result in the setting of a date for an NLRB-supervised, secret ballot election. The NLRB will then certify the result: whether or not the union has secured a majority vote. (Employers who are dissatisfied with the Regional Director's decision have the option of appealing to the central NLRB for review.)

A union will be certified as bargaining representative for the unit if it wins the votes of a majority of the voters (not a majority of those eligible to vote). But the election will not be valid unless a "representative number" of eligible employees actually voted. There is no bright-line test for whether the number of voters was representative. Many factors, such as the voter turnout, adequacy of the employees' notice of the election and opportunity to vote, and the presence or absence of unfair practices by the employer, are considered if the size of the electorate is challenged.

18.4.3 Electioneering and Communications

During a certification campaign, it is important to understand the extent to which the employer can communicate its point of view to the employees, and the extent to which the employer can require union organizers and sympathizers to express their viewpoints somewhere other than within the workplace itself. The employer is considered a "person" entitled to exercise the right of free speech, but subject to limitations of accuracy and fairness. Overreaching by the employer can mean that election results are set aside (so the employer has to go through the whole process over again, perhaps with more employee sympathy for the union).

Examples of inappropriate practices are benefits announced on election day, explicit promises of benefits if the union loses, or threats to withhold benefits if the union wins. (However, it is permissible to delay pay raises until after the election, as long as only timing is the issue, and the raises will be paid no matter who wins the election.) It can also be unfair to announce new benefits during the critical period (to show that the employer offers a better deal than the union), unless the benefits were decided before the representation petition was filed, or there is economic justification for providing them at that time.

In egregious cases, the employer might have to answer charges of an unfair labor practice. On the other side, unfair practices by the union can also invalidate an election, as in the case where the union representative promised to throw "the biggest party in Texas" if the union won.

The time between the filing of a representation petition and the election itself is called the "critical period." The NLRB will take note of the conduct of both sides during this time, and perhaps the election will be invalidated (even if the conduct is not serious enough to constitute an unfair labor practice). The employer is also responsible for the conduct of its agents, including its lawyers and labor relations consultants.

➠ **TIP**

An employer can avoid liability for an inappropriate statement by an agent if it repudiates the statement promptly, admitting that it was out of line, restating it in proper form, and giving at least as much publicity to the retraction as to the original communication.

Certification elections are supposed to be pure enough to represent "laboratory conditions" for workplace democracy. (For a runoff or rerun election, the critical period begins at the first election, and even conduct before the certification petition was filed might be considered relevant in determining the fairness of the election.)

Employers are forbidden to conduct pre-election polls, or even to ask employees their opinions of unionization if the inquiry is too close to the time of the election. However, it is accepted labor law that the employer can call a meeting of workers on company time so the management can express its arguments against unionization. If the union is permitted to solicit employees during their meals and other breaks, then the employer can call the mass meeting without giving the union equal time to reply.

However, during the 24-hour period just before the election, neither management nor union is permitted to make speeches to massed employees on company time. If the employer does so, it is not an unfair labor practice, but could lead to invalidation of the election. Nevertheless, the employer is permitted to distribute printed materials to workers during this time. The employer can also conduct anti-union meetings away from the workplace during the 24-hour period, as long as the meetings are held on the employees' own time and attendance is voluntary. However, anyone who remembers high school assemblies should be cautious about the value of getting a bunch of workers together and making them listen to speeches as a method of making them feel more positive about the employer and its viewpoint.

The right to free speech extends to employees in the workplace to the extent that workers must be permitted to wear union buttons, even to the poll (even though such blatant electioneering would be improper in a political election). Wearing union insignia is protected by NLRA §7, and interfering with this right violates §8(a)(1), unless the union materials cause a real safety hazard, or there is a real risk of violence between union supporters and opponents. (The mere possibility of violence isn't enough.)

There is a partial exception: employees who work with the public, and who are required to wear a uniform, can be forbidden to wear all kinds of jewelry (including union buttons) and can be required to wear the standard uniform (and not a union t-shirt). But the employer must be careful to communicate the uniform policy, and to enforce it across the board, not just penalize union insignia.

18.4.4 Access by Non-Employees

In most instances, the workplace is private property, not a public space. Therefore, union organizers do not have a right to leaflet or distribute literature if this is contrary to the wishes of the employer or other owner of the property. An exception might occur in the "company town" situation, where in effect all property is owned by the employer, and the union has no public space where it can distribute literature. Another exception might be in a location that is so remote geographically that the union has no reasonable prospect of communicating with employees unless they can be reached at the workplace.

The Third Circuit has found that the NLRA is not violated when an employer denies access to its property to union representatives who want to distribute handbills accusing the employer of using underpaid non-union labor. In this context, the employer's property rights clearly prevail over the union's free speech right—especially because general information to the public, and not an actual certification election, was involved. The employer also has a right to control the use of in-plant bulletin boards (used for employer notices, social events, items for sale by employees, etc.) and to forbid the posting of union materials on those boards.

Can businesses located in a shopping mall forbid the distribution of union literature in that mall? The Eighth Circuit says that a business that is just a tenant (and therefore does not have exclusive rights to the corridor outside its business location) can't forbid union handbilling. But the Sixth Circuit says that it's permissible for a mall *owner* to ban solicitation by non-employee union representatives, even if other kinds of solicitation (e.g., the Red Cross and the Sierra Club) are allowed.

18.4.5 Election Procedures

Usually, the election will be held at the workplace, because that is accessible to all employees. However, if there is good cause shown to hold the election elsewhere, or to allow balloting by mail, the NLRB will supervise the out-of-plant election. It is held by secret ballot; potential voters enter the voting location, have their employee status checked, and then mark their ballots in a closed booth where their selections are not visible. The ballots are collected for later tallying.

Before a certification or deauthorization election (see below), the employer must post an election notice in conspicuous workplace locations for at least three full working days before 12:01 A.M. of the day scheduled for the election. Failure to post the notice can result in setting aside the election results. The notice must give the date, time, and place of the election, and must show a sample ballot so employees will know how to mark it to indicate their choice.

If there are objections to the eligibility of certain voters, or to the mechanics of the election, the employer or union can file the objections with the NLRB within seven days of the ballot tally. However, there is no absolute right to demand a post-election hearing. The Regional Director decides whether one is needed.

If an invalid election is carried out, and the employer relies on the results of the election to change policies within the workplace, the Ninth Circuit says that the appropriate remedy is to hold a new election. A bargaining order is improper unless there is proof that it would be impossible to hold a valid election.

18.4.6 Voter Eligibility

The simple answer is that all "employees" in the "bargaining unit" are entitled to vote in a representation election, although, as discussed below, it can be difficult to determine the appropriate bargaining unit, and there are some questions about who retains employee status.

A worker who has taken a voluntary leave of absence is entitled to vote unless the relationship with the employer has been severed. If the employee on leave retains seniority and is still in the employer's pension and benefit plans, he or she is probably an eligible voter. Employees on sick leave or maternity leave are entitled to vote, unless they have been actually or constructively terminated from employment.

For laid-off workers, the question is whether they have a reasonable expectation of recall (determined as of the date of the election, not the date of the NLRB pre-election hearing). Laid-off workers with no such reasonable expectation can't vote in an election about whether the union from the old plant can continue to represent workers after the employer's move to a smaller, more automated plant.

A person who was lawfully fired before the date of the election is not eligible to vote, but someone who is unlawfully discharged for union activity retains employee status, and therefore is entitled to vote.

Economic strikers who have not been replaced as of the date of the election are entitled to vote. (See page 366 for a discussion of how to characterize strikes, and page 367 for striker replacements.)

During the 12 months after the beginning of an economic strike, economic strikers are still entitled to vote if they have been replaced, even if they are not entitled to immediate reinstatement after the strike ends. Employees who are on the preferential reinstatement list are also entitled to vote. However, if the election is held more than 12 months after the beginning of a strike, replaced economic strikers are not entitled to vote, even if they still have a reasonable expectation of recall.

Replacement workers hired during an economic strike are entitled to vote in the election, but only if they were employed before the eligibility cutoff date for the election. In contrast to the situation for economic strikers, unfair labor practice strikers are always eligible to vote in representation elections; their replacements are never entitled to vote.

18.5 PREVENTIVE LABOR RELATIONS

In essence, employees are responsive to an organizing drive for many reasons. The more positive the employees' feelings about the company they work for, and the more truthful and candid they believe employer communications to be, the less likely they are to favor a representation election. If one is held, favorable feelings about the employer (perhaps in combination with negative feelings about the union) are more likely to mean that the organizing drive will fail.

Employers can promote positive feelings by making employees feel valued and wanted, listening to their suggestions and implementing the most valuable of them, and by offering a grievance procedure at least as beneficial as a union would provide under a collective bargaining agreement. If an employer constantly increases the compensation of its top executives, while claiming that it is unable to afford raises or benefits for employees, real discontent is likely.

Although employers are not permitted to lie to employees, threaten them, coerce them, or interfere with their desire to organize and bargain collectively, they are permitted to make an honest statement of their own case. The basic case for a non-union workplace is that it will be more harmonious and less contentious, and that employees will be economically better off than they would be after deduction of union dues. In effect, the employer's argument is that joining a union is simply a bad investment for workers.

The stakes for employers are high. Union workers earn basic compensation about 20% more than non-union workers. (Part of this is due to the fact that unions typically organize fairly skilled workers rather than minimum-wage-level workers, so much of the higher compensation is due to characterization of the workers rather than to union efforts.)

In the summer of 1997, the average wage was about $12 an hour, versus about $16 for unionized employees. But the most dramatic difference was in fringe benefits (a cost area that an employer often finds it very hard to control): the union fringe benefit package can be worth two to four times as much as a non-union benefit package. When all elements of compensation are taken into account, union workers earn about $22.50 per hour, as compared to slightly over $15 per hour for all workers. Furthermore, only 57% of all workers—but 85% of unionized workers—have health insurance at work. As Chapter 9 shows, health plans are a very expensive compensation element for the employer.

If the employer faces heavy competition (locally, nationally, or internationally), the union may oppose installing new technology that may cause some short-range job loss but that promotes long-range competitiveness. The employer may also have (or be able to get, through legitimate research methods) information about the union that wants to organize the operation. Union seniority rules may operate as a disadvantage to ambitious workers who can't get promotions when less skillful, energetic workers with more seniority block the way. Employees should know if the union has a documented history of improprieties, bad management, or simple bad judgment that has harmed other employees (e.g., by calling an injudicious strike that resulted in ignominious defeat for the union).

It also makes sense to adopt and implement a non-discriminatory "no solicitation" policy, forbidding solicitation not only for unions but also for charities, employees' small businesses, etc. This not only promotes efficiency but defuses accusations that the employer has discriminated against union organizing campaigns.

18.6 THE COLLECTIVE BARGAINING PROCESS

Under the NLRA, the whole purpose of certifying a union is so that there will be an ongoing process of collective bargaining between employer and union, dealing with important work-related issues. The major product of the process is the union contract, or Collective Bargaining Agreement (CBA); but even after a CBA is in place, it may be necessary to bargain on "mandatory" issues, and allowable to bargain on "permissible" issues. See 29 United States Code §158(a)(5).

> ⇒ **TIP**
>
> _____
>
> Bargaining is also illegal on some subjects. For instance, it is illegal to implement a closed shop, even if both employer and union are willing.

Bargaining must be done in good faith, not simply a sham; but neither side is obligated to make concessions or give in where it thinks it would be imprudent to surrender. If the bargaining process comes to an impasse (i.e., neither side is introducing new proposals or yielding on proposals already on the table), the employer can lawfully cease negotiating and simply put its own proposals into place.

Once a collective bargaining agreement expires, there is nothing left to be enforced under contract law. However, labor law (NLRA §8(a)(5)) says that the employer must maintain the status quo, at least until an impasse is reached and the employer can start implementing its own proposals unilaterally.

18.6.1 The Obligation to Bargain

In a unionized environment, the employer is obligated to bargain in good faith about certain issues; other issues are management prerogatives that can be set unilaterally by the employer without consulting the union. Mandatory bargaining subjects are those that materially or significantly affect the terms or conditions of employment, while issues that have a remote or incidental effect on the work environment are permissible subjects of bargaining. Where bargaining is required, the employer has a duty to meet with the union at reasonable times to confer over the terms and conditions of employment (such as wages and hours). Refusal to bargain is an unfair labor practice.

The first year after a union is certified is referred to as the "certification year," during which time no rival union can hold another election and the employer cannot claim that the union lacks majority status and thus refuse to bargain with it.

According to the NLRB, the employer cannot eliminate its existing comprehensive health plan and substitute a managed care program unilaterally, without bargaining, because the managed care system is an entirely new delivery system that is not part of the plan the union agreed to. Although the employer reserved the right to amend or modify the plan, this right does not extend to terminating one plan and substituting another.

Mandatory bargaining subjects include:

- Drug testing
- Dues checkoff (the employer's practice of deducting union dues from paychecks, then forwarding these amounts to the union)
- Work rules
- Bans on moonlighting by employees
- Transfers of work out of the bargaining unit
- Contracting out work done by bargaining unit employees (but not work done by non-unionized employees)
- Bonuses
- Medical insurance
- No strike/no lockout clauses.

It can often be difficult to determine whether an issue requires bargaining, or is a management prerogative. Simple relocation of bargaining unit work is probably a managerial decision, but even if the employer has the right to make the decision without union involvement, it has to engage in "effects bargaining," i.e., it must notify the union that the decision has been made, and bargain about the effects the change will have on union members.

Managerial prerogatives include:

- Complete termination of operations
- Sale of an entire business
- A partial closing that has business motivations, and is not the result of anti-union animus
- Relocation of unit work motivated by a basic change in the nature of the employer's operations, where the work at the new location is significantly different from the work at the old one.

The basic rule is that bargaining is required if a decision is undertaken to save labor costs, but the exception to this rule is that bargaining will be excused if the employer undertakes a program of modernization or environmental compliance that costs more than could potentially be saved via union concessions on labor costs.

Changing the methods of production is considered an employer prerogative, although employees who believe that they are adversely affected by the change can file a grievance or ask for effects bargaining about the change.

The Seventh Circuit says that the management rights clause permits the employer to unilaterally impose a policy controlling employees' use of drugs and alcohol both on and off the job. Although in general drug testing is a mandatory bargaining subject, the Fifth Circuit allows the employer to impose its policy unilaterally after a bargaining impasse.

18.6.2 Appropriate Bargaining Unit

A union cannot be certified, even after winning an election, unless it is organized as the appropriate bargaining unit for the enterprise. One area of uncertainty is that neither the employer nor the union can tell in advance what will be considered the appropriate bargaining unit, or how large it will be. A union can be organized by employer, craft, or plant (or by a subdivision of one of these categories).

⟫ TIP

A union decision to organize a craft unit is legally protected: the NLRB lacks the power to determine that a different unit would be more appropriate.

Under NLRA §9(b), the NLRB has power to determine the appropriate bargaining unit. The basic standard is whether there is a community of interest among unit members, as distinct from employees in general. (There's nothing unique about the desire to get a raise or better benefits, for instance.)

The appropriateness of a bargaining unit depends on the duties, skills, and working conditions of the employees who are supposed to have common interests. If there are competing proposed same bargaining units, their relative popularity with employees is highly significant.

Employees and supervisors cannot be in the same bargaining unit. (In many instances, supervisors cannot unionize at all, because they are considered a part of management.) In general, professionals and nonprofessionals cannot be included in the bargaining unit, but this rule can be waived if a majority of the professional employees vote to be included. (The non-professionals don't get veto power over inclusion of professionals.)

Determination of professional status does not depend entirely on job title. The factual determination is whether the work is predominantly intellectual, is not routine, requires discretion and independent judgment, mandates specialized knowledge, and cannot be standardized as to time. None of this means that professionals cannot be unionized—only that they must consent to inclusion in a non-professional bargaining unit instead of having their own.

If plant guards are unionized, they must have their own bargaining unit; they can't be organized with other employees, for the obvious reason that the employer would not feel very secure during a strike if several of the security guards were union activists, and one of them was the shop steward!

18.6.3 Typical CBA Clauses

Although naturally each CBA will be drafted to respond to the bargaining process, and to the nature of the workplace and its workforce, these are some of the major issues that are usually covered in CBAs:

- Description of the bargaining unit

- Management rights

- Workday and work week, including overtime

- Classification of jobs for wage purposes

- Compensation, bonuses, benefits

- Fringe benefits—health insurance for employees and dependents; benefit formulas including "caps"; pension plans; life insurance; etc.

- Paid time off—who is eligible; scheduling time off; who must be notified; paid holidays

- Sick leave—amount; how to compute it; waiting period; doctors' notes and other reporting provisions; discipline for misusing sick leave

- Seniority—whether service counts for the whole company, within the workgroup, department, bargaining unit, or plant; what constitutes a break in continuous service; and the effect of transitions in corporate ownership on seniority

- Subcontracting

- Plant closing and successorship

- Severance pay

- Union security and hiring hall

- Access to premises by non-employee union staff

- Progressive discipline—steps such as reprimands, conferences, and written warnings that will be provided before an employee is discharged

- Drug testing—whether random tests will be permitted, or whether there must be suspicion to test a particular person; which substances will be tested for; method used for initial and confirming tests; what level of detected substances will be considered a positive reading; what happens if an employee refuses to take a test; safeguarding employee rights; confidentiality of test results; records of testing; employee discipline subsequent to a positive reading

- Grievance procedures—scope of disputes covered; how employees can present complaints; steps in settling a grievance; whether grievances must be submitted to binding arbitration.

18.6.4 *Required Notices and Disclosures*

The employer must notify the union whenever it intends to terminate or modify a CBA, and must also notify the Federal Mediation and Conciliation Service of its intended action. Sixty days before the contract is scheduled to expire (or 60 days before the employer seeks to terminate or modify the terms of a contract that has no expiration date), the employer must notify the union, inviting it to negotiate a new or amended contract. Notice to the FMCS is due 30 days after the notice to the union, and 29 U.S.C. §158(d) provides that not giving the required notice is an unfair labor practice.

The sixty-day notice period is also referred to as the "cooling-off" period, because the contract remains in effect during this period, and neither strikes nor lockouts are permitted.

As an essential part of the bargaining process, the employer must disclose to the union whatever information the union requests that is required for it to represent the employees effectively. (Employers merely have to respond to requests; they don't have to volunteer.) Information is presumed relevant if it relates to wage rates and job descriptions. However, disclosure of confidential or privileged information is not required, nor is disclosure of material that is irrelevant to the bargaining process.

If the union seeks access to the employer's financial information, it must show specific need for the information (unless, of course, the employer is a public corporation that has to publish such data). But if the employer claims that it can't afford to increase wages, the union can see the financial data, because the employer has put its own financial condition into issue. In case of dispute, the NLRB determines what must or need not be disclosed.

18.6.5 *The Effect of an Impasse*

Sometimes both sides will bargain in good faith, as required, but will be unable to agree. At that point, a factual judgment can be made that further negotiations would be futile, based on factors such as how long bargaining has continued, the parties' bargaining history, their conduct during negotiations, and the importance of the issue.

Once impasse is reached on a mandatory bargaining subject, the employer is permitted to stop bargaining. It can implement its own proposals on that subject unilaterally, until the impasse is resolved, and if the employer proposals were raised before the impasse. The employer cannot take advantage of an impasse to unilaterally impose new provisions, or any more favorable to its own cause than those on the table during negotiations.

18.7 UNION SECURITY

Closed shops (i.e., where no one except union members can be hired) are illegal. The NLRA also forbids "preferential hiring" situations, under which the employer is required to hire only union members unless the union is unable to supply enough qualified workers for all the vacancies. However, the LMRA permits "union shops," where all current employees must be union members, and new hires can be required to join the union after hiring (within seven days in the construction industry; within 30 days in other industries), and "agency shops" where payment of initiation fees and union dues is mandatory, but actual membership is optional. These union security alternatives are available if the union is the bona fide bargaining representative of the employees in the bargaining unit, and there has not been a deauthorization election certified in the year preceding the effective date of the union security agreement.

If the union wants "automatic dues check-off" (deduction of dues from the paycheck, instead of billing the member for the dues), it must get the union member to provide a written assignment which is not permitted to last more than one year or until the union contract expires (whichever is earlier).

The converse is that a state can pass a "right to work" law, under which employees cannot be compelled to join unions or pay dues if they are unwilling to do so. The states that have adopted right to work laws are Alabama, Arizona, Arkansas, Georgia, Louisiana, Mississippi, Nebraska, Nevada, North Dakota, South Carolina, Texas, Utah, and Virginia.

18.7.1 Hiring Halls

In the union security options discussed above, the employer retains the right to select who will be hired, although the union may be able to get those who are hired to join or pay dues. A hiring hall works differently: it is a mechanism under which the union selects workers and sends them to the employer, based on needs identified by the employer (e.g., for six plasterers and two electricians). The union decides which union or non-union workers will be referred to the employer.

An exclusive hiring hall is a relationship under which the employer gets all of its workers through such union referrals. Because it is not considered a union security arrangement, it is legal in the right-to-work states. A non-exclusive hiring hall makes union referral only one of multiple sources for new workers. The NLRA provides that hiring halls are unlawful if they give preference to union members over equally qualified non-members. Operations that seem to be valid can become unlawful if they are managed in a discriminatory manner.

➡ **TIP**

Operation and structure of a hiring hall is a mandatory bargaining subject.

18.8 OTHER ELECTIONS

The NLRB can order and supervise other kinds of elections, although they are far less common than elections to determine whether a union should serve as the bargaining representative for a group of workers. Federal labor law allows a rerun or runoff election to be held to redress an improper election. Once a union is in place, employees can ask that it be deauthorized or decertified. The employer has the right to challenge a union's majority status.

A rerun election is held if there were election improprieties, or if two unions competed for representation; the ballot included a "no union" choice; and "no union" got as many votes as the other alternatives. (If there is only one union on the ballot, a tie vote means that the union loses, because it failed to attract a majority of the voters.)

A runoff election is held when no choice gets a majority (e.g., there are two unions and a "no union" option on the ballot). Only one runoff election can be held, although there could be both a rerun and a runoff election in the same organizing campaign.

A deauthorization petition is filed by a group of employees who want to remove the union's authority to enter into a union shop contract.

➠ **TIP**

There are no deauthorization petitions in the right-to-work states, because there aren't any union shop agreements there either.

If a majority of the bargaining unit (not just a majority of the voters) vote for deauthorization, they are no longer compelled to pay union dues, although the union is still the authorized bargaining representative for the employees.

On the other hand, the objective of a decertification petition is to remove the union's bargaining authority. It can be filed by an employee, a group of employees, or someone acting on behalf of the employees. The employer does not have the right to file a decertification petition, but it does have a free speech right to inform employees that they have a right to remove a union that they feel has done a poor job of representing them. A decertification petition requires a showing of interest by 30% of the employees in the bargaining unit. A successful petition requires a majority of those voting (rather than a majority of eligible voters) to ask for removal of the union. Most such petitions that are filed result in decertification of the union.

There are certain times during which decertification petitions are not allowed: one year after certification of a union; a reasonable time after an employer's voluntary recognition of a union; or within 12 months of another decertification petition.

Although it cannot file a decertification or deauthorization petition, the employer can petition the NLRB to determine that the union has lost its majority status. The employer must offer objective evidence of the change, such as employee turnover so heavy that few of the original pro-union workers remain in the bargaining unit; the union's failure to process employee grievances; or a strike that yielded no benefits for employees.

⟹ TIP

A 1996 Supreme Court case, *Auciello Iron Works Inc. v. NLRB*, #75-668, 116 S.Ct. 1754, says that it is an unfair labor practice for an employer to enter into a contract, then disavow it based on doubts about the union's majority status, if the doubts come from information that the employer already had when it entered into the contract. In other words, the appropriate action would have been to refuse to enter into the contract in the first place, not enter into the contract then repudiate it.

The Supreme Court has another majority status case on its calendar, *Allentown Mack Sales v. NLRB*, #96-795, challenging the NLRB's policy that an employer needs objective evidence creating a reasonable doubt as to a union's majority status before it can poll the employees about their level of support for the union. As of late December 1997, the case had not yet been decided.

In most cases, no union election can be held while a collective bargaining agreement is in force. (This is sometimes called the "CBA Bar.") However, if there has been a substantial increase in personnel since the contract was signed, a new election may be proper if the union no longer represents a majority of workers.

18.9 LABOR ARBITRATION

As page 517 shows, arbitration is often used to process employees' claims of employment discrimination. This often-controversial process evolved from the universally accepted use of alternative dispute resolution (mediation and arbitration) when a strike is threatened. The Labor-Management Relations Act is drafted to favor arbitration.

By agreeing to arbitrate an issue, in effect the union agrees not to strike over that issue; the employer agrees not to take unilateral action. The two main types of labor arbitration are grievance arbitration (also known as rights arbitration), when there is disagreement about how to interpret an existing contract, and contract or interest arbitration, invoked when the parties are not sure which provisions should be included in a new, renewed, or reopened collective bargaining agreement.

According to three Supreme Court cases known as the "Steelworker's Trilogy" (decided in 1960; the opinions begin at 363 U.S. 564), if it's not clear whether a company has agreed to submit a particular issue to arbitration, then the issue is arbitrable. If a CBA contains both an arbitration clause and a no-strike clause, any dispute that involves the application and interpretation of the CBA is arbitrable unless arbitration is specifically ruled out by the contract terms.

However, because of a later Supreme Court case it's up to the court system, and not the arbitrator, to decide if a party agreed to arbitrate a particular type of dispute, in any situation where there is no clear, unmistakable evidence of the parties' intentions.

➠ TIP

If the NLRB has already considered a particular issue in an unfair labor practice proceeding, then there's no right to arbitrate the issue all over again.

Under the Steelworker's Trilogy, arbitrators begin by considering the language of the CBA, but this is not the only factor in their analysis. They can also use the "law of the shop"—practices that have evolved in the particular operation. It's appropriate for arbitrators to consider factors such as the effect of their decisions on productivity, morale, and tensions within the workplace.

18.9.1 Potentially Arbitrable Issues

Many issues have been found to be subject to arbitration—in fact, the list is rather similar to the issues that are subjects for mandatory bargaining between employer and employee, because the processes of collective bargaining and arbitration are complementary.

- Sale of a business
- Relocation of operations
- Contracting out bargaining unit work
- Temporary shutdowns
- Discharge of a particular employee
- Layoffs
- Who will be recalled after a layoff
- Disputes about work assignments (including supervisors assigned to bargaining unit work)
- Work schedules

- Classification of work
- Compensation (including bonuses, overtime pay, incentive pay, severance)
- Employer contributions to pension and benefit plans
- Vacation, sick leave, and holidays
- Seniority systems
- Safety disputes
- No-strike clauses.

18.9.2 The Process of Arbitration

Usually, arbitration is automatic when management and union hit a deadlock over a grievance or dispute. However, depending on needs and comparative bargaining power, the arbitration clause might be drafted to allow only the union to invoke arbitration; employees might also be given the right to invoke arbitration in situations where the union declines to press an employee grievance.

⇒ TIP

Even if there is no formal arbitration clause in the CBA, management and union can, on a one-time basis, sign a "submission agreement" agreeing to be bound by the arbitration decision.

Arbitration clauses are usually written to call for the involvement of either the Federal Mediation and Conciliation Service (FMCS) or the American Arbitration Association (AAA), although the parties can agree on other ways to resolve disputes if they choose. Arbitration begins with a "demand": either side invokes the contract's arbitration clause and notifies the appropriate agency.

Either the employer or the union can ask the Federal Mediation and Conciliation Service (FMCS) to assist in the negotiating process. The FMCS can also offer its services, but cannot demand to be made part of the process. FMCS will not, however, mediate a dispute that has only minor effect on interstate commerce if other conciliation services are available, e.g., a state agency.

In June, 1997, the FMCS published long-awaited rules to speed up labor arbitration by introducing a streamlined, expedited process for simple cases: see 62 *Federal Register* 34175 (6/25/97). To get an arbitration panel, parties to a labor dispute must submit FMCS Form R-43. The arbitrator must now draft an award no later than 60 days after the case is closed; individuals can lose their place on the arbitration panel if they are consistently late in preparing awards. Where a request is unsuitable for arbitration ("overly burdensome or otherwise impractical"), FMCS can refer the parties to an FMCS mediator to help them work out a compromise.

FMCS can also refuse to intervene on behalf of parties who have a record of non-cooperation with arbitration, including failure to pay arbitration fees.

If both parties agree, they can use the new expedited procedure. Deadlines are shortened, and instead of having 60 days to prepare a fully-argued award, the arbitrator must draft a brief award within seven days. (Cases that require a lot of research are not suitable for the expedited procedure.)

The new rules implement user fees for FMCS services: $30 for each request for a panel of arbitrators; $10 and 10 cents a page for a list of local arbitrators. Arbitrators pay $100 for being listed in the official directory.

Once an arbitration award is rendered, it is usually final, binding, and not subject to judicial review by any court. In other words, agreeing to submit to arbitration is a very significant decision that cannot be undertaken casually; it will probably be impossible to get any kind of review or have the decision set aside. (A serious irregularity in the process, such as proof that the arbitrator was not impartial, may be sufficient.)

18.10 STRIKES

The management-union relationship always includes the threat of a strike (if a new contract cannot be negotiated, or based on the union's claim that working conditions have deteriorated enough to justify a walkout). Sometimes the threat has a minor or major element of bluff, because the union's rank- and- file workers don't want a strike or are unwilling to face a lengthy spell without work. At other times, the strike can actually be beneficial to the employer, if it allows the employer to save payroll, shut down an unproductive location, move to an area of lower labor costs, or replace marginal or dissatisfied employees with "striker replacements." (See page 367 for a discussion of situations in which employers are or are not justified in discharging and replacing workers who strike.)

The NLRA gives employees the right to engage in "protected concerted activities"—joining together to organize, protest, and otherwise assert their interests in a lawful manner. However, violence, sabotage, and threats are not protected activity. If a threatened strike would imperil the national health or safety, the President of the United States can order the U.S. Attorney General to petition the appropriate federal court for an 80-day cooling off period, during which the strike is enjoined.

Secondary strikes and secondary boycotts, i.e., actions taken against one employer to put pressure on a different employer that does business with the first, are banned by NLRA §8(b)(4). A company that is the victim of a secondary strike or boycott can sue for damages under LMRA §303. When a union posted a sign, "This building is full of rats" near a hospital that was a neutral second party (referring to a construction subcontractor accused of failing to pay prevailing wages, not to rodents) an injunction on the basis of fraud was granted, because of the likelihood of misleading hospital patients.

18.10.1 Classifying Strikes

There are three situations in which employees can lawfully engage in a work stoppage: if they have an economic dispute with the employer; if they claim that the employer has committed unfair labor practices; and if they feel that workplace conditions are so unreasonably dangerous that they should not be required to work in such hazardous situations.

An unfair labor practices strike is caused in whole or part by unfair labor practices committed by the employer. There must be a causal connection between the strike and the employer practices. Furthermore, the practices must not be simply cost-related (such as shift changes), because then the strike should be characterized as an economic strike. But if a strike begins as an economic strike, it can be converted to an unfair labor practices strike if the employer acts unfairly or refuses to accept legitimate offers for return to work.

The main difference between an economic strike and an unfair labor practices strike is the extent of employees' reinstatement rights after the strike ends and they want to go back to work. Certain issues are considered to fall within the exclusive discretion of management, so employees cannot lawfully go on strike to challenge management decisions on these areas.

Technically, a work stoppage caused by dangerous conditions is not a strike; 29 United States Code §143 makes it a protected concerted activity for employees to refuse to work when there is measurable, objective evidence (not just a subjective feeling) of undue hazards. The employees must also articulate goals that the employer can respond to, e.g., replace a defective machine or install guard rails, not just "make the workplace safer." See Chapter 21 for a discussion of the employer's obligations under the Occupational Safety and Health Act.

A sympathy strike, when workers outside the striking bargaining unit refuse to cross a picket line, is probably protected concerted activity as defined by the NLRA—at least if the underlying strike is protected.

In contrast to those protected activities, a sitdown strike, which involves an illegal takeover of the employer's premises, or even a part of the premises, is unlawful. A wildcat strike, which is one called by the rank-and-file without authorization from the union, is not protected activity if the workers want to usurp the union's bargaining authority. (Remember, recognition of a union makes it the sole bargaining representative for the workers; they can no longer negotiate individually on their own behalf.)

A collective bargaining agreement can lawfully be drafted to include a no-strike clause. An economic strike (but not an unfair labor practices strike) in violation of a no-strike clause does not constitute protected concerted activity, and therefore the employer can legitimately fire the strikers and deny them reinstatement after the strike ends.

18.10.2 Employer Activities

The lockout is the employer's counterpart to the union's strike. In a strike, the employees refuse to come to work; in a lockout, the employer refuses to let them in. The employer can hire replacement workers if it undertakes a lockout for business reasons, and can enter into a temporary subcontract during the lockout, but cannot use the lockout to permanently contract out work formerly performed by employees.

Although the lockout is an accepted tactic available to the employer (e.g., to protect a bargaining position even if an impasse has not occurred), lockouts are lawful if and only if they have a business motivation, not if the employer intends to prevent the workers from organizing a union, or to avoid bargaining with an incumbent union. However, a lockout is justified if employees strike in violation of a CBA no-strike clause.

Lockouts are analyzed to see if they are inherently destructive of the rights of employees. If so, the employer has committed an unfair labor practice. There is also an unfair labor practice if the employer institutes a lockout without legitimate economic business justification that goes beyond the mere convenience of the employer.

> ⇒ **TIP**
>
> A lockout during collective bargaining might be treated as an unlawful refusal to bargain; and the mere possibility of a strike if contract negotiations break down is not a sufficient economic justification. Outside of the strike context, the union's economic power is weaker, so there is less need for the employer to counterbalance it. Therefore lockouts will be analyzed more stringently.

Employers have the right to close a business, or go through a temporary shutdown, based on economic motivations. But doing so to harm unionization is an unfair labor practice. A "runaway shop" (transferring work between existing locations, or opening a new location) is an unfair labor practice if it is based on antiunion motivation rather than a desire to enhance profitability. A partial closing motivated by discouraging unionization in another part of an integrated enterprise is an unfair labor practice, but not a partial closing that makes sense economically.

During a strike, the employer is not permitted to alter the terms and conditions of employment that affect strikers. However, once a CBA expires, the employer is allowed to change those terms as they affect striker replacements.

18.10.3 Striker Replacements

Employers are entitled to keep their operations open by hiring replacements during a strike; employers can always hire replacements for jobs that are described as temporary stopgaps until the strike ends. The question is whether the employer can hire permanent replacements, outsource functions formerly performed by employees, and have to get rid of the replacement workers and give strikers their old jobs back.

Strikers lose their employee status, and therefore their protection under the NLRA, under certain circumstances, and discharging them under these circumstances is not an unfair labor practice. NLRA protection is limited to "lawful" strikes that are conducted in a lawful manner, are called for a protected purpose, and are authorized by the bargaining unit representative (if there is one). A strike is lawful if it occurs after the expiration of a collective bargaining agreement, if it is either an economic strike or a response to the employer's unfair labor practices, or if it demands concessions from the employer.

Employee status is lost when there is a "wildcat" strike (not authorized by the union), or when a strike violates a collective bargaining agreement's no-strike clause. However, a strike is lawful in response to any unfair labor practice by the employer. Sitdown strikes are never considered lawful. "Excessive" violence removes employee status, although a minor instance of violence would not prevent the perpetrator from being considered an employee.

In an economic strike, the employer can permanently replace the strikers, and keep the replacement workers after the end of the strike. However, strikers are entitled to reinstatement after the strike if they have not been replaced, and delay in reinstating them counts as an unfair labor practice. The economic striker is still considered an employee after being replaced.

If the former economic striker makes an unconditional application for reinstatement, the employer must reinstate him or her if the replacement worker quits or is terminated. If no jobs are available at the time of the application, the employer must reinstate the ex-striker when a job becomes available.

There are two exceptions to this rule: if the economic striker gets regular and substantially equivalent employment somewhere else, or if the employer has a legitimate business reason not to rehire the ex-striker (e.g., violence or sabotage during the strike). If the job itself has been eliminated (for instance, because of the adoption of new technology), it is not required that the former striker be reinstated.

According to the NLRB (a position that has been upheld by the Seventh Circuit), the question is whether the replacement workers have a reasonable expectation of being recalled after they are laid off. If there was no reasonable expectation of recall, strikers would be entitled to reinstatement, unless the employer has proved that the job is vacant or has a good reason not to rehire the striker. A so-called "Laidlaw vacancy," otherwise known as a "genuine job vacancy," occurs if the replacement workers cannot reasonably expect recall after layoff; in that situation, strikers are entitled to reinstatement.

A reinstated economic striker must be treated equally with nonstrikers and permanent replacements, with the same benefits, including paid vacations and accrual of seniority, unless there is a legitimate and substantial business reason to depart from this rule.

Normally, reinstatement should return the worker to status quo, but it is permissible to demote the ex-striker based on legitimate business reasons, for example, if returning him or her to the previous job would create a risk of sabotage.

18.10.4 Subcontracting

When a strike is imminent, employers can subcontract out work that was performed by the bargaining unit, thus displacing employees—as long as there is a pressing business reason, and as long as the employer acts out of business reasons rather than to pursue an anti-union animus.

The D.C. Circuit ruled in early 1997 that it was not an unfair labor practice for an employer to subcontract some bargaining unit work (plant maintenance) during a lockout. During this time, the employer brought in workers from other mills and hired a maintenance subcontractor. This saved so much money that the employer entered into a permanent subcontract and bargained to outsource this function permanently.

A violation of NLRA §8(a)(3), which penalizes employer actions that intend to discourage union membership, can be inferred even without direct proof of the employer's anti-union motivation, but only if the employer's action is inherently destructive of important employee rights. The court deemed contracting out the maintenance work to have too minimal an effect on the rights of employees to be "inherently destructive." Furthermore, subcontracting is considered a mandatory bargaining subject, and thus the employer is entitled to act unilaterally once a bargaining impasse has been reached.

18.11 THE WARN ACT

Under federal law, employers have an obligation to notify employees of events that will result in large-scale job loss. The obligation stems from the Worker Adjustment Retraining and Notice Act, 29 U.S.C. §2101, popularly known as the "WARN Act." Covered employers are those with 100 or more full-time employees (or a combination of full-timers and part-time employees totalling at least 100 people and 4000 work hours a week). Before any plant closing or mass layoff, the employer must give at least 60 days' notice to employees, unions, and the federal government. The Act defines a plant closing as employment loss (termination, prolonged layoff, serious cutback in work hours) to 50 or more workers during a 30-day period.

A mass layoff has a lesser effect on the individual workers (e.g., potential for recall), and affects 500 people or one-third of the work force. People rehired within six months, and employees who elected early retirement, should not be counted in determining if a mass layoff has occurred.

If an employer fails to give the required notice, each affected employee is entitled to receive up to 60 days' back pay and benefits. A federal civil penalty of up to

$500 per day that the failure to give notice continued can also be imposed. Unions have the right to sue for damages on behalf of union members. The calculation of back pay uses work days, not calendar days.

> **➡ TIP**
>
> If a violation occurs with respect to workers who are paid by the hour, an allocation can be done to determine the actual hours involved during the period when WARN Act notice was supposed to be given but was not given. However, if the employees involved were salaried employees (who could have been ordered to work weekends or overtime without additional compensation), they can receive two months' salary for a 60-day WARN Act violation; the employer is not entitled to allocate.

18.12 GRIEVANCES AND DISCIPLINE

Presenting grievances to the employer is one of the clearest cases of protected concerted activity, whether or not the employees are unionized. However, they must in fact act in concert, or one employee must present a shared grievance; one person pressing his or her own agenda is not protected under the NLRA. For NLRA purposes, a grievance must be something that relates directly to the terms and conditions of employment. Once they have made a complaint, employees are required to return to work within a reasonable time.

Sometimes the employer will be unclear on the facts of a situation, or will want the employee to get a chance to put his or her own version of the facts on the record. If there is a reasonable likelihood that such an "investigatory interview" will lead to dismissal or lesser forms of employee discipline, the employee has the right to bring a union representative along. (Non-unionized employees do not have the right to bring a representative to a meeting; this is one of the union's selling points.) However, if the meeting is simply a review of work rules, or is used to give additional training (in other words, the employee can't get into any trouble), there is no right of representation.

18.13 SHARED LIABILITY

There are many instances in which two nominally (or even actually) separate companies will be deemed to be the same for labor law purposes, or under which one company's activities will be ascribed to the other. Liability can be shared when it comes to penalizing unfair labor practices, enforcing a collective bargaining agreement, or defining an appropriate bargaining unit.

What happens if, as a result of a merger or a takeover, Company B now owns the business formerly operated by Company A? In these situations, it's common for most or all of Company A's employees to be retained. Is Company B now the "employer" of the workers, and is it bound by the old employer's union contract and other promises to employees? The answer is a factual one that looks at whether or not real operational changes were made.

In connection with collective bargaining agreements, a "successor company" is one which continues the same business and hires at least half of the old employees. A successor employer is not bound by the contracts (after all, it didn't have any input in negotiating them), but is obligated to "recognize" and "consult" with the union. The Supreme Court has ruled that a new company becomes a successor if it is perfectly clear that all the former employees will be retained. A company can also be treated as a successor employer if it fails to give employees enough information about the new wages and working conditions to make a meaningful choice about whether to sign on with the new employer.

After a merger or purchase of a business, the successor has a duty to bargain collectively (but only if the union asks; the successor need not volunteer) and can be liable for unfair labor practices committed by the predecessor if there is "continuity of identity" with the former employer, such as:

- Use of the same facility
- The labor force is the same or substantially the same
- The job descriptions, working conditions, supervision, equipment, and production methods are unchanged despite the corporate transition
- The products and services of the two are identical.

An alternate test is whether there is a new corporate entity to replace the predecessor, whether there was a hiatus in the enterprise's operations, and whether the employment relationship with the prior workforce was terminated. The "perfectly clear" doctrine is also a factor. If it's perfectly clear that the new owner of a business will hire all of the existing workforce, then the incoming employer has a duty to consult with the union about wage scales. It can't unilaterally implement cuts. If there is no consultation in such a case, it is presumed that negotiations would have continued the prior wage scale.

If the corporate transition occurs through the sale of all of one corporation's stock to another corporation, the second corporation becomes an employer of the first corporation's workforce if operations remain the same after the transition.

Another possibility is that two or more enterprises might be deemed to be "alter egos" (substitutes) for one another, even if they are not formally under common control. Alter egos may be held liable for each other's unfair labor practices. The test is whether transferring business from one alter ego operation to another benefits the transferor by eliminating labor relations obligations. The alter ego theory became part of labor law to prevent "double-breasting": the practice of pairing commonly-owned firms, one with a union and one non-unionized. If the double-breasted firms are actually alter egos, a federal district court can require the non-union firm to abide by the union firm's labor agreements, even if there has been no NLRB unit determination.

Two or more entities might be treated as a "single employer," even though they are organized as legally separate entities, if they are really structured as an integrated enterprise. The presence of an integrated enterprise affects the bargaining unit that is valid, what the company's "business" is for NLRB jurisdictional purposes, and who will be blamed for unfair labor practices. Under this theory, the factors that determine integration include:

- Common ownership
- Integrated business operations
- Common management
- Centralized control of labor relations.

These tests are similar to the tests used to see if companies are alter egos. The difference between the alter ego and single employer concepts is that the two alter egos are not considered a single "enterprise," and therefore all the employees are not necessarily in the same bargaining unit.

A parent company and its subsidiary would probably be treated as a single employer if they are fundamentally in the same industry or business enterprise. This would be manifested by their sharing supervisory, technical, and professional personnel, sharing workforce and equipment, having common officers and directors, and operating under the same labor relations policies.

Separate entities might be grouped together by the NLRB as "joint employers" if they "codetermine" (i.e., make decisions jointly) about essential terms and conditions of employment. Under this theory, the crucial factor is not whether the companies have overlapping ownership, but whether they make joint decisions about hiring and firing, working conditions, compensation, and supervision of employees.

18.13.1 Agents of the Employer

An employer company will be liable based on the actions of anyone who is an "agent" of the employer, acting in the employer's interests. For instance, a labor consultant hired by the employer is considered the employer's agent, but a Chapter 7 bankruptcy trustee is not. The test of whether someone is the employer's agent is quite similar to the test of whether someone is a common-law employee. Once again, the employer's degree of control is crucial: the right to hire and fire the agent; prescribing what the agent will do and how; furnishing tools and materials. Actual agency is explicitly granted. In contrast, apparent authority exists where a principal says that the agent can speak for it, or knowingly lets the agent exercise authority. (The difference between apparent authority and ratification is that ratification occurs after the fact.)

An employer is responsible for actions performed by a supervisor (see page 346 for a definition of " supervisor") in the course of his or her actual or apparent authority. Even if a supervisor acts without authority, the employer can become liable by ratifying the supervisor's action (offering support for it after the fact). The general rule is that the employer is NOT responsible for the activities of non-employees, or for non-supervisory employees, unless the employer initiates, promotes, or ratifies that conduct.

Under circumstances under which it would otherwise be liable, the employer can be relieved of liability if its agent's improper conduct was an isolated, unpremeditated act, or if the employer repudiates the conduct.

Generally, a finding of agency is crucial if the NLRB is to blame the employer for an unfair labor practice committed by some other party. But in a representation proceeding, a finding of agency is NOT required to set aside an election if the circumstances surrounding the election were improper enough to prevent employees from making a rational, unforced choice.

18.13.2 Agents of the Union

Employers are not the only party potentially guilty of unfair labor practices. A union is liable for those of its own agents, including actions taken by rank-and-file union members to further union goals. Unions are often held responsible for acts performed by picketers, unless the union takes preventive or corrective action to stem inappropriate picket-line behavior.

18.14 EMPLOYER DOMINATION

In Europe, it is quite common for union representatives to collaborate closely with management, and for joint management-labor committees to have an important decision-making role. In the United States, employers who want to implement "co-determination" (as it is called) have two problems: reaching a mutually tolerable resolution with the union, and avoiding NLRA violations. NLRA §8(a)(2) makes employer domination of a labor organization an unfair labor practice. Although originally enacted to bar "sweetheart unions" (formed or taken over by the employer), the provision has been applied more broadly.

According to the Sixth Circuit, for instance, a plant council was created just after an election was held (resulting in a victory for the employer). The plant council met during working hours to discuss work rules, wages, and benefits. The council, consisting of five employees and three management representatives, reviewed ideas from the company's suggestion box and made proposals to management, some of which were adopted.

The DOL challenged the council as an inappropriately employer-dominated labor organization; the NLRB and the Sixth Circuit agreed, because it fit into the statutory definition: it represented employees, dealt with the employer, and was concerned with conditions of employment. Employer domination was present because management created and could disband the committee; it met during working hours; and always had management representatives present.

In 1992, the NLRB ruled that an "action committee" created by the employer in response to employee dissatisfaction was improperly employer-dominated. The NLRB considered it a labor organization, not a communications device, because its purpose was to find bilateral solutions to employee grievances, and because the employee members acted in a representative capacity. The agency was upheld by the Seventh Circuit in 1994.

In 1993, the NLRB found that six joint labor-management safety committees, and a joint committee on fitness, were also labor organizations, because their purpose was to deal with the employer, and because they were concerned with important issues such as safety, incentive awards, and facilities for employees to work out.

Management consultant Glenn L. Dalton says that worker teams have a "honeymoon" of about a year and a half to three years, at which time disenchanted workers may raise complaints.

To avoid NLRB characterization of a work team or quality circle as an unduly dominated "labor organization," the employer should consider these steps:

- Limit the use of the employer's facilities. Perhaps the local City Hall or Rotary club could provide a neutral meeting place away from the workplace.

- The membership of the team should rotate, involving as many people as possible. (This is also useful in getting new viewpoints.)

- The focus of the team should be on productivity and workplace issues rather than compensation; the team should not be used as a way to avoid regular contract negotiations.

- The bylaws should be drafted by employee representatives, not by the employer.

18.15 NLRB JURISDICTION

The National Labor Relations Board has the power to get involved in a situation if:

- It is a labor dispute—i.e., there is any controversy about conditions of employment or representation of workers. Strikes, walkouts, picketing, and employer refusals to bargain are all deemed to be labor disputes.

- It affects interstate commerce. The threshold is so low that virtually any business will be deemed to affect interstate commerce.

- Employers and employees (e.g., not independent contractors and their clients) are involved.
- One or more of a broad spectrum of working condition issues are at stake.

When it has issued a complaint or filed an unfair labor practices charge, the NLRB can ask a federal District Court to issue a temporary injunction. (An injunction is a court order telling a party to do something or to stop doing something.) In fact, the agency has an obligation to seek an injunction if it alleges unlawful secondary activity (striking one employer to put pressure on a different employer), some forms of improper picketing, or certain boycotts.

Permanent injunctions are quite rare in labor law, because a Depression-era statute, the Norris-LaGuardia Anti-Injunction Act, forbids most permanent labor injunctions. (The statute was passed because courts often made it almost impossible for unions to strike, by issuing injunctions forcing them back to work; labor law is supposed to maintain a balance between the union's weapon of lawful strikes and the employer's weapons, including lawful lockouts.)

Theoretically, the NLRB has jurisdiction over all unfair labor practice claims that require interpretation of a CBA that is still in effect. However, in many circumstances the NLRB will decline to exercise its jurisdiction, permitting the parties to proceed with ongoing arbitration, to use the contract's grievance arbitration machinery, or to enforce an arbitration award. However, it's up to the NLRB to intervene or stay out: the employer and union can't deprive the NLRB of jurisdiction by agreeing to arbitrate.

➠ TIP

For 25 years it was simply assumed that the NLRB had the power to order an employer to reimburse the union for negotiating and litigating expenses after a determination that the employer committed unfair labor practices during collective bargaining. But the Court of Appeals for the District of Columbia Circuit ruled in July, 1997 that the National Labor Relations Act is not specific enough on this point to deviate from the regular American rule that litigants have to pay their own litigation costs.

18.16 LMRA PREEMPTION

Labor law, like the law of employee benefits, is heavily dominated by federal law. The Labor-Management Relations Act (LMRA), most specifically §301(a), which gives federal District Courts jurisdiction over suits for violations of a collective bargaining agreement (as well as suits by one union against another) is often applied to bring labor questions to the federal courts (and keep them out of state courts when issues such as wrongful termination and allegedly unfair employee discipline are raised).

➡ **TIP**

Plaintiffs who bring LMRA §301 claims (for instance, that an employer's assignment of jobs violated the CBA) are entitled to demand a jury trial.

The central inquiry in determining if LMRA preemption exists is the relationship between the controversy and the collective bargaining agreement. If it is necessary to interpret the CBA, then state laws are preempted. However, the Supreme Court decided in 1994 that a mere need to refer to the CBA is not enough for preemption; it must be necessary for the underlying dispute really to involve contract terms.

In 1996, two Circuits found that state laws that penalize employers for late payments of wages are preempted by LMRA §301, in one case because the CBA had to be interpreted (raises take effect for the first payroll period after ratification of a contract), in the other because the state law, which allows suits for back wages against shareholders and officers as well as the employer corporation, was deemed to be an "end run" around the limits imposed by the LMRA.

Preemption was found in a 1994 case involving alleged failure to rehire and negligent and intentional infliction of emotional distress, because assessing the validity of the claims depended on interpreting the CBA seniority provisions.

Similarly, a claim that an employee was denied reinstatement after a period of disability because she had filed a Worker's Compensation claim was deemed preempted, because resolving the claim required interpreting the CBA "management rights" clause (which gives the management the exclusive right to hire and fire). State law claims that the employer failed to promote the plaintiff because of his race, and as retaliation for his protected labor activity, were also preempted, because the CBA covers promotion, seniority, and training, and the employer's defense would no doubt involve construing the CBA language.

The following situations have been found *not* to be preempted by §301, because contract interpretation was not required:

- Retaliatory discharge
- Discharge of an employee for a reason that violates public policy

- False imprisonment (when an employee was unreasonably detained by a security guard)

- Claims dealing with oral contracts other than the CBA (e.g., alleged promises of lifetime employment)

- Claims on implied contracts

- Claims made pursuant to state anti-discrimination statutes about issues that are not normally bargained away during CBA negotiations.

The fact that an employee is permitted to bring one of these claims in state court doesn't mean that he or she will win; all it means is that the charge can't be dismissed on the theory that it should be brought in federal court under LMRA §301.

The LMRA itself can be preempted by other statutes. In a Sixth Circuit case, employees and a union sued under LMRA §301 to recover non-guaranteed pension benefits. The court ruled that ERISA, not the LMRA, governed, because of 1987 ERISA amendments that make the employer liable to the PBGC for benefits that are unfunded at the time a plan terminates.

If the CBA includes a contractual grievance or arbitration provision (as most do), then potential plaintiffs have to exhaust their remedies (complete the entire procedure) before bringing suit under §301.

18.17 LABOR LAW IMPLICATIONS OF BANKRUPTCY FILINGS

Usually, merely filing for bankruptcy protects the company that files, because there is an "automatic stay" that prevents other parties from suing the bankruptcy filer. However, because the NLRB is considered a unit of the federal government exercising its regulatory powers, NLRB unfair labor practices hearings are exempt from the automatic stay. However, the bankruptcy court has the power to enjoin the NLRB from doing anything that would prevent it from expediting the reorganization of the bankrupt company.

Part of the bankruptcy process is a decision about which executory contracts (i.e., contracts to be performed in the future) will be retained by the company and which can and should be rejected. The company filing for bankruptcy protection can petition the court to allow it to assume or reject a collective bargaining agreement, because it is an executory contract. The court's standard for granting a rejection request is whether it would be fair to permit the rejection, or whether the union unreasonably refused to accept contract modifications proposed by the employer.

➠ **TIP**

The employer is not required to prove that the bankruptcy reorganization will fail if it is forced to maintain the contract.

If the collective bargaining agreement expires during the pendency of bankruptcy proceedings, the whole issue becomes moot, because there is nothing for the employer to either accept or reject.

Chapter 19

UNEMPLOYMENT INSURANCE

19.1 INTRODUCTION

Unemployment compensation is a state-administered insurance system, under which employers make contributions to a fund. The state agencies are referred to as State Employment Security Agencies (SESAs). They receive federal funding, but in order to get the funds, they have to do various things, including finding out which claimants are likely to exhaust regular unemployment benefits, and will need reemployment assistance, such as job search assistance services provided at the federal or state levels. The Unemployment Compensation Amendments of 1993, P.L. 103-152, sets the obligations that SESAs must meet to get funding. (This follows on several other federal statutes including the Employment Security Amendments of 1970 and the Unemployment Compensation Amendments of 1976 and 1992.)

Each state accumulates and administers a fund (the Unemployment Insurance Trust Fund), deriving from employer contributions. In a very few states, employee contributions are also required; but, unlike FICA, where the employer and employee have equal and substantial burdens, unemployment tax is almost exclusively a responsibility of the employer. The theory is that in good times, unemployment will be low, and the fund will accumulate a surplus, which can be invested in government securities and used to pay benefits in the bad times of higher unemployment.

19.2 ELIGIBILITY FOR BENEFITS

Whether a former employee qualifies for unemployment benefits depends on factors such as whether he or she worked long enough before termination of employment and the reason for termination. The base period is the period of time used to calculate if pre-termination employment was adequate to justify payment of benefits.

Usually the base period is the first four of the preceding five completed calendar quarters, although some states allow the four most recent quarters of employment to be counted. The difference is whether the most recent months of employment (which might have higher earnings) will be counted. States set a minimum amount that must be earned by eligible employees during the base period, but this is usually so low it can be assumed that all employees will meet it.

The purpose of the unemployment insurance fund is to provide benefits when employees, through no fault of their own, are laid off or otherwise do not receive a salary. (However, in this context, "no fault of their own" can include firings that were justifiable on the part of the employer—for instance, if an employee is not very competent, but is not guilty of theft or other wrongdoing.)

The general rule is that unemployment benefits are not available to those who quit voluntarily without good cause, although states vary as to whether the denial is total or just for a period of time. Abusive actions by the employer that would constitute constructive discharge would constitute good cause to quit, but so would some situations in which the employer is not at fault. For instance, many states interpret good cause to include quitting a job to follow a spouse who has been employed in another city or state.

Benefits are also denied to those who are guilty of "misconduct detrimental to the best interests of the employer." Misconduct is interpreted in an industrial, not a moral, sense, and activities that are not tantamount to crime might easily be considered employee misconduct that bars benefit eligibility. However, simple incompetence would not rise to the level of misconduct unless it demonstrated gross negligence or willful disregard of the employer's best interests.

Depending on the state, disqualifying misconduct might also have to be work-related. For example, excessive absence might be treated as misconduct, as might insubordination. Being intoxicated on business premises almost certainly would be deemed misconduct. If the employee actually provokes the employer to discharge him or her, that would probably be treated as voluntary resignation that would bar benefit eligibility.

For benefits to continue, the claimant must make a serious search for work. Eligibility will be terminated if the claimant refuses a legitimate job offer of suitable work.

Benefits are also unavailable in any week in which the claimant receives a pension, annuity, retirement pay, or any other private or government payment paid based on past work history. However, benefits can be paid in a week where the claimant receives a distribution from a profit sharing plan, because that is not compensation for work.

The employer is responsible for unemployment benefits if it makes a material change in working conditions, and the employee has a valid reason for inability to perform according to the new conditions. A published job description can be evidence of the original nature of the job and, therefore, of any material change. For instance, a job can be described as a day-shift position; a change to a night or swing shift might well be considered material.

The actual benefit will be computed either based on the claimant's average weekly wage, or by the wage earned in the quarter of the base period in which wages were highest. For partial weeks of unemployment, a reduced benefit will be available, although states use different methods for its calculation.

If and when an ex-employee files for unemployment compensation benefits, the employer will be notified and asked to give a reason for the termination. The employer will be given a certain number of days to contest the claim, and will lose the right to protest once this period of time elapses.

The state department that administers unemployment benefits will assess the matter; the decision can be appealed to an Administrative Law Judge, an administrative board, and finally through the court system.

⇒ **TIP**

Some states require employers to report all separations from service. The forms usually explain the language to be used. The point is to furnish enough detail to characterize the termination, yet to avoid defamation: for instance, stating that an employee removed materials from a worksite without permission and without paying for them, not drawing a conclusion that the employee "stole" (i.e., committed a crime).

Appeal of a state official's denial of unemployment benefits has to go through the state court system; employees can't go to federal court to challenge the denial.

19.3 DURATION OF BENEFITS

Calculations are usually made on the basis of an individual 52-week benefit year for each claimant, beginning when the claim is filed and running for a year. (Some states use the same benefit year, similar to a fiscal year, for all claimants.) There is usually a one-week waiting period before benefits become payable.

The typical maximum benefit period for the basic benefit is 26 weeks, although a few states permit 30 weeks. Once claimants use up the basic benefit, they must wait until the next benefit year before starting another base period and therefore qualifying for unemployment benefits all over again. Therefore, someone who receives benefits in a particular benefit year will have to be re-employed and work for at least a second base period, before qualifying for a second benefit period.

In addition to the basic benefits, extensions are available under certain circumstances. The Employment Security Amendments of 1970 created a program of Federal-State Extended Benefits, covering benefits during weeks 27-39 of a spell of unemployment.(Other federal programs have been enacted but expired, such as the Emergency Unemployment Compensation program that expired in early 1994, and the Supplemental Compensation program that ended in 1985.) A few states (Alaska, California, Connecticut, Hawaii, Minnesota, and Oregon) have extended benefit funds that are completely state-funded, with no federal involvement.

19.4 EXPERIENCE RATING

Employers must have input into the process for one simple reason: the unemployment insurance rate that employers pay is based in part on their "experience" (the number of claims against them), and the more claims, the higher the insurance rate. In particular, seasonal businesses often have a regular cycle of laying off workers, who collect unemployment benefits until the need for their services recurs and they are rehired.

Some states have a broad spread between the highest insurance rates, paid by employers who have a lot of claims, and the lowest rates, by companies with few worker claims. Other states have a narrower spread—with the result that companies with better claims experience in effect subsidize those with worse.

The standard rate is 5.4%, although many employers qualify for a more favorable experience rate. States vary in their treatment of new employers. They may impose a higher rate at first, until the new employer can demonstrate favorable experience (and has filed all required reports and paid all required taxes). In contrast, some states have a special *low* rate for new employers until they demonstrate bad claims experience. In fact, some states allow a "zero" rate (no tax at all) for companies with exceptionally good records. However, if the state suffers from a high rate of unemployment, with a consequent low balance in the fund, then all employers may have to pay the standard rate anyway, and might be subject to a duty to make additional "subsidiary contributions" to increase the fund balance.

States use four basic methods for experience rating (and some states have hybrid methods): calculations could be based on variations in a company's payroll over time (reflecting an increased or reduced workforce), a reserve ratio, a benefit ratio, or a ratio of benefits to wages.

It's common for states to allow joint filing and risk pooling. That is, a group of employers pay jointly and get a combined experience rate for the entire group. Of course, each employer hopes that the group rate will be lower than the rate they could achieve individually (they can't all be right!)

➠ **TIP**

Many states allow companies to make additional voluntary contributions to the state fund, thus lowering their experience rates.

A further refinement is the distinction between "charging" and "noncharging" claims. Certain claims are not charged against the last employer's experience rating: for instance, claims for very brief periods of unemployment, or cases where the employee's sojourn at his or her last employer (as compared to other employers) was very brief. Furthermore, some states do not charge an employer for benefits paid after a period of disqualification for misconduct or voluntary quitting, or when a claimant's benefits are terminated for failure to seek suitable work. The theory is that employers should not be penalized for situations beyond their control.

Another variable is whether all employers in the base period, or only the last one in the series, will be charged with the claim. If several employers are charged, they might be charged in reverse order (the most recent first), or charging might be proportionate to the amount of wages they paid during the base period.

19.4.1 *Collateral Estoppel*

There are two related legal doctrines: res judicata and collateral estoppel. Res judicata means a thing already tried: in other words, if one court has already dealt with a case, another court with appeals powers may survey what the first court did, but a different court, which is not in the same line of authority, won't decide a matter that has already been decided. Res judicata involves not only the same legal issues but the same or closely related parties: in other words, if Smith sues the Jones Company alleging racial discrimination, that won't be res judicata when McTavish sues the Acme Company alleging racial discrimination. However, McTavish's suit against the Acme Company could have collateral estoppel effect when Timberlake brings a race discrimination suit against the Acme Company, because the same basic issues (Acme Company's racial policies at a particular time) have already been decided.

The reason to mention this in the context of unemployment insurance is that if you contest one worker's unemployment insurance claim, and lose, it could harm you in a later lawsuit. So what to do? Do you let the claim go through unopposed (thus raising your insurance premium), or do you contest it, lose, and be in a bad litigation position? It's a decision that requires personalized legal advice.

Collateral estoppel can be used by either side: the employer saying in a later court case that the unemployment decision proves the employee was guilty of misconduct, and therefore could not have been wrongfully terminated; or the employee asserting that receiving unemployment benefits already proves that he or she didn't quit and wasn't guilty of misconduct.

As noted above, an unemployment case has to go through several levels of administrative review before reaching the court system. Probably the administrative decisions will have collateral estoppel effect in later litigation, but in some jurisdictions, only a court decision can have this effect.

See Chapter 27 for an extensive discussion of what leads up to a discrimination suit, and what happens along the way. If an employee files a Title VII charge with the EEOC, and, as is normal practice, the EEOC refers it to a state anti-discrimination agency, and if the agency finds there was no discrimination and a state court affirms that judgment, the federal courts must give full faith and credit to the state judgment. This is provided, however, that the administrative proceedings gave the charging party a full, fair chance to litigate the issues raised in the federal case.

19.5 UNEMPLOYMENT TAX COMPLIANCE

The Federal Unemployment Tax Act (FUTA) imposes an obligation on employers (but not employees) to pay an amount that funds a federal program of unemployment benefits. The FUTA tax rate is 6.2% (the same as the basic FICA rate)—but with the dramatic difference that the tax is due only on the first $7,000 of wages, not the first $68,400, and there is no additional tax that is a counterpart of the Medicare tax.

> **➥ TIP**
>
> Although the federal FUTA base is only $7,000, some states impose unemployment tax on a higher base amount.

Employers are subject to FUTA if, in the current year or the year before, the employer had one or more employees in at least part of one day in 20 different weeks, or pays wages of $1,500 or more in any calendar quarter. (In other words, there's just about no way for an employer to escape.)

For FUTA purposes, employees are common-law employees, subject to the employer's direction and control as to the details and means of accomplishing tasks, not just the tasks to be performed. Therefore, a corporate officer is an employee for FUTA purposes, as are some salespersons.

The 6.2% rate consists of a base rate of 6%, plus a surcharge of 0.2% that was supposed to be temporary when it was enacted in 1977, but which keeps getting renewed (most recently as part of the Taxpayer Relief Act of 1997; current law calls for it to expire in 2007, so the base rate of 6%, and a net federal rate after credit of 0.6%, will prevail).

For most employers, the 6.2% rate is purely theoretical, because most of them qualify for a 5.4% credit for state unemployment taxes they have already paid. See Code §3302. This is sometimes referred to as the "normal credit" or the "90% credit." So, for practical purposes, the effective federal rate is 0.8% of the initial $7,000 in compensation. In fact, if the employer's experience rating is good (see above), it may pay even less than 0.8% as a federal rate, because the company often qualifies for an additional credit against FUTA, equaling the difference between the basic state rate of 5.4% and the employer's actual experience rate. (The full credit can be claimed only in states that the Department of Labor has certified as complying with federal requirements for SESAs, and employers must make all their state contributions by January 31, the due date for the Form 940, to claim the full credit.)

The employer reports its FUTA liability on IRS Form 940 or 940-EZ.

➠ **TIP**

The IRS mails pre-addressed forms to employers who are on record as FUTA filers; if you don't get your form, you can call 1-800-TAX-FORM (1-800-829-3676). The short form, 940-EZ, can be used by an employer, no matter how large its work force, who makes unemployment tax contributions to only one state; the state taxes are paid no later than the due date for the federal form, and all FUTA-taxable wages are also subject to state unemployment tax.

➠ **TIP**

Some states exempt the pay of corporate officers from state unemployment tax, so companies in those states can't use the 940-EZ.

The employer determines how much it owes in FUTA taxes each quarter. That amount must be deposited with Form 8109 at the local Federal Reserve Bank or other authorized financial institution. Due dates for the deposit are April 30, July 31, October 31, and January 31.

If taxes are underpaid, the IRS is entitled to collect interest and, often, penalties. Code §6321 and the laws of the various states impose a lien on the company's real and personal property for taxes that remain unpaid after the taxing authority files a payment demand, plus interest and penalties.

If taxes are overpaid, the company is entitled to file Form 843 to apply for a refund.

➠ **TIP**

A suit against the IRS seeking a refund will be dismissed for lack of jurisdiction; first, you have to file the refund claim with the IRS.

19.5.1 Other Tax Issues

Persons who receive unemployment benefits can direct the state to withhold federal and/or state income tax from the benefits; this change was made by P.L. 103-463, the Uruguay Round Agreements Act, also known as GATT (the General Agreement on Taxes and Tariffs). There are technical issues about what forms of compensation count for FUTA purposes, but they are fairly irrelevant because it is virtually inevitable that any employee—even a part-timer—will earn more than $7,000 a year.

Supplemental Unemployment Benefit funds—SUBs—are private employer funds that are maintained by employers to supplement unemployment benefits so that workers (typically laid-off workers) will receive a higher income replacement level when they are out of work. When an individual receives SUB benefits, the question then becomes twofold: What portion of the SUB benefit constitutes taxable wages? Is the individual truly unemployed or receiving payments that bar unemployment insurance eligibility because they are wage equivalents? Most of the states take the position that SUB benefits are not compensation, so unemployment benefits can be received at the same time.

Alabama, Alaska, California, Connecticut, Georgia, Hawaii, Illinois, Indiana, Maryland, New Hampshire, North Carolina, Ohio, Virginia, and West Virginia are the states that have laws dealing with SUB accounts, so consult state law if you have operations in those states.

For federal tax purposes, SUB benefits are not wages if the employer funds the benefits through deposits into a fund with an independent trustee, and the employee has no right or title in the fund until he or she is laid off. Furthermore, payments must be linked to unemployment insurance, and only periodic payments, not lump-sum payouts, are permitted. Payments from a collectively bargained SUB arrangement are not taxable wages.

Payments that merely return to the employees amounts that have already been included in taxable income are not taxed again, and are not subject to withholding. However, the taxable portion does require the employer to withhold when employees are temporarily or permanently separated under a RIF, or when a plant or operation is discontinued. SUB withholding is based on the number of withholding exemptions claimed on the ex-employee's W-4 form.

> ⇒ **TIP**
> _____
>
> For more guidance on SUB withholding, see IRS Publication 525, "Taxable and Nontaxable Income."

IRS Private Letter Ruling 9525054 deals with a corporation's contributions to a trust to provide benefits linked to receipt of state unemployment compensation. The payments were not FICA or FUTA wages, and income tax withholding was not required. This tax treatment prevailed even for employees who received benefits from the trust when they were ineligible for state unemployment benefits (because the waiting period had not yet expired; because they didn't have enough wage credits; or because they had exhausted the state benefits).

However, benefits received at a time the employee has another job, or has turned down work permitted under a union agreement are taxable. Furthermore, the benefits from the trust do become taxable wages if, when added to all other remuneration including the state unemployment benefit, the total exceeds the individual's weekly pay when he or she was still employed.

As noted above, pension payments reduce entitlement to unemployment compensation. But when distributions from one qualified plan are rolled over to that plan or to an IRA, the claimant has not received the money (it went directly into the retirement account), and therefore it is not necessary to reduce the benefits. Furthermore, reduction is necessary only for amounts based on the claimant's own past work history—not if a person receiving benefits gets a distribution as a surviving spouse.

Also see 61 *Federal Register* 2214 (January 25, 1996), proposed Regulations under Code §3306(r) defining when amounts deferred under or paid from a nonqualified deferred compensation plan are FUTA wages.

A SESA's claim for reimbursement of a bankrupt company's unemployment compensation liability gets priority in the company's Chapter 11 case as an "excise tax." Worker's Compensation is not treated as an excise tax, because of the availability of private insurance options under the Comp system that do not exist for unemployment insurance.

19.6 BENEFIT OFFSETS

This question occurs in two contexts: whether there is any reason to reduce a person's unemployment benefits (because of other income received); and whether the unemployment benefits offset other amounts that would otherwise be received by the person.

As noted above, unemployment compensation is reduced by retirement benefits based on the employee's own work, including IRA and Keogh plan benefits. However, the offset is limited to a plan maintained or contributed to by the company that was the employer during the base payment period, or the employer that is chargeable. In other words, if the pension was earned at Company A, but the person was working for Company B when he or she became unemployed, the Company A pension will not operate as an offset.

About half the states deny unemployment benefits in weeks in which Worker's Compensation benefits are also received, or consider the Comp benefit income that reduces the benefit. (There is also a question of whether someone ill or injured enough to get Comp benefits is "ready and able" to work, even if willing.)

Vacation pay also generally offsets unemployment benefits, although there might be an exception if the claimant is deemed to be on vacation involuntarily rather than voluntarily choosing to take time off.

The general rule is that back pay awarded to a successful Title VII plaintiff will not be reduced by unemployment insurance. However, some courts, like the

Second Circuit, say that the court that hears the Title VII case has discretion to decide whether or not to reduce the award to account for unemployment insurance received.

19.7 DOL PROPOSAL FOR EXPANDED ELIGIBILITY

In May, 1997, the Department of Labor issued a request to the states to expand eligibility for unemployment benefits to new groups, including part-time workers and employees who voluntarily quit a job. As page 80 discusses, close to 20% of the workforce now consists of part-time employees, so their exclusion from unemployment benefits has a major impact.

The proposal pleased neither employers (who would have to pay billions of dollars in additional taxes to fund the expanded benefits) nor the SESAs (who saw the proposal as a step toward an unwelcome unification around a federal standard, thus reducing the state flexibility and discretion that currently prevail.

19.8 PLANNING MEASURES TO REDUCE UNEMPLOYMENT TAX LIABILITY

The unemployment insurance system is designed to stabilize employment, and therefore provides disincentives to employers who dislocate workers unnecessarily. It can be a lot easier for a terminated employee to get a new job if records indicate that he or she quit (instead of being fired), so the termination negotiations may include an agreement to say that the employee quit.

Given the right circumstances, this can be a win-win situation: a more satisfied terminating employee, and a lower experience rate for the employer. But if the employee relies on getting unemployment benefits, this will be a real problem. It is therefore necessary to clarify with employees how their termination will be treated for unemployment compensation purposes.

Some measures that can reduce your company's experience rating and therefore its unemployment tax liability:

* Understand the nature and interaction of the federal and state payroll taxes
* Reduce your FUTA payments appropriately to compensate for state tax payments
* Make sure taxes are paid when due
* Make sure the experience records are accurate; there might be errors, or you might mistakenly be charged with experience of another company with a similar name
* Understand the experience rating system and the claims appeal procedure

- If possible, transfer employees within your operation instead of terminating them, because termination could rise to unemployment claims
- Analyze your operations: could you add additional products, services, or equipment so you could have more consistent, less seasonal, operations (and fewer layoffs)?
- Fire unsatisfactory employees quickly, before they attain eligibility
- When employees quit, do an exit interview to find out why—and whether there are sources of discontent that could be eliminated
- Because all the states provide benefits for partial weeks of unemployment, try to schedule layoffs for Fridays, not earlier in the week
- Make sure you have adequate documentation of misconduct (which will also be useful if the terminated employee alleges discriminatory or other wrongful discharge)
- Monitor all benefit claims, and appeal claims that you believe to be unfounded (e.g., voluntary quits represented as involuntary terminations).

Chapter 20

WORKER'S COMPENSATION

20.1 INTRODUCTION

The worker's compensation (WC) system is administered by the states as a means of providing income for individuals who are unable to work because of injuries and illnesses caused by their past employment history. (Like unemployment insurance, the benefits are funded by insurance-based payments made by the employer.)

> ⇒ **TIP**
>
> Generally speaking, WC payments are not considered taxable income for the employee, nor are the WC insurance premiums paid by the employer. Therefore the employer has no obligations to withhold on the amounts, or to withhold or pay FICA or FUTA taxes. However, WC benefits will be taxable in a limited range of situations: for instance, if they are paid to a person who has returned to work and been assigned light duties; if the WC benefits reduce Social Security benefits; or if the state law calls for payment of non-occupational disability benefits. (For a discussion of the related topic of disability payments provided as a fringe benefit, see Chapter 10.)

It's estimated that there were 11 million work-related injuries in 1997, requiring the Comp system to provide $111 billion for medical expenses and lost wages. The average injured employee was a 34-year-old male who suffered a musculoskeletal injury such as a wrenched back or injured elbow.

According to the Bureau of Labor Statistics, in 1993 there were about 2.75 million WC claims for Repetitive Stress Injuries (RSIs), adding up to more than $20 billion, with five times as much indirect impact in that employers had to replace injured workers and suffer reduced productivity. The average RSI claim is about $8,000, or twice the average Comp claim. Also in 1993, about one-quarter of the 615,000 lost-time injuries were caused by RSIs. The vast majority were either back injuries (65%) or injuries to arms and hands (32%).

The WC system balances the interests of employers and employees. Employees have an interest in having a stream of continuing income (even if they had some responsibility for the incident that caused the injury). Employers have an interest in having claims resolved quickly, by an administrative system that does not have juries; therefore large jury awards arising out of sympathy are not a risk the employer must face.

Employers have a compensating duty to make prompt reports of accidents to the agency administering the Worker's Compensation system. If an employee claims job-related injury or illness, the claim is heard by a Worker's Compensation tribunal (depending on the state, it may be referred to as a board or a commission), which determines if the claim is a valid one for occupational illness or injury.

If it decides it is, the worker is awarded benefits: reimbursement of medical expenses, plus weekly income. This is usually limited to half to two-thirds of the pre-accident wage, with fixed minimum and maximum payments which are often keyed to the state's average income, and an overall limitation on payments. Some states make additional payments available if the injured worker has dependent children; this is especially common in cases where the work-related incident caused the worker's death. (Death cases also involve a burial benefit of between $1,000 and $5,000, depending on the state.)

Compensation benefits do not begin until a waiting period, typically three to seven days, has elapsed. This serves to distinguish genuine temporary disability from a minor incident without lasting consequences. However, most state WC laws also provide that if a disability continues for a period of time (which could be set by the state at anywhere from five days to over seven weeks), retroactive payments dating back to the original date of the injury will be granted.

If the claim is uncontested (i.e., the employer agrees that the injury or disease is work-related, and accepts the employee's characterization of its seriousness), most states follow the "agreement system" under which a settlement is negotiated by the parties (or by the employee and the employer's Worker's Compensation insurer).

⇢ **TIP**
_____

In some states, the agency that administers compensation claims must approve the settlement, even if it was uncontested.

Contested cases are heard and decided by the agency administering the system. Appeal rights are available if either the employee or employer is dissatisfied with the result. After exhaustion of administrative remedies (appealing the ruling within the Compensation system), the case can be taken to court.

20.2 CLASSIFICATION OF BENEFITS

If the initial tribunal accepts the contention that the worker is genuinely disabled and the disability is indeed work-related, then benefits are awarded based on the type and degree of disability. There are four categories: permanent total disability, permanent partial, temporary total, and temporary partial. (Most claims involve temporary total disability.)

A "schedule injury" is the loss of a finger, toe, arm, eye, or leg. The schedule determines the number of weeks of benefits payable for the loss of each member. Death benefits are also available to the survivors of individuals killed in work-related incidents. For injuries such as lifting-related back strains, the tribunal must make a case-by-case determination of the number of weeks of disability that can be anticipated, and the seriousness of the disability.

➡ TIP

Sometimes entitlement to compensation is suspended during any period of time when the employee refuses to undergo a medical examination ordered by the tribunal or requested by the employer or insurer. However, protective state laws provide that information not related to the case will be kept confidential. They also permit the employee to have his or her own doctor present at the examination and entitle him or her to see the examination report.

20.3 ADMINISTRATION OF WORKER'S COMPENSATION (WC)

Participation in the WC system is usually mandatory for employers, although Texas and New Jersey allow private employers to opt out of the system entirely, as long as they notify the Compensation Commission and their employees that they have left the system. Some states allow employees to opt out of WC coverage, in writing, within a reasonable time after starting a new job, and before any accident or injury has occurred. The officers of a corporation are often given the option to leave the WC system.

In about a third of the states, the state itself runs the worker's compensation fund. In these states, employers have three choices for handling their compensation responsibilities: pay into the state fund; buy insurance from a private carrier; or self-insure (i.e., maintain a segregated fund that contains enough money to handle expected compensation claims). In states with no state fund, employers can either buy insurance or self-insure. The insurance premium depends on the degree of risk: a coal mine is clearly much more likely to have occupational injury claims than a boutique. The nationwide average premium is about 2.5% of compensation.(See below for a more detailed discussion of insurance alternatives.)

In a few states (e.g., Texas) worker's compensation is optional. An employer can lawfully opt out of the system altogether, but the tradeoff is that injured employees can then bring a tort suit against the employer (a risk that employers could avoid by participating in the system.)

The general rule is that employees are obligated to notify the employer within a short time (typically, about five days) after an injury or the onset of an illness.

⇒ **TIP**

Encourage employees to report *all* incidents; you need this information for many purposes, including WC, OSHA reporting, and improving in-house safety conditions. In some Comp systems, the employer notifies its WC insurer, which then files the report; in other systems, the employer, whether it has insurance or is self-insured, is responsible for notifying the compensation board. If the employer fails to make the necessary report, the employee will probably be given additional time to bring his or her claim.

20.3.1 Compensable Injuries

Whether an incident is covered by WC depends on several factors:

- Whether the injured person is a common-law employee (not an independent contractor; top corporate managers may be denied benefits on the theory that they are the corporation's alter ego, not ordinary employees)

- If the injury arises out of employment (e.g., is not an illness or hurt that could happen to anyone, employed or not)

- If the injury arises in the course of employment (e.g., not during commuting or when the employee was out "goofing off")

- If the injury is deemed an "accident" (an unexpected occurrence that can be linked to a definite time, place, and occasion)

- If the injury is exempt from statutory coverage for some reason (e.g., the employee's drunkenness or drug impairment was a significant causative factor).

A final question is whether exclusivity applies to an incident that has been established as a compensable injury (see below).

Employees can receive benefits for illness and injury suffered in the course of employment. Therefore, coverage will not be available if there is no relation between work and the incident. The simplest case is an injury or illness occurring within the workplace itself and which therefore must be covered. An employee might be covered if he or she was sent by the employer to work somewhere else (or to perform deliveries or errands), and the injury occurred at that place or en route.

Injuries occurring in non-work contexts, however, such as lunchtime pickup softball games or horseplay, are probably not compensable. But if the employer sponsors athletics, or if the injury occurs during a company picnic or holiday party, it probably would be compensable.

⇒ TIP

For a recent example, see a 1997 Minnesota case in which WC was held to cover (and to be the exclusive remedy) for an employee who slipped and fell at a party for staff and vendors held at the company CEO's house.

Injuries occurring on company premises during scheduled breaks (for instance, slipping on the cafeteria floor) would probably be compensable, although they might be treated as happening on the employee's own time and thus not compensable. Employees take unscheduled breaks at their own risk.

One of the most vital factors is the employer's degree of control over the employee's activities. A recent Missouri case says that a job applicant who was injured during training had not become an "employee," and thus was not covered by WC. The potential employer didn't require her to get the training; didn't control her activities during the training period; and in fact didn't even guarantee her a job if she completed the training successfully.

Generally, Worker's Compensation doesn't cover injuries during normal commuting (either to or from the workplace), but a recent Maryland case provides an exception. It does hold a temporary services agency responsible for injuries occurring on a private bus, furnished by the agency only for its employees, on the theory that the agency benefited by the bus service because employees were more likely to arrive at work on time (enhancing the agency's reputation) if they were furnished with transportation.

At-work assaults raise difficult questions. The general rule is that injuries caused by assaults are compensable if they result from work-related increases in the risk of encountering dangerous people: for instance, convenience store clerks are at risk of being assaulted or even killed by robbers. But if someone is the target of assault for personal reasons (e.g., an abusive spouse), the fact that the assault happened to occur at work rather than in another setting will not necessarily render the injury a compensable one, if it is not work-related in any way. (Remember, the WC system is basically a no-fault system, so it will not be necessary to determine if the employer's poor security system facilitated the assault.)

20.3.2 Classifications and MMI

Compensable injuries might be permanent and total; permanent and partial, temporary and total, or temporary and partial. Benefits can be granted for either "disability" or "impairment"; the difference is that disability is defined to mean loss of wages, whereas impairment is permanent partial disability that does not cause wage loss.

In the case of temporary disabilities, the concept of Maximum Medical Improvement, or MMI, comes into play. MMI is a doctor's opinion that there is no reasonable medical probability of further improvement in function (assessed based on factors such as current and proposed treatment, history of improvement, and preexisting conditions). Most states impose an obligation on the employer to notify the employee that MMI has been reached, and that the employee probably will lose benefits within 90 days unless he or she returns to work or finds other employment. However, WC benefits can be extended past the MMI if the claimant makes an honest effort yet cannot find suitable work.

Permanent disability payments could be based on wage loss, earning capacity, physical impairment, or some combination of the three.

In addition to making wage-based payments, the employer must provide the employee with reasonable and necessary medical treatment, continued as long as the injured employee's medical condition requires. Most states include chiropractic in the definition of medical care; many include home health attendants as well.

20.4 WC EXCLUSIVITY

The system gives employers the protection of "worker's compensation exclusivity." In other words, in the normal work-related injury or illness case, the employee's only remedy against the employer is to collect compensation benefits; lawsuits are not permitted. However, exclusivity applies only to suits against the employer. If the employee is injured by a manufactured product that is manufactured by the employer, the employee can sue the employer in its capacity as manufacturer.

Suits against other manufacturers, or non-employer parties responsible for hazardous conditions at the workplace, may also be a possibility. Such litigation is not merely an option for the injured employee: the employer itself can sue the third party in order to recover the medical benefits that the employer provided on behalf of the worker.

Basically, Worker's Compensation is a no-fault system, and negligence by any party is simply irrelevant. However, in some states, a worker's failure to use safety equipment can reduce (but not eliminate) the benefits that would otherwise be payable for the consequences of failing to use that equipment.

Compensation benefits will be granted only if the employee has medical evidence of the connection between the job and the disabling condition. See, e.g., *Hanten* v. *Palace Builders, Inc.*, 1997 SD 3 (1997), where an employee who underwent surgery for tendinitis, returned to work, and sought Worker's Compensation benefits for a syndrome she claimed was related to keyboard use. Her claim was denied, because her medical witness said the syndrome was "possibly" work-related; there must be testimony that the symptoms are at least *probably* connected to work for the employee to be awarded benefits.

Furthermore, the employee must be actually and totally incapacitated (i.e., unable to work): benefits will not be awarded to a stoical employee who insists on continuing to work despite pain. Courts are split as to whether a claimant is permanently, totally disabled only if there is absolutely no job he or she can perform, or whether "human factors" such as availability of jobs within reasonable commuting distance must be considered.

Sometimes the employer's wrongdoing will take the case out of WC exclusivity. For instance, the employer might be subjected to ordinary tort claims if it intentionally conceals information about workplace hazards (although not all courts will rule this way).

Few employees have been successful in suing their employers for intentional infliction of mental anguish in the context of sexual harassment cases: the mental anguish claim is usually, although not always, considered to fall under WC exclusivity.

However, a 1997 Washington State case says that WC is not the exclusive remedy in a case alleging negligent infliction of emotional stress. The plaintiff was an Asian-American worker who claimed that racial harassment caused him to suffer physical consequences such as stress, nausea, weakness, and insomnia. A contemporary Wisconsin case also found that state fair employment act claims of sexual harassment were not preempted by WC, because in this reading WC is supposed to deal with physical injury, not discrimination.

20.5 DISEASE IN THE WC SYSTEM

Compensation benefits are also available if the employee develops a disease rather than an injury in the workplace. However, occupational diseases create some extremely difficult analytic problems. They are covered only if there is a close connection between the disease and the work environment. This is fairly clear in the case of "brown lung" and cotton mills, but more difficult in the case of passive smoking when non-smoking employees are exposed to cigarette smoke from customers and co-employees who do smoke.

Some states take the position that workers are entitled to compensation benefits if conditions in the workplace aggravated a disease they already had. In states such as

California, Florida, Kentucky, Maryland, Mississippi, North Dakota, and South Carolina, benefits are available but will be reduced to compensate for pre-existing conditions. (In other words, if the worker's condition was 25% due to workplace factors, 75% due to the preexisting condition, only 25% of the full benefit will be payable.)

Perhaps the most difficult problem of occupational disease is the "long tail" question. It may take years, or even decades, for symptoms caused by occupational exposure to chemicals, dust, fumes, etc., to manifest themselves. During this time, the employee may have moved to another job in the same industry, to a completely different job, or engaged in behaviors that cause or contribute to disease (e.g., asbestosis complicated by cigarette smoking).

The general rule is that claims are timely if they are filed within a reasonable time after the individual first experiences disability or symptoms, and could reasonably be expected to draw a connection between work exposure and illness. However, the employee could experience symptoms long after changing jobs. For instance, a worker might be exposed to a dangerous substance in 1995; quit his or her job in 1999; and experience symptoms in 2001. Thus, the employer may have to face claims long after the termination of employment—another reason for long-term maintenance of health records.

> ⇒ **TIP**
>
> Sometimes occupational disease claims, even if brought in good faith, are not well-founded in fact. The employer should appoint a multi-disciplinary investigation team (including legal and medical professionals and industrial hygienists) to evaluate the claim. The team should review the toxicology literature to see if there is a connection between the illness claimed and the substance the employee alleges exposure to.

Another question is whether the employee's dosage was high enough to trigger the claimed symptoms. The epidemiology (disease pattern) for similar exposures should be studied to see if the employee's alleged experience is typical. Furthermore, one disease claim by an employee could trigger a wave of related claims from other employees who actually are ill, believe themselves to be ill because they have developed psychosomatic symptoms, or who just hope for easy money.

20.5.1 Psychological Injuries

Although by and large the WC system concerns itself with palpable physical injuries and diseases, under some circumstances mental illnesses can be compensable. Emotional and mental injuries are analyzed in three categories: mental-physical (i.e., physical impact of mental conditions, such as chest pains and high blood pressure); physical-mental (such as suffering a phobia after being involved in an accident; "AIDS-phobia" after receiving a needle-stick injury); and mental-mental injuries with no physical component.

In all states, mental-physical and physical-mental injuries are potentially compensable as long as a causal connection can be established between the two. Compensability of mental-mental injuries is less clear-cut. Some states, including Alabama, Florida, Georgia, Kansas, Minnesota, Montana, Nebraska, Ohio, Oklahoma, and South Dakota refuse to compensate mental-mental injuries where there is no physical trauma involved. In the other states, compensability may depend on whether the onset was gradual or sudden; a connection with a severe, unpredictable event may have to be shown. But see *Everingim* v. *Good Samaritan Center*, 552 NW2d 837 (SD 1996), holding that a nursing home employee, who had a past history of being sexually abused, could get WC for post-traumatic stress disorder after being touched offensively by a patient, on the theory that sexual battery constitutes physical injury.

The stress of having too much work, leading to a nervous breakdown, is not a compensable "accident," according to a Nebraska court; but a contemporary New York case says that suicide after the corporation's merger led an employee to depression is compensable. Most states hold that suicide is not an "intentional act," and therefore wrongful death compensation is payable, if the employee committed suicide while depressed, and the depression was the legacy of a workplace accident.

A 1997 Wyoming case finds that it is not a violation of the Constitutional guarantee of equal protection for a WC system to impose a higher standard of proof for mental than for physical injuries. A legitimate state interest is at stake, because mental injuries are easier to fabricate than physical ones, which leave detectable evidence.

20.6 ALTERNATIVES FOR INSURING WC

Outside of the few states that require coverage to be purchased from the monopolistic state funds, nearly all WC policies purchased from any other source will follow the form of the "standard policy"—the Worker's Compensation and Employers' Liability Policy developed by the National Council on Compensation Insurance (NCCI). In 1996, the total of all WC premiums was close to $25 billion. Interestingly, this is 20% below the 1991 level; total premiums decreased because of factors such as increased self-insurance, the creation of high-deductible plans, the growing role of state WC funds, and increased competition within the commercial market.

Depending on the state and the employer's own risk categorization and financial status, some or all of these methods may be available for coping with the WC obligation:

- Purchasing insurance from the monopolistic state fund that is the sole source of WC coverage within the state
- Purchasing insurance from a commercial carrier

- Purchasing insurance from a "state fund" that competes with commercial carriers
- Self-insurance (nearly always combined with third party administration and/or reinsurance)
- Insurance through a captive insurer owned or "rented" by the employer
- Participation in the assigned risk pool (which can be compelled or a voluntary choice, depending on circumstances).

Employers can often keep their premium under control by participating in a high deductible program.

⇒ TIP

If the employer company goes bankrupt, the Tenth Circuit has ruled that unpaid Worker's Compensation premiums are not entitled to priority status under Bankruptcy Code §507(a)(4), even though contributions to an employee benefit plan do get priority when creditors divide up the assets of the bankrupt company. The court's rationale is that priority is limited to wage substitutes that the employees bargained to receive (and gave up other forms of compensation to get). WC premiums don't fall into this category because paying them is a statutory requirement, so they really benefit the employer, not the employees.

20.6.1 State Funds

Monopolistic state funds are maintained in North Dakota, Ohio, Washington, West Virginia, and Wyoming: i.e., all covered employers must purchase their coverage from the fund. Nevada was originally part of this group, but as of July 1, 1997, although the state fund will continue, it will compete with the commercial insurers that are permitted to offer coverage in the state.

Where the state fund is competitive (as in Arizona, California, Colorado, Idaho, Louisiana, Maine, Maryland, Michigan, Minnesota, Montana, New Mexico, New York, Oklahoma, Oregon, Pennsylvania, Rhode Island, Texas, and Utah), each employer analyzes the overall cost of state versus commercial coverage. Often the state funds can offer very attractive prices, because they spend very little on marketing. In these states, the competitive fund decides which applications to accept, and sets its own rate card.

20.6.2 Assigned Risk Pools

In any situation in which people or organizations are legally compelled to maintain insurance, some of them are not insurable under normal underwriting principles, and there is likely to be an assigned risk pool. This is true in both automobile liability and the WC market. For WC, in about half the states, the NCCI is responsible for administering the National Worker's Compensation Reassurance (assigned risk) Pool.

However, the WC assigned risk pool has some unusual features. For one thing, commercial insurers have an obligation to pay "residual market assessments" of about 14 cents on every premium dollar they receive, to support the assigned risk pool. This heavy assessment makes commercial insurers less willing to grant discounts—and thus drives more employers to see the assigned risk pool as an attractive source of coverage.

Furthermore, when commercial insurers don't get the rate increases they request from state insurance regulators, they may deny insurance to the weakest prospects, driving them into the assigned risk pool as well. As a matter of fact, about 25% of all employers are insured under the NCCI-managed pool, which makes it the largest single WC insurer in the country.

The day-to-day operations of the pool are unusual, too. "Servicing carriers" issue the actual policies (in fact, some employers think they are insured by the servicing carriers; they don't even know they have coverage under the assigned risk pool) and pay the claims, then turn to the NCCI for reimbursement. Sometimes all the servicing carriers share in the losses; at other times, the state randomly matches up assigned risks and servicing carriers, who then are required to insure them.

20.6.3 Self-Insurance

All the states (except North Dakota and Wyoming) permit employers who satisfy certain criteria to self-insure, but in practice self-insurance is usually not practical except for very large companies. But, because of these scale factors, about one-third of the WC market is now self-insured.

A company would not be considered a candidate for self-insurance unless its annual WC premium is in six or even seven figures, or unless it operates in several states and has WC obligations in each. (Of course, there's no way to guarantee that all the states will have compatible requirements for self-insuring employers.)

> ⇒ **TIP**
>
> If your company switches to self-insurance, the company that sells your umbrella liability insurance coverage should be notified, and an appropriate endorsement should be added to the umbrella policy. Don't forget that incidents occurring this year could have repercussions in many future years (including years when you have commercial coverage).

To satisfy state requirements, the company must be financially capable of paying all WC claims that arise in the course of its operations, and must post bond or establish escrows to prove this. Furthermore, the company's cash flow must be stable enough to support a claim at any stage in its cash cycle.

Typically, the state law will require self-insured companies to purchase excess coverage (reinsurance); more than half the states impose this requirement. Even if it is not required, it is prudent. Generally, the employer will also have to show that it has made arrangements for claims administration, employee communications, and safety programs. These functions are typically delivered via a Third Party Administration (TPA) arrangement.

A good WC TPA takes an active stance toward claims investigation (to deter and detect fraud), steers appropriate cases toward the Second Injury Fund (to reduce the burden on the employer), and actively pursues rehabilitation and return-to-work programs, for the same reason.

An effective TPA should have 24-hour-a-day claim service, low turnover (experienced representatives do a much better job than novices), a high proportion of employees with professional certification in loss control, and a low average final cost per claim combined with quick settlement of claims.

Self-insurance can be pure (the employer pays all claims out of the reserves it has established for this purpose), group (several companies join forces; each is jointly and severally liable for all Comp claims within the group), or limited. Under limited self-insurance, the employer is responsible for the SIR (Self-Insured Retention), roughly equal to a deductible; excess insurance pays the rest.

Excess coverage is written in several ways: per occurrence, per loss, as an aggregate amount for the year, or per accident per payment year. (After all, an injury could have consequences that stretch over several years.)

Specific excess insurance limits the employer's liability for claims for any occurrence where the exposure exceeds the SIR. Aggregate excess insurance copes with a bad year: the employer has to pay the amount in the aggregate retention or loss fund, usually expressed as a percentage (e.g., 125%) of the premium set by the re-insurer for the year. Aggregate excess coverage usually stops at $1 million or $2 million, so on the off-chance that there is a greater exposure, the employer will once again be at risk. It's much easier to get specific excess insurance than aggregate insurance, which is also more expensive.

The majority of the states permit group self-insurance; nationwide, there are more than 250 pools that represent over $1.5 billion in premiums.

➠ **TIP**

Self-insurance is considered a privilege, which the state can revoke if the employer fails to file necessary reports, doesn't maintain the required level of excess insurance, or otherwise fails to keep up its end of the bargain. A change in corporate ownership might also lead to revocation of the privilege, even if the corporate structure remains the same.

Self-insurance carries a cost burden. The company must file an application, asking the state for permission to self-insure; this usually costs $100–$1,000. If the company has to post a letter of credit as security, the lending bank will impose fees. Excess insurance and TPAs each cost anywhere from 8-13% of what would otherwise be the premium for WC insurance. There is also a state tax, the equivalent of 1–4% of either the manual premium, incurred losses, or paid losses, depending on the way the state law is drafted.

20.6.4 High-Deductible Plans

A high-deductible plan is a kind of combination of insurance and self-insurance: the employer reduces its premium obligation by accepting a higher deductible, typically somewhere between $100,000 and $1 million, although policies are available with deductibles up to $5 million. Any employer can purchase a high-deductible policy; it is not necessary to meet state-imposed financial qualifications, as it would be to self-insure.

Operations are somewhat unusual. When a claim is made, the insurer pays the full claim, then goes back to the policyholder (usually on a monthly basis) to collect any payments made that actually fell within the deductible. Generally, employers who purchase such policies must create an escrow fund equal to about three months' potential payment of losses, and must put up a letter of credit in an amount equal to the deductible (the amount which the insurer might have to advance on behalf of the employer).

At the end of the first year of the high-deductible coverage, the letter of credit is adjusted upward or downward, as experience suggests. Paid losses are billed until all claims have been closed. Sometimes high-deductible insurers require indemnification or a hold-harmless agreement that will permit them to come back if, for example, legislation is passed that subjects them to increased losses that fall within the deductible.

20.6.5 Captive Insurers

A captive insurance company is one that, instead of doing business with the public, does business only with one company that is its sole shareholder, or a limited number of companies that agree to participate in a "rent-a-captive" arrangement. The new owner or "renter" of the captive insurance company deposits enough money for estimated WC losses for the following year. (In many states, direct insurance via the captive is not permitted; a fronting company, which receives a commission, must be involved.)

The advantage to the employer is the ability to retain the underwriting income (the premium equivalent deposited, minus the expenses) as well as the investment income on deposited but unused funds. Remember, payments on a

Comp claim can extend for many years, so investment income can become a serious factor. Furthermore, the premium-equivalent payments are tax deductible.

Once again, this option is available to companies that cannot satisfy state requirements for self-insurance.

> ⇥ **TIP**
> _____
>
> A captive insurer can be used to reinsure the deductible under a high-deductible plan.

20.7 SETTING THE WC PREMIUM

The basic level of WC premium that an employer will have to pay for its insurance is the "manual rate" for the relevant industry classification. (There are 600 industry classifications, each identified by a four-digit number.) The manual rate is the average cost of WC coverage for the classification, based on the number of claims of injuries serious enough to cause lost work time in the past three years. It is sometimes expressed as a percentage of total payroll, but is usually defined as a certain number of dollars per $100 of payroll.

But the manual rate is only the beginning of the employer's rate. Experience rating (the employer's actual claims experience for the preceding two years) can be used to increase or decrease the base premium that will be imposed in the future. Retrospective rating is an alternative that states can adopt: past losses are used to adjust the premium already charged for a particular year, resulting in a refund to the employer or a demand for additional payments.

> ⇥ **TIP**
> _____
>
> Large employers may be entitled to a discounted premium, because administrative expenses stay fairly stable no matter what the size of the policy.

WC policies operate with certain frequent exceptions to the basic rules. There are general inclusions to the policy (so-called because they recur in a large percentage of all industries): workers in employee cafeterias, people who manufacture packing containers, in-house printing departments, and repair and maintenance crews. There are also general exclusions which are "written out" of ordinary industry classifications: new construction activities performed by employees (as distinct from contractors), aviation, running a sawmill, and one that is much less exotic—having an employer-operated day care center.

It should also be noted that the amount the employer pays as WC premiums is tax deductible; so are loss amounts paid by a self-insured employer. On the other hand, reserves maintained in order to satisfy the deductible under a WC policy are *not* tax-deductible.

Sometimes a premium quote will be inaccurate, and the premium can be reduced by the simple expedient of:

- Checking to see payroll is stated accurately; the higher the presumed payroll, the higher the premium
- Making sure employees are assigned to the lowest risk classification that accurately reflects their duties
- Having your insurance agent review the calculations.

In particularly egregious cases, the employer can appeal to the state's rating agency—which, in most cases, will be delegated to the NCCI central office in Boca Raton, Florida.

20.8 BAN ON RETALIATION

Thirty-eight states have passed statutes making it illegal to retaliate against an employee, either specifically for filing a Worker's Compensation claim or for filing any "wage claim" or "wage complaint," a classification broad enough to encompass WC. The states are Alabama, Arizona, California, Connecticut, Delaware, Florida, Hawaii, Idaho, Illinois, Indiana, Kansas, Kentucky, Louisiana, Maine, Maryland, Mississippi, Michigan, Minnesota, Missouri, Montana, New Hampshire, New Jersey, New Mexico, New York, North Carolina, North Dakota, Ohio, Oklahoma, Rhode Island, South Carolina, South Dakota, Texas, Vermont, Virginia, Washington, West Virginia, Wisconsin, and Wyoming. Even in the minority states that lack such statutes, employers are not necessarily free to retaliate: it's very likely that state courts will deem retaliatory discharge a violation of public policy.

It has also been held that a retaliatory *demotion*, resulting in lower pay for the employee, is wrongful and can give rise to a lawsuit.

However, the employee will not always be allowed to use the state courts to press claims of retaliatory discharge. In a unionized workplace, according to the First Circuit, §301 of the Labor-Management Relations Act preempts a claim that the employee was not rehired after a period of disability because she filed a WC claim. The court reached this result because the collective bargaining agreement's "management rights" clause gives management the sole right to hire and fire, so assessing the validity of the retaliation claim requires interpretation of the collective bargaining agreement, which in turn falls under §301. (See page 375 for more discussion of §301 preemption.)

This contrasts with the Eighth Circuit's 1995 decision that an employee's claim of unlawful retaliatory discharge *cannot* be removed from state to federal court, because the collective bargaining agreement does not have to be interpreted, and therefore state remedies are not preempted.

20.9   OTHER STATE LAWS INVOLVING WC

WC is an area in which states frequently amend their laws. In the past few years, various states have passed laws dealing with WC issues such as:

- Denial of WC benefits to employees who were intoxicated at the time of the injury (although the employee must be given the right to rebut the presumption that a high concentration of alcohol in the blood, or a positive post-accident drug test, was the cause of the accident)

- Employers' ability to combine with other employers as "common self-insurers," in order to achieve economies of scale

- Authorizing employers to use managed care organizations to coordinate and centralize care and rehabilitation of injured employees

- Discounted WC premiums for employers who implement and sustain an effective drug-free workplace program

- Utilization review in WC cases

- Clarification of who is an "independent contractor" and not an employee entitled to WC coverage

- Premium discounts for attending an OSHA-approved program about cost containment

- Higher penalties imposed on employers who fail to make WC payments as they fall due.

20.10   WC IN RELATION TO LAWS ON OTHER SUBJECTS

An individual who claims a compensable injury may also assert claims under other statutes, so it becomes necessary to determine how the statutes work together. Unfortunately, in many cases new statutes were added to the legal system without careful consideration of interactions with other laws, so seemingly simple questions can be hard to answer, and results that seem inequitable may prevail.

20.10.1   The ADA

Sometimes the same individual may, at the same or different times, claim disability discrimination and also claim eligibility for WC benefits. ADA/WC interface problems also arise when an employer interviews a job applicant who appears to have some physical limitations, which might have been caused by an earlier compensable injury.

As page 17 explains, job interviews are not appropriate venues for discussing an employee's injury history (or health status in general). During the interview, however, the interviewer can inform the applicant of the essential and peripheral duties involved in doing the job, and can find out whether the applicant is capable of performing the essential duties, with or without reasonable accommodations made by the employer. Inquiries about past WC claims are barred because they are considered to be disability-related.

Once an employer is prepared to extend a conditional job offer to an applicant, however, it can ask about past WC claims—as long as the question is posed to all recipients of conditional offers, not just to those who appear to have some impairment. Fear that employing someone with a prior injury will increase current WC costs is not a valid reason for denying a job to a qualified applicant.

As for current employees who suffer an injury and are partially recovered, it probably violates the ADA to maintain a policy that employees cannot return to work until they are 100% fit to resume all of their old duties. If an employee wants to return to work (which would certainly offer better value for money to the employer than continued receipt of disability benefits!), the ADA requires the employer to offer assignment to a light-duty job when this would be a reasonable accommodation to the employee's disability. However, the employer is not required to create new jobs merely to assist recuperating employees; nor is it necessary to "bump" another employee to accommodate disability. The ADA preempts state laws that permit the "100% or nothing" policy.

Referring an injured person to a vocational rehabilitation program is not considered a reasonable accommodation, if the employee could return to work with accommodations that do not constitute a hardship to the employer.

The fact that a person receives WC benefits does not prove that he or she is disabled under the ADA definition, because the statutes serve different purposes: WC replaces income lost because of job-related incidents; the ADA protects disabled people against discrimination that would keep them out of jobs they are qualified to perform.

It has been held that the Americans with Disabilities Act (ADA) does not preempt state case law that denies worker's compensation to someone who was hired in substantial part because of pre-employment lies about physical condition, if that condition is causally connected to the injury. There is no ADA preemption because the ADA allows pre-employment inquiries about the applicant's ability to do the job, and even if the employer asks improper questions, lying is not an appropriate response. Nevertheless, some states might make compensation benefits available to an employee who lied on the application, on the theory that there was no connection between the false statement and the injury—only between the false statement and the employer's decision to hire the applicant.

Of course, employees' medical records are confidential, but it is appropriate to ask employees for permission to contact their treating physicians so you can discuss the ADA's definition of "disability" with the physician, then ask about the extent of the employee's limitations and his or her ability to perform specific work tasks. Also use the conference to ask the physician which accommodations he or she suggests will facilitate the employee's work.

20.10.2 FMLA

Although many people think of the Family and Medical Leave Act (FMLA) in terms of leave to provide child care or elder care, unpaid leave under the FMLA is also available to employees who require medical care themselves. One approach that satisfies the employer's various legal obligations is to issue an FMLA notice whenever employees are injured.

Make sure that they know their rights—but also make sure that they are advised that you will count their WC leave toward their "ration" of 12 annual weeks of unpaid FMLA leave. Let them know that after the 12 weeks have been used up, you will assess whether they have become qualified individuals with a disability for ADA purposes. If so, explore whether reasonable accommodations can be made at acceptable cost to return the employee to work.

20.10.3 Second Injury Funds

Although they predate the ADA, in a sense state "second injury funds" also represent a legislative purpose, which is to promote the employment of disabled people. In states that do not have such a fund, an employer who hires a person who has already suffered an illness or injury, which becomes worse because of occupational factors arising on the job, would be responsible for the full burden of that employee's compensation benefits, even though the occupational factors may be comparatively less important than the preexisting condition. Second injury funds deal with the situation in which a permanent disability is compounded to become either a permanent partial disability that is more serious than before, or a permanent total disability.

If there is a second injury fund in the picture (as is true, for instance, in California, Missouri, New Jersey and Washington State), however, the employer merely pays the economic consequences of the new injury. The publicly funded second injury fund assumes the rest of the economic burden. The first injury must have been serious enough to be compensable, but need not actually have come under the WC system. For instance, the second injury fund would come into play if a work-related injury aggravated an existing condition that was caused by a non-work-related automobile accident, or a birth defect.

➥ TIP

To collect from the fund, the employer may have to certify that it was aware of the preexisting condition at the time of hiring. To get this information without violating the ADA, the employer must be careful to defer questions about prior injuries until after a tentative job offer has been made—and, preferably, should make it clear to the potential new hire that the purpose of the query is merely to prepare for a potential second injury fund claim, not to screen out job offerees with a history of Comp claims.

20.10.4 ERISA

The general tenor of court decisions on this issue is that WC benefits can legitimately be used to offset accrued benefits that derive from the employer's contribution to a pension plan—but only if a statute specifically provides this, or if the plan has been drafted to include this specific provision. ERISA will preempt state WC laws to the extent that the laws "relate" to the plan.

In 1992, the Supreme Court decided that a state law "relates" to an ERISA plan if it refers to or has a connection with the plan even if the effect is indirect—and even if the law was not designed to affect the plan. Therefore, a law requiring employers to provide health insurance to employees receiving or eligible for WC benefits was preempted by ERISA. (See page 329 for a discussion of when a matter "relates" to a pension plan, thus triggering ERISA preemption.)

20.10.5 Social Security Disability

In many states, the Social Security Disability Income system (SSDI) is considered the primary payer for any injured employee whose condition is serious enough to constitute total disability under the Social Security Administration's stringent definition. The states following this system are Alaska, Arkansas, California, Colorado, Florida, Louisiana, Maine, Massachusetts, Michigan, Minnesota, Missouri, Montana, Nevada, New Jersey, New York, North Dakota, Ohio, Oregon, Utah, Washington, and Wisconsin.

If SSDI is involved, the payments reduce the WC benefit dollar-for-dollar, until the combined SSDI and WC benefit reaches the level of 80% of the worker's pre-accident earnings. However, SSDI reduces only the portion of the benefit that represents lost income, not the part that goes to medical care or legal fees.

In the states mentioned, employers sometimes actually hire attorneys to represent injured workers in their Social Security Disability cases, because that way, the employer's Worker's Compensation experience will be charged with a much lower claim. (Self-insured employers have to actually pay WC claims themselves, so they have an even stronger rationale for furthering the employee's claim.)

20.11 RESPONDING TO AN ACCIDENT

What should you do if an accident occurs? Before the first accident, make sure that you have an effective procedure in place, and that everyone on premises has been drilled in using it. Employees should have free access to first aid for minor incidents, and for immediate medical treatment in more serious cases.

Somebody must be responsible for driving the injured worker to the doctor's office or the hospital emergency room, or summoning an ambulance when one is needed. Have plenty of employees who have training in first aid and CPR; have an adequate number of first aid kits with fresh supplies (including disposable airways and latex gloves, to safeguard persons performing first aid) in convenient locations. Someone must be responsible for filing the initial accident report (and an OSHA incident report, if required: see page 420). (Some insurers maintain 24-hour telephone lines; the insurer uses the information for WC and OSHA reporting, and to assign a case manager so the case can be reviewed for utilization and rehabilitation potential.) The HR department must monitor compliance.

The employer's involvement had better not end there, either. Part of what determines if an injured employee can be rehabilitated, or how quickly, is the employee's attitude. If the employee genuinely wants to return to work soon (or seek alternative employment), then he or she will cooperate better with the sometimes difficult and painful work of rehabilitation.

Informing workers about compensation as a routine part of corporate communications (even before any accidents occur) creates a beneficial "halo effect": employees who do suffer injuries are more satisfied with their treatment and rehabilitation, and return to work sooner and are less likely to hire a lawyer or attempt to sue or contest the Comp award.

On the other hand, if the employee is so hostile that he or she sees the injury as a gravy train to be ridden as long as possible, the employer will wind up with a long-term Comp case or a contested hearing. Making the employee feel genuinely valued goes a long way toward establishing a positive attitude.

⟹ **TIP**

Inform employees if their treating physicians will bill the insurer directly; employees will appreciate not having to make out-of-pocket payments at a time when family income has dropped. Having a network of preferred providers helps both employer (by cutting costs) and employees (by giving them access to qualified doctors and saving them a "research project" in finding appropriate medical aid).

The company can also provide injured workers with a referral list of doctors who have a documented history of beginning rehabilitation right away, and pursuing it actively. Employees may feel pressured to select one of these physicians, but they may also be grateful to know which doctors have the best record in treating work-related injuries; otherwise, they might end up with a doctor who isn't aware of the latest developments in physiatry (rehabilitation medicine).

In addition to immediate accident reports, some states require a cumulative annual report of all workplace incidents, similar to the OSHA annual report (see page 420). Follow-up status reports may also be required on individual accidents. Employers who fail to make mandated reports may be subject to fines or even imprisonment.

20.12 WC HEARINGS AND SETTLEMENTS

There is no real controversy in most WC cases. For one thing, since fault is basically irrelevant, it isn't necessary to apportion fault. For another thing, it's usually pretty obvious that an injury has indeed occurred, and often there is no real dispute about its seriousness. (Disease claims are more likely to involve controverted allegations.) Generally, the employer is given a certain number of days to contest a claim; if this time passes without notice, the claim is deemed uncontested.

Thus, many WC cases are settled: the employee claims benefits and the employer agrees that they should be paid. Most settlements involve payment of ongoing benefits at a continuing rate (a percentage of either the employee's pre-accident income or of average monthly income within the state). However, there is an increasing trend to settle WC cases in return for payment of a lump sum. Depending on state practice, the settlement may require approval by the Comp board, but the approval may be more or less automatic; or, the board may turn down any settlement that gives the worker less than he or she would receive under the statute.

Uncontested cases can be handled either by "direct payment" or "agreement." In a direct payment case, the employer or insurer initiates the process, by making the initial installment payment prescribed by statute to the employee. Under this option, the employee doesn't have to sign anything or agree to anything. Agreement systems are more common: employer and employee enter into a written agreement.

Settlements cover only the matters specifically discussed in the agreement, so it's important to draft any such agreement to cover all permissible items. However, employers must not overreach: they are allowed to settle claims that have already accrued, but not future claims (such as claims for future medical expenses), because no one can know how large the future claims will be and therefore cannot decide what constitutes a fair settlement.

The general rule is that the settlement between employer and employee is final, although there may be legal reasons why the parties can have it set aside. Possible grounds include fraud, mutual mistake of fact (both parties believe something about the employee's condition that proves to be incorrect), or mistake of law (one side or the other misinterprets the legal rules and their consequences). The fact that an employee was not represented by counsel probably will not be enough to invalidate a settlement (unless, perhaps, the employer prevented the employee from seeking legal advice).

> ⇒ **TIP**
>
> It could still be worthwhile to inform employees that they have the right to have an attorney represent them.

Contested claims don't necessarily go straight to the Comp board. Some states make mediation an option that is available (but does not become binding until both sides agree that it will be); others make it compulsory. In mediated cases, a neutral mediator will meet with the parties at least once, in an informal manner. Sometimes the meeting will be off the record, so both sides can speak freely, without fearing that what they say will influence later legal proceedings. If necessary, the mediator arranges more meetings, until either the parties reach a settlement (facilitated by the mediator) or it is clear that an impasse has been reached.

In some states, when mediation fails, binding arbitration can be applied; in other states, the case is sent to the Comp board for adjudication.

Once the Comp board reaches a decision in a contested case, the parties get a period of time to file for an appeal; 30 days is most usual, although it could be anywhere from 10 days to a year. Grounds for appeal include improprieties in the process, and changed circumstances that were unknown at the time of the original award (e.g., unexpected, pronounced improvement or deterioration in the employee's condition).

> ⇒ **TIP**
>
> If the employer is late in making the required payments, many state laws entitle the employee to an additional 10-20% payment. Civil fines may also be imposed, and the unpaid amounts could operate as a lien on the employer's assets.

20.13 CONTROLLING WORKER'S COMPENSATION COSTS

In any employer-funded system, employers will have an interest in keeping costs down and improving their claims experience (thus reducing their payment rates). Improving the safety of the workplace not only reduces the likelihood of an OSHA citation (see Chapter 21) but reduces (although it can never entirely eliminate) the risk of disease and accident on the job.

Obviously employers will benefit from efforts to rehabilitate injured workers, so that they can return to at least some form of productive and wage-earning work rather than remaining lifelong "Comp cases." For example, a construction worker who becomes a paraplegic in a fall can't return to his former job. But with additional training or academic education, and with paratransit or a specially equipped car or van, he could be retrained (for instance, to work at a telephone help desk doing consumer support).

This easy-to-believe proposition gets academic support from a study performed by Axiomedics Research Inc. on behalf of San Francisco's Paradigm Health Corporation. The sooner the case was referred to a rehabilitation specialist, the more likely a catastrophically injured worker was to get back to work eventually. Cases referred within one week of the injury generally resulted in re-employment of the ex-employee; cases referred more than one year after the injury seldom returned to productive work.

Managed care is also making inroads into the WC market. For example, in 1996 New York State passed a law that permits the use of Preferred Provider Organizations (PPOs) to treat non-unionized employees who have filed for compensation benefits, on condition that the PPOs be completely independent of insurance companies, which cannot have a financial interest in them. (In a unionized workplace, PPO involvement in comp cases is a mandatory subject of bargaining.)

The PPOs are subject to all requirements covering commercial insurers, including quality standards. However, the state insurance fund, the insurer of last resort for companies whose record is too bad to get private insurance, does not have the option of using PPOs to treat ill or injured workers.

In some states (e.g., Connecticut, Florida, Ohio), managed care involvement in WC cases is compulsory, not just an economical option. As of February 15, 1997, for example, all Ohio employers were required to select a Managed Care Organization from the Health Partnership Program, a list of 56 providers who are approved to handle the medical management of Comp claims. The Health Partnership Program began to handle new-injury claims on March 1, 1997; the intention is that all Comp claims would be subject to the Program's medical management by January 1, 1998.

Many other states have laws authorizing managed care as an option in Comp cases: Arkansas, California, Georgia, Kentucky, Massachusetts, Minnesota, Missouri, Montana, Nebraska, Nevada, New Hampshire, New Jersey, New York, North Carolina, North Dakota, Oregon, Pennsylvania, Rhode Island, South Dakota, Utah, Washington.

HR policies that are associated with lower WC rates include:

- Increasing employee involvement (e.g., through the use of quality circles). The more involved employees are, the more careful they will be about identifying potentially dangerous conditions, finding ways to correct them—and the more motivation they will have to return to work quickly after an injury.

- Strengthening grievance and conflict resolution procedures if dangerous conditions are alleged, or to resolve claims of occupational disease and injury

- Reducing turnover; the rate of injury is higher among novice workers than among those who are more experienced and better adapted to the company's work methods

- Better training, especially in lifting and safe handling of hazardous materials

- Health maintenance and wellness programs.

According to the National Institute of Occupational Safety and Health (NIOSH), the Comp cost of musculoskeletal disorders of the upper extremities are $2.1 billion a year, and an even more startling $11 billion a year for back injuries. NIOSH's publication, "Elements of Ergonomics Programs," available by calling (800) 356-4674, defines three areas in which employers can be proactive to cut comp costs:

- Engineering controls, e.g., workstation layout, choice of tools, work methods; in essence, to design the job to fit employee capacities and limitations

- Administrative controls,—e.g., more rest breaks, training, task rotation, to reduce risk exposure

- Personal Protective Equipment (PPE)—although there is no scientific consensus as to which devices work.

20.13.1 Worker Leasing to Cut Comp Costs

As noted above, an employer's insurance rate (if it is not self-insured) has a lot to do with its past experience. The smaller the workplace, the greater the impact that a few claims (especially a few very large claims) will have on its experience rating. One response is to shift from a workforce of common-law employees to one composed in part or in whole of leased employees.

Leasing companies can qualify for low rates in their initial years, because any company's record will initially be clean until there has been enough time for accidents to happen. Furthermore, a leasing company can offer the services of a broad range of workers, some of them in very low-risk occupations such as office work. (On the other hand, a large leasing company won't qualify for small-business discounted rates.)

Abuses of the system are possible: the Acme Leasing Co. starts up in Year 1, qualifies for low rates, then dissolves as soon as WC claims begin to accrue, starting up again in Year 3 or 4 as the Beta Leasing Co.

Just for this reason, several states (e.g., Arizona, California, Colorado, Florida, Nevada, New Hampshire, New Mexico, Oregon, South Carolina, Texas, and Utah) disregard the presence of leasing companies, and still require the underlying employer to buy WC insurance and maintain its own experience rating.

The National Association of Insurance Commissioners (NAIC) has drafted an Employee Leasing Registration Model Act under which leasing firms must register with the state before they purchase WC insurance. At the time of registration, they must disclose their ownership and their past WC history. Registration will not be permitted if the company has had policies terminated in the past for failure to pay premiums.

Furthermore, state courts may decide that the leasing company or temporary agency's client is the actual employer, because it is the company that has real control over the worker's activities and therefore is legally responsible for compensation for injuries. Or both companies might be treated as co-employers.

Yet another possibility: if the underlying employer claims that the leasing company is the true employer, it becomes a third party who can be sued for tort claims, and who cannot claim WC exclusivity. The underlying employer might be sued for negligence or for violating established safety rules, and might be forced to pay heavy damages (including punitive damages). It would also not be able to use the employee's WC benefits to reduce the amount it would have to pay.

Chapter 21

OSHA

21.1 INTRODUCTION

Most workplaces never have an OSHA inspection; many of them never have a serious accident. High-risk industrial settings can be managed, not to eliminate all risk, but to bring risk within tolerable limits.

In 1992, the last year for which complete statistics are available, the cost of occupational injury and illness was on a par with the cost of cancer or heart disease, and even greater than the cost of very serious public health problems such as AIDS and Alzheimer's Disease. There were about 6,500 workplace accidental deaths in 1992, a number far overshadowed by over 13 million occupational injuries, over 60,000 occupational illness deaths, and almost 900,000 illnesses caused by occupational factors.

The mandate of the federal Occupational Safety and Health Act (abbreviated as OSHA or the OSH Act), enforced by the Occupational Safety and Health Administration (confusingly, also abbreviated as OSHA), is to protect employees against unreasonably hazardous workplaces. In addition to specific requirements known as "standards" imposed in certain circumstances (especially affecting the construction industry), employers must satisfy the "general duty standard" of maintaining a workplace that is reasonably free of recognized dangers.

Employers are not held to the impossible requirement of a danger-free workplace in which nothing ever goes wrong. However, they must take into account known hazards (of disease and chemical toxicity as well as accident), and use reasonably available methods and technology to keep the dangers within bounds.

21.2 OSHA POWERS

The OSH Act gives OSHA authority to inspect workplaces, order that violations be corrected, and impose penalties if correction does not occur or does not occur fast enough.

➠ TIP

It has been held that it is not a violation of the OSH Act (or of the Fourth Amendment ban on unreasonable searches and seizures) for an OSHA compliance officer to videotape a construction site from across the street before going to the site and presenting his credentials. The theory is that merely looking at a site (to determine if fall protection techniques were adequate) is not a "search," so no warrant is required.

The Act also requires employers to keep records of workplace injuries, and to use this information to generate annual reports (which must be disclosed to the workforce as well as being submitted to OSHA).

All employers whose operations "affect commerce" among the states are subject to OSHA; there is no minimum number of employees. However, some reporting requirements are relaxed for operations that are small-scale or low risk.

➠ TIP

OSHA has a procedure under which an employer who would be damaged by full compliance has the right to petition the Secretary of Labor for a temporary or permanent "variance" that will excuse the employer from noncompliance penalties. (For a temporary variance, the employer sets up a schedule for getting into full compliance.) However, variances are limited to the company that applies for them—it's no defense that another company in a similar situation received one.

In addition to the simplest, basic issues of OSHA compliance, employers must be aware of the way that OSHA works with other laws. For instance, it is probably a violation of public policy to discharge a worker on the grounds that he or she suffered an occupational injury, then filed a Worker's Compensation Claim, or to retaliate against a worker who "blew the whistle" on unsafe conditions to OSHA, or who cooperated in an OSHA investigation.

Under federal labor law (see Chapter 18), a walkout premised on unsafe working conditions is not treated as a strike. Furthermore, employee complaints about workplace safety conditions are treated as "protected concerted activity," so it is unlawful for the employer to use them as a premise for employee discipline.

On the other hand, state courts will not necessarily consider an OSHA violation relevant evidence of negligence if the employer is sued. A March, 1997 case from Mississippi, for instance, says that OSHA regulations do not have the "compulsory force" under state law that would make a violation of the federal regulation proof that the employer was negligent. (A state law says specifically that OSHA regulations do not have compulsory force.)

21.3 OSHA REGULATIONS

The main authority for federal regulation of workplace safety comes from the OSH Act itself. Because OSHA is a federal agency, its rules can be found in the Code of Federal Regulations. In addition to its powers under the General Duty Clause, OSHA has set out more specific guidance for employers in the General Industry Standards (covering most industrial workplaces) and the Construction Standards.

The topics covered by the General Industry Standards (in great detail) include:

- Condition of floors in the workplace ("walking/working" standards)
- Number and design of entrances and exits
- Noise control
- Radiation safety
- Proper handling of hazardous materials ("hazmats"; toxic chemicals and toxic wastes)
- Personal protective equipment (PPE) such as respirators, hard hats, steel-toed shoes, work gloves, etc.
- Fire prevention and safety
- On-site first aid and medical treatment
- Requirements for guards on machinery
- Proper use of hand-held equipment (e.g., tools)
- Welding and cutting
- Controlling electrical hazards
- Design and maintenance of lifts and powered platforms
- Access to employees' health records.

The Construction Industry Standards overlap with the General Industry Standards. The two rules sometimes treat the same topics, although somewhat different (usually more stringent) rules are imposed in the construction context. In particular, the construction standards deal with control of asbestos, welding and cutting, scaffolding, steel construction, and the use of masonry and concrete in construction.

> **➡ TIP**
>
> OSHA and the National Association of Home Builders (NAHB) have developed a 26-page pictorial guide to instruct workers in the basics of safety in residential construction. The booklet deals with matters such as fall protection, personal protective equipment, onsite housekeeping, scaffolds and ladders, and fire safety. Single copies are free from your local OSHA office (the national OSHA office doesn't carry the publication) or can be ordered from the NAHB, 1201 15th Street NW, Washington, DC, 20005, (800) 223-2665.

21.4 RECORDKEEPING REQUIREMENTS

The OSH Act requires employers to make an ongoing log of incidents of injury and illness as they occur. A summary annual report must be made incorporating these logs, and the logs themselves must be retained for at least five years.

The OSHA-200 form, Log of Occupational Injuries and Illnesses, is the basic reporting form for recording serious incidents as they occur.

> **➡ TIP**
>
> Collecting the OSHA-200 information is mandatory, but use of the actual form for this purpose is not; other recordkeeping forms, on paper or on computer, can be used to gather the raw data, as long as the column numbers on the Form 200 are used.

It is not necessary to record minor injuries such as small cuts that merely require antiseptic and a bandage; it is necessary to record serious injuries that require medical treatment or hospitalization. Injuries must also be logged if they cause loss of consciousness, if they restrict the employee's work or motion, or if the employee must be transferred to another job as a result.

> **⤑ TIP**
> _____
>
> In these instances, the employee might also become a "qualified individual with a disability" for ADA purposes, thus triggering the employer's obligation to offer reasonable accommodation to the disability (see page 480).

Occupational illness is also reportable. It's defined to include poisoning, repetitive trauma, and skin and lung disease due to dust, inhaling toxic substances, and the like. Illnesses are reportable even if the work environment is merely one of several contributory factors, or if it exacerbated a condition the employee already had.

The OSHA-200 form has another use: compiling the year's record for submission to OSHA and disclosure for employees. The employer simply totals up each column, then signs and dates the certification that the form is complete and correct. The annual summary form must be completed in February, covering incidents of the past year. The employer has an obligation to post the annual summary in a conspicuous location in the workplace (where notices are usually posted) and keep it there during the entire month of February of the year after the year whose injury/illness record is summarized on the form.

Employers with 10 or fewer employees are exempt from this requirement, as are larger operations in the Department of Commerce Standard Industrial Classifications (SICs) 52-54, 70, 75-76, and 79-80. These classifications cover retail stores, service industries, the finance industry, and other workplaces where there are comparatively few industrial hazards.

OSHA-200 is a three-part form. The first part calls for a description of the individual who was hurt (name; job title; department where he or she works; date of the injury or illness). The second part classifies on-the-job injuries as fatal or nonfatal and logs the amount of time lost due to the injury (lost work days do not have to be consecutive to be reportable). The third part does the same tasks for occupational illnesses.

The form refers to seven categories of occupational illness; each incident must be assigned to only one:

- Skin disorders (e.g., contact dermatitis or oil acne)
- Lung diseases caused by dust (e.g., asbestosis; silicosis; byssinosis)
- Toxic-based respiratory conditions (illnesses caused by exposure to gas, fumes, chemicals, or dusts)
- Poisoning (deleterious effects of lead, carbon monoxide, solvents, etc. on the body)
- Illnesses caused by physical agents that are not chemicals (e.g., exposure to heat and radiation)

- Traumatically induced illness (e.g., bursitis caused by constant strain on the shoulder)

- A catch-all category for occupational disease that doesn't fit any of the other categories.

> ⟾ **TIP**
>
> Employers have an obligation to update logs as the employee's condition changes. (Thus, the logs should be retained for at least five years.) For instance, a serious incident could prove fatal; or a condition that seemed mild might prove to be more serious than originally diagnosed. An asterisk is used to highlight illnesses resulting in permanent transfer or termination of an employee.

The general rule is that on-premises injuries are considered occupational, even during breaks or meal periods, as long as the employee is on premises for a reason related to his or her job status. It doesn't matter if the injury is compensable by Worker's Compensation, or whether the negligence of one or more people (including the worker) was involved in the injury. Certain off-premises injuries are also reportable—e.g., while the employee was traveling on business; while the employee is performing a delivery for the employer.

When a reportable accident or injury occurs, a Supplementary Record Form (OSHA-101, or comparable in-house, Worker's Compensation, or published form) must be completed within six working days after the incident. These forms are then collated to create the summary OSHA-200.

An incident report within eight hours is required when there is any incident serious enough to cause death, or to impel the hospitalization of three or more workers. (The employer who doesn't learn about the incident right away is required to report within eight hours of finding out.)

> ⟾ **TIP**
>
> Some cases say that this means admission of three or more workers to the hospital; treatment and release at the Emergency Room doesn't count. The initial report should be made by telephone, then backed up with a simple written report (when and where the incident occurred; what happened; number of employees involved; contact person who can discuss the incident with OSHA).

In states with an approved state plan, the report is made to the state agency; in the other states, it goes to the regional OSHA office. The report is simply the number of fatalities, the extent of injuries, and how the injuries and fatalities came about. Although non-work-related incidents do not have to be reported, work-related incidents away from the employer's premises might be reportable—for instance, if the employee was working for the employer at the remote location, or if the employee was either traveling to the workplace or somewhere else for work-related reasons.

OSHA forms don't work the same way as other government forms. The employer is not supposed to submit the completed forms to OSHA, but retain them in case OSHA wants to consult them at a later date. Employees also have an absolute right to inspect the safety records whenever they want; they don't need authorization, much less a warrant.

OSHA Form 200-S is sent to a sample of employers each year by the Bureau of Labor Statistics. The employers who get the form are obligated to complete it within 30 days and submit it to the BLS, even if they had no reportable injuries or illnesses during the year in question. The form is compiled based on the employer's existing OSHA logs and summaries.

In addition to these official survey forms, OSHA may seek to collect other information, but its power to do so is not infinite. OSHA sent a survey form to employers, notifying them that participation in the survey of illness and injury data was mandatory and noncompliance could result in citations and penalties. But a federal district court ruled in early 1997 that OSHA has to issue an official regulation, complying with the Administrative Procedures Act, if it seeks to penalize noncompliance. The agency can't just decide unilaterally that a survey is mandatory.

OSHA's response was to get the survey approved by the Office of Management and Budget (OMB), so the survey requirement is now a properly-promulgated regulation, 29 CFR §1904.17 (see 62 *Federal Register* 6434). Thus, employers are now required to respond or face penalties.

Employers can be subject to civil penalties if they fail to create and maintain the proper records. The penalty goes up to a fine that can reach $10,000 and/or six months' imprisonment if the employer falsifies an OSHA record.

21.5 USE OF PERSONAL PROTECTIVE EQUIPMENT

The use of Personal Protective Equipment (PPE) is key to workplace safety. If possible, the employer should eliminate hazards directly, by reducing the likelihood that employees will fall, slip, be struck by falling objects, burned, exposed to chemicals, etc. But it isn't always possible to remove these hazards, and even reducing them can be inefficient in terms of the cost and effort of achieving a comparatively minor improvement.

In such situations, the employer has a duty to provide PPE, and employees have a complementary duty to use it. The employer must provide suitable PPE, in sizes that fit the workers, and must train them how to use it. Whether or not there is a legal obligation to provide and use such equipment depends on whether a reasonable person (who was familiar with workplace conditions and industry practices) would do so. Furthermore, the industry standard is not a defense if the employer knew or should have been aware that dangerous conditions were present—for instance, if injuries had occurred in the past under similar circumstances.

21.6 LOCKOUT/TAGOUT

OSHA's lockout/tagout rule applies in non-construction situations where workers deal with machinery that has potentially dangerous moving parts. In certain circumstances, the employer has a duty to immobilize the machinery while it is being serviced, cleaned, repaired, etc. (The rule does not apply to normal operation of the machinery, because in those situations presumably the equipment and work routines will be designed to prevent contact between workers' bodies and moving parts of machinery.)

As an example, machinery could be equipped with a trip control (a "panic button") so it can be shut down quickly in an emergency. Blades and other dangerous parts of the machine should be protected with guards that shield workers' bodies from contact, and prevent scrap materials from becoming projectiles. If guards are impractical, the machinery could be equipped with sensing devices that turn off the machine if a body part goes beyond a certain point. Or the machine could be designed so that the operator must use two hands—and therefore cannot place a hand within reach of moving parts.

OSHA rules require that employees must be trained to understand the safety procedures, and the machinery must be inspected at least once a year.

21.7 CONTROLLING EXPOSURE TO HAZARDOUS CONDITIONS

OSHA contains rules about Permissible Exposure Limits (PELs) for certain hazardous substances such as asbestos and lead. A PEL is a level of contact with the substance that a worker can encounter without being endangered. The employer has an obligation to monitor the plant environment to determine the levels of the regulated substance, to provide appropriate safety equipment (e.g., face masks and respirators), and to train employees in safety techniques.

OSHA rules require that employees have access to showers, changing rooms, eye baths, first aid, and other measures for preventing long-term contamination. Where necessary, the employer must provide protective clothing, and appropriate containers for collecting contaminated clothing for treatment or disposal. Employees must not be permitted to smoke or eat in any environment where asbestos, lead, etc. are present, and warning signs must be posted in danger areas.

The employer's basic job is to keep employee exposure below the PEL. In some instances, this will be impossible, and exposure will reach what OSHA defines as the "action level." Once it is attained, the employer must take additional steps, such as periodic medical testing of employees to see if they have suffered environmental injury or illness.

> ⇒ **TIP**
>
> When hazardous materials are present, the employer organization also has responsibilities (and potential liability) under other laws, e.g., environmental laws and the laws that require community notification of the routine presence and accidental release of hazardous substances. The company must have a plan for responding to emergencies, and working with fire departments and other community resources.

Hazardous substances must be stored properly, and employees must be warned about their presence and taught how to handle the materials safely. Furthermore, hazardous wastes must be disposed of appropriately. Although these topics are outside the scope of this book, they should be considered whenever controls on employee exposure to such substances are reviewed.

In addition to regulating these hazardous substances, the OSH Act deals with hazardous conditions, such as excessive noise. In workplaces where the noise level routinely exceeds 85 decibels per 8-hour shift, the employer has an obligation to set up and maintain a comprehensive program for hearing conservation. The environmental noise level must be monitored; employees' hearing must be tested (a baseline reading within six months of initial exposure to high occupational noise levels, and an annual checkup after that); and they must be trained to protect themselves against hearing loss. If any audiometric test shows that an employee's hearing has deteriorated, the employer's obligation is to notify that worker within 21 days and thereafter make sure that the worker uses hearing protection devices.

Records of noise exposure must be maintained by the employer for two years; records of hearing tests must be retained as long as the individual continues to be an employee. Furthermore, employees, ex-employees, and employees who are assigned to tasks that expose them to hazardous substances are entitled to access to the employer's records that identify health and safety risks, including reports of monitoring workplace exposure levels. Exposure monitoring records and medical surveillance records for asbestos and lead should be retained by the employer for at least 30 years after the individual's employment terminates.

> ⇒ **TIP**
>
> A New York court said in 1997 that if an employee sues for work-related hearing loss, the statute of limitations begins to run on the date of exposure to the damaging noise.

Asbestos monitoring records should indicate:

- For each affected employee, his or her name, Social Security number, and extent of exposure
- If a respirator was worn, and what kind
- Date the asbestos level was monitored
- The workplace operation or process that was monitored
- How samples were taken and evaluated; evidence supporting the scientific validity of that method
- How long the sampling process lasted; how many samples were taken; sampling results.

For each employee subject to medical surveillance, the medical record should indicate the name and Social Security number of the employee; employee reports of asbestos-related medical conditions; and a written opinion from the doctor who performs the surveillance as to whether the employee is in fact suffering effects of asbestos exposure.

If the tested substance is lead rather than asbestos, the employer has an obligation to maintain written records of tests that determine if the ambient lead level is lower than the PEL. The test record should include:

- The name and Social Security number of each monitored employee
- The date of the test
- The area within the workplace that was monitored
- Previous airborne lead readings taken at the same place
- Employee complaints that might be related to lead exposure
- Any other evidence suggestive of lead exposure.

⇒ TIP

In most instances, it is illegal to force workers to retire at age 65, if they are willing to continue working and the job does not have any physical requirements (especially requirements for the safety of others) that the worker is unable to satisfy. Also, some people find that retirement bores them, or they can't live on their pensions and Social Security, so they get a post-retirement job. Senior citizen workers have a lower rate of accidents than their younger colleagues, perhaps because they are more experienced or more cautious. They also have less absenteeism, probably because of different attitudes toward work.

However, according to Bureau of Labor Statistics figures dating from 1992–1993, the rate of FATAL accidents among over-65 workers is close to four times as high as the fatality rate for younger workers. Even after a non-fatal accident, recuperation time may be much longer, or bones may be too brittle to heal properly; infection risk is greater. Older workers have a particularly high incidence of falls, which have more serious consequences for them than for younger workers, so you should be particularly careful about fall protection if you have workers aged 65 and older.

21.8 ERGONOMICS

Ergonomics is the study of the mutual adaptation between tools and the human body. An ergonomically correct machine will cause less stress and fewer injuries than one which is less well-suited to the body. However, determining the optimum ergonomic solution is not a simple matter, and employers are often called upon to make expensive workplace modifications whose benefits are controversial or uncertain.

It has frequently been proposed that OSHA adopt general ergonomics standards, but it has not taken this step, in part because industry opposition to ergonomics standards has been transmitted to Congress. Sometimes the appropriations that Congress votes to fund the DOL actually include provisions forbidding OSHA to adopt an ergonomics standard, or to adopt one that Congress thinks is too broad and is not appropriate to real industry conditions.

The Occupational Safety and Health Review Commission issued a decision in April, 1997 that is the first statement that the Secretary of Labor can properly cite ergonomic hazards under the general duty clause.

Thus, 27 willful lifting-hazard violations were upheld against the employer. However, the Secretary did not propose any feasible means of abatement, so the 175 willful repetitive-motion violations could not be sustained. Furthermore, penalties cannot be imposed on a per-employee basis for ergonomic hazards. (They can't be imposed on a per-employee basis for general duty violations, either, so large employers don't have to fear very large penalties if ergonomic, general duty, or other non-specific violations are found.)

One of the most controversial ergonomic issues is the effect of conventional computer keyboards. These keyboards have often been implicated in RSI (repetitive stress injuries), but the scientific evidence is ambiguous. In early 1997, NIOSH did a two-day study of keyboards, and found no significant differences in levels of discomfort and fatigue between users of standard keyboards and those identified as "ergonomic." (Many commentators said that the study was far too brief, and that differences, if any, would emerge over time.)

In July, 1997, NIOSH released a study, "Musculoskeletal Disorders and Workplace Factors," indicating a strong correlation between job activities and injury to the musculoskeletal system of the back, neck, and upper arms.

> ➠ **TIP**
> _____
>
> You can place a phone order for a copy of the report, at (800) 356-4674, or see it on the NIOSH site, **http://www.cdc.gov/niosh/ergoscil.html.** NIOSH also has a primer, "Elements of Ergonomics Programs," about preventing further injuries.

OSHA is using this report to develop an ergonomics standard, tailored to workplaces with the highest risk levels, yet for which effective protective measures have already been identified. OSHA also announced that it would have regional meetings on ergonomics in late 1997 and early 1998.

A related issue is prevention of slip-and-fall injuries which, according to the Bureau of Labor Statistics, account for more than one-third of workplace accidents. Depending on the industry, this is either the leading or secondary cause of accidents. Half of slips are caused by unsafe or unclean floor surfaces, almost one-quarter by inappropriate footwear, 9% by inadequate identification of hazards, and 7% by inadequate training of employees. New floor care products have been developed that make floor surfaces non-slippery even when they are freshly washed and still wet.

The National Technical Information Service (NTIS) publishes a catalogue, "Health and Safety Highlights," available by calling (703) 487-4650. NTIS publications deal with issues such as cumulative trauma disorder, risk factors and prevention of workplace violence, and OSHA's very comprehensive safety and health outreach program for the construction industry (which includes over 900 pages of instructional material).

21.9 DIVISION OF RESPONSIBILITY

For OSHA purposes, companies are responsible for the safety of their "employees"; but a company that has no employees (e.g., all work is done by leased employees or independent contractors) will not be subject to OSHA unless the arrangements are only a subterfuge to avoid liability. Courts will examine the economic reality of the work relationship, e.g., the degree of control over the work, who signs the paychecks, and whether individuals are paid a regular salary or a per-project amount. The power to change working conditions or fire the employee is considered especially significant.

If an individual might be deemed to have several employers (such as a temporary employment agency and also that agency's clients), then OSHA responsibility will be allocated based on actual job performance and working conditions.

Construction sites often involve several contractors, or a general contractor and various subcontractors. The basic rule is that the general contractor has primary OSHA responsibility for the site.

⇒ TIP

If there's any doubt, OSHA will simply cite all the parties who might be responsible, and wait for the innocent ones to get themselves off the hook. And if there are multiple companies involved at a site where hazards are present, both the company creating the hazard and the actual employer of the employees who were exposed to the hazard (i.e., were not protected by their employer) may be found liable.

OSHA liability of general contractors can derive from several theories:

- A provision in the construction contract under which the general contractor agrees to provide safety equipment
- Because the general contractor is in charge of the site and controls its conditions
- Because the general contractor is the only party involved with the specialized knowledge to abate the hazards
- Because the general contractor is actually aware of the hazards (either by observation or by notice from a subcontractor) and therefore has a duty to cope with them.

21.10 OSHA ENFORCEMENT

Unlike the ERISA field (where federal jurisdiction preempts the state role), OSHA enforcement is coordinated between the states and the federal government. States have discretion to shape the extent of their enforcement role in the occupational safety and health field. They can choose to draft their own regulatory plans for approval by the Department of Labor. The plan becomes an "approved state plan" if, in the DOL's judgment, it is adequately protective of worker safety.

Almost half the states have approved state plans: Alaska, Arizona, California, Connecticut, Hawaii, Indiana, Iowa, Kentucky, Maryland, Michigan, Minnesota, Nevada, New Mexico, New York, North Carolina, Oregon, South Carolina, Tennessee, Utah, Vermont, Virginia, and Washington. (However, the plans in Connecticut and New York are limited to coverage of state employees, not private-sector workers.)

In the other states, OSHA has primary responsibility for safety enforcement, but the state governments are allowed to regulate issues that the OSH Act does not cover (such as boiler and elevator safety), and issues that are broader than worker safety (such as fire safety in buildings that are open to the public). One important function of state OSH agencies is offering free on-site consultations. (Even where there is no approved state plan, the state agency may have received a grant from the federal OSHA to provide this service.)

The consultation is a simulated inspection, but the inspector is only authorized to point out problem areas and suggest solutions, not to issue citations or penalize the company. The consultation begins with an opening conference with the employer, proceeds to a walk-through and identification of safety problems, and a closing conference to discuss ways to solve those problems.

21.10.1 Inspections

The inspection process is central to OSHA's enforcement function: someone must go to the worksite and actually observe safety conditions. OSHA inspections can occur either on a routine basis ("programmed inspections" of workplaces chosen randomly from a list of establishments whose injury rates are above the average for comparable locations) or based on a complaint.

Employees, former employees, and their representatives (such as attorneys and union staff) are entitled to complain in writing to an OSHA area director or Compliance Officer (CO) that there are safety violations at a workplace. OSHA investigates the complaint and sends a copy of the complaint to the employer. (The complaining employee has a right to request that his or her name be withheld on the employer's copy). Depending on the nature of the complaint, OSHA might send the employer a letter describing the alleged hazard and giving a date by which to abate it, or an inspection might be scheduled. (If the employer ignores OSHA's letter or if there is evidence of additional safety problems, the inspection probably will be scheduled.)

OSHA is supposed to respond to a complaint of imminent danger within one day, to an allegation of a serious hazard (reasonable expectation that death or irreversible bodily injury or illness could be caused by the hazard) within five working days, or within 30 working days to a complaint of less serious conditions.

The general rule is that OSHA inspections are supposed to be made on an unannounced basis, so the CO will see the normal state of affairs and not a "gussied-up" workplace that returns to unsafe conditions as soon as the CO leaves.

➠ **TIP**

Employers are entitled to notice if the alleged safety problem creates an imminently dangerous situation (because abatement is more important than detecting violations), or if special arrangements are needed for the inspection, or if the inspection will take place outside of normal working hours.

The drill is for the CO to arrive at the workplace, show credentials, and ask permission to inspect. If permission is refused, then the CO must get an administrative search warrant from a court to be permitted to search. Courts will not grant a warrant unless OSHA has some reason to believe that violations (of the general duty clause or of a specific requirement) have occurred. However, the standards of proof for an administrative search warrant are much less rigorous than those for a criminal search.

Usually the employer will grant permission, so no warrant is needed. The CO has an "opening conference" with the employer, explaining the procedure. Next is the "walk-through," (employer and employee representatives are entitled to participate and give their input), when the CO views the workplace and takes notes on hazardous and non-compliant conditions. Finally, there is a "closing conference" at which the CO reveals his or her findings as to potential OSHA violations.

⇒ **TIP**

If the inspection is based on a complaint, the employer has the right to review the complaint document and to instruct the CO to limit the inspection just to issues raised by the complaint. Employers who choose this option should create a written record of the scope of the authorized inspection based on the complaint, and should give one copy to the CO and retain the other for the company's records.

During the walk-through, the CO often points out trivial violations that can be corrected on the spot: for instance, a pool of water can be mopped up; piles of debris can be cleared up; employees who are not wearing required PPE can be sent to put it on. At this stage, the CO usually asks to see the business' logs, summary reports, exposure records, training records, and other safety-related paperwork.

The CO's powers do not include issuing citations during the inspection. The CO has to return to the OSHA office and confer with the Area Director as to what level of citations (if any) should be issued in response to each perceived deficiency.

In the construction industry, a "targeted inspection" is a short-form inspection that concentrates on the major hazards to construction workers' safety: falls, being struck by vehicles or falling objects, electrical hazards.

The CO decides whether to do a focused or a full inspection during the opening conference. A focused inspection will be done at sites where the general or prime contractor (or equivalent) has a workable plan for preserving safety and health, and designates someone who can work with OSHA.

⇒ **TIP**

During the opening conference, the employer can request performance of a focused rather than a comprehensive inspection.

Citations can be issued during a focused inspection if there are serious violations, or non-serious violations that are not abated immediately. A CO who begins a focused inspection can switch to a comprehensive inspection if he or she believes that poor safety conditions prevail.

21.10.2 OSHA Consultation

Although it may not seem that way to beleaguered employers, faced with a Himalayan mountain of paperwork and a handful of pettifogging citations, OSHA's real job is to prevent accidents by making workplaces safer—not to harass employers. If the agency and employers can cooperate to reduce injuries and illness, everyone benefits. Therefore, state OSH agencies, working with grants from federal OSHA, offer free on-site consultation services to identify and eliminate potential safety problems before they become real ones.

The consultation system centers around the workplace, but the consultants are available by telephone for advice and discussions. If there are more requests than the system can handle, priority goes to small companies in potentially high-risk industries (because they are at the highest risk of industrial accident, but have the fewest resources to promote safety).

When a company participates in the consultation system, the consultant begins by learning about the company, its operations, and its employees. The consulting visit is structured like an OSHA inspection (although the employer has the right to ask that the scope of the visit be expanded or reduced). The on-site visit is followed up with a written analysis of the hazard status of the workplace and recommendations for correction. Employers must give the consultants free access to employees so the consultant can ask them about working conditions.

> **➡ TIP**
>
> Consultants are pledged to confidentiality. Not only do they have to maintain trade secrets, they are not allowed to report unsafe conditions found in the course of consultation to OSHA unless the employer fails to correct known dangers. The consultants themselves do not have the authority to impose penalties, but participating employers agree to take steps to correct whatever problems are uncovered by the program. Employers who are ordered to abate hazards during an OSHA inspection can use the consultation system to get advice about the best way to correct the problems that have already been identified.

Consultations can't take place while an OSHA inspection is already underway, but if a consultation is scheduled, there's a good chance that OSHA will cancel a scheduled inspection (unless a fatality or serious incident is under investigation, or imminent danger to employees is suspected). An employer who has completed a consultation, who makes corrections based on the recommendations, and who posts a notice of correction where employees can see it has the right to request immunity from scheduled OSHA inspections. The immunity lasts for one year from the consultant's visit.

To find a consultant, call the nearest OSHA office or look in the State Government section of the telephone directory for the state program.

21.10.3 *Voluntary Programs*

Under the title of Voluntary Protection Programs (VPP), OSHA maintains three incentive programs for employers with good safety records; these companies are supposed to serve as an example for others. Participants in the Star, Merit, or Demonstration programs (or their counterparts in states that have approved state plans) qualify for the program by proving that they maintain safe workplaces and have ongoing efforts to inform and train workers about safety issues. In return, the authorities refrain from doing programmed inspections at those companies (although inspections will still be made if a complaint is registered).

Employers can apply to OSHA for VPP certification. They must complete applications that demonstrate their qualifications for participation, and OSHA will send an inspector to check the company's safety records and site conditions. VPP applicants can get assistance from a private company, the Voluntary Protection Programs Participants' Association, which can be reached at (703) 761-1146.

21.10.4 *OSHA Citations*

Comments made by a CO during an inspection are not official OSHA pronouncements. The employer cannot be penalized for failing to respond to them, until and unless it receives a written citation that is sent no later than six months after the date of the alleged violation that is cited. The citation lists the nature of the violations and classifies them by seriousness. The OSHA Area Director issues the citation, computing a schedule of penalties and setting a date for abating each violation. Form OSHA-2, sent by certified mail, is the usual method of communicating a citation (although other forms can be used).

➠ TIP

It's no defense that a company terminated all its operations and fired all its employees after receiving a citation; what counts is the company's status on the date of the alleged violation.

Generally, OSHA violations are characterized as de minimis (trivial), non-serious, or serious (although there is a category of "other" for situations that don't fit comfortably into a category). Willful or repeated violations (i.e., when the same violation was cited within the previous three years) carry heavier penalties, because they show that the employer is flouting the OSH Act's compliance objective. In the very worst cases, such as those resulting in a preventable death of a worker, criminal penalties might be imposed, including heavier fines and imprisonment of the corporate officials most responsible for the violations.

If the violation is adjudged nonserious, the standard penalties run from $0 to $1000. For serious violations, the maximum penalty is also $1000, but a minimum penalty of at least $100 must be assessed. If the employer is culpable for repeated or willful violations (which will seldom be charged until at least two final orders have already been issued for similar violations), then the penalty runs from $0 to $10,000. Within this range, the Area Director sets a penalty level using factors such as the size of the employer, the degree of good or bad faith it has displayed, the seriousness of the violation, and the company's past history of OSHA compliance.

A recent Fifth Circuit case says that the number of employees exposed is *not* the correct measure for general duty clause violations; the appropriate standard is per-violation (although the number of employees at risk is relevant in the size of the penalties).

A little later, the Fifth Circuit also found that it is inappropriate for OSHA to "stack" general duty clause violations in order to increase the potential penalty; an explosion exposing 87 employees to hazard is still only one violation, not 87.

➡ TIP

In the case of a "de minimis" violation (where, technically, rules were broken but employees were not really endangered), violations will be cited but monetary penalties will not be applied. Penalties are not assessed against an employer that has ten or fewer workers, and that went through an on-site consultation and made reasonable efforts to follow the consultant's recommendations. Even a larger employer will be issued a citation with an abatement date for a first offense nonserious violation, but penalties will not be imposed unless there were at least ten violations.

A stricter penalty schedule is imposed if the workplace conditions resulted in a worker's death. The penalty for a first violation is up to $10,000, six months' imprisonment, or both, and is doubled for a second violation. A non-OSH Act federal law, the Criminal Fine Enforcement Act, defines the maximum penalty to the corporation as $100,000 and $500,000 (depending on whether a misdemeanor or a felony led to a death); corporate officers and other responsible individuals can be fined up to $100,000 (if a misdemeanor punishable by six months' imprisonment or more results in death) or up to $250,000 (if a felony causes death).

According to the Seventh Circuit, imposing an instance-by-instance fine after an employer had already been convicted in criminal court and fined for willful violations that led to the deaths of three employees constitutes unlawful double jeopardy. In this instance, the administrative fine is punishment, not a remedy, because it goes to the government, not survivors of the decedents.

According to the Tenth Circuit, a fine cannot constitute punishment if it is less than the cost of investigation and prosecution, but the Seventh Circuit disagrees with this analysis. The way the Seventh Circuit sees it, administrative fines could have been imposed in addition to the criminal fines as part of the same proceeding (which would be one instance of jeopardy, with multiple punishments), but the constitutional ban on double jeopardy makes it impossible to impose administrative fines in a separate proceeding that follows the criminal case.

21.10.5 1997 Abatement Rule

On March 31, 1997, a new rule on the abatement of safety and health hazards was published in the *Federal Register*. The rule, effective May 30, 1997, requires employers to notify both OSHA and the employees when hazards are abated. However, employers no longer have to submit certification documents attesting to the abatement, if the abatement actually occurs in the course of an OSHA inspection. Employers are relieved of the obligation to document correction of minor violations (and even some serious violations).

The new policy reduces the number of follow-up inspections OSHA will do to verify abatement of hazards; OSHA and state administrators estimate that this change in policy will save $4.5 million a year.

21.10.6 OSHA Appeals

Employers are not obligated to accept the judgment of the OSHA citation. The OSH Act includes a structure of several steps that can be taken to appeal a decision administratively. (However, administrative remedies must be exhausted before litigating.)

If the employer challenges the citation, OSHA has to prove that the employer failed to live up to some applicable standard—and, furthermore, that feasible corrective measures existed that could have brought the employer into compliance. If the standard has a durational element (e.g., the noise exposure standard) OSHA also has to prove that the condition existed long enough and intensely enough to constitute a violation.

OSHA's burden is proving that the employer knew about the condition, or would have been aware of the condition by exercising due diligence; it is not necessary to prove that the employer was aware of the standard and deliberately chose to violate it. The knowledge of a supervisor or foreman is usually attributed to the employer, unless the employer maintained work rules that satisfied the OSHA standard, communicated those rules to employees, and enforced the work rules. OSHA is entitled to a presumption of knowledge (i.e., does not have to prove actual knowledge) in various situations:

- Another employee has already been injured by the same hazardous condition
- Multiple written employee complaints have already been made to OSHA
- The employer knows that employees habitually omit safety equipment, or otherwise allow hazardous conditions to occur and continue
- The employer doesn't provide enough training or enforcement of its own safety rules
- The hazards would easily have been discovered if the employer had performed an adequate inspection.

An employer that receives an OSHA citation has 15 days to file a Notice of Contest, disputing that there was a violation, demanding a fair period of time to abate the violation, or challenging the size of the penalty. If the employer is not sure whether or not to contest, it can schedule an informal conference with the OSHA area director to discuss OSHA's position on workplace conditions and when and how to improve them.

There is no official form for the Notice of Contest; it is simply a letter stating in plain English that the employer does not agree with the citation and wants to contest some or all of the violations noted there, to ask for a smaller penalty, and/or ask for more time to comply.

⇒ TIP

If the Notice of Contest is not filed within the required 15 days, the citation becomes final, and no court has the power to reverse it or even review it. (An informal conference with the CO who issued the citation doesn't count as a Notice of Contest and doesn't extend the 15-day period.) That might suggest that the proper strategy is to file a Notice of Contest in every case. If the employer files the notice in good faith (honestly believing that the citation is defective), then the time schedule for abating the violations is delayed until the whole administrative challenge process is completed.

On the other hand, if the employer appeals in bad faith, when it knows that the citation is valid, then the whole period of time until resolution of the challenge will be treated as a period of non-compliance, with additional penalties for each day.

Another factor is how the OSHA allegations will be treated in other cases—say, if the injured employee is able to sue and is not precluded by Worker's Compensation. (For instance, an employee of Company A who is injured on Company B's premises may be able to sue Company B, even though a suit against Company A would be preempted.) Some courts allow the OSHA citation, especially if it was not contested, to be introduced as evidence of dangerous conditions within the workplace. Contesting the violation can have the effect of clearing the employer's name.

After a notice is filed, an OSHA Administrative Law Judge (ALJ) will set a date for an informal hearing. (Nevertheless, the Federal Rules of Evidence still govern the hearing.) The ALJ's decision becomes final 30 days after it is rendered, if it is not contested. If the employer is dissatisfied with the ALJ's decision, further appeals are permitted.

All Notices of Contest, and all ALJ decisions, are automatically passed along to the Occupational Safety and Health Review Commission (OSHRC). OSHRC has the power to order review of part or all of an ALJ decision. The employer (or any other party adversely affected by the decision) can file a Petition for Discretionary Review (PDR).

⇒ **TIP**
_____

OSHRC seldom raises the level of a violation, so if the employer has a good-faith argument, it has little to lose by filing a PDR. However, it sometimes happens, as in a recent case where the level of a fall protection violation was raised from serious to willful because the employer had two prior citations from other sites. There were no safety belts or nets to protect workers from a potential 35-foot fall. The totality of the circumstances (lack of a safety program; inadequate training of employees; lack of fall protection equipment) demonstrated the employer's indifference to safety issues. Where the employer's pre-inspection conduct is willful, adding safety devices after the inspection won't alter the violation level.

There are many arguments that an employer can raise to avert or restrict the scope of OSHA enforcement:

- The CO simply got the facts wrong

- The employer did not know, and was not required to know, of the existence of the violation

- The inspection itself was improper (e.g., the inspection was really a search, and a warrant was required but not obtained)

- OSHA applied the wrong standard
- The standard itself was not properly promulgated, or was so vague that employers could not reasonably be expected to understand it and comply with it
- Employee misconduct beyond the employer's control was the real cause of the violation, but is unlikely to recur
- Complying with the OSHA requirement actually INCREASED rather than decreased hazards to employees, but the employer was unable to get a variance (page 440).

⟹ **TIP**

The argument that OSHA harassed the employer, or singled it out for enforcement when other, equally violative, companies, were not targeted, has not been very successful. As long as the hazardous conditions that were cited actually existed in that particular workplace, comparable or even worse conditions in other workplaces will not extenuate this particular employer's responsibility.

OSHRC will consider the employer's arguments and defenses, and will issue its own order. The employer has 60 days from the date of the OSHRC order to file a further appeal. By this time, administrative remedies have been exhausted, and the employer has the right to go to federal court. In fact, the employer is allowed to bypass the District Court (the lowest tier in the federal court system where federal cases normally begin) and appeal to the Court of Appeals for the Circuit where the violation is alleged to have occurred, or to the District of Columbia Circuit.

21.10.7 E-Z Trial

For small businesses, and cases that are not egregious (proposed penalties under $10,000; no allegation of willfulness; no fatalities; not many violations cited; the hearing is not expected to last longer than two days), an expedited procedure called E-Z Trial is available. Initially created as a pilot project, E-Z Trial got two extensions, the second until July 1997. Proposed Rules were published on June 24, 1997 for revised E-Z Trial rules: see 62 *Federal Register* 34031.

The employer can apply to have the case heard under the program, or the judge assigned to the full scale hearing on the case can divert it into the less formal program. E-Z Trial decisions can be appealed to OSHRC just as full-scale hearing decisions can be. However, under OSHRC proposals to revise the program, E-Z trial should not be used if a fatality occurred or if repeat violations are alleged, and the chief ALJ should have the discretion to assign uncomplicated cases in the $10,000-$20,000 range of proposed penalties to this program.

21.11 ABATEMENT

The theoretical reason behind the entire OSHA process is abatement: removal of hazardous conditions. An uncontested citation, a citation for which the time to contest has expired, or a citation where the employer's challenge was partially or wholly unsuccessful, all give rise to abatement responsibilities.

The general rule is that abatement must take place within 30 days, although if the problem takes a long time to correct, the employer may have to submit a progress report to OSHA every 30 days until it is corrected.

> ⇒ **TIP**
>
> If a citation notes several violations, and the employer contests some but not others, the appropriate action for the uncontested violations is to correct the situation, send a letter notifying the local OSHA area director that correction has occurred, and pay the fine imposed for the uncontested violations. With respect to the contested citations, abatement and payment of fines will be suspended until the OSHRC final order is issued.

OSHA will re-inspect the premises and, if the same conditions still are present, penalties of up to $1,000 a day can be imposed. However, the employer can contest penalties in the same way as an original citation.

> ⇒ **TIP**
>
> If you want to abate hazards, but are financially unable to do so, the Small Business Administration has the power to make loans to small companies facing OSHA problems.

A Petition for Modification of Abatement (PMA) can be filed where even a good-faith effort to abate is blocked by factors beyond the employer's control. PMAs are filed with the OSHA Area Director on or before the first working day after the scheduled abatement date. The PMA explains what the employer has done to cure the problem, why and how much additional time is required, and what the employer will do to protect employees until full abatement is achieved. The PMA must be posted and served on the employer's workforce, because they have the right to contest it.

If the PMA is uncontested, the Secretary of Labor has the power to approve it. OSHRC holds a hearing on contested PMAs, to determine if the employer did in fact act in good faith and was really unable to achieve full compliance. The employer does not have to comply with the underlying citation during the time that the PMA is under consideration.

21.12 VARIANCES

Sometimes it's a lot easier for someone at General Staff Headquarters (or in an ivory tower) to dream up requirements than for the people on the front line to carry them out. In recognition of this fact, the OSH Act permits employers to petition for variances that will exempt them from having to comply with requirements that are particularly onerous, as long as granting the variance does not expose employees to undue risk or danger.

Although the CFR includes rules for "national security variances" and "experimental variances," most of the variances granted are classified as either "temporary" or "permanent." Grounds for a temporary variance are that the company will eventually comply with a newly enacted regulation, but cannot do so by the scheduled effective date because of a shortage of staff, materials, or equipment. (Being unable to afford to comply is *not* considered good cause to grant a variance.) A temporary variance lasts up to one year; it can be renewed twice, for up to 180 days at a time. The application must demonstrate that the employer is doing everything it can to come into compliance as soon as it can, and that employees are being protected from undue hazards in the interim.

A permanent variance is granted to an employer whose work methods are unconventional but still provide employees with at least as much safety protection as the conventional methods embodied in OSHA regulations.

> ⇒ **TIP**
>
> A company seeking a permanent variance can also apply for an interim variance so it can retain its work methods until the permanent application is adjudicated.

The Assistant Secretary of Labor for Occupational Health and Safety (headquartered in Washington, D.C.) is the official charged with reviewing variance applications and granting or denying them. Variance applicants must notify their workforce of the application, because the employees will be affected by any change in the safety rules, and employees can ask that a hearing examiner conduct a hearing on the employer's application. Employees (or, for that matter, employers) who are affected by a variance after it is granted can petition for modification or revocation of the granting order; the employer who gets the variance can petition to have it renewed or extended after it ends.

> ➡ **TIP**
>
> The original plus six copies of the variance application and supporting documents must be filed. The documents must be signed either by a representative of the company that applies, or by a lawyer or other authorized representative.

21.13 PENALTY FACTORS

At times, the employer will concede that a violation did occur, and that some level of penalty is appropriate—but will take the position that the level assessed in the citation is unjust or unaffordable. Exceptional circumstances must be present for a penalty to be canceled or reduced more than 20%; but within limits, one might be reduced based on a showing of good faith, where there are few or no previous violations, and/or the employees were not really endangered by the violations. Reduction of penalties is more likely for small businesses than for large ones.

How serious a violation is depends in large part on the real danger to employees as opposed to mere technical violations. This is based on factors such as the number of affected employees, how long the exposure lasted, whether precautions (however ineffective) were taken, and how likely it was that an injury would occur as a result of the conditions. The more the employer could have predicted injury, the more seriously the violation will be treated.

Employer good faith is demonstrated by factors such as a well-planned and consistently applied safety program, prompt action to correct all non-contested violations, and a history of good communications and good relations with the local OSHA office.

21.14 EMPLOYEE COMMUNICATIONS

OSHA publishes an official poster that explains, in simple language, what OSHA does and what employee rights are. Employers have an obligation to get these posters and display them prominently in the workplace. (The posters are free, and you can get them directly from OSHA Publications, Room N3101, 200 Constitution Avenue NW, Washington, D.C. or from the state safety agency; you can also buy them from various publishers that specialize in human resources materials.) Employers are mandated to display the posters in a "conspicuous place," and if an OSHA inspector finds that the posters are missing, a fine can be imposed.

If an employer receives an OSHA citation, a copy of the citation must be posted near each place where a violation occurred. The copy must be left in place for three working days or until the violation is corrected (whichever comes first). Posting must also be done if the employer contests the citation or files a petition for modification of abatement. Failure to make these postings can result in a $1,000 fine.

During the month of February in each year, the employer is further obligated to post an annual summary of occupational injuries and illnesses that occurred in the preceding year.

21.15 EMPLOYEE TRAINING

Many of the individual OSHA rules refer to training of employees: for instance, those that deal with PPE, working with hazardous chemicals, operating power presses, and upgrading technology within a workplace. The construction standards impose training requirements about tool use, avoiding falls, using heavy equipment, and using explosives safely. Although training can be expensive (especially if outside firms have to be hired, or if computer and kiosk applications have to be developed), it can provide immediate dividends in the form of increased efficiency and reduced waste.

OSHA has issued guidelines that take the position that employees must be trained whenever they are unfamiliar with particular equipment or aren't sure how to perform particular tasks. A concentration of injuries often shows either defective equipment or misuse by employees who don't understand proper use.

⇒ TIP

If employees put suggestions in the Suggestion Box expressing confusion about equipment or techniques, more training is probably called for. Or you can give employees an oral or written quiz to test their understanding, then follow up with additional training if comprehension is poor. Follow-up studies should also be done to see if the training was effective in improving work and safety habits.

Training is always worthwhile. Employees who don't understand their machinery and equipment, or who use it carelessly, are likely to get sick or injured—and are also likely to damage the equipment and produce low-quality work. Employees should understand:

- Safe working practices
- How to collect and store scrap materials so they don't become a stumbling block or fire hazard; how to re-use scrap materials when appropriate
- When they must use PPE; how PPE should fit; when equipment is defective and must be repaired or replaced
- What to do when an injury occurs; where first aid materials, showers, and eye-baths are located

- How to handle hazardous materials (including how to dispose of contaminated materials and work clothes)
- Which areas are safe for eating, smoking, etc.; which are not safe (employees can't eat in areas that contain radioactive materials, for example)
- What to do when a hazardous substance is released
- How to react in an emergency (fire, flood, etc.).

Some OSHA requirements do not merely require the employer to provide formal training sessions, but also to document when the sessions occurred, who was present, and what was discussed.

Despite the importance of the subject, employees may react poorly to safety training (just as airplane passengers tend to ignore the cabin attendants' safety demonstration—at least unless there's been a major crash in the news recently). Many independent consulting companies have prepared visually exciting safety materials, available in booklet, poster, and video form and, increasingly, as computer programs and on the Internet.

21.16 PREVENTION AND PLANNING

Preventing occupational injury and illness has to be done in two ways. From the "top down" there has to be management commitment to safety and recommendations from industrial hygienists and other professionals. It also has to be from the "bottom up": employees should be able to report bottlenecks and potential hazards without fear of reprisal, and with the expectation that legitimate suggestions will be implemented.

To reduce the risk of repetitive stress injuries, schedule the job with adequate rest breaks. If possible, workers should rotate tasks, so different joints and muscles will be used at different times of the day, relieving stress on body parts that might otherwise be vulnerable to injury. Wherever possible, office and factory furniture should be adjustable. Get professional advice on appropriate lighting levels and filters to prevent glare.

Hearing loss is a fairly common occupational injury, but one that occurs over a long time and is hard to detect. An effective hearing conservation program in a noisy factory requires issuing earplugs, headphones, or other devices to damp noise (and making sure that employees use them), monitoring of workplace noise levels, hearing tests, and records.

> ➠ **TIP**
>
> For Worker's Compensation purposes, the test of compensable occupationally-related hearing loss is the inability to function in the worker's customary family and social activities.

21.17 HIV EXPOSURE ISSUES IN THE WORKPLACE

Under most circumstances, the fact that an employee or job candidate is HIV positive does not pose a risk to others, because HIV is not spread by casual contact with infected people. However, as page 480 discusses, it may be necessary under the Americans with Disabilities Act or Family and Medical Leave Act to offer accommodation to employees with AIDS or who are HIV positive: for instance, they may need special work schedules or time off to get medical care, and they may need additional protective equipment to prevent colds and other infections that would be hazardous to a person with a compromised immune system.

HIV issues also arise if an employee is exposed to contaminated needles and other medical equipment; there is a small but not non-existent risk that a health care worker or sanitation worker who is stuck with a needle, cut with a scalpel, etc., will become HIV positive and perhaps develop AIDS.

Even employees who do not suffer physical illness may make claims based on the emotional stress of being exposed to contaminated items. Some states do not allow these "AIDS-phobia" claims unless the employee can prove HIV infection, or at least that the contact created a plausible channel for infection. The New Jersey test comes from a case in which a cleaning woman was stabbed by a lancet (a device used to draw blood for blood tests) and sued the doctors whose office she cleaned for negligent infliction of mental distress. The New Jersey court found that an employee can sue if the employer's negligence (i.e., improper handling of contaminated sharp instruments) was the direct cause of genuine and substantial emotional distress, and a reasonable person, armed with the level of general knowledge about AIDS prevailing at the time of the injury, would have been worried.

Chapter 22

PRIVACY ISSUES

22.1 INTRODUCTION

For the employee, a significant portion of the day is spent in the workplace, and the employer takes on some of the roles of the government. Does that mean that employees have the same civil rights with respect to their employers as citizens have with respect to their governments? In some ways, the answer is "yes," but Congress, state legislatures, and the courts understand that it is necessary to balance the employer's need for honesty, sobriety, and efficiency in the workplace against the employees' desire for privacy. Furthermore, many if not most Constitutional rights are limitations on government power, not the power of private entities such as employers.

Unlike many of the topics discussed in this book, where federal laws either control the whole field or are dominant, state laws are very significant in the issue of employer rights versus employee privacy. For instance, most states have some legislation on access and copying of personnel files (letting employees view and copy their own files, but restricting access of persons who do not have a need to know). Most also protect privacy of medical records, especially those involving genetic testing or reports of substance abuse treatment, and have legislated limitations on the extent to which employers can collect and record information about employees' lawful off-premises activities. For instance, many states make it illegal to investigate what religious, political, or social organizations employees belong to.

22.2 POLYGRAPHS IN THE WORKPLACE

There are many problems with using polygraphy ("lie detector tests") in the workplace setting. For one thing, this testing is expensive and not very reliable; the real test is whether the employee is nervous, and a practiced liar may be far less nervous than a timid but honest employee.

Some states prohibit outright the use of polygraph testing in the workplace: Massachusetts, Michigan, Minnesota, and Oregon, so in those states it isn't an issue. Alaska, Connecticut, Delaware, Hawaii, Maine, Nebraska, New Jersey, New York, Rhode Island, West Virginia, and Wisconsin forbid employers to require, request, or even suggest testing. In one of these states, if you cannot demand a polygraph test as a condition of employment, it would violate public policy to fire someone for refusing to take the test. Illinois, Maine, Michigan, Nevada, New Mexico, and Virginia require polygraph operators to be licensed.

The Federal Employee Polygraph Protection Act of 1988 (P.L. 100-347, 29 United States Code §2001) forbids most private employers from using polygraph tests for preemployment screening. In the workplace itself, it's permissible to polygraph employees but only in the course of an ongoing investigation about economic loss or injury to the employer's business. (For this purpose, drug tests and written or oral "honesty tests" are not considered polygraph examinations.)

Under the federal law, an employee can be asked to submit to polygraph testing only if:

- He or she has access to the property involved in the inquiry
- The employer has a reasonable suspicion about the employee's involvement
- Before the examination, the employer provides the employee with a specific written statement about the nature of the investigation and the basis for the employer's suspicion of the employee.

➠ **TIP**

The employer must keep these statements on file for three years after they are issued.

The employer must advise the employee of his or her rights:

- to refuse the test or stop it after it has begun;
- to seek representation by a lawyer or other person (such as a union representative);
- to review the questions before the test;
- to review the results before the employer uses them as a premise for adverse employment action.

The employee must be notified that test results may be turned over to prosecutors.

22.3 DRUG USE IN THE WORKPLACE

Drug use in the workplace is a serious problem for many reasons. Some drug users are able to restrict their substance abuse to off-work hours and off-premises locations, and some of them are able to pay for drugs by legitimate means. Even so, drug residues are likely to affect their physical dexterity and judgment during working hours.

> **➡ TIP**
>
> That's why many states provide that, if a worker was drunk or drug-impaired at the time of the accident, either Worker's Compensation will be denied, or it will be presumed that substance abuse was the cause of the accident, unless the worker can prove otherwise.

Many, if not most, drug users are unable to use such moderation in their drug consumption. They cause even greater problems for the employer, because they are likely to be impaired during working hours. They may use or even deal drugs in the workplace, and probably cannot support their drug use on their legitimate salaries, so the employer is at great risk of product theft, embezzlement, and industrial espionage. Employees who are already committing serious crimes by using illegal drugs may lose their inhibitions against committing other crimes as well.

It's been estimated that drug-using employees are absent more often than their non-drug-using counterparts, use about twice as much in medical benefits, and make about twice as many Worker's Compensation claims. So reducing or eliminating drug use among your workforce will provide many indirect benefits.

Employers also encounter problems caused by legal substance abuse, such as alcohol abuse and overuse and misuse of psychoactive prescription drugs. The problems can be less acute, because the employees are not breaking the law and don't have trouble financing their habit, but they are problems nonetheless, and Employee Assistance Programs should be sure to make help available for those who want to tackle such a problem.

The Federal Drug-Free Workplace Act, 41 United States Code §701, is designed to jolt employers out of complacency if they feel that they have no drug problem or that it is under control. Companies that have federal procurement contracts in excess of $25,000 (and a large proportion of companies are federal contractors) must certify to the contracting agency that they will provide a drug-free workplace. (If they don't make the certification, the contract can't be awarded.) The obligations of the contractor-employer are to:

- Notify employees that using, possessing, and selling drugs is prohibited; notify employees of what the penalties will be if these rules are violated
- Set up a drug-free awareness program
- Order employees to abide by the program and notify the employer if they are convicted of a drug offense (even one occurring off-premises)
- Notify the contracting agency within 10 days of receiving such a report from an employee
- Impose penalties on all employees convicted of drug violations that are related to the workplace
- Continue to make a good-faith effort to keep drugs out of the workplace.

If the employer is a defense contractor, it must do regular drug tests on employees in "sensitive positions," i.e., those with access to classified information.

Department of Transportation rules on drug testing have been held to be intended to protect the public, not transportation workers. Therefore, employers have a perfect right to delegate the administration of the testing program to an outside company. If the outside company mixes up urine specimens, it is liable for the mistakes; the employer that hired the company is not.

Pre-employment drug testing is more likely to be upheld by the courts than testing of current employees, which is more likely to be viewed as an invasion of a right of privacy legitimately expected by the employees.

A California case from early 1997 permits the employer (in this case, a government agency) to require urine testing for drugs of individuals who have received conditional job offers, but not of employees who are under consideration for promotions. (The nature of the job to which they might be promoted doesn't matter.) The California Supreme Court takes the position that the Fourth Amendment allows drug testing that is not connected to specific suspicion, but only if there is a special need and the employee's privacy is impaired only minimally, as compared to the special interests of public employers.

An earlier California case says that it does not violate public policy to discharge a worker based on his or her refusal to take a drug test. A 1997 Arizona case is similar, taking the position that although the state constitution includes a guarantee of the right to privacy, it does not provide for private suits against employers.

It is probably inappropriate to impose a drug testing requirement that covers lawful prescription and over-the-counter medications. The Tenth Circuit granted an injunction against an employer's drug policy that required its employees to notify, and get permission from, their supervisors if they used prescription medications. The court said that the requirement violates the Americans with Disabilities Act (ADA), because it is a forbidden inquiry about a person's disability.

> ⇒ **TIP**
> ───
> The ADA's function is to protect "qualified" disabled people against discrimination. But if a prescription medication has side effects that makes it unsafe for a person to perform a particular job (such as falling asleep or losing coordination), then that person is not qualified for ADA purposes.

If a third party performs the test, it might be treated as a "credit report" or "investigative credit report" for purposes of the federal Fair Credit Reporting Act (see below). However, if the employer performs the test itself, the FCRA is not involved, because the statute does not apply to transactions between the consumer and the entity that makes the report. Therefore, an employee fired after testing positive for marijuana on a urine test could not use the FCRA to sue the employer that performed the test.

Yet another possible issue is the situation in which law enforcement officers get involved in a workplace drug case. Then the inquiry becomes whether the search was to further the employer's own anti-drug policy rather than general police activity. If the purpose was private and employer-related, the Fourth Amendment doesn't come into play, even if police dogs and Drug Enforcement Administration personnel were present at the workplace search.

22.4 CREDIT CHECKS

A federal law, the Fair Credit Reporting Act, 15 USC §1681, governs the access of businesses to credit reports. Although, as the name suggests, credit reports are usually used by lenders and sellers of merchandise to decide whether to grant an application for a loan or credit sale of merchandise, it is also fairly common for potential employers to run a credit check before making an offer of employment to an applicant. Under the FCRA, employers must notify applicants *before* they seek credit information as part of the application process; a civil penalty is imposed for ordering the credit check without the mandatory notification. The employer must also notify applicants and employees before any negative employment-related action is taken on the basis of an investigative credit report. See page 19 for more discussion of credit checks in the hiring process.

Under the FCRA, credit reporting agencies are allowed to disclose the information they have gathered to companies that want it for "employment purposes," i.e., evaluating the subject of the credit report for employment, promotion, retention as an employee, or reassignment. The reporting agency is allowed to furnish a credit report to employers, discussing the employee's creditworthiness, standing, character, and reputation.

There are some inherent limitations, of course: someone can be very good at paying bills but very bad at being an engineer, secretary, executive, or whatever position he or she has applied for; and the credit reports get much of their information by asking neighbors, who may be spiteful or who may be short on accurate information.

➡ **TIP**

Effective September 30, 1997, job applicants and employees became entitled to a greater measure of disclosure and protection, because of the FCRA amendments embodied in the Consumer Credit Reporting Reform Act of 1996, P.L. 104-208.

In addition to federal regulation of the use of credit reports, some states (Arizona, California, Connecticut, Florida, Kansas, Kentucky, Maine, Maryland, Massachusetts, Montana, New Hampshire, New Mexico, New York, Oklahoma, and Texas) impose additional requirements on employer use of credit reports.

22.5 GENETIC TESTING

More than half the states make it unlawful to impose a requirement of genetic testing (e.g., for sickle cell trait; susceptibility to cancer) as a condition of employment, as a condition of insurance, or as a factor used to increase insurance premiums. (Approximately 450 genetic tests already exist, although they are too expensive to be used widely.) Several bills are pending before Congress to limit or forbid employment-related genetic testing.

The various state laws have different emphases. Some make the result of genetic testing confidential; others limit the extent to which insurers can deny coverage or make it more expensive as a result of genetic test results; others are more hiring-oriented.

These state laws are not popular with the insurance industry (which could be forecast!) but also have triggered concerns in drug companies, who are afraid that the greater the confidentiality given to genetic test results, the more difficult it will be for them to research new drugs and new treatments for illnesses that have identifiable genetic markers.

22.6 SEARCHES AND SURVEILLANCE

Most of the Constitutional law protections against searches and seizures protect individuals against public action: actions taken by the police, the military, or other public agencies. However, an employer's surveillance activities might constitute an invasion of privacy which could become the subject of a suit brought by an employee.

An employer can legitimately order a workplace search if there is a good reason in the first place (such as getting evidence of embezzlement, theft of products, or other work-related misconduct) and if the scope of the search is appropriate to satisfying that purpose. But get legal advice if a search is planned; personal items such as handbags and briefcases might be immune from search unless the employee gives consent for the search. After all, the employer owns or controls the workplace, but the employee controls the personal items.

There is no general federal or state law ban on video surveillance of areas within the workplace that are open to the public, or open to the inspection of other employees, and therefore are not private. The First Circuit says that it does not violate the Fourth Amendment for a public employer to use silent video cameras for surveillance of the work area. In this case, the work environment was an open space with no assigned offices, cubicles, work stations, or desks, so the court concluded that it would not be reasonable to assume that privacy would be available in such an environment.

However, in a unionized company, it might be an unfair labor practice to install surveillance devices, at least without the consent of the union. In 1997, the NLRB decided that installation of hidden surveillance cameras is a mandatory subject of bargaining. The agency didn't accept the employer's claim that surveillance is a managerial decision involving entrepreneurial control; to the NLRB, only subjects like product lines and capital investment are in that category. The cameras pertain to the employment relationship because they are used to investigate misconduct by employees; hence bargaining, rather than unilateral decision, is required.

Employees may be able to sue the employer for invasion of privacy, if a reasonable person would be offended by the employer's intentional intrusion into locations or matters that are reasonably expected to be private. However, in a unionized workplace, employees would probably not be able to bring invasion of privacy suits in state court. §301 of the Labor-Management Relations Act would probably preempt the suit because interpretation of the Collective Bargaining Agreement is essential to deciding the case. (See page 375 for more about LMRA §301 preemption.)

22.6.1 Workplace Wiretapping

Wiretapping, and other forms of interception of wire, oral, and electronic communications, including e-mail (or electronic or mechanical interception of conversations), are covered by the federal Omnibus Crime Control and Safe Streets Act of 1968, 18 United States Code §2511 et.seq. Interceptions by the employer are regulated, and are prohibited but only if the employee had a reasonable expectation that the communication would not be subject to interception.

If, for instance, the employee is a telephone salesperson and has been told from the outset that contact with customers is subject to monitoring, there would be no reasonable expectation of privacy. However, even if interception of calls is legitimate, the employer must cease the interception if it is clear that a particular call is personal rather than business-related. One of the parties to the communication has a right to intercept it; so does anyone who has explicit or implicit consent to intercept.

The federal statute imposes penalties for improper interception which can be as high as $10,000. Punitive damages can be imposed if the employer acted wantonly, recklessly, or maliciously. An Eighth Circuit case refused to impose punitive damages where the employer did intercept personal phone calls (which was wrong), but it was part of the investigation of a major theft, and the employer was not reckless because it got advice (however inaccurate) from a police officer who said that companies are entitled to tap their own telephones.

Part V

COPING WITH CHARGES OF DISCRIMINATION AND WRONGFUL TERMINATION

Chapter 23

TITLE VII

23.1 INTRODUCTION

Both state and federal law forbid employers to discriminate against applicants and employees (and, sometimes, former employees) on the basis of various characteristics. The laws determine the proper method for employees to assert such claims. Employers can defend themselves by showing that the claim was invalid or unfounded, or that it was improperly asserted (at the wrong time, in the wrong form, brought before the wrong agency).

Perhaps the most significant antidiscrimination act is the federal Title VII: so-called because it is Title VII of the Civil Rights Act of 1964. It forbids discrimination on the basis of race, religion, sex, color, nationality, or pregnancy. This chapter discusses the kinds of employer conduct that constitute Title VII violations, and the conduct that is permissible. The other chapters in this Part discuss other discrimination statutes (covering disability discrimination, leave for personal or family health needs, and age discrimination); the procedures for bringing or combating a discrimination suit; and employee charges of wrongful termination.

How big a threat to corporate success are discrimination charges? The most obvious threat is the multi-million-dollar verdict, although these are quite rare. (See page 542 for a discussion of the Civil Rights Act of 1991 cap on damages that can be received per winning plaintiff.) Consulting firm Jury Verdict Research found that the median (i.e., the point at which half the verdicts were above, half below) for sexual harassment cases was $38,500; the median for age discrimination cases was $218,000.

Furthermore, a jumbo-sized jury verdict may very well be reduced by the trial judge, who views it as excessive, or could be reduced or even dismissed on appeal. One dramatic instance of this was the early 1997 reduction of a 1995 $50 million jury verdict in a sexual harassment case: first to $5 million (by the judge) and then

455

to $350,000 (by the Eighth Circuit). In many cases, after the noisy pretrial and trial periods, the case is quietly settled before the appeal, for a much smaller figure.

However, there are hidden costs and threats: the amount of time and attention senior managers must devote to fighting the suit; legal fees and expenses (which can run into millions of dollars); and bad publicity. The perception that a company is biased can harm recruitment, and can turn away potential customers. A chain store or franchise can suffer a nationwide loss of reputation even if only a few—or even if only a single unit—practices or is perceived to practice bias.

23.1.1 USERRA Rights

The Uniformed Services Employment and Reemployment Rights Act protects military personnel from job discrimination when they return to civilian life. A person who was in the military for five years or less and makes a prompt application for re-employment with his or her former civilian employer is entitled to re-employment unless the employer can demonstrate:

- It would be impossible to reinstate the veteran because of a change in the employer's circumstances

- It would constitute an unreasonable hardship on the employer to reinstate the veteran, because of the veteran's disabilities or lack of qualifications

- The civilian job formerly held by the veteran was explicitly described as a temporary one with no re-employment rights.

A prompt application for re-employment means one made within 90 days of discharge—or less, if the veteran was in the military service for less than 180 days. In fact, service with the military is considered "service" in the ERISA context, so the veteran is entitled to receive pension and profit sharing benefits that would have accrued if he or she had been working for the employer rather than enlisted in the service.

In addition, military service members have continuation coverage rights (similar to COBRA rights—see page 142) in the employer's group health plan while they are serving in the military.

It may be necessary for the employer to deposit make-up contributions into the plan when the service member becomes reemployed. The Small Business Job Protection Act of 1996 makes it clear that these make-up contributions will not impair the plan's qualified status, even though they may exceed the amounts that would otherwise be legitimate contributions.

If the plan includes employee contribution or elective deferrals (for instance, a 401(k) plan), the reemployed veteran must be given a chance to make additional deferrals or contributions when returning to work; the extra payments must be allowed during the time period that starts when the veteran is reemployed, and ends either five years later or after a period of time equal to three times the period of military service. However, the veteran can't contribute or defer more than he or she could have done by working for the employer instead of going into military service.

23.2 TITLE VII COVERAGE

The Civil Rights Act of 1964 is a very wide-ranging document—so wide-ranging, in fact, that the Supreme Court has found it necessary to rein it in, and Congress has adopted several modifications (some pro-employee, some pro-employer) since its original enactment. The Civil Rights Act is also a very long document, so for ease of reference it is divided into Titles (major section headings). Title VII (42 United States Code §2000e) forbids bias in the employment context.

It covers businesses with 15 or more employees. (Although it is outside the scope of this book, it should be noted that many state anti-discrimination laws apply to enterprises that are too small to be subject to the federal law.) In early 1997, the U.S. Supreme Court clarified the method of calculating the number of employees: what counts is the number of persons on the payroll, even if some of them are part-time employees.

23.2.1 Forbidden Acts

Title VII is a descendent of Civil War statutes aimed at giving former slaves civil rights, so it bars racial discrimination.

> **➠ TIP**
>
> The plaintiff in a racial discrimination termination case does not have to prove that he or she was replaced by someone of a different race, only that racial factors entered into the discharge decision.

Title VII also bars sex discrimination (defined to include pregnancy discrimination and sexual harassment) and discrimination on the basis of national origin. (But see page 13: employers are not only permitted but required to ascertain that employees are legally entitled to work in the United States.)

Religious discrimination is barred, and employers are also required to make reasonable accommodation to the religious practices and observances of employees—e.g., employers should not assign employees to work on a Sabbath or holy day if this can easily be avoided. In a sense, religious discrimination is treated similarly to disability discrimination: if a qualified individual can do the job, the employer must take reasonable steps to make it possible.

Title VII bars these types of discrimination in many employment contexts: job applications and interviews, hiring, retention, promotion, compensation and benefits, and dismissal. However, as long as it is neutral and does not manifest discriminatory intent, a bona fide seniority system can be maintained, and can be used to provide different wages or terms and conditions of employment for various employees based on their seniority. This is permissible even if the seniority system has the effect of maintaining past discrimination. See 42 United States Code §2000e-2(h).

It is also unlawful for an employer to retaliate against an employee who exercises rights under Title VII (e.g., by filing a complaint with an anti-discrimination agency). According to the 1997 Supreme Court case, for this purpose a former employee is an "employee" for Title VII purposes, and thus is entitled to bring a retaliation action.

⇒ **TIP**

A sustainable retaliation claim must involve an "ultimate employment decision" such as termination or demotion. A verbal threat of firing, or a so-called "final warning" is not adequate to support a retaliation suit if the firing never actually ensued.

Title VII does not contain any reference to discrimination on the basis of sexual orientation or gender dysphoria, although some state statutes do bar sexual-orientation discrimination and/or discrimination against transvestites and transsexuals.

Title VII forbids both "disparate treatment" and "disparate impact." Disparate treatment is the use of overt, intentional classifications that favor one group over another—e.g., insisting on three years' experience for black applicants, versus only one year's experience for white applicants. Disparate impact is the use of facially neutral practices (not necessarily adopted for discriminatory reasons) that have the effect of disfavoring one group. For instance, requiring that applicants be at least six feet tall has disparate impact on women and members of ethnic groups that are not characterized by a great average height.

23.2.2 The EEOC's Role

As discussed in more depth in Chapters 24 and 27, the Equal Employment Opportunity Commission is in charge of enforcing Title VII and the Americans with Disabilities Act (ADA). It also enforces the Equal Pay Act (EPA) and Age Discrimination in Employment Act (ADEA), although the enforcement provisions for these laws are somewhat different because they derive from the Fair Labor Standards Act. The EPA complaint process does not require an EEOC charge; rules for ADEA charges are found at 29 CFR §1626.4.

The general enforcement scheme is that individuals who believe that they have been the victims of discrimination file charges with the EEOC. The EEOC's job is to work with state anti-discrimination agencies, and to use methods ranging from informal persuasion to litigation to get employers to comply with the law and eliminate any discriminatory practices prevailing within the workplace.

The EEOC can intervene in a suit brought by an employee, or can bring its own lawsuits against employers. The EEOC has the power to collect data, investigate allegations of discrimination, go to workplaces to view conditions, interview workers, and inspect records. It can also advise employers on how to comply with the law, subpoena witnesses and documents, bring suits, and supervise collection of damages that employees have been awarded or that the employer has agreed to pay under a settlement.

23.2.3 The BFOQ Concept

Certain conduct that might be discriminatory at first glance is permissible if it falls under the bona fide occupational qualification (BFOQ) exception to Title VII and other anti-discrimination laws. It might be a BFOQ to be male or female (e.g., because of authenticity, for an actor or actress; for privacy, for a restroom attendant), to be under 40 (e.g., a job where public safety depends on youthful physical reactions), or even to belong to a particular religion (e.g., to work in a kosher slaughterhouse). In the disability context, not posing a safety risk to one's self or others is a BFOQ. However, the BFOQ defense is not accepted in cases of alleged racial discrimination.

If safety and efficiency are involved, it may be possible to show that a discriminatory practice is actually acceptable because it is a business necessity.

23.2.4 Race Discrimination

Laws against racial discrimination were the first equal opportunity laws: the Civil Rights Act of 1866, enacted at 42 United States Code §1981, was passed to give former slaves the same rights as "white citizens." Unlike Title VII, §1981 suits can be brought against an employer of any size; there is no minimum number of employees, the plaintiff can sue as soon as he or she believes there has been a violation (charges need not be filed with the EEOC or a state anti-discrimination agency); jury trials are allowed; and there is no limitation on the amount of compensatory or punitive damages that can be awarded under this ruling.

For many years, it was unclear how the Civil War anti-discrimination statutes interacted with Title VII, and some commentators believed that Title VII was supposed to replace the nineteenth century statutes. However, in 1991 Congress decisively put an end to this argument. The Civil Rights Act of 1991 generally requires plaintiffs to proceed under §1981 if they have claims of racial discrimination, before using Title VII. Furthermore, compensatory and punitive damages will not be available under Title VII for any plaintiff who can get such damages under §1981.

23.2.5 Sex Discrimination

Discrimination on account of sex is unlawful, except in the situations where belonging to a particular gender is a bona fide occupational qualification (BFOQ). Being male or female is a BFOQ in a limited range of biologically-based jobs, as well as instances in which the privacy of patients, customers, clients, etc. might be violated: store detectives who patrol dressing rooms, for instance. However, even privacy arguments probably will not prevail if a qualified male seeks a health-care job caring for females, or if a qualified female seeks a job as a prison guard in a men's prison. Comparatively few pure sex discrimination cases are brought these days, although sexual harassment is a very active litigation area (see page 461).

In 1983, the Supreme Court decided that it constitutes sex discrimination for a plan to provide less comprehensive benefits to male employees and their spouses than to female employees and their spouses.

Executive Order 11246 forbids sex discrimination by government contractors and subcontractors, a category that includes many manufacturing businesses. The Executive Order is enforced by the Office of Federal Contract Compliance Programs (OFCCP), and violators can be barred from federal contracting.

⇒ TIP

A contractor charged by the OFCCP with sex discrimination has to exhaust its remedies within the administrative system before suing the OFFCP in federal court.

23.2.6 The Pregnancy Discrimination Act (PDA)

Title VII has also been amended by the Pregnancy Discrimination Act (PDA, 42 United States Code §2000e(k)), which bars discrimination on the basis of pregnancy or related conditions. Although the PDA does not require employers to provide health coverage if they would not otherwise, it does require coverage of pregnancy-related conditions if there is a health plan, on a basis comparable with comparable non-pregnancy conditions.

If pregnant employees are covered by the plan, the pregnant wives of employees must be covered (in a plan with dependent coverage), and vice versa. However, it is permissible to exclude the pregnancy-related conditions of dependents who are not employees' spouses, as long as the exclusion is applied equally for male and female employees and their dependents.

> ⇒ **TIP**
> _____
>
> 29 CFR Part 1604, Question 17, says that if the employer has a policy of continuing benefits for employees who are on leave, benefits must be continued for pregnancy-related leave as well as for other forms of leave (e.g., when an employee is injured, or when an employee is fulfilling a military reserve commitment).

In 1978, the EEOC published a series of Questions and Answers on the PDA, stating the agency's viewpoint. Under these guidelines:

- If there is a health plan at all, it must cover female employees for pregnancy-related conditions

- A percentage limitation on reimbursement for pregnancy-related conditions is permissible, as long as the percentage limitation is the same as for non-pregnancy-related conditions

- Female employees can get more pregnancy coverage than the wives of male employees, but wives of male employees must get as much pregnancy coverage as the husbands of female employees get for non-pregnancy-related conditions.

Like the later Americans with Disabilities Act, the PDA focuses on the ability of a particular pregnant woman to work. Under the PDA, normal pregnancy itself cannot be treated as a disability; if an individual woman does have disability related to a particular pregnancy, the employer must give individualized consideration to her case. Disparate impact PDA cases, not just disparate treatment ones, are possible.

It violates the PDA to fire an employee for contemplating having an abortion, or even having an abortion, because the PDA prohibits all forms of discrimination on the basis of reproductive capacity, except in the very limited situation where reproductive capacity is relevant to the job. The employee's prima facie case (and the case the employer has to defend against) is that a non-pregnant employee who had a similar capacity to work was favored over the pregnant plaintiff.

23.3 SEXUAL HARASSMENT

Sexual harassment is the subjection of an employee to unwanted sexual contact, propositions, or innuendoes. It is considered a form of sex discrimination, and therefore is forbidden by Title VII. The EEOC has adopted a two-part test: conduct is unwanted if the employee did not solicit or initiate the conduct, and the employee finds it undesirable or offensive.

Since 1990, the number of complaints of sexual harassment recorded by the EEOC has increased greatly, from approximately 6,000 in 1990 to about 15,000 in 1996. This could reflect many trends (or a combination of trends): greater incidence of harassment, greater consciousness of legal remedies by victims, or higher incidence of unfounded complaints. Whatever the reason, few of those complaints have resulted in a resolution in favor of the complainant: about one-third of the complaints in 1990, but only about one-seventh of the complaints in 1996. In fact, the number of pro-plaintiff resolutions in 1996 was scarcely higher than the number in 1990, although the number of complaints had more than doubled. Nevertheless, although the gross number of settlements is not large, the amount of money involved in settlements is quite meaningful. In 1990, the total amount of funds involved in all EEOC settlements was about $7 million. In 1993, settlements added up to $25 million, and totaled about $27 million in 1997.

The law recognizes two forms of sexual harassment: "quid pro quo" harassment and "hostile environment" harassment. The ban on quid pro quo harassment is not particularly controversial. In this type of case, a supervisor either threatens an employee with dismissal or other adverse job action, or promises some form of advantage, if the target employee provides some kind of sexual services to the supervisor.

Very few people would argue that employees should be subjected to pressures of this kind in the workplace. Of course, only a human being and not a corporation can seek gratification, so it may seem paradoxical that only the corporation, and not the insensitive person who demands sexual favors, can be sued!

Although it may be unprofessional, it is not unlawful for a supervisor to date or have sexual relations with a subordinate. The essence of harassment is continued pressing of unwanted sexual attentions. There can be very different responses as to when attentions are unwelcome, however, and whether the undesirability of the attentions was communicated to the person soliciting a sexual relationship. Sexual harassment may also occur if a supervisor imposes penalties on a subordinate who terminates or wishes to terminate a relationship that was voluntary at its outset.

Employers have several defenses when charged with quid pro quo harassment by a supervisor. First, the supervisor's threats may have never been carried out, and thus the plaintiff suffered no real harm or damage. The employer can also defend by showing that it maintained a strong anti-harassment policy and a reasonable grievance procedure, which the plaintiff either knew about or should have known about.

It is fairly clear that a quid pro quo harassment claim can be maintained by male plaintiffs as well as females. Quid pro quo harassment of a male by a female is actionable. The legal status of same-sex harassment is a more complex matter. At first, courts tended to say that such actions were not discriminatory or not carried out "on account of sex," but more and more courts are recognizing this cause of action, and the Supreme Court has agreed to hear a case in which both the complainant and the alleged harassers are male.

Hostile environment harassment is far more controversial, in part because it is much harder to define. A hostile work environment is one where actions are taken to make the employee feel unwelcome. In the racial context, this might consist of racist jokes and remarks, posters for white supremacy organizations, and other statements made by members of one race implying that members of other races are inferior or should not be employed there. Hostile work environment sexual harassment cases have been permitted for over a decade, starting with the Supreme Court case of *Meritor Savings Bank* v. *Vinson*, 477 U.S. 57 (1986).

In the sexual context, the work atmosphere may be inappropriately sexualized in an unwelcome way—through pin-ups, innuendo, jokes, and horseplay. The intellectual difficulty with analyzing these cases is that they can involve a wide range of motivations (from attempting to drive women out of a conventionally all-male workplace, to enlivening a dull workday with repartee that is expected to be amusing, to making statements and performing actions that are expected to be offensive to the recipient).

Furthermore, it is true in almost all cases that the perpetrator of quid pro quo harassment must be a supervisor or other person with power over the victim—not merely a co-employee who cannot enforce the sexual proposition. But in hostile work environment cases, the alleged perpetrators are frequently co-employees.

There is also a far greater subjective element. Nearly everyone would agree that quid pro quo sexual harassment in effect attempts to get its target to engage in immoral sexual conduct (and, indeed, fornication and adultery may violate state laws that are still on the books, so the target is also solicited to commit a crime). But whether a nude pin-up, a dirty joke, or locker-room horseplay is offensive or not is very much dependent on the values and attitudes of the recipient. Conduct is assessed by both an objective test (what a reasonable person would perceive) and a subjective one (the plaintiff's viewpoint).

The totality of circumstances is examined, including factors such as:

- Frequency of incidents
- Their severity
- Whether the employee's work performance suffered unreasonable interference.

It is often, but not necessarily, the case that hostile environment sexual harassment claims involve conduct by men that violates the sensibilities of women, but it is perfectly possible for a man to be shocked and offended by conduct by women. Furthermore, there have been many cases questioning whether offensive conduct is cognizable as sexual harassment where both the perpetrators and the targets are males.

Some courts take the position that the ban on hostile environment sexual harassment was enacted to protect women, who are more vulnerable than men, and therefore claims by men are not valid. Other courts find that conduct perpetrated by some heterosexual males against other heterosexual males could not have been carried out "on account of sex." Another theory is that if the harassment is based on the target's real or perceived homosexuality, then Title VII is not involved because that law does not cover discrimination on the basis of sexual orientation.

Another recent line of cases finds that conduct that might be described as horseplay (such as incidents of removing a male worker's clothing, touching his genitals) does not create a hostile work environment unless there were repeated incidents extending over a significant amount of time. However, some courts do find such conduct actionable—especially if the target has been subjected to outright sexual propositions by other males.

Dramatic court-to-court differences exist about how conduct will be analyzed. There is an increasing trend to dismiss cases, on the theory that the conduct the plaintiff complains of was insufficient in severity or duration to constitute a hostile work environment. Brief incidents of vulgar joking have been held insufficient to create a hostile environment, as have offensive vocal comments extending only over a period of hours and not accompanied by physical touching, and, in like manner, one isolated instance of sexually explicit epithets.

23.3.1 The Employer's Responsibility

According to the Eleventh Circuit, the employer is liable only if it had actual knowledge of the harassment, or if the hostile environment was so pervasive as to constitute constructive knowledge on the part of the employer. The Eighth Circuit requires the judge to instruct the jury that the employer's liability depends on whether it knew or should have known about sexual harassment. The mere fact that the harasser is an agent of the employer isn't enough to put the employer in the "hot seat."

⇒ TIP

In a Second Circuit case, the employee reported racial and sexual harassment by her immediate supervisor, but asked her manager to keep the report confidential. The manager did so—with the result that the employer was relieved of liability, because it could not remedy a situation it was not aware of.

In contrast, the Seventh Circuit applies common law agency principles to make the employer liable for both quid pro quo and hostile environment harassment, even though the harassment does not benefit the employer, and even if the victimized employee fails to use the employer's procedure for reporting the harassment.

The Tenth Circuit says that the employer is liable if the supervisor was able to commit harassment because of real or apparent authority to control the harassed person's work environment; it is not necessary that the employer provide actual or implied authority to harass the victim.

The EEOC's position is that the employer is liable for harassment by co-workers if the employer knew or should have known of the harassment (based on EEOC charges, complaints to management, or observation of workplace conditions) and failed to take prompt corrective action. The employer is presumed to know about harassment that is "open" or "well-known among employees." Under this theory, the employer is also liable if it failed to maintain and communicate an effective anti-harassment policy and workable complaint procedure. Failing this test makes the employer liable, even if it did not know about the harassment.

What to do when the harassment arises outside of the company? The EEOC's position (expressed in 1980 and 1984 Guidelines) is that employers have a duty to take immediate action if the company, its agents, or its supervisors, are aware of the non-employees' conduct. Some courts have agreed, but they have not set out clear principles that employers can follow once they do become aware of such harassment.

⟱ TIP

Certainly, a regular customer can be politely requested to desist, or the victim of harassment could be transferred to a situation where the troublesome non-employees will not be encountered. The employer corporation should not ignore complaints, and certainly should not discipline or retaliate against the employee for reporting harassment.

A recent case permits employees to sue for hostile environment sexual harassment premised on harassment directed against them as women, even though the hostile remarks were sexist rather than sexual in nature, on the theory that men would not have been subjected to equivalent conduct.

Employees often seek to combine federal and state claims: for instance, a state law claim of intentional infliction of emotional stress. A 1995 Pennsylvania case says that that state's employment discrimination law specifically rules out these emotional distress claims.

23.3.2 Required Employer Response

Of course, corporations don't have sexual desires, so individuals who commit sexual harassment do it for their own gratification, not to advance the corporate agenda. (In contrast, executives who bribe officials or illegally dump toxic wastes are furthering corporate objectives.) Nevertheless, Title VII makes employers responsible for workplace harassment unless the employer takes reasonable steps to respond to sexual harassment charges, to investigate the facts, and to take prompt action to eliminate improper conduct.

Several cases have been reported of harassment occurring at Christmas and other office parties, perhaps because excessive alcohol consumption "dissolved" the inhibitions of the harasser. It would certainly be improper for the corporation to hire strippers or scantily-clad cocktail waitresses for an office function, and if it is deemed necessary to give "gag" presents, these should be selected so that they will not be offensive even to strait-laced employees. Some companies find that a day-time alcohol-free event, with employees' spouses and children present, creates fewer problems (and is less expensive) than an evening event with an open bar.

The party itself should be supervised, and if incidents of propositions or improper touching do occur, a corporate representative will immediately protect and take the side of the employee subject to harassment, and immediately rebuke the harasser.

Immediate and appropriate corrective action by an employer, whether in the context of corporate entertainment or of ordinary day-to-day operations is necessary and appropriate. Such action would include:

- informing employees that the company is opposed to sexual harassment;
- creating an atmosphere in which employees are comfortable reporting their complaints and concerns, knowing that they will not be subject to retaliation;
- an investigation procedure done by neutral individuals (often from the HR department) that is thorough yet discreet;
- a bypass procedure in case the person who would normally receive the report is the alleged harasser;
- real, appropriate penalties against the harasser if the complaint is found to be accurate.

The employer must also monitor the procedure to make sure that complaining employees and employees who are witnesses do not become the subject of retaliation.

Depending on the circumstances, appropriate sanctions against the harasser could be counseling, a fine, a reprimand, a suspension, reassignment, or even termination. Because the alleged harasser and alleged victim are likely to feel uncomfortable working together, a transfer may be a good idea. Yet it can be hard to find an appropriate job slot for either of them. The company must be careful to avoid transferring the alleged victim into a position with inferior pay, status, or other unfavorable conditions of employment, because this creates an inference that the victim has been subjected to retaliation for making a complaint.

Once a harassment claim has been investigated, the complainant's personnel file should be examined to see if any retaliatory negative comments have been placed there; if so, the file should be annotated to explain the comments and the outcome of the investigation.

If the individual found to have committed harassment is fired or otherwise disciplined, he (or, in rare cases, she) may charge the company with discrimination or wrongful termination. Even if the person found to have committed harassment has a contract, or works under a corporate policy, where termination requires "good cause" or "just cause," the employer will probably be safe as long as it acts after a factual investigation and based on a reasonable and good-faith belief that the terminated individual did commit harassment.

23.3.3 Outside Investigators

Some companies rely on their outside attorneys to investigate harassment charges. However, this is not always a good strategy: the same person is not allowed to act both as a company's attorney and as a witness on its behalf, and the employer will certainly want the investigator to testify that the employer ensured a prompt, effective investigation. In fact, the attorney-investigator's whole law firm may be disqualified from working for the employer—which means the employer will have to hire a new law firm to do whatever the firm was doing.

Another risk is that the plaintiff will be able to question the attorney-investigator about his or her findings; it might be ruled that the attorney's investigative role was primary, so attorney-client privilege does not apply to what the attorney learned during the investigation.

In addition to its arbitration activities, the American Arbitration Association has a program under which it will send a two-person fact-finding team (consisting of either one man and one woman or two women) to investigate. The process usually takes two days; it costs $250-$600 per investigator per day, plus a $200 filing fee. Contact the AAA at (212) 484-4000, or your local regional office, for more information. Bringing in neutral observers from a respected organization can be an efficient and cost-effective way to resolve complaints, especially if widespread harassment is alleged, and the objectivity of the company's management might be called into question.

23.4 RELIGIOUS DISCRIMINATION AND THE ISSUE OF REASONABLE ACCOMMODATION

Except in the limited cases where religious tests are truly applicable (certain religious beliefs can be reasonably expected before hiring someone as a priest or minister!), religious beliefs are irrelevant to hiring, and cannot be used as a hiring criterion. Employers are not supposed to prefer one religion over another, or even to prefer organized religion over atheism or agnosticism.

At the same time, however, employers have a duty to make reasonable accommodations so that employees can carry out what they conceive to be their religious duties. (EEOC guidelines hold that all sincerely held moral and ethical beliefs are entitled to the same protection as religious beliefs.)

In 1986, the Supreme Court held that employers are not obligated to accept the *employee's* characterization of what would constitute a reasonable religious accommodation; it is sufficient for the employer to make its own reasonable suggestion of how to accommodate the employee's belief.

In the context of religious accommodation, like the context of accommodation to disability (see page 480), it is not necessary for the employer to undergo undue hardship. In fact, in 1977 the Supreme Court decided that if the employer invests more than a minimal amount of expense in accommodation, it is actually offering an illegal preference to the employee who receives the accommodation.

One context in which religious accommodation may be required is union security (see page 359): the National Labor Relations Act (29 United States Code §169) provides that if an employee belongs to a religion that has traditionally objected to unions, then the employer cannot require the employee to join or support a union even if the employer maintains an agency shop or other union security arrangement.

However, the employee's religious objection can be accommodated by requiring him or her to contribute an amount equivalent to the union initiation fee and dues to a charitable organization that is neither a union nor religious in nature. That way, the employee does not benefit financially from the anti-union belief, but is not required to perform a religiously repugnant act.

Employers will probably have to permit employees to wear forms of dress, jewelry, and hairstyles required by their religion. The exception might be a situation in which the employer can show a genuine safety hazard that cannot be accommodated in another way; for instance, an employer's "no-beard" policy would not be valid against an employee whose religion requires him to grow a beard, unless the beard is unsanitary (e.g., in food preparation), creates a hazard (e.g., getting caught in machinery)—and, further, there is no method of securing the beard that would cope with these asserted hazards.

Probably the most common issue of religious accommodation involves work assignments at times when the employee is supposed to observe a Sabbath, or is supposed to be attending religious services, Bible study, teaching religious school, etc. The consensus of court cases is that employers do not have to accommodate employees' personal desires for religious observance (e.g., feeling a call to preach), only observances required by the employee's religion (e.g., the religion teaches that it is sinful to work on the Sabbath, or that it is mandatory to attend services at particular times). The EEOC considers it unlawful discrimination to set overtime rates in a way that disadvantages employees who observe a Sabbath other than Sunday.

The EEOC's Guidelines on religious accommodation are found at 29 CFR Part 1605. According to the EEOC (which often requires more of employers than courts will uphold), acceptable accommodations include voluntary substitution of one employee for another, swapping shifts, lateral transfers, changes of job assignment, and flextime (i.e., the employee makes up the time devoted to religious observance).

However, employers are not obligated to accommodate religious observance by violating the seniority rights of a non-observant employee. In the view of the EEOC, it would be an undue hardship for the employer to pay other employees overtime to cover for the religious employee, or to have an untrained or inexperienced employee covering for the religious employee.

⇒ TIP

It's unconstitutional (as an establishment of religion) for a state to pass a law that gives employees an absolute right to get their Sabbath day as a day off. However, an employee who is fired for refusing to work on his or her Sabbath day is entitled to collect unemployment benefits. Some state laws, (such as New York's Human Rights Law), make it clear that if employees get time off for religious observances, they must make up the time at other, religiously acceptable, times.

Once again, the employer is caught between two fires: what if an employee asserts that his or her faith requires preaching and seeking converts at work, and other employees are perfectly satisfied with their own religion (or lack of religion) and are angry, disturbed, or threatened by the preaching?

A recent case (involving a police dispatcher who claims that she was fired because her born-again boss insisted that she share his religious views) suggests that unwanted proselytizing could create a "hostile religious environment" in the workplace, similar to a climate of racial hostility or sexual harassment.

It should also be noted that a ban on preaching in the workplace doesn't prevent employees from inviting fellow-employees to a church service, prayer meeting, Bible study group, etc., that takes place outside the workplace, so a person who feels called to share his or her beliefs with others can do so in many other settings.

On August 14, 1997, the Clinton administration promulgated religious accommodation guidelines for federal employees. Private employers cannot be penalized for failing to meet these guidelines, but they do give some suggestions about how to deal with the often-murky subject of religious accommodation. The guidelines require federal agencies to accommodate religious dress (such as head coverings and crucifixes) and to permit employees to read religious literature during their breaktimes. Perhaps surprisingly, they must be given access to conference rooms to hold prayer meetings for voluntary participants during breaks.

23.5 THE EQUAL PAY ACT (EPA)

The Equal Pay Act, 29 U.S.C. §206, is related to the Title VII provisions that forbid sex discrimination. The EPA, which covers all employers with two or more employees (the other employment anti-discrimination laws are limited to coverage of businesses with more employees), forbids discrimination in compensation (including all forms of benefits) on the basis of sex, if the jobs are of equal skill, effort, and responsibility and performed under similar working conditions. In other words, this statute does not apply to "comparable worth" claims under which women claim that a typically female job is of greater value to society than a higher-paid but different job typically performed by men (e.g., child care center workers and parking lot attendants).

Unlike most statutes, the EPA does *not* permit a cost-based defense: under 29 CFR §216(b), even if it costs more to provide benefits to women than to men, the employer must either eliminate the benefit or provide it to everyone. See page 510 for a discussion of cost issues in benefits for older employees.

An employer who loses an EPA case can be subjected to civil penalties, and possibly even criminal penalties as prescribed by Fair Labor Standards Act §216(a). Punitive damages are not allowed, but double back pay is; a winning plaintiff can get costs and attorneys' fees.

23.6 DISCRIMINATION SUIT PROCEDURAL ISSUES

In most areas of civil law, anyone who feels aggrieved can simply file a complaint and sue the party who is supposedly responsible for the grievance. However, Congress has created a very different set-up for the adjudication of Title VII cases. Employees who feel they have a claim are not permitted to file an immediate lawsuit. Instead, they must pursue administrative remedies, by filing a complaint with the EEOC and/or the state anti-discrimination agency. The agency(ies) must investigate the complaint and attempt to conciliate (i.e., to get the employer and employee to agree on the facts of the case and a mutually acceptable remedy).

Only after the completion of the investigation and the failure of conciliation will the employee be permitted to litigate. If the employee fails to conform to the requirements of the system (for instance, by missing a filing deadline or failing to provide necessary evidence), the defendant corporation will have the right to have the case dismissed.

Furthermore, if the employee has agreed to arbitrate discrimination claims in lieu of litigating them, and if this requirement is either accepted by the employee or challenged by the employee but upheld by the court, then the employee will not be permitted to go to litigation.

The litigation process is a lengthy one, and seldom an agreeable one for the plaintiff. The employer has the right to search out evidence of the plaintiff's work-related wrongdoing, or of misrepresentations made during the application process, and can use these facts to show that the employee is neither credible nor entitled to a large-scale recovery.

Sometimes the employer has to fight on two fronts. The EEOC has a dual role. It investigates charges brought by employees, but it can also litigate as a plaintiff. The theory is that the EEOC acts as plaintiff to preserve the rights of all the employees within the workplace. The EEOC always has a right to investigate and, where it believes a cause of action exists, to litigate. So if a terminated employee signs a release of claims against the employer as part of the outplacement process, or if the company negotiates a settlement with the employee, that settlement will prevent the employee from filing a lawsuit against the employer, but will not prevent the EEOC from filing its own suit.

> ⇒ **TIP**
>
> Waivers and releases are void as against public policy if they try to bar employees from helping the EEOC in its investigation, as distinct from filing cases seeking relief and damages for themselves. For further discussion of waivers and releases, see page 556.

23.6.1 Tolling

The statute of limitations can be tolled (suspended) in a limited class of situations where it would be unjust to insist on strict observance of the time limitations. However, most plaintiffs who apply for tolling of the statute of limitations will be denied, because this is supposed to be a last-ditch defense, not an ordinary litigation tactic. Some situations in which tolling may be permitted include:

- The employer was guilty of some form of deception or other wrongdoing that prevented the employee from asserting Title VII rights (for this purpose, it doesn't count if the employer honestly but inaccurately reported what it believed to be the law)
- The employee did try to institute a lawsuit in time, but the pleading was rejected as defective
- The employee filed a lawsuit in time, but went to the wrong court.

In most of these situations, tolling is considered a defense—so it's up to the plaintiff to prove that it was available.

Another possibility is that the plaintiff will be able to prove that there was not just one discriminatory act, but a series. In that situation, the plaintiff's case will be timely as long as the LAST discriminatory act occurs within the required time frame.

The plaintiff will probably have to prove that all the discriminatory acts were linked by a policy of discrimination (or that the employer allowed discrimination to continue so long that the effect was the same as a policy of discrimination).

Otherwise, if the acts are truly separate, the plaintiff should have brought separate suits for each act, and should have been more prompt in filing with respect to the earliest acts in the series.

Sometimes the term "tolling" is used to cover two different but related concepts. "Equitable tolling" allows a delayed case to continue because, even though the delay was caused by the plaintiff's excusable ignorance or oversight, the delay is not prejudicial to the plaintiff (does not harm the plaintiff's interests). "Equitable estoppel" prevents the defendant from complaining about a delay that is caused in whole or in part by the defendant's deceit or other conduct that is prejudicial to the plaintiff's interests.

23.7 AFFIRMATIVE ACTION

Reasonable people may differ about the validity of affirmative action and preferences as a remedy for past discrimination. One theory is that, unless traditionally disfavored groups are given hiring preferences, there will never be a critical mass that makes up for the former inequalities within the workplace. Furthermore, since most promotions take place from within a company's ranks, a company will never have a group of women and minorities with management experience who qualify for promotions, unless they have entry-level women and minority staff.

The opposite point of view is that justice calls for truly neutral hiring: the employer should always hire the best-qualified individual, even if the result is a continuing preponderance of white males with good jobs. Under this theory, a white male should not be denied job opportunities because of past inequalities which he did not perpetrate. Furthermore, this view says that traditional labor law concepts such as seniority should be upheld, so it would be wrong to "bump" a more senior white male to give a job to a minority-group member or woman.

In 1977, the Supreme Court decided that it is unlawful to perpetuate the present effects of past discrimination, although bona fide seniority systems can be left in operation. Under this approach, preferential hiring of women and minorities might be acceptable, to correct an imbalance in the workforce that results from past discrimination. It might also be acceptable to set goals to remove past discrimination, and to remove the barriers that existed in the past to prevent racially neutral hiring, but the hiring system must not exclude white applicants.

In the past two decades, affirmative action has been most prominent in the context of government contracts, rather than in strictly private-sector operations. However, because government procurement is a major economic sector, many companies have been subjected to affirmative action requirements at one time or another.

In 1995, the U.S. Supreme Court decided that race-based preferences in government contracting are permissible only if the actual contractor has been the victim of discrimination—not merely if he or she is a member of a group that has historically been economically disadvantaged.

The Supreme Court agreed to hear the case of *Piscataway Township Board of Education* v. *Taxman*, #96-679, involving the important issue of whether it is legitimate for an employer to use layoffs (in this case, of a well-qualified white employee) as a tool to promote diversity in the workforce. However, before the High Court could decide the case (and render a decision that would make at least one side angry!) the two sides reached an out-of-court settlement on November 20, 1997.

California, which is a particularly large and economically influential state, has passed a law called Proposition 209, which forbids affirmative action in hiring and state public contracts. The Ninth Circuit upheld Proposition 209 in April, 1997, finding that it is not unconstitutional. The Supreme Court refused to hear the case, so the law remains valid.

The traditional principle is that a voluntary affirmative action program (as distinct from a quota program that actually excludes white males) is permissible if it is temporary, if it eliminates a manifest imbalance in traditionally segregated job categories, and if it is fair to non-minorities. The affirmative action plan should end once the manifest imbalance is eliminated; it should not be maintained afterwards in order to maintain a balanced work force.

Affirmative action programs have not been popular with the courts of the late 1990s. (This is understandable, given the large numbers of judges appointed during the Reagan and Bush administrations, when economic conservatives were more likely to be appointed than economic liberals.)

Recent cases say that employers should *not* set up an affirmative action program merely to enhance diversity within the workplace. However, if the court deems that there is a history of racism in a particular industry, an affirmative action program might be an acceptable corrective method.

23.7.1 Executive Order 11246

Under this Executive Order, government contractors and contractors on federally assisted construction projects worth over $10,000 must have a policy of furthering equal employment opportunity. If a contractor or subcontractor has over 50 employees, and the contract is worth over $50,000, the company must have a formal affirmative action program which must be submitted to the Office of Federal Contract Compliance (OFCCP) within 30 days of the OFCCP's request to see the program.

Contracts over $1 million require a preaward audit of the affirmative action program. See 41 CFR Part 60. There are separate, slightly different, rules for construction contractors. The policy must be disseminated both within and outside the firm, and a senior executive must be named as EEO director. The program must be reviewed and updated each year. The program must include a policy statement, dated and signed by the establishment's top official, to the effect that the company is committed to equal employment opportunity in recruitment, hiring, training, and promotion, and that selections will not be made based on race, color, religion, sex, or national origin unless a BFOQ is present.

The contractor company has to perform "utilization analysis": i.e., analyze each category of its workers to see if women and minorities are underrepresented as compared to the relevant local workforce. If so, the company must set goals and reasonably attainable targets, and make a good-faith effort to meet them. There must be an audit and reporting program to see if the plan is working, and statistics about EEO performance must be compiled and maintained.

In May, 1997, the Clinton administration announced a change in the way federal contracts would be awarded. Some race-based preferences would be eliminated, in favor of broader procurement policies. The new policy looks to studies of 80 industries done by the Department of Commerce to find economic sectors in which racial discrimination still exists, and also areas in which minority preferences should be scaled back because of over-representation of minority-owned firms.

If a company is charged with reverse discrimination because of its affirmative action program, it can cite as a defense that it just followed the EEOC's Guidelines on Affirmative Action. To qualify for this defense, the employer must have a written plan, and must act reasonably, i.e., taking reasonable action, based on reasonable self-analysis that leads to a reasonable conclusion that job bias problems actually exist and require correction. The employer's plan of action (e.g., improved recruitment; training so minority employees in low-level jobs can qualify for advancement) must be tailored to eliminate inequality, and must last only as long as it takes to eliminate the effects of past discrimination.

Chapter 24

THE AMERICANS WITH DISABILITIES ACT (ADA)

24.1 INTRODUCTION

The Americans with Disabilities Act of 1990 (42 USC §12101; regulations at 29 CFR §1630.1) forbids discrimination against a qualified individual with a disability. In addition to public accommodations requirements for handicap accessibility, the ADA covers discrimination in employment, employment-related practices, and benefits or other privileges of employment (including training, leave, and layoffs). Employers are not required to prefer disabled individuals in hiring; they must select on the basis of qualifications, but without discriminating against individuals with real or perceived disabilities.

There is no individual liability under the ADA: only the employer company is liable if and when discrimination occurs. Two federal agencies (the EEOC and the Department of Labor) share enforcement responsibilities for the statute.

➡ **TIP**

Employers are required to display posters explaining ADA rights in the workplace. These posters, like mandatory OSHA and FLSA postings (see page 441) are available without charge from the relevant enforcement agency.

An ADA plaintiff can win even if the decision to terminate him or her involved factors other than disability. In other words, a mixed-motive ADA case is possible, because the statute bans disability discrimination, not just discrimination solely on the basis of disability.

ADA charges must be filed with the EEOC or the state agency (see page 526 for an explanation of the process). The charge must be filed within 180 days of the last discriminatory act (in non-deferral states), or within 300 days of the last act (in deferral states). The Title VII investigation and conciliation procedures will be followed, and the ADA remedies are equivalent to Title VII remedies, with the distinction that reasonable accommodation can be ordered as an ADA remedy.

A District Court has ruled that an ADA hostile environment case can be maintained (in this case, by an asthmatic employee who charged that smoking rendered the work environment hostile) on the theory that the ADA derives from Title VII and therefore Title VII concepts are applicable. However, it has been held (by the Northern District of New York) that medical expert testimony about Multiple Chemical Sensitivity is not scientifically accepted enough to be introduced in an ADA case. MCS is a controversial syndrome involving a variety of symptoms allegedly caused by an immune system collapse triggered by excessive chemical exposure,

In the view of the Eleventh Circuit, only a current, and not an ex-employee, can assert ADA claims. In this view, subjecting a former employee to a cap on AIDS-related health benefits meant that the alleged discrimination occurred after termination of employment, at a time when he was too sick to work and thus no longer qualified within the ADA definition.

As of 9/30/96, the EEOC had received a total of 72,600 ADA charges. As of that date, the largest ADA award, in the case of *EEOC* v. *Complete Auto Transit*, was $5.5 million awarded by a Detroit jury. In that case, the plaintiff couldn't keep his old job as an auto hauler because of epilepsy. The Department of Transportation ruled that he would not be allowed to drive for six months. After he completed six months free of seizures, he applied to be reinstated in a job that did not involve driving, but was turned down. In the jury's view, he was capable of doing yard work. They awarded him $191,000 in back pay, close to a million dollars in compensatory damages, and over $4 million in punitive damages.

However, because of CRA '91's cap on compensatory and punitive damages (see page 542), he was only allowed to retain $491,000 plus interest. In other words, the jury's verdict was more a slap on the wrist than a financial disembowelment for the defendant company—but the company was still required to pay close to half a million dollars, which is no trivial amount.

Readers of this book are almost certainly subject to the ADA, because it covers employers who have 15 or more employees. Employers also face coverage under state laws forbidding handicap discrimination. It should also be noted that many state insurance codes forbid disability discrimination in insurance, including EGHPs.

The EEOC has published numerous hard-copy and on-line documents explaining its positions on ADA compliance. The Technical Assistance Manual is particularly detailed in its treatment. The EEOC has a technical assistance program (kept separate from its enforcement power) that will answer employers' questions about ADA duties and specific techniques for compliance. Before formal employee complaints arise, employers can apply to the EEOC for the use of Alternative Dispute Resolution (ADR) techniques to resolve disputes and keep them outside the court system.

24.1.1 The Rehabilitation Act

The ADA was preceded by the Rehabilitation Act of 1973, 29 United States Code §793 et.seq. The Rehab Act applies to federal contractors and subcontractors whose government contract involves more than $2,500, and to federal programs and federal grantees; it does not apply to the many businesses that are not involved in government contracting. Rehab Act §503 protects qualified handicapped applicants against discrimination in employment practices. However, the Act does not contain a private right of action: handicapped persons who charge that they were discrimination victims cannot sue the alleged discriminators. Another section, §504, does carry a private right of action, but its coverage is limited to discrimination solely on account of handicap in a federally financed program or activity.

Rehab Act §503 imposes an affirmative action requirement: federal contractors must have goals for hiring and promotion of qualified handicapped individuals. However, the Department of Labor does not have the power to enforce this requirement by bringing an administrative prosecution against companies that violate it.

24.2 UNDERSTANDING THE DEFINITION OF DISABILITY

The ADA defines a disability as a physical or mental impairment that substantially limits at least one major life activity. A record of such an impairment—or even the perception of having such an impairment—can trigger rights under the ADA even if, in fact, no limitation on activities actually exists.

A qualified individual with a disability is one who has the experience, education, and other criteria to be able to perform the essential functions of the job, either with or without accommodations made by the employer. Determinations must be made by considering the individual applicant or employee, not by forming or participating in assumptions about what a group of people (e.g., the blind, people with epilepsy) can do.

The statute is explicit: *current* drug use (or alcohol abuse) is not a disability, although employers are forbidden to discriminate against now-sober individuals who have abused substances in the past. According to the Fourth Circuit the ban on job discrimination is limited to "persons who have refrained from using drugs for some time"; drug use during the weeks and months prior to discharge is considered current, even if on the actual day of discharge the plaintiff is abstinent or even enrolled in a rehab program.

The Northern District of Texas took a somewhat different viewpoint, allowing an employer to bar former substance abusers from the jobs the employer deemed to be safety-sensitive (about 10% of all jobs). In this reading, a blanket ban is permissible if the employer can prove that it is impossible, or at least impractical, to make individual judgments about suitability for the job.

According to the EEOC's Website (**http://www.eeoc.gov**), determining which functions are essential to the job is a complex process involving several factors, e.g.,

- Expertise or skill needed to do that task
- Other employees available to perform that function (as individuals or as a team)
- If that function is the entire rationale of the job
- Time spent on that particular function
- Qualifications of people who held the same job in the past
- What would happen if a particular employee did *not* perform the function in question
- What the Collective Bargaining Agreement (if there is one) says about the function as it relates to the job.

24.3 PREEMPLOYMENT INQUIRIES

Employers are not allowed to ask job applicants about their disabilities, although it is permissible to tell the applicant what tasks the job entails, and elicit information about the applicant's ability to perform these tasks, with or without accommodation. In other words, it is illegitimate to ask "Have you ever had any back problems?" but it is legitimate to say that the job frequently calls for lifting 25-pound weights, and sometimes involves lifting weights of up to 100 pounds, and then to ask if the applicant can handle that.

At this stage, it's up to the applicant to request that the employer make a reasonable accommodation to the applicant's disability. If the need for the accommodation is not visibly obvious, the employer can legitimately ask for documentation of the disability from an objective health professional such as a physician or a psychiatrist.

The situation changes once the employer is prepared to extend a job offer to an applicant. At this stage, it is permissible to impose a uniformly-applied requirement that all new hires submit to a medical examination and/or answer questions about their disabilities. In other words, the employer cannot demand a medical examination until and unless it is prepared to hire the applicant. (Mental and physical disabilities are treated in the same way for this purpose.) If the medical examination results in withdrawal of the job offer (or the decision not to extend a previously contemplated job offer), the employer may face ADA charges and should prepare for its defense by proving that not hiring the applicant was a job-related decision necessary to business efficiency.

Furthermore, the employer can ask general questions about health status; the inquiry does not have to be tailored to the tasks encountered on the job. However, if the employer uses this information to screen out disabled potential employees, then it's up to the employer to be able to prove that there is a business necessity for the exclusion, and that it would not be practical to accommodate the potential employee's disability.

If the employer wants to impose a requirement of HIV testing, it must be applied uniformly to everyone who applies within a particular job category. It is not permissible to identify some applicants as appearing to be at risk of AIDS, and therefore requiring them (but not others) to take an HIV test. Even if results are positive, the employer cannot withdraw its conditional job offer on this basis, unless being HIV positive renders the applicant unable to perform the central functions of the job.

> ⇒ **TIP**
>
> 42 U.S. Code §12112 also requires employers to maintain the confidentiality of HIV test results which must be kept separate from other employee records (and even from other medical records). Access must be restricted to individuals with a real need to know: i.e., managers and supervisors who may have to offer reasonable accommodation to the needs of an HIV positive or AIDS-symptomatic employee; first aid personnel who may have to treat the HIV positive worker; and government officials who are assessing the company's record of compliance with the ADA.

Still other factors come into play once an applicant becomes an actual employee. The employer is permitted to make inquiries and demand medical examinations when there is objective evidence that the employee has a medical condition limiting the ability to perform essential job functions, or when the employee is dangerous enough to pose a direct threat. However, the scope of the inquiry or examination must be restricted to the employee's ability, or lack of it, to carry out essential job functions with or without reasonable accommodation.

The employer must keep disability-related information (whether voluntarily disclosed by an employee or applicant, or elicited by a permissible inquiry or medical examination) separate from other personnel files. In general, the employer must maintain the confidentiality of such material, although supervisors can be informed about necessary accommodations and any restrictions on the employee's work. Where a disability could call for emergency treatment, first aid and safety personnel can be warned in advance. Of course, information about disabilities must be disclosed in connection with the investigation of an ADA claim, and information can be released for insurance purposes or in connection with the investigation of a Worker's Compensation claim.

24.4 REASONABLE ACCOMMODATIONS

The employer is guilty of discrimination if it fails to make reasonable accommodations, although employers are not obligated to undergo undue hardship or make requested accommodations that are not reasonable. (For instance, employers don't have to relax their quality or quantity standards for productivity to help out disabled employees: see 29 CFR §1630.2(n).)

Employees can't demand accommodation in the abstract; *Willis* v. *Conopco Inc.*, 65 LW 2671 (11th Cir. 3/25/97) holds that the disabled individual must identify a specific accommodation that would make it possible to do the job, then show that it is reasonable. Even if the employer failed to investigate possible accommodations, the plaintiff still has to prove that reasonable accommodations were available. The claimant must prove his or her ability to carry out the essential job functions with accommodation; the employer merely has to show that following the employee's suggestion would impose undue hardship.

The ADA says that reasonable accommodations can include making the existing workplace accessible, or using job restructuring, part-time or modified work schedules, reassignment to a *vacant* position, use or modification of equipment or devices, providing qualified readers or interpreters (e.g., a reader for a blind person; a sign language interpreter for a deaf person).

24.4.1 Typical Accommodations

As an example of an accommodation that may be required, the Second Circuit cites providing a parking space for an employee whose mobility is limited. According to the Northern District of Illinois, an employee failed to show that a voice-activated computer system and split keyboard were reasonable accommodations to a carpal tunnel syndrome disability. The court accepted the employer's argument that split keyboards have not been proved helpful in this context, and voice activation would cost far more than the benefits it would provide.

An employee request for accommodation can be spoken rather than written; and the words "reasonable accommodation" need not be used by the employee.

⮕ TIP

The employer must retain records about requests for accommodation for one year after the request or personnel action, whichever is later. See 29 CFR §1602.14.

Reasonableness of a proposed accommodation depends on factors such as:

- the amount of work and money involved to make an accommodation;

- the financial resources of the employer;
- the number of people employed at the facility where accommodation is requested;
- how the proposed accommodation will affect other employees;
- how the operation where the accommodation is proposed relates to other facilities in a multi-facility operation.

> ➠ **TIP**
>
> The Department of Labor runs the Job Accommodation Network, which provides free consultations about how to implement accommodations on a case-by-case basis. JAN's toll-free telephone number is 1-800-ADA-WORK. Agencies that serve the disabled, and organizations concerned with vocational rehabilitation, can also provide insights into accommodations and assistive technologies.

The ADA is supposed to level the playing field, so qualified people can undertake jobs despite problems that limit their performance of major life activities. But employers are not required to impair their own business operations, or operate in order to create jobs for the disabled. The EEOC's position is that an accommodation, even if reasonable, generates undue hardship if it is a source of undue cost, is extensive, substantial, or disruptive, or would fundamentally alter the nature or operation of the business.

> ➠ **TIP**
>
> If the problem is cost, the EEOC's position is that it is incumbent on the employer to seek grant or other funding; the disabled applicant or employee should also be given the opportunity to provide the accommodation (e.g., bring his or her own specialized computer equipment) or pay the portion of the cost that exceeds what would be reasonable for the employer.

24.4.2 Effect on Other Employees

In a unionized workplace, the terms of the collective bargaining agreement are relevant in determining which functions are essential to which jobs, and what will be considered a reasonable accommodation. However, employers must not use the union contract as a pretext for avoiding required accommodations to the disabled. A couple of courts have looked at the obvious question: what happens if a disabled person wants to be transferred into a position held by someone who has more seniority under the collective bargaining agreement?

The Seventh and Eighth Circuits have favored the collective bargaining agreement, saying that employers do not have to "bump" more senior employees in order to accommodate disabled applicants or workers. On the other hand, the Ninth Circuit has said that some alterations in transfer preferences might have to be made to accommodate their needs.

If there is a job vacancy that the disabled person can handle, then transfer to that position can be an excellent way to meet the burden of accommodation. However, employers do not have a duty to create new jobs tailored to the capacities of disabled employees; nor do they have to promote disabled employees merely because of difficulties they have with job tasks.

Job restructuring is one way to accommodate employees, but once again, employers are not subjected to unreasonable burdens. It may be necessary to change the job description to shift marginal job functions to someone else, but there is no necessity to reassign the central functions of the job because if this were necessary, then the disabled job applicant or employee would not be qualified for the job. Furthermore, non-disabled employees are not required to pick up the slack by, in effect, doing part of the disabled person's job while receiving no additional compensation.

One possibility is to reassign the employee to a simpler job, carrying a lower grade or rating, that he or she can handle. But it is not reasonable for an employee to demand to retain the same grade or rating while being unable to perform the tasks that justify the rating. Nevertheless, it may be necessary to alter supervisory policies, for instance, by instructing a supervisor to give additional guidance or feedback to a disabled employee.

Courts usually take the position that showing up for work regularly, on the normal schedule, is central to what employment is all about. Therefore, it would probably not be necessary to institute a special flexible schedule, or allow work at home and telecommuting, just for disabled employees. If a disabled person is able to predict absences (e.g., chemotherapy every third Wednesday from 10 A.M. to 4 P.M., including travel and recovery time), it would probably be necessary to offer some flexibility in terms of allowing the employee time off that would have to be made up at another time. (If it's essential that someone be at the job during these hours, then the employee might not be qualified.)

On the other hand, if the employer has a track record of allowing flextime (to accommodate non-disabled employees' child care needs or simply for their convenience), or of allowing non-disabled employees access to part- or full-time telecommuting, then it will be hard for that employer to claim that such accommodation for a disabled employee is an undue burden.

Several cases treat leave of absence as a reasonable accommodation, at least given reasonable likelihood that the employee will recuperate during the leave and will be able to return to work.

Another issue that often arises is the question of expense. According to the President's Committee on Employment of People with Disabilities, the most common cost of accommodating disability is $200; more than half of accommodations cost less than $500. But, at the other end of the scale, accommodation can be very expensive: altering a production line or computer system, or hiring interpreters, for instance.

Theoretically, employers are supposed to consult with disabled applicants and employees and find out what accommodations they think are appropriate; on the other hand, the statute and regulations do not include any penalties for *not* engaging in this "informal, interactive process."

In 1996, two federal courts (the Second and Seventh Circuits) ruled that reasonable accommodation does not include transferring an employee so he or she would no longer have to report to a supervisor who is considered a cause of stress. In this view, the ADA is not required (or even able) to eliminate the strains inherent to employment, including working with distasteful colleagues.

Once an accommodation is made, employers don't have to worry that it will be set in stone. It's legitimate for an employer to terminate an accommodation if it becomes clear that even with it the employee will not be able to perform essential job functions.

24.5 WHAT CONSTITUTES DISABILITY?

The ADA's focus is on serious problems, not minor ones, so an impairment constitutes a disability if, and only if, it is severe enough and persistent enough (in the EEOC's view, lasting at least several months) to limit the performance of a major life activity.

A common and seemingly minor condition, such as nearsightedness, can be treated as a disability: see *Wilson* v. *Pennsylvania State Police Dept.*, 65 LW 2654 (E.D. Pa. 3/26/97), which permits a very nearsighted applicant for a state trooper position to pursue an ADA claim, based on the state of his eyesight without his powerful eyeglasses. The District Court for the District of Columbia deemed an IRS revenue officer to be disabled by being legally blind without glasses, although his corrected vision was 20/20. The District Court adopted the EEOC position that disability should be assessed without considering mitigating measures.

In late 1996, the Fourth Circuit ruled that an inability to lift 25 pounds is not a restriction in a major life activity. Therefore, it was legitimate to fire an employee who could not satisfy the lifting requirement.

Although morbid obesity (e.g., being 100 or more pounds over the weight deemed desirable for the individual's height) is likely to be treated as a disability for ADA purposes, ordinary overweight probably would not.

A late-1996 Eleventh Circuit case says that an employee was not disabled under the ADA definition because of cancer chemotherapy. The treatment was given only every three weeks and was well-tolerated; the employee's doctor said he was not disabled, and even the employee admitted that he was able to work.

⇛ **TIP**
_____

A better way to handle the situation might have been unpaid intermittent leave under the FMLA.

Infertility is a controversial case. Some courts hold that infertility is an impairment in the major life activity of reproduction, while others treat it as a normal physical variation that is in any case part of a personal decision to have children or avoid having children, and too personal for employer involvement.

The Fourth Circuit has decided that a person who is HIV positive but asymptomatic is not covered by the ADA. Such a person does not have an impairment, because he or she can carry out all major life activities.(This is certainly not the EEOC's position; the agency interprets the ADA to cover people who either have or are perceived to have an impairment, and sees the ADA as a major weapon against AIDS-related discrimination against qualified employees.)

The EEOC takes the position that the degree of impairment should be adjudicated by considering what the individual's functioning is like *without* medication or adaptive devices (which, of course, enlarges rather than restricts the number of individuals considered disabled). However, there are court decisions disagreeing with this view.

24.6 DISABILITY AND THE BENEFIT PLAN

Under the ADA, employers are permitted to make benefit plan decisions that are consistent with "legitimate underwriting or classification of risks based on sound actuarial principles, or actual or reasonably anticipated experience." However, otherwise legitimate risk-based practices are not allowable if they are used as a subterfuge to evade the ADA. If an employer does not provide an EGHP or other form of health insurance, there is no requirement that special insurance coverage be provided for the disabled, or that a plan be added to cover the employees, disabled and non-disabled alike.

The Act's legislative history and EEOC Interpretive Guidelines 1630.2(m) say that employers are not permitted to fire or refuse to hire a qualified individual with a disability because of the benefit plan's exclusions or limitations. Adverse employment decisions must not be based on anticipated cost increases in the benefit plan that result from an applicant's or employee's (or dependent's) health care needs. In other words, an employer cannot refuse to hire a designer on the grounds that the designer has a chronically ill child whose coverage will increase the cost of the group health plan.

The ADA legislative history permits employers to set preexisting condition limitations, limits on which treatments and procedures are covered, and limitations on the kind, extent, and levels of coverage set by risk classifications. If the health plan includes a limit on the number of doctor's office visits or treatments, and if that limitation is applied uniformly to all employees, it does not violate the ADA even if the effect is to cover less than all the visits or treatments required by disabled employees. (But see page 148 for generalized constraints on preexisting condition limitations, enacted by the Health Insurance Portability and Accountability Act of 1996.) Rate differentials can be imposed if they are based on legitimate underwriting factors.

A May 11, 1995 EEOC Notice (No. 915.002) permits a company's disability retirement plan to offer less favorable terms than its standard ("service") retirement plan—within limits. The benefits under the service plan can increase based on longer service, as long as ADA-eligible employees who are eligible for both disability and service retirement are not forced to choose the less favorable of the two retirement formulas. The Notice permits an employer to offer cost of living increases in the service plan but not in the disability plan. However, it is not permissible to have COLAs in both plans, but to adjust the benefit more frequently in the service plan than in the disability retirement plan.

In several cases, employees have been unsuccessful in using ERISA to challenge a "cap" (e.g., a limitation of $100,000 or $1 million) on health benefits payable for treatment of AIDS-related illnesses. Courts have found that there was no ERISA violation in imposing a cap only on HIV-related health care, or on capping HIV-related treatment at a lower level than treatment of other expensive illnesses.

The ADA does not specifically define the benefit plan's requirements with respect to HIV+ plan participants, although the general ADA rule is that disability cannot be used to deny access to health insurance coverage. If the plan has a uniformly applied exclusion of experimental treatments, it is legitimate to exclude experimental AIDS treatments. Interim EEOC guidelines, N-915.002, published in 1993, say that caps on AIDS treatment violate the ADA (although, as noted above, courts say that the caps do not violate ERISA).

However, a cap on AIDS-related benefits might be acceptable if the cap was not only necessary to prevent the insurance plan from becoming insolvent but was the only feasible step the employer could have taken for this purpose. A drastic increase in premiums, such that all or nearly all employees would lose coverage or would be unable to afford their copayments, might also justify a cap that was limited to AIDS-related benefits.

Courts are split on whether, before the effective date of the 1996 statute requiring parity in health plans for mental and physical conditions (see page 116), employers were guilty of ADA violations by imposing stricter limits on mental than physical disabilities in the company's long-term disability plan.

According to *Parker* v. *Metropolitan Life Ins. Co.*, 99 F.3d 181 (6th Cir. 10/25/96), having different durations for mental and physical disabilities in a LTD plan does violate the ADA unless the differential can be justified based on, e.g., experience (including reasonable predictions), actuarial factors, or bona fide risk classifications.

In contrast, *EEOC* v. *CNA Insurance Co.*, 96 F3d 1039 (7th Cir. 9/27/96), says that the ADA is not violated by a LTD plan that allows only two years of benefits for mental disability but no limit for physical disability. The court's rationale is that all employees, whatever their mental condition, were subject to the same limitations, and the employee sought relief under the wrong statute, in that the claim was really an ERISA allegation that the plan *should* have offered parity.

In some instances, a managed care organization (MCO) that provides a benefit plan may fit within the ADA definition of "employer," and thus become a potential defendant in an ADA suit. "Covered entities" are forbidden to discriminate against qualified individuals with a disability. From the employer's viewpoint, this is actually a positive development, because it is better for any liability to be shared among several defendants so that the employer doesn't have to shoulder the full burden.

Guidelines issued by the EEOC state that it considers MCOs to be employers because they provide fringe benefits (health insurance) and enter into contracts with employers (two key concepts within the ADA statute). The EEOC Guidelines say that an employer is liable whenever a disabled employee suffers discrimination resulting from the employer's contracts with an insurer, HMO, third party administrator, or any other organization that provides or administers the employees' health insurance. Another possibility is that the MCO will be sued under another part of the ADA: not the part relating to employment, but the part relating to public accommodations.

24.7 EMPLOYEE DISCIPLINE

It is justifiable for employers to set and maintain standards of conduct and performance, and to hold all employees (including those with ADA disabilities) to the same standards. For example, theft, vandalism, or workplace fights might be caused by a personality disorder. Although the employer cannot discriminate on the basis of the presence of the disorder, it can lawfully discipline any and all employees who violate standards of conduct that are related to the actual job and are consistent with business necessity.

Once again, the employer must apply the standards uniformly and objectively—not, for example, penalizing employees who have a psychiatric disability for conduct that would not cause sanctions if another employee acted the same way. The EEOC Guidance on mental disability takes the position that the employer can only enforce standards that are work-related: an employee's disheveled appearance and anti-social tendencies are relevant if the job involves customer contact, but not if the employee works in a back office or warehouse and is not in contact with the public. Also see *Palmer* v. *Circuit Court of Cook County*, 66 LW 1039 (7th Cir. 6/26/97), which says that the ADA does not protect violent or threatening acts, even if it could be argued that these acts are the results of a mental disability.

24.8 "DIRECT RISK" AS AN ADA DEFENSE

There is no obligation for employers to undergo risk in order to accommodate a disabled employee. A person who is dangerous to himself or to others (a category that includes not just a mentally unstable person who could commit violence in the workplace, but someone whose diabetes or seizure disorder causes him or her to black out while driving or operating a forklift) is not qualified and therefore need not be accommodated under the ADA.

An employer that wants to use the "direct threat" defense against an ADA claim must be prepared to explain how long the risk lasted, how likely it was to occur, how many people were affected, the potential seriousness of the risk, and related factors. Furthermore, the employer must be consistent, and must not consider conduct acceptable when performed by non-disabled employees, but dangerous and risky when performed by the disabled.

The EEOC Guidance on mental disability says that an individual poses a direct risk if an individualized assessment is made based on reasonable medical judgment, the most current medical knowledge, and/or the best available objective evidence. More specifically, the mere fact that a person has a history of psychiatric disability, or is currently under psychiatric treatment, is not enough to render that person a direct threat.

For people who take prescribed medications that can affect concentration or coordination, reasonable medical judgment must be applied to determine the likelihood of future safety problems (e.g., when driving or operating machinery). If a significant risk of substantial harm is present, the employer must attempt to control the risk via reasonable accommodations, if any are possible.

24.9 INTERACTION WITH OTHER STATUTES

Unfortunately, when the ADA was drafted, Congress failed to give appropriate attention to the way it would work with other statutes. So there are some very knotty problems involved when two or more employment statutes join (or collide). For example, the ADA doesn't say in so many words that employees can demand paid or unpaid leave as an accommodation. It isn't clear if they can require employers to permit them to use vacation time when they need time off for disability reasons or to get medical treatment.

The few cases that deal with the issue seem to suggest that the more likely the employee is to make a full recovery (given adequate rest or adequate time for treatment), the more likely it is that the employer will be required to grant the leave.

The EEOC has issued extensive guidance about the ADA, especially in 1997. However, it should be noted that Guidance represents the EEOC's position, which may be far more employee-oriented than courts would support. Thus, although an employer can't get into trouble by conforming to EEOC policy statements (and will certainly avert trouble from the EEOC by listening to it!), EEOC Guidance statements and EEOC internal policy manuals do not have the force of law. Therefore, it is quite possible that an employer can maintain policies that are not as extreme as the EEOC would suggest, without violating the statute and without being subjected to liability in court.

A February 12, 1997 EEOC Notice, Number 915.002, sets out the EEOC's rationale for stating that employees and ex-employees can legitimately make ADA claims (based on the assertion that they are qualified to perform essential job functions) at the same time that they apply for disability benefits (premised on inability to do gainful work). In the EEOC view, the two positions are not necessarily contradictory, because the ADA assumes that disabled people can work; disability programs assume that they can't.

According to the EEOC, the ADA's whole purpose is to call for individualized consideration of each individual's capacities, while Worker's Compensation, Social Security disability, and other disability programs focus on classes of disabled people (e.g., by drafting schedules of impairments), and the concept of accommodation is not involved. Nor do the disability-related programs distinguish between essential and marginal job tasks.

Depending on the facts of the case and state-law requirements, a person might be found eligible for Worker's Compensation as totally disabled (because he or she cannot do any kind of work for which there is a reasonable market) even though that person could perform the essential functions of certain jobs. As to those jobs, that person could be a qualified individual with a disability, and thus a potentially successful ADA plaintiff. The Social Security system has a special disability category for blind persons—even though, for ADA purposes, they are capable of performing many jobs, with or without accommodation.

A further complicating factor is that a person may apply for disability benefits under a welfare benefit plan offered through the job, and then be required to apply for Worker's Compensation or Social Security disability benefits as a condition of receiving benefits under the welfare plan. That way, the welfare plan can reduce its costs by offsetting the government benefits against the amount it would otherwise have to pay.

The EEOC's position is that even representations of disability made in a Worker's Compensation or disability hearing may not prevent the person making those representations from filing an ADA claim, because the questions posed at that hearing may be imprecise, or may focus on inability rather than employability. Furthermore, an individual may in effect be driven out of the workforce by outright discrimination or by the employer's refusal to make the reasonable accommodations that would have permitted continued employability. Yet another possibility is that, at the time the individual applied for disability benefits, he or she was in fact unable to work, but at an earlier or later time cited in the ADA claim, he or she could have worked if disability discrimination had not been exercised.

The EEOC also takes the position that it can be proper for workers to bring ADA claims not only on their own behalf, but in order to expose and correct workplace discrimination in a way that benefits others.

Some courts accept the EEOC argument that disability benefits and an ADA claim can coexist, because their purposes and standards are different. However, there is authority in the courts requiring potential plaintiffs to pick one position and stick to it: such courts take the position that a disability claim rules out an ADA claim.

24.9.1 The Special Case of Psychiatric Disabilities

A later EEOC Notice, also identified as 915.002, was issued on March 25, 1997, to explain the EEOC's position on the ADA status of psychiatric disabilities. The question is a significant one; a footnote to this report states that about one-eighth of the ADA charges filed with the EEOC from July 1992-September 1996 related to psychiatric impairments. The ADA regulations define mental impairment as developmental disability, learning disabilities, organic brain syndrome, and neurological disease (conditions seldom found in the workplace) and also mental or psychological disorders such as emotional or mental illness, which do affect many employees. The examples given by the EEOC are major depression, bipolar disorder, panic disorder, obsessive-compulsive disorder, post-traumatic stress disorder, schizophrenia, and personality disorders.

The first step in identifying mental disorders is the psychiatric profession's official compendium, *The Diagnostic and Statistical Manual of Mental Disorders*, 4th Edition (DSM-IV). However, consulting the DSM doesn't end the inquiry, because it covers quite a few disorders, some of which are not also covered by the ADA. The ADA specifically excludes current drug and alcohol abuse, compulsive gambling, some sexual disorders, and kleptomania, although these are discussed in the DSM-IV. (As noted above, a past history of substance abuse by a person who is now sober does constitute an ADA-covered condition.) Furthermore, individuals who are troubled but not classically mentally ill may seek treatment (e.g., family therapy); such individuals are not impaired for ADA purposes. An impairment may be present yet not covered by the ADA, if it is mild enough so that it does not substantially limit the impaired person's ability to work and carry out other major life activities.

The EEOC Guidance devotes a good deal of space to the subject of what is a mental impairment under the ADA. Mere traits and behaviors (e.g., stress, anger, unpunctuality, bad judgment), taken by themselves, are not mental impairments, although in some cases they are its result.

The Guidance deals with a question that frequently arises in the context of psychiatric disabilities: impairment of the major life activity of interacting with others. The test is whether, compared to an average person in the general population, the employee is significantly restricted in human interactions because of severe problems such as "consistently high levels of hostility, social withdrawal, or failure to communicate when necessary," with a long-term or potential long-term duration. Similar considerations are applied in assessing an alleged disability of substantial limitation in the ability to concentrate, or in the ability to get adequate sleep or care for one's self.

It's no exaggeration to say that the EEOC Guidance has been controversial. Negative articles appeared in both the *New York Times* and the *Wall Street Journal,* noting that employers were fearful of being accused of discrimination although they have no clear way of judging which employees have a psychiatric disability or what would constitute a reasonable accommodation. Furthermore, people who are not ill but are guilty of ordinary bad behavior might attempt to claim that they are qualified disabled individuals entitled to protection and insulation from the ordinary consequences of their conduct.

Chapter 25

THE FAMILY AND MEDICAL LEAVE ACT (FMLA)

25.1 INTRODUCTION

The Family and Medical Leave Act of 1993, 29 USC §2601, requires employers to provide up to 12 weeks' unpaid leave in each "leave year" (which can be a calendar year, plan year, or a 12-month period since the employee's last exercise of FMLA rights) when the employee is ill or is needed to care for a family member who is ill.

> ⇒ **TIP**
>
> If the employer changes its method of calculating the leave year, employees must be given at least 60 days' notice of the change.

FMLA leave can also be used by new parents (whether the family was enlarged by birth or adoption) and both parents can take FMLA leave. It's not just "maternity leave." It can also be taken for adoption or foster care hearings, but not for custody hearings.

> ⇒ **TIP**
>
> If the parents are unmarried, or if they are married but work for separate employers, then each is entitled to the full 12 weeks of FMLA leave. But if they are married and work for the same employer, it is not a violation for the employer to grant only a single 12-week leave for the couple, and require them to allocate it between them.

However, the 12-week limit applies per year, not per illness, so an employee who uses up his or her allowance is not entitled to demand additional leave if he, she, or a family member suffers another health problem later in the same year.

FMLA leave can be taken on account of one's own illness, or that of a spouse, child, parent, or step-parent. The federal law does not require granting leave to take care of a parent-in-law, although some state laws do. If you're reading this book, the FMLA probably covers your company: every employer that has 50 or more employees in each working day during each of 20 or more workweeks during the leave year is subject to the FMLA.

If, as a result of state law, a collective bargaining agreement, or company policy, the employee would be entitled to a certain amount of paid leave, that paid leave can legitimately be used to reduce the amount of FMLA leave the worker would otherwise be entitled to. The FMLA itself allows employers to require that employees use accrued vacation days, personal leave, or family leave before claiming FMLA leave. However, some state laws forbid this requirement to be imposed on a worker who has suffered a temporary disability, so check your applicable local rules.

25.2 NOTICE REQUIREMENTS

Employers must provide written notice of FMLA rights (see the standard EEOC notice, which must be posted in an easily visible workplace location). You can get copies of the notice from your local Wage and Hour Division office, or copy it from 29 CFR Part 825, Appendix C. The copy that is posted must be at least $8^1/_2 \times 11$". A cash penalty is imposed for failure to post. If a substantial portion of your workforce is not literate in English, the notice must also be translated into their own language and posted in that form as well.

FMLA information must also be included in the employee handbook, if the company has one. If this notice is defective, the employer can cure this fault by giving adequate written notice at the time an employee actually requests leave. Even if there is no handbook, employees are entitled to a written explanation of their rights when they request a leave.

According to 29 CFR §825.301(b)(1), the employer's notice to employees must include at least this much information:

- That the requested leave reduces the employee's "bank" of FMLA leave for the year
- Whether medical certification of the serious health condition will be required; consequences if the certification is not provided
- The fact that the employee has a right to substitute paid leave (if he or she is entitled to any) for FMLA leave; the extent to which the employer chooses to substitute paid leave; under what conditions

- The employee's right to reinstatement post-leave in a comparable job
- How the employee can pay health premiums while on leave
- Explanation of the employee's obligation to pay back premiums if he or she does not return to work after the leave
- Any requirements of getting a fitness-for-duty certificate before returning to work
- Limitations on the reinstatement right (if the employee is a key employee).

⇒ **TIP**

Although it is not a substitute for the required notice, employees can be referred to the DOL's toll-free FMLA hotline, (800) 959-FMLA, which provides a recorded explanation of FMLA rights and a mechanism for ordering pertinent publications. Employees who have Web access at home or in the office can view **http://www.dol.gov** for more FMLA information.

25.3 EFFECT OF LEAVE

The DOL's Wage and Hour Division published a Compliance Guide to the FMLA in June, 1993 (Wage and Hour Publication 1421). The Guide says that it's the employer's responsibility for designating paid leave as FMLA leave (i.e., reducing the amount of unpaid leave available in the balance of the year). Furthermore, this must be done, if at all, before the leave is completed; the employer can't re-characterize it later.

It constitutes a violation of the FMLA to count qualifying leave for any attendance policy where absences can lead to discipline or discharge. To avoid inadvertent violations, the Clark Boardman Callaghan Employment Alert recommends that line supervisors should be trained to refer all matters to the Human Resources department when a worker cites health factors as a reason for absence.

That way, the HR department can check with the employee to see if the leave qualifies as paid leave, if the employee wants to use vacation or comp time, or if the time off qualifies for FMLA status and the employee wants to use it as such. (It's possible that the employee will prefer simply to forgo pay for the leave time, if he or she has already exhausted the FMLA allocation or expects to need further time off during the FMLA leave year.) In FMLA situations, the HR department can instruct the employee to complete a medical certification form, preferably DOL Form WH-380 (certificate of health care provider).

Of course, employees can't provide advance notice of emergencies, but under the FMLA, employers can require 30 days' advance notice of predictable future needs for leave, e.g., parenthood leave or leave related to medical procedures scheduled in the future.

⇒ **TIP**

The Wage and Hour Division says that if the employee fails to give the 30 days' notice of a foreseeable leave, and has no excuse for the failure, the employer can legitimately refuse to let the leave begin until 30 days after the notice is finally given.

Nor is the employer required to accept the employee's unsupported word that a serious medical condition is present: the employer is entitled to ask for medical certification which is supposed to contain evidence of these facts:

- Scheduled date(s) of medical treatment
- Amount of time the treatment takes
- Recovery time associated with the treatment.

Under 29 CFR §2613(a), the best time to ask for certification is at the time the employee requests the leave. However, the employer can defer it for up to two days. Once the employer makes the request, the employee has 15 days to provide it.

Where the employee requests intermittent leave (see page 497 below) rather than taking a certain number of days off, the certification should also include the doctor's statement that intermittent leave is medically necessary, or at least will promote the employee's or family member's recovery from the underlying serious health condition.

As a general rule, the employer can make a reasonable demand for re-certification of the continuing serious nature of the health condition, although demanding certification more often than once every 30 days will be considered unreasonable unless:

- The employee requested an extension of the leave
- Circumstances have changed, so the initial certification is no longer accurate
- The employer has learned something that makes the original certification seem suspicious.

The Wage and Hour Division's compliance guide says that employees have a responsibility to try to schedule planned medical treatments (e.g., physical therapy; cancer chemotherapy) in a manner that will not unduly disrupt the employer company's operations.

There is an official form for the certification (Appendix B to 29 CFR Part 825), but its use is not mandatory. Employers or doctors can draft their own forms, but the employer can't require more information than the official form requires.

25.4 FMLA LEAVE AND BENEFITS

During leave, the general rule is that the employee does not accrue seniority or additional benefits, but the employer cannot deprive the employee of benefits that had already accrued prior to the leave (even if the benefits were informal and not part of an ERISA welfare benefit plan, or even a plan at all). Benefits continue to accrue if the FMLA leave runs concurrently with paid leave. Benefits under ERISA plans do not accrue during unpaid FMLA leave (although they do during concurrent paid leave), but the FMLA leave is not considered a break in service when pension eligibility is determined.

EGHPs must maintain the coverage, at the original level, for employees who are on FMLA leave. If the plan is contributory (employees must pay part of the premium), it's permissible for the plan to mandate continued contributions during FMLA leave. If the employee is more than 30 days late in paying the premium, health insurance coverage can legitimately be terminated.

> ⇒ **TIP**
>
> If this is done, but the employee returns to work and is reinstated, the re-employed person is entitled to immediate reinstatement in the EGHP, with no need to satisfy the plan's eligibility requirements a second time.

It's not uncommon for employees to quit instead of returning after leave (especially after parenthood leave). If that happens, the employer is entitled to recover the health premiums expended on the employee's behalf during the leave. However, if an employee files a health claim for treatment during the leave period, an otherwise allowable claim cannot be denied by reason of the employee's termination of employment.

Once an employee completes a period of FMLA leave, the statute mandates that the employer reinstate the employee in the old job, or provide another job with equivalent duties, pension rights, and benefits. An offer of re-employment unrelated to the original employment, or inferior in compensation, is not acceptable.

Just as there is an ADEA exemption for highly paid policy-makers, (see page 502), there is an FMLA reinstatement exception: it is not necessary to offer post-leave reinstatement to an employee who is a member of the highest-paid 10% of the workforce, if the employee decides not to return to employment after receiving notice from the employer; if the employer gives adequate notice of intention not to reinstate, or if the employer would suffer substantial economic harm as a result of the reinstatement.

See page 147 for a discussion of the way COBRA and the FMLA interact.

25.5 FMLA LITIGATION AND REMEDIES

The statute forbids employers to interfere with FMLA leave, or to retaliate against employees who do exercise their legal right to leave. According to the Department of Labor, of more than 6000 FMLA-related complaints received by the agency between the law's effective date and early 1997, the most prevalent cause for complaint was employer refusal to reinstate after a period of leave. About 90% of those complaints were resolved by the agency without litigation, usually after a single telephone call to the employer. (Overall, 95% of FMLA complaints are resolved by the employer coming back into compliance with the statute.)

In situations where conciliation is impossible, employees who are denied their FMLA rights are entitled to sue for damages or equitable relief, plus attorneys' fees and costs, up to a maximum of twice twelve weeks' compensation (defined to include benefits as well as straight salary) plus interest. The employee can sue without following the Title VII conciliation procedure, and without filing an administrative complaint. The FMLA statute of limitations is two years from the last violative event—three years, if the violation was a willful one.

If the employer did not act in "good faith," it may become liable to pay additional liquidated damages. There is no statutory definition of "good faith," so the Western District of Missouri adopted the FLSA standard: whether the defendant made a good-faith effort to determine and observe the rights of the plaintiff. This is a tough test to satisfy, and means that in the comparatively few litigated FMLA cases, there is a strong likelihood that liquidated damages will be awarded.

Although most of the remedies are equitable ones, the Southern District of Georgia says that jury trial is available in FMLA cases because the statute was drafted to resemble the Fair Labor Standards Act. (Actually, the FLSA doesn't say in so many words that jury trial is available to enforce it, but courts have interpreted it that way.)

An employer lost a 1996 District Court case because the employee handbook said that unpaid parenthood leave could be as long as 16 weeks, but failed to disclose that the right to reinstatement ended with the 12-week period of FMLA leave. The court deemed that the employer's inadequate notice served to entice employees into extending their leave and forfeiting their FMLA rights.

See page 517 for a discussion of mandatory arbitration of employee claims of discrimination and wrongful termination. This issue is just as controversial in the FMLA context as for other statutes. According to a recent Southern District of New York case, employees can litigate FMLA claims (and ADA claims) despite a provision in the employment contract mandating arbitration for any claim or controversy about the agreement. The court's reading was that this wording was not specific enough to put employees on notice about their FMLA and ADA claims.

In contrast, a Northern District of Texas case from about the same time holds that "any controversy or dispute" covering employment or the employment contract does cover FMLA claims. In the unionized workplace, *Smith* v. *CPC Foodservice*, 1997 WL 101756 (N.D. Ill. 3/5/97) says that a collective bargaining agreement statement that FMLA leaves will be granted in accordance with the law in effect "plugs in" the FMLA to the CBA's grievance and arbitration mechanism, thus precluding lawsuits.

According to *Petsche* v. *Home Federal Savings Bank*, 1997 WL 61270 (N.D. Ohio 2/4/97) the burden-shifting analysis used in Title VII cases (see page 536) also applies to the FMLA. Once the employee makes it seem that the employer has violated the FMLA, it's the employer's turn to deploy the evidence in its possession to demonstrate that the employee was not the victim of retaliation for exercising FMLA rights.

⇒ **TIP**

In a recent case, a jury (upheld by the Fourth Circuit) believed the plaintiff when she said she was fired for exercising her FMLA rights and taking maternity leave—but refused to award her any damages, because she didn't make any reasonable effort to find another job.

In addition to suits brought by employees, employers are at risk of suits filed by the DOL. (When the DOL sues, the employee rather than the agency receives the damages.) By May, 1997, the DOL had already received 8,000 complaints of employer non-compliance with the FMLA, and employees benefited by close to $6 million in FMLA-related damages.

25.6 INTERMITTENT LEAVE

Employees are entitled to a great deal of flexibility under the FMLA. As long as they give the appropriate notice of non-emergency conditions, and as long as they provide the required medical certification, employees can get not only conventional leave but "intermittent leave." In other words, an employee who has cancer doesn't have to stop working and claim disability and/or FMLA leave. He or she can take leave on every Tuesday afternoon and Wednesday morning, giving time to take chemotherapy treatment and time to recover.

Employees are entitled to the equivalent of 12 weeks of work: i.e., up to 480 hours a year for full-time workers, and an equivalent prorated amount for part-time workers (240 hours a year for a half-time employee). For hourly employees, the proration depends on scheduled hours of work. The FMLA regulations refer to, for exempts, the actual number of hours the employee usually works in a week (or in an average week, if the schedule varies). So an exempt worker who regularly puts in 45 or 50 hours a week (and, of course, doesn't earn overtime for the extra hours) will be entitled to additional intermittent leave because of this history.

All FMLA leaves have the potential for serious inconvenience to the employer; intermittent leaves are more inconvenient yet, because they impose extra burdens of tracking and recordkeeping. (On the other hand, when employees are present and working part of the time, the employer loses less productivity than if they were absent and had to be replaced.)

The rules for intermittent FMLA leave are slightly different from those for regular leave. It's against the law for employers to refuse parenthood leave, but they don't have to grant intermittent parenthood leave unless the child has a serious health condition, or unless a pregnant employee has severe morning sickness or needs time off for prenatal care. Employees can't get intermittent leave for voluntary treatments or procedures (cosmetic plastic surgery or dermatology treatments, for instance). Employers have an obligation to grant intermittent leave only if there is medical need for the leave, and intermittent leave or a reduced work schedule is the best way to handle it. (Of course, employers can voluntarily agree to grant intermittent leave even under circumstances where they could not be compelled to do so.) However, if an employee takes outright leave, the employer can require the employee to submit a medical report about his or her fitness for work; that can't be required during intermittent leave.

Employers are allowed to mandate a temporary transfer during the intermittent leave period, to a job that is more compatible with the leave periods than the employee's original job. The employee has to get the same hourly rate after the transfer as before, but not necessarily the same total salary (because hours have changed), and the duties of the transfer job do not have to be equivalent to those of the prior job. (An employee who is reinstated after a full-time leave must be offered a job with equivalent duties to the old job.) But once the need for intermittent leave ends, the transferred employee must be offered reinstatement in the old job or a comparable job. Furthermore, it is a violation of the FMLA for employers to use the transfers deliberately as a way to discourage the use of FMLA leave or to punish those who use it. See 29 CFR §825.205.

⟹ TIP

The employer can set the minimum span of intermittent leave as the shortest period (but not more than one hour) that the employer's payroll system can accommodate. If your payroll system is not sufficiently flexible or sophisticated enough to cope with absences of less than a day, it's OK to add up the periods of intermittent leave until they total a full day, then deduct a day's pay from the worker's pay check. But give employees advance written notice if this is your policy, and make sure they sign the notice so they are on record as being aware of this policy.

Originally, there was a "glitch" in the system: the DOL took the position that if the employer allowed partial-day FMLA leave, it therefore converted its exempt employees into non-exempts entitled to payments of up to two years' worth of back overtime. However, the FMLA text now reads (at 29 U.S. Code §2612(c)) that allowing partial-day leave, or even docking the exempt worker's pay for the time taken, does not convert him or her into a non-exempt, potential recipient of overtime pay.

Once you analyze the entitlement to FMLA leave, the job is not necessarily over. State law may impose even greater requirements for intermittent leave. If the employee is also a qualified person with a disability for ADA purposes (see page 483), then it may be necessary to grant even more than the equivalent of 12 weeks' intermittent FMLA leave as a means of reasonably accommodating the employee's disability.

Leave time around the time of childbirth could be related to a pregnancy-related disability, or could be used to get the home ready for the new baby and to care for the infant. Wage and Hour Division regulations say that it is not acceptable to take FMLA leave after taking a disability leave for pregnancy-related complications. However, if there is a period before or after delivery when the mother is physically unable to work, that period can be counted as leave for a serious illness even though it is also parenting leave. (This is especially significant if both parents work for the same employer, and would otherwise have to split a single 12-week leave period.)

25.7 FMLA INTERFACE WITH OTHER LAWS

In states that have laws requiring employers to provide paid maternity leave, or maternity leave at a reduced rate of pay, the entitlement to unpaid FMLA leave is over and above the entitlement to paid leave under state law. If the state requires employers to grant leave for purposes similar to but not covered by the FMLA (such as caring for an elderly person who is a friend or parent-in-law rather than one's own parent), the state-required leave does *not* reduce the entitlement to 12 weeks of FMLA leave, because the state-mandated leave was taken for non-FMLA purposes.

See 29 CFR §§825.701 and .702 for a discussion of the relationship between the FMLA and the ADA. For example, an employer could satisfy both statutes by offering a reduced work schedule to a disabled employee until he or she used up the 12 weeks of FMLA leave. After FMLA leave, employees are entitled to reinstatement in a job equivalent to the original job (including equivalent health benefits). However, if the disability makes it impossible for the employee to perform the original job, the employer can lawfully offer the employee a reasonable ADA accommodation in the form of a part-time job, with benefit entitlement equivalent to other part-time workers rather than equivalent to the original job.

The FMLA permits the employer to demand a physical exam to determine if a worker is able to be reinstated after an FMLA leave related to his or her own health condition. To satisfy the ADA as well, the examination must be job-related, not a comprehensive inventory of all physical conditions.

Chapter 26

THE AGE DISCRIMINATION IN EMPLOYMENT ACT (ADEA)

26.1 INTRODUCTION

A few years after the initial enactment of Title VII, another statute, the Age Discrimination Act of 1967 (ADEA), 29 USC §621 et.seq., was passed to protect older workers who are still able to carry out vital job functions. Employers with 20 or more employees are forbidden to discriminate against persons over 40 in hiring, compensation, or other employment-related areas.

In a limited range of situations, being under 40 is a bona fide occupational qualification. In other cases it may be possible to take adverse employment action against an older person based on an allowable RFOA (Reasonable Factor Other than Age). However, in most instances, the inquiry must be the individual's ability to perform the tasks involved in the job, not his or her age.

Employers are forbidden to fail or refuse to hire on the basis of age, discriminate as to compensation or the terms, conditions, or privileges of employment, or retaliate against employees who exercise ADEA rights. The statute has been interpreted as being broad enough to encompass an age-based failure to promote.

Merely asking questions to ascertain when an older employee plans to retire is not tantamount to pressure to force an involuntary retirement, so there has been no ADEA violation. If there is a good reason for a discharge or reduction in force (for instance, that the employee is unpleasant and difficult to work with), it does not violate the ADEA to urge him or her to accept retirement instead of being fired or RIFed. According to the Sixth Circuit, the company is offering a dignified exit, not committing discrimination.

In technical legal terms, the ADEA is a hybrid between civil rights law and labor law. This hybrid nature helps explain why there are still some unanswered questions about ADEA procedures and employer liability, and why it took so long for some of the answered questions to be resolved. Furthermore, there are a number of situations in which different courts have reached different answers to similar or apparently identical ADEA questions. A major conceptual problem: Title VII covers discrimination based on unalterable characteristics such as age and race; the ADEA covers discrimination based on the inevitable process of aging, under which everyone begins as a young person and eventually ages.

ADEA issues seem timely in an aging society, as lifespans are increasing and the proportion of the populace over age 65 (and especially over age 75) is at an all-time high. Interestingly enough, although one might predict that demographics, the ADEA (and more favorable tax treatment for people who retire late) would motivate employees to defer retirement long past the traditional age of 65, in fact the proportion of senior citizens in the workforce is actually declining, and early retirement (before 65, or even before 62) is becoming an increasingly popular choice.

At one time, it would have been accurate to say that the ADEA covered only hiring, firing, and salary, but not employee benefits. This analysis would have been based on a Supreme Court case, *Public Employees Retirement System of Ohio* v. *Betts*, 492 U.S. 158 (1989). In 1990, however, Congress stepped in and passed a statute, the Older Workers Benefit Protection Act, to make it clear that the ADEA *does* cover all terms and conditions of employment, including the full compensation package. (See page 559 for a discussion of OWBPA requirements for a valid release of an ADEA claim.) Thus, it becomes important to discover how the ADEA interacts with ERISA, insurance laws, and other statutes affecting compensation and benefits. There is also a troubled relationship between the ADEA and employer incentive programs for early retirement.

> ⇒ **TIP**
>
> Employers can usually defend against state law claims involving pensions and early retirement programs by raising the defense of ERISA preemption and getting the case removed to federal court. (See page 208 for a discussion of employers' pension obligations to older employees; page 191 for information about early retirement programs; and page 329 about the extent to which ERISA preempts state law claims.) However, if the plaintiff charges fraud rather than ordinary matters of plan administration, state law claims might be appropriate.

26.2 ADEA EXCEPTIONS

It's not surprising that the ADEA permits employers to discharge over-40 employees for good cause, such as poor work performance or dishonesty. Given employee misconduct, the employer is justified in taking negative actions, and is not acting with a discriminatory motive.

There is a minor exception to ADEA coverage for instances in which being under 40 is a bona fide occupational qualification (BFOQ): 29 U.S.Code §623(f)(1); 29 CFR §1625.5). These instances usually involve public safety (e.g., patrol officers and firefighters who need physical strength and quick reaction times) and therefore are of limited applicability in the private sector.

A more useful exception is the one for decisions made based on "reasonable factors other than age" (RFOAs). The employer must prove that it used objective, uniformly applied, job-related criteria to make the decision. There has been an increasing tendency for courts to accept employer's arguments that the decision was not, strictly speaking, based on age, but on other factors that tend to go along with age. Employers have also had some success in asserting the defense that older workers or applicants were overqualified, and would not be satisfied in an inferior job, or would decamp as soon as a better job presented itself.

For instance, an employee might be discharged in a cost-cutting drive. Because the oldest employee also had the longest employment history and the highest salary, discharging that employee saved more money than discharging a lower-paid (and, coincidentally, younger) person. The EEOC Regulations say that if the RFOA has a disparate impact on workers over 40, the employer has to prove that there was a business necessity for applying the criteria.

Employers are insulated against ADEA liability for actions taken in compliance with a bona fide seniority system or employee benefit plan: see 29 USC §623(f)(2) and Regulations at 29 CFR §1625.8. But this defense cannot be used to impose involuntary retirement or to justify failure to hire.

One group of employees can be subjected to compulsory retirement, even if they are still capable of performing the job: a person who has reached his or her 70th birthday, who was a bona fide executive or held a high policy-making position, for at least the two years prior to retirement.

Furthermore, for this exception to apply, the individual must have had immediate nonforfeitable annual retirement benefits of at least $44,000 for this exception to apply. An interesting 1991 case says that it can violate the ADEA to *increase* someone's pension to put him or her "over the top," even though in a sense the employee has been benefited rather than harmed by the employer's decision. The legislative history for the ADEA says that this exception is supposed to be quite narrow, permitting involuntary retirement only of a small group of top executives, not of ordinary middle managers.

The EEOC's Guidelines (see 29 CFR §1625.12(d)) define a bona fide policymaker this way:

- The person manages a whole enterprise, or at least a customarily recognized department or subdivision

- He or she directs the work of at least two employees

- The job regularly involves exercising discretionary power

- At least 80% of the employee's time (or 60%, in a retail or service business) is spent on managing the business rather than on other, lower-echelon tasks.

⇒ TIP

A federal District Court has ruled that it is *not* an ADEA violation to demote someone who would be forced to retire because of the executive exception if the demotion did not occur. The court said that the demotion came closer to satisfying the ADEA's objectives (enhanced employment opportunities for qualified older workers) than maintaining the individual's job level and discharging him.

26.2.1 International Issues

The coverage of the statute is limited to acts of discrimination that occur within the United States; even if a policy is created within the United States, by a U.S. company, and carried out elsewhere, it is not ADEA-covered. On the other hand, if a foreign company does business within the United States, its actions within this country are subject to the ADEA.

26.2.2 Non-Employees

ADEA cases are limited to the employment context, and do not cover all aspects of economic life. Thus, it could not be an ADEA violation to use age to refuse an automobile dealership to a graduate of a car company's Minority Dealership Development Program. The Fourth Circuit reached this decision because the would-be dealer was not employed by the car company (even though he received a stipend during the training program) and if he had been granted a dealership, that would have been a business contract rather than an employment relationship.

If a salesperson is genuinely an independent contractor and not an employee, then he or she is not covered by the ADEA. On the other hand, the Second Circuit has ruled that members of a corporation's Board of Directors who work full time as corporate managers or officers, and report to senior board members, are entitled to the protection of the ADEA.

Most ADEA cases are disparate treatment cases, i.e., the plaintiff charges that age was a (not necessarily the only) determining factor in subjecting him or her to adverse employment action. However, a disparate impact ADEA case is also permitted, at least by some courts, as is a hostile work environment claim (on the theory that the ADEA is based on Title VII, which permits hostile work environment claims).

Consult your attorney if you are confronted by a disparate impact ADEA claim: in 1996 and 1997, several federal Circuit Courts questioned or limited their validity. According to the Tenth Circuit, the Civil Rights Act of 1991 could have, but failed to, authorize disparate impact ADEA claims, thus showing that Congress doesn't believe such cases should be brought. The ADEA statute itself refers to a defense of "reasonable factors other than age" (a provision that is not paralleled in other anti-discrimination statutes), and some courts believe that this allows employers to maintain employment practices that do not intend discrimination, but do have a disparate impact on older workers.

Although the ADEA statute refers to "employees," it has been held that retirees (charging their union with violating the ADEA by amending the health plan to exclude retirees who are over 65 and thus Medicare-eligible) have standing to sue even though they are no longer current employees.

In a RIF situation, the employer is trying to reduce the number of people on its payroll, so the ADEA plaintiff's contention is that he or she was selected for termination based on improper age-related reasons—and was not replaced by anyone.

> ⏩ **TIP**
>
> An employee is not "replaced" if his or her job is eliminated completely, or if job tasks are assigned to one or more other employees in addition to their other work. An employee is replaced if, and only if, someone else takes over all the functions of the original employee's job.

Although employees may prefer to sue in state courts (where it can be quicker to get the case before a jury, and where remedies can be broader), attempts to sue in state court for age-based wrongful discharge will probably be unsuccessful, because the federal and state statutes dealing specifically with age discrimination preclude the possibility of wrongful termination suits.

26.3 THE ADEA PLAINTIFF'S BURDEN OF PROOF

In other termination situations, the over-40 employee *is* replaced. In 1996, the Supreme Court resolved the question of whether success in the ADEA action depends on proof of replacement by someone under 40 (i.e., not in the protected group). In *O'Connor v. Consolidated Coin Caterers Corp.*, #95-354, 116 S.Ct. 1307 (1997) the Supreme Court said that it is possible (although difficult) to win an ADEA case by showing replacement by someone else over 40, as long as improper age-related motives are shown (e.g., that the replacement was selected precisely because he or she will soon retire, thus "purging" the workplace of older people).

The ADEA plaintiff does not have to prove that the employer knew the plaintiff's exact age.

As you have seen, the problem of who has to prove what in a discrimination case is a tough one. Like a basketball game, each side switches frequently from offense to defense. By and large, proof is the plaintiff's problem, but if an employer claims a BFOQ, that is an affirmative defense—and the party asserting an affirmative defense also has the responsibility of proving it.

In 1993, the Supreme Court set a new standard for proving ADEA cases based on age-related factors rather than on pure age itself. What if, for instance, an employee charges that he was subjected to adverse employment action not precisely because he is 57 years old, but because his long tenure with the company and many promotions entitle him to an extremely high salary and generous benefit package, and the company replaced him with a newcomer who has less experience and therefore works less expensively?

The key case is *Hazen Paper Co.* v. *Biggins*, 507 U.S. 604 (1993), which requires the plaintiff to prove that age (and not just age-related factors) influenced the employer's decision. Age-related factors are not the same as age. For instance, a 30-year-old can't have 30 years' employment experience with the same company—but an employee with 20 years seniority might be only 38, and therefore have more seniority than a 50-year-old who has only worked for the company for 10 years. In that example, the 38-year-old would be more expensive in terms of the allegedly age-related factors of higher salary and benefits.

A recent article provides guidance about two important issues: how to defend against an age discrimination plaintiff's case that is statistically based, and how to make it clear to a court that age-biased remarks cited by the employee were casual utterances that did not influence the employment decision.

According to the Eleventh Circuit, laid-off older workers don't always have to be rehired or offered a transfer to a new job, but they must at least be considered for rehiring, not rejected on the basis of age. Therefore, a prima facie case is made out when a younger employee is hired or transferred to replace an older employee who was RIFed.

In a disparate treatment age discrimination case, the plaintiff can succeed by having an adequate amount of either direct or indirect evidence, but the burden of proof, and the way it shifts, is different for direct and indirect evidence. Direct evidence of discrimination doesn't require the judge or jury to use any presumptions or make any inferences. Indirect evidence requires an interpretation of the employer's actions and statements.

Another key Supreme Court case, *Price Waterhouse* v. *Hopkins*, 490 US 228 (1989) says that plaintiffs who have direct evidence of discrimination can force employers to prove that they would have fired or otherwise acted against the plaintiff even without discrimination. But without direct evidence, the conventional three-step pretextuality analysis applies. That is to say, first the plaintiff produces a prima facie case (i.e., enough evidence of discrimination to make that inference believable). Next, the defendant corporation steps up to bat, and demonstrates a legitimate non-discriminatory reason for the action. But the plaintiff still has another chance: he or she can prove that the stated non-discriminatory reason is merely a pretext for discrimination.

Hopkins also covers mixed-motive cases, those in which the employer had several motivations, and allegedly age discrimination was one of them. To win an ADEA case, *Hopkins* requires the plaintiff to show that age is a substantial factor in the decision, but not necessarily the only one or even the most salient one. But the employer can offer a defense (by a preponderance of the evidence, not necessarily beyond a reasonable doubt) that it would have taken the same employment decision against the older employee even if age had not been used as a criterion.

➠ TIP

The Civil Rights Act of 1991 (see page 542) overruled *Hopkins* with respect to Title VII plaintiffs, but not for ADEA plaintiffs.

St. Mary's Honor Center v. *Hicks*, 113 S.Ct. 2742 (1993) says that the plaintiff always has the "ultimate burden of persuasion." So if the judge or jury (whichever is responsible for determining the facts of the case) don't believe the employer's explanation why its conduct was legitimate, the plaintiff could still lose—if the plaintiff simply fails to offer enough evidence. (This builds on an earlier Supreme Court case, *Texas Department of Community Affairs* v. *Burdine*, 450 U.S. 248 (1981), which says that the defendant can win just by creating a genuine issue of fact; the jury doesn't have to believe that the asserted legitimate, nondiscriminatory motives were actually applied by the defendant, merely that the plaintiff has not ruled them out.) The *Hicks* standard is sometimes called "pretext-plus": the plaintiff has to do more than show the defendant's excuses are a mere pretext for discrimination.

26.3.1 The ADEA Prima Facie Case

The basic prima facie case for an ADEA lawsuit is:

- The plaintiff belongs to the protected group (i.e., is over 40)
- The plaintiff was qualified for the position he or she held or applied for
- The plaintiff was discharged, not hired, demoted, deprived of a raise, or otherwise disfavored because of age
- (In appropriate cases) The plaintiff was replaced—especially by someone under 40 (although, as you've seen above, it is not absolutely necessary that the replacement be outside the protected group). Plaintiffs who charge a

discriminatory RIF have to show that age was a factor in choosing them for termination (although they need not prove that age was the *only* factor), or at least that the employer was not age-neutral in selecting employees to be RIFed. However, it's pretty simple for employers to defend against discriminatory RIF accusations, merely by showing good economic reason for cutting back.

⇒ **TIP**

The employer just has to show that reducing the workforce made good economic sense. It doesn't have to claim that it was at the brink of bankruptcy without the reductions.

- Depending on the type of case, where it is heard, and the individual facts, the plaintiff may have to prove that his or her own qualifications and/or job performance were satisfactory—or *better* than the performance of younger employees or of the replacement worker.

Direct evidence of age discrimination is hard to find—not least because even if employers do practice discrimination, they usually have enough sophistication to conceal it. Therefore, as a practical matter, most age discrimination plaintiffs will introduce (or attempt to introduce) statistical evidence to support the discrimination claim, will cite remarks by executives and supervisors as evidence of discrimination, or both. Statistics are especially useful in proving a disparate impact case (one where the plaintiff charges that a policy that appears to be neutral and non-discriminatory actually has an unfair impact on a protected group of employees).

However, the trend in recent court cases has been to reduce the amount of credence given to statistics, for various reasons. In a very small workplace, for instance, it is impossible to derive a statistically valid sample. If there were only 25 employees to start with, and the plaintiff and three other employees were discharged, the sample is simply too small to come to any meaningful conclusions. Even a workplace with several hundred employees may be too small to generate valid statistics. Furthermore, the statistics must compare groups that are truly comparable. Employment actions taken with respect to clerical workers don't prove much about the treatment of professional scientists, and vice versa.

Plaintiffs frequently want to introduce testimony about age-related statements in the workplace, similar to sexual harassment plaintiffs' intention to introduce testimony about sexually hostile remarks in the workplace. The current trend is for courts to treat many age-related statements as "stray remarks" that are not evidence of discrimination, unless the statements were made by someone with a real role in making employment decisions, and unless the remarks show real hostility to the plaintiff, not just cliches or truisms about the aging process. Remarks remote in time from the employment decision are less likely to be admissible than ones close in time.

Don't forget that a 1995 Supreme Court case, *McKennon v. Nashville Banner Pub. Co.*, #93-1543 (1/24/95), allows employers to use "after-acquired evidence" of employee misconduct. In other words, if an employee is terminated and later charges the employer with discrimination, the employer can investigate what the employee really did during his or her tenure, and whether there were any lies on the job application or other misconduct. Then evidence of this misconduct (e.g., irregularities in expense accounts; sloppy work) can be introduced at the trial. The after-acquired evidence can't be used to dismiss the plaintiff's case without a full hearing, but it can reduce the remedies he or she can get.

26.4 THE ADEA AND SEVERANCE PAY

If many employees are terminated at once, based on economic needs of the employer, they probably will be offered severance pay based on their length of service. What if some of these employees are eligible for retirement, and will begin to collect pensions immediately? Is it legitimate for the employer to deny them severance pay, or to use the amount of severance pay to reduce the pension obligation?

The Older Workers Benefit Protection Act (OWBPA) allows employers to use retirement-related sums to reduce the amount of severance pay when the severance benefits are offered because of an event that is not related to age (for instance, when a plant closing occurs). The employer can reduce severance benefits by:

- Supplemental unemployment insurance benefits
- Additional pension benefits offered solely because of the severance event, to people who are eligible to retire with a full pension at the time of the event
- Retiree health benefits payable to people who qualify for a full pension at the time of the severance event.

It could be difficult to calculate the value of benefits, so the OWBPA includes a formula. When retiree health benefits are offered for an indefinite period, the benefit is deemed to be worth $24,000 for those over 65, $48,000 for those under 65. If benefits are offered for a limited period, the employer can offset $750 per year (employees over 65) and $3000 per year (younger employees), respectively. If the employer uses insurance to provide the benefits, the insurance premium reduces the amount that the employer can offset against severance benefits.

> **⮕ TIP**
>
> If the employer says that retiree health benefits will be provided, and offsets their value against the severance pay, but fails to provide them, there is a statutory provision (29 USC §623(l)(2)(F)) that allows the employee to sue for specific performance (i.e., to make the employer provide the benefits). This right is in addition to any other remedies the individual might have.

However, according to the Eleventh Circuit, Social Security benefits should not be used to reduce back pay under the ADEA (and neither should unemployment compensation). However, if the employee applies for Social Security benefits, that might be evidence that the employee didn't try hard enough to get another job—and *that* could be grounds for reducing the back pay award.

26.5 PENSION AND BENEFIT ISSUES

Even if the company never fires or demotes people because of their age, it may run into problems because of the way it handles pension and benefit issues. Since 1987, defined benefit plans have been obligated to continue to accrue benefits on behalf of all active participants. Contribution accrual on behalf of older participants cannot be slowed down or stopped merely on account of the participant's age.

In fact, even the participant's reaching normal retirement age is not a legal justification to terminate or reduce benefit accrual or contributions. However, it *is* permissible to cut back or stop once the participant has reached the maximum number of years of creditable service that the plan allows. This might seem like a meaningless distinction if you assume that everyone works for the same employer for the whole of his or her career—but it's a very meaningful distinction if, for instance, someone doesn't join your company until age 43, and the plan allows for a maximum of 30 years of creditable service.

> **⮕ TIP**
>
> If a plan subsidizes early retirement, it does not violate the ADEA to stop accruing additional benefits toward early retirement.

Originally, plan participants were given the option to remain at work as long as they wanted, collecting a salary but deferring the onset of their pension payments. In 1986, the rule was changed, and participants were penalized for failure to receive "minimum distributions" from their pension plans. The minimum distribution rules required pension payouts to begin no later than April 1 of the year following the year in which the participant attained age $70^1/_2$.

In 1996, the SBJPA eliminated the minimum distribution requirement for rank-and-file plan participants. However, the rule does remain in effect for IRAs, and for individuals who are 5% owners of the corporation sponsoring the plan. Under the SBJPA, older employees who continue to remain in the workforce can defer their initial pension payment until their actual retirement (whenever that may be); the size of the eventual payout must be adjusted actuarially to compensate for the delay.

Once the participant has reached normal retirement age, the actuarial equivalent of in-service distributions made to that participant is used to determine if the plan has satisfied its actuarial requirements. If the participant continues to work past normal retirement age, and the pension has not been placed into pay status but benefits are not suspended because of employment, any adjustment because of the deferred payout is applied in determining whether the accrual requirements have been met.

⟹ TIP

Although it may be presumed that everyone will retire at normal age, the presumption is not conclusive, and can be rebutted by the plaintiff. In a 1997 Eighth Circuit case, for example, an employee who was subjected to a discriminatory RIF just before reaching age 64 was awarded three years' back pay plus three years' front pay. She was in good health and needed to keep working to support herself, and she continued to look for work after the RIF, so the presumption of age-65 retirement was refuted.

26.5.1 Health Insurance

If the employer maintains a group health plan, the plan must cover over-65 employees on equal terms with younger employees: either the cost per employee must be the same, irrespective of age, or the employer must offer equal benefits. (The second approach is likely to be more costly than the first.) See page 154 for a discussion of the situations in which the EGHP remains the primary payer even though the employee is old enough to be eligible for Medicare.

Under ADEA §3(f)(2), an employer can abide by the terms of a bona fide employee benefit plan without violating the ADEA or the OWBPA. A bona fide plan is one which existed before the challenged employment action occurred; the terms of the plan must be observed; the plan cannot be used to force anyone into undesired retirement; and (unless the plan is a voluntary early retirement plan) the costs incurred, or the benefits paid, on behalf of older and younger employees must be equivalent.

The EEOC has expanded on these requirements in the Regulations appearing at 29 CFR §1625.10. To be bona fide, a plan must pay substantial benefits; the plan must actually pay benefits according to its own terms; and the employees must be given an accurate written description of the plan terms. (Meeting the ERISA Title I notification requirements will comply with the latter two requirements.)

Employers are not allowed to give themselves a windfall: even if it's legitimate to reduce the benefits available to older workers, the benefits must not be reduced more than the cost differential would justify. *Lyon* v. *Ohio Educational Association* permits an early retirement plan that gave the same benefit to young retirees who had accumulated 20 years of service as to older retirees. The court treated the greater cost of benefits to young retirees as a function of the plan's actuarial arrangements—not deliberate age discrimination.

The Regulations at §1625.10 give the employer two methods of comparing the costs of benefits for older and younger employees: for the whole "benefit package," or on a benefit-by-benefit basis. Within limits, the employer can choose whichever gives the more favorable results. The benefit-by-benefit approach cannot be used to substitute a new form of benefit from an existing benefit within the package.

On the other hand, the benefit package approach cannot be used for:

- Plans that are not subject to ADEA §4(f)(2)
- Pension or retirement plans
- Health insurance reductions greater than those justified by the benefit-by-benefit calculation
- Any change greater than the benefit-by-benefit analysis would allow, unless the employer adds a new benefit to compensate
- Any change that cannot be justified by significant age-related cost considerations, based on valid and reasonable cost data. Preferably this will come from the employer's own data over a representative number of years, but sometimes reasonably comparable data from other employers can be used.

Under ADEA §4(f)(2), the employer is allowed to compare costs quoted on the basis of five-year age brackets (e.g., employees aged 30–35). But the comparisons must be made using adjacent age brackets: you can't compare the costs of employees 65–70 with those 20–25.

- The ADEA allows employers to draw a distinction between compulsory plans (those for which employee participation is a condition of employment) and voluntary ones. A voluntary plan can require a greater contribution from older employees, just as long as the older employees pay the same proportion of the overall premium cost as younger employees do. In other words, if older employees generate 40% of the overall premium cost, they can be required to pay that 40%. In an employee-pay-all plan, the employer can legitimately require each employee to pay the full premium or other cost of the benefit (even if older employees have to pay a lot more than their younger counterparts, e.g., for long-term care insurance).

In an employer-pay-all plan, the employer would violate the ADEA if it chose to pay for younger employees but required older employees to contribute. In a contributory plan, the required contributions can lawfully increase with age, but the percentage of the premium paid must not increase (e.g., everyone pays 20% of the premium attributable to him- or herself). Older employees can also be given the choice of retaining the same level of benefits as younger employees, at the cost of contributing more to the plan.

ADEA §4(l)(3)(B) permits long-term disability benefits to be reduced by pension benefits for which the plaintiff is "eligible" at age 62 or normal retirement age. (The LTD benefit cannot be reduced by benefits that derive from voluntary employee contributions.) The Ninth Circuit interprets this to mean whatever benefits are payable at the same time the disability benefits are received—not the benefits an active worker would receive if he or she actually retired. Also see the Regulations at 29 CFR §1625.10(f)(1)(ii): the EEOC says that it will not pursue an ADEA claim in situations where disability benefits stop at 65 for disabilities occurring before 60, or stop five years after a disability that occurred after age 60.

The Supreme Court took the position in 1993 that age and years of service have to be analyzed separately for legal purposes. The implication that follows is that ADEA and ERISA issues also have to be analyzed separately. For instance, if an employer decides to fire everyone who has 20 or more years of service, that is not necessarily a matter of age discrimination (because someone who was hired at age 18 could have 20 years' service at age 38, while a 68-year-old worker could have been hired only five years earlier). If an employer fires an employee to prevent his or her pension from vesting, that violates ERISA . . . but not necessarily the ADEA.

This case also says that, for an employer to be guilty of a "willful" violation (and subject to liquidated damages), the employer must have known that its conduct violated the ADEA, or recklessly disregarded whether or not the conduct was violative. Under this test, an employee may have to pay simple damages, but not additional liquidated damages, in a case of a good-faith error in interpreting the statute.

PROCEDURE FOR DISCRIMINATION SUITS

27.1 INTRODUCTION

It is quite common for job applicants, employees, and ex-employees to believe that they have suffered some form of unlawful discrimination in the workplace. Some undeterminable percentage of the unhappy employees will consult a lawyer, file a union grievance, or otherwise attempt to pursue discrimination claims. A smaller percentage will actually file a discrimination claim with the applicable state or federal agency. Some of these claims will be abandoned; others will proceed to court.

However, as discussed below, many employees have voluntarily agreed not to bring lawsuits but to submit to arbitration instead; others are covered by contracts or subject to employer policies of mandatory arbitration. Finally, even cases that get to court are often dismissed by the court or turned down by a jury, because the employees are unable to satisfy the stringent standards of proof.

A lot of media attention goes to multi-million dollar judgments or jury verdicts in employment discrimination cases, but these are a very small percentage of all cases ever instituted or that could have been instituted. Most cases "wash out" along the way, or the judge or jury finds in favor of the employer, not the employee.

27.2 POTENTIAL CAUSES OF ACTION

Nevertheless, employers don't have to be paranoid to feel that they are forced to fight on many fronts. From the plaintiff's point of view, it makes sense to make as many claims as can be justified by any stretch of the legal imagination; after all, some of them may stick. Employees might charge that the employer was guilty of one or more of these improprieties:

- Violation of Title VII of the Civil Rights Act of 1964, i.e., discriminating against an employee on the grounds of race, sex, nationality, color, or pregnancy; sexual harassment is considered a type of sex discrimination

- Violation of the Pregnancy Discrimination Act (PDA), an addition to Title VII which forbids treating a qualified pregnant employee on less favorable terms than a non-pregnant employee who is otherwise similarly situated

- Violation of the Age Discrimination in Employment Act, i.e., discriminating against an individual who is age 40 or over, in any term or condition of employment (e.g., hiring, firing, promotion, salary, benefits)

- Wrongful refusal to reemploy a military veteran

- Violation of the Equal Pay Act: paying women less than men for *the same job*; this law does not permit "comparable worth" claims that charge that a typically female job is actually more valuable than a different job typically done by men.

- Retaliation against an employee who has filed a discrimination claim or cooperated in an investigation

- Wrongful discharge for a reason other than one of the above, for instance, discharging someone who "blew the whistle" on corporate wrongdoing

- Violation of labor law, e.g., firing or imposing other negative employment consequences on an employee who is carrying out protected labor activity (such as being a union activist, or trying to organize a union). Employees who bring labor law claims in state court often find that their claims are either dismissed or removed to federal court, because in nearly all cases where a union contract must be interpreted, federal law preempts state law.

- Breach of contract, either an explicit, written contract such as an employment contract or a union contract, or of an implied contract. Here's where employers get into trouble, when the employee handbook or a job application contains material that employees interpret as contractual (such as a promise that no one will be discharged except for good cause, after a disciplinary process).

- Defamation, e.g., if the employer gives an unfavorable reference or makes unfavorable statements about a person in the press, and cannot assert the truth of the statement as a defense

- Interference with contractual relations, e.g., the employer prevents the ex-employee from getting a new job or setting up a successful business

- Infliction of emotional distress (either negligent or intentional), e.g., the employee charges that she has suffered nervous symptoms ever since a traumatic firing or incident of sexual harassment.

In general, the employee plaintiff's lawyer will figure out every charge that could reasonably be brought, and will bring them all at once (unless there is a strategic reason to concentrate on some of them and forgo the rest). Important legal questions may arise: which court the charges should have been brought in; whether all the prerequisites to bringing a charge have been satisfied; whether some of the claims are clearly improper from the legal standpoint and can be dismissed immediately without even assessing their factual validity.

If the case mixes tort and contract charges, the defendant may be able to get at least some of the charges dismissed. The statute of limitations (time period within which claims must be brought) is usually shorter for torts than for breach of contract actions.

The general rule is that the statute of limitations begins to run when the employee is actually terminated (or other negative employment action is taken) although it might start even earlier if the plaintiff is aware that the negative action will definitely occur in the future.

In a wrongful discharge case, specific performance of the employment agreement via reinstatement is not an available remedy. The normal remedy is back pay; front pay may also be available. However, an arbitrator might be able to offer reinstatement.

27.3 ARBITRATION AND ADR

If charges are filed, what is the proper mechanism for the employer to contest them and defend itself? There's a lot wrong with the court system—from every viewpoint. Litigation takes a long time, is very expensive, and does less than nothing to improve the smooth functioning of the workplace and a harmonious relationship between employers and employees!

There's a great deal of interest in finding ways to settle employer-employee conflicts faster, cheaper, and with less hostility. Alternative Dispute Resolution (ADR) methods are designed to meet these objectives. The Civil Rights Act of 1991 and the Americans with Disabilities Act both include language indicating that ADR is a worthwhile tool for handling discrimination charges.

ADR methods are supposed to be informal, and governed more by justice and fairness than by strict rules of legal procedure. Depending on the method of ADR, a knowledgeable, trustworthy person (or panel of such people) either makes a decision or helps the opponents work out a mutually acceptable decision together. Arbitration involves decision-making by the trustworthy person(s); mediation involves getting the parties to make their own agreement that they can both accept. It's been estimated that it takes an average of two and a half years to resolve an employment lawsuit, versus only one year to resolve a case through arbitration, and 90% of arbitration hearings are completed within two days or less.

> **⇒ TIP**
> _____
>
> All consequences of ADR systems must be considered. For instance, the Eighth Circuit has held that, when the employer adopts a mandatory arbitration policy, that shifts the operation away from strict at-will employment, and employees cannot be discharged without the employer showing "discernable cause" for the termination.

The employer and employee may have agreed that the ADR decision is final, and can be enforced by the court system but can't be challenged there. On the other hand, they may have agreed that the ADR is only a preliminary stage, and litigation is possible if one or both are dissatisfied with the ADR decision.

That's how ADR is supposed to work. But ADR systems are a little like computer systems: the temptation to add more complexities, bells, and whistles is irresistible. So some ADR systems have grown almost as complex and costly as litigation.

> **⇒ TIP**
> _____
>
> If an employee refuses the employer's offer to arbitrate, that could show that the employer was acting in good faith, with the result that the employee might not be able to collect damages for breach of the covenant of good faith and fair dealing.

27.3.1 AAA Arbitration

The American Arbitration Association has long been respected for its work in dispute resolution. In 1993, the AAA promulgated a major set of rules for mediation and arbitration with non-union employees, the *National Rules for the Resolution of Employment Disputes*. They were amended in 1996, to give employees additional due process protections.

> **⇒ TIP**
> _____
>
> If you want employee disputes to be handled under AAA rules and procedures, you can say that AAA rules will govern in employment applications, the employee handbook, and/or employment contracts. Approximately three million workers are subject to these arbitration plans.

Arbitration provisions can be drafted in many ways. Predispute arbitration occurs based on an agreement to arbitrate made before there was any dispute (e.g., as part of the employment contract); it can be either voluntary or mandatory. If voluntary, it is just one option available for resolving a later dispute; if mandatory, the employee is blocked from suing the employer. Postdispute arbitration is also a possibility: i.e., when a claim, such as a claim of discrimination or wrongful termination, is made, both parties agree to submit it to arbitration and thus bypass the court system.

Since 1996, AAA arbitrators have had the power to order discovery. In other words, either the employer or the employee can be ordered to produce documents, answer interrogatories (written lists of questions), or be deposed (appear and answer questions posed by an attorney). In the nature of things, employers have more documents that employees want to see (and more documents containing trade secrets and confidential matters) than employees have documents that employers want to see!

Under the new rules, any party can be represented by an attorney, so arbitration is not necessarily all that informal. The arbitrator has a duty to decide and make a written award within 30 days of the end of the hearing. The arbitrator has the power to award any remedy that he or she thinks is just, including ordering one side to pay the other side's costs and attorneys' fees.

The arbitrator has to be paid. In addition, the AAA charges a fee to administer the case. The fee depends on the size of the claim or counterclaim when it is filed (not based on any amendments made later).

As a general rule, the AAA will administer arbitration even if the employer unilaterally imposed the arbitration requirement as a condition of employment. However, the organization reserves the right to refuse to enforce unfair arbitration policies—those that do not provide basic due process protection to employees.

27.3.2 Securities Industry Arbitration

In a sense, the securities industry is a "test case" for arbitration, because over half a million industry employees had to sign the U-4 employment agreement as a condition of working in the industry (the only entire industry to have a uniform arbitration requirement), and it includes a mandatory arbitration clause. There have been some major sexual harassment lawsuits against brokerage firms, but they were brought by support staffers who were not required to sign the U-4 before being hired.

However, on August 7, 1997, the National Association of Securities Dealers (NASD) voted to eliminate mandatory arbitration of employment discrimination claims involving federal and state anti-discrimination statutes brought by registered brokers. The NASD proposal is that the U-4 form should be redrafted to let brokers either agree to mandatory arbitration or retain the right to bring discrimination suits. Any brokerage that entered into arbitration agreements with its employees would have to specify a forum that complies with the standards of the American Bar Association's Due Process Protocol. The change is scheduled to take effect one year after the SEC approves the change.

At about the same time, the EEOC ruled that it was unlawful for securities firm Smith Barney to impose mandatory arbitration on its employees, because arbitration deprived employees of certain rights available in litigation (such as keeping embarrassing or unfavorable material about the employee confidential).

27.3.3 EEOC ADR

The EEOC's position on alternative dispute resolution (ADR) and mandatory arbitration, in the context of employee claims against the employer, is discussed on page 524. However, at times the EEOC itself will engage in ADR with employers and employees, as an alternative to the normal charge processing methods. The EEOC has not published formal regulations on this subject, but did issue two policy statements in 1997.

Under these policy statements, the EEOC says that ADR is not appropriate in some cases. Examples are: a really important test case where the EEOC needs a published court decision to establish policy or set a precedent; if the dispute has significant implications for people who are not parties to the individual charge (for instance, other employees or employees of other companies in the same industry); or if the EEOC has to maintain an ongoing presence to monitor the situation.

The EEOC's position is that ADR is appropriately fair if:

- it is voluntary (not compelled);
- the EEOC offers help to employees who are confused about the process;
- decisions are made by a truly neutral arbitrator or mediator;
- the proceedings are confidential;
- the outcome of the process is an enforceable written agreement.

27.3.4 Factors that Favor Successful ADR

Successful ADR systems usually have several steps, including in-house procedures for resolving grievances before any outside party is involved. In-house resolutions can be speedy and inexpensive; there is always some degree of delay and expense involved in using a mediator or arbitrator, even though litigation would be much more time-consuming and expensive. The ADR system should specify whether the matter will be heard by one mediator or arbitrator or by a panel (usually three, although it could be another odd number to prevent even splits).

The ADR policy should specify not only the number but the qualifications of the mediators or arbitrators who will decide cases. It should also be clear which employees may use ADR to handle disputes, and which will be obligated to do so.

Which disputes are covered should also be spelled out —all employment related disputes? all federal statutory discrimination claims? only certain federal claims? claims that would be tried in state court if they were litigated?

An appropriate ADR policy should be fair to employees, providing them with the same degree of due process (although not the same level of formality) as litigation. They should have an adequate opportunity to make claims, to get evidence of employer actions, and to receive adequate remedies if the mediator or arbitrator decides in their favor.

The American Bar Association's "Due Process Protocol" includes these standards for fairness in mandatory arbitration claims:

- The employee is aware of the arbitration requirement and accepts it voluntarily
- The employee can be represented at arbitration by a lawyer, union representative, etc.
- The arbitrator has the power to order the employer to pay the employee's costs related to the arbitration. (Some courts take the position that since the employer was the party that wanted arbitration, the employee should not have to undergo any costs when arbitration is actually carried out.)

➠ TIP

Another possibility is for the system to be set up so that the employee never has to pay more than 50% of the cost of arbitration, or never has to pay more than one day's fee for the arbitrators.

- The employee has access to a full range of remedies.

27.3.5 Cases About Arbitration

Ironically (for a process that is supposed to be an informal alternative to litigation), there are many court decisions about arbitration and especially about arbitration clauses in employer-employee contracts. The "Steelworkers' Trilogy" of Supreme Court cases sets the basic principles:

- Courts, not arbitrators, determine issues of substantive arbitrability
- There is a presumption in favor of arbitrability: an issue will be arbitrable unless it can be proved that there's a good reason why it shouldn't be
- A court can't review the merits of an arbitration decision; all the court can do is decide whether the arbitration award "draws its essence" from the arbitration agreement.

Since then, however, the issue of arbitrability has frequently arisen in the courts. It's one thing for two businesses of roughly equal bargaining power to think it over and decide that, on the off-chance that they might have a problem with their business contract, the problem should be resolved by an arbitrator.

It's something else entirely when an employer unilaterally drafts an employment contract or an employee handbook clause that requires arbitration of grievances. If a union contract is involved, at least representatives of the employees were involved in drafting, but that doesn't mean that each individual employee likes every provision of the collective bargaining agreement.

Therefore, while many employers find it worthwhile to include arbitration clauses in their agreements and handbooks, they don't always find smooth sailing, and they can't always bypass the court system just because they want to. The advantages of arbitration are a quicker resolution of the question (with less potential for bad publicity threatened by a major lawsuit), lower legal fees, and, often, a lower recovery if the employee wins the case.

That's because some state law causes of action permit punitive damages and attorneys' fee awards that are usually ruled out in arbitration. Arbitrators are selected from the business and professional communities, and are less likely to succumb to emotional appeals than lay juries. Furthermore, some claims may be too late for arbitration, but would be allowed in the court system, so the employer can get the claims dismissed if they are arbitrated but not if they are litigated.

The Supreme Court *Gilmer* v. *Interstate/Johnson Lane Corp.* decision, 500 U.S. 20 (1991) says that arbitration requirements can be valid in the employment context as long as there is a neutral arbitrator who makes a written award, and discovery and adequate remedies are available via arbitration. (Before the Supreme Court issued its decision, arbitration clauses in employment agreements weren't illegal, but didn't protect the employer either, because courts would never enforce arbitration clauses against employees who signed the clauses but who wanted a court to hear their claims.)

After this watershed case, courts have usually upheld agreements that impose a predispute requirement of arbitration as long as the agreements themselves are fair, nothing prevents the arbitration process from being carried out fairly, and the employer was not greedy or "overreaching" in imposing the arbitration requirement.

A D.C. Circuit case says that it's all right for an employer to impose mandatory arbitration of employment claims as a condition of hiring, as long as the *Gilmer* tests are met, and as long as the employer pays all the costs and fees involved in arbitration.

According to the Fifth Circuit, mandatory arbitration of age discrimination claims is permissible, and does not violate the Older Worker's Benefit Protection Act (OWBPA; see page 559). The Fourth Circuit believes that Congress intended FMLA claims to be arbitrable, and enforced an arbitration clause in an employment contract. Although the contract says that agreeing to arbitration is a condition of continued employment, the employer can still use the arbitration clause after the claimant ceases to be an employee.

A 1997 Ninth Circuit case says that, where an employer unilaterally drafted the employee handbook to include an arbitration clause, the employee did not waive the right to bring ADA charges by signing a statement that he read and understood the handbook. First, there was no informed, voluntary waiver of ADA rights; second, "understanding" a document is not the same as agreeing to be bound by its provisions.

In another handbook case, the employee was permitted to litigate because, although the employee handbook included a mandatory arbitration provision, the employer retained the right to amend the handbook at will. The court interpreted this to mean that the employer did not intend to be bound by the original terms of the handbook, and therefore the employee could not be bound either. But an arbitration clause found in an employee handbook was upheld in another case, even though the employer also retained the right to amend or modify at any time, and the employer disclaimed any treatment of the handbook as an employment contract. The deciding factor was the separate "acknowledgment form" that the employee signed, acknowledging the obligation of binding arbitration in lieu of litigation; in the court's view, this separately signed document put the employee on notice that important issues were involved.

A job *application* that says that the employer won't consider hiring someone unless he or she agrees to arbitrate job-related claims is void because there is no consideration (exchange of value). The employer didn't promise to do anything (including give serious consideration to the application) if the applicant *did* agree to arbitration. The situation would be different if an actual job offer were being made, contingent on signing the arbitration agreement.

In 1996, the Fourth Circuit said that a collective bargaining agreement that mandates arbitration of claims of sex discrimination and disability discrimination can be enforced against a union member who wants to sue for violations of Title VII and the ADEA. The District Court for the District of Connecticut decided that a 42 USC §1981 claim of race-based job bias (see page 459) was a "federal law discrimination claim" and therefore, because of the CBA, must be arbitrated.

But, in contrast, the Seventh Circuit decided in 1997 that a collective bargaining agreement can't compel employees (who may have been opposed to part or all of the agreement's terms) to arbitrate their statutory federal discrimination claims. Even back in 1994, the Ninth Circuit did not require arbitration of sex discrimination claims, on the grounds that a boilerplate arbitration clause buried within a contract was not conspicuous enough to warn employees that important rights were forfeited

Of course, if the employee is the one who initiates the arbitration, he or she will be bound by the arbitrator's decision; the controversial part is what happens to employees who are forced to arbitrate their cases when they'd rather go to court.

Arbitration, although somewhat less formal than litigation, is still a formal system with defined rules and an outside decision-maker. An employer's internal grievance procedure does not constitute arbitration, and therefore, in the view of a California court, an employee can pursue a claim of wrongful termination based on race and sex discrimination in the court system, because agreement to use the internal grievance procedure did not constitute consent to arbitration.

An arbitration clause imposed by one employer can operate for the benefit of its successors. An agreement signed by an employee with the owner of a hospital barred an Americans with Disabilities Act suit against a later purchaser of the same hospital, on the grounds that the new employer inherited the old employer's arbitration clauses as well as liability for its actions vis-à-vis employees.

In 1996, the Second Circuit ruled that a company was not guilty of retaliation merely because it had a policy of terminating its internal grievance procedures and sending the file to the corporate legal department as soon as an employee claim became the subject of an agency charge or litigation, because referring the file to the legal department did not harm the complaining employee.

Fraud can entitle employees to litigate their claims rather than go through the arbitration procedure. Such a situation arose in a mid-1997 California case. An HMO claimed that its arbitration procedure was "speedy" when in fact getting a claim to an arbitrator took much longer than purported (in this case, two years instead of two months, by which time the patient had died).

27.3.6 1997 EEOC Guidance

The EEOC's view is that arbitration should be a choice available to employees; they should not be forced to arbitrate workplace claims if they believe that litigation would offer better results. On July 10, 1997, the EEOC released a document (designed as internal policy guidance for its offices) telling its workers to continue processing discrimination charges, and even to take them to court in appropriate instances, even if the complaining employee works in an industry or operation that imposes mandatory arbitration. (According to the EEOC, mandatory arbitration is common in retail trade, restaurants and hotels, health care, and communications, as well as in the securities industry.)

The EEOC opposes mandatory arbitration because it values the role of courts in setting precedents that extend beyond the practices of one employer. Arbitration also lacks the public disclosure effect of a discrimination suit (fear of bad publicity could encourage some employers to eliminate discrimination). Also, employers use the arbitration system repeatedly, so they gain sophistication that helps them present their case; and arbitrators may be influenced by a desire to favor employers, who might give them more business in the future.

27.3.7 Handling Grievances in the Unionized Workplace

Most of today's collective bargaining agreements (CBAs) lay out the grievance procedures, leading up to binding arbitration, that must be followed to discipline an employee. For instance, the employee's supervisor may think that a warning, or a suspension with or without pay is justified; the employee doesn't think this is fair.

Or the employee may charge the employer with doing something unfair, such as requiring the employee to work unwanted overtime hours, or not permitting the employee to work overtime hours he or she has bid for. Usually the contract protects the employees against discharge unless good cause is present.

⇒ **TIP**

Some non-union companies voluntarily adopt similar grievance procedures, on the theory that employees will have far less incentive to unionize if they are protected against arbitrary discharge with no need to pay union dues.

Typically, the first grievance step is for the employee to approach his or her supervisor, or for the supervisor to initiate disciplinary proceedings. The employee can usually ask to be represented by the shop steward or other union representative. The supervisor then makes a decision about the question and records it in writing. If the employee is not satisfied, the grievance provision should indicate a clear action path. The process can be set up so that a company employee (such as a senior manager, especially one within the HR department) makes decisions; there is a committee to interpret and handle decisions made by the first-level supervisor; or a neutral arbitrator could have this power.

Neutral arbitrators can be supplied by the AAA or the Federal Mediation and Conciliation Service. By and large, the decision-maker's role is to interpret company policy and see if the employee has violated it. The decision-maker probably won't be able to add to or modify the corporate policy. The general rule is that the employer company pays the full cost of the grievance procedure.

When a unionized company's Collective Bargaining Agreement (CBA) provides for final and binding arbitration of grievances, then the employee will have to abide by the results of the arbitration process, and will not be able to bypass the procedure or sue without first going through the mandated procedure. (However, the legal system recognizes an exception, if the union breaches its duty of fair representation.)

According to the Supreme Court, employees get a choice of how to handle claims that involve employment discrimination (rather than other sources of dispute within the workplace). The employee certainly has a right to use the grievance procedure in the CBA. However, the mere fact that the CBA has a grievance procedure doesn't keep the employee from suing; it doesn't act in the same way as an arbitration clause that specifically rules out lawsuits. Many later cases expand on this Supreme Court decision; for instance, it has been held that a mandatory arbitration clause doesn't prevent employees from suing under the federal anti-discrimination laws unless they have individually agreed to arbitration, and have authorized the arbitrator to resolve their claims.

An arbitrator's ruling interpreting the CBA does not bar a subsequent Title VII suit for wrongful termination.

27.3.8 Non-Arbitral ADR

Although arbitration is the highest-profile form of ADR, it is far from the most common. Appointment of a corporate ombudsman, someone who can investigate complaints made by employees and supervisors, is the most common form. The job of the ombudsprogram is to find out what really happened, report to management, and help the parties reach an accommodation that they find mutually acceptable.

Many employers claim that they maintain an open-door policy, where employees can freely discuss their grievances and, if necessary, join with a management representative in meeting with an expert third party who can investigate the situation and resolve the problem.

Peer review systems create internal "jury" panels with representatives from both management and staff. Usually employees dominate: the typical composition is three employees and two management representatives. (An odd number is better than an even number, to avoid 2–2 or 3–3 splits.) The peer review panel is given the power to make a final, binding decision on grievances; management surrenders the option of overruling the panel if it adopts this option.

Mediation is a more formal procedure (yet less formal than arbitration) under which the disputants turn to a trusted, neutral party who helps them reach a decision that they both can accept. Like arbitration, mediation involves a third party, but the difference is that the arbitrator renders a decision, which the parties are required to accept and live by. The mediator does not make a decision, but instead concentrates on helping the parties resolve their differences and agree on what should be done. Although mediation awards do not have the status of a binding contract, they are nevertheless likely to be carried out because the parties have reached the decision themselves instead of having a decision imposed on them from outside.

Adopting an innovative ADR alternative could lead to labor law problems. National Labor Relations Act (NLRA) §8(a)(2) forbids employee representation committees that are "dominated" by the employer. In a 1997 case, the employer set up two employee committees, one dealing with safety, productivity and quality issues, and the other one concerned with wages, benefits, and work rules. The National Labor Relations Board said that the first committee passed muster, but the second was unacceptable—especially because there had just been a representation election (see page 348) and the union lost. The NLRB, upheld by the Sixth Circuit, required the second committee to be disbanded and a new union election to be held.

27.4 THE EEOC CHARGE PROCESS

Any employee who gets into federal court has to be patient, dogged, and really angry, because he or she must undertake many difficult procedural steps before getting to court. Both the EEOC and state agencies have a role in investigating an employee's allegations of discrimination, so charges can initially be filed with either the EEOC or the state or local anti-discrimination agency.

However, if the employee goes to the EEOC first, it generally "defers" to the state or local agency. That is, it sends it the paperwork, and allows the state or local agency a 60-day deferral period to resolve the complaint.

See 29 CFR §1601.74 for a list of state and local agencies that are deemed to have enough enforcement power to handle a discrimination charge. Furthermore, some agencies are "certified" by the EEOC (this time, the list is found at 29 CFR §1601.80) based on having been a deferral agency for at least four years, during which time the EEOC found its work product to be acceptable.

Title VII and ADA charges must be filed with the EEOC within 180 days of the time of the alleged discrimination (if there is no deferral agency in the picture) or within 300 days of the alleged discrimination, or 30 days of the time the deferral agency terminates processing of the charge (if a deferral agency is involved).

In cases involving a deferral agency, the filing period is really only 240 days, because of the 60-day period when the EEOC steps out and lets the deferral agency handle the matter. However, most deferral agencies have what is called "work sharing" agreements with the EEOC; in the jurisdiction of those agencies, an employee's complaint is timely if it is made more than 240, but less than 300, days after the alleged discrimination occurred. At any rate, once the EEOC gets a charge, by whatever circuitous route, it is required to notify the charged party (nearly always, this will be the employer corporation; the ability to sue human individuals for discrimination is quite limited) and to try to conciliate (get the parties to agree on a view of what happened in the past and what should be done in the future).

There can be some difficult technical legal issues in determining when the final act that violated the law occurred. The problem gets even harder if the employee alleges more than one, single, discriminatory action: for instance, a continuing violation (one that lasts a long time) or a series of related violations. In that case, the timing requirements probably run from the latest action in the series. There may also be two separate violations, such as discriminatory refusal to promote and retaliation against the employee for filing discrimination charges.

Where the employer is accused of adopting a seniority system for intentionally discriminatory reasons (e.g., a desire to prevent women or minorities entering the workplace from gaining a foothold), the time to file the EEOC charge is the time at which the employee becomes injured by application of the seniority system to his or her particular case. This seems innocuous enough, but it had to be added to Title VII by the Civil Rights Act of 1991, which aimed at reversing a 1989 Supreme Court case that said that the time ran from the date the seniority system was *adopted*. Of course, in most cases that would be before the employee was hired by the company—often, before the employee was even born.

27.4.1 Tolling the Time Limits

The timing requirements are fairly absolute, although there are limited circumstances under which employees will be allowed to press an untimely claim.

Usually, "tolling" (suspension of the regular time limit) depends on the employer's having done something wrong: failing to post the required EEOC poster, for instance, or actually deceiving the employee about his or her rights, or doing something active to hinder the employee from pressing charges. (Merely defending against charges is legitimate, and will not toll the time limits.)

If an employee's Title VII suit is dismissed because the charge was untimely, but the employee can assert another charge based on other facts, he or she can file a suit based on the second charge—as long as this one is filed on time.

27.4.2 EEOC Investigation

If the EEOC can't settle a charge informally, its next step is to investigate the facts and determine if there is reasonable cause to believe that the employee's complaint is well-founded. See 29 CFR §1601.24(a). If it makes such a "reasonable cause" determination, it has an obligation to attempt to conciliate, i.e., to get the employer to improve its equal opportunity policies, sign a compliance agreement, and compensate the employee. The EEOC can't close its case file until it has evidence that the employer is indeed complying with the conciliation agreement.

If the EEOC believes that the employer is blocking the process, it sends it a written notice giving it another chance to (literally) get with the program. Title VII §706(c) gives the EEOC discretion to sue the employer if an acceptable conciliation agreement cannot be reached within 30 days after the end of the period when the EEOC defers to state agency jurisdiction, or 30 days of the date a charge is filed with the EEOC. There is no statute of limitations on suits brought directly by the EEOC; they can sue for events even in the remote past.

If and when the EEOC concludes that there is no reasonable cause to believe that the facts are as charged by the employee, it will inform the charging party of this determination. In Title VII and ADA cases (but not EPA or ADEA cases), the charging party can still go to federal court and sue the employer, but he or she must get a "right to sue" letter from the EEOC. Usually, the EEOC gets 180 days to attempt conciliation, but the employee can ask for earlier termination of the EEOC's involvement, and earlier issuance of a right to sue letter. (However, the employee can't bypass the conciliation process entirely.)

Once the right to sue letter is issued, the employee has only 90 days to file the federal suit. If 90 days pass without the employee filing such a suit, it might be possible for the EEOC to bring its own suit, on the theory that its own rights have been reinstated because of the potential private plaintiff's inaction.

⇒ **TIP**

See page 529 for a discussion of the ADEA procedure, which is similar but not identical to the Title VII procedure.

Grievance procedures in a collective bargaining agreement have no impact on Title VII suits. That is, the employee doesn't have to use those procedures before filing an EEOC charge or bringing suit, but ongoing grievances under the CBA will not prevent or delay a Title VII suit. The same is true of company-sponsored grievance procedures in a non-union enterprise.

A "no reasonable cause" determination does not prevent the employee from suing, and does not limit the lawsuit, what the employee can try to prove, or even the remedies he or she can receive. The judge or jury makes a separate inquiry into the facts, without influence from the EEOC investigation. However, the EEOC will not intervene in the suit or bring its own suit if it makes a "no reasonable cause" determination.

The EEOC might intervene in a private suit brought by an employee, or might bring its own suit. Suits with the EEOC as plaintiff are limited to matters investigated as a result of a charge, not matters outside the investigation for which conciliation was attempted. In other words, if the EEOC tries to conciliate one charge, the employer doesn't have to worry about being clobbered by unrelated charges.

In practical terms, EEOC suits are a distinctly minor threat, because the agency is swamped with work. For instance, in 1995 alone, the EEOC received 95,000 charges of all kinds, but resolved only about 33,000 cases and had a backlog of 100,000 cases. The snowed-under agency needs more than a year to process and investigate a charge. The magnitude of the workload puts pressure on the agency to settle cases, not litigate them, and reduces the likelihood that the agency will bring cases as a plaintiff. In the first nine months of 1996, the EEOC filed only 161 suits: 105 under Title VII, 36 under the ADA, 12 under the ADEA, two under the Equal Pay Act, and six involving multiple charges. By September, 1996, the agency's backlog was reduced to "only" 80,000 cases, thanks to improved efficiency in the agency's processing system.

27.5 ADEA PROCEDURE

ADEA procedure is much like a simplified Title VII procedure (see page 527). Yet even the ADEA procedure is complex, and provides many pitfalls that can be used by the employer to dismiss employee charges that are incorrectly drafted, incorrectly filed, or are not timely.

A person who believes him- or herself to be a victim of age discrimination must file an administrative charge with the EEOC or the relevant state anti-discrimination agency. In effect, potential plaintiffs have to go through enforcement procedures at both the state and the federal level. However, if the federal charge is filed on time, the complainant doesn't have to complete the state enforcement process (see page 530). He or she merely has to file a charge within the state system.

The federal law requires that, in a state that has an anti-discrimination statute and an enforcement agency, potential plaintiffs have to file charges within both systems. The federal/state enforcement relationship revolves around the concepts of "referral" and "deferral."

Referral means that the state has a work-sharing agreement with the EEOC, as provided by 29 CFR §1626.9. When an age discrimination complaint is made to the state agency, the state agency refers it to the EEOC . If the state charge is dismissed, the EEOC has the power to conduct an independent investigation. The referral states are Alaska, California, Connecticut, Delaware, Florida, Georgia, Hawaii, Idaho, Illinois, Iowa, Kentucky, Maryland, Massachusetts, Michigan, Minnesota, Montana, Nebraska, Nevada, New Hampshire, New Jersey, New Mexico, New York, Oregon, Pennsylvania, South Carolina, Utah, West Virginia, and Wisconsin.

A further group of states (Arizona, Colorado, Kansas, Maine, Ohio, Rhode Island, South Dakota, and Washington) are "conditional referral" states. They do have anti-discrimination statutes, but their provisions are quite different from the federal ADEA. So there is the possibility that employees in these states will bring claims that are covered by the state law but not the federal law; in such instances, the state-only claims will not be referred to the EEOC. Claims that are covered only by federal law must be filed directly with the EEOC, within 180 days of the discriminatory act.

The "deferral" concept means that the EEOC defers to the state and does not process the charge for a period of 60 days after the referral, so that the state agency can take action. Once it receives a charge, the EEOC has an obligation (see 29 USC §626(d)) to notify everyone named in the charge. The EEOC is supposed to use "informal methods" of conciliation, conference, and persuasion to eliminate unlawful discriminatory practices.

Except in a deferral state, plaintiffs must file the charge no later than 180 days after the discriminatory act (or the latest discriminatory act that forms part of a pattern). In deferral states, the latest permissible filing date is the earlier of either 300 days after the discriminatory act/last discriminatory act, or 30 days after the state agency dismisses the charge and notifies the complainant of the dismissal. The simplification comes about because suit can be brought right after completion of the administrative proceedings (Title VII plaintiffs have to wait 180 days) and ADEA plaintiffs do not have to get a right to sue letter from the EEOC.

Conciliation is so important to the federal ADEA system that 29 USC §626(d) does not allow age discrimination claimants to file federal suits unless they have filed a charge with the EEOC (or filed a state charge referred to the EEOC) and waited for the 60-day conciliation period to lapse.

Courts have reached different conclusions about what to do if the plaintiff does *not* wait the 60 days. The Sixth Circuit says the case should be dismissed (but without prejudice, so it can be refiled later), but the Eighth Circuit says the case should not be dismissed, just suspended pending the administrative disposition of the complaint.

During this period, the EEOC's task is to determine if it has a "reasonable basis to conclude that a violation of the Act has occurred or will occur." If the answer is in the affirmative, the EEOC makes what is called a "good cause" finding, i.e., the employee had good cause to complain. Then the EEOC will probably issue a Letter of Violation, but the mere fact that no letter is issued does not prove that the EEOC did not find any violations. Next, the EEOC tries to get the company into compliance by informal persuasion.

If the company and the EEOC reach an agreement which the agency believes will eliminate the discrimination, then the agreement will be written down and signed by the EEOC representative, a company representative, and the employee who charged discrimination. If the charging party doesn't like the agreement, he or she can withdraw the charge, but the EEOC has independent authority to settle on behalf of other employees affected by discrimination.

On the other hand, if conciliation fails and no agreement is reached (possibly because there has been no discrimination and therefore the employer is unwilling to admit culpability and "eliminate" discrimination which never occurred in the first place), the EEOC and/or the charging party might sue. (As noted above, the charging party's suit may be blocked by an EEOC suit.) The charging party's suit must be brought within 90 days of his or her receipt of notice from the EEOC that conciliation has failed, but it is not necessary for a would-be plaintiff to get a formal "right to sue" letter from the EEOC. (See page 528: Title VII plaintiffs do need a right to sue letter.)

27.5.1 ADEA Litigation by the EEOC

The EEOC itself also has the power to file suit as a plaintiff; it seldom does so, and the cases selected are usually large-scale cases involving egregious practices, many employees, or a pattern or practice of discrimination. The agency can bring a suit even if no employee of the company has filed timely charges of age discrimination. The EEOC's involvement further complicates the extent to which the employer might be held liable to one or more individual employees who complain of age discrimination.

If the EEOC files suit *after* an employee has already sued based on the same employer conduct, the earlier individual suit can proceed, but an individual who wants monetary relief such as back pay cannot file suit after the EEOC starts its own suit, because the EEOC litigates on behalf of all affected employees.

But if the EEOC complaint covers a pattern or practice of discrimination lasting up to "the present time," this means the date the EEOC filed its complaint, so an individual can file a private suit charging that the employer committed discrimination AFTER the filing of the EEOC complaint.

The EEOC doesn't need written consent from employees to file a suit on their behalf, and the EEOC can seek relief for all employees based on a charge filed by one employee who only reported discrimination against himself or herself. The EEOC can also undertake only one conciliation effort, as long as the employer is notified that the charge covers more than one complainant.

No employee who has already sued the employer can get back pay or other individual relief from an EEOC suit involving the same facts.

However, if an employee tried to sue, but the case was dismissed because of untimely filing, then the EEOC can bring a suit to get an injunction against the employer—even if the EEOC's case is based on the same facts as the suit that was dismissed.

⇒ **TIP**

As a general rule, a company's bankruptcy filing entitles it to an "automatic stay," a period of time during which lawsuits against the company cannot proceed. However, a suit by the EEOC is considered an exercise of the government's regulatory/policing function, so it can proceed even during the automatic stay.

27.5.2 ADEA Statute of Limitations Questions

At its initial enactment, the ADEA carried a statute of limitations of two years from the last discriminatory act, or three years from the last willful discriminatory act. The Civil Rights Act of 1991, however, dramatically changes the timing. Suit must be brought within 90 days of the time the EEOC either makes a ruling or dismisses the charge. Given the EEOC's large workload and small staff, in many cases this is in effect a longer statute of limitations than the prior one: many charges take far more than two years for resolution.

The question of limitations (which has the practical consequence of determining which lawsuits can be dismissed without even discussing their merits, because they were filed too late) also involves the question of "accrual," i.e., when the plaintiff was actually subjected to discriminatory conduct. The earlier the cause of action is deemed to accrue, the earlier the charge will have to be filed—and the more likely it is that the plaintiff will miss this deadline and that the case can be dismissed.

If the alleged discriminatory act is the firing of the employee, then there is a single act of discrimination. Most cases hold that the discriminatory act occurs on the date the plaintiff is unambiguously informed that he or she will be fired. The salient date is the date of notice, *not* the first warning the plaintiff receives of impending termination, and *not* the last day the employee works for the employer or the last date he or she is on the payroll. The notice doesn't have to be formal or even written, but it does have to be a definite statement that a final decision has been made to fire the employee.

Other alleged acts of discrimination are harder to place on a time continuum. It has been held that a claim of failure to promote accrues when the employee knows or should have known about the facts that support the claim—probably, that a younger individual got the promotion that the plaintiff wanted.

If there is only a single decision, there is only a single act that might be discriminatory. However, some courts allow a plaintiff to argue that there was a continuing violation lasting over a period of time, i.e., that the plaintiff was allowed to keep his or her job, but was constantly denied merited promotions because of age discrimination. If the court accepts the "continuing violation" theory, the cause of action accrues on the *last* discriminatory act in the series.

An employee who charges a continuing violation has to file with the EEOC within 180 or 300 days (depending on which is the relevant time period; see page 530) of at least one act of discrimination in the series. But a filing that is timely for one act of discrimination will be timely for all of the discriminatory acts in the series.

A bad performance appraisal that makes the employee more vulnerable to being laid off or RIFed (but does not constitute an actual threat of dismissal unless performance improves) is not considered an employment action that could give rise to an ADEA claim. Therefore, employees are not required to file charges that the appraisals were discriminatory within 300 days of the date of the evaluation.

Courts reach different conclusions about when the cause of action accrues when the charge is a discriminatory layoff. One theory is that accrual occurs on the date of the layoff itself; the other is that the cause of action accrues later, when the possibility of reinstatement disappears because the employer has filled the last job for which the plaintiff might have been recalled.

Discrimination claims related to retirement plans often require interpretation of the employer's seniority system. In 1989, the U.S. Supreme Court rendered a controversial decision in a Title VII case. It said that the cause of action for discrimination in a seniority system accrues when the system is adopted, with the result that almost no claims can ever be brought on a timely basis, simply because most employees are hired years or even decades after the adoption of the system, and do not become aware of what they believe to be discriminatory practices until some time after their hiring.

Congress tried to overrule this case by adopting §112 of the Civil Rights Act of 1991, which says that for Title VII purposes, the statute of limitations for a seniority system accrues when the system is adopted; when an employee becomes subject to it; or when the plaintiff is injured by it—whichever is latest. (Typically, the injury will be the last of the three events, so the cause of action will accrue then.) But Congress didn't enact a similar provision relating to the ADEA, so some courts continue to apply the "plan adoption" standard, thus foreclosing employee claims. (See page 527 for a general discussion of tolling (suspending) the statute of limitations in employment discrimination cases.) Specifically in the ADEA context, improper employer conduct may give the employee additional time to litigate the claim.

Many cases define instances of employer conduct that is not wrongful and will *not* toll the statute of limitations, such as:

- Putting an employee on "special assignment" until termination takes effect

- Offering a severance benefits package; on the other hand, offering a lavish severance package but requiring the employee not to discuss it with other employees was held to discourage employees from vindicating their legal rights, and therefore serious enough to toll the statute of limitations.

Even if tolling is available, it probably cannot last past the point at which the employee who took reasonable steps to investigate would have been aware of the discrimination.

A special form of tolling is available when employers fail to post the notice of ADEA rights required by 29 U.S.C. §627. If the notice is duly posted (free copies are available from the EEOC and Department of Labor; posters can also be purchased from many publishers), then the court will presume that the employee could have learned about his or her rights under the ADEA through this medium.

However, if the employer *fails* to post the information, the court may conclude that the employer deprived the employee of access to information about older employees' rights, and consequently the statute of limitations should be tolled. On the other hand, some courts say that the real test is the employee's awareness or lack of awareness of the ADEA's provisions. If the employee knew his or her rights, the lack of a poster in the workplace won't entitle the employee to extra time to file.

The statute of limitations is not tolled, and continues to run, while the employee is going through the employer's internal grievance procedures.

➠ TIP

However, it's been held that a collective bargaining agreement provision is invalid if it terminates an employee's right to bring a grievance once he or she files age discrimination charges with the EEOC or the local anti-discrimination agency. The clause is void because it retaliates against employees who exercise legal rights.

27.5.3 ADEA Class Actions

If a timely charge was filed by a named plaintiff in a class action, non-filing complainants have the right to opt in, but they have to file written consent to opting in before the statute of limitations expires on the potential plaintiff's individual claims. Failure to do so will permit the employer to have the potential plaintiff's case dismissed. The same case also says that ADEA opt-in class actions use the tolling rules prescribed by the FLSA, not those of Title VII.

Later the same year, however, the Eleventh Circuit made it somewhat easier for ADEA class actions to be maintained: when plaintiffs are dismissed from a class action (because they were not "similarly situated" to the other plaintiffs), the 90-day ADEA statute of limitations is tolled (suspended) until a final judgment has been rendered in the underlying class action. Usually, that takes years. The court's theory is that the District Court could change its mind about allowing the would-be plaintiffs to join the class action, or they could appeal and the District Court could be reversed.

If one employee sues the employer, based on a charge referring only to discrimination he or she personally experienced, that charge does not put the employer on notice of claims by other employees. Therefore, other employees who have not filed ADEA charges are not allowed to intervene in the first employee's suit against the employer. The flip side is that if you ever receive one employee's charge that refers to discriminatory conduct that affects other older employees, there is a real possibility of additional suits (or the addition of other plaintiffs to this suit).

When the EEOC files suit, employees do not have the power to opt out of the suit, and they can't file their own suit (unless they have already filed a timely claim) if they don't like the terms on which the EEOC settles with the employer.

27.5.4 State Laws Banning Age Discrimination

Most of the states have some kind of law prohibiting age discrimination in employment. However, Alabama has none, and Missouri, Oklahoma, and Wyoming have general anti-discrimination laws that don't go into detail about age claims. In Arkansas, Mississippi, and South Dakota, state employees, but not private-sector employees, are covered by the state ADEA. North Carolina says that age discrimination violates public policy, but there is no comprehensive anti-discrimination law.

Some of the state laws cover all employers, some are limited to employers of 4-25 workers (the limit depends on the state). In other words, some small companies are subject to state ADEAs but not to the federal law. But the Indiana statute applies ONLY to situations that are excluded by federal law.

> ➠ **TIP**
>
> Violating the anti-discrimination statutes of Georgia, Nebraska, New Hampshire, and South Dakota can trigger criminal penalties, not just civil liability.

Although procedure varies from state to state, usually a person who claims to be the victim of age discrimination begins the state enforcement process by filing a charge with the state human rights/equal employment opportunity agency, within the time frame set out by the statute. (The period ranges from 30 days after the alleged discriminatory practice to one year plus 90 days of the time the complainant discovered the employer acted illegally.)

Most of the states, like the federal government, have a dual system of agency enforcement and private litigation. The agency investigates the charge and issues either a finding of good cause or a no-cause finding. If the agency deems that the charge is founded, then it tries to conciliate (get the employer and employee to agree on remedies to settle the matter) or brings a lawsuit against the employer. On the other hand, if it makes a no-cause finding, or can't resolve the matter prompt-ly, the employee has the right to sue the employer in state court (basing the com-plaint on the state anti-discrimination law). However, in some states, there is no agency enforcement; employers are at risk only of private suits.

Other states (Massachusetts, Michigan, New York, Ohio, Pennsylvania) have a different dual system; complaining employees get a choice. They can file a state court suit right away, without going to the anti-discrimination agency, or they can file an administrative complaint. But election of remedies is usually required: i.e., once an employee sues in state court, he or she can't go back and initiate the administrative process. Complainants in these states are entitled to take advantage of the 300-day filing period available in deferral states.

27.6 PROVING (AND DEFENDING) THE TITLE VII CASE

A Title VII case is very unlike most other civil cases. Most civil cases involve simple facts: was the merchandise delivered on time? Whose fault was the delay? Did the merchandise satisfy the contract specifications? Was the driver of the Buick exceed-ing the speed limit? In contrast, a Title VII case involves exploration of motivations and perceptions (and perhaps unconscious assumptions about groups of people).

Over time, various courts have explored many subtle issues of statutory and Constitutional law; a full discussion of the evolution of the Title VII case, and who has to prove what in what situation, is beyond the scope of this book. In the Civil Rights Act of 1991, Congress stepped in to modify the effect of a number of Supreme Court decisions that it deemed to be unduly pro-employer.

The basic Title VII case is a three-step process. The plaintiff establishes a prima facie case, basic facts that are suggestive of discrimination. If the prima facie case is not good enough that the plaintiff would win if the defense didn't put in a case, the defense can get the plaintiff's case dismissed right away. But if the prima facie is good enough to keep the case going, the defendant employer then gets a chance to rebut the plaintiff's charge of discriminatory conduct. It can do this by proving legitimate, non-discriminatory reasons for the action that it took (e.g., dis-charging the plaintiff; not promoting him or her, or not giving a raise), or by prov-ing that the controversial action was impelled by business necessity. The third step is the plaintiff's again: the plaintiff then gets to show "pretextuality"—that the employer's asserted non-discriminatory reasons are fabrications, and the true motive was indeed discriminatory.

The kind and amount of evidence the plaintiff has to introduce to make a prima facie case depends on two factors: the kind of case (sex discrimination, sex-ual harassment, age discrimination, racial discrimination, etc.) and whether the plaintiff charges disparate treatment or disparate impact. Disparate treatment is a practice of intentional discrimination against a group or an individual, whereas disparate impact is a practice that seems to be neutral and non-discriminatory, but has a heavier negative impact on some groups than on others.

Furthermore, if the plaintiff charges that an employment practice has a disparate impact, and the employer responds by showing business necessity for that practice, the plaintiff can nevertheless win by proving that there was an alternative practice that would also have satisfied business necessity, and the employer refused to adopt that practice.

If there are many factors that go into a workplace decision (for instance, promotion could be based on educational attainment, objective measures such as sales performance or departmental profitability, written tests, interviews, and assessments by several supervisors) and the plaintiff challenges more than one of those criteria, the plaintiff has to be able to prove that each of the factors caused disparate impact (and therefore harmed the plaintiff). If the various elements can't be separated and analyzed separately, then the whole decision-making practice can be treated as a single employment practice.

The "mixed motive" case is somewhat different. It arises out of the situation in which the employer has several motivations that influence a decision, and some of them are lawful and others are discriminatory. In the mixed motive case, the plaintiff can win by showing that the discriminatory motive was influential; he or she doesn't have to prove that there were *no* legitimate motives behind the decision. However, if the employer would have acted the same way with or without the discriminatory motive being present, this will reduce the remedies that the plaintiff can get.

To make out a prima facie case the plaintiff might have to prove that he or she belonged to a protected class (women, racial or religious minorities), had the necessary qualifications for the job, or was doing an adequate job if hired but later discharged, denied a raise, or not promoted. Disparate treatment cases are usually proved by direct or indirect evidence of explicit discrimination; disparate impact cases usually turn on statistics (e.g., it looks really bad if, in 20 years in which 3,227 minority group members applied for jobs, the company claims it could not find any qualified applicants).

Once the plaintiff establishes the prima facie case, and produces enough evidence to raise a genuine issue of fact as to pretextuality, the employer will not be able to terminate the case early by getting summary judgment or judgment as a matter of law: the case will have to be tried fully, and will have to go to the jury (or to the judge, if there is no jury in the case).

The job of the defense counsel, of course, is to show that the plaintiff's evidence is not strong enough to constitute a prima facie case, that there are methodological problems with the statistics introduced by the plaintiff, or that the plaintiff's witnesses (especially the plaintiff him- or herself) are not credible, and to prove that the employer acted in a legitimate manner based on business necessity.

27.7 LITIGATION

Frequently, the employer's litigation objectives include removing the case from state court to federal court. Federal courts are often more sophisticated, and less inclined to make awards based on emotive factors. Furthermore, a plaintiff is often entitled to a broader array of remedies if his or her state law case can be maintained than if the case goes to federal court.

For instance, the employee may be entitled to damages for intentional or negligent infliction of emotional distress; and there are more circumstances under which state courts can grant punitive damages than can federal courts. Some important federal laws "cap" damages that successful plaintiffs can obtain; state fair employment practices laws seldom include such caps. There are also instances in which employees cannot sue in federal court, but can in state court: for instance, if their employer is too small to be covered by federal law; if they are suing for a reason (such as sexual orientation) that is covered by state but not federal law.

In many instances, federal law preempts state law, i.e., in some areas, such as pensions and benefits, the federal law prevails over states' attempts to regulate those issues. Thus, if the employee does not have a valid cause of action under federal law, or if the time to bring the case has expired, then getting the case removed to federal court is tantamount to getting it dismissed.

During the discovery process (court-supervised exchange of documents) it may be possible to uncover "after-acquired evidence," such as evidence that the employee lied on the job application. Although after-acquired evidence does not prevent the plaintiff from winning a discrimination case, it can limit the available remedies. For instance, it may be possible to subpoena former employers of the plaintiff in order to find out if the plaintiff's statements about employment history and the reason for leaving past jobs were accurate.

> **⇒ TIP**
>
> The Ninth Circuit says that after-acquired evidence can *only* be introduced if the employer can prove that the employee's misconduct was serious enough so that it would have led to discharge, and not just a reprimand or other form of discipline, if the employer had known about it while the employee still worked there.

Some of the plaintiff's claims may be so badly pleaded that they can be dismissed at an early stage of litigation. If, assuming that the facts are as stated by the plaintiff, there is still no legal ground for relief, then the claim can be dismissed.

27.8 SETTLEMENT OF A DISCRIMINATION SUIT

It may seem odd that settlement negotiations can continue even after the judge and jury have spoken. In litigation, however, the game truly "ain't over till the fat lady sings": as long as there are still appeal rights that could be exercised, the case is still open for negotiations. The most usual negotiations take place before the case is even filed. The employee's objective is to collect at least some money, as soon as possible, instead of having to wait for years for an uncertain result. Emotional vindication is often very important to plaintiffs. Indeed, there are situations in which years of litigation could have been avoided by a simple—but timely—apology.

There are many delicate considerations involved in the negotiation process. At a very early stage, the matter might be resolved by an agreement to let the employee resign instead of being fired and receive severance pay, and perhaps some other benefits, in exchange for releasing the employer from all liability. Both sides must agree on how the matter will be treated for purposes of unemployment insurance—and both must consult attorneys to make sure that their agreement doesn't violate unemployment insurance law!

Then there is the situation in which the employer acknowledges that the plaintiff has a valid case, or at least that the claims have some validity. The employer knows that it is likely to lose at trial, and wants to settle early to limit the amount of its possible exposure and the risk of bad publicity.

Finally, there are cases where the employer thinks that the plaintiff's claims are entirely fabricated, or have little legal validity (even though they are sincerely asserted)—but nevertheless wants to settle, because of the sheer cost and effort involved even in *winning* a major discrimination suit.

What usually happens is that cases are settled somewhere around halfway between the plaintiff's demand and the defendant's counter-offer. Of course, both sides know this, which influences what they will offer. It's also a rule in negotiating that "the first one to mention a number, loses," which can be a real problem in conventional business negotiations. However, in a litigation-related negotiation, it's only natural for the plaintiff to "open the bidding," and for the employer to respond with its counter-offer. No one should ever go to the negotiating table without authority actually to settle the case, and without a range of acceptable settlement figures.

If the employer is completely unwilling to settle on any terms that the plaintiff might accept, there's no point in extensive negotiations; all that will be achieved is an unnecessary increase in hostility in an already tense situation. Furthermore, an infuriated employee representative might be goaded into saying something that is very much against the employer's best interests ("If they'd only listened to me at that meeting, and gotten rid of all you people, we wouldn't be having this problem")

⇒ **TIP**
_____

If the case is settled quickly, it's very likely that it will be settled within the policy limits and thus that the insurer will assume the entire cost of settlement. Moreover, if the employer performs a prompt investigation, negotiates in good faith, and does not unduly delay the settlement, then the plaintiff will have no grounds for demanding punitive damages (because the employer has not acted outrageously and has not violated the norms of public policy).

Also, some statutes (such as California's Civil Procedure Code §998) penalize plaintiffs who reject fair settlement offers. If the judge or jury awards less than a settlement offer made in accordance with the statute, the plaintiff may have to pay the defendant's costs for the lawsuit. (After all, the suit could have been avoided by settling it on reasonable terms.)

If a settlement can be reached, then there are two major legal documents to be prepared: a court order dismissing the suit with prejudice (i.e., in a way that prevents it from being re-filed later) and a release containing the terms of the settlement. This time, the rule is the opposite from money negotiations: instead of responding to the other fellow's offer, you want to be the one who drafts the documents for approval by the other side. That way, you control the basic form of the documents and therefore the basic form of the transaction.

There are other advantages to the employer of making a reasonable settlement offer. For one thing, a settlement can be offered without admitting culpability. Also, under 29 CFR §1601.20(a), the EEOC has the power to dismiss an employee's discrimination charge if the employee rejects a written settlement offer from the employer that is a legitimate offer of "full relief," i.e., adequate compensation for the discrimination suffered by the employee. The EEOC sends the employee a strongly worded form letter that gives the employee only two choices: to accept the settlement offer promptly, or to have the EEOC charge dismissed. (This doesn't mean that the employee can't sue; it only means that the EEOC will not have any involvement in the case.)

Full relief means that the employee gets full back pay, plus any out-of-pocket expenses stemming from discrimination (such as moving expenses for an employee who was wrongfully dismissed, or psychological consultation for a stressed-out employee). Compensation must also be included for non-monetary losses such as loss of sleep, anxiety, and indigestion.

However, the employer should be aware that settling with one employee is not necessarily the end of the problem. It is against public policy (and a court might very well issue an injunction to forbid) to include a provision in a settlement agreement that forbids a current or former employee to cooperate with an EEOC investigation. The settlement can prevent a person from pursuing his or her own claims against the employer; but the EEOC continues to have a right to investigate workplace conditions, and pursue claims on its own behalf (or help other employees assert their claims).

27.9 REMEDIES

The nature of the "remedies" available to the successful plaintiff depends on the claim or claims asserted. Of course, it's in the plaintiff's best interest to assert as many claims, of as many types, as he or she can possibly justify by the most liberal interpretation of the laws, with the result that the employer often finds itself fighting on many fronts simultaneously. (Lawyers and clients can be punished for pursuing abusive claims.)

Some employment discrimination claims fit into the "breach of contract" category, but most of them are "tort" claims. A tort is any kind of wrongdoing committed against a party, where the injured person can sue the "tortfeasor." The difference between a tort and a crime is that a crime is considered an injury against the state, so it is prosecuted by the state. In many instances, the same conduct is both a crime and a tort.

The importance of the tort/contract distinction is that the remedies are different for the two categories. If a plaintiff proves breach of contract, the court's job is to put the plaintiff back in the position he, she, or it would have been in if the contract had been carried out. In the context of an employment contract (or implied contract), that probably means earnings and fringe benefits that were lost because of the breach, and perhaps out-of-pocket expenses of seeking and getting a new job.

Back pay is not limited to simple salary; it includes benefits, overtime, shift differentials, merit raises, and the like. However, if the employer can prove that the employee would have been laid off, or was unavailable for work, back pay damages will not have to be paid for that time the employee would not have been working anyway.

> ➠ **TIP**
>
> In this context, fringe benefits are valued at the cost the employee would encounter to replace the benefits, not the (probably lower) cost the employer would pay to provide them. In the breach of contract context, employees are required to mitigate their damages—undertake steps, such as collecting unemployment benefits and looking for a new job, that will improve their financial condition.

These mitigating amounts reduce what the ex-employer will have to pay in damages. On the other hand, to the extent that the plaintiff proves that the employer committed one or more torts, the successful plaintiff can be awarded back pay, front pay (moving from the end of the trial forward), lost earnings, medical expenses, the value of pain and anguish, and emotional distress. The plaintiff's spouse might be granted an award for loss of consortium (marital services that were not rendered because of the employer's wrongdoing). In most states, interest on the judgment, running from the time the case is decided, can also be ordered—which mounts up quickly if the award is in six or seven figures.

Sometimes front pay and reinstatement can be combined, i.e., if the remedies don't overlap, chronologically or economically. Front pay can be awarded to get the employee to the "point of employability," at which point he/she can be reinstated.

One of the most controversial questions is the matter of punitive damages. In a few cases, judges or juries have awarded a small or fairly small sum in compensatory damages (to compensate the plaintiff for actual losses that are attributed to the fault of the defendant), but have accompanied them by enormous punitive damage awards. Theoretically, punitive damages are supposed to be quite rare, ordered only in those cases where the defendant's conduct was outrageous, not merely negligent or improper. There must have been malice, or willful or reckless acts undertaken to vex, injure, or annoy the plaintiff, or at least conscious disregard of the plaintiff's rights.

There are not many instances in which very large punitive damages have actually been paid. Such awards are vulnerable to being reduced on appeal. Or the plaintiff may feel both emotionally vindicated and sick of litigating the case, and may settle the case after the trial for quite a bit less than the theoretical award. Nevertheless, a company can suffer a real public relations disaster if it is ordered to pay millions of dollars as a punishment, even if the order is never actually carried out.

The general rule is that unemployment benefits received will not reduce the amount of back pay available to a successful Title VII plaintiff. However, in the Second Circuit, courts have the discretion to offset unemployment compensation against the back pay award.

27.9.1 Title VII and the CRA

The basic rule is that Title VII provides equitable remedies for successful plaintiffs. That is, the defendant company that is found to have discriminated can be ordered to hire or reinstate a plaintiff (plus back pay for the time the plaintiff would have been working absent discrimination, but not more than two years' worth), and can be enjoined from further discrimination. Authorization for back pay and injunctions comes from 42 U.S.C. §2000e-5(g).

If the plaintiff further succeeds in proving disparate treatment (as distinct from facially neutral practices that have a disparate impact on the protected group the plaintiff belongs to), then compensatory damages can be awarded to the plaintiff as reimbursement for costs (e.g., job hunting; psychotherapy) incurred directly as a result of the discrimination. However, in cases of racial discrimination, the plaintiff must look to the Civil Rights Act of 1866, 42 USC §1981, and not to Title VII, for compensatory and punitive damages. If the alleged discrimination consists of failing to accommodate a disability, the employer will not have to pay compensatory damages if it made a good-faith effort at reasonable accommodation, even if its offer of accommodation was later deemed inadequate.

The court can also award attorneys' fees if the plaintiff wins. This can be the case even if the jury agrees that there was some kind of violation, but the plaintiff is only entitled to nominal damages such as a symbolic $1, and even if the employer acted in a good-faith belief that it was complying with the law.

In especially egregious cases of corporate misconduct, punitive damages can be ordered to punish the defendant company. The basic rule is that the defendant must have acted maliciously, or at least with "reckless indifference" to the plaintiff's statutory rights to work without discrimination. (But see *Kilstad* v. *American Dental Association*, 65 LW 2623 (D.C. Cir. 3/21/97) allowing a punitive damage award in cases of intentional discrimination, even if they are not exceptionally outrageous.)

According to 1992 Guidelines published in the EEOC Compliance Manual, these are appropriate factors in deciding if the employer acted with malice or reckless indifference:

- If the conduct was egregious or merely somewhat unacceptable
- The nature, severity, and extent of harm suffered by the complaining employee
- The duration of the conduct; a practice that persists for years is more serious than one that is terminated after a short period of time
- If the employer acted similarly in the past; if so, how often (i.e., was there an extensive pattern of discriminatory conduct, or merely one or a few isolated incidents?)
- If, once the employer became aware of the situation, it took corrective steps (a positive factor)—or, on the other hand, if a cover-up was attempted or achieved (a negative factor)
- If retaliation against complainants and witnesses was threatened or practiced.

The Civil Rights Act of 1991 (P.L. 102-166) imposes a cap on total damages that any successful Title VII plaintiff can receive. The damage cap depends on the size of the defendant corporation, not the number or seriousness of the charges against it. The cap covers all punitive damages and nearly all compensatory damages. However, medical bills and other monetary losses that the plaintiff incurred before the trial are not subject to the cap.

For companies that have 15–100 employees (remember, Title VII does not apply to companies with under 15 employees), the damage cap is $50,000. For the target audience of this book, the damage caps are significantly higher. The cap is set at $100,000 for companies with 101–200 employees, $200,000 for 210–500 employees, and $300,000 for companies with more than 500 in the workforce.

> ⇒ **TIP**
> ──
> *Luciano* v. *Olsten Corp.*, 65 LW 2624 (2nd Cir. 3/21/97) allows an award of the *maximum* permitted punitive damages even without a showing that the employer's conduct was particularly egregious.

The Civil Rights Act of 1991 made it somewhat easier to prove Title VII cases statistically, and overruled some earlier Supreme Court decisions by permitting "mixed motive" cases to be brought successfully. In a mixed motive case, the plaintiff charges that he or she was subjected to adverse employment action for several reasons, and at least one of the reasons was discriminatory. (It's also possible for an employee to charge discrimination on more than one basis, e.g., a 54-year-old black male charges race and age discrimination; a white female charges sex and pregnancy discrimination.)

Employees can win a mixed motive case by proving that discrimination was <u>a</u> motivating factor in the employer's decision; it is not necessary to prove that it was the sole or even the predominant factor. CRA '91 §107(b) limits relief in mixed motive cases: plaintiffs can get injunctive and declaratory relief, but not damages.

But this limitation doesn't apply to Title VII retaliation claims, because the statute does not refer specifically to such claims. To prove retaliation, it is necessary to prove that the employer's improper motive had "a determinative effect" on its action. The Second Circuit says that if the employer defends itself by asserting a legitimate reason for the discharge, it has to prove two things: not just that it would have fired the plaintiff if the discriminatory motive had not been present, but that it would have fired him or her at that time rather than later.

27.9.2 Tax Factors in Settling Discrimination Cases

Settling a case might require paying damages for some claims, while the plaintiff agrees to drop other claims. Because the plaintiff wants financial compensation, tax factors are important, and the plaintiff will want to structure the settlement to be able to keep as much as possible after taxes.

The basic division is between damages for breach of contract, which are taxable income because, in essence, they are a delayed payment of compensation that the employee would have received earlier if the contract had not been breached, and tort damages for personal injury. Because the employee will want the amounts to be characterized as personal injury damages (which are not taxable), it becomes necessary to determine which claims, under which statutes, resemble personal injuries and which resemble taxable back pay. In 1992, the Supreme Court ruled that Title VII damages are included in taxable income, because they are not similar enough to traditional tort recoveries (e.g., for injuries sustained in a car accident) to be excluded.

In like manner, the Supreme Court has held that the back pay and liquidated damages that a successful ADEA plaintiff receives are not close enough to the tort damages received for personal injuries for the plaintiff to be able to exclude them from income.

Clearly, back pay settlements and awards have always been taxable. The Small Business Job Protection Act of 1996 clarified the application of the relevant Internal Revenue Code section, §104(a)(2). As of August 21, 1996, damages received for "personal physical injuries" and physical illness will be tax-free (i.e., if the plaintiff became physically ill as a result of the employer's wrongful conduct), but damages for emotional distress will be taxable except to the extent of medical expenses for therapists and other treatment of emotional distress.

The IRS' version of the new statutory requirement is found in Rev.Rul. 96-65, 1996-53 IRB 5. Amounts received before August 21, 1996, or received later under a written agreement, decree, or award that was in effect on September 13, 1995 [not 1996], are not taxable to the extent that they represent emotional distress damages. But amounts received under a post-8/21/96 judgment or agreement can be excluded from income only if they represent physical illness or medical expenses to treat emotional distress.

➥ **TIP**

Taxable damages that are wage replacements may be subject to withholding requirements, and may be FICA wages. See IRS Publication 957: Reporting Back Pay to the Social Security Administration (for Title VII, ADEA, FLSA, NLRA, etc.)

WRONGFUL TERMINATION AND AT-WILL EMPLOYMENT

28.1 INTRODUCTION

Diamonds, they say, are forever, but that's not always true of employees. Employees always have the right to quit their jobs, no matter how inconvenient their departure may be for the employer. (The employer may be able to negotiate an agreement under which the employee agrees not to disclose the employer's proprietary information, and agrees not to compete with the employer or solicit its customers and other employees.) The employer's right to fire the employee is not quite so simple and clear-cut.

Some employees work under a written contract that specifies exactly the circumstances under which they can be terminated. Unionized employees are covered by a collective bargaining agreement (CBA). Some top executives or creative personnel also have written employment agreements. If the agreement sets out a termination procedure (e.g., a warning, then a chance for the employee to respond to charges, a suspension, and only then termination), then it is a breach of contract to terminate the employee without following the procedure.

Contracts are not always a bad idea, from the employer's perspective: the contract can spell out the employee's duty to avoid competing with the employer or soliciting its customers and employees, which can be very helpful in an industry where valuable employees often quit to set up their own businesses. (These covenants not to compete will not be enforceable unless they are reasonable, in both their duration and the geographic area they cover.)

As will be discussed in detail later, employers may also subject themselves to responsibilities under implied contracts. If conduct, written documents, or even oral statements are considered to create a legally enforceable contract, then the employer will have to abide by that contract. For instance, even if the employee is not a union member, and does not have a written employment contract, there may be statements in the employee handbook or job application that create a contract under which employees can only be discharged for good cause.

⇒ **TIP**

If an employee is discharged for good cause, the employer will probably not have to provide severance pay—unless, of course, there is an implied contract to do so.

The vast majority of employees have no written contract; they are "at-will" employees who work "at the will of the employer." At-will employment is a traditional legal doctrine that has been greatly modified by twentieth-century statutes and court cases. The employer still retains significant discretion, but cannot discharge employees for discriminatory reasons or for reasons contrary to public policy.

Furthermore, even if termination is justifiable, the employer must carry it out in a reasonable manner. Intentional infliction of emotional suffering on an employee, for instance, is not permissible. Even subsequent to termination, the employer must behave appropriately. There's a fine line to walk between misrepresenting the employee's tenure in a derogatory way (which is actionable defamation: see page 569) and depriving another employer of the information needed to make a rational hiring decision.

Proper communications with terminated employees can make the difference between those who understand the need for their termination, and who accept their severance packages . . . and plaintiffs who cause endless trouble even if their suits are eventually dismissed for lack of validity.

Many employee terminations are based on a need to downsize, rather than on the employee's individual poor performance. When employees are RIFed (become part of a Reduction in Force), it should be clarified that they are not at fault, and that the company will give them an excellent reference. Downsizing also affects a company's public profile, and its ex-employees can either become good-will ambassadors or quite the opposite.

HRMagazine editor Elaine McShulskis points out that employees who are finally laid off have probably experienced a prolonged period of anxiety; when the actual notice comes, they may be too shell-shocked to understand it properly. So it makes sense to distribute a brochure that answers questions about why the layoffs were necessary, the likelihood or unlikelihood of being recalled, the employee's COBRA rights and other benefits issues, and the availability of severance pay and outplacement assistance.

If conditions in the workplace are intolerable enough, and the employer has acted wrongfully enough, even an employee who quits might be able to sustain a wrongful termination case, under a legal theory called "constructive discharge." In other words, the conditions were tantamount to discharge.

To prove constructive discharge, the employee doesn't have to prove that the employer intended to force a resignation—only that it was reasonably foreseeable that an ordinary, non-saintly employee would quit under the same circumstances. There is no specific length of time that the conditions must continue before the employee's constructive discharge claim will be subject to rejection (i.e., if conditions were intolerable, the employee could not have tolerated them over the long run). It's a factual matter of reasonableness.

28.2 WHO SPEAKS FOR THE EMPLOYER?

Supervisors are representatives of the employer. If the supervisor is acting in the scope of his or her job, in a situation in which he or she is authorized to act, then what the supervisor says or does will have legal implications for the employer. The supervisor's negligence or outrageous conduct (such as humiliating an employee, causing him or her emotional distress) will be treated as if the employer had committed it.

In fact, in many instances the employer is legally responsible for the supervisor's conduct, and can be penalized for it, but the supervisor him- or herself can't be. Nearly all cases say that employees' discrimination suits are brought against the employer only. The supervisor can't be sued, even though people commit sexual harassment and corporations don't. Supervisors (as long as they are operating within the scope of their authority) can't be sued for inducing a breach of contract, either.

28.3 EMPLOYEE TENURE

The courts of some states (California is an example) may treat the fact that an employee has worked for an employer for a long time as an implied promise that the employee can continue to work there. Especially if the employee's tenure has been really long—say, a decade or more—the state may impose an "implied covenant of good faith and fair dealing." This has been done in Alaska, Arizona, California, Connecticut, Idaho, Massachusetts, Montana, Nevada, New Hampshire, New Jersey, New Mexico, and South Carolina.

A covenant is a promise; this line of cases deems the employer to have implied a promise to the employee that he or she will be treated fairly, and that the employer will not act in bad faith. Further, this implied covenant has been held to invalidate the firing of some long-term workers, at least without the corporate equivalent of due process of law.

However, one basic theme that runs through this book is the lack of uniformity in the way different jurisdictions treat the same issue. Courts in Florida, Kansas, Michigan, Minnesota, Missouri, Nebraska, New York, Oklahoma, Texas, and Washington have *rejected* the implied covenant theory. A 1994 Wyoming case says that in order to sue for breach of the implied covenant of good faith the plaintiff must prove that there was a special relationship of trust and confidence, over and above ordinary employee status.

Everyone involved in the hiring process should understand the employer's policies and how they should be implemented. For instance, interviewers should discuss positions as involving "regular" or "full-time" employment; calling a job "permanent" might be treated as a promise of continued tenure.

28.4 PROMISSORY ESTOPPEL

Another legal theory that may come up in employment cases is promissory estoppel. This is the contention that the employer made a promise to the employee, and is estopped (prevented) from disavowing that promise. This theory typically arises when an employee has "undergone detrimental reliance" (encountered problems after relying on something the employer said or implied).

The classic example is the top executive recruited from another company. The executive gives up a highly-paid, prestigious job, perhaps sacrificing the chance to become CEO of a major company, losing stock options, and other financial incentives. Maybe he or she moves cross country, unsettling the family. It could be that the luxurious home in the other part of the country has to be sold at a loss. All this is acceptable if there is a long, productive relationship with the new company— but not if, as soon as the new executive arrives, he or she is told that there has been a change in plans and his or her services will not be required!

In a 1994 Alabama case, the plaintiff won a claim for fraud in the inducement of contract because the employer lied about the facts she relied on in quitting her old job and going to work for the defendant company. A year later, another Alabama case imposed another requirement for the plaintiff to prevail: the employer must have made its promises with intention to deceive the plaintiff.

A Colorado case involved an employee who was recruited by a competitor of her then-employer to open a new office. She hesitated about leaving an established operation for a start-up, so they promised her that her new job would be much better in the long run than the old one. The new office closed in two months, and she was fired. The court decided that she was promised a "reasonable" term of employment, which the court interpreted to mean one year.

However, a more recent Wyoming case refused to apply the concept of promissory estoppel to a plaintiff who relied on verbal assurances of continued employment when she moved to a city that had no other jobs available for her after the termination of the job with the defendant company. She was not allowed to claim promissory estoppel because the job application and employee handbook both described the job as at-will employment, and the written documents control verbal statements. A 1995 Wisconsin case says that there is no breach of contract if an oral offer of at-will employment for an indefinite period is made and then withdrawn before the potential employee starts work.

Promissory estoppel has been applied in other contexts, too. For instance, when an oral promise of continued employment was made to induce an employee to remain at her job during a merger, to assist the transition team, her continued service with the company and her giving up the opportunity to find a new job were found to create an implied contract.

On the other hand, Illinois says that even if a contract is created with an employee who listens to the employer's promises of long-term employment and therefore fails to pursue an opportunity with another company, an oral "contract" cannot be enforced. A traditional concept called the Statute of Frauds says that contracts that last more than a year must be in writing to be enforceable, and this "contract" involved multiple years of employment.

The employee may argue that he or she provided consideration for a promise of lifetime employment, by staying on the job and not pursuing other job opportunities. But this argument won't persuade every court: some of them say that an employee can only hold one job at a time anyway, and therefore doesn't give up anything that would support a promise of lifetime employment.

After-acquired evidence of resume fraud has been held to bar all claims of breach of implied contract (failure to follow handbook procedures) and promissory estoppel, as long as the fraud was material and would have prevented an objective employer from hiring the perpetrator of the fraud. (In this case, a job applicant failed to mention a job from which she had been fired—and where she had sued, and settled with, the employer.)

28.5 PUBLIC POLICY

There's a whole line of cases that permits employees to sue when they were fired for reasons that are contrary to the public policy of the state. In other words, if an employee does something that is generally accepted as permissible or even admirable, the employer cannot fire the employee for that reason. For instance, no matter how inconvenient the timing is for the employer, it is not permitted to fire an employee for serving on a jury.

As discussed at page 329, ERISA §510 forbids employers to fire employees merely in order to prevent their access to pension benefits. In May, 1997 the Supreme Court extended this prohibition to discharges undertaken to prevent access to ERISA welfare benefits. Even though pension benefits can vest and welfare benefits can't, the correct response is to amend the plan to reduce the benefits, not to terminate the employees.

One fairly common argument is that states maintain a policy of promoting equal employment opportunity, and consequently a discriminatory discharge would have to violate state policy. However, this argument is seldom successful: for instance, a 1996 Oklahoma case says that the statutory remedies for age discrimination make it impossible for a discharged employee to sue for wrongful termination on this ground.

28.5.1 Whistleblowers

The case of the "whistleblower" employee is more complex. In many instances, employees (often employees who were dissatisfied for other reasons) go to the press, or file complaints with enforcement agencies, about some aspect of corporate conduct that they find unsatisfactory. Some states have statutes extending specific protection to whistle-blower employees (but some of these statutes are limited in their application to government workers, not employees of private-sector companies). The increasing trend in the courts (many of which have a majority of conservative, business-oriented judges) is to limit the situations in which an employee will be treated as a protected whistle-blower.

For instance, a drug company director of research was fired for insisting that some test results had to be reported to the FDA, when company officials did not think that the research demonstrated a serious risk (the standard for reporting incorporated into the FDA regulations). The director of research lost his case when he sued the ex-employer for wrongful discharge in violation of public policy. In the court's view, there had simply been a difference of opinion, and the employer could legitimately fire someone it believed to have used poor judgment.

In a Colorado case from early 1997, an employee was fired for sending a letter to a newspaper criticizing the employer's business practices. Colorado does have a statute that makes it unlawful to discharge anyone for lawful activity carried on outside the workplace, but that statute has an exception for bona fide occupational qualifications.

The federal District Court for the District of Colorado read this to mean that employers have a right to an implied right of loyalty in public communications. The employee didn't count as a whistleblower, because he failed to use the internal grievance procedure (which he probably would have done if he had a good-faith objective of solving the problem) and because customer service quality, not public safety, was at issue.

Furthermore, wrongful "discharge" means just that: a Washington State court found that there was no cause of action for wrongful *transfer* with no loss of salary or benefits, allegedly because the plaintiff reported what she perceived to be patient abuse to the state nursing home regulators. In this analysis, the plaintiff didn't lose any money, and therefore no legally enforceable rights had been violated.

It is certainly not the case that employees always prevail in these situations; there are various legal theories that come to the employer's aid. For instance, if the person reporting the alleged violation works for a government agency, the Civil Service Reform Act's whistleblower provisions preempt First Amendment claims of wrongful termination.

28.6 PREEMPTION

Preemption is a legal doctrine under which passage of a federal law will limit or eliminate the power of the states to regulate a particular subject. The federal law is said to preempt state enactments in part or entirely. In 1990, the U.S. Supreme Court ruled that ERISA, the federal pension and benefit statute (see Chapter 12), preempts state wrongful termination claims that involve an employee allegation of termination to prevent the employer from having to pay pension benefits. All such claims must be brought in federal court, under ERISA §510, and not in state court. (See page 329 for more discussion of ERISA preemption.)

According to the Massachusetts Superior Court, because OSHA has no private right of action, it does not preempt state claims that an employee was wrongfully discharged for reporting safety violations.

The Family and Medical Leave Act (FMLA) preempts common-law claims of retaliatory discharge (the employee claimed that the discharge was punishment for taking FMLA leave).

Employers can take advantage of the preemption argument in the state law context, too. If the state has an anti-discrimination law that covers the employee, and that is not in its turn preempted by federal anti-discrimination law, the employer may be able to get an ex-employee's wrongful termination suit (or wrongful termination claims within the suit) dismissed on the grounds that the employee should be bringing (or should have brought) a discrimination suit, not one for wrongful termination. From the employer's viewpoint, the best-case scenario is that the employee has waited too long, and can no longer bring discrimination charges, so the matter can be disposed of completely.

28.7 EMPLOYMENT CONTRACT TERMS

If the employer offers, or agrees to, a written employment contract, it should cover issues such as:

- Duration of employment
- How the contract can be renewed when it ends (including notice to be given)
- The rights of each party to terminate the contract, under specified circumstances
- The duties the employee will perform
- Promotion possibilities for the employee
- Compensation and benefits (including circumstances under which bonuses will be paid and stock options awarded; extent to which compensation is dependent on results)
- Who has the rights in inventions and other intellectual property developed by the employee during the contract term (especially intellectual property that is developed during the contract term but not during working hours, or not of a type that the employee was hired to produce)

- Ban on employee competing with the employer, or soliciting its employees and customers, even after termination of employment. (Any such restriction must be reasonable in both duration and geographic scope.)

- Severability, i.e., if any contract provision is invalid, it will be discarded, and the rest of the contract will continue in effect

- Alternative Dispute Resolution: whether the contract will be interpreted by an arbitrator, mediator, or other non-court decision-maker.

If the employee does have a written employment contract, all disputes with the employer have to be handled by suing for breach of that contract; the employee can't sue for wrongful termination, which is limited to at-will employees.

A 1995 Georgia case allows a suit for breach of contract when a one-year contract was terminated before the end of the year. However, if the only irregularity was failure to follow the termination procedure outlined in the contract, the damages would be only trivial. On the other hand, significant damages would be awarded only if vital rights under the contract were breached.

28.8 EXECUTIVE SEVERANCE PACKAGES

Major corporations, especially those that are financially troubled, often undergo lengthy searches to find a CEO or another top manager. Once recruited, the new hire will probably demand an employment contract; and that contract will probably require a significant amount of money and stock to be paid if the employee is dismissed before the contract expires.

In 1996 and 1997, there were a number of multi-million-dollar settlements with CEOs whose Boards of Directors in essence fired them for extremely poor performance. In turn, executives below the CEO level are using these large payouts as a reason to seek severance packages in their own contract negotiations.

Typical elements of an executive severance package include:

- Make-whole compensation, i.e., the salary, stock options, other deferred compensation, and non-qualified plan benefits that the executive forfeited by leaving the former job

- Up to three years' worth of compensation that the executive expects will be lost if he or she is fired and has to look for another job.

Furthermore, once a board has decided that a major executive must be replaced, the employment contract is only the starting point for the negotiations. The executive may be asked to resign, but might refuse to do so unless additional incentives are provided.

> ⇒ **TIP**
>
> It could be bad publicity for your company—or just an incentive for your other executives and job candidates to raise their demands!—if a big settlement is reported. So a typical severance agreement provision calls for confidentiality; if the exiting executive discloses the nature and size of the compensation package, he or she will have to pay back the severance benefits, plus the ex-employer's legal fees for the negotiation.

28.9 NEGOTIATED RESIGNATIONS

In some cases, an employee has been guilty of such serious misconduct that he or she must be removed immediately, or the corporation itself will be placed at hazard (large-scale embezzlement or securities fraud, for instance). In other cases, it will be less clear that employment must be ended. There might be a degree of ambiguity about the employee's conduct or its implications. In such a situation, the motto could be "Don't go away mad . . . just go away." Both parties benefit if they negotiate a resignation: the employee leaves on a stipulated date, and releases the company from all claims of employment-related discrimination.

A resignation agreement is a contract, and therefore is subject to ordinary contract law rules. For instance, if the employer deliberately misleads the employee or subjects him or her to undue influence, the resignation agreement will be void and will not be enforceable against the employee.

> ⇒ **TIP**
>
> First-line supervisors should not be allowed to negotiate employee resignations; either a corporate attorney, or a trained HR staffer, should take on this responsibility.

The agreement should deal with issues such as these:

- The employee promises that he or she has not already filed any charges, or instituted any litigation against the employer. (If legal action is already pending, settlement discussions or conciliation by the anti-discrimination agency are in order, but it's too late to negotiate a simple resignation agreement.)
- The employee waives all claims against the employer. The release must be carefully drafted by your corporate legal department or outside counsel, and should conform to the Older Worker's Benefit Protection Act (OWBPA) if the employee is aged 40 or over.

- The employee should agree to treat the resignation as a voluntary one, and therefore will not apply for unemployment compensation

- The employer should state that it does not admit liability of any kind; the agreement is merely a clarification of issues

- The employer should specify the kind of reference it will give the employee, and how it will handle reference checks by potential future employers

- The employee should waive receiving any merit-based bonuses that would otherwise be payable for the year of the resignation

- The employee should agree to return all materials in his or her possession that contain trade secrets or other proprietary materials of the employers, and should agree not to use the employer's proprietary/trade secret information in any later employment

- If a covenant not to compete is desired, it should be approved by the employer's attorney, and should be reasonable in both duration and geographic scope; it should prevent unfair competition with the ex-employer, but should not prevent the signing employee from earning a living

- The employee should agree not to recruit other employees to leave the company

- The employee should agree to keep the terms of the agreement confidential.

28.10 RELEASES

An employee who has already brought discrimination charges may be willing to settle those charges, receiving some consideration in exchange for releasing the employer from further threat of suit by that employee. (However, a suit by another employee, or by the EEOC, is still a risk.) Or, during the period of negotiations and disclosure before an employee is terminated, the employer and employee might agree on a severance package (see page 554) that settles their relationship, making it clear that the soon-to-be-ex-employee will not bring any charges of discrimination.

> ⇒ **TIP**
>
> If the terminating employee is a major executive or creative person, and the risk of lawsuit, unfair competition, or solicitation of your employees or customers is a significant one, it might make sense to meet the threat head-on by offering the employee a consulting agreement after termination. That way, at least he or she will be on your team instead of an enemy.

28.10.1 Forms for Releases

A release is a contract, a legal agreement under which the employee agrees to give up whatever claims he or she may already have. Releases can be quite general, merely referring to "all claims," or quite specific, spelling out a whole laundry list of claims.

There are trade-offs for each. If the release is too general, courts might refuse to enforce it, claiming that it is not specific enough to inform employees of their rights. On the other hand, if the release is too detailed, it could put ideas into the heads of employees who had no real intention of suing—or who didn't know the vast and exotic variety of ways they could make trouble for the employer!

The release document can deal with issues other than discrimination suits. The agreement can include provisions obligating the ex-employee not to disclose your company's trade secrets or other proprietary information that came into his or her possession during employment.

The terminating employee can be asked to agree not to compete with the employer, or not to solicit its customers or other employees. These "covenants not to compete" have some legal problems, but they should in all probability be upheld as long as the agreement serves reasonable interests of the employer, and is reasonably limited. If the covenant is so comprehensive and wide-ranging that it prevents the ex-employee from earning a living at all, or restricts legitimate opportunities, it probably will not be upheld. But if it makes sense in terms of the employer's business, without being too harsh on the ex-employee, then it is likely to be upheld.

Another issue that should be spelled out is intellectual property: if the terminating employee was a scientist, writer, designer, or other creative person, conflicts are likely to arise about how much of the intellectual property developed during the term of employment belongs to the employer.

Even if there was a clear work-for-hire agreement, the terminating employee might claim that the work at issue was really done on his or her own time, was submitted to the employer and rejected, or is so remote from the employer's business that it would be unjust to make the employer the owner of the intellectual property. Reasonable minds may differ about these issues, but it makes sense to try to resolve them during a moderately calm, rational discussion, instead of in the extremely hostile atmosphere of litigation.

Before payments of pensions and benefits begin, the plan might require the potential participant or beneficiary to sign a release to the effect that the plan has computed the amount of benefits correctly, or that the participant or beneficiary waives all claims against the plan *except* the right to receive benefits as specified by the plan.

Courts are split as to whether these mandatory releases are enforceable. As the next section discusses, if all participants and beneficiaries are required to sign, the release becomes part of ordinary plan administration, and there is no additional consideration for signing the release. The employer gets something (freedom from claims and suits) but doesn't give up anything in return (the benefits would be available under the plan anyway).

28.10.2 Consideration

A release is a contract, and all contracts require consideration in order to be enforceable. Consideration means that each party must receive something under the contract. In the typical release situation, the employer offers the employee some additional benefits (such as outplacement assistance, early retirement incentives, or additional severance pay).

> ⇒ **TIP**
>
> The employee really must get something extra—if all he or she gets is normal severance pay, the employer has not given any consideration for the release.

The employee offers the employer a release of all claims, thus sparing the employer the anxiety of having to defend against charges. As long as each party got something, courts probably won't worry about exact equivalence—and as long as the parties knew their rights and understood all the implications of the release.

28.10.3 Scope of Release

A general release covers all claims in existence at the time of the release; a limited release covers only the types of claims named in the release itself.

> ⇒ **TIP**
>
> If the release covers an injured worker who is entitled to Workers Compensation, then the release has to be approved by a Workers Compensation judge to be valid. It must be worded with special care in this situation: if the worker releases claims relating to the compensable *physical* injury, he or she will still have the right to bring suit on other grounds, for example, claims that the employer acted in bad faith or intentionally inflicted emotional distress on the employee.

States take varying approaches about what can be covered by a general release. Some states say that it can cover all claims, known or unknown, but other states say that a general release is not effective for claims that the employee did not know about or suspect at the time the release was signed. Under this theory, people can only give up claims that they know about and decide are worth less than the benefits under the release.

28.10.4 Basic OWBPA Rules

Under the Older Workers Benefit Protection Act, it is clearly permissible for employers and employees to negotiate and agree on the terms of a release under which the employee agrees not to press discrimination claims. The OWBPA's requirements are fairly simple and common-sense, aimed at assuring that employees will make a knowing and voluntary waiver of rights if they do choose to sign a release.

A valid release must:

- Refer specifically to the ADEA, so that workers know just what it is they are surrendering
- Give the employee at least 21 days to consider the release—at least 45 days if the release is offered in connection with a large-scale termination program rather than an individual termination
- Give the employee at least seven days during which the release can be withdrawn if the worker decides that signing it was a bad idea
- Inform workers that they can seek legal counsel before signing the release, which is a legal document.

⇒ **TIP**

It's a good idea to draft the release with a separate signature line so that employees who were NOT represented by counsel can indicate that they knew they could have legal representation, but chose to forgo it and sign the release without consulting a lawyer.

According to the Eleventh Circuit, there is no specific number of days that employees must be given to sign a release, although the 24 hours required by the company was clearly insufficient because there was no emergency. In this analysis, all that really counts is whether the employees had enough information and enough time to make a valid decision.

28.10.5 EEOC Guidance

On March 10, 1997, the EEOC issued a proposed regulation that would amend the OWBPA to explain proper release procedure for ADEA claims. The proposal appears at 62 *Federal Register* 10790, and affects 29 CFR Part 1625. An estimated 14,000 employees per year would be affected by the EEOC proposal.

Under the proposal, an acceptable waiver must:

- Be knowing and voluntary

- Not be the product of material mistake, omission, or misstatement in the materials provided by the employer

- Be made in writing

- Be in plain language that the employee (or the group of employees eligible for the exit incentive) can understand

- Be accurate and candid; it must not mislead or misinform employees, or deprive them of necessary information

- Mention the ADEA by name

- Not waive rights that arise after the waiver is signed. However, it is allowable for the waiver to obligate the employee to perform "future employment-related actions" such as taking early retirement or otherwise ceasing to be an employee as of a particular date in the future.

- Provide new consideration to the employee. In other words, in return for signing, the employee must get something he or she would not otherwise be entitled to. (However, if several employees are being terminated, and they all sign waivers, employers do *not* have an obligation to provide more consideration to employees over 40 than to those who are younger—even though only the over-40 employees have an ADEA cause of action that they can waive.)

If the employer eliminated some benefit in a way contrary to law, returning that benefit is not adequate consideration.

- Employment termination programs such as exit incentives can be either voluntary or involuntary; in either case, the employee must be given 45 days from the date of the employer's final offer to decide about a waiver. (This is longer than the general requirement of 21 days to decide whether or not to accept the waiver.) If the employer materially changes its offer, then the 21-day or 45-day period starts over again when the changes are made (unless the employees agree to abide by the earlier date). However, minor, trivial changes don't require re-starting the time period.

The proposal discusses two kinds of termination programs: exit incentives and others. An exit incentive program is voluntary, offered to a group of employees who can get extra consideration if they agree to resign and provide a waiver. The other programs cover employees who, after an involuntary termination, are asked to sign a waiver, usually in connection with a standardized formula or benefit package.

Usually, the employer makes a standard offer: the employees don't have the option of negotiating their own individual deals. In this context, an employer's offer can be a "program" even if it is not formal enough to constitute a "welfare benefit plan" for ERISA purposes.

Information about the program must be disclosed to every employee within the "decisional unit," which is a category or grouping of employees affected by a program. In this case, the decision refers to the employer's decision as to how to classify employees and determine which ones are eligible for the program. For most RIFs, the decisional unit is the facility; but it can also be a subgroup of the workforce, if that is the only one involved in the program. Decisional units can also be divisions, departments, groups of workers who report to a particular executive, or job categories.

The determination of the decisional unit can be difficult. If there are many small facilities in an area, with interrelated functions and employees, all of them together might constitute a decisional unit; or a function such as accounting may be dispersed over various facilities, yet form a decisional unit. There could be several decisional units within a single facility.

The Guidance is quite specific about how information should be provided. Age-group information should be reported according to the age of each person chosen or eligible for exit incentives, and everyone not chosen or eligible. Exact ages must be reported, not "age bands" such as 30-40. If the employees who will be terminated are at different grade levels or other subcategories, the information must also be broken down in this way. It must also be provided cumulatively if the termination program takes place over a period of time rather than in a single action.

The Guidance also makes it clear that if a waiver has been given, but its validity is later disputed by the signing employee, the party asserting its validity (which would nearly always be the employer) has the burden of proving to the court that the waiver was given knowingly and voluntarily. The party challenging the waiver (nearly always the employee) doesn't have to prove that the waiver was defective.

ADEA waivers are not permitted to bar individuals from "filing a charge or complaint, including a challenge to the validity of the waiver agreement" with the EEOC. Even waiving employees can still participate in EEOC investigations and proceedings. Waivers cannot impose penalties or other limitations on workers who do file an EEOC charge or assist the EEOC in an investigation.

This proposal is unusual because it was developed by the EEOC in collaboration with employer and employee representatives. The proposal does not cover the issue of whether or not employees who challenge a release must first tender back the consideration they received for signing the release. This is not because the question was deemed unimportant, but rather because the conferees could not reach an agreement.

EEOC guidance issued in April, 1997, as part of the agency compliance manual (see 65 LW 2678) says that the right to sue can be waived, but not the individual's right to file charges under the civil rights acts enforced by the EEOC. The agency's theory is that individuals can give up their own right of private recovery, but can't refuse to cooperate with the EEOC's duty to find discrimination and seek relief that benefits the public and other employees who have not waived their rights. EEOC investigators are trained to process claims even if the charging party has signed a waiver. This guidance also expresses the EEOC's position that employee handbook provisions mandating ADR instead of litigation are void as against public policy.

28.10.6 *Tender Back*

The question is whether an employee can challenge the validity of a release while retaining the benefits. "Ratification" is a traditional legal concept: in other words, some actions by one party can correct or make up for mistakes by the other party. For instance, if an employee willingly signs a release, and the release is technically deficient, some courts say that the employee can make the release valid by the action of accepting consideration from the employer in exchange for signing the release.

The Fourth and Fifth Circuits says that accepting benefits ratifies the release. The District Court for the District of Columbia says that even an employee who doesn't sign a release can ratify the release by accepting consideration.

However, the Third, Sixth, Seventh and Eleventh Circuits disagree, saying that employees can properly sue to challenge what they think is an invalid release, while still retaining the consideration paid for that release. In this analysis, they can always be ordered to give back the consideration if the court's judgment is that the release was valid all along. Some employers feel that it is especially unfair for plaintiffs to keep the release money (and use it to pay a lawyer!) but the Third Circuit specifically said that it is much more likely that ex-employees will need the release money for living expenses, so it is equitable to let them hang on to it, at least for the time being.

The Southern District of New York has yet another approach, to equalize the situation by placing both parties at some degree of financial risk. A plaintiff who sues for discrimination despite having given a release has to sign a formal undertaking that, if the release is found valid, the plaintiff will return the consideration for the release to the employer, no matter who wins the Title VII case.

The Supreme Court's docket for the October, 1997 term includes an OWBPA case, *Oubre* v. *Entergy Operations, Inc.*, #96-1291, but the issue is a narrow one: whether an employee who signs a release that does *not* satisfy the OWBPA can bring an ADEA suit without returning the consideration paid for the release. So the decision in this case will not resolve the question of tender back for cases in which the release was OWBPA-compliant.

28.10.7 *Waivers Under Other Statutes*

The OWBPA was passed to clarify the difficult issue of waiving ADEA rights. Even that wasn't enough to solve the problem! There is no specific statute governing waiver of Americans with Disabilities Act claims. A case from Spring, 1997, *Rivera-*

Flores v. *Bristol-Myers Squibb Caribbean, Inc.*, 65 LW 2719 (1st Cir. 4/25/97), finds that ADA waivers, unlike ADEA waivers, are interpreted under general contract principles. The existence of a waiver by the employee is an affirmative defense, so the employer has to prove that, based on the totality of the circumstances, the employee's waiver was made knowingly and voluntarily.

The relevant factors include:

- The degree of the plaintiff's education and business sophistication
- The extent (if any) to which the plaintiff had negotiating power to influence the text of the waiver (which might happen in the case of a top executive who was represented by influential counsel)
- The amount of time the employee was given to examine the waiver
- The participation of legal counsel or other independent advisors for the plaintiff
- Consideration given for the release.

Even if the employee claims that he or she was under a psychiatric disability, the test is the presence or absence of capacity to execute a knowing, voluntary waiver.

28.11 REDUCTIONS IN FORCE

The termination of a single employee is usually related to something about that employee: misconduct, poor work performance, creative differences, or simply personality conflicts. However, in many situations, the employer finds it necessary to reduce its force by laying off or terminating many workers at once. You might think that the presence of a business-related mass termination would protect the employer from discrimination claims: if 200 people are being let go, it's probably not because of animus against a particular individual or even a group.

However, employees frequently assert claims relating to RIFs (Reductions in Force). They charge that the RIF has been adopted to eliminate employees in disfavored classes, and the asserted need to reduce the payroll is only an excuse. Or they may acknowledge the legitimacy of the RIF as a whole, but say that conscious or unconscious prejudices determined which employees were chosen to be terminated.

In essence, there are three kinds of RIF:

- Complete elimination of operations, such as going out of business or moving a plant
- Elimination of a particular department or operation
- Making the overall workforce smaller.

A legitimate RIF can be based on either objective standards such as seniority or subjective (an assessment of the employees' qualifications and performance). It's important to train the supervisors who make decisions about layoffs to avoid assumptions based on prejudice. For instance, it is improper (and could be very expensive for the employer!) if an employee with a documented record of good performance is terminated instead of being offered a transfer, based on the supervisor's assumption that a married woman with children would not be willing to relocate.

Corporate counsel have some advice to offer about how to perform a RIF or downsize without violating laws or creating a public relations disaster:

- Set objective criteria for whose job will be eliminated
- Review these criteria to make sure they do not have a disparate impact on workers within a protected group
- Review the employee handbook to see if it contains explicit or implicit employment contract provisions
- Make sure any procedure for RIFs in the handbook is followed; try to meet employees' expectations about implied contract provisions
- Give WARN Act notice, if necessary (see page 369)
- Review the company's loan agreements: some are drafted to provide that reducing the workforce below a certain point accelerates loan obligations
- Offer employees as much notice as possible of impending job losses; on the other hand, reassure employees who will not be terminated that their jobs are secure
- Have your attorney prepare a legally valid release agreement; give employees plenty of time to review it, and do not discourage them from seeking legal representation if they want it.

28.12 PROGRESSIVE DISCIPLINE

The typical collective bargaining agreement (CBA) in a unionized operation will spell out a system of "progressive discipline": employees whose work performance is unsatisfactory will be warned, offered guidance and training, and subjected to a series of less stringent but escalating penalties before being fired. Progressive discipline is also used, albeit less frequently, in non-unionized enterprises.

It's not surprising that employees who are disciplined often resent it, or blame someone else (including "the system") for failings that have been charged to them. In some cases, a discharged or otherwise disciplined employee will file discrimination charges. Thus, an important HR function is creating a legally sustainable system of progressive discipline—and making sure that supervisors understand the system, and apply it with objectivity.

A progressive discipline system can also be a productivity tool. Sometimes the employee is simply at fault, and must either improve his or her attitude or look for work somewhere else. But other bottlenecks are caused by:

- insufficient staffing
- defective equipment that has to be replaced
- defective materials purchased from an inferior supplier
- employees who need more training to do an effective job
- employees who have disabilities that require accommodation from the employer. (See page 480 for a discussion of ADA issues.)

Once an employer establishes a system of progressive discipline, whether explicitly in a written contract or implied (by descriptions in the employee handbook, or even by course of conduct), that system becomes the equivalent of the company's legal system, and employees are entitled to some degree of "due process of law" before being demoted, having wages docked, and especially before termination.

Arbitrators will examine the "step formula" created by the employer, and will see if it was followed. If not, there's a good chance that the arbitrator will reverse the decision, or substitute a lesser penalty—and there's also a good chance that courts will uphold the arbitrator.

However, an Iowa case from early 1997 deals with a disciplinary procedure set out in the employee handbook. The handbook included explicit disclaimers saying that the handbook provisions did not create a contract. Therefore, it did not constitute wrongful termination to fire the employee without going through all the steps included therein.

The progressive discipline system must make clear to employees what is expected of them: sometimes flexible working hours are just fine, but in other operations, presence at defined hours is mission-critical. Employees should also know in advance what the employer intends to do if the rules are violated. It's not fair to terminate employees immediately under circumstances that they have been led to believe will generate only an oral reprimand.

Once employees know what they're doing wrong, they should be given a reasonable amount of time to correct it, and there should be a monitoring process to sort out which employees have made adequate progress and which have not (or whose performance has deteriorated). However, the time period should be neither too short (usually 30 days is the minimum) or too long (or the arbitrator may feel that the employer was throwing together distant, unrelated incidents to make its case). A 90-day "window" is probably the practical maximum.

A legally-sustainable disciplinary system should be:

- Consistent—not only must discrimination be avoided, but employees should not be subjected to supervisors' whims or penalized when the supervisor has a bad day

- Well documented—an arbitrator or court should be able to see that every step in the process was carried out according to the employer's own rules

- Clear—employees should know that if they don't meet X goals in Y days, they will be put on probation, lose wages, or be terminated

- Appropriate—applying the same sanctions to an employee who deals drugs at the workplace, or whose negligence endangers many people's safety, as to an employee who has a dusty desktop and uses paper coffee cups instead of reusable mugs, would hardly be fair!

- Reciprocal—employees should get a chance to state their side of the story to an objective decision-maker who is not already committed to management's viewpoint.

It can be very helpful to hire employees for an initial probationary period. During this time, the employer will have more leeway to terminate them than if they were long-term employees with some expectation of permanence. However, even probationary employees should be given clear guidance and explicit warnings if their behavior is likely to lead to dismissal, or to an extension of the probationary period.

28.13 HANDLING A DISCHARGE FOR CAUSE

In any operation, a proportion (let's hope it's a tiny one!) of employees will be larcenous, incompetent, drug-addicted, perpetually late, or simply ineffective. Employers are fully justified in making employment decisions based on poor work performance or misconduct (although they must apply equality of treatment: it is impermissible to fire black employees for persistent lateness if the same infraction by white employees is not penalized).

Sometimes the employer has made an explicit or implicit promise that discharges will occur only after a system of progressive discipline; in which case, it's important for the employer to document that the process was followed but the employee did not make the improvement necessary for retention.

Even if there is no such promise, it may make sense for the employer to try to salvage the situation. Firing one employee can damage the morale of a whole department even if there is no lawsuit in the picture. Time has to be taken to recruit a replacement, interview the candidates, and bring the new hire up to speed. The problems get even bigger if an employment agency or headhunter's fees are involved, or if the new hire has to be trained during a particularly busy period for the business.

When challenged, the employer has to be able to document the reason for the discharge. This is only one reason why the employee assessment program must offer real, hard-hitting criticisms and not just be a popularity contest. Many employers have lost suits because employees got repeated excellent evaluations (even though their performance was in fact mediocre or worse). When the time came to discharge the employee, there seemed to be no legitimate reason for the decline from lavish praise in past evaluations to condemnation in the final evaluation.

It may make sense to carry out and document an internal investigation of the facts of the situation. However, you must be aware that the information uncovered by the investigation is not necessarily confidential. If the discharged employee does sue, the court may give him or her access to all of this information (which may contain some not favorable to the employer).

Some recent examples of cases that find the employer legitimately discharged the employee for cause:

- A paramedic could be fired for insubordination after his second drug test that showed a positive for marijuana. Although he only smoked marijuana off-duty, the continuing effects of the drug during working hours justified his discharge.

- Even if the employee is entitled to an implied contract of discharge for good cause only, the employer can lawfully act on a reasonable, good faith belief that the plaintiff was guilty of sexual harassment—even if the harassment did not actually occur as charged.

28.14 THE EMPLOYMENT LITIGATION PROCESS

When the employer is named in a charge of discrimination or other employment-related wrongdoing, an important first step is an internal investigation to determine the extent to which the charges are valid. If the charges *are* valid then it probably makes sense to settle them immediately. In many instances, the anti-discrimination agency will close the file without imposing any penalties, based on the employer's assurance that the situation will be corrected.

Depending on the nature and egregiousness of the conduct, the charging employee may be willing to settle for a simple apology; it's more likely that some degree of compensation (e.g., reinstatement, a promotion, money damages) will be required. However, at an early stage, it may be possible to resolve the matter fairly amicably, at limited cost, and without incurring adverse publicity and large legal fees.

It has been held that there is no tort of "wrongful failure to promote."

An important issue in litigation is how wrongful termination suits (which are typically brought in state court) interact with discrimination suits (typically brought in federal court; see Chapter 27). Although some cases let employees sue for wrongful discharge if there is a reason why they can't sue for discrimination (e.g., because the company is so small that it is exempt from Title VII, the EPA, etc.), the more recent trend is to shut the cases out of the state courts too.

For example, in 1994 California said that employees of a company that is too small to be covered by the state age discrimination law can't claim that an age-based discharge is wrongful in that it violates state public policy against age discrimination.

The interaction of various employment laws is also important. In 1997, for instance, the Tenth Circuit found that an earlier case that the employee had already lost, alleging wrongful termination on the basis of race, disability, and in retaliation for filing a Worker's Compensation claim, prevented the employee from bringing a later ERISA charge of improper denial of severance pay. The legal doctrine of res judicata (matters already decided) prevented the second suit from being pursued because the court believed the allegations were so close to the original charges that they should all have been consolidated into a single suit.

In California, the statute of limitations for a wrongful discharge case runs from the actual termination date, not the earlier date on which the employee is informed he or she will be discharged in the future. In a constructive discharge case, the statute of limitations runs from the date the employee actually leaves, not the time at which conditions become intolerable.

In Tennessee, the rule is just the opposite: the statute of limitations starts to run on the date of notice, not the last day at work. This rule is more favorable to employers, because it means that more cases can be dismissed as untimely.

Chapter 29

CORPORATE COMMUNICATIONS

29.1 INTRODUCTION

Although there are many types of corporate communications, both within the staff and between the corporation and the public, the focus of this chapter is on those that might be potential sources of liability. The problematic area is defamation: hostile or unflattering statements about an applicant, employee, or former employee that the individual alleges to be damaging.

As the balance of this chapter shows, there are several circumstances under which the corporation can make negative statements without becoming liable. For one thing, the statements might be demonstrably true, they might have been made without malice, or they might have been made in a privileged context. This chapter also explores broader implications of privilege for corporate communications about HR topics.

29.2 DEFAMATION

Slander is defined as communicating a defamatory statement orally or otherwise informally; libel is communicating a defamatory statement more broadly ("publishing" it). A defamatory statement is one that attributes serious misconduct to someone else. The victim of slander or libel can sue and obtain tort damages. Sometimes an employer's statements about an employee are legally considered slanderous or libelous; however, they may also be privileged (thus preventing the employee from winning a suit).

To support a suit, the alleged slander or libel must be statement of fact, not a mere opinion or a general, imprecise statement ("Marcia is hard to work with"; "Steve seems to be working through some problems in his life.") A pure opinion can't be defamatory, because it is not a statement of fact, but a statement of fact backing up that opinion can be defamatory.

Truth is always a defense to a defamation charge; although it is not flattering to an employee to say that he or she was fired for stealing office supplies, it is not defamatory if that's what happened. If the employer believes a statement is true, and the statement is communicated without malice, then the employer is entitled to a defense for that reason. (It's up to the jury, not the judge, to decide if malice was present or absent.)

A statement has not been "published" to the point that a libel charge can be made if it is just communicated to the plaintiff, or to someone who is acting on behalf of the plaintiff (including a friend or investigator who calls just to find out what the employer is saying about the employee!). Courts differ in their reaction to the situation in which all the communication is within the employer corporation. It might be considered that this is so narrow that no publication has occurred; on the other hand, the court may accept the plaintiff's argument that dissemination was broad enough to constitute libel.

The doctrine that communication within the corporation can't be defamatory, because the corporation is "talking to itself," has been adopted in Alabama, Georgia, Louisiana, Missouri, Oklahoma, Tennessee, Washington, and Wisconsin. It used to be the rule in Nevada, but it was changed at the beginning of 1997.

On the other hand, the Restatement of Torts 2nd §577 states that expression within a corporation clearly constitutes publication, and this is the position taken by the states of California, Connecticut, Florida, Illinois, Indiana, Kansas, Massachusetts, Michigan, Minnesota, New York, Nevada, and Oregon. These states view the entire purpose of defamation law as protecting reputation within the business community, so an intraoffice communication could certainly endanger reputation.

A corporation can definitely be liable for statements made by its employees and agents, as long as they were acting in the scope of their employment.

29.2.1 Defamation Per Se

In the average, common-or-garden defamation case, the plaintiff doesn't just have to prove that defamation occurred: he or she must also prove that some actual damages were suffered by the plaintiff because of the defamation. But there are some statements so negative that it is automatically presumed that they will harm the reputation of the person about whom they are made. If the plaintiff charges such "defamation per se," he or she can win without proving actual damages (concrete injury attributable to the defamation).

29.3 PRIVILEGED STATEMENTS

Some kinds of communication are essential to the operation of businesses and the legal system, so they are afforded special treatment; they are referred to as "privileged" statements, and by definition they cannot be defamatory.

For instance, a 1993 case from California holds that a supervisor's statements made in an employee's performance review generally cannot be considered defamatory unless the supervisor falsely accuses an employee of criminal conduct, lack of integrity, incompetence or reprehensible behavior. In other words, to lose the privilege, the supervisor must actually lie, not just be wrong about the employee. Even unjustified or bad-faith statements might be treated as privileged if they are opinions held by the supervisor.

Restatement of Torts 2nd §596 permits a privilege when the publisher and the recipient of the information share a common interest, e.g., both are interested in making sure that qualified, honest individuals are hired and retain their jobs.

In addition to general privilege, "qualified" privilege exists in some circumstances. If a corporation has an audit committee, discussions of possible embezzlement or securities violations are probably entitled to qualified privilege as long as they remain within the committee, and are not disclosed (unless, of course, they are disclosed to law enforcement officials—which is the subject of another privilege). If there has been an investigation (e.g., to determine the source of inventory shrinkage), disclosing the results of the investigation to the employees at large would probably also be privileged.

Even though they are not, strictly speaking, law enforcement officials, the EEOC and unemployment officials are similar enough so that communications to them are privileged. There is at least a qualified privilege to make statements in the course of processing a union grievance or issuing dismissal letters required under a collective bargaining agreement; the privilege is made absolute by the statutes of Michigan, New Mexico, Louisiana, and Missouri.

Some state laws spell out a privilege. California, for instance (Civil Code §47(c)) gives employers a qualified privilege for statements made without malice and on the basis of credible evidence. Alaska presumes (Statute §09.65.160) that employers are in good faith when they discuss their employees with other prospective employers. However, if the employer acts recklessly, maliciously, or contrary to the employee's civil rights, the privilege is no longer available.

⟫ TIP

If the employer asserts a qualified privilege, it has the burden of proving that it is entitled to the privilege.

Employers are probably entitled to a qualified privilege when they make good-faith comments on employee performance to someone who has a legitimate right to the information. That in itself is a cause for caution: not all co-workers necessarily have a legitimate interest in the performance appraisal.

There is a qualified privilege to protect the safety of employees who might hurt themselves, or might be hurt by others. Thus, an employer was held not to have violated the employee's privacy by telling managers that the company's Employee Assistance Program thought that the employee was suicidal. (By the way, if a communication is privileged in the context of a defamation suit, it is probably also privileged if the employee sues for violation of privacy instead of, or in addition to, defamation.)

However, even if a privilege initially exists, it can be sacrificed—most typically, by failure to act in good faith, or by making statements without proof and with reckless disregard as to whether or not they are true.

29.3.1 Lawyer-Client Privilege

In order to do a good job, lawyers have to know all the facts of the situation— the ugly ones as well as the ones that make their clients look good. But clients will have little incentive to come clean if they know their lawyers will have to disclose the unfavorable facts. Therefore, the U.S. legal system allows certain information to be privileged: clients can tell their lawyers, and the lawyers not only can't be forced to disclose the information, they can't even disclose it if they want to. (In really drastic situations, where the lawyer would be able to prevent a crime by disclosing the information, the information loses its privileged status.)

> ⟼ **TIP**
>
> Just to be on the safe side, mark documents "Confidential" if their circulation should be restricted. Furthermore, although it is considered unethical for plaintiffs' attorneys to contact the defendant corporation's managers and supervisors outside of the litigation process, it makes sense to warn managers to say "No Comment" if an improper contact does occur.

These are the factors that determine the availability of attorney-client privilege:

- The client went to the lawyer to get legal advice (as distinct from a casual chat, or when the lawyer is playing another role, such as giving business advice or serving on the client company's Board of Directors)
- The lawyer is acting as a lawyer, not as a director or business advisor
- The communication relates to the lawyer-client relationship
- The client intends for the communication to be confidential
- The client didn't do anything (whether deliberately or inadvertently) to remove the privilege—for instance, material will lose its privileged nature if the corporation distributes it.

There are subtle questions involved in the treatment of corporate documents. For example, a report might be confidential *only* if it was prepared specifically as a confidential document for transmission to the attorney. Probably, if a communication's primary purpose is to get legal advice, secondary business advice won't take away the privilege. However, the privilege is waived (surrendered) if the corporation voluntarily distributed the document to non- attorneys, or disclosed or allowed the disclosure of a significant part of the document. For instance, if a corporation issues a press release about a development, or sends an employee to read a technical paper at an industry conference, it will be impossible to argue that the release and the technical paper are confidential documents.

> ⇒ **TIP**
> _____
>
> A statement made by an employee who is not acting as an agent of the employer, but who is simply an independent witness to an event, probably will not be confidential, no matter why the statement was prepared. Let's say a company is determining whether or not to discharge Edward Hayes, a supervisor who has been the subject of repeated sexual harassment complaints from subordinates. The investigation includes asking the complainants and other employees about Hayes' actions. A secretary's statement that she observed Hayes fondling a data entry worker would not be privileged.

Where outside counsel (not attorneys who were also company employees) did an investigation of an allegation of sexual harassment, the employer waived the attorney-client privilege by asserting the thoroughness of the investigation to show that the employer had adequate remedial measures and was not tolerant of harassment.

Perhaps because so many legislators are lawyers, there is a separate "work product" privilege contained in the laws of evidence. Work product is material prepared by attorneys, and agents working for attorneys, in the course of representing a client. Work product is also confidential and immune from discovery.

29.3.2 Self-Critical Analysis

One way that companies can eliminate job discrimination is to take a long, hard, objective look at their actual employment practices, then improve hiring and personnel practices. Reasonably enough, the results of these studies are often written down. The question becomes whether discrimination plaintiffs can require the company to disclose these documents. The plaintiff's objective is to use the document (which was created to *eliminate* discrimination) to prove that the company was guilty of discrimination at the relevant time.

Several federal courts have ruled that there is a "self-critical analysis privilege": in other words, that these documents are internal documents which should not have to be revealed to plaintiffs, because companies should be encouraged to be candid about their discrimination problems instead of suppressing what they know to avoid embarrassing disclosures in lawsuits.

The contrary view is that the documents were prepared as part of the company's Title VII compliance program, would eventually be reported to the EEOC, and therefore could not reasonably be described as privileged. Even under this argument, a distinction might be drawn between a self-critical analysis voluntarily undertaken by a company, and one that is mandated by the EEOC (or by agencies determining whether government contractors practice discrimination). Or the court might require the company to produce hard information like statistics about workplace diversity, but permit the analytical part of the report to remain confidential.

Of course, it helps to control dissemination of sensitive documents: the fewer people have access to the document, and the more they agree that the company needs to analyze its performance in order to correct it, the less likely they are to disclose the document in a way that is harmful or embarrassing to the corporation.

29.3.3 *Corporate Ombudsman*

An ombudsman is a neutral outsider whose job it is to hear complaints and assess the performance of a system; it's a "watchdog" function. Some corporations employ ombudsmen to gather facts about disputes and workplace problems (and, if possible, iron them out). There is a professional group, the Corporate Ombudsman Association, and its ethical code requires confidentiality of communications with the ombudsman.

An employer that had a corporate ombudsman tried to get federal law to recognize that communications with an ombudsman are privileged, and therefore cannot be discovered by employees who sue. (In this case, the claim was age discrimination.) But the Eighth Circuit refused to recognize this privilege, finding that the public need to know outweighs the corporation's interest in using ombudsmen to resolve claims. In the court's view, the employer didn't prove that an ombudsman did a better job than an arbitrator or mediator, or that the ombudsman would be prevented from doing an effective job if his or her records could be discovered by an employee plaintiff.

29.4 DUTY TO COMMUNICATE

The flip side of situations in which the employer is not supposed to communicate material adverse to the employee occurs when the employer is held liable for *not* communicating such material. For instance, there might be a duty to disclose dangerousness, so other employers will not hire someone who puts their other employees or customers at risk. Or a subsequent employer may sue if the first employer fails to reveal relevant information, such as an applicant's dismissal for stealing or selling drugs at the workplace.

Employers have a duty to protect customers and co-workers, so they are negligent if they know that someone is dangerous but still hire or retain him or her as an employee. This is true even if the risk is of conduct outside the scope of employment. An employer who knows that an employee has violent tendencies can be liable because of workplace assaults committed by that person—even if the assaults are not only not part of the job, but are contrary to the employer's policy and work rules. (However, if the injured person is also an employee, it's quite likely that the employee's only remedy will be through the worker's compensation system—see page 396.)

Employers can be sued for negligent hiring or negligent entrustment if they hire someone for a safety-critical job, but fail to check that person's references. In some contexts (for instance, hiring an employee for a nursing home or day care center), there may also be a duty to consult a special database maintained by the state or a licensing organization to list individuals who have been convicted of crimes and are therefore ineligible for employment.

An employer will probably be exempt from liability for negligent hiring if a thorough investigation is performed before hiring; but if an employer fails to discover information that would have been disclosed by an ordinary background check, liability is a possibility.

Discrimination plaintiffs sometimes tack on a negligent hiring claim. Their theory is that the employer was negligent in hiring and/or retaining a supervisor who was racist, sexist, or otherwise prone to engage in discriminatory conduct. The advantage to the plaintiff is that, although the discrimination claim is subject to the CRA '91 limits on damages (see page 542), the negligent hiring claim is not. Also, it's hard to introduce evidence into a discrimination case about acts of discrimination or harassment carried out against others, but much easier in the negligent hiring context.

The employer might also be liable for negligent supervision, if the court or jury accepts the argument that the supervisor would not have been able to carry out the act of discrimination or harassment if the employer had managed the facility better. However, in the sexual harassment context, some courts have refused to let employees sue the employer if the alleged harassment merely had psychological implications and did not include battery or physical injury to the employee.

➡ TIP

To stave off allegations of negligent supervision, make sure your organization has, communicates, and lives up to a policy of doing a prompt, thorough, and fair internal investigation of discrimination and harassment charges.

29.5 RESPONSES TO REFERENCE CHECKS

Obviously, the employer must steer between two hazards: on one side, the employer must avoid committing defamation against employees and ex-employees. On the other side, it must disclose whatever information is mandatory. One approach that often works is simply to confirm the date of the employee's tenure at your company, then say that it is against company policy to discuss ex-employees. Another possibility is to disclose only information that is fully documented by personnel files.

> ⇒ **TIP**
>
> Many states allow employees to review these files and make their own comments; if your state is one of them, make sure that anyone responding to an inquiry includes the employee's comments. For instance, he or she might say "Ms. Jones was dismissed for excessive lateness and poor performance. However, she said that other people were late at least as often, and we should have been more sympathetic about her performance because her mother had just died." That way, the questioner gets both sides of the story.

If an employee's resignation or termination is being negotiated, one area of negotiation is what will be said in response to reference checks.

A frustrating possibility: an employer may maintain a strict policy of disclosing only the fact of past employment, start date, and termination date. Even then, the employer may be sued by an ex-employee who charges "compelled self-publication," i.e., because the past employer said so little, the employee was forced to spill the beans to the potential new employer, and thus had to make the negative revelation personally. Some courts have penalized the former employer for forcing the terminated employee into this position: see, e.g., *Churchey* v. *Adolph Coors Co.*, 759 P.2d 1336 (Colo. 1988); *Neighbors* v. *Kirksville College of Osteopathic Medicine*, 694 S.W.2d 822 (Mo.App. 1985).

On the other hand, some courts have rejected this theory, perhaps because they know that the employer restricts its communications precisely in order to avoid defamatory statements: *Gore* v. *Health-OK Inc.*, 567 So.2d 1307 (Ala.Sup. 1990); *Layne* v. *Builders Plumbing Supply Co.*, 210 Ill.App.3d 966, 569 N.E.2d 1104 (1991); *Wieder* v. *Chemical Bank*, 202 A.D.2d 168, 608 N.Y.S.2d 195 (1994).

It may be easier to get reference check information by asking what the job candidate did that was *good* and what his or her strengths were as an employee, than to ask explicitly or implicitly that you're looking for a hatchet job that will give you good reason to avoid hiring the candidate. There's less fear about disclosing positive than negative information, because nobody is going to sue for defamation for being described as "effective," "creative," "incredibly hard-working," or "honorable and completely trustworthy."

Chapter 30

INSURANCE COVERAGE FOR CLAIMS AGAINST THE EMPLOYER

30.1 INTRODUCTION

What if someone slips and falls on the employer's business property, and breaks a leg? There's a simple answer: the sensible manager will make sure that the business has adequate liability insurance. However, if the question changes to ask what happens if an employee or ex-employee charges the employer with discrimination, harassment, or wrongful termination, the answer is much more complex. Whether insurance can be purchased, or whether an existing policy will pay claims based on employment-related incidents and allegations, is a difficult question to answer. The response depends on understanding insurance law and practice, employment discrimination law, and the way they work together.

30.2 THE CGL

For most businesses, the Commercial General Liability policy (the CGL) is the basic way to get liability coverage. In fact, for most of them, the CGL is the only coverage they have against liability to third parties.

The CGL has two basic purposes: first, to provide a defense (i.e., supply a lawyer who will investigate, negotiate, and settle or try the case), and second, to take over the insured company's obligation to pay a settlement or judgment to a successful plaintiff. The insurer doesn't have to start paying until the insured satisfies its obligation to pay a deductible, and the insurer doesn't have to pay any more than the maximum amount provided in the policy.

Furthermore, the insurer only has to pay for claims that are covered under the policy, not for those that are excluded. So, to determine if the CGL will cover an employment-related claim, you must see what it covers and what it excludes. (The

Insurance Standards Organization, or ISO, has published a very influential model for CGL policies, but insurance companies have the option of tailoring this model as they see fit, so CGL policies are not really uniform.)

There's a trend for recently-written policies to have a straightforward exclusion for *all* claims related to the plaintiff's employment by the defendant, based on ISO's "Employment-Related Practices Exclusion." That pretty much takes care of that (although a legal loophole can be found in just about any brick wall: for instance, a court might take the position that the real injury to the plaintiff occurred *after* he or she was fired and therefore stopped being an employee).

What about CGL policies that do not have a specific exclusion for employment-related claims? In many cases, the language of the policy will prevent the employer from collecting insurance benefits under the policy.

30.2.1 Bodily Injury and Personal Injury

Coverage A of the CGL provides liability insurance when the insured becomes liable to someone who has suffered "bodily injury." Usually, of course, plaintiffs in employment cases don't claim that they suffered physically, but that they lost economic benefits (such as salary and pension) because of wrongful conduct by the employer. If the plaintiff only charges breach of contract or other economic consequences, then it's clear that the CGL will *not* cover the charges.

For this and other reasons, plaintiffs often ask for damages based on their emotional suffering, and their complaints allege pain and suffering, intentional infliction of emotional distress, or negligent infliction of emotional distress. (Whether they can bring these charges depends on whether they are in the state or federal system; there are also variations from state to state.)

Most courts that have dealt with this question say that there is no "bodily injury" in an emotional suffering case unless the plaintiff can prove that there was at least some physical consequence of the emotional injury: an ulcer or high blood pressure, for instance. Even if there are physical consequences, they might be treated as incidental to what is basically an economic case—one which falls outside the CGL.

The CGL's Coverage B deals with liability that the insured encounters for "personal injury" (such as libel or slander) or advertising injury (such as defaming another company's products in your ads). Coverage B might get involved in an employment-related case if, for instance, the plaintiff claims that the employer not only fired the plaintiff, but also "blacklisted" him or her and used a campaign of lies to prevent the ex-employee from getting another job or establishing business relationships.

30.2.2 Occurrences and the Problem of Intention

Coverage under the CGL Coverage A depends on there being an "occurrence," which is defined as an accident which was neither intended nor expected by the insured. (Coverage B does not have an occurrence requirement, but it does exclude coverage of personal injuries that stem from a willful violation of the law, committed by or with the consent of the insured company.)

It would seem, then, that employment cases could never be covered under the CGL, because the employee or former employee who brings the case charges that someone deliberately injured him or her. After all, there's no form of corporate Alzheimer's that allows companies to fire or underpay their employees in a fit of absent-mindedness.

But the picture is more complex than that. As discussed on page 455, some discrimination charges claim "disparate treatment" (roughly speaking, intentional discrimination), while others claim "disparate impact" (policies that have subtle negative effects on a protected group of employees). If the employer deliberately adopts a policy or publishes an employee manual, those deliberate actions might have unintended consequences, which might perhaps be treated as occurrences under the CGL. However, intentional discrimination would not be; and courts often treat some conduct (such as sexual harassment) as being so likely to have bad consequences for their victims that the consequences are presumed to have been intended, or at least expected, by the insured company.

Employment discrimination plaintiffs usually want the insurance company to be involved, because they know that liability insurance is another potential source of payment if they settle or win the case. So in this instance, they're on the same side as the employer: they both want the CGL to cover the employee's claims. One simple strategy is for plaintiffs to add claims of negligent supervision by the employer, or negligent infliction of emotional distress, in the hope that these charges of negligence will be treated as covered "occurrences." However, this tactic usually fails: the negligence charges are treated as purely incidental to more important charges of intentional conduct.

The CGL exclusion of "intentional" conduct does not apply to conduct that is negligent, or even grossly negligent. Although facts and legal interpretations differ from case to case, in most instances termination, even wrongful termination, does not involve the intention or expectation of harm, so the insurer will probably have a duty to defend.

There are some conceptual problems because, naturally, corporations rely on human agents to carry out their policies. A corporation's management is deemed to expect or intend acts that it knows about and condones. The corporation's management is responsible for adopting unlawful policies.

CGL personal injury coverage often excludes damage resulting from the willful violation of a penal statute or ordinance, if the violation is committed by or with the insured's knowledge or consent. Civil rights laws are not considered "penal statutes" for this purpose. Even if the actions are "willful" for Title VII purposes, this will not trigger the criminal law exclusion.

> ⇒ **TIP**
> _____
> Some CGL policies offer (at additional cost, of course) an endorsement or rider that WILL cover discrimination and harassment claims, often by broadening the underlying policy's definition of personal injury.

Another typical CGL exclusion is bodily injury to the employee, arising out of and in the course of employment, whether the employer is liable as an employer or in other capacities. But that is probably included in the policy simply for coordination with Worker's Compensation. The insured may succeed in arguing that intentional tort claims made by employees do not arise out of or in the course of the employment relationship. Supervisors are not hired to commit discrimination or harassment! This fact may at least impose a duty to defend on the insurer. Furthermore, occupational injuries may be considered a known risk that employees are aware of; discrimination and harassment are not risks of the same category.

30.2.3 Public Policy Issues

Suppose you were really angry at someone, so you bought a liability insurance policy, paid a premium or two, then deliberately and maliciously destroyed your enemy's property or physically injured him—then sat back and waited for your insurance company to bail you out! Obviously, that wouldn't be fair, so there's a basic principle of insurance law that you can't buy insurance to protect yourself against *intentional* wrongdoing. In fact, until 1994, New York State considered it illegal to sell liability insurance covering employment-related claims. (That practice has since been changed.)

Nowadays, and in most states, the usual interpretation is that it does not violate public policy for companies to buy insurance to cover employment-related liability, because the benefit to injured employees (who are more likely to collect whatever they win, if insurance is involved) is greater than the risk that companies will engage in worse employment practices because they know they have insurance.

A related policy question is whether insurance can cover punitive damages. About two-thirds of the states that have decided cases about this question say yes, but punitive damages for intentional wrongdoing cannot be insured, and most punitive damages are imposed precisely to punish a defendant for intentional wrongdoing that shocks the conscience, not just a defendant that was exceptionally careless.

30.3 NON-CGL POLICIES

Every CGL policy has limits: maximum amounts of coverage obtainable under particular circumstances. If your company already has maximum CGL coverage, but feels that more is necessary, there are two related ways to supplement it. The first is "follow-form" excess liability insurance, which increases the amount of coverage available under your CGL (and other insurance, such as Worker's Compensation and Business Automobile Liability coverage), but is subject to the same terms and exclusions. This coverage would work if you had to pay an amount that was covered under the CGL or a related policy, but was greater than the limitation of that policy.

For many companies, an "umbrella" policy is a better choice, because it is more broadly defined and may cover situations that were excluded by the underlying policy. (NOTE: If you are entitled to "gap" coverage of this kind, the coverage will probably be reduced by a "retained limit," which is just a fancy name for a deductible.)

Umbrella policies offer coverage in more situations because their coverage definitions are based on a definition of "personal injury" that is broader than Coverage A or Coverage B of the standard CGL. A typical provision includes both bodily injury and mental injury, mental anguish, shock, sickness, disease, discrimination, humiliation, libel, slander, defamation of character, and invasion of property—so many employment-related claims would fit within this definition but not within CGL Coverage A.

30.3.1 Worker's Compensation Policies

Separate Worker's Compensation coverage is available to deal with the employer's obligation to pay benefits to employees who are injured in job-related situations. Of course, because of WC exclusivity (see page 396), the employer doesn't have to worry about ordinary liability actions from injured workers, although there may be special situations where the employer, or someone else (such as the manufacturer of unsafe factory machinery) can be sued even if Worker's Compensation is involved. In a WC employment liability policy, Worker's Compensation is Coverage A; the employment liability is Coverage B.

The Insurance Standards Organization (ISO) has not drafted a standard for these policies, so there are wide variations from insurer to insurer. Some policies combine WC coverage with employer liability coverage for non-WC common-law claims for injuries resulting to employees (e.g., bodily injury that is not subject to WC exclusivity).

⇒ TIP

If the charges you face involve an injured worker (for instance, one who claims disability discrimination after an injury), your Worker's Compensation insurer may have a duty to defend you because of the possibility that you may be able to dispose of the case by claiming WC exclusivity.

30.3.2 *Directors' and Officers' Liability (D&O)*

D&O Insurance covers the situation in which a corporation's directors and officers get not only themselves but the corporation into trouble. Frequently, executives won't agree to serve as directors or officers unless the corporation first promises them indemnification, i.e., that the corporation will pay the executive whatever amount he or she has to pay because of liability incurred while acting as a director or officer.

D&O insurance, in turn, reimburses the corporation for whatever it spends on indemnification (up to the limit of the policy, of course, and subject to a deductible).

30.3.3 *Errors & Omissions (E&O)*

Errors and Omissions insurance pays, on behalf of the insured, all loss for which the insured person is not indemnified by the insured organization if the person has to pay because of any wrongful act he or she committed or attempted. In general, committing disparate treatment discrimination will be considered a wrongful act that can be covered under the policy, unless the policy definition covers only *negligent*, and not intentional, acts and omissions.

In many companies, E&O insurance is complemented by D&O insurance which covers the company for the losses it incurs when it indemnifies directors and officers acting in that capacity.

An important issue is whether or not administrative actions (such as state agency and EEOC proceedings) are considered "claims or suits" for insurance purposes. The insurer is also likely to advance the argument that back pay awarded to a prevailing plaintiff is equitable relief rather than "damages" eligible for plan coverage.

However, many courts have rejected this argument and required liability insurers to handle back-pay awards against their policyholders. E&O insurers may also resist paying back pay if the policy excludes amounts owed under a "contractual obligation," but here again, the insured will probably prevail if a back pay award is made.

Another insurance form covers plans, administrators, and trustees against allegations of impropriety. Many employment-related claims involve ERISA allegations, so the employer should at least consider adding this coverage to its insurance portfolio.

30.3.4 *Employment Practices Liability Insurance (EPLI)*

Since about 1990, EPLI, or Employment Practices Liability Insurance, has been available precisely for the situations in which the CGL does not offer coverage. EPLI is designed to cover damages, judgments, settlements, defense costs, and attorneys' fee awards in the employment liability context. The EPLI policy excludes penalties, punitive damages, and any amounts deemed to be uninsurable under relevant state law.

Events included under the EPLI are discrimination, sexual harassment, and wrongful termination, but not "golden parachutes" (payments to top managers who lose their jobs because of corporate mergers and acquisitions) or contractual obligations to make payments to terminated employees.

As of late 1996, coverage with a $1 million limit was available for about $7,500 a year. (Although $1-$5 million is the usual limit, "jumbo" policies with up to $100 million in coverage are offered by some of the 20 or so insurers that offer EPLI.) At that time, about $100 million a year in EPLI insurance was sold, but the potential market was estimated at $1 billion a year by 2000, and $2 billion by 2006.

> ⇒ **TIP**
>
> In addition to coverage, the policy may offer access to valuable loss prevention consulting services and compliance advice that would otherwise carry a high price tag.

An EPLI "claim" is a suit or other proceeding brought against the covered employer, or a written claim or demand that seeks to hold the covered employer civilly liable for a wrongful employment practice (employment discrimination, sexual harassment, wrongful termination). Criminal charges are excluded from the policy. It covers reasonable and necessary expenses of defending against or settling a claim, including attorneys' fees and interest. However, most policies exclude fines and punitive damages.

30.4 THE DUTY TO DEFEND

A lesser-known, but perhaps more important, part of the liability insurance policy is the insurer's duty to defend. That is, whenever a "claim" is made against the employer, the insurer has to provide a lawyer and take care of the case. That is a very valuable provision: at a time of crisis, the insured knows that an experienced insurance defense lawyer will get to work right away. It won't be necessary for the house counsel to hurriedly get up to speed on insurance and tort law, or to retain another lawyer with the appropriate expertise.

As usual, this advantage is balanced by a downside. Generally speaking, the insurer will be in control of the litigation. That is, it will decide how good your case is and how vigorously to defend it. Suppose it thinks that it makes sense to settle the case quickly, and you want to fight to the last ditch to defend your good name: well, too bad for you, unless you can persuade the insurance company lawyer to see it your way, or unless your policy specifically returns control of the litigation to you.

In fact, the typical business policy is drafted so that, if the insured company settles the case without consent and participation of the insurer, the insured company will not be able to recover any part of the settlement costs from the insurer.

The duty to defend is much broader than the duty to indemnify (pay amounts that the insured is ordered to pay by a court, or as part of a settlement). This makes sense—if the charge against an insured company is invalid, or can't be proved, then the liability insurer's role is to get the charge dismissed, even though the insured doesn't have any liability exposure.

The basic legal rule is that if an employee's or ex-employee's complaint mixes charges that are covered by liability insurance with those that are not, the insurer has a duty to defend against *all* the charges, not just the covered one(s). (The legal theory is that it makes sense to deal with all the related allegations at once, instead of splitting them up into a series of smaller cases.)

Generally speaking, the insurer's duty to defend is triggered by a "claim" made against the insured employer. This is usually interpreted to mean filing of a complaint with a court. If the claim involves employment discrimination, the plaintiff probably had to go through agency proceedings with the EEOC or a local agency (see page 470) before getting the right to sue. The EEOC or local agency proceedings are not generally considered "claims," so you're on your own for a significant part of the process, before the duty to defend kicks in.

30.5 QUESTIONS OF TIMING

Even if an employment-related claim makes it through all those filters, and is entitled to a defense or to reimbursement under a liability policy, there are still some legal questions to be resolved about whether coverage will be available for timing reasons (or *which* policy, of several, will have to provide coverage).

Liability policies are divided into "occurrence" and "claims-made" policies. If there is an "occurrence" covered by the policy, *all* the occurrence policies in force at that time have to pay up. (No, you don't get five times the amount of your liability if you have five policies. The coverage is coordinated, or divided among the five so you don't get a windfall.)

If you are accused of a pattern or practice of discrimination, rather than a single discriminatory act, it becomes necessary to determine what took place during the effective dates of each policy. This becomes particularly crucial if you drop one policy and replace it with another.

➠ **TIP**

It may be a false economy to replace a liability insurance policy, if you have a new waiting period in the new policy, leaving you with a period without coverage.

In contrast, a claims-made policy covers only claims that are made during the policy term, and for events that happened during the policy term. In other words, if you get sued in 2003 for something that happened in 1999, a claims-made policy won't cover you unless it was in force in both years. Because this can be a difficult standard to meet, claims-made policies are often extended to cover events after the "retroactive date" specified in the policy. There may also be an "extended reporting period" after the policy expires, where events are covered if they occurred while the policy was still in force, and were reported later.

30.6 DUTIES OF THE INSURED

Your insurance company might not have to pay your claim, if you failed to satisfy your obligations to the insurer. The most obvious one is paying your premiums! There is also a less obvious requirement contained in the liability policy: you must notify the insurer, as soon as possible, if you become the subject of a "claim." As noted above, it can be pretty tough to determine what, short of an actual lawsuit, constitutes a claim. Get legal advice about how to respond to all charges, and whether the insurer must be notified. There is, of course, a temptation to push complaints under the rug, and to avoid mentioning them to the insurer in case the result is a higher premium or denial of renewal coverage—but it's vital to make all necessary reports and make sure that the insurer doesn't have an excuse for not paying you.

Notes

Chapter 4 — Work-Family Issues

Page 44   Relative cost of family-friendly measures: Elaine McShulskis, "Work/Life Programs Increase Employee Retention," *HRMagazine* June, 1997 p. 32.

Page 44   Reducing turnover: Michelle Neely Martinez, "Work-Life Programs Reap Business Benefits," *HRMagazine* June, 1997 p. 110.

Page 44   Dissatisfaction of single employees: Gillian Flynn, "Backlash: Why Single Employees Are Angry," *Personnel J.* 9/96 p. 59.

Page 45   Adoption assistance: Marilyn Manewitz, "Employers Foster Assistance for Adoptive Parents," *HRMagazine* May 1997 p. 97.

Page 46   Time requirements of caregiving: Employee Benefits Alert, 6/4/97 p. 5.

Pages 46–7   Corporate impact of elder care: Maureen Minehan, "The Aging of America Will Increase Elder Care Responsibilities," *HRMagazine* July, 1997 p. 184.

Pages 46–7   Recent survey on cost of caregiving: "The MetLife Study of Employers Costs for Working Caregivers," published by the National Alliance for Caregiving; free copies of the report are available by calling (301) 718-8444.

Pages 46–7   Beliefs about the future of elder care: summary of survey results, *Personnel J.* August, 1996 p. 16.

Chapter 5 — Diversity in the Workplace

Page 52   Downside of diversity training: Alex Markels, "A Diversity Program Can Prove Divisive," *Wall St. J.* 1/30/97 p. B1; Michael Delikat and Ruth Raisfeld, "Litigation Over Corporate Diversity Programs," *N.Y.L.J.* 7/14/97 p. S5.

Page 53   Working around prejudices: Claudia H. Deutsch, "Diversity Training: Just Shut Up and Hire," *N.Y.T.* 12/1/96 p. E4.

Page 53   EEOC guidelines: 29 CFR §1606.7.

Page 53   Ninth Circuit decision on English-only rules: *Garcia* v. *Spun Steak Co.*, 998 F.2d 1480 (1993).

Page 53   Pending lawsuits: e.g., *EEOC* v. *Long Life Home Care Service Inc.*; see Mirta Ojito, "Bias Suits Increase Over English-Only Rules," *N.Y.T.* 4/23/97 p. B1; Ann Davis, "English-Only Rules Spur Workers to Speak Legalese," *Wall St.J.* 1/23/97 p. B1.

Page 53   Workplace English classes: Andy Newman, "Shop Talk: English at Work," *N.Y.T.* 5/18/97 p. NJ1.

Page 54   Premium for extra languages? Peter Fritsch, "Bilingual Employees Are Seeking More Pay, and Many Now Get It," *Wall St. J.* 11/13/96 p. A1.

Chapter 6 — The Role of the Computer in HR

Page 59   Meta-indexes: Mike Frost, "Technology Solutions," *HRMagazine* July, 1997 p. 30.

Page 60   Internet job searches: Mike Frost, "The Internet's Hire Purpose," *HRMagazine* May, 1997 p. 30.

Page 61   Creating a corporate intranet: Elaine McShulskis, "HRM Update," *HRMagazine* June, 1997 p. 20; Martha I. Finney, "Harness the Power Within," *HRMagazine* January, 1997 p. 66.

Page 63   E-mail as protected communication under NLRA: *Timekeeping Systems Inc.* v. *Lawrence Leinweber*, 323 NLRB No. 30, 1997, discussed in Note, "NLRB Case Adds Protected Activity Issue to Debate over Employer E-Mail Policies," 66 LW 2019 (7/8/97).

Page 63   Gaming and other non-work uses: Amy Harmon, "On the Office PC, Bosses Opt for All Work, and No Play," *N.Y.T.* 9/22/97 p. A1.

Chapter 7 — Compensation Planning

Page 69   Merit increases: Hewitt Associates survey, quoted in Joann S. Lublin, "Don't Count on that Merit Raise This Year," *Wall St. J.* 1/7/97 p. B1.

Page 69   Value-based pay: Joseph B. White, "The 'In' Thing," *Wall St. J.* 4/10/97 p. R10.

Page 70   Broadbanding: Karen Jacobs, "The Broad View," *Wall St. J.* 4/10/97 p. R10.

Page 71   Benefits at large vs. small companies: Quoted in Elizabeth MacDonald, "Slim Pickings," *Wall St. J.* 5/22/97 p. R6.

Page 71   Severance pay trends: Elaine McShulskis, "HRM Update," *HRMagazine* May 1997 pp. 20, 23.

Page 72   Disclosure requirement depends on "serious consideration": *Pierson* v. *Hallmark Marketing Corp.*, 66 LW 1063 (E.D. Pa. 6/24/97).

Page 73   Taxation of parachute payments: William J. Canan, Welfare Benefits (West 1997) §18.5.

Page 74   Capitalization of severance payments: TAM 9326001, TAM 9527005, Rev.Rul. 94-77, 1994-2 CB 19.

Page 76   Direct deposit implications: Steven Greenhouse, "When Direct Deposit Shifts into Reverse," *N.Y.T.* 3/3/97 p. B4; Martha Nolan McKenzie, "Turning Direct Deposits into Direct Withdrawals," *N.Y.T.* 3/23/97 p. F12.

Chapter 8 — Wage and Hour Issues

Page 80   Flexible work hours: Bureau of Labor Statistics, quoted in *N.Y.T.* 6/15/97 p. F9.

Page 80   Rehiring downsized workers: Louis Uchitelle, "More Downsized Workers Returning as Rentals," *N.Y.T.* 12/8/96 p. A1.

Page 80   Determination of employee status: *Parsons* v. *Public Employees Insurance Agency*, 1997 WL 207633 (Washington App. 1997).

Page 80   Size of temporary work force: Rob Turner, "Putting Temp Stocks to Work," *Smart Money* March '97 p. 38; Glenn Burkins, "Temp Workers May be Able to Join Unions," *Wall St. J.* 12/2/96 p. A3; Mary Jane Fisher, "Closing the Benefit Gap for Temps and Contingent Workers," *National Underwriter* 4/14/97 p. S-4.

Page 81   Options for staffing: Thomas C. Greble, "A Leading Role for HR in Alternative Staffing," *HRMagazine* February, 1997 p. 99.

Page 83   Avoiding unwanted characterization as co-employer: Lin Grensing-Pophal, "When Things Go Wrong with Temps," *Personnel J.* August, 1996 p. 44.

Page 83   Professional part-timers: Phaedra Brotherton, "For Many Part-Timers, Less is More," *HRMagazine* June, 1997 p. 102.

Page 83   Stability of part-time workforce: Michael M. Phillips, "Part-Time Work Issue is Greatly Overworked," *Wall St. J.* 8/11/97 p. A1.

Page 83   Other rationales for part-time hiring: see John Kador, "Managing the Flex Force," *Beyond Computing* April 1997 p. 18.

Page 83   Data about part-time workers: "Part-Time Employment," 6 *Work-Family Roundtable* (The Conference Board) No. 1; see *HRMagazine* June 1997 pp. 105-106.

Page 83   General information on part-time work: Elaine McShulskis, "'Blended Workforce' Gives Companies an Edge," *HRMagazine* July, 1997 p. 20. For a free copy of a major report on part-time work, call Olsten's Brigid Deegan, (516) 844-7950.

Page 85   Managing shift work: Elaine McShulskis, "HRM Update," *HRMagazine* June, 1997 p. 22

Page 85   Compressed work week: Michelle Neely Martinez, "Work-Life Programs Reap Business Benefits," *HRMagazine* June 1997 p. 110.

Page 86   30/40 and related schedules: Susan J. Wells, "Honey, They've Shrunk the Workweek," *N.Y.T.* 6/15/97 p. F9.

Page 87   Base information about telecommuting: Susan J. Wells, "For Stay-Home Workers, Speed Bumps on the Telecommute," *N.Y.T.* 8/17/97 Section 3 p. 1; Bernadette Fusaro, Here's How," *PC World* February 1997 p. 238; Debra Galant, "My Office, Myself," *N.Y.T.* 2/9/97 Section 13 p. 1.

Page 90   Payment for lunch breaks: *Reich* v. *Southern New England Telecommunications Corp.*, 66 LW 1105 (2nd Cir. 7/31/97).

Page 91   Police officers exempt despite threat of docked pay: *Auer* v. *Robbins*, 117 S.Ct. 905 (1997).

Page 95   Garnishment for IRS judgment OK: *U.S.* v. *Sawaf*, 74 F.3d 119 (6th Cir. 1/26/96).

Page 96   New Hires database: see Robert Pear, "Vast Worker Database to Track Deadbeat Parents," *N.Y.T.* 9/22/97 p. A1.

Page 101   Used car salespersons: *Springfield* v. *Comm'r*, 88 F.3d 750 (Tax Court 1996); also see IRS's ruling IR-96-44, "Independent Contractor or Employee."

Page 106   Choice between keeping job and making payments: *Howard* v. *U.S.* 711 F.2d 729 (5th Cir. 1983); *Brounstein* v. *U.S.*, 979 F.2d 952 (3rd Cir. 1992); *Roth* v. *U.S.*, 779 F.2d 1567 (11th Cir. 1986); *Greenberg* v. *U.S.*, 46 F.3d 239 (3rd Cir. 1994).

Page 106   Check-writing manager can be penalized: *Gephart* v. *U.S.*, 818 F.2d 469 (6th Cir. 1987); *Munley* v. *U.S.*, 161 F.R.D. 430 (D.Nev. 1995).

Page 107   Duty to investigate past omissions: *Hutchison* v. *U.S.*, 962 F.Supp. 965 (N.D. Tex. 1997).

Page 107   Lender takes over company finances: *Bradshaw* v. *U.S.*, 83 F.3d 1175 (10th Cir. 1996); *Lee* v. *U.S.*, 951 F.Supp. 79 (W.D. Pa. 1997); *Rykoff* v. *U.S.*, 40 F.3d 305 (9th Cir. 1994).

Page 107   Responsible person penalties re trust fund taxes: Note, "Unpaid Withholding Taxes and the 100% Penalty: How to Ruin the Rest of Your Life," *Clark Boardman Callaghan Employment Alert* 7/10/97 p. 1; Note, "Enforcing Responsibility for Paying Withholding Taxes," *CCH Standard Federal Tax Reports* 11/26/96 p. 1.

Chapter 9 — Employee Group Health Plans (EGHPs)

Page 116   Handling mental health issues: For more information, see Michael T. O'Mahoney, "Holding the Line on Behavioral Health Costs," *Best's Review* (Life/Health edition) November 1996 p. 88.

Page 117   Infertility treatment: *Krauel* v. *Iowa Methodist Medical Center*, 95 F.3d 674 (8th Cir. 9/11/96).

Page 118   Prevalence of domestic partner benefits: Alice M. Starcke, "Equitable Plans Help Balance Work and Life," *HRMagazine* 5/97 p. 53.

Page 118   Limited utilization of domestic partner benefits: Barbara Whitaker, "Partner Benefits Have a Surprising Lack of Takers," *N.Y.T.* 4/27/97.

Page 119   Tax on domestic partner benefits: PLR 9717018.

Page 119   For information on dental benefits, see EBRI, *Fundamentals of Employee Benefit Programs* (5th ed., 1997).

Page 121   Discussion of ERISA preemption: see Thomas A. Moore and Matthew Gaier, "HMO Liability Part III—ERISA Preemption," *N.Y.L.J.* 9/2/97 p. 3.

Page 123   "Any willing provider" laws: *Texas Pharmacy Ass'n* v. *Prudential Insurance Co.*, 65 LW 2545 (5th Cir. 2/14/97); *CIGNA Healthplan of Louisiana* v. *Louisiana*, 82 F.3d 642 (5th Cir. 1996).

Page 123   Gatekeeper functions limited: *Prudential Insurance Co.* v. *National Park Medical Center Inc.*, 65 LW 2552 (E.D. Ark. 1/31/97).

Page 123   Nontraditional care: *Washington Physicians Service Association* v. *Gregoire*, 65 LW 2737 (W.D. Wash. 5/2/97).

Page 123   State laws on HMO malpractice: Sam Howe Verhovek, "Texas Allowing Suits Against H.M.O.'s," *N.Y.T.* 6/4/97 p. A16; Frank Bass, "HMOs in Texas to Be Made Liable for Malpractice," *Wall St. J.* 5/23/97 p. B12.

Page 124   NLRB ruling on modifying health plan: *Loral Defense Systems-Akron*, 320 NLRB No. 54 (1/31/96).

Page 124   Negotiations at impasse: *Grondorf, Field Black & Co.* v. *NLRB*, 65 LW 2648 (D.C. Cir. 3/7/97).

Page 124   Abuse of discretion to deny without sufficient information: *Booton* v. *Lockheed Medical Benefit Plan*, 65 LW 2728 (9th Cir. 4/11/97).

Page 124   Vesting once treatment begins: *Wheeler* v. *Dynamic Engineering Inc.*, 62 F.3d 634 (4th Cir. 1995).

Page 124   Waiver eliminates plan's obligation: *T.J. Kennedy* v. *Connecticut General Life Ins. Co.*, 924 F.2d 698 (7th Cir. 1991).

Page 125   OK to add escape clause: *Musto* v. *American General Corp.*, 861 F.2d 897 (6th Cir. 1988), *cert.denied* 490 U.S. 1020 (1989).

Page 125   COB applied to self-insured plans: *PM Group Life Insurance Co.* v. *Western Growers Assurance Trust*, 953 F.2d 543 (9th Cir. 1992).

Page 125   Interface of ERISA plan and auto insurance: *Auto Owners Inc.* v. *Thorn Apple Valley*, 31 F.3d 371 (5th Cir. 1994), *cert.denied* 115 S.Ct. 1177 (1995).

Page 125   Preemption of state laws against subrogation: *FMC Corp.* v. *Holliday*, 498 U.S. 52 (1990).

Page 126   Quoted $3,915 cost figure: Bureau of Labor Statistics, cited in Ron Winslow, "Health-Care Costs May be Heading Up Again," *Wall St. J.* 1/21/97 p. B1 and David Wessel, "Firms Cut Health Costs, Cover Fewer Workers," *Wall. St. J.* 11/11/96 p. A1.

Page 126   Comparison of 1988 and 1996 for under-200 employee firms, compiled by KPMG Peat Marwick: Nancy Ann Jeffrey, "Health-Care Costs Rise for Workers at Small Firms," *Wall St. J.* 9/8/97 p. B2.

Page 126   Reduction in equipment purchases: David Wessel, "Health-Cost Trims Hold Inflation Down," *Wall. St. J.* 6/30/97 p. A1.

Page 126   HMO premium increases: Laurie Joan Aron, "HMO Price Hikes Hit Businesses," *Crain's N.Y. Business* 6/9/97 p. 28.

Page 128   Higher copayments: Jeffrey A. Tannenbaum, "Health Costs at Small and Midsize Firms Decline," *Wall St.J.* 9/11/97 p. B2.

Page 128   BLS figures: cited in EBRI, "Fundamentals of Employee Benefits Programs, 5th ed. 1997.

Page 129   Coverage of HMOs and POS plans: EBRI, *Fundamentals of Employee Benefit Programs*, p. 235.

Page 131   Non-capitated HMO services: EBRI *Fundamentals of Employee Benefit Programs*, Chapter 23.

Page 131   POS plan coinsurance: Nancy Ann Jeffrey, "Bills and Costs Lurk Within HMO Options," *Wall St. J.* 12/2/96 p. C1.

Page 131   Carve-out plans: Barbara Benson, "Getting a Fix on Prices," *Crain's N.Y. Business* 5/12/97 p. 11.

Page 131   Cost comparison among managed care types: Elaine McShulskis, "Managed Care Lowers Health Care Costs, but Which Plan is Best?" *HRMagazine* January 1997 p. 26.

Page 131   Unavailability of fee-for-service plans: Robin Toner, "Harry and Louise Were Right, Sort Of," *N.Y.T.* 11/24/96 Section 4 p. 1.

Page 131   Segments where indemnity plans remain: Leslie Werstein Hann, "Indemnity's Last Stand," *Best's Review* November 1996 p. 47.

Page 131   1988–1994 trends: discussed in Peter T. Kilborn, "Workers Getting Greater Freedom in Health Plans," *N.Y.T.* 8/17/97 p. A1.

Page 131   Preventive services: Discussed in Nancy Ann Jeffrey, "To Your Health," *Wall St. J.* 12/12/96 p. R27.

Page 133   Factors in plan choice: Howard Tarre, "Checking HMO Quality Without Going Broke," *National Underwriter* 4/14/97 p. S-8.

Page 135   Consulting costs: Barbara Benson, "Consultants Flexing Their Muscles," *Crain's N.Y. Business* 1/27/97 p. 26.

Page 136   Regulation of MCOs: Milt Freudenheim, "H.M.O.'s Cope with a Backlash on Cost Cutting," *N.Y.T.* 5/19/96 p. A1; Laurie McGinley, "State Legislators Push for Safeguards for Patients Covered by Managed Care," *Wall St. J.* 1/14/97 p. A3; Note, "More States Join Nationwide Trend of Regulating Managed Care Networks," 66 LW 2026 (7/8/97); Milt Freudenheim, "Pioneering State for Managed Care Considers Change," *N.Y.T.* 7/14/97 p. A1; Jonathan Rabinovitz, "Connecticut Seeks to Appeal Managed Health Care Denials," *N.Y.T.* 5/22/97 p. A1.

Page 138	Third Party Administration: Kerry Murtha, "Companies' Self-Insured Health Plans Get the Bargaining Power of Networks," *Crain's N.Y. Business* 6/9/97 p. 34.
Page 138	Provider-controlled plans: Bob Gough, "Bypassing the Managed-Care Maze," *HRMagazine* July, 1997 p. 99.
Page 144	Disabled employees: HIPAA §421(d), effective 1/1/97.
Page 146	Election indefinite if 60-day period not disclosed: *Branch* v. *G. Bernd Co.*, 955 F.2d 1574 (11th Cir. 1992).
Page 146	Oral waiver OK: *Hummer* v. *Sears, Roebuck & Co.*, 1994 WL 116117 (E.D. Pa. 1994).
Page 147	IRS notice: Notice 94-103, IRB 1994-51 p. 10; also available as Appendix E for 29 CFR Part 825.
Page 153	MSA tax issues: HIPAA §301(c); Code §§106, 125(f), new 4980E.
Page 155	MSP for independent contractor: *Therkelsen* v. *Shalala*, 839 F.Supp. 661 (D.Minn. 1993).

Chapter 10 — Fringe Benefits

Page 157	Microsoft case: *Vizcaino* v. *Microsoft Corp.*, 97 F.3d 1187 (9th Cir. 1996); this decision was upheld by the entire Ninth Circuit in 1997: see Charles McCoy and David Bank, "Microsoft Loses Appeal in Worker-Benefits Case," *Wall St.J.* 7/25/97 p. A3.
Page 158	Fifth and Fourth Circuit cases; Ann Davis, "Employee Benefits at DuPont Don't Extend to Temp Workers," *Wall St.J.* 1/16/97 p. B4.
Page 158	Increased prevalence of stock options: Beth Kobliner, "Buy Your Company's Stock Plan and Get a 'Captive Broker,' Too," *N.Y.T.* 12/22/96 p. F6.
Page 165	Golden handcuffs: Alok K. Jha, "The Price of Disloyalty," *Wall St. J.* 4/10/97 p. R13.
Page 169	Living benefits: Allison Bell, "Living Benefits Become Typical in Group Life," *National Underwriter* 4/14/97 p. S-4.
Page 175	Increased stress and higher disability claims: Nancy Ann Jeffrey, "Disability Claims Mirror Rising Job Cuts," *Wall St. J.* 11/21/96 p. A2.
Page 178	Prolonged mental-illness disability claims: Nancy Ann Jeffrey, "Mental-Health Ruling Alarms Employers and Insurers," *Wall St. J.* 1/22/97 p. B10; Linda Koco, "Disability Workshop Eyes Group Trends," *National Underwriter* 6/16/97 p. 31.
Page 178	List-billed disability plans: Barbara Whitaker, "A Less Burdensome Path to Safeguard the Future," *N.Y.T.* 8/3/97 p. F10.
Page 178	Former employees must use internal remedies: *Kinkead* v. *Southwestern Bell Corp.*, 65 LW 2695 (8th Cir. 4/9/97).
Page 184	Vacation allotments: Leah Beth Ward, "Working Harder to Earn the Same Old Vacation," *N.Y.T.* 5/11/97 p. F12.
Page 185	Use or lose vacation days: Brenda Paik Sunoo, "Vacations: Going Once, Going Twice, Sold," *Personnel J.* August, 1996 p. 72.
Page 187	When there is a "plan": *Donovan* v. *Dillingham*, 688 F.2d 1367 (11th Cir. 1982).
Page 187	Writing not required for a plan: *Hollingshead* v. *Burford Equip. Co.*, 747 F.Supp. 1421 (M.D. Ala. 1990).

Chapter 11 — Early Retirement Plans

Page 192   Normal retirement age can be over 65: *Lindsay* v. *Thiokol Corp.*, 65 LW 2706 (10th Cir. 4/18/97).

Page 192   Work for predecessor employer doesn't count: *Hunger* v. *A.B.*, 12 F.3d 118 (8th Cir. 1993).

Page 192   Early retirement offer is not constructive discharge: *Christopher* v. *Mobil Oil Corp.*, 950 F.2d 1205 (5th Cir. 1992).

Page 192   No preemption because of retirement: *Warner* v. *Ford Motor Co.*, 46 F.3d 531 (6th Cir. 1995).

Page 193   No preemption of fraud claims: *Farr* v. *United States West, Inc.*, 50 F.3d 1361 (9th Cir. 1995); also see *Forbus* v. *Sears, Roebuck & Co.*, 64 LW 2178 (11th Cir. 9/2/94).

Page 193   Eleventh Circuit finds fraud claim preempted: *Sanson* v. *GM*, 966 F.2d 618 (11th Cir. 1992).

Page 193   Availability of benefits not fiduciary issue: *Fletcher* v. *Kroger Co.*, 942 F.2d 1137 (7th Cir. 1991).

Page 193   Benefit committee members are fiduciaries: *Siskind* v. *Sperry Retirement Program*, 795 F.Supp. 614 (S.D.N.Y. 1992).

Page 193   Package can be made available later: *Barnes* v. *Lacy*, 927 F.2d 539 (11th Cir. 1991), *cert.denied* 112 S.Ct. 372.

Page 193   "Last chance" statement inadvisable: *Wilson* v. *Southwestern Bell*, 55 F.3d 399 (8th Cir. 1995); *Pocchia* v. *NYNEX Corp.*, 81 F.3d 275 (2nd Cir. 1996); *Maez* v. *Mountain States Telephone & Telegraph, Inc.*, 54 F.3d 1488 (10th Cir. 1995).

Page 194   Promissory estoppel theory: *Diehl* v. *Twin Disk Inc.*, 65 LW 2472 (7th Cir. 12/12/96).

Page 194   Plaintiff has to prove he/she would have bought insurance: *Miller* v. *Taylor Insulation Co.*, 39 F.3d 755 (7th Cir. 1994).

Page 195   Retirees are not "employees": *Chemical Workers* v. *Pittsburgh Plate Glass Co.*, 404 U.S. 157 (1971).

Page 195   Employer can change policy despite course of conduct: *Frank D. Gentile* v. *Youngstown Steel Door Co.*, CCH Pension Plan Guide ¶23,718V (6th Cir. 1986).

Page 195   SPD is major information source: *Moore* v. *Metropolitan Life Ins. Co.*, 856 F.2d 488 (2nd Cir. 1988).

Page 196   Union benefits don't have to be maintained: *LTV Steel Co.* v. *UMW*, 945 F.2d 1205 (2nd Cir. 1991).

Chapter 12 — The Substantive Law of Pensions

Page 208   Rights of returning veterans: Small Business Job Protection Act §1704(n), enacting new Code §414(u) and amending ERISA §408(b)(1).

Page 211   RogersCasey study: Ellen E. Schultz, "Executives See Trouble in Employees' Nest Eggs," *Wall St.J.* 3/27/96 p. C1.

Page 215   Automatic enrollment: Sana Siwolop, "When Saving for Retirement Comes With the Job," *N.Y.Times* 5/18/97 p. F4.

Pages 215–6   After-tax contributions to 401(k) plans: Michael Brush, "Why a 401(k) Option May Deserve a Look," *N.Y. Times* 11/24/96 p. F6.

Page 216   Self-managed 401(k) accounts: Sana Siwolop, "The Widest of 401(k) Options: Invest It Yourself," *N.Y. Times* 5/12/96 p. F3.

Page 216   Safe harbor for post-1998 plan years: Small Business Job Protection Act §1433; Code §401(k)(12).

Page 217   Waiver of excise tax: TRA '97 §1507(b), effective for tax years beginning after 12/31/97.

Page 223   Separate account requirement: Reg. §1.404(a)-12(b)(1).

Page 225   Employee preferences for plan type: see *HRMagazine* June, 1997 p. 126.

Page 229   Leased employees: see SBJPA §1454, amending Code §414(n)(2)(C).

Page 242   Popularity of various plans: "Private Pensions: Most Employers That Offer Pensions Use Defined Contribution Plans," GAO Report Number GAO/GGD-97-1, October 1996.

Page 243   Aggregate plan assets and cost per hour worked: Employee Benefits Research Institute figures, quoted in David Cay Johnston, "Pension Concerns Move to the Picket Line," *N.Y. Times* 8/10/97 p. F11.

Page 245   Abuse of discretion standard: *Bruch* v. *Firestone Tire & Rubber*, 489 U.S. 101 (1989).

Chapter 13 — Plan Administration

Page 252   Effect of conflict of interest: *Anderson* v. *Blue Cross/Blue Shield of Alabama*, 907 F.2d 1072 (11th Cir. 1990); *Baker* v. *Big Star Division of Grand Union*, 893 F.2d 288 (11th Cir. 1989).

Page 252   Full and fair review not provided: *Crocco* v. *Xerox Corp.*, 65 LW 2567 (D.Conn. 2/5/97).

Page 252   Experimental treatment exclusion: *Martin* v. *Blue Cross/Blue Shield*, 66 LW 1063 (4th Cir. 6/23/97).

Page 253   Calculating investment costs: Timothy G. Murphy, "Comparison Shopping for the Best 401(k) Plan," *HRMagazine* June 1997 p. 130; Carole Gould, "Funds Watch," *New York Times* 12/10/96 p. F6.

Page 256   Underfunding penalty in bankruptcy: *U.S.* v. *Reorganized CF & I Fabricators of Utah Inc.*, #95-325, 116 S.Ct. 2106 (6/20/96).

Page 258   Court can overturn actuarial assumptions: *Rhoades, McKees & Boer* v. *U.S.*, 43 F.3d 1071 (6th Cir. 1995).

Page 260   Single notice for all missed payments: RIA Employee Benefits Alert, 6/4/97 p. 5.

Chapter 14 — Plan Disclosure

Page 277   Distributing plan literature gives employer discretionary authority: *Curcio* v. *John Hancock Mutual Life Ins.*, 33 F.3d 226 (3rd Cir. 1994).

Page 277   Revisions to 5500-series forms: Judith Burns, "Simpler Forms for Firms' Plans," *Wall St. J.* 6/20/97 p. A5A.

Page 282   For increased penalties, see 62 *Federal Register* 40696, 7/29/97, effective for violations occurring after that date.

Chapter 15 — Distributions From the Plan

Page 295 Proof the second plan will accept the rollover: Reg. §1.401(a)(31)-1.

Page 298 1997 Fourth Circuit case on post-retirement QDROs: *Hopkins* v. *AT&T Global Information Systems*, 105 F.3d 153 (4th Cir. 1997); this case is discussed in Mervin M. Wilf, "'Vesting' of Beneficiary's Retirement Benefit for QDRO and Disclosure Purposes," *Estate Planner's Alert* June, 1997 p. 8.

Page 299 Beneficiary can be a trust: Prop. Reg. §1.401(a)(9)-1.

Page 300 Will is not a QDRO: *Boggs* v. *Boggs*, #96-79, 65 LW 4418 (Sup.Ct. 6/2/97).

Page 300 Attachment of embezzler's benefits forbidden: *Guidry* v. *Sheet Metal Workers National Pension Fund*, 493 U.S. 365 (1990); but a much later statute, the Taxpayer Relief Act of 1997, does allow reduction of pension benefits in this "bad boy" situation.

Page 300 Pension plan claim can't be used as offset: *Herberger* v. *Shanbaum*, 897 F.2d 801 (5th Cir. 1990).

Page 300 Limited circumstances justifying offset: *Coar* v. *Kazmir*, 990 F.2d 1413 (3rd Cir. 1993); *Trucking Employees of North Jersey Welfare Fund Inc.* v. *Colville*, 16 F.3d 42 (3rd Cir. 1994).

Page 300 Attachment of checks held by plan: *Hoffman Chevrolet Inc.* v. *Washington County National Savings Bank*, 297 Md. 691, 467 A.2d 758 (1983); *National Bank of North America* v. *IBEW*, 69 A.D.2d 679, 419 N.Y.S.2d 127 (1979).

Page 300 Attachment OK before, not after, retirement: *U.S.* v. *Smith*, 47 F.3d 681 (4th Cir. 1995).

Page 301 Plan benefits out of bankruptcy estate: *Anderson* v. *Raine*, 907 F.2d 1476 (4th Cir. 1990).

Page 301 Plan benefits in estate: *In re Lichstrahl*, 750 F.2d 1488 (11th Cir. 1985); *Matter of Goff*, 706 F.2d 574 (5th Cir. 1983); *In re Graham*, 726 F.2d 1268 (8th Cir. 1984); *In re Daniel*, 771 F.2d 1352 (9th Cir. 1985).

Page 301 ERISA preempts anti-garnishment laws: *Mackey* v. *Lanier Collection Agency*, 486 U.S. 825 (1988).

Chapter 16 — Termination of a Plan

No notes.

Chapter 17 — ERISA Enforcement

Page 319 Malpractice suits OK: *Custer* v. *Sweeney*, 89 F.3d 1156 (4th Cir. 1996).

Page 321 Real estate investments: *Metzler* v. *Graham*, 65 LW 2754 (5th Cir. 5/13/97).

Page 323 Benefits for laid-off workers: *Aminoff* v. *Ally & Gargano*, 65 LW 2400 (S.D.N.Y. 11/21/96).

Page 323 Misappropriation of plan assets: *Jacobson* v. *Hughes Aircraft Co.*, 65 LW 2498 (9th Cir. 1/23/97).

Page 325 When future changes must be disclosed: *Ballone* v. *Eastman Kodak Co.*, 65 LW 2626 (2nd Cir. 3/21/97); *Hockett* v. *Sun Company Inc.*, 65 LW 2641 (10th Cir. 3/24/97). Also see *Vartanian* v. *Monsanto Co.*, 65 LW 2616, (D.Mass. 2/20/97), finding that there was no duty to disclose a new plan that was not under serious consideration until several weeks after the plaintiff retired.

Page 325 Definition of "plan documents": *Board of Trustees of CWA/ITU Negotiated Pension Plan* v. *Weinstein*, 65 LW 2579 (2nd Cir. 2/24/97); *Bartling* v. *Fruehauf Corp.*, 29 F.3d 1062 (6th Cir. 1994).

Page 326 Duty to speak where beneficiary could be harmed: *Jordan* v. *Federal Express Corp.*, 66 LW 1037 (3rd Cir. 6/19/97).

Page 326 Plan's right to sue: *Massachusetts Mutual Life Insurance* v. *Russell*, 473 U.S. 134 (1985).

Page 328 Knowing but failing to remedy: *Free* v. *Brody*, 732 F.2d 1331 (7th Cir. 1984).

Page 328 Only equitable remedies against non-fiduciary: *Mertens* v. *Hewitt Associates*, 508 U.S. 248 (Sup.Ct.1993).

Page 329 Preemption of employee benefit claims: *Wilcott* v. *Matlack Inc.*, 64 F.3d 1458 (10th Cir. 1995).

Page 329 Emotional distress claims preempted: *Burks* v. *Amerada Hess Corp.*, 8 F.3d 301 (5th Cir. 1993).

Page 329 State business tax not preempted: *Thiokol Corp.* v. *Roberts*, 64 LW 2558 (6th Cir. 2/23/96).

Page 329 Case can't be removed to federal court: *Kemp* v. *IBM*, 65 LW 2673 (11th Cir. 4/8/97).

Page 329 Availability of jury trial: *Adams* v. *Cyprus Amax Mineral Co.*, 65 LW 2560 (D.Colo. 2/7/97).

Page 335 Colorable claim to benefits or employment: *Firestone Tire & Rubber* v. *Bruch*, 489 U.S. 101 (1989).

Page 335 People who would have been participants: *Adamson* v. *Armco*, 44 F.3d 650(8th Cir. 1995), *cert.denied* 116 S.Ct. 85.

Page 335 Plan administrator must be named: *Fisher* v. *Metropolitan Life Insurance Co.*, 895 F.2d 1073 (5th Cir. 1990).

Page 335 No suits against non-fiduciary under §502(a)(3): *Mertens* v. *Hewitt Associates*, 508 U.S. 248 (1993).

Page 336 Lies about benefit security: *Varity Corp.* v. *Howe*, #94-1471, 116 S.Ct. 1065 (3/19/96).

Page 337 Wrongful termination suit preempted: *Ingersoll-Rand* v. *McClendon*, 498 U.S. 133 (1990).

Page 337 ERISA §510 applies to welfare benefit plans: *Inter-Modal Rail Employees* v. *Atchison, Topeka & Santa Fe Railroad*, #96-491, 65 LW 4319 (Sup.Ct. 5/12/97).

Page 337 Firing because of beneficiary's claim: *Fitzgerald* v. *Codex Corp.*, 882 F.2d 586 (1st Cir. 1989).

Page 337 Altered records: *Bishop* v. *Osborn Transportation Inc.*, 838 F.2d 1173 (11th Cir. 1988).

Page 337   A determining factor: *Pacificare* v. *Martin*, 34 F.3d 834 (9th Cir. 1994).

Page 338   Order of proof: *Dister* v. *Continental Group Inc.*, 859 F.2d 1108 (2nd Cir. 1988).

Page 340   Punitive damages generally unavailable: *Mertens* v. *Hewitt Associates*, 508 U.S. 248 (1993); *Massachusetts Mutual Life Insurance* v. *Russell*, 469 U.S. 816 (1984).

Chapter 18—Labor Law

Page 343   Percentage of unionized employees: BLS statistics quoted in CBC Employment Alert 3/6/97 issue p. 8.

Page 347   Technical directors not supervisors: *Telemundo de Puerto Rico* v. *NLRB*, 65 LW 2816 (1st Cir. 5/15/97).

Page 347   No-moonlighting policy OK: *Architectural Glass and Metal Co.* v. *NLRB*, 65 LW 2575 (6th Cir. 2/14/97).

Page 347   No-moonlighting policy must be neutral: *H.B. Zachry Co.* v. *NLRB*, 886 F.2d 70 (4th Cir. 1989).

Page 347   Paid union organizer can be protected employee: *NLRB* v. *Town & Country Electric Inc.*, 116 S.Ct. 450 (Sup.Ct. 1995).

Page 347   Protection of volunteer union organizer: *NLRB* v. *Fluor Daniel*, 1996 WL 725505 (6th Cir. 1996).

Page 348   NLRB must prove anti-union animus:*Schaeff Inc.* v. *NLRB*, 65 LW 2816 (D.C.Cir. 5/27/97), interpreting *Office of Workers' Compensation Programs* v. *Greenwich Collieries*, 512 U.S. 267 (Sup.Ct. 1994).

Page 350   Promised party invalidates election: *Trencor, Inc.* v. *NLRB*, 110 F.3d 268 (5th Cir. 1997).

Page 351   Premises as "company town": *Lechmere* v. *NLRB*, 111 S.Ct. 1305 (Sup.Ct. 1991); *United Food and Commercial Workers, Local 880* v. *NLRB*, 74 F.3d 292 (D.C. Cir. 1996) permits a business to forbid union representatives who are not employees to distribute union literature to the business' customers on the business premises.

Page 352   OK to bar handbilling: *Metropolitan District Council of Philadelphia* v. *NLRB*, 68 F.3d 71 (3rd Cir. 1995).

Page 352   Union materials can be kept off bulletin boards: *Guardian Industries Corp.* v. *NLRB*, 49 F.3d 317 (7th Cir. 1995).

Page 352   Mall tenant can't ban handbilling: *O'Neil's Markets* v. *United Food & Commercial Workers*, 95 F.3d 733 (8th Cir. 1996).

Page 352   Mall owner can ban solicitation: *Cleveland Real Estate Partners* v. *NLRB*, 95 F.3d 457 (6th Cir. 1996); *Riesbeck Food Markets Inc.* v. *NLRB*, 91 F.3d 132 (4th Cir. 1996).

Page 352   Bargaining order only if valid election impossible: *Gardner Mechanical Services* v. *NLRB*, 89 F.3d 586 (9th Cir. 1996).

Page 353   Workers can't vote without reasonable expectation of rehire: *Hughes Christensen Inc.* v. *NLRB*, 101 F.3d 28 (5th Cir. 1996).

Page 354   Reasons for higher union compensation: BLS Economic Policy Institute figures, quoted in David Cay Johnston, "On Payday, Union Jobs Stack Up Very Well," *N.Y.T.* 8/31/97 Sec. 3 p. 1.

Page 355 Substitution of managed care plan invalid: *Loral Defense Systems* v. *Akron*, 320 NLRB No. 54 (1/31/96).

Pages 356–7 Unilateral substance abuse policy: *Chicago Tribune Co.* v. *NLRB*, 974 F.2d 933 (7th Cir. 1992).

Page 357 Drug testing policy OK after impasse: *Steelworkers* v. *ASARCO, Inc.*, 970 F.2d 1448 (5th Cir. 1992).

Page 363 Interpreting parties' intentions: *First Options of Chicago, Inc.* v. *Kaplan*, 115 S.Ct. 1920 (Sup.Ct. 1995).

Page 365 Charge that "rats" are present: *San Antonio Community Hospital* v. *Southern California District Council of Carpenters*, 65 LW 2828 (9th Cir. 6/4/97).

Page 368 Recall rights of strikers v. replacement workers: *Aqua-Chem Inc.* v. *NLRB*, 910 F.2d 1487 (7th Cir. 1990).

Page 369 Demotion OK for legitimate business reasons: *Diamond Walnut Growers* v. *NLRB*, 65 LW 2769 (D.C. Cir. 5/20/97).

Page 369 Subcontracting OK after impasse: *International Paper Co.* v. *NLRB*, 66 LW 1025 (D.C. Cir. 6/27/97).

Page 369 Early retirees, rehired workers not counted for WARN Act purposes: *Rifkin* v. *McDonnell-Douglas Corp.*, 78 F.3d 1277 (8th Cir. 1996).

Page 370 Unions can sue on behalf of members: *United Food & Commercial Workers* v. *Brown Group*, 80 F.3d 1220 (8th Cir. 1996).

Page 370 Back pay based on work days: *Saxion* v. *Titan-C Mfg. Inc.*, 64 LW 2788 (6th Cir. 1996).

Page 370 Damages for salaried employees: *Ciarlante* v. *Brown & Williamson Tobacco Co.*, 65 LW 2536 (E.D. Pa. 12/18/96).

Page 371 A new company becomes a successor: *NLRB* v. *Burns International Security Services Inc.*, 406 U.S. 272 (1972).

Page 371 Lack of information for meaningful choice: *Canteen Corp.* v. *NLRB*, 1997 WL 4580 (7th Cir. 1/17/97).

Page 371 When new owner must consult: *New Breed Leasing Corp.* v. *NLRB*, 111 F. 3d 1460 (9th Cir. 1997).

Page 373 Management domination of labor council: *NLRB* v. *Webcor Packaging Inc.*, 66 LW 1074 (6th Cir. 7/11/97).

Page 374 Disapproval of action committee: *Electromation, Inc.*, 309 NLRB No. 163 (1992); 35 F.3d 1148 (7th Cir. 1994).

Page 374 Safety and fitness committees: *E.I. DuPont de Nemours*, 311 NLRB No. 88 (1993).

Page 375 NLRB can't order payment of litigation costs: *Unbelievable Inc.* v. *NLRB*, 66 LW 1074 (D.C. Cir. 7/18/97).

Page 376 Mere reference to CBA is not enough: *Lividas* v. *Bradshaw*, 512 U.S. 107 (1994).

Page 376 State wage payment laws preempted: *Antol* v. *Esposito*, 100 F.3d 1111 (3rd Cir. 1996); *Atchley* v. *Heritage Cable Vision Association*, 101 F.3d 495 (7th Cir. 1996).

Page 376 Failure to rehire, emotional distress claims require CBA interpretation: *Weisbarth* v. *Hawaiian Tug & Barge Corp.*, 1994 U.S.App. LEXIS 13061 (9th Cir. 1994).

Page 376 Worker's Compensation claim preempted: *Martin* v. *Shaw's Supermarkets, Inc.*, 65 LW 2528 (1st Cir. 1/28/97).

Chapter 19 — Unemployment Insurance

Chapter 20 — Worker's Compensation

Page 397	Obligation to consider human factors: Compare *Spady Brothers* v. *Industrial Claim Appeals Office of Colorado*, Colo.App. No. 96CA089 (Colo.App. 2/6/97)—no possible job—with *Brush Greenhouse Partners* v. *Ernesto Godinez*, No. 96CA0266 (Colo.App. 12/27/96)—human factors count.
Page 397	Non-exclusivity for emotional stress: *Chea* v. *Men's Wearhouse, Inc.*, No. 38312-4-1 (Wash.App. 3/17/97).
Page 397	WC not designed to deal with discrimination: *Byers* v. *Labor & Industry Review Comm'n*, 561 NW2d 678 (Wis. 1997).
Page 399	Overwork, suicides: *Dyer* v. *Hastings Industries Inc.*, 252 Neb. 361, 562 N.W.2d 348 (1997); *Miller* v. *IBEW*, 654 N.Y.S.2d 460 (A.D. 1997); *Food Distributors* v. *Estate of Ball*, 24 Va.App. 692, 485 S.E.2d 155 (1997).
Page 399	OK to have higher standard of proof for mental injuries: *Frantz* v. *Cambell County Memorial Hosp.*, 1997 WL 71067 (Wyoming 2/21/97).
Page 400	Bankruptcy treatment of unpaid premiums: *State Insurance Fund* v. *Mather*, 66 LW 1127 (10th Cir. 7/28/97).
Page 405	Retaliatory demotion wrongful: *Brigham* v. *Dillon Cos., Inc.*, 935 P.2d 1054 (Kan.Sup. 4/18/97).
Page 405	LMRA preemption: *Martin* v. *Shaw's Supermarkets Inc.*, 65 LW 2528 (1st Cir. 1/28/97).
Page 406	Retaliatory discharge claim can't be removed: *Humphrey* v. *Sequentia Inc.*, 58 F.3d 1238 (8th Cir. 1995)
Page 407	Lying by applicant is wrongful:*Caldwell* v. *Aarlin/Holcombe Armature Co.*, 65 LW 2565 (Ga. Sup. 2/17/97)
Page 409	1992 Supreme Court case: *District of Columbia* v. *Greater Washington Board of Trade*, 506 U.S. 125 (1992).
Page 413	Referrals to rehab specialists: unsigned news item, *Wall St.J.* 6/12/97 p. A1.
Page 413	Quick referral speeds return to work: Elaine McShulskis, "Early Intervention in WC Cases Beneficial," *HRMagazine* June, 1997 p. 30.
Page 413	PPOs in comp cases: Barbara Benson, "Managed Care Regulations for Workers' Comp Pass," *Crain's NY Business* 3/31/97 p. 7.
Page 413	Mandatory managed care: CCH Workers' Compensation Coordinator Newsletter 1/7/97 p. 194.
Page 415	Leased employees: *JFC Temps Inc.* v. *W.C.A.B.*, 680 A.2d 862 (Pa. Sup. 1996); *State* v. *Industrial Commission of Ohio*, 673 N.E.2d 1301 (Oh.Sup. 1997); see Darryl Van Duch, "Hiring Temps Not Always a Bargain," *Nat.L.J.* 3/17/97 p. B1.

Chapter 21— OSHA

Page 417	1992 statistics: Research published in the July, 1997 issue of the Archives of Internal Medicine, discussed in an unbylined news item in the *New York Times*, 7/28/97 p. A9.
Page 418	Videotaping of construction site OK: *Sec'y of Labor* v. *L.R. Willson & Sons Ltd.*, 65 LW 2631 (OSHRC 3/11/97).
Page 419	OSHA violation as proof of negligence: *Sumrall* v. *Mississippi Power Co.*, 65 LW 2728 (Miss.Sup. 3/6/97).

Page 423   Surveys require APA compliance: *American Trucking Ass'n* v. *Reich*, 65 LW 2530 (DDC 1/31/97).

Page 425   Statute of limitations for noise exposure: *Martzloff* v. *New York City*, 65 LW 2728, (N.Y.A.D. 4/1/97).

Pages 426–7   Injury risk to senior citizen employees: Michael Moss, "Gray Area: For Older Employees, On-the-Job Injuries Are More Often Deadly," *Wall St. J.* 6/17/97 p. A1.

Page 427   Ergonomic hazards can be cited under General Duty clause: *Sec'y of Labor* v. *Pepperidge Farm Inc.*, 65 LW 2725 (OSHRC 4/26/97); also see *Reich* v. *Arcadian Corp.*, 110 F.3d 1192 (5th Cir. 1997). These cases are discussed by Robert Davis in his Employment Law column in the 6/9/97 issue of the *National Law Journal*, p. B4.

Page 428   Regional meetings on ergonomics: Ellen Byerrum, "NIOSH Review Finds 'Compelling Support' for Job-Related Musculoskeletal Disorders," 66 LW 2043 (7/15/97).

Page 428   Preventing slip and fall injuries: CCH Employment Safety & Health Guide newsletter #1360, 4/21/97.

Page 433   Status on date of alleged violation: *Sec'y of Labor* v. *Jacksonville Shipyards, Inc.*, CCH Employment Safety & Health Guide ¶31,216 (11th Cir. 1996); *Meridian Contractors Inc.*, CCH Employment Safety & Health Guide ¶31,347 (OSHRC 1997).

Page 434   Per-violation, not per-employee standard: *Metzler* v. *Arcadian Corp.*, 65 LW 2722 (5th Cir. 4/27/97).

Page 434   Stacking of violations improper: *Reich* v. *Arcadian Corp.*, 110 F.3d 1192 (5th Cir. 1997); also see 66 LW 2073 for OSHA's decision not to appeal the case.

Page 435   Double jeopardy analysis: *S.A. Healy Co.*, CCH Employment Safety & Health Guide ¶31,239 (7th Cir. 1997); *U.S.* v. *Hudson*, 92 F.3d 1026 (10th Cir. 1996).

Page 437   For procedural changes in how to file with OSHRC, see CCH Employment Safety & Health Guide ¶13,038.

Page 438   E-Z Trial procedure: CCH Employment Safety & Health Guide ¶13,024.

Page 444   AIDS-phobia: see *Williamson* v. *Waldman*, 66 LW 1088 (N.J. Sup. 7/21/97).

Chapter 22 — Privacy Issues

Page 447   Worker's Compensation denial for impaired workers: *Recchi America Inc.* v. *Hall*, 692 So.2d 153 (Fla. 1997).

Page 448   Mistake by third-party testing company: *Carroll* v. *Federal Express Corp.*, 113 F.3d 163 (9th Cir. 1997).

Page 448   Pre-employment testing preferred over employee testing: *Loder* v. *Glendale, California*, 65 LW 2461 (Cal.Sup. 1/6/97).

Page 448   No suit against employer when discharged for refusal to take drug test: *AFL-CIO* v. *California Unemployment Insurance Appeals Board*, 23 Cal.App. 4th 51, 28 Cal.Rptr.2nd 210 (1994); *Hart* v. *Seven Resorts Inc.*, 1997 WL 211647 (Ariz.App. 1997).

Page 448   Prescription drugs: *Roe* v. *Cheyenne Mountain Conference Resort Inc.*, #96-1086 (10th Cir. 9/3/97).

Chapter 23 — Title VII

Page 462   Resolution of sexual harassment charges: EEOC figures, quoted in Jennifer
                 Steinhauer, "If the Boss is Out of Line, What's the Legal Boundary?" *N.Y. Times*
                 3/27/97 p. D1.

Page 462   Total aggregated in EEOC settlements: EEOC figures, quoted in Barbara B.
                 Buchholz, "After the Talk or the Touching Gets Too Personal, Where to Turn?"
                 N.Y. Times 3/2/97 p. F11.

Page 462   Harassment after termination of consensual relationship: *Prichard* v. *Ledford*, 57
                 EPD ¶41, 018 (D.Tenn. 1980).

Page 462   Employer defenses: *Karibian* v. *Columbia University*, 63 EPD ¶42,825 (2nd Cir.
                 1994); *Gary* v. *Long*, 66 EPD ¶43,660 (D.C. Cir. 1995).

Page 462   Male/male quid pro quo: *Tiegen* v. *Brown's Westminster Motors Inc.*, 921 F.Supp.
                 1495 (ED Va. 4/18/96); *Fredette* v. *BVP Management Associates*, 65 LW 2791 (11th
                 Cir. 5/22/97). See David E. Rovella, "Same-Sex Harassment Suits on the Rise,"
                 Nat.L.J. 2/10/97 p. A1 and Michael Delikat and Rene Kathawala, "Same-Sex
                 Harassment and Title VII," *N.Y.L.J.* 9/8/97 p. 1. The Supreme Court case is *Oncale*
                 v. *Sundown Offshore Services Inc.*, #96-568, 65 LW 3814 (6/9/97).

Page 463   Factors in analyzing conduct: *Harris* v. *Forklift Systems, Inc.*, 62 EPD ¶42,611
                 (Sup.Ct. 1993).

Page 463   Heterosexual males: *McWilliams* v. *Fairfax County Board of Supervisors*, 72 F.3d 1192
                 (4th Cir. 1/9/96).

Page 464   Actual or perceived homosexuality of target: *Quick* v. *Donaldson Co.*, 90 F.3d 1372
                 (8th Cir. 7/29/96), finding that a charge of over 100 incidents of insults and
                 unwanted touching premised on the plaintiff's supposed but not actual homo-
                 sexuality, can be pursued in court.

Page 464   Horseplay not tantamount to hostile environment: *Hopkins* v. *Baltimore Gas &
                 Electric Co.*, 77 F.3d 745 (4th Cir. 3/5/96).

Page 464   Male-male hostile environment actionable: *Gerd* v. *UPS*, 934 F.Supp. 357 (D.Colo.
                 8/19/96); *Wrightson* v. *Pizza Hut of America*, 99 F.3d 138 (4th Cir. 10/31/96); *Yeary*
                 v. *Goodwill Industries-Knoxville*, 65 LW 2556 (6th Cir. 2/24/97).

Page 464   Seventh Circuit case on heterosexual male harassment: *Doe* v. *Belleville, Inc.*, 66
                 LW 1070 (7th Cir. 7/17/97); also see *Cummings* v. *Koehnen*, 556 N.W.2d 586
                 (Minn.App. 1996, noting that the Minnesota Human Rights Act forbids unwant-
                 ed same-sex sexual comments, physical gestures, and sexual touching, without
                 inquiry into the sexual orientation of either alleged perpetrator or alleged victim.

Page 464   Brief incidents of vulgarities not actionable: *Baskerville* v. *Culligan International
                 Inc.*, 50 F.3d 428 (7th Cir. 1995); *Black* v. *Zaring Homes*, 1997 WL 9853 (6th Cir.
                 1997).

Page 464   Limited duration of offensive comments: *Jones* v. *Gatzambide*, 940 F.Supp. 182
                 (N.D. Ill. 9/16/96).

Page 464   Isolated instance of foul language: *Galvez* v. *Means*, 65 LW 2272 (S.D.N.Y.
                 8/26/96).

Page 464   Agency not enough: *Davis* v. *Sioux City*, 66 LW 1022 (8th Cir. 6/18/97).

Page 464   Confidentiality relieves employer of liability: *Torres* v. *Pisano*, 65 LW 2807 (2nd Cir.
                 6/3/97).

Page 464	Employer liable for quid pro quo and hostile environment: *Ellerth* v. *Burlington Industries, Inc.*, 65 LW 2391 (7th Cir. 11/27/96).
Page 465	Authority to harass not required: *Harrison* v. *Eddy Potash Inc.*, 65 LW 2799 (10th Cir. 5/8/97).
Page 465	Harassment by customers, etc.: Jeffrey S. Klein and Nicholas J. Pappas, "Liability for Sexual Harassment by Non-Employees," *N.Y.L.J.* 6/2/97 p. 3.
Page 465	Sexist comments: *Smith* v. *St. Louis University*, 1997 WL 134586 (8th Cir. 1997). See Jennifer Steinhauer, "If the Boss Is Out of Line, What's the Legal Boundary?" *N.Y. Times* 3/27/97 p. D1, covering allegations of hostile environment sex discrimination in cases involving vulgarity and disparaging, though not necessarily sexually oriented, remarks.
Page 465	No emotional distress claims: *Tronoski* v. *Murphy*, 65 FEP Cases 1121 (E.D. Pa. 1995.)
Page 466	Guidelines for avoiding harassment at corporate events: Allan H. Weitzman and Kathleen M. McKenna, "Employment Law," *Nat.L.J.* 12/9/96 p. B5.
Page 467	Implications of firing a harasser: Gary R. Siniscalco and Nancy M. Lee, "Employment Law," *Nat. L.J.* 9/22/97 p. B5, discussing cases such as *Agugliaro* v. *Brooks Brothers*, 927 F.Supp. 741 (S.D.N.Y. 1996) and *Southwest Gas Corp.* v. *Vargas*, 901 P.2d 693 (Nev. 1995).
Page 467	Investigation by attorneys: Janice Goodman, "Investigating Sex Harassment Claims," *N.Y.L.J.* 4/21/97 p. 9.
Page 468	Employer determines reasonableness of accommodation: *Ansonia Board of Education* v. *Philbrook*, 41 EPD ¶36,565 (Sup.Ct. 1986).
Page 468	Excessive expense can be illegal preference: *TWA* v. *Hardison*, 432 U.S. 63 (1977).
Page 468	Only religious mandates need be accommodated: Jeffrey S. Klein and Nicholas J. Pappas, "Accommodation of Religious Observances—Part I," *N.Y.L.J.* 3/3/97 p. 3.
Page 469	State can't pass law requiring Sabbath day off: *Estate of Thornton* v. *Caldor, Inc.*, 37 EPD ¶ 35,312 (Sup.Ct. 1985).
Page 469	Employee can collect unemployment insurance: *Hobbie* v. *Unemployment Appeals Commission of Florida*, 480 U.S. 136 (S.Ct. 1987).
Page 469	Hostile religious environment: *Venters* v. *City of Delphi*, 1997 U.S.App. LEXIS 22360 (8/19/97); see Dominic Bencivenga, "Religion at Work: When Accommodation Becomes Harassment," *N.Y.L.J.* 9/11/97 p. 5.
Page 471	Employees can't waive assistance to EEOC: *EEOC* v. *Astra USA Inc.*, 94 F.3d 738 (1st Cir. 9/6/96).
Pages 471–72	Filing re a series of acts: Evan H. Krinick and Joseph J. Ortego, "Tolling Statute of Limitations Period in Discrimination Suits," *N.Y.L.J.* 5/12/97 p. S8.
Page 472	Seniority system can stay in place: *Teamsters* v. *U.S.*, 431 U.S. 324 (Sup.Ct. 1977).
Page 473	Individual contractor must have suffered discrimination: *Adarand Constructors Inc.* v. *Pena*, 513 U.S. 1108(1995).
Page 473	1997 Supreme Court case: see Harvey Berkman, "Supremes May Get Other Affirmative Action Cases," *National Law J.* 12/8/97, p. B10.

Page 473   Proposition 209 upheld: *Coalition for Economic Equality* v. *Wilson*, 65 LW 2650 (9th Cir. 4/9/97) *cert. denied* #97–369, 11/3/97. See Edward Felsenthal and G. Pascal Zachary, "Supreme Court Refuses Case on Preferences," *Wall Street Journal.* 11/4/97 p. A24.

Page 473   Basic standards for affirmative action: *United Steelworkers of America* v. *Weber*, 20 EPD ¶30,026 (Sup.Ct. 1979); *Johnson* v. *Transportation Agency of Santa Clara County*, 42 EPD ¶36,831 (Sup.Ct. 1987).

Page 473   Correcting a history of racism: *Eldredge* v. *Carpenters Joint Apprenticeship and Training Committee*, 94 F.3d 1366 (9th Cir. 1996).

Page 474   Clinton administration policy: John M. Broder, "U.S. Readies Rules Over Preferences Aiding Minorities," *N.Y.T.* 5/6/97 p. A1.; Eva M. Rodriguez, "Justice Department Abandons Effort to Reverse Affirmative-Action Ruling," *Wall St. J.* 6/6/97 p. A4.

Chapter 24 — The Americans With Disabilities Act

Page 475   Company, not individuals, liable: *Mason* v. *Stallings*, 82 F.3d 1007 (11th Cir. 5/9/96).

Page 475   Mixed-motive ADA case OK: *McNely* v. *Ocala Star-Banner Corp.*, 99 F.3d 1068 (11th Cir. 1996).

Page 476   Hostile environment ADA case OK: *Hendler* v. *Intellicom U.S.A. Inc.*, 95-CV-2490 (E.D.N.Y. May, 1997).

Page 476   Testimony about multiple chemical sensitivity: *Frank* v. *New York*, 66 LW 1128 (N.D.N.Y. 7/17/97).

Page 476   No ADA claims by ex-employees: *Gonzalez* v. *Garner Food Service*, 89 F.3d 1523 (11th Cir. 8/2/96).

Page 476   Information on ADA awards: Barbara C. Neff, "Reasonable Accommodations" Under the ADA: Employers' Duties and Defenses," *Defense Law J.* January, 1997 p. 110.

Page 477   No DOL administrative prosecution: *American Airlines* v. *Metzler*, 65 LW 2685 (N.D.Tex. 4/8/97).

Page 477   Individual, not group, assessment: *EEOC* v. *Chrysler Corp.*, 917 F. Supp. 1164 (E.D. Mich. 3/6/96)[improper to refuse to hire individuals with elevated blood-sugar levels, without considering individual capacity]; *EEOC* v. *Kinney Shoe Corp.*, 917 F.Supp. 419 (W.D.Va. 2/14/96)[firing epileptic suffering from seizures is legitimate, because it was based on actual danger, not generalized beliefs about epilepsy].

Page 477   Fourth Circuit on drug abuse coverage: *Shafer* v. *Preston Memorial Hosp. Corp.*, 65 LW 2572 (4th Cir. 2/26/97).

Page 477   Former substance abusers can be barred: *EEOC* v. *Exxon Corp.*, 66 LW 1016 (N.D. Tex. 5/13/97).

Page 478   Permissible and forbidden interview questions: 42 USC §12112(d)(2); 29 CFR 1630.13(a); also see EEOC's 1995 Guidance, "Preemployment Disability-Related Questions and Medical Examinations."

Page 478   Business necessity; 42 USC §12112(b)(6).

Page 478   Uniform or no HIV testing: 42 U.S.Code §12112(d)(3).

Page 478   Direct threat: 42 U.S.Code §12112(d)(4); 29 CFR §1630.14(c).

Page 478   Confidentiality and disclosure: 42 USC §12112(d)(3)(B); 29 CFR §1630.14(b).

Page 480   Plaintiff has to prove availability of accommodations: *Moses* v. *American Nonwovens Inc.*, 97 F.3d 446 (11th Cir. 1996).

Page 480   Employer just has to show undue hardship: *Monette* v. *EDS Corp.*, 90 F.3d 1173 (6th Cir. 1996).

Page 480   Parking space as accommodation: *Lyons* v. *Legal Aid Society*, 68 F.3d 1512 (2nd Cir. 1996).

Page 480   Computer system accommodations not proved reasonable: *Garza* v. *Abbott Labs*, 940 F.Supp. 1224 (ND Ill. 1996).

Page 481   Definition of undue hardship: Web document, "The ADA: Your Responsibilities as an Employer."

Page 482   Bumping not a required accommodation: *Eckles* v. *Consolidated Rail Corp.* , 94 F.3d 1041 (7th Cir. 1996); *Benson* v. *Northwest Airlines Inc.*, 62 F.3d 1108 (8th Cir. 1995); *Wooten* v. *Farmland Foods*, 58 F.3d 382 (8th Cir. 1995).

Page 482   Transfer preferences might have to change to accommodate: *Buckingham* v. *U.S.*, 998 F.2d 735 (9th Cir. 1993).

Page 482   Creating new jobs not required: *White* v. *York International Corp.*, 45 F.3d 357 (10th Cir. 1995).

Page 482   Change in grade or rating: *Bolstein* v. *Reich*, 1995 WL 46387 (D.D.C. 1995).

Page 482   Flexible schedule probably not required: *Tyndall* v. *Natl Education Centers*, 31 F.3d 209 (4th Cir. 1994).

Page 482   Leave of absence as accommodation: *Vande Zande* v. *Wisconsin Dept of Administration*, 44 F.3d 538 (7th Cir. 1995); *Vializ* v. *NYC Board of Education*, 1995 WL 110112 (S.D.N.Y. 1995); *Schmidt* v. *Safeway Inc.*, 864 F.Supp. 991 (D.Ore. 1994); *Dutton* v. *Johnson County Board*, 1995 WL 337588 (D.Kan. 1995).

Page 483   Accommodating stress: Frances A. McMorris, "Worker's Transfer Plea Against is Rejected," *Wall St. J.* 1/21/97 p. B5.

Page 483   Termination of accommodation: *Holbrook* v. *Alpharetta, Georgia*, 65 LW 2767 (11th Cir. 5/11/97).

Page 483   Legally blind IRS officer: *Fallacaro* v. *Richardson*, 66 LW 1007 (D.D.C. 6/6/97).

Page 483   Lifting requirements:*Williams* v. *Channel Master*, 65 LW 2438 (4th Cir. 11/27/96).

Page 483   Cancer chemotherapy: *Gordon* v. *Hamm*, 65 LW 2390 (11th Cir. 12/4/96).

Page 484   Infertility as impairment: e.g., *Pacourek* v. *Inland Steel Co.*, 916 F.Supp. 979 (N.D. Ill. 2/16/96).

Page 484   HIV positive status and the ADA: *Runnebaum* v. *Nationsbank*, 95 F.3d 1285 (4th Cir. 9/19/96) and 66 LW 1119 (4th Cir. 8/15/97).

Page 484	EEOC view: *Canon* v. *Clark*, 883 F.Supp. 718 (S.D. Fla. 1995); *Sarsycki* v. *UPS*, 862 F.Supp. 336 (W.D. Okla. 1994). Cases under the Rehab Act contrary to EEOC view, and requiring consideration of medication/adaptive devices in the assessment: *Mackie* v. *Runyon*, 804 F.Supp. 1508 (M.D. Fla. 1992); *Chandler* v. *City of Dallas*, 2 F.3d 1385 (5th Cir. 1993), *cert.denied* 114 S.Ct. 1386).
Page 485	Employees lose ERISA cases on benefits cap: *McGann* v. *H&H Music Co.*, 946 F.2d 401 (5th Cir. 1991), *cert.denied* 113 S.Ct. 482; *Owens* v. *Storehouse, Inc.*, 948 F.2d 394 (11th Cir. 1993).
Page 486	Managed care organizations: David Manoogian, "Health Care" column, *Nat. L.J.* 3/17/97 p. B6.
Page 486	Conduct standards: 42 U.S.Code §12112(b)(6); 29 CFR §§1630.10, 1630.15(c).
Page 487	Employees who create risk are not qualified: 42 U.S.Code §12113(b).
Page 487	Probability of recovery: *Myers* v. *Hose*, 50 F.3d 278 (4th Cir. 1995); *Hudson* v. *MCI Telecommunications Corp.*, 87 F.3d 1167 (10th Cir. 1996); *Rogers* v. *Int'l Marine Terminals Inc.*, 87 F.3d 755 (5th Cir. 1996).
Page 488	Failure to accommodate creates inability to work:*Labonte* v. *Hutchins & Wheeler*, 65 LW 2734 (Mass.Sup.Jud.Ct. 5/5/97).
Page 488	Combined disability and ADA claims: *Swanks* v. *Washington Metro Area Transit Authority*, 66 LW 1038 (D.C. Cir. 6/20/97); *Mohamed* v. *Marriott International Inc.*, 944 F.Supp. 277 (S.D.N.Y. 1996); *D'Aprile* v. *Fleet Services Corp.*, 92 F.3d 1 (1st Cir. 1996); also see *Whitbeck* v. *Vital Signs Inc.*, 66 LW 1039 (D.C. Cir. 6/20/97) making a similar point about private disability benefits paid in the interim until SSDI becomes available. For a good review of the subject, see Wayne N. Outten and Jack A. Raisner, "EEOC Resolves 'Untenable Choice' for Disabled Employees, Or Does It?" *N.Y.L.J.* 4/21/97 p. 9.
Page 489	ADA and disability claims can't be combined: *McNemar* v. *The Disney Store*, 91 F.3d 610 (3rd Cir. 1996); *August* v. *Offices Unlimited*, 982 F.2d 576 (1st Cir. 1992); *Bonnano* v. *Gannett Co.*, 934 F.Supp. 113 (S.D.N.Y. 1996); on a related issue, see *Simon* v. *Safelite Glass Courts Corp.*, 65 LW 2327 (E.D.N.Y. 10/28/96), finding that a plaintiff is estopped from both claiming SSDI, premised on being too disabled to work, and bringing an ADEA suit, premised on age-based denial of a position for which the plaintiff was qualified.
Page 489	ADA regulations on mental impairment: 29 CFR §1630.2(h)(2).
Page 490	Claims of mental disability: Ellen Joan Pollock and Joann S. Lublin, "Employers Are Wary of Rules on Mentally Ill," *Wall St. J.* 5/1/97 p. B1.

Chapter 25 — The Family and Medical Leave Act

Page 491	Notice of changed leave year: 29 CFR §825.200(d).
Page 491	Custody hearings don't count: *Kelley* v. *Crossfield Catalysts*, 1997 WL 80960 (N.D. Ill. 2/21/97).
Page 492	Cure of defective notice: *Fry* v. *First Fidelity Bancorporation*, 67 EPD ¶43,943.
Page 493	Referral to HR department: Note, "Employers Face FMLA Compliance Pitfalls," *Employment Alert* 1/23/97 p. 1.

Page 494	Recertification: 29 United States Code §2613(a); 29 CFR §825.308.
Page 496	Definition of good faith: *Morris* v. *VCW, Inc.*, 1996 WL 740544 (W.D. Mo 1996).
Page 496	Availability of jury trial: *Helmly* v. *Stone Container Corp.*, 1997 WL 138304 (S.D.Ga. 3/24/97).
Page 496	Employee handbook provision: *Fry* v. *First Fidelity Bancorporation*, 64 LW 2503 (E.D. Pa. 1/30/96).
Page 496	Southern District of N.Y. permits litigation: *Hoffman* v. *Aaron Kamhi, Inc.*, 927 F.Supp. 640 (S.D.N.Y. 1996)
Page 497	N.D. Texas on arbitrability: *Satarino* v. *A.G. Edwards & Sons Inc.*, 941 F.Supp. 609 (N.D.Tex. 1996).
Page 497	No damages for employee who didn't look for another job: *McDonnell* v. *Miller Oil Co.*, 110 F.3d 60 (4th Cir. 1997).
Page 497	FMLA regulations on workweek: 29 CFR §825.205(b).
Page 498	Administration of intermittent leave: Michael Faillace and Richard Lang, "Intermittent Leave: Guide to the Minefield," *Nat. L.J.* 5/12/97 p. S6.
Page 499	Interface of disability and pregnancy: see 58 *Federal Register* 31802 (6/4/93) and 60 *Federal Register* 2201 (1/6/95).

Chapter 26 — The Age Discrimination in Employment Act

Page 501	ADEA covers failure to promote: *Kauffman* v. *Kent State University*, 815 F.Supp. 1077 (N.D. Ohio 1993).
Page 501	Asking about retirement date is not unlawful: *Woythal* v. *Tenn-Tex Corp.*, 65 LW 2759 (6th Cir. 4/25/97).
Page 501	Unpleasant personality: *Crabbs* v. *Copperweld Tubing Products Co.*, 1997 WL 25514 (6th Cir. 1997).
Page 502	Fraud cases might be appropriate in state court: *Ingersoll-Rand* v. *McClendon*, 111 S.Ct. 478 (1990).
Page 503	Overqualified older workers: *EEOC* v. *Insurance Company of North America*, 49 F.3d 1418 (9th Cir. 1995); *EEOC* v. *Francis W. Parker School*, 41 F.3d 1073 (7th Cir. 1994).
Page 503	Increasing pension can violate ADEA: *Passer* v. *American Chemical Society*, 935 F.2d 322 (D.C. Cir. 1991).
Page 504	Demotion didn't violate ADEA: *Koprowski* v. *Wistar Inc.*, 819 F.Supp. 410 (E.D. Pa. 1992).
Page 504	Discrimination within the U.S.: *Cleary* v. *United States Lines Inc.*, 728 F.2d 607 (3rd Cir. 1984); *Zahourek* v. *Arthur Young & Co.*, 750 F.2d 827 (10th Cir. 1984).
Page 504	Foreign company doing business in the U.S.: *EEOC* v. *Kloster Cruise Ltd.*, 888 F.Supp. 147 (S.D. Fla. 1995).
Page 504	Auto dealership: *Mangram* v. *GM Corp.*, 65 LW 2679 (4th Cir. 3/6/97).

Page 504   Independent-contractor salespersons not covered: *Oestman* v. *Nat'l Farmers Union Inc.*, 958 F.2d 303 (10th Cir. 1992); *Caruso* v. *Peat, Marwick Mitchell & Co.*, 664 F.Supp. 144 (S.D.N.Y. 1987).

Page 504   Corporate directors covered: *EEOC* v. *Johnson & Higgins Inc.*, 91 F.3d 1529 (2nd Cir. 8/8/96).

Page 504   Disparate impact and hostile environment claims: *Crawford* v. *Medina General Hospital*, 96 F.3d 830 (6th Cir. 9/24/96); *Spence* v. *Maryland Casualty Co.*, 995 F.2d 1147 (2nd Cir. 1993); *Young* v. *Will County Dep't of Public Aid*, 882 F.2d 290 (7th Cir. 1989).

Page 505   Doubt cast on disparate impact theory: *Ellis* v. *United Air Lines*, 73 F.3d 999 (10th Cir. 1997); also see *Rhodes* v. *Guiberson Oil Tools*, 75 F.3d 989 (5th Cir. 1996); *Fobian* v. *Storage Technology*, 959 F.Supp. 742 (E.D. Va. 1997).

Page 505   RFOA defense may justify disparate impact: Jeffrey S. Klein and Ross E. Morrison, "Courts Rethink ADEA Disparate-Impact Claims," *Nat. L.J.* 6/30/97; also see Frances A. McMorris, "Age-Bias Suits May Become Harder to Prove," *Wall St.J.* 2/20/97 p. B1.

Page 505   Retirees have standing to sue: *McKeever* v. *Ironworkers' District Council*, 65 LW 2608 (E.D. Pa. 3/7/97).

Page 505   Statutory causes of action prevent wrongful termination suit: *List* v. *Anchor Paint Mfg. Co.*, 910 P.2d 1011 (Okla.Sup. 1/9/96).

Page 505   Replacement by worker over 40: also see *Greene* v. *Safeway Stores*, 98 F.3d 554 (10th Cir. 10/15/96).

Page 506   Employer need not know exact age: *DePriest* v. *Safeway Food Town Inc.*, 543 F.Supp. 1355 (D.Mich. 1982).

Page 506   Proof of affirmative defenses: *Western Air Lines Inc.* v. *Criswell*, 472 U.S. 400 (1985).

Page 506   Recent article on defense techniques: "Age Discrimination Litigation: RIFs, Statistics and Stray Remarks," *Defense Counsel J.* 88 (January 1997).

Page 506   Transfer of younger worker: *Jameson* v. *Arrow Co.*, 75 F.3d 1528 (11th Cir. 1996).

Page 506   Direct and indirect evidence: *Torrey* v. *Casio Inc.*, 42 F.3d 825 (3rd Cir. 1994).

Page 508   Stray remarks: see, e.g., *EEOC* v. *Texas Instruments, Inc.*, 100 F.3d 1173 (5th Cir. 1996); *Renz* v. *Grey Advertising, Inc.*, #96-7775 (2nd Cir. 8/8/97).

Page 510   No offset for Social Security benefits: *Dominguez* v. *Tom James Co.*, 65 LW 2815 (11th Cir. 5/15/97); the earlier case on unemployment benefits is *Brown* v. *A.J.Gerrard Manufacturing Co.*, 715 F.2d 1549 (11th Cir. 1983).

Page 510   Accrual must continue: 29 USC §623(i)(1)(A).

Page 511   Presumption of retirement at normal age: *Curtis* v. *Electronics & Space Corp.*, 66 LW 1031 (8th Cir. 5/28/97).

                 Lyon case: 53 F.3d 135 (6th Cir. 1995).

Page 512   Reduction of disability benefits: *Kalvinskas* v. *California Institute of Technology*, 96 F.3d 1305 (9th Cir. 9/27/96).

Page 513   Age and years of service are distinct: *Biggins* v. *Hazen Paper Company*, 507 U.S. 604 (1993).

Chapter 27—Procedure for Discrimination Suits

Page 517 Speed of arbitration: Agnes J. Wilson, "Resolution of Employment Disputes," *N.Y.L.J.* 5/1/97 p. 3.

Page 518 Mandatory arbitration implies termination for cause only: *PaineWebber Inc.* v. *Agron* , 49 F.3d 347 (8th Cir. 1995).

Page 519 Coverage of AAA arbitration: Agnes J. Wilson, "Resolution of Employment Disputes," *N.Y.L.J.* 5/1/97 p. 3.

Page 519 Mandatory arbitration under the U-4: see John C. Coffee Jr., "Sex and the Securities Industry," *N.Y.L.J.* 5/29/97 p. 5.

Page 519 Change in NASD arbitration policy: see 66 LW 2105.

Page 520 EEOC position on securities industry arbitration: Margaret A. Jacobs and Patrick McGeehan, "Wall Street's Forced Arbitration of Bias Claims Set Back by EEOC," *Wall St.J.* 9/12/97 p. B19.

Page 520 Standards for enforcing predispute arbitration requirements: Jay M. Waks, John Roberti and Rachem H. Yarkon, "Predispute ADR Raises Fairness Issue," *Nat.L.J.* 6/30/97 p. B8.

Page 522 D.C. Circuit case: *Cole* v. *Burns International Security Services*, 65 LW 2526 (D.C.Cir. 2/11/97).

Page 522 Fifth Circuit allows mandatory arbitration of age claims: *Williams* v. *CIGNA Financial Advisors Inc.*, 56 F.3d 656 (5th Cir. 1995).

Page 522 Arbitration clause can be enforced post-termination: *O'Neil* v. *Hilton Head Hospital*, 66 LW 1019 (4th Cir. 6/13/97).

Page 523 ADA rights not waived: *Nelson* v. *Cyprus Bagdad Copper Corp.*, 66 LW 1054 (9th Cir. 7/10/97).

Page 523 Handbook clauses: compare *Heurtebise* v. *Reliable Business Computers Inc.*, 550 N.W.2d 243 (Michigan 1996), *cert.denied* 117 S.Ct. 1311, saying the employer did not intend to be bound, to *Patterson* v. *Tenet Healthcare Inc.*, 65 LW 2733 (8th Cir. 5/17/97), enforcing the handbook provision.

Page 523 Job application: *Brooks* v. *Circuit City Store*, 65 LW 2823 (D.Md. 5/30/97).

Page 523 Arbitration enforceable for Title VII, ADEA: *Austin* v. *Owens-Brockway Glass Container, Inc.*, 78 F.3d 875 (4th Cir. 3/12/96).

Page 523 §1981 claim has to be arbitrated: *Almonte* v. *Coca-Cola Bottling Co. of NY*, 65 LW 2622 (D. Conn. 3/11/97).

Page 523 Employees can still sue for statutory claims: *Pryner* v. *Tractor Supply Co.*, 65 LW 2622 (7th Cir. 3/20/97).

Page 523 1994 Ninth Circuit case: *Prudential Insurance Co.* v. *Lai*, 42 F.3d 1299 (9th Cir. 1994).

Page 523 Voluntary initiation of arbitration by employee: *Nghiem* v. *NEC Electronic Inc.*, 64 EPD ¶43,075 (1994).

Page 523 Grievance procedure isn't arbitration: *Cheng-Canindin* v. *Renaissance Hotel Associates*, 50 Cal.App.4th 676, 57 Cal.Rptr.2d 867 (1996).

Page 524   Successor owner: *Jones* v. *Tenet Health Network Inc.*, 65 LW 2815 (E.D.La. 4/7/97).

Page 524   Referral to legal department: *U.S.* v. *N.Y. Transit Authority*, 97 F.3d 672 (2nd Cir. 10/8/96).

Page 524   Arbitration delays can be fraudulent: see *Wall St. J.* item, "California High Court Says HMO Members Opt Out of Arbitration," 7/1/97 p. B8.

Page 524   EEOC's position on mandatory arbitration: Nancy Montwieler, "EEOC Policy Guidance Reaffirms Opposition to Mandatory Arbitration," 66 LW 2055 (7/22/97). The online version of the EEOC statement can be found at (**http://www.eeoc.gov/docs/mandarb.txt**). Also see Margaret A. Jacobs and Patrick McGeehan, "Wall Street's Forced Arbitration of Bias Claims Set Back by EEOC," *Wall St. J.* 9/12/97 p. B19.

Page 525   Supreme Court on grievance procedures: *Alexander* v. *Gardner-Denver*, 415 U.S. 36 (Sup. Ct. 1974).

Page 525   Personal agreement to arbitrate: *Brisentine* v. *Stone & Webster Engineering Corp.*, 66 LW 1070 (11th Cir. 7/21/97).

Page 525   Arbitrator's interpretation of CBA: *Tang* v. *Rhode Island Dep't of Elderly Affairs*, 904 F.Supp. 69 (D.R.I. 1995).

Page 526   Information on non-arbitral ADR: see C.C. Harness III and Jonathan R. Mook, "ADR: The Privatizing of Employment Dispute Resolution," 23 *Employment Relations Today* No. 4 (Winter '97) p. 51; Dominic Bencivenga, "Extending ADR's Reach," *N.Y.L.J.* 5/29/97 p. 5.

Page 526   Wage/benefit committee unacceptably employer-dominated: *NLRB* v. *Webcor Packaging Inc.*, 1997 WL 380413, 66 LW 1074 (6th Cir. 1997).

Page 527   Timing for seniority systems: CRA '91, P.L. 102-166 §706(e)(2), overruling *Lorance* v. *AT&T Technologies Inc.*, 109 S.Ct. 2261 (1989).

Page 528   Second, timely charge: *Criales* v. *American Airlines Inc.*, 65 LW 2551 (2nd Cir. 1/21/97).

Page 529   No need to use CBA grievance procedure: *Alexander* v. *Gardner-Denver Co.*, 415 U.S. 36.

Page 529   EEOC caseload: Bill Leonard, "Executive Briefing," *HRMagazine* 5/97 p. 10; also see *CBC Employment Alert* 12/26/96 p. 1 and Evan Ramstad and Louise Lee, "Race Issues Create Divide in Corporate Cultures," *Wall St. J.* 11/18/96 p. B1.

Page 530   Dismissal or suspension of case: *Chapman* v. *City of Detroit*, 808 F.2d 459 (6th Cir. 1986); *Wilson* v. *Westinghouse Electric Corp.*, 838 F.2d 286 (8th Cir. 1988).

Page 531   EEOC litigates for all employees: *EEOC* v. *Pan Am World Airlines*, 897 F.2d 1499 (9th Cir. 1990), *cert.denied* 498 U.S. 815; *Burns* v. *Equitable Life Assurance Society*, 696 F.2d 21 (2nd Cir. 1992), *cert.denied* 464 U.S. 933; *EEOC* v. *Wackenhut*, 939 F.2d 241 (5th Cir. 1991).

Page 531   Private suit OK re discrimination after filing of EEOC pattern or practice suit: *Verschuuren* v. *Equitable Life Assurance Society*, 544 F.Supp. 1188 (S.D.N.Y. 1983).

Page 531   Consolidated conciliation efforts OK: *EEOC* v. *Home Insurance Co.*, 553 F.Supp. 704 (S.D.N.Y. 1982); *EEOC* v. *Rhone-Poulenc Inc.*, 677 F.Supp. 264 (D.N.J. 1988).

Page 532   Past plaintiffs can't recover under EEOC suit: *EEOC* v. *U.S. Steel*, 921 F.2d 489 (3rd Cir. 1990).

Page 532   Injunction OK on same facts as dismissed suit: *EEOC* v. *Harris Chernin Inc.*, 10 F.3d 1286 (7th Cir. 1993).

Page 532   EEOC can sue bankrupt company: *EEOC* v. *McLean Trucking Co.*, 525 F.2d 1007 (4th Cir. 1987).

Page 532   Definite statement of final decision: *EEOC* v. *Home Insurance Co.*, 553 F.Supp. 704 (S.D.N.Y. 1982); *Leite* v. *Kennecott Copper Corp.*, 720 F.2d 658 (1st Cir. 1983); *Cada* v. *Baxter Healthcare Corp.*, 920 F.2d 446 (7th Cir. 1990), *cert.denied* 111 S.Ct. 2916.

Page 532   Timing of failure to promote case: *Coleman* v. *Clark Oil & Ref. Co.*, 568 F.Supp. 1035 (E.D. Wis. 1983); *Conor* v. *Hodel*, 36 FEP Cases 362 (D.D.C. 1984).

Page 533   Continuing violation accrues at last act: *Miller* v. *Beneficial Management Corp.*, 977 F.2d 834 (3rd Cir. 1992).

Page 533   Filing is timely for all acts in series: *Snead* v. *Harris*, 22 FEP Cases 1434 (D.D.C. 1980).

Page 533   Charges re bad appraisals: *Colgan* v. *Fisher Scientific Co.*, 935 F.2d 1407 (3rd Cir. 1991), *cert.denied* 112 S.Ct. 379; *Gustovich* v. *AT&T Communications Inc.*, 972 F.2d 845 (7th Cir. 1992).

Page 533   Accrual of layoff cause of action: *Morris* v. *Frank IX & Sons*, 486 F.Supp. 728 (W.D. Va. 1980); *Cutright* v. *General Motors Corp.*, 486 F.Supp. 590 (W.D. Pa. 1980); *Elliott* v. *Group Hospital Service*, 714 F.2d 556 (5th Cir. 1983), *cert.denied* 467 U.S. 1215.

Page 533   Accrual of seniority case: *Lorance* v. *AT&T Technologies Inc.*, 490 U.S. 900 (1989).

Page 533   Plan adoption standard continues for ADEA: *EEOC* v. *City Colleges of Chicago*, 944 F.2d 339 (9th Cir. 1991); *Thompson* v. *Prudential Insurance Co. of America*, 993 F.2d 226 (3rd Cir. 1993).

Page 533   Special assignment: *E. Kingsley Mull* v. *Arco Durethane Plastics Inc.*, 784 F.2d 284 (7th Cir. 1986).

Page 534   Severance benefit package: *Dillman* v. *Combustion Engineering*, 784 F.2d 57 (2nd Cir. 1986).

Page 534   Ban on discussion: *Felty* v. *Grays Humphrey's Co.*, 785 F.2d 516 (4th Cir. 1986).

Page 534   Duration of tolling: *Cada* v. *Baxter Healthcare Corp.*, 920 F.2d 446 (7th Cir. 1990), *cert.denied* 111 S.Ct. 2916; *Olson* v. *Mobil Oil Co.*, 904 F.2d 198 (4th Cir. 1990).

Page 534   Not posting required information tolls the statute: *Holly* v. *Naperville*, 571 F.Supp. 668 (N.D. Ill. 1983); *Jacobson* v. *Pitman-Moore Inc.*, 573 F.Supp. 545 (D.Minn. 1983).

Page 534   No tolling if employee had actual knowledge: *Templeton* v. *Western Union*, 607 F.2d 89 (5th Cir. 1979); *Hageman* v. *Phillips Roxane Lab. Inc.*, 623 F.2d 1381 (9th Cir. 1981).

Page 534   No tolling during grievance proceedings: *Sanders* v. *Duke University*, 538 F.Supp. 1443 (N.D.N.C. 1982); *Vaught* v. *R.R. Donnelley & Sons Co.*, 745 F.2d 407 (7th Cir. 1984).

Page 534   Grievance must be allowed after charges filed: *EEOC* v. *Board of Governors of State Colleges*, 957 F.2d 424 (7th Cir. 1992).

Page 534   Consent to opting in required: *Grayson* v. *K-Mart Corp.*, 79 F. 3d 1086 (11th Cir. 4/9/96).

Page 534   Tolling until class action resolved: *Armstrong* v. *Martin Marietta Corp.*, 93 F.3d 1505 (11th Cir. 9/11/96).

Page 535   Intervention not permitted: *Anson* v. *University of Texas Health Science Center*, 962 F.2d 539 (5th Cir. 1992).

Page 535   Employees dissatisfied with EEOC can't file own suit: *EEOC* v. *Con Edison*, 557 F.Supp. 468 (S.D.N.Y. 1983).

Page 535   Summary judgment unavailable: *Sheridan* v. *DuPont*, 65 LW 2372 (3rd Cir. 11/14/96).

Page 538   Difference between state and federal courts: Robert M. Wolff, "Making the Leap to State Courts," *Nat.L.J.* 6/30/97 p. B8.

Page 538   After-acquired evidence must justify firing: *O'Day* v. *McDonnell-Douglas*, 79 F.3d 756 (9th Cir. 3/26/96).

Page 540   Settlement doesn't bar cooperation with EEOC investigation: *EEOC* v. *Astra USA Inc.*, 94 F.3d 738 (1st Cir. 9/6/96).

Page 542   Combining front pay and reinstatement: *Selgas* v. *American Airlines, Inc.*, 104 F.3d 9 (1st Cir. 1997).

Page 542   Unemployment benefit offset: *Craig* v. *Y&Y Snacks Inc.*, 721 F.2d 77 (3rd Cir. 1983); *Brown* v. *A.J. Gerrard Mfg. Co.*, 715 F.2d 1549 (11th Cir. 1983); *Dailey* v. *Societe Generale*, CCH Unemployment Insurance Reporter ¶22,175 (2nd Cir. 3/5/97). Also see *Gaworski* v. *ITT Commercial Finance Corp.*, 17 F.3d 1104 (8th Cir. 1994), holding that unemployment insurance does not reduce ADEA back pay.

Page 544   Proof of retaliation: *Woodson* v. *Scott Paper Co.*, 65 LW 2775 (3rd Cir. 4/3/97); *Tanca* v. *Nordberg*, 65 LW 2329 (1st Cir. 10/28/96).

Page 544   Employee would have been fired then, not later: *Sagendorf-Teal* v. *Rensselaer County, N.Y.*, 65 LW 2344 (2nd Cir. 11/12/96).

Page 544   Title VII damages: *U.S.* v. *Burke*, 504 U.S. 229 (1992).

Page 545   ADEA back pay is taxable income: *Commissioner of Internal Revenue* v. *Schleier*, 115 S.Ct. 2159 (1995).

Chapter 28—Wrongful Termination and At-Will Employment

Page 548   Written communication desirable: Elaine McShulskis, "Communicate Clearly During Staff Reductions," *HRMagazine* January, 1997 p. 22.

Page 548   Duration of conditions: *Turner* v. *Anheuser-Busch*, 7 Cal.4th 1238, 32 Cal.Rptr.2d 223, 876 P.2d 1022 (1994).

Page 549   Relationship of trust and confidence required: *Wilder* v. *Cody County Chamber of Commerce*, 868 P.2d 211 (Wyo. 1994).

Page 550   Sacrifice to take new job: *Choate* v. *TRW, Inc.*, 14 F.3d 74 (D.C.Cir. 1994).

Page 550   Lies to new hire: *Kidder* v. *American South Bank, N.A.*, 639 So.2d 1361 (Ala. 1994); *National Security Insurance Co.* v. *Donaldson*, 664 So.2d 871 (Ala. 1995).

Page 550   Reasonable term of employment guaranteed: *Pickell* v. *Arizona Components Co.*, 1997 WL 27173 (Colo. 1/27/97).

Page 550   Written statements control: *Davis* v. *Wyoming Medical Center Inc.*, 1997 WL 118453 (Wyoming 1997).

Page 550   Oral offer withdrawn: *Heinritz* v. *Lawrence University*, 194 Wis.2d 607, 535 N.W.2d 81 (Wis.App. 1995).

Page 551   Implied contract: *Rinck* v. *Association of Reserve City Bankers*, 676 A.2d 12 (D.C. App. 1996).

Page 551   Statute of Frauds: *McInerney* v. *Chater Golf Inc.*, 176 Ill.2d 482, 680 N.E.2d 1347 (1997).

Page 551   One job at a time: *Bynum* v. *Boeing Co.*, 1997 Westlaw 177431 (Wash.App. 1997). See "The Strange Law of Lifetime Employment Contracts," (no by-line), CBC *Employment Alert* 8/21/97 p. 1.

Page 551   After-acquired evidence of fraud: *Crawford Rehab Services Inc.* v. *Weissman*, 66 LW 1009 (Colo.Sup. 6/9/97).

Page 551   Welfare benefits: *Inter-Modal Rail Employees* v. *Atchison, Topeka & Santa Fe Railroad*, #96-491, Supreme Court (May 1997).

Page 551   Statutory remedies prevent age discrimination wrongful termination suit: *List* v. *Anchor Paint Mfg. Co.*, 910 P.2d 1011 (Okla.Sup. 1/9/96).

Page 552   Difference of opinion: *Chelly* v. *Knoll Pharmaceuticals*, 295 N.J. Super. 478, 685 A.2d 498 (N.J. Super. 1996). Also see *Whitney* v. *Xerox Co.*, 9 IER Cases 1425 (E.D. Pa. 1994) holding that it is not unlawful to discharge a whistleblower who was not obligated to report illegalities.

Page 552   Failure to use internal grievance procedure: *Marsh* v. *Delta Air Lines Inc.*, 65 LW 2558 (D.Colo. 2/7/97); the statute is Colorado Revised Statutes §24-34-402.5.

Page 552   Transfer is not a discharge: *White* v. *State of Washington*, 1997 WL 7264 (Washington 1/9/97).

Page 552   Government agency: *Grisham* v. *U.S.*, CCH Employment Safety & Health Guide ¶31,214 (5th Cir. 1997).

Page 553   OSHA doesn't preempt wrongful discharge claims: *Antlitz* v. *CMJ Management Co.*, 1997 WL 42396 (Mass.Super. 1/30/97).

Page 553   FMLA preempts state claims: *Hamros* v. *Bethany Homes*, 894 F.Supp. 1176 (N.D. Ill. 1995).

Page 554   Breach of contract only: *Claggett* v. *Wake Forest University*, 486 S.E.2d 443 (N.C. App. 1997).

Page 554   Premature termination of contract: *Savannah College of Art and Design* v. *Nulph*, 265 Georgia 662, 460 S.E.2d 792 (1995).

Page 554   Severance packages: Judith H. Dobryznski, "Growing Trend: Giant Payoffs for Executives Who Fail Big," *N.Y.T.* 7/21/97 p. C1.

Page 555   Tactics for negotiations: Lee T. Paterson, *Negotiating Employee Resignations*, Parker & Sons Pubs. Inc., (1990).

Page 559   24-hour period too short: *Puentes* v. *UPS*, 86 F.3d 196 and 65 LW 2060 (11th Cir. 6/20/96).

Page 562	Ratification of release: *Blistein* v. *St. John's College*, 74 F.3d 1459 (4th Cir. 1/26/96); *Blakeney* v. *Lomas Information Systems*, 65 F.3d 482 (5th Cir. 1995); *Wamsley* v. *Champlin Ref. & Chemicals Inc.*, 11 F.3d 534 (5th Cir. 1993).
Page 562	Consideration ratifies even unwritten release: *Somerville* v. *Baxter Healthcare*, 66 LW 1048 (D.D.C. 6/4/97).
Page 562	Release not ratified by acceptance of consideration: *Raczak* v. *Ameritech*, 1997 WL 5921 (6th Cir. 1997); *Howlett* v. *Holiday Inns*, No. 95-6236 (6th Cir. 8/5/97); *Long* v. *Sears-Roebuck & Co.*, 105 F.3d 1529 (3rd Cir. 2/6/97); *Oberg* v. *Allied Van Lines Inc.*, 11 F.3d 679 (7th Cir. 1993), *cert.denied* 114 S.Ct. 2104; *Forbus* v. *Sears-Roebuck & Co.*, 958 F.2d 1036 (11th Cir. 1992).
Page 562	Obligation to return consideration: *Kristoferson* v. *Otis Spunkmeyer*, 66 LW 1048 (S.D.N.Y. 6/4/97). This subject is discussed in Ronald M. Green and William J. Milani, "The 'Tender Back' Controversy," *N.Y.L.J.* 4/21/97 p. 9.
Page 564	Advice on downsizing: Beth Duncan, "Corporate Counsel Share Tips on Downsizing, Use of Mediation," LW 7/8/97 p. 2031.
Page 565	Not necessary to follow all steps, because of disclaimer: *Phipps* v. *IASD Health Services Corp.*, 1997 WL 24836 (Iowa 1/22/97).
Page 565	Systems of progressive discipline: Paul Falcone, "The Fundamentals of Progressive Discipline," *HRMagazine* February, 1997 p. 90.
Page 567	Marijuana: *D.C.* v. *Davis*, 1996 WL 7264 (Washington 1/9/97).
Page 567	Reasonable belief sexual harassment occurred: *Cotran* v. *Rollins Hudig Hall Int'l.*, 65 LW 2273 (Cal.App. 9/26/96).
Page 567	No tort of failure to promote: *Mintz* v. *Bell Atlantic Systems Leasing Int'l*, 183 Arizona 550, 905 P.2d 559 (Ariz.App. 1995).
Page 568	State age claim foreclosed: *Jennings* v. *Maralle*, 63 LW 2119 (Cal. 8/1/94); also see *List* v. *Anchor Paint Mfg. Co.*, 910 P.2d 1011 (Okla.Sup. 1/9/96), which holds that, given statutory remedies for age discrimination available to at-will employees, they can't sue in state court for tort of wrongful discharge, and *Brown* v. *Ford*, 905 P.2d 223 (Okla. 1995), ruling out sex discrimination wrongful discharge suits against companies too small to be covered by state or federal laws.
Page 568	Earlier suits bar suit over denial of severance: *King* v. *Union Oil Co.*, 1997 U.S.App. LEXIS 16107 (10th Cir. 1997).
Page 568	Termination date, not notice date, counts: *Romano* v. *Rockwell Int'l*, 14 Cal.4th 479 (1996).
Page 568	Date of leaving, not deterioration of conditions, counts: *Mullins* v. *Rockwell Int'l Corp.*, 65 LW 2793 (Cal.Sup. 5/19/97).
Page 568	Tennesee starts statute of limitations on notice date: *Weber* v. *Moses*, 72 FEP Cases 1584 (Tenn. 1996).

Chapter 29 — Corporate Communications

Page 569	Pure opinion not defamatory: *Williams* v. *Garraghty*, 249 Va. 224, 455 S.E.2d 209 (1995).

Page 570   Publication: *Maynard* v. *Vanderbilt U.*, 1993 Tenn. App LEXIS 351 (1993), *Friel* v. *Angell Care Inc.*, 113 N.C.App. 505, 440 S.E.2d 111 (1994).

Page 570   Nevada rule: *Simpson* v. *Mars, Inc.*, 1997 WL 4818 (Nev. 1/5/97).

Page 570   1993 California case on privilege: *Jensen* v. *Hewlett-Packard Co.*, 14 Cal.App.4th 958.

Page 571   EEOC and unemployment officials: *Stockstill* v. *Shell Oil Co.*, 3 F.3d 868 (5th Cir. 1993); *Thompto* v. *Colwin's Inc.*, 871 F.Supp. 1097 (N.D. Iowa 1994).

Pages 571–72 Qualified privilege to prevent harm: *Davis* v. *Monsanto Co.*, 627 F.Supp. 418 (S.D.W.V. 1986).

Page 572   Loss of privileged status: *Samaritan Foundation* v. *Goodfarb*, 176 Ariz. 497, 862 P.2d 870 (1993)which imposes a subject-matter test: a confidential communication initiated by employee to counsel, for legal advice, is privileged, but if the company initiates the investigation, factual statements by employee to counsel are privileged only if they concern the employee's own conduct in the scope of employment, and are made to help the counsel assess the legal consequences of the conduct to the corporation.

Page 573   Waiver of privilege re outside counsel: *Harding* v. *Dana Transportation Inc.*, 914 F.Supp. 1084 (D.N.J. 1996).

Page 573   Self-critical analysis privilege: see "Employment Law" column by Eric J. Wallach, Leslie Reider, and Anthony C. Ginetto, *Nat.L.J.* 6/16/97 p. B9; Michael Delikat and Ruth Raisfeld, "Litigation Over Corporate Diversity Programs," *N.Y.L.J.* 7/14/97 p. S5. Cases that recognize the privilege include *Banks* v. *Lockheed-Georgia Co.*, 53 F.R.D. 283 (N.D. Ga. 1971), *Troupin* v. *Metropolitan Life Insurance Co.*, 169 F.R.D. 546 (S.D.N.Y. 1996); cases that either say that there is no such privilege, or that it can't be applied to the particular case at hand, include *U.S.* v. *Adlman*, 68 F.3d 1495 (2nd Cir. 1995); *Georgia-Pacific Corp.* v. *GAF Roofing Mfg. Corp.*, 1996 U.S. Dist. LEXIS 671 (S.D.N.Y. 1/24/96); *Spencer Savings Bank* v. *Excell Mortgage Corp.*, 1997 Westlaw 106390, (D.N.J. 3/7/97); *Dowling* v. *American Hawaii Inc.*, 971 F.2d 423 (9th Cir. 1992), *Cloud* v. *Superior Court*, 65 LW 2369 (Cal.App. 11/21/96).

Page 574   Ombudsman privilege not recognized: *Carman* v. *McDonnell Douglas Corp.*, 65 LW 2826 (8th Cir. 6/11/97).

Page 575   Duty to discover information from background check: *Randi W.* v. *Muroc Joint Unified School District*, 60 Cal.Rptr.2nd 263 (1994).

Page 575   Preventing negligent supervision claims: Eric J. Wallach and Mark E. Greenfield, "Negligent Hiring and Supervision Claims: The New Look," *Nat.L.J.* 5/12/97 p. S9.

Page 576   Eliciting positive information: No by-line, "Getting Former Employer to Give Useful Information During Reference Checks," *CBC Employment Alert* 9/4/97 p. 1.

Chapter 30 — Insurance Coverage for Claims Against the Employer

Page 583   Market for EPLI policies: Leslie Scism, "More Firms Insure Against Worker Suits," *Wall St.J.* 11/15/96 p. A2.

Index